SOUTHERN ITALY

LINDA SARRIS & LAURA THAYER

Contents

Discover Southern Italy 6
  10 Top Experiences 10
  Planning Your Time............... 18
  • If You Like... 21
  • If You Have...................... 23
  Best of Southern Italy 25
  • From Ruins to Romanesque...... 27
  • Southern Italian Beach 101 29
  • Best Road Trips 31
  • Outdoor Adventures 32
  Tasting Southern Italy 33

Naples and the Ruins 35
  Itinerary Ideas 40
  Sights 42
  Sports and Recreation............. 59
  Entertainment and Events.......... 60
  Shopping 61
  Food 64
  Bars and Nightlife 69
  Accommodations 70
  Information and Services 72
  Getting There 73
  Getting Around.................... 75
  Pompeii.......................... 78
  Herculaneum 87
  Vesuvius 92

**Sorrento, Capri, and
  the Amalfi Coast** 96
  Itinerary Ideas 104
  Sorrento 105
  Positano 120
  Amalfi 141
  Ravello.......................... 158
  Salerno 167
  Capri 180

**Puglia and the
  Best of the South** 202
  Itinerary Ideas 207
  Bari 210
  Around Bari...................... 220
  The Salento 240
  Matera.......................... 259
  Highlights of Calabria and Basilicata . . 267

Palermo and Western Sicily ... 269
  Itinerary Ideas 275
  Sights 277
  Sports and Recreation............. 285
  Entertainment and Events.......... 288
  Shopping 291
  Food 292
  Bars and Nightlife 300
  Accommodations 302

Information and Services 303
Getting There 304
Getting Around 305
Vicinity of Palermo 306
Trapani and the West Coast 314
Agrigento and the Southern Coast . . . 322

Catania, Northeastern Sicily, and the Aeolian Islands 330
Itinerary Ideas 334
Catania 336
Taormina 354
Mount Etna 362
The Aeolian Islands 375

Syracuse and Southeastern Sicily 394
Itinerary Ideas 399
Syracuse 402
Around Syracuse 417
Ragusa 424

Background 437
The Landscape 437
Plants and Animals 439
History 441
Government and Economy 449
People and Culture 450

Essentials 455
Transportation 455
Visas and Officialdom 461
Festivals and Events 463
Recreation 464
Food 465
Shopping 468
Accommodations 468
Health and Safety 470
Conduct and Customs 471
Practical Details 472
Traveler Advice 476

Resources 479
Glossary 479
Italian Phrasebook 480
Suggested Reading 483
Suggested Films 485
Internet and Digital Resources 486

Index 488

List of Maps 498

Although every effort was made to make sure the information in this book was accurate when going to press, research was impacted by the COVID-19 pandemic and things may have changed since the time of writing. Be sure to confirm specific details, like opening hours, closures, and travel guidelines and restrictions, when making your travel plans. For more detailed information, see page 456.

Southern Italy

Things move at a different speed in Southern Italy, where a slow pace and easy living are almost always the keys to happiness, whether you're sailing into Amalfi's harbor, wandering the ruins of Magna Graecia in Sicily, or watching pasta experts hand-making orecchiette in front of their homes in Bari.

Though plenty ties the people, landscape, and culture of this region together—from the midday siesta, pre-dinner aperitivo, and evening passeggiata, to the excellent gastronomy and importance of the sea—each part has its own distinct character, too.

On the Amalfi Coast, it's pastel-hued homes clinging to the cliffs between mountain and sea, tempting beaches lined with colorful umbrellas, and postcard-worthy views in every direction. Just a short distance away you'll find sunny Sorrento, Paestum and its incredibly well-preserved Greek temples, and the ancient cities of Pompeii and Herculaneum frozen in time. When you're ready for a burst of energy, head to Naples where, amid the buzz of scooters and backdrop of Neapolitan songs, there lies a city that was meant to be uncovered.

In Sicily, think dipping into salty, cool, crystal-blue water from rocky beaches

Clockwise from top left: Grotta della Poesia in the Salento; procession at the Festival of Sant'Andrea in Amalfi; gulf of Cefalù; beach on the Aeolian island of Lipari; fresh sea urchin in Puglia; Positano.

on hot summer days, the constant, looming presence of Mount Etna, biting into a crispy fried arancina on the lively streets of Palermo, and small Baroque towns built into hillside cliffs.

Meanwhile, at the southeastern heel of Italy's boot, Puglia's long coastline lures travelers from around the world. The region is known for cucina povera—making miraculous food with simple, inexpensive ingredients—usually with a big glug of high-quality extra virgin olive oil to finish a dish.

Get ready to experience a place that captures your heart and leaves you longing for more. One thing is for sure: You'll have travel memories to relive for a lifetime.

Clockwise from top left: Marina Grande in Capri; Duomo di Amalfi; Sorrento's Marina Grande; cheesemaking in Puglia.

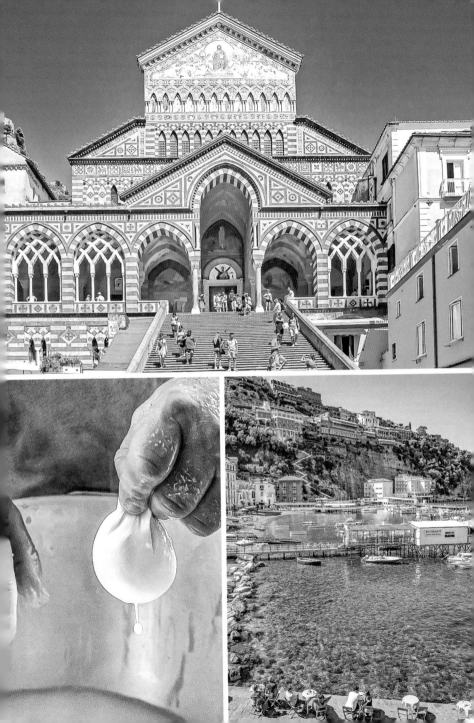

10 TOP
EXPERIENCES

1 Finding your own personal paradise at one of **Southern Italy's best beaches,** from chic beach clubs dotted with colorful umbrellas to secluded rocky coves (page 29).

2 Eating **pizza in Naples,** the birthplace of Neapolitan pizza, where it's truly a gastronomic art (page 66).

3 **Climbing Mount Etna,** Sicily's beating heart and the most active volcano in all of Europe, where you can grab a glass of volcanic wine after your hike (page 364).

4 Walking the streets of **Pompeii** (page 78) and **Herculaneum** (page 87), two Roman cities frozen in time by the eruption of Vesuvius in AD 79, offering a somber and fascinating look at life in ancient Rome.

^
^
^
5 **Cruising on a boat around Capri,** through turquoise blue waters and past stunning grottoes (page 192).

6 Seeking out Spanish-influenced Baroque architecture in Puglia and Sicily, from **Lecce** (page 241), known as the "Florence of the South," to the UNESCO World Heritage Site of **Noto** (page 419).

7 Snacking on crispy, salty, sinfully good **street food in Palermo** (page 296).

8 Following in the footsteps of the ancient Greeks, from the magnificent Doric temples of **Paestum** (page 177) to the eight majestic temples of the **Valle dei Templi** (page 322).

9 Marveling at the cave dwellings of the **Sasso Caveoso** in Matera, one of the oldest continually inhabited settlements in the world (page 260).

10 Hiking in the mountains above the Amalfi Coast on the **Pathway of the Gods,** where the scenery leaves little doubt as to how the hike got its name (page 129).

Planning Your Time

Where to Go

Naples and the Ruins

The largest city in Southern Italy, **Naples** buzzes with a vibrant energy and magnetism truly its own. How could you not fall for a city with royal **palaces,** world-class **museums,** and some of Italy's tastiest **street food?** Around every corner there's something unexpected to discover, and it's also a great base for day trips to famous archaeological sites as well as Capri and Sorrento.

Mount Vesuvius looms over the Gulf of Naples and the archaeological sites of **Pompeii** and **Herculaneum,** thriving Roman cities that were destroyed by the violent eruption of the volcano in AD 79. Walking through the streets of Pompeii and Herculaneum is a unique chance to see **ancient Roman culture** firsthand.

Sorrento, Capri, and the Amalfi Coast

Sorrento is a popular spot for travelers looking to explore all the top destinations in the area thanks to its convenient setting between Naples and the Amalfi Coast. With **panoramic views** across the Gulf of Naples, a **historic center** full of shops and restaurants, and picturesque **Marina Grande harbor,** this vacation setting combines beauty, charm, and convenience. It's one of the main gateways to the justifiably famous island of **Capri.** Expect crowds on the island, especially in the high season, when the iconic **Piazzetta** and the **chic shopping streets** are bustling. Yet there's a quieter side of Capri if you ride a chairlift to **Monte Solaro,** the island's highest point, or

the Duomo di Amalfi

ITALY

© MOON.COM

get lost in narrow pathways past **bougainvillea-draped villas.**

To the west, on the southern side of the Sorrentine Peninsula, you'll be captivated by the Amalfi Coast's **rugged coastline** and rocky, **secluded beaches. Positano's** cascade of pastel-colored buildings and seemingly unreal beauty makes it one of the most visited spots on the Amalfi Coast. **Amalfi,** the coastline's namesake town, has a scenic port and a fascinating history as Italy's first maritime republic, dating back to the Middle Ages. And set high in the mountains, the town of **Ravello** is a big draw, with its lovely gardens and

romantic views. Plus, just east of the coast lies the city of **Salerno,** with its attractive lungomare (waterfront) and maze of medieval streets in its historic center. It's a good home base in this area for travelers who enjoy a bigger city vibe.

Puglia and the Best of the South

Puglia, the heel of Italy's boot, is still less visited by international tourists, but its long coastline promises Italian adventures that touch on history, food, slow living, and relaxation. Most visitors start in the central, regional capital of **Bari,** with one of the area's main airports (the other, the Aeroporto del Salento, is located outside Brindisi, farther south). The surrounding area is known for its cultivation of grapes and olives, **hilltop villages** and **coastal towns,** and diverse **national parks.** Breathtaking cities like **Lecce,** the "Florence of the South," and **Gallipoli,** "the beautiful city," show off Puglia's romantic side.

Just west of Puglia, in the province of Basilicata, don't miss captivating **Matera,** whose distinctive cave dwellings have been inhabited continuously for at least 3,000 years, now converted into charming restaurants and B&Bs.

Palermo and Western Sicily

Start your trip to Sicily in the fascinating capital city of **Palermo,** whose history is marked by waves of conquerors, from the Greeks to the Romans, Arabs, Normans, French, and Spanish. Each one has left its mark and influenced the architecture, culture, landscape, customs, and culinary traditions of the island. Palermo is a hub of Sicilian art, culture, and gastronomy. The **centro storico** is filled with art museums, folksy puppet performances, noble palaces, flourishing **outdoor markets,** and some of Italy's best **street food.**

Nearby, don't miss the **Aegadian Islands,** just a stone's throw from the coastal towns of **Trapani** and **Marsala.** Farther south, the **Valle dei Templi** archaeological site rivals anything you might find in Greece.

Catania, Northeastern Sicily, and the Aeolian Islands

Under the shadow of Mother Etna, **Catania**'s proximity to Sicily's largest airport, Catania-Fontanarossa, makes it a no-brainer stop on any trip to Sicily. This intricate black rock city was rebuilt with lava stones after two devastating volcanic eruptions, but the vivacious **A' Piscaria** fish market shows the town to be very much alive. Within an easy drive, you can climb the slopes of **Mount Etna,** sip volcanic wines, live large in glamorous, historic **Taormina,** or head off the grid to the **Aeolian Islands,** top destinations for pristine beaches and fresh seafood.

sailing to Sicily's Aeolian Islands

If You Like...

PURE RELAXATION

- **Capri:** With views of the Bay of Naples in almost every direction, it's hard not to feel serene on Capri, whether you're boating around its famous grottoes or dining on a terrace surrounded by fragrant flowers (page 180).

- **The Amalfi Coast:** The beaches and picturesque coastal towns of the Amalfi Coast are famous for a reason, perfect for the ultimate seaside vacation (page 120).

HISTORY

- **Naples:** Go underground to see the ancient urban plan of the city, and don't miss the stunning Baroque churches, royal palaces, and world-class museums (page 35).

- **Archaeological sites:** Lovers of Greek and Roman history will be spoiled almost anywhere they go in Southern Italy, from Pompeii (page 78) and Herculaneum (page 87), to Paestum (page 177), to Valle dei Templi in Sicily (page 322).

- **Baroque towns:** In Puglia, Lecce's highly embellished Baroque architecture has earned it the nickname "The Florence of the South" (page 241), and the towns of Noto (page 419), Modica (page 432), and Ragusa (page 424) in Sicily also feature this charming architectural style.

- **Matera:** Thought to be one of the oldest continually inhabited places on the planet, the cliff dwellings of Matera are a can't-miss stop on the way to Puglia (page 259).

FOOD

- **Cetara and Catania:** Seafood is a gastronomic highlight of the entire region, but the anchovies of Cetara (page 166) and Catania's A' Piscaria seafood market (page 341) stand out.

the Baroque town of Modica in Sicily

- **Palermo:** In one of the world's street food capitals, urban foodies are spoiled for choice (page 269).

- **Puglia:** The heel of Italy's boot is known for its cucina povera, in which fresh ingredients combine to make simple dishes in the cheapest possible way, often topped off with a glug of locally made olive oil (page 202).

AVOIDING CROWDS

- **The Salento:** The southern tip of Puglia is a seemingly endless coast of remote beaches and hidden swimming spots, each more secluded than the next (page 240).

- **Aeolian Islands:** In this tiny archipelago off the island of Sicily, many of the beaches are only accessible by boat (page 375).

Syracuse and Southeastern Sicily

Get a glimpse into Sicily's Greek history in Syracuse, originally founded by the Corinthians in 734 BC. Its Parco Archeologico della Neapolis is home to an impressive Greek theater and a Roman amphitheater, and the island of Ortigia jutting just off the city's coast is the perfect combination of historic architecture, the sea, and delicious food. Then, venture out to the villages of Modica, Noto, and Ragusa, living pieces of art with their beautiful Baroque townscapes.

When to Go

With Southern Italy's plentiful beaches and Mediterranean climate, the Amalfi Coast region is a top choice for travelers looking for a relaxing summer holiday, and Puglia and Sicily can be visited year-round. High season runs from Easter-October in all three regions, and July and August are the busiest months, with the caveat that some establishments in Sicilian cities may be closed in August, when the heat can get unbearable and people tend to head to the beach. Visit during this peak period if your primary object is a beach vacation, though you can expect higher prices for accommodations and even rentals for sun beds and umbrellas at some beach clubs (stabilimenti balneari).

The shoulder seasons are gorgeous throughout Southern Italy and are probably the best all-around times to visit. Try planning your trip for April or May, before things get too warm and busy; the weather usually stays very nice through October and November as well.

Low season runs from November-Easter, when Southern Italy is much quieter but still offers beautiful landscapes. Many accommodations and restaurants will close for a period, especially in the places most dependent on tourism; ferry service around the Amalfi Coast stops in low season. If you'd prefer cooler temperatures for sightseeing and hiking, a shoulder season may be preferable. Though it can be a bit rainy off-season, more so on the Amalfi Coast and Sicily than in Puglia, it usually doesn't last for long and there are many clear, crisp days.

Note that the impact of high and low season will be less noticeable in larger cities like Salerno, Naples, and Palermo. Accommodations and restaurants in these regional hubs are usually open all year, with the Christmas holiday time being very popular.

Before You Go

Passports and Visas

For travelers visiting Italy from the United States, Canada, Australia, and New Zealand, there are currently no visa requirements for visits of fewer than 90 days. You'll only need a passport that is valid at least three months after your planned departure date from the European Union. For stays longer than 90 days, you will need to apply for a visa at the Italian embassy in your home country before you travel.

For EU citizens, or citizens of the non-EU member states of the EEA or Switzerland, there are no visa requirements for traveling to Italy. You can enter Italy with your passport or National Identity Card. After Brexit, UK citizens can enter Italy with a UK passport without a visa for visits of fewer than 90 days within any 180-day period. Passports must be less than 10 years old and valid for at least six months beyond the travel dates.

Travelers from South Africa will need to

If You Have...

- **Three Days:** Pick a town or two in one area—**Naples,** the **Amalfi Coast, Puglia,** or the western or eastern coast of **Sicily**—to truly hunker down and enjoy what's special about each of these unique regions.

- **Five Days:** With two extra days, you can add on a day trip to the island of **Capri** or Pompeii and Herculaneum from Naples or the Amalfi Coast, the **Aeolian Islands** from northeastern Sicily, or ancient **Matera** from Puglia.

- **One Week:** If you have a full week, you should be able to visit two Southern Italian regions, whether you choose to visit **Puglia** on a road trip from the **Amalfi Coast,** hop on a quick

flight from Puglia to **Sicily,** or ride the overnight ferry from **Naples** to **Palermo.**

- **Two Weeks:** Two weeks is enough time for a whirlwind tour of Campania, Puglia, and Sicily. Base yourself in **Naples** for a few days, before heading to the **Amalfi Coast** for three days of R&R. Road trip to Puglia for three days or so, exploring the area around **Bari** before driving down toward **Lecce** and finally toward the Airport of the Salento to catch a quick flight to **Palermo** or **Catania.** With 3-4 days, prioritize either the western or eastern coast of Sicily—the west coast is known for its authentic culture and Greek archaeological sites, while the Baroque towns and seaside resorts of the east coast are justifiably famous.

procure a Schengen Visa to enter Italy. This currently costs €60 for adults (€35 for children ages 6-12, and free for children younger than 6).

You can check for the latest information on visa requirements and other restrictions, such as current **COVID-19 measures,** at Italy's Farnesina website (http://vistoperitalia.esteri.it).

Transportation
BY AIR
The **Aeroporto Internazionale di Napoli,** also referred to as **Capodichino,** is the largest airport in the region, and it's well connected with flights from across Italy as well as international flights from more than 80 cities. Direct flights from North America, however, are limited, and are only available May-October. The airport is only about 3.7 miles (6 km) northeast of Naples city center.

Similarly, there are no direct flights from North America to Sicily's **Palermo** and **Catania-Fontanarossa** airports, but both are well-connected to airports across Europe and Italy. Though it is possible to travel to Sicily by train, bus, and rental car from the Puglia and the Amalfi Coast areas, travelers with limited time

should consider quick, frequent, and cheap domestic flights.

BY TRAIN
Naples and Salerno are major stops for trains operated by the Italian national railway company **Trenitalia** (www.trenitalia.com), with Regional, InterCity, and high-speed trains connecting the region to destinations across Italy. The private company **Italotreno** (www.italotreno.it) also offers high-speed trains to both Naples and Salerno from Torino, Milan, Venice, Bologna, Florence, Rome, and many other smaller cities. The **Circumvesuviana** train line (www.eavsrl.it) connects Naples with Pompeii, Herculaneum, and Sorrento. The closest train stations to reach the Amalfi Coast are in Salerno and Sorrento.

Traveling by train between Campania, Puglia, and Sicily is possible, but it's not the quickest way to travel Southern Italy. That said, there is a relatively quick train from Rome to Puglian hub Bari run by Trenitalia. Most major cities and towns in Puglia and Sicily have train stations, but train service is generally a bit less frequent and reliable.

BY FERRY

Ferries offer an excellent way to move around the Amalfi Coast and Sorrentine Peninsula, are necessary to reach Capri and Sicily's Aeolian Islands, and can be an adventurous way to travel from Naples to Palermo. The **Porto di Napoli** (Port of Naples) is one of the largest in Italy. Ferry service from Salerno and along the Amalfi Coast runs seasonally from Easter-October.

BY BUS

Bus companies like **Flixbus** (www.flixbus.com) offer service to most major cities in Southern Italy from across Italy. Local buses provide an inexpensive option to get around. Since ferry service along the Amalfi Coast is seasonal, buses are the best way to get around during the off-season (Nov.-Easter).

BY CAR

Given the famously chaotic traffic of Naples, the narrow and curvy Amalfi Coast Road, and congested island roads, driving is not recommended in this area. This is much less the case in **Puglia** and **Sicily,** at least outside larger cities like Palermo and Bari, where roads are much less crowded, generally easy to drive, and offer the most flexibility for road-trip-type vacations.

What to Pack

When packing for Southern Italy, think relaxed yet elegant resort wear. Puglia and Sicily are much more casual. For women, a scarf can come in handy for layering, and to use as a shoulder wrap to use when you visit churches, where modest dress is recommended and tank tops and short skirts or shorts are not considered appropriate attire.

Beachwear and swimsuits are a must if you're traveling during the summer. Cover-ups are a good idea, too, as it's not permitted to walk around most towns (even beachside towns) only wearing swimwear. Pack sun protection and a hat for beach days.

Considering the sometimes steep and often cobblestone roads throughout Southern Italy, comfortable shoes are a must. If you plan to hike, bring good footwear with plenty of support. For the rocky beaches, a pair of flip-flops or water shoes will save your feet.

Pack a European **plug adapter** and **converter** for your electronic devices. You'll also want to bring plenty of memory cards or film for photos, as the endless fine views and landscape will inspire you to snap more photos than you expect.

Best of Southern Italy

You could spend a lifetime wandering Southern Italy's well-known sights, charming villages, and secluded beaches, but two weeks are just enough to get a taste of this beautiful, culturally rich region. This itinerary is broken up into three of Southern Italy's most distinctive and worthwhile areas: Naples and the Amalfi Coast, Puglia, and Sicily. Theoretically, the three regions could be visited in any order—say, if you find a good deal on a flight to a Sicilian or Apulian hub—though note that Naples's airport is the largest in the region. You could also leave out a leg of this trip to opt for more time in just one or two areas—each of which truly merits a trip in its own right. Just keep in mind that when it comes to transport between the areas, road-trip-friendly Puglia can be reached from Naples and the Amalfi Coast on a relatively easy drive; to get to Sicily, a quick domestic flight is likely the best option.

Naples and the Amalfi Coast
DAY 1: NAPLES

Start your first morning in **Naples** at the **Museo Archeologico Nazionale,** where you can explore one of the world's most important archaeological collections. Then, enjoy a walk down **Spaccanapoli,** a straight street named for the way it cuts right through the historic center. Take a left on **Via San Gregorio Armeno,** where you can see artisans creating traditional nativity scenes. Not far away, stop in the **Duomo di Napoli** to see the city's most important church. Next, head over to Piazza del Plebiscito to admire the elegant **Palazzo Reale.** Stop for true Neapolitan espresso at the **Gran Caffè Gambrinus** at the edge of the piazza. Cross the Piazza Trieste e Trento and go inside the **Galleria Umberto I** shopping center to admire the soaring glass dome. Watch the sunset from the **Castel dell'Ovo** with fine views of the Gulf of Naples.

Galleria Umberto I in Naples

For dinner, have a traditional **Neapolitan-style pizza.**

DAY 2: DAY TRIP TO POMPEII
Take an excursion to the ruins of **Pompeii,** easily reached by the Circumvesuviana train in about 45 minutes. Plan on about three hours to explore the museum and archaeological site to see the highlights and really experience what life was like in an ancient Roman town, stopping for a light lunch at the café onsite. Don't miss the experience of standing in the center of Pompeii's ancient **Amphitheater** where gladiators once battled or exploring the **Villa of the Mysteries,** named for its captivating and enigmatic frescoes. After returning to Naples, take time to explore your neighborhood and enjoy some Neapolitan **street food,** like the classic fried pizza.

DAY 3: AMALFI
Today you'll head to the Amalfi Coast. Make your way first to sunny **Sorrento** by ferry or the Circumvesuviana train, where you can explore the **centro storico,** largely pedestrian-only and lined with shops and restaurants, enjoy beautiful views over the Gulf of Naples from the **Villa Comunale** gardens, and stop somewhere with a view for a light lunch. If it's summer, you can take the scenic ferry to **Amalfi,** your base for the next two nights; otherwise, you'll need to take a bus.

Once arrived, sip a coffee and nibble a freshly baked sfogliatella in **Piazza Duomo,** visit the **Museo della Carta** to learn more about Amalfi's fascinating history of papermaking, shop along the town's main street, and climb the steps to the **Duomo di Amalfi.** Then, take a leisurely evening stroll along the harbor or savor a sunset aperitivo before a relaxed dinner overlooking the sea.

DAY 4: POSITANO
Start your second day on the Amalfi Coast by catching a ferry or bus to **Positano.** By ferry, you'll arrive right on the **Spiaggia Grande** beach with the **Chiesa di Santa Maria Assunta** in the middle. Climb the steps to visit the church and see its much-loved Byzantine icon. From the Spiaggia Grande, follow the

Sorrento

Positano

From Ruins to Romanesque

From what remains of the luxurious villas of Herculaneum to the striking black-and-white-striped Duomo di Amalfi, chances are that in Southern Italy, you'll be bowled over by architecture around every corner. Below is a brief primer on some of the architectural styles you'll find throughout the region.

GREEK

The Greek archaeological sites found throughout Southern Italy rival those found in modern-day Greece. Much of the region was once known as Magna Graecia, named for the high concentration of Greek settlers who founded cities here between 750 BC- AD 400. Looking at the extremely proportional design and well-preserved columns at Paestum (page 177), south of Salerno, and Segesta (page 321), Selinunte (page 321), and the Valle dei Templi (page 322) in western Sicily, it's easy to see how influential the ancient Greek architectural style is to this day.

ROMAN AND ROMANESQUE

Temple of Segesta in Sicily

The Roman ruins of Pompeii (page 78) and Herculaneum (page 87) need no introduction, and you can learn about how the ancient Roman elite lived at sites like Villa Jovis (page 183). You can see the influence of Roman architecture in Southern Italy's Romanesque structures, especially common in Puglia. The rounded arches of the Cattedrale di Salerno (page 168) and Basilica di San Nicola in Bari (page 213) emerged in medieval times, but they borrowed from Roman design.

TRULLI AND SASSI

In Puglia and the neighboring region of Basilicata are two architectural styles found almost nowhere else in the world. Trulli (page 236), found around Alberobello, are distinctive huts with conical roofs, used in ancient times for agricultural purposes and today housing boutique B&Bs. Just a few hours to the west, the cave dwellings known as the Sassi di Matera (page 260) have been inhabited since Paleolithic times.

GOTHIC

When the Angevin dynasty was kicked out of Sicily by the Spanish in the 13th century, they moved their capital to Naples, and brought with them Gothic architecture, characterized by pointed arches, flying buttresses, and massive, open, airy interiors. Prime examples include the Complesso Monumentale di Santa Chiara (page 46) and the Duomo di Napoli (page 48).

BAROQUE

Baroque architecture, characterized by elaborate, theatrical ornamentation on everything from interiors to facades, took root in Lecce (page 241) when the Catholic church tried to reassert its power after Turkish invasions throughout Puglia in the 17th and 18th centuries, and in Sicilian towns like Noto (page 419) after devastating earthquakes allowed the Spanish rulers of the time to rebuild lavishly decorated palaces and churches.

A LITTLE BIT OF EVERYTHING

Some of Southern Italy's most distinctive architecture was repeatedly rebuilt and renovated in the styles of the time over the centuries. The Duomo di Amalfi (page 141), the peculiar Castel del Monte in the hills of Puglia (page 227), and Palermo's massive Palazzo dei Normanni (page 282) all have Arab, Norman, Romanesque, Byzantine, Gothic, and Baroque architectural elements—a mixture that embodies what makes this part of Italy special.

the Terrace of Infinity at the Villa Cimbrone in Ravello

olive groves around Andria in Puglia

cliff-hugging Via Positanesi d'America pathway over to **Spiaggia di Fornillo,** a very scenic and quieter spot for a swim. Rent a sun bed and enjoy a fresh lunch at a beachside restaurant. Later in the afternoon, head back to Positano's town center to explore the streets lined with tempting boutiques before catching the last evening ferry back to Amalfi.

DAY 5: RAVELLO
On your last day on the Amalfi Coast, head into the mountains above the beaches on the City Sightseeing open-top bus to **Ravello.** Visit the town's elegant central piazza and stop in the **Duomo** before taking a pleasant walk through the quiet streets of Ravello to reach the **Villa Cimbrone.** Stroll along the wisteria-covered pathway to the **Terrace of Infinity,** where the blue sea and sky blend into one breathtaking vista. Enjoy shopping for ceramics in Ravello's town center before having evening cocktails or dinner on a romantic terrace overlooking the coastline. Catch a late bus or taxi back down to Amalfi.

Puglia
DAY 6: POLIGNANO A MARE
Today, leave the Amalfi Coast by bus to **Salerno,** where you can pick up your rental car for the 3-hour drive to **Puglia.** En route, consider stopping near the town of **Andria** for an olive oil tasting or lunch featuring Puglia's famous burrata cheese. You're heading straight for the tiny seaside village of **Polignano a Mare,** home to one of the most recognizable beaches in Puglia. Spend a few hours relaxing on the **Spiaggia di Lama Monachile** and wandering the picture-perfect cobbled streets, before driving to a luxurious countryside accommodation, such as **Borgo Egnazia,** for the night. Enjoy dinner at your hotel's restaurant, or, for something more adventurous, visit the commune of **Savelletri** to try some fresh-shucked ricci di mare (sea urchin) from a seafood shack.

DAY 7: ALBEROBELLO AND LECCE
Get an early start today to see the iconic trulli of **Alberobello,** conical huts that have become a symbol of the Apulian countryside. Afterward,

Southern Italian Beach 101

With a rugged coastline dotted with picturesque swimming spots, the beaches of Southern Italy lure summertime visitors from around the world. If you're dreaming of soaking up the Mediterranean atmosphere and diving into the turquoise sea, here's what to expect and how to make the most of your time.

BEACH CLUBS

Much of the coast in this region is quite rocky, and most beaches are pebbly rather than sandy. Bring a pair of beach flip-flops or water shoes to make walking on the beach easier. To make lounging on the rocks more comfortable, many of the beaches have at least one stabilimente balneare (beach club), wooden structures built right on the beach that offer sun beds and umbrella rentals for rent (usually around €10 per person), as well as showers, changing rooms, bathrooms, and usually a snack bar or even a full restaurant. A few stabilimenti balneari also offer kayaks for rent.

FREE AREAS

Although the beach clubs are the most comfortable way to spend a day at the beach, nearly all beaches also have a free area (spiaggia libera), where you can throw down a towel and relax. This is where locals usually are, sometimes fully outfitted for the day with their own umbrellas, chairs, and picnics.

WHEN TO GO

The best time to head to the beach depends on when the sun hits it, but mornings are often nicest, when the beaches are less crowded and the water clearer. The sun is hottest in the early afternoon; if you're going that time of day you might want to rent an umbrella, especially in the hottest months of July and August. In general, beach season begins in late spring and stretches through October—this is when most stabilimenti balneari are open.

BEST BEACHES

- **Amalfi Coast:** Beautiful beach spots are around every corner of the Amalfi Coast, where

Spiaggia di Lama Monachile

you'll find everything from rows of multicolored umbrellas and sun beds to secluded rocky beaches (page 130).

- **Capri:** Enjoy a day at the chic beach clubs that dot the rocky seaside at the base of the Faraglioni (page 187) or soak up the charm of the island's Marina Piccola beach that's popular with locals and visitors alike (page 187).

- **Puglia:** Polignano a Mare's Spiaggia di Lama Monachile (page 229) is picture-perfect, sheltered in a narrow cove, and swimming spots and secluded beaches are around every corner on the Salento coast (page 254).

- **Sicily:** In Sicily a beach is never far away, even in larger cities like Palermo and Taormina, but some of the best stretches of sand are more far-flung, heading west toward Trapani (page 318), and south of Syracuse on the east coast (page 410).

continue south toward the Baroque town of **Lecce** in the heart of the Salento peninsula, your base for two nights. Known as the "Florence of the South," this is where you'll see layers of history as you wander the second-century **Roman Amphitheatre** and the deliriously ornamented 17th-century **Basilica di Santa Croce.** In the evening, enjoy dinner and drinks, sampling this university town's vibrant dining and nightlife scene.

DAY 8: THE SALENTO

Today you'll make a day trip from Lecce to the Salento coast, starting in seaside **Otranto,** Italy's easternmost town. Visit the **Castello Aragonese,** typical of many castles in this region, built to guard the town from attacks by sea, and grab a fresh seafood lunch, followed by a visit to some of Puglia's best beaches and swimming spots, such as the 13-foot-deep (4-m-deep) **Grotta della Poesia.** Sun-kissed and refreshed from your beach day, return to your hotel in Lecce for the night.

Sicily
DAY 9: CATANIA

Drop off your rental car in **Brindisi,** a 35-minute drive from Lecce, and catch a 2-hour flight to Catania-Fontanarossa Airport, where you'll pick up your rental car for the Sicilian portion of your trip. In **Catania,** wake up your senses at the **A' Piscaria** seafood market, not far from the town's **Piazza del Duomo** and impressive **Cattedrale di Sant'Agata.** Admire the basalt architecture of this city built in Mount Etna's shadow, strolling past ancient Roman sites including a theater and thermal baths, to **Villa Bellini,** surrounded by many excellent cafés and bars for getting a pastry or aperitivo.

DAY 10: MOUNT ETNA

Take an excursion to **Mount Etna** today, an hour's drive north of Catania. Depending on your tastes, you can hike to the **volcanic crater** from the Etna Sud visitor center, or sample some volcanic vino at one of the many **wineries** on the volcano's slopes. Consider booking a **wine tour**

---

volcanic crater at Mount Etna

Best Road Trips

Zooming through golden hills and along dramatic coastlines in a tiny Italian car—this is the stuff vacation dreams are made of. Though the legendary traffic and chaotic driving in cities like Naples and Palermo scare many potential road trippers off, there are some beautiful places to drive in Southern Italy, and these are a few of the best.

THE AMALFI COAST ROAD

You've been warned—the twisty, narrow road along the Amalfi Coast, often congested with traffic in the summer, is not for every driver. Still, it's known as one of the world's most beautiful roads for a reason, connecting the picturesque towns and villages built into the cliffs of the coast with stunning views around every turn.

A few tips if you decide to drive this route in your own car: Start out early, or even better, drive in the off-season, when the vistas are just as dramatic. Feel free to take your time, and to pull over where possible to let faster drivers pass; there's no shame in stopping to enjoy the view. If you're lucky enough to be traveling with another experienced driver, take turns so each of you can have time to look out the window. Call ahead with your accommodation to inquire about parking, which can be difficult in summer. And if all else fails, rent a scooter! These maneuverable vehicles are easy to drive and can whisk past traffic.

THE SALENTO

The relatively uncrowded roads of Puglia, connecting tiny hilltop towns through olive and citrus groves, are ideal for a road trip. This is true perhaps nowhere more so than on the Salento coast, where isolated swimming spots and

the Salento coast

tiny villages are impossible to access by public transportation.

COASTAL SICILY

Like Puglia, Sicily's public transportation is a bit less frequent and reliable than in other parts of Italy, and outside of cities, its roads are mercifully uncongested, making this another great place to rent a car for maximum flexibility. Driving along the coast south of Palermo toward Trapani, and south from Syracuse, you'll pass regional parks protecting untouched nature, and secluded beaches that look more Caribbean than Italian.

if you go the latter route. Return to Catania for your final night on Sicily's eastern coast.

DAY 11: VALLE DEI TEMPLI
Today you'll drive 2 hours across the island, making a beeline for the dramatic ruins of the ancient Greek city of Akragas, known as **Valle dei Templi.**

Among the remains of seven impressive temples spread out over 3,000 acres (1,200 ha), the **Temple of Concordia** is the best preserved. Be sure to stop by the **Giardino della Kolymbetra,** built to supply the city of Akragas with water, still a fertile garden to this day. Fifteen minutes' drive from here, the dramatic, terraced limestone beach of **Scala dei**

Outdoor Adventures

There's more to Southern Italy than eating your weight in pasta and hitting the beach. From summiting two of the volcanoes that have dominated the history of the region (and maybe even skiing down one), to kayaking along the Amalfi Coast, hikers will find plenty of great reasons to stretch their legs.

VOLCANIC SLOPES

After indulging on too much pizza and Naples, one of the best ways to get your heart rate up a little is the moderate hike up to Mount Vesuvius (page 94), where you'll get stupendous view of the Bay of Naples and Pompeii and Herculaneum, the settlements that the volcano destroyed in AD 79.

Farther south, you may be surprised to find yourself shivering at the top of Mount Etna, where snow often blankets the slopes and craters. Hike to the almost 11,000-foot (3,000-m) summit (page 364) with a guide, or visit in winter (usually Nov.-Mar. or Apr.) to ski (page 367) at one of two resorts.

HIKING THE AMALFI COAST

Leave the sunbathers and jet-setters far below on some of the Amalfi Coast's most beautiful hikes, such as the Pathway of the Gods (page 129)—so named for the heavenly vistas.

KAYAKING

See vibrant Naples (page 59), captivating Sorrento (page 114), and the Amalfi Coast (page 130) from a different perspective by renting a kayak, floating past grottos and beaches invisible from the main roads.

Turchi is a great place to meditate on all the history that this part of Sicily has seen. For dinner and a much-needed night's sleep, head to the regional hub of Agrigento, a 20-minute drive from the beach.

DAY 12: PALERMO

Three days into your visit to Sicily, you're heading to Palermo, the island's buzzing, vibrant capital, a 2-hour drive north from Agrigento. Get the lay of the land at Quattro Canti, or the "Four Corners," a beautiful Baroque landmark at the main crossroads of Palermo's old town. Nearby, stroll through Piazza Pretoria and the Byzantine church known as La Martorana, before walking south to Mercato di Ballarò for a deep dive into Palermitan street food. Spend the afternoon in the fascinating Palazzo dei Normanni before finding a nearby wine bar for an aperitivo and enjoying dinner at a tucked-away trattoria.

DAY 13: MONREALE CATHEDRAL

A 20-minute drive from Palermo's city center, the stunning Cattedrale di Monreale is a can't-miss UNESCO World Heritage Site, built in the 12th century, when Sicily was under Norman rule. Continue driving west into the Monreale DOC winemaking region, where you can schedule tastings at wineries like Alessandro di Camporeale or Tenuta Sallier de La Tour. Return to Palermo in the early evening with a typically Sicilian passeggiata along the waterfront Foro Italico, heading to Mercato Vucciria just as its alleyways start to bustle with young people drinking, dancing, and snacking on Palermitan street food delicacies.

DAY 14: JOURNEY HOME

Begin your last day in Sicily with breakfast at the oldest coffee roaster in Palermo, Casa Stagnitta, before starting your journey home. For most, this will mean a flight back to Naples or Rome, but the adventurous may want to travel back to Naples by ferry, or perhaps continue their Southern Italian adventures elsewhere.

Tasting Southern Italy

Southern Italy is rich with delicious gastronomic experiences. Stroll through lemon groves, go in search of the best pizza in Naples, or watch pasta being made by hand on the streets of Bari.

Lemons and Lemon Products

The Amalfi Coast's distinctive lemons grow on terraced groves along the coastline and are ubiquitous in the region's cuisine, from pasta sauces to desserts. In Amalfi, the **Amalfi Lemon Experience** tour and cooking classes give you the chance to visit lemon gardens and see **limoncello** being made (page 149).

Neapolitan Pizza

It's no exaggeration to say that pizza today would not exist as we know it—essentially, flatbread topped with tomatoes and cheese—if it weren't for Neapolitan pizza, invented in Naples in 1889. Finding your favorite means stopping in a few of the most iconic pizzerias, like **L'Antica Pizzeria da Michele** (page 65), as well as some of the newer top-ranked spots in the city such as **Pizzaria La Notizia** (page 69).

Seafood

Seafood is the area's true gastronomic specialty, one you'll find highlighted in nearly every restaurant. On the Amalfi Coast, a very localized seafood specialty can be found in Cetara on the Amalfi Coast: alici, or **anchovies,** served fresh and preserved with oil (page 166). You'll find fresh-shucked **ricci di mare** (sea urchin) on Puglia's coast (page 233), and a highlight of a visit to Sicily is Catania's **A' Piscaria fish market** (page 341).

Wine

Wine is grown throughout Southern Italy, but perhaps the most unique place to taste vino is on the slopes of **Mount Etna** (page 368), where the volcanic soil and high elevation lends unique

fried pizza in Naples

ash, sand, and minerals to the grapes. To the west, taste **marsala** in its namesake town (page 322), where this fortified wine is experiencing a resurgence.

Baked Goods

Sweet tooths will be spoiled in Southern Italy. In Naples, start your day with a classic Neapolitan **sfogliatella,** a shell-shaped pastry with citrus-infused ricotta filling (page 68). In Puglia, try hyper-local baked goods like Lecce's cotognata leccese, a quince-paste sweet served at **Bar Cotognata Leccese** (page 247). In Sicily, many bakeries keep alive centuries-old recipes perfected by nuns cloistered in convents; give them a try at **I Segreti del Chiostro** (page 294) or **Pasticceria Maria Grammatico** (page 320).

Street Food

The street food of choice in Naples is, perhaps unsurprisingly, pizza-related; try **pizza fritta,** or fried pizza, at **Sorbillo** (page 65). Street food is a serious business in Palermo, from irresistible **panelle** (fried chickpea fritters) to the more adventurous **pani cà meusa** (spleen and lung sandwich) (page 296). Across the island, Catania has its own street food specialties, including **arancini** (fried rice balls) and **cipolline** pastries stuffed with onions, mozzarella, ham, and tomatoes (page 346).

Cucina Povera

Perhaps nowhere else in Italy is as closely linked to cucina povera, or the philosophy of "poor cooking," than Puglia. Based on creating delicious food with the simplest, best-quality ingredients, see this cooking tradition in action watching pastai (pasta experts) making **orecchiette** by hand in Bari (page 215) or visiting olive groves to sample **olive oil** fresh from the presses (page 226).

tasty treats in Sicily

orecchiette pasta being handmade in Bari, Puglia

Naples and the Ruins

Often described as tumultuous and gritty,

Naples is a fascinating city teeming with vibrant energy and, yes, a touch of chaos. Travelers who get to know this city's dynamic culture and layers of history often find it captures their heart when they least expect it. From royal palaces to castles, world-class museums, and some of Italy's best street food, Naples is unexpected in the best possible ways.

Naples is a city of too many contrasts to describe. One moment you're gazing up at the impressive glass dome of the Galleria Umberto I or admiring Roman statues in the Museo Archeologico Nazionale, and the next scooters are zipping past you down impossibly narrow alleyways as you discover artisans continuing centuries-old craft traditions.

Itinerary Ideas 40

Sights 42

Sports and Recreation. . 59

Entertainment
   and Events. 60

Shopping 61

Food 64

Bars and Nightlife 69

Accommodations 70

Information
   and Services 72

Getting There 73

Getting Around 75

Pompeii 78

Herculaneum 87

Vesuvius 92

Highlights

Look for ★ to find recommended sights, activities, dining, and lodging.

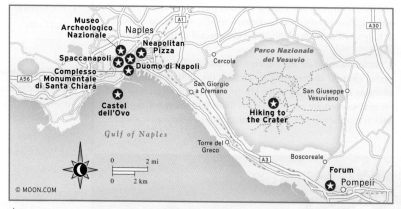

★ **Museo Archeologico Nazionale:** This museum is a must, as it houses one of the finest archaeological collections in the world, including treasures uncovered at the ancient Roman cities of Pompeii and Herculaneum (page 42).

★ **Spaccanapoli:** Walk down this characteristic and vibrant street in the centro storico. Its name means "Split Naples" after the way it cuts a straight line through the historic center (page 46).

★ **Complesso Monumentale di Santa Chiara:** This Gothic church was built by the Angevin rulers of Naples. Don't miss the excellent museum, ancient Roman archaeological site, and famous cloister featuring 18th-century majolica tiles (page 46).

★ **Duomo di Napoli:** The Cathedral of Naples includes the earliest baptistery in the Western world and the Chapel of San Gennaro, the patron saint of Naples (page 48).

★ **Castel dell'Ovo:** The oldest castle in Naples is set right on the waterfront on an islet near the picturesque little harbor of Borgo Marinari (page 52).

★ **Neapolitan Pizza:** Naples is famous as the birthplace of pizza. Enjoy a true Neapolitan experience with a classic pizza Margherita cooked to perfection (page 66).

★ **Forum, Pompeii:** Stand in the middle of what was Pompeii's city center and imagine what everyday life was like for the people who lived here (page 80).

★ **Hiking to the Crater, Vesuvius:** Hike to the summit of Vesuvius to take in panoramic views of the Naples area and the Sorrentine Peninsula (page 94).

What's that delicious scent? There's no need to worry about going hungry in Naples, because no matter where you turn, you won't be far from a pizzeria or the sweet scent of sfogliatelle (shell-shaped pastry filled with citrus infused ricotta) or strong Neapolitan coffee.

While Naples has enough captivating sights and experiences to fill a vacation, it's also a great jumping-off point to explore other popular destinations such as Pompeii and Herculaneum: two of the world's most important archaeological sites, frozen in time by the explosive eruption of Mount Vesuvius in AD 79.

ORIENTATION

Set on the Gulf of Naples, the city of Naples stretches out from the waterfront and flat centro storico (historic center) up into the surrounding hilly landscape.

Centro Storico

The centro storico (historic center) of Naples is rich with beautiful Gothic and baroque churches and fine museums like the **Museo Archeologico Nazionale.** Located over the heart of the ancient Greek and later Roman city, the centro storico runs roughly from Via Toledo (running from Piazza Dante down to the grand Treiste e Trento in the San Ferdinando neighborhood) east to the area around the **Duomo di Napoli.** Among this tight grid of narrow streets, **Spaccanapoli** cuts a straight line through the center of the city. **Napoli Centrale Stazione** is to the east, about 1 mile (1.5 km) away.

In the hills north of the city center, the **Capodimonte** neighborhood is noted especially for its fine **Museo di Capodimonte,** surrounded by a wooded park.

San Ferdinando

Where Via Toledo ends (or starts) to the south of the centro storico lies the San Ferdinando neighborhood, the setting for the grandiose **Galleria Umberto I,** and the **Piazza del Plebiscito.** This has been the political and administrative center of Naples for centuries and the Porto di Napoli is just about half a mile (600 m) to the east. Go from the depths of the city in **Napoli Sotterranea** (Naples Underground) to the heights of Bourbon dynasty at the **Palazzo Reale.**

Waterfront, Chiaia, and Vomero

The waterfront of Naples stretches west from the **Castel dell'Ovo** to the harbor at **Mergellina,** is one of the loveliest spots in the city. South of Piazza del Plebiscito lies the Santa Lucia neighborhood with elegant buildings overlooking the sea, and Castel dell'Ovo and its tiny harbor of Borgo Marinari. Heading west is the stylish **Chiaia** neighborhood, which stretches from the Villa Comunale gardens up the slopes until Vomero. The **Vomero** neighborhood offers bird's-eye views from the **Castel Sant'Elmo** and **Certosa di San Martino.** Several funicular trains connect the Vomero with Chiaia and the historic center.

Pompeii, Herculaneum, and Mount Vesuvius

The ancient ruins of **Pompeii** are fairly evenly situated between Naples and Sorrento, about 20 miles (30 km) southeast of Naples and 15 miles (25 km) northeast of Sorrento. It's easily reached by train from either city. Smaller but equally worth visiting, **Herculaneum** is farther north up the coast of the Gulf of Naples from Pompeii, closer to Naples and also accessible by train. Towering **Mount Vesuvius** is always looming in the distance, whether you're exploring the archaological sites or wandering the streets of Naples; tourist buses connect visitors to the volcanic slopes

---

Previous: view of the city of Naples with famous Mount Vesuvius in the background; ancient Roman ruins at Herculaneum; Gothic revival façade of the Duomo di Napoli.

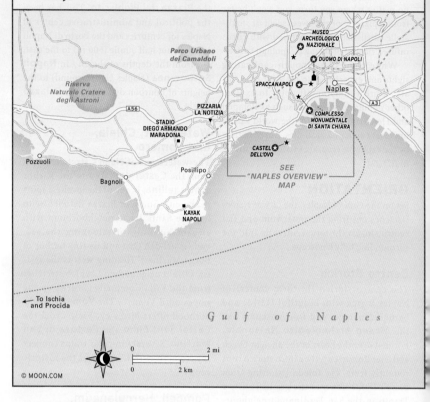

Naples and the Ruins

Parco Urbano dei Camaldoli

Riserva Naturale Cratere degli Astroni

A56

MUSEO ARCHEOLOGICO NAZIONALE

DUOMO DI NAPOLI

SPACCANAPOLI

Naples

A3

PIZZARIA LA NOTIZIA

STADIO DIEGO ARMANDO MARADONA

COMPLESSO MONUMENTALE DI SANTA CHIARA

CASTEL DELL'OVO

Pozzuoli

Posillipo

SEE "NAPLES OVERVIEW" MAP

Bagnoli

KAYAK NAPOLI

To Ischia and Procida

Gulf of Naples

0   2 mi
0   2 km

© MOON.COM

from both Pompeii and Herculaneum's train stations.

PLANNING YOUR TIME

With more than 2,700 years of history and culture to explore, Italy's third-largest city deserves at least two to three days for you to cover just the top sights. Whether you're just visiting for a day or for longer, allow time to explore the centro storico, walk along **Spaccanapoli,** visit the churches and layers of history underground, and enjoy the best pizza in Italy. A longer stay means you'll also have time to explore the city's incredible museums, and time to take the funicular train up to **Vomero** to see the Castel Sant'Elmo and sweeping views across the city and Gulf of Naples.

From the waterfront with romantic views across the gulf to the narrow alleys of the historic center, Naples is a city to be explored. It's also a city that is best seen on foot to get a feel for all its little quirks and its soul. Plan also to spend some time in the **Chiaia** area with its chic shopping and explore the fine collection at the **Museo di Capodimonte.**

That said, in Naples there are plenty of transportation options right at your fingertips, which makes it a convenient base to explore the entire region. You can spend easily up to a week if you plan day trips to popular destinations nearby, such as Pompeii, Herculaneum, Sorrento, or the island of Capri. Ferries depart regularly from Naples's

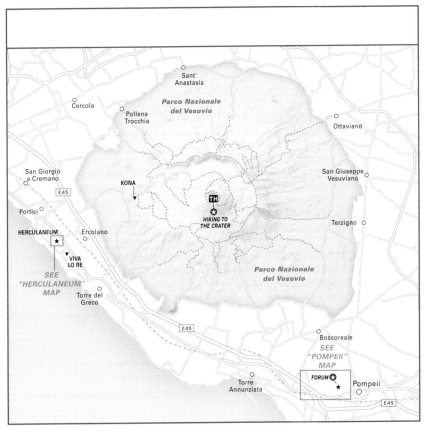

port for Capri and Sorrento, or you can reach Sorrento on the Circumvesuviana commuter train, which includes stops at **Pompeii** and **Herculaneum.**

Though both archaeological sites can be visited in one day, this requires a good deal of walking and there's a lot of ground to cover, especially if you're getting around on public transportation. It's a good idea to take two days of sightseeing if your travel schedule allows, or elect to visit only one of the sites. Pompeii is the popular choice if time only permits one site, because its larger size offers a more complete look at an ancient Roman city. However, Herculaneum has many historical gems and usually less crowded. A visit to either archaeological site can be combined with a visit to Mount Vesuvius.

Sightseeing Passes

The **Campania Artecard** (www.campaniartecard.it) is an excellent sightseeing pass for Naples and sights throughout Campania. It covers many art and cultural sights in Naples, including museums, archaeological sites, churches, and more. The pass also includes access to nearly all public transportation systems. A three-day **Naples Card** (€21 adults, €12 youth ages 18-25) covers only sights in the city, whereas a three-day **Campania Card** (€32 adults, €25 youth age 18-25) covers Naples and all of the region; the latter is the better bet if you plan to visit the archaeological cities of Pompeii and Herculaneum. For longer visits, a seven-day Campania Card (€34 adults) is also available. All of the cards provide free entry to the first two to five sights, depending on the card selected, and then discounts of up to 50 percent are given for admission to subsequent sights. If you plan to visit many sights in Naples or the surrounding area, the Campania Artecard quickly pays for itself.

Itinerary Ideas

In a city with such an extensive history, seeing all the sights in Naples would require a lifetime. Yet the highlights of the city can be enjoyed in a 48-hour tour that covers the essential sights, panoramic views from the best vantage points, and the gastronomic delights of Naples.

TWO DAYS IN NAPLES

Day 1

Day 1 starts with a walking tour through the centro storico (historic center), a stop for pizza for lunch, and a visit to the remarkable Museo Archeologico Nazionale. This neighborhood is incredibly rich with historic sights and rewarding museums. So put on some comfortable walking shoes and set off to discover Naples!

1 Start the day with a walk down **Spaccanapoli** through the most characteristic area of Naples.

2 Stop in **Scaturchio** for a shot of strong Neapolitan espresso.

3 Take a left on Via Duomo to visit the **Duomo di Napoli** (Naples Cathedral) with its sumptuous chapel dedicated to the city's patron saint, San Gennaro.

4 Detour down **Via San Gregorio Armeno** to see artisans selling presepi (nativity scenes).

5 Stop for a pizza break at **Sorbillo** along Via dei Tribunali.

6 After lunch, stop by the **Museo Cappella Sansevero** to see the *Cristo Velato* (Veiled Christ) statue by Giuseppe Sanmartino.

7 Go down Via Santa Maria di Costantinopoli to the world-class **Museo Archeologico Nazionale.**

8 Enjoy an aperitivo and people-watching in **Piazza Bellini,** where nightlife options abound.

Day 2

Day 2 begins high in Vomero and continues down to Piazza del Plebiscito, Palazzo Reale, and the waterfront castles of Naples.

1 Make your way to the **Castel Sant'Elmo** in the Vomero neighborhood for panoramic views.

2 Stop for lunch at **Borbonika Napulitan Restaurant** and enjoy a dish of pasta with traditional genovese (meat) sauce.

3 Head to Piazza Ferdinando Fuga to take the **Funicolare Centrale** train down to the Augusteo stop at the bottom on Via Toledo.

Itinerary Ideas

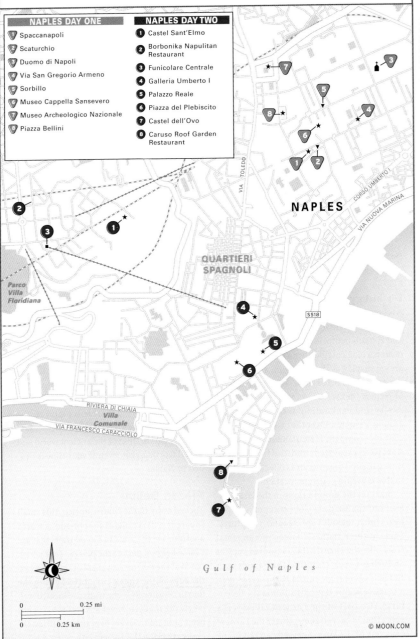

NAPLES DAY ONE
- Spaccanapoli
- Scaturchio
- Duomo di Napoli
- Via San Gregorio Armeno
- Sorbillo
- Museo Cappella Sansevero
- Museo Archeologico Nazionale
- Piazza Bellini

NAPLES DAY TWO
1. Castel Sant'Elmo
2. Borbonika Napulitan Restaurant
3. Funicolare Centrale
4. Galleria Umberto I
5. Palazzo Reale
6. Piazza del Plebiscito
7. Castel dell'Ovo
8. Caruso Roof Garden Restaurant

NAPLES

QUARTIERI SPAGNOLI

Parco Villa Floridiana

VIA TOLEDO

CORSO UMBERTO I

VIA NUOVA MARINA

SS18

RIVIERA DI CHIAIA
Villa Comunale
VIA FRANCESCO CARACCIOLO

Gulf of Naples

0   0.25 mi
0   0.25 km

© MOON.COM

4 Cross Via Toledo and see the **Galleria Umberto I** and stop for a traditional sfogliatella pastry at La Sfogliatella Mary.

5 Across Piazza Trieste e Trento, visit the **Palazzo Reale,** the stunning royal palace of Naples.

6 Admire **Piazza del Plebiscito** and continue along the waterfront to the Borgo Marinari.

7 Climb to the top of **Castel dell'Ovo** for incredible views of the Gulf of Naples with Vesuvius and the island of Capri in the distance.

8 Relax and watch the golden glow of sunset from the **Caruso Roof Garden Restaurant** at the Grand Hotel Vesuvio with views overlooking the gulf and the charming Borgo Marinari below.

Sights

CENTRO STORICO
★ Museo Archeologico Nazionale

Piazza Museo 19; tel. 848/800-288; www. museoarcheologiconapoli.it; 9am-7:30pm Wed.-Mon.; €10

For history lovers, a visit to the Museo Archeologico Nazionale, before or after exploring the ancient Roman towns of Pompeii and Herculaneum, is a must. A treasure trove of archaeological finds from the ancient world are on display at this museum, and many of the objects are here thanks to Bourbon kings of Naples who were fascinated with the discovery and exploration of the ancient sites around Vesuvius. Over the course of the 18th century, Pompeii, Herculaneum, and other sites were excavated, and the finest pieces were gathered together in a collection housed in this museum's current location.

Start on the ground floor in the large galleries of the Farnese Collection of antiquities, which includes spectacular sculptures. Some of these statues are on a monumental scale, like the *Farnese Bull*, a Roman copy of an earlier Greek sculpture that stands over 12 feet (3.7 m) high, or the *Farnese Hercules*, a massive statue dating from the third century. Also part of the Farnese galleries is a collection of carved gems, where the Farnese Cup, one of the largest carved cameos in the

world, is not to be missed. Spread over the ground floor and the first and second floors, the collection of pieces from Campania's archaeological sites is also on display, including mosaics, frescoes, sculptures, the numismatics collection, and a unique room called the Gabinetto Segreto (Secret Cabinet) entirely dedicated to ancient art with an erotic theme. There's also dedicated space with artifacts from prehistoric and protohistoric time, as well as galleries that tell the story of ancient Naples. On the lower level, you'll find a fine Egyptian collection as well.

From exquisitely detailed Roman mosaics to awe-inspiring marble sculptures, the Museo Archeologico Nazionale offers a fascinating exploration of the ancient world and is well worth a visit, even if your time is limited in Naples.

Piazza Bellini

Tucked away in the centro storico, this small square is a lively nightlife spot and is worth a visit to see the ancient Greek walls that are visible below a part of the piazza. Take a look down at the defensive walls that once marked the edge of the Greek city of Neapolis in the fourth century BC. The walls are located well below the modern street level, as the city has been built up in layers over the centuries, literally covering the ancient city.

Naples Overview

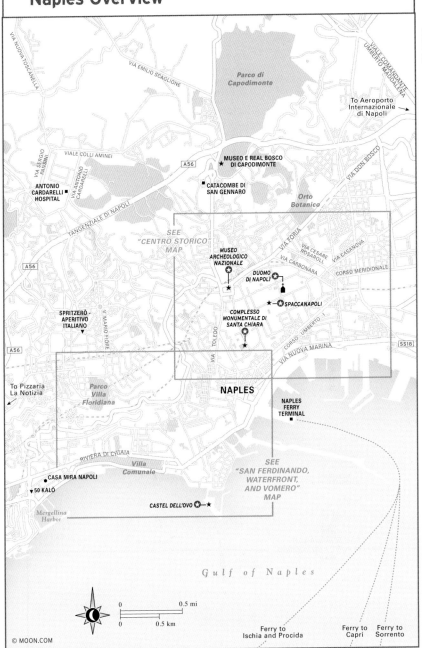

Centro Storico

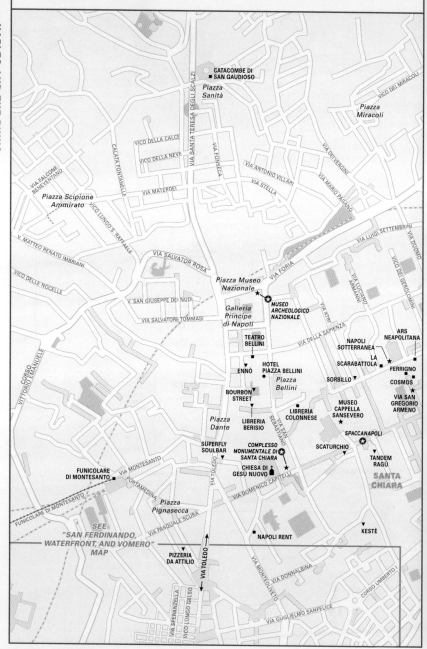

CATACOMBE DI
SAN GAUDIOSO

Piazza
Sanità

Piazza
Miracoli

VICO DEI MIRACOLI

CALATA FONTANELLE

VICO DELLA CALCE

VICO DELLA NEVE

VIA SANTA TERESA DEGLI SCALZI

VIA FONSECA

VIA ANTONIO VILLARI

VIA STELLA

VIA DEI VERGINI

VIA MARIO PAGANO

VIA FALCONE
BENEVENTANO

VIA MATERDEI

Piazza Scipione
Ammirato

VICO LUNGO S. RAFFAELE

V. MATTEO RENATO IMBRIANI

VIA SALVATOR ROSA

VIA LUIGI SETTEMBRINI

VICO DEL MIRACOLI

VIA DUOMO

VICO DELLE NOCELLE

V. SAN GIUSEPPE DEI NUDI

VIA SALVATORE TOMMASI

Piazza Museo
Nazionale

VIA FORIA

VIA LUCIANO
ARMANNI

VICO DE GEROLOMINI

Galleria
Principe
di Napoli

MUSEO
ARCHEOLOGICO
NAZIONALE

VIA ATRI

VIA DELLA SAPIENZA

NAPOLI
SOTTERRANEA

ARS
NEAPOLITANA

TEATRO
BELLINI

ENNÒ

HOTEL
PIAZZA BELLINI

Piazza
Bellini

LA
SCARABATTOLA

SORBILLO

FERRIGNO

COSMOS

CORSO VITTORIO EMANUELE

BOURBON
STREET

Piazza
Dante

LIBRERIA
BERISIO

LIBRERIA
COLONNESE

VIA SAN SEBASTIANO

MUSEO
CAPPELLA
SANSEVERO

VIA SAN
GREGORIO
ARMENO

SPACCANAPOLI

SUPERFLY
SOULBAR

COMPLESSO
MONUMENTALE DI
SANTA CHIARA

SCATURCHIO

FUNICOLARE
DI MONTESANTO

VIA MONTESANTO

PORTAMEDINA

CHIESA DI
GESÙ NUOVO

TANDEM
RAGÙ

SANTA
CHIARA

FUNICOLARE DI MONTESANTO

Piazza
Pignasecca

VIA PASQUALE SCURA

VIA DOMENICO CAPITELLI

VIA TOLEDO

SEE
"SAN FERDINANDO,
WATERFRONT, AND VOMERO"
MAP

NAPOLI RENT

VIA MONTEOLIVETO

KESTÈ

PIZZERIA
DA ATTILIO

VIA TOLEDO

VIA DONNALBINA

VIA GUGLIELMO SANFELICE

CORSO UMBERTO I

VIA SPERANZELLA

VICO LUNGO GELSO

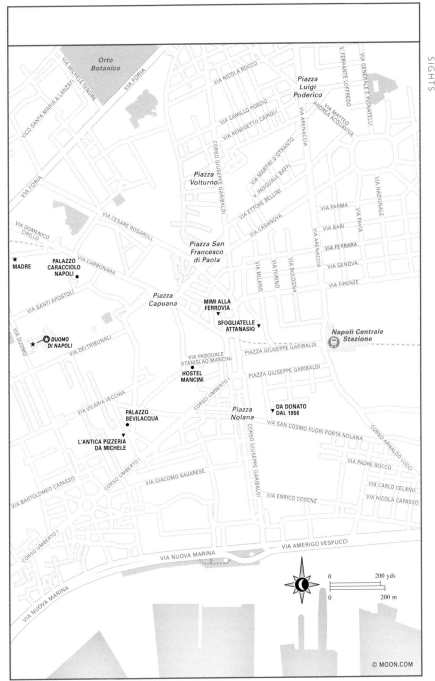

Orto Botanico

VIA MICHELE TENORE

VICO SANTA MARIA A LANZATI

VIA FORIA

VIA FORIA

VIA NICOLA ROCCO

Piazza Luigi Poderico

V. FERRANTE LOFFREDO

VIA GENERALE F. PIGNATELLI

VIA CAMILLO PORZIO

VIA MATTEO ANDREA ACQUAVIVA

VIA BENEDETTO CAIROLI

CORSO GIUSEPPE GARIBALDI

VIA ARENACCIA

Piazza Volturno

VIA MARTIRI D'OTRANTO

V. PASQUALE BAFFI

VIA ETTORE BELLINI

VIA NAZIONALE

VIA DOMENICO CIRILLO

VIA CESARE ROSAROLL

VIA CASANOVA

VIA PARMA

VIA PAVA

VIA BARI

VIA FERRARA

VIA ARENACCIA

VIA GENOVA

Piazza San Francesco di Paola

VIA CARBONARA

VIA MILANO

VIA TORINO

VIA BOLOGNA

VIA FIRENZE

★ MADRE

★ PALAZZO CARACCIOLO NAPOLI ●

VIA SANTI APOSTOLI

Piazza Capuana

MIMI ALLA FERROVIA ▼

SFOGLIATELLE ATTANASIO ▼

🅿 **Napoli Centrale Stazione**

VIA DUOMO

★ ✪ DUOMO DI NAPOLI

VIA DEI TRIBUNALI

PIAZZA GIUSEPPE GARIBALDI

VIA PASQUALE STANISLAO MANCINI

HOSTEL MANCINI ●

PIAZZA GIUSEPPE GARIBALDI

VIA VICARIA VECCHIA

CORSO UMBERTO I

Piazza Nolana

▼ **DA DONATO DAL 1956**

PALAZZO BEVILACQUA ●

CORSO ARNALDO LUCCI

VIA SAN COSMO FUORI PORTA NOLANA

L'ANTICA PIZZERIA DA MICHELE ●

CORSO GIUSEPPE GARIBALDI

VIA PADRE ROCCO

CORSO UMBERTO I

VIA GIACOMO SAVARESE

VIA ENRICO COSENZ

VIA CARLO CELANO

VIA NICOLA CAPASSO

VIA BARTOLOMEO CAPASSO

VIA NUOVA MARINA

VIA AMERIGO VESPUCCI

CORSO UMBERTO I

VIA NUOVA MARINA

| 0 | 200 yds |
| 0 | 200 m |

© MOON.COM

★ Spaccanapoli

Via Benedetto Croce and Via San Biagio dei Librai,
from Piazza Gesù Nuovo to Via Duomo

Running through the heart of Naples's historic center, Spaccanapoli is the popular name for a very straight and long street. Literally meaning "Split Naples," it takes its name from the way it cuts down the middle of the city. Starting in Piazza del Gesù Nuovo, the street now is labeled Via Benedetto Croce, which then becomes Via San Biagio dei Librai until it crosses Via Duomo. Spaccanapoli is the lower, or southernmost, of the three decumani, or main streets that date back to the Greek and Roman city. The two parallel streets, Via dei Tribunali and Via Sapienza/Via Anticaglia, form the upper two decumani, and all three are crossed by a grid of streets that form the backbone of the ancient city that is still visible today. A stroll down Spaccanapoli is a must, not only to take in the ethos of Naples that is so perfectly captured here but also to see many of the city's most important churches and historic monuments in a very short distance. The streets in the historic center are narrow and can be crowded, especially during the lead up to the Christmas season with so many people heading toward Via San Gregorio Armeno to see the Christmas nativity workshops.

Chiesa di Gesù Nuovo

Piazza del Gesù Nuovo 2; tel. 081/557-8111; www.
gesunuovo.it; 7am-1pm and 4pm-8pm daily; free

The beautiful Piazza del Gesù Nuovo is one of the city's loveliest, with its ornate Guglia dell'Immacolata (Spire of the Immaculate, an 18th-century decorative obelisk), elegant palazzos, and the very striking facade of the Chiesa di Gesù Nuovo. Its dark gray stone facade is almost completely covered with carved pyramid-shaped projections, an imposing design that reflects the building's origins as a private palazzo in the 15th century. The Jesuits later confiscated the building, completely gutted the inside, and transformed the space into an architectural and artistic treasure. Inside you'll find artworks by some of the most important Neapolitan artists of the 17th century, including Luca Giordano, Francesco Solimena, and Giovanni Lanfranco. The church is free to visit and worth the time to admire the resplendent interior and explore the highly decorated chapels.

★ Complesso Monumentale di Santa Chiara

Via Santa Chiara 49c; tel. 081/551-6673; www.
monasterodisantachiara.it; 9:30am-5:30pm
Mon.-Sat. and 10am-2:30pm Sun.; €6

At the edge of Piazza del Gesù Nuovo sits the monumental religious complex of the Basilica di Santa Chiara. Built in the early 14th century, the basilica has a stark Gothic facade that stands in striking contrast to the Chiesa di Gesù Nuovo across the piazza. Near the entrance stands a tall bell tower, which also dates from the 14th century yet shows baroque decorations from a later restoration. The church itself was also restored during the baroque period, yet was unfortunately almost completely destroyed by World War II bombardments. After the war, the church was rebuilt in a style to recapture the majestic beauty of the original Gothic design. The chapels along the nave hold tombs of aristocratic Neapolitan families and Angevin sovereigns from the 14th-15th centuries. Behind the main altar is the intricately carved Gothic-style tomb of King Robert of Anjou, created by Florentine sculptors Giovanni and Pacio Bertini in the 14th century.

The monastery features three cloisters. The most remarkable is the Chiostro Maiolicato (Majolica Cloister), which was designed by Domenico Vaccaro from 1739 to 1742 and includes beautiful hand-painted majolica tiles on the 64 octagonal pillars and benches throughout the cloister. Look closely at the benches, which feature a series of scenes from daily life in the 18th century. Off the cloister, look for the room with the large Neapolitan presepe (nativity) from the 1700s-1800s.

Beyond the cloister is the Museo

1: orange trees in the courtyard of Complesso Monumentale di Santa Chiara 2: Chiesa di Santa Chiara and Piazza del Gesù Nuovo

dell'Opera, which houses a collection of religious artworks saved from the church and archaeological finds from excavations on the site. Part of the museum includes ruins of a Roman bath complex, dating from the first century AD, that were discovered during restorations after World War II.

Museo Cappella Sansevero

Via Francesco De Sanctis 19/21; tel. 081/551-8470; www.museosansevero.it; 9am-7pm Wed.-Mon.; €8

For its intensity and artistic masterpieces, the small Cappella Sansevero is a jewel of Neapolitan baroque design. With pride of place in the center of the chapel is the remarkable *Cristo Velato* (Veiled Christ) statue by Giuseppe Sanmartino. This marble sculpture from 1753 depicts Christ after being taken down from the cross and covered with a sheet. It is so finely carved as to capture the pain and suffering of Christ through the incredible lightness of the sheet. While this fine statue is utterly captivating, the rest of the museum, featuring works by the most prominent 18th-century sculptors and artists, is no less worthy of attention.

★ Duomo di Napoli

Via Duomo 147; tel. 081/449-087;

www.chiesadinapoli.it; 8:30am-1:30pm and 4:30pm-7:30pm daily; free to enter cathedral, €2 to visit baptistery

In a city with no shortage of impressive religious sights, the Duomo (Cathedral of Naples) holds an important place not only as the largest and most important church in the city, but also for its strong connection to Neapolitan traditions and life. Behind the Gothic-revival facade designed by Neapolitan architect Errico Alvino at the end of the 1800s lies a church with layers of history dating back to the 13th century, when the Gothic cathedral was built. Over the centuries the cathedral was rebuilt, expanded, and decorated in a variety of different styles that blend together to tell the story of art in Naples from the 13th to the 19th century. The central nave soars to about 157 feet (48 m) and combines Gothic elements with later baroque decorations and a coffered and gilded 17th-century ceiling with painted panels. On the upper band of the nave are paintings by celebrated Neapolitan artist Luca Giordano depicting the Apostles and Doctors of the church, and on the lower band are round portraits of important patron saints of Naples.

To the left of the entrance is a large chapel that was once the Basilica of Santa

the dome of Duomo di Napoli

Underground Naples

Descend deep down below the busy streets of Naples and you can explore layers upon layers of history. There is so much history here that there are not one, but two, great tour companies in the city just waiting to take you beneath the surface: one under Piazza San Gaetano in the centro storico, which was built on the exact location of the Greek agora and later the Roman forum of Neapolis; and one located not far from Piazza Trieste e Trento and the historic Bar Gambrinus. You can see caves excavated in the fourth century BC by the Greeks, later used for cisterns for the city's water supply; the remains of a Roman theater and city; World War II air raid shelters; and more. Tours last about an hour and include steps, and some passageways can be quite narrow and dark. Comfortable shoes are a good idea. Advance reservation is not necessary.

- **Napoli Sotterranea:** Piazza San Gaetano 68; tel. 081/296-944; www.napolisotterranea. org; tours 10am-6pm daily; €10

- **Napoli Sotterranea, L.A.E.S.:** Vico S. Anna di Palazzo 52; tel. 081/400-256; www. lanapolisotterranea.it; first tour 10am Sat.-Sun., noon Mon.-Fri. daily.; €10

Restituta dating to the fourth century, offering an interesting look at early Christian architecture. Don't miss the **Battistero di San Giovanni in Fonte,** a Byzantine baptistery that is the oldest surviving in the Western world. The baptistery is open 8:30am-12:30pm and 2:30pm-6:30pm Monday-Friday, and 8:30am-1pm Sunday. As in much of the centro storico, the history below the Duomo dates back to Greek and Roman times. Archaeological excavation has uncovered a Greek street made of tufa with traces of cart wheels carved into the stone, beautiful Roman mosaics, and architectural ruins. Unfortunately, the archaeological area below the Duomo is closed indefinitely for restoration.

The heart and soul of the Duomo is the gleaming **Reale Cappella del Tesoro di San Gennaro,** a sumptuous baroque chapel built in the early 17th century. Dedicated to the city's patron saint and protector San Gennaro, the chapel holds artifacts, reliquaries, and the much-treasured vial of the saint's blood that, faithful say, miraculously liquefies three times a year (first Sun. in May, Sept. 19, and Dec. 16). Besides the chapel, take time to visit the **Museo del Tesoro di San Gennaro** (Via Duomo 149; tel. 081/294-980; www.museosangennaro.it; 9am-4:30pm Mon.-Fri., 9am-5:30pm Sat.-Sun.; €5) to see

the collection of exquisite religious silver objects, textiles, jewels, sculptures, and artwork.

Madre

Via Luigi Settembrini 79; tel. 081/197-37254; www. madrenapoli.it; 10am-7:30pm Mon. and Wed.-Sat., 10am-7:30pm and 10am-8pm Sun.; €8

Located in the 19th-century Palazzo Donnaregina, the Madre (Museo d'Arte Contemporanea Donnaregina) museum has a fine collection of contemporary art. The permanent collection, exhibitions, and educational spaces are spread across three floors and 77,500 square feet (7,200 square m). With a unique juxtaposition of historic and modern architectural styles, the collection includes works by the biggest names in Italian and international art from the past 50 years, including Mimmo Paladino, Richard Serra, Sol LeWitt, Francesco Clemente, Jeff Koons, Anish Kapoor, and many more.

CAPODIMONTE

Once a rural area in hills north of Naples, the Capodimonte area saw many changes during the 18th century, including the construction of the royal palace and development of expansive gardens and woods. Despite the treasures housed in the Museo di Capodimonte and the tranquility of the setting, the area was not particularly well connected to the city center until the early 1800s, when a long, straight road and bridge were built over the Sanità neighborhood. Today a visit to Capodimonte is a must for art lovers, but don't miss exploring the area's catacombs as well.

Museo e Real Bosco di Capodimonte

Via Miano 2; tel. 081/749-9111; www. museocapodimonte.beniculturali.it; 8:30am-7:30pm Thurs.-Tues.; €10

In the hills above Naples, the Museo e Real Bosco di Capodimonte was built in the 18th century by the Bourbon king Carlo III as a royal palace set amid a lush forest perfect for hunting. It was also intended from the beginning as the setting for the marvelous art collection belonging to Elisabetta Farnese, the mother of Carlo III. Today the Farnese Collection is the heart of the museum, which includes works by Titian, Botticelli, Raphael, and Caravaggio, to name only a selection of the highlights. One of the largest art museums in Italy, Capodimonte also houses an excellent collection of paintings and sculptures from the 13th-18th centuries. Decorative art enthusiasts will enjoy the elegant Royal Apartments and extensive porcelain collection, as well as the remarkable Salottino di Porcellana, an 18th-century rococo-style salon decorated with delicately painted porcelain. To complete the incredible walk through art history, the museum also includes a gallery dedicated to the 1800s and a contemporary art collection.

SAN FERDINANDO
Castel Nuovo

Piazza Municipio; tel. 081/795-7722; www.comune. napoli.it; 9am-7pm Mon.-Sat.; €6

Sitting grandly on the waterfront, the imposing Castel Nuovo, also called the Maschio Angioino, is a castle dating from the late 13th century. Built by the French King Charles I of Anjou, it was later expanded under the Aragonese control of the city. The stunning Triumphal Arch with marble bas-reliefs at the entrance dates from the Aragonese period. Entering through the massive bronze gates, look for the cannonball still embedded in one of the gates, a reminder of the battles this castle has seen over its long history. The view inside the courtyard is an impressive sight. Don't miss the **Cappella Palatina** from the 14th century, **Sala dell'Armeria** (armory), and the **Museo Civico** (Civic Museum), displaying artwork from the medieval period to the late 1800s.

Palazzo Reale

Piazza del Plebiscito 1; tel. 081/580-8255; www. beniculturali.it/luogo/palazzo-reale-di-napoli; 9am-8pm Thurs.-Tues.; €6

Occupying appropriately fine waterfront real estate, the Palazzo Reale is the royal palace of Naples and was built starting at the beginning of the 17th century for Spanish royalty. Originally designed by noted architect Domenico Fontana, the palace has changed in many ways over the years, including the addition of the grand entrance staircase. Standing in the immense Scalone d'onore (Staircase of Honor), it's hard to imagine an entryway more impressive with its multiple types of marble, soaring ceiling, and sober yet regal neoclassical design. Following the grand hallways, it's possible to visit the 17th-century Cappella Palatina (Palantine Chapel) and a series of grand royal apartment rooms, including the throne room, all beautifully decorated with historic furniture and artwork from the days of Bourbon rule in Naples. With its frescoes and outstanding sculptural work, the court theater is a sparkling gem, designed by architect Ferdinando Fuga to celebrate the marriage of Ferdinand IV to Maria Carolina of Austria in 1768. An audio guide, available in English, is included with the ticket price and brings the history of the state apartments and richness of the decor and artwork on display to life.

1: Piazza del Plebiscito and the Basilica di San Francesco di Paola 2: Palazzo Reale 3: Castel Nuovo 4: glass domed shopping center Galleria Umberto I

Piazza del Plebiscito

The largest piazza in Naples, and one of the largest in Italy, Piazza del Plebiscito is where much of the city's history has played out over the centuries. Opening from Piazza Trieste e Trento, the large piazza is an impressive sight with the **Palazzo Reale** on the left and a glimpse of the sea in the distance. Two large equestrian statues stand in the piazza, one representing Bourbon king Carlo III and the other his son Ferdinando I. While firmly rooted in the city's royal past, the name Piazza del Plebiscito today refers to the referendum, or plebiscite, in 1860, when the Kingdom of Two Sicilies was annexed to the Kingdom of Italy during the unification. While the Piazza del Plebiscito is occasionally the setting for concerts and events, the rest of the time the large open piazza is a popular spot for kids to run and play, and for locals to enjoy a walk away from the traffic and hustle and bustle of the city.

Galleria Umberto I

Via San Carlo 15; www.comune.napoli.it; open 24 hours

The distinctive soaring glass and metal ribbed dome of the Galleria Umberto I is an arresting sight amid the urban landscape of Naples. Built at the end of the 19th century, the Galleria was a key part of the city's revival and regeneration, called the Risanamento (Restoration), which saw massive changes in the historic center. Located across the street from the Teatro di San Carlo, the Galleria was envisioned as a public space that would bring together shops, cafés, and living with private apartments on the upper floor. The architectural style is reminiscent of the Galleria Vittorio Emanuele II in Milan. The glass dome rises to 187 feet (57 m) and is an impressive sight, especially when you stand below the central dome where a large mosaic in the floor depicts the zodiac signs. The ground level has shops and simple restaurants and cafés.

The best way to experience the Galleria is to find a spot and simply look up to admire the incredible level of architectural detail and the richness of the decor, with its decorative arched windows, rows of columns, and ornate friezes and sculptures. The Galleria was built to impress in the late 19th century and is still a splendid sight today.

Galleria Borbonica

Vico del Grottone 4; tel. 081/764-5808; www. galleriaborbonica.com; tours Fri.-Sun.; €10-15

Built in the mid-19th century at the request of King Ferdinando II, this massive tunnel was created to connect the Palazzo Reale to the military barracks and sea on the other side of Monte Erchie. Opened in 1855 after three years of work that was all done by hand with picks, hammers, and wedges, the tunnel has served many purposes over the years. During World War II, the tunnel and nearby cisterns were used for shelter by 5,000-10,000 Neapolitans during the extensive German and Allied bombings of the city. It's possible to visit the tunnel on four different themed tours, from a standard tour offering a glimpse of the highlights to an adventure tour complete with helmet and flashlight, or a speleological tour for a unique experience deep underground in Naples. Tours are available throughout the day and last 1-1.5 hours. The standard tour doesn't require reservations, but more specialized tours need to be booked in advance. Tickets can be purchased online.

WATERFRONT
★ Castel dell'Ovo

Borgo Marinari; tel. 081/795-4592; www.comune. napoli.it; 9am-7:30pm Mon.-Sat. (closes 6:30pm in winter), 9am-2pm Sun.; free

One of Naples's most scenic and historic spots, the Castel dell'Ovo sits on an islet jutting out into the gulf south of Santa Lucia. The earliest Greek settlers landed on this spot and named the island Megaride. Over the centuries it has been a lavish Roman villa, a monastery in the fifth century, and the castle we see today. Legend says the name, meaning Castle of the Egg, comes from the story that the Roman poet Virgil buried an egg below where the castle stands today. The legend says as long as the egg remains unbroken the castle will stand and Naples will be safe. The castle itself is a fascinating amalgam of styles as it was modified by many rulers of the city since it was first built by the Normans in the 12th century. The castle today largely dates from the Aragonese rulers of Naples in the 15th century. Climb to the top of the castle's terraces for a panoramic view of the Gulf of Naples.

A small causeway leads out to the Castel dell'Ovo and offers an extraordinary up-close view of the castle and the charming **Borgo Marinari,** a small harbor at the base of the castle. An old-world fishing village atmosphere, with boats bobbing in the harbor and seaside restaurants, makes this an especially romantic spot for dinner.

Villa Comunale

Via Francesco Caracciolo and Riviera di Chiaia from
Piazza Vittoria to Piazza della Repubblica

Stretching along the waterfront in Chiaia from just west of the Borgo Marinari to Piazza della Repubblica, this large public garden along the **lungomare** (waterfront) offers green space and a place to stroll by the sea. The sprawling gardens were originally designed by Carlo Vanvitelli from 1778-1780 for the private use of the royal family of King Ferdinand IV. Following the unification of Italy, the gardens were opened to the public and renamed the Villa Comunale in 1869. The gardens are dotted with statues, sculptures, and an ornate art nouveau cast-iron and glass bandstand designed by Errico Alvino in 1887. In the center of the gardens you'll find the **Stazione Zoologica Anton Dohrn** (tel. 081/583-3111; www.szn.it; closed for maintenance), which was founded in 1872 and houses the oldest aquarium in Europe.

Mergellina

Mergellina Harbor

At the base of the hill leading up to Posillipo, this small harbor is a picturesque spot along the waterfront in Naples. Once a small fishing village, it was absorbed into the city as it expanded in the 17th century. As the beach area that once ran along the Villa Comunale was transformed into gardens and eventually paved for Via Francesco Caracciolo, the fishing boats once located along the beach were moved toward the Mergellina marina. Now more of a seaside tourist spot than a place for fishing boats, this area is lovely for a stroll along the harbor to enjoy the excellent view of the Naples waterfront with Mount Vesuvius in the distance. A great viewpoint is from the **Fontana del Sebeto,** a large fountain originally designed by Cosimo Fanzago in 1635. At the heart of the statue is an old man representing the Sebeto river, the ancient river that flowed through Naples.

The harbor is also a departure point for ferries to Ischia, Sicily's Aeolian Islands, and the Pontine islands of Ponza and Ventotene.

VOMERO
Castel Sant'Elmo

Via Tito Angelini 22; tel. 081/558-7708; www.musei.
campania.beniculturali.it; 8:30am-7:30pm daily; €5

Sitting atop the San Martino hill, the Castel Sant'Elmo is perfectly situated to take in views of the city of Naples and the entire Gulf of Naples. Naturally, with such a fine view, it has been the spot for an overlook for centuries. The original construction on this site goes back to the 1200s when the Normans built a fortified residence called Belforte. Expanded and modified many times, the unique hexagonal star-shaped design we see today dates from the 16th century under Spanish rule. From 1860 to 1952, the castle was a military prison and then continued to be used for military purposes until 1976. After an extensive restoration, the castle was transformed into a space for the public to enjoy and visit. It's possible to explore many areas of the castle, which often hosts art exhibitions and events. The **Museo del Novecento** (9:30am-5pm Wed.-Mon.) in the castle is dedicated to 20th-century Neapolitan art. Don't miss the views overlooking the Certosa di San Martino and the Gulf of Naples

San Ferdinando, Waterfront, and Vomero

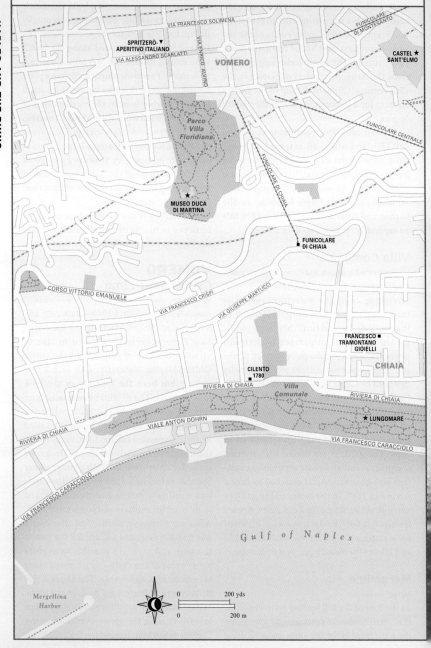

VIA FRANCESCO SOLIMENA

FUNICOLARE DI MONTESANTO

SPRITZERÒ-
APERITIVO ITALIANO
VIA ALESSANDRO SCARLATTI

VIA ENRICO ALVINO

VOMERO

CASTEL ★
SANT'ELMO

Parco
Villa
Floridiana

FUNICOLARE CENTRALE

FUNICOLARE DI CHIAIA

MUSEO DUCA ★
DI MARTINA

FUNICOLARE ■
DI CHIAIA

CORSO VITTORIO EMANUELE

VIA FRANCESCO CRISPI

VIA GIUSEPPE MARTUCCI

FRANCESCO ■
TRAMONTANO
GIOIELLI

CHIAIA

CILENTO ■
1780

RIVIERA DI CHIAIA

Villa
Comunale

RIVIERA DI CHIAIA

RIVIERA DI CHIAIA

★ LUNGOMARE

VIALE ANTON DOHRN

VIA FRANCESCO CARACCIOLO

VIA FRANCESCO CARACCIOLO

Gulf of Naples

Mergellina
Harbor

0   200 yds

0   200 m

55

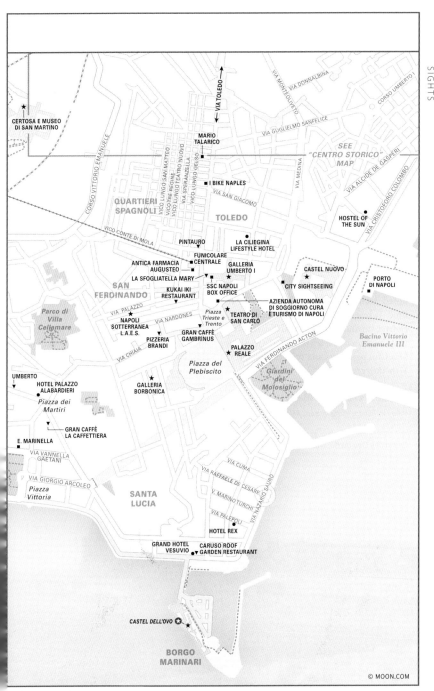

from a variety of different lookout points on the castle walls.

Certosa e Museo di San Martino

Largo San Martino 5; tel. 081/229-4503; www. musei.campania.beniculturali.it; 8:30am-7:30pm Thurs.-Sat. and Mon.-Tues., 8:30am-5pm Sun.; €6

Easily spotted atop Vomero hill next to the Castel Sant'Elmo, the Certosa di San Martino is a former Carthusian monastery, now a museum with a remarkable art collection. Visit to explore excellent examples of work by important Neapolitan painters from the 1800s, decorative arts, and historic presepi (nativities), and to admire the spectacular view over the Gulf of Naples. Although founded in the 14th century, the Certosa has a baroque design that dates to the mid 1600s and is the work of Cosimo Fanzago, the most noted architect working in Naples at the time. Take a stroll around the stunning large cloister surrounded by 60 marble arches and visit the church that is a museum in itself with beautiful paintings and sculptures from the 17th-18th centuries.

Museo Duca di Martina

Villa Floridiana, Via Cimarosa 77; tel. 081/578-8418; *www.musei.campania.beniculturali.it; 9:30am-5pm Wed.-Mon.; €4*

For decorative arts enthusiasts, a visit to the Museo Duca di Martina is a special experience while in Naples. This small house museum is located in the Villa Floridiana, a stunning neoclassical villa built on the slopes of Vomero for Lucia Migliaccio, the Duchess of Floridia, who was the second wife of King Ferdinand I. Surrounded by a lush park, the villa is at its most impressive on the south side, where a grand staircase leads down into the gardens with a view to the sea. Since 1931, the villa has been the home of the Museo Duca di Martina, which houses one of the finest collections of decorative arts in Italy. Created by Placido de Sangro, Duke of Martina, the massive collection of more than 6,000 objects dating from the 12th-19th centuries was donated to the city of Naples in 1911. The museum's collection is spread across three floors of the villa and includes Chinese porcelain and eastern objects on the lowest level; ivories, corals, and majolica from the Middle Ages to the Renaissance and baroque periods on the ground floor; and an incredible collection of 18th-century porcelain on the first floor.

Castel dell'Ovo on the waterfront of Naples

The Best of Ischia and Procida

Marina Corricella in Procida

Slightly less known than Capri, their glamorous sister to the south, the islands of Ischia and Procida sit just over 20 miles (about 30 km) west of Naples. These small, rugged islands—Ischia measures 18 square miles (about 50 square km), while tiny Procida is just 1.4 square miles (3.7 square km)—are known for their rugged natural beauty and historic charm, great alternatives to Capri for a relaxing holiday surrounded by nature.

HIGHLIGHTS

On **Ischia,** exploring the medieval **Castello Aragonese** (tel. 081/992-834; www.castelloaragoneseischia.com; 9am-sunset daily; €10) and the seaside village of **Sant'Angelo** are unforgettable experiences, but it's the **thermal spas** that have been bringing visitors here for centuries. The **Giardini Poseidon Terme** (Via Giovanni Mazzella 338; tel. 081/908-7111; www.giardiniposeidonterme.com; 9am-7pm daily mid-Apr.-Oct. 1, 9am-6:30pm daily Oct. 2-31; from €35 per person) offers the most pools, with private beach access and beautiful gardens.

A short ferry ride away, the small island of **Procida** is easily explored on a day trip from Ischia or Naples. Meander through the medieval **Terra Murata** village at the island's highest point and enjoy leisurely lunches among the pastel-hued buildings and fishing boats of **Marina Corricella.**

GETTING THERE

With ferries arriving from Naples, Sorrento, and other islands in the Gulf of Naples, Ischia is easy to reach. The majority of ferries arrive in **Ischia Porto,** though they also go to the towns of **Casamicciola Terme** and **Forio.** Ferry companies serving Ischia include **Caremar** (www.caremar.it), **SNAV** (www.snav.it), **Medmar** (www.medmargroup.it), **Alilauro** (www.alilaurogruson.it), and **Alicost** (www.alicost.it). It's possible to bring your rental car to Ischia, but you should check in advance with the rental agency before taking your car on a ferry. That said, it's often easier to hop around the island by taxi or on public buses operated by **EAV** (www.eavsrl.it). All ferries to Procida arrive from Ischia in the island's **Marina Grande** port.

For more information, the **Azienda Autonoma Di Cura Soggiorno e Turismo delle Isole di Ischia e Procida** (Via Iasolino 7; tel. 081/507-4231; www.infoischiaprocida.it; 9am-1:30pm and 3pm-8pm daily May-Oct., 9am-1:30pm Mon.-Fri. Nov.-Apr) is the main tourist office serving all of Ischia and Procida, located right in Ischia Porto, where ferries arrive.

Visiting the Catacombs of Naples

inside the Catacombe di San Gennaro

While in many places the traces of early Christianity have long since been covered with layers upon layers of history, in Naples the catacombs offer a chance to see some of the earliest records of its arrival in the city. The majority of the city's catacombs are located between the historic center and Capodimonte in the Rione Sanità neighborhood, and near the Museo di Capodimonte. Both of the catacombs below are managed by the Catacombe di Napoli organization, and the €9 entrance fee covers both sights. You pay at the first one you visit, and your ticket gives you free access to the other sight. Guided tours are available in English hourly, and written information in English is also available at both catacombs.

CATACOMBE DI SAN GENNARO
Via Capodimonte 13; tel. 081/744-3714; www.catacombedinapoli.it; 10am-5pm Mon.-Sat., 10am-2pm Sun.; €9, includes admission to San Gaudioso
Located below the Basilica della Madre del Buon Consiglio, the Catacombe di San Gennaro is one of the oldest and most important catacomb sites to visit. The paleo-Christian burial area held a strong religious significance when San Gennaro was buried here in the fifth century. Divided into two levels and carved out of tufa rock, the catacombs offer the chance to see the different types of tombs, early chapels, and artwork from pagan designs, from second-century works to Byzantine paintings from the 9th-10th centuries.

CATACOMBE DI SAN GAUDIOSO
Basilica Santa Maria della Sanità, Piazza Sanità 14; tel. 081/744-3714; www.catacombedinapoli.it; 10am-1pm Fri.-Sun.; €9, includes admission to San Gennaro
Inside the Basilica Santa Maria della Sanità is the entrance to the fascinating Catacombe di San Gaudioso. Dating from the fourth-fifth centuries, these catacombs are the second largest in Naples, after the Catacombe di San Gennaro. The catacombs contain preserved frescoes and mosaics from the fifth-sixth centuries, displaying early Christian symbols, including the lamb, fish, and grapevines. Abandoned during the late Middle Ages, the catacombs were rediscovered and used as a burial site again in the 16th century. To preserve and honor the location, builders constructed the basilica above in the early 17th century with a beautiful baroque design by Fra Nuvolo.

Sports and Recreation

There are fun biking and kayaking tours for those looking for more active ways to explore the urban landscape or enjoy views of the city from the Gulf of Naples. Soccer is the main sport in Naples and one the Neapolitans are very passionate about. For soccer enthusiasts, catching a game with the locals can be an exciting experience.

BIKING

I BIKE NAPLES

Via Toledo 317; tel. 081/419-528; www.ibikenaples.it; tours daily; from €40 per person

Though Naples is known for its chaotic traffic, don't let that stop you from exploring the city on two wheels if you enjoy a biking adventure. I Bike Naples offers small-group tours for 5-15 people. Tours that travel through the heart of Naples include a 2.5-hour basic tour and a 6-hour excursion with a stop for lunch. Tours are family-friendly, but children must be older than 14. For safety, the tours take place in pedestrian areas and helmets are included. Bike tours in English take place daily throughout the year, but advance booking is required.

KAYAKING

KAYAK NAPOLI

Via Posillipo 68 and Via Posillipo 357; tel. 331/987-4271; www.kayaknapoli.com; tours from €25 per person

Located just west of Naples's historic center, the Posillipo coastline with its caves and beautiful seaside villas is the nicest area to kayak. Kayak Napoli offers both kayak and stand-up paddleboard rentals, as well as guided kayak tours along the coast. From Bagno Sirena (Via Posillipo 357), the Naples and its Villas tour offers a close-up look at some of the historic villas of the area. The Wild Posillipo tour highlights the natural landscape, archaeological ruins, and marine-protected area of Gaiola. Tours are offered with an English-speaking guide throughout the year, weather permitting. The 140 bus from the center of Naples runs along Via Posillipo and passes the starting points for both tours.

FOOTBALL (SOCCER)

SSC NAPOLI

Stadio Diego Armando Maradona, Piazza Giorgio Ascarelli; tel. 081/509-5344; www.sscnapoli.it; from €25 per person

If there's one thing that is deep at the heart of Neapolitans, it's their love for the local Napoli soccer club. Founded in 1926, the Napoli team has boasted many of the world's best soccer players, including the Argentinian player Diego Maradona from 1984-1991. The Napoli team plays at the highest level (Serie A) of soccer in Italy and is regularly one of the top teams. The soccer season runs August-May, for a total of 38 games. The Stadio Diego Armando Maradona is the home stadium for Napoli and is located west of the historic center of Naples.

To enjoy a game at **Stadio Diego Armando Maradona,** your best bet is to buy tickets in person in Naples. Advance ticket sales are tricky to come by, given the regulations around sales. You'll find tickets for sale at various points around Naples, including the **Box Office** (Galleria Umberto I 17; tel. 081/551-9188; 10am-6pm Mon.-Sat.) or at the stadium in advance of a game. Bring your passport when purchasing tickets because your name will be printed on the ticket. You'll also need your passport as identification to get into the stadium, and the name must match the name on your ticket.

Entertainment and Events

The music and theater scene in Naples has a tremendous history, and for generations it has influenced scores of musicians from Italy and around the world. It's hard to find travelers who aren't familiar with the strains of popular Neapolitan songs like "O Sole Mio." Traditional Neapolitan music is very much alive; it's treasured by the locals and enjoyed by visitors. Naples also offers resplendent opera houses like Teatro di San Carlo and Teatro Bellini, and with so many locals dedicated to preserving music traditions, there are plenty of ways for visitors to experience Neapolitan music.

Tradition is also very much at the heart of the biggest religious events throughout the year. Whether it's a festival dedicated to the city's patron saint and protector San Gennaro or a celebration of the city's much-revered pizza, joining the locals in honoring their traditions is a moving experience in a city as full of passion as Naples.

THE ARTS
Centro Storico
TEATRO BELLINI

Via Conte di Ruvo 14; tel. 081/549-9688; www. teatrobellini.it

Located off of Via Toledo in the centro storico, Teatro Bellini is one of the city's important historic theaters. Inaugurated in 1878, the theater was restored in the 1980s, bringing back the original splendor of its six tiers of box seats, frescoed ceiling, and 19th-century details. A wide variety of theatrical, musical, and dance performances take place throughout the year.

San Ferdinando
TEATRO DI SAN CARLO

Via San Carlo 98/F; tel. 081/797-2331; www. teatrosancarlo.it; performances throughout the year

Founded in 1737, the Teatro di San Carlo is the oldest opera house in Europe in continuous use since it first opened. The grand theater

Teatro di San Carlo

was built at the behest of King Carlo III adjacent to the Palazzo Reale. The glittering gold and red theater seats up to 1,379 people with its 184 boxes, including a lavish royal box. It's an extraordinary setting to enjoy an opera, dance, or concert performance. The Teatro di San Carlo welcomes visitors outside of performance times with **guided tours** (€10; English-language tours are limited and reserving in advance is best), which include a visit to **MeMus** (tel. 081/797-2448; www.memus.org; 9:30am-1pm and 2pm-6pm Mon.-Tues. and Thurs.-Friday, 9:30am-3pm Sun.), the museum and archive of the Teatro di San Carlo.

FESTIVALS AND EVENTS
NAPOLI PIZZA VILLAGE
Lungomare Caracciolo; tel. 081/404-089; www.pizzavillage.it; June

Every year at the beginning of June along the waterfront, the Napoli Pizza Village celebrates the city's most famous gastronomic contribution. More than 50 pizzerias are present, and there are competitions, events, and live music as well. This is the chance to sample some of the best pizza from Italy's top pizza makers on a festive and fun summer evening in Naples.

FESTA DEL CARMINE
Piazza del Carmine 2; tel. 081/201-196; www.santuariocarminemaggiore.it; July 15

One of the most historic religious celebrations in Naples is also one of the most explosive.

The Festa del Carmine takes place July 15, the evening before the festival celebrating the Madonna del Carmine (Our Lady of Mount Carmel). After evening Mass in the Santuario del Carmine Maggiore, fireworks are set off from all over the bell tower of the church to create the impression that the bell tower is on fire. Only the arrival of a celebrated portrait of the Madonna del Carmine stops the fire. At 246 feet (75 m) tall, the bell tower is the tallest in Naples. The festival is very popular with Neapolitans, who pack the Piazza del Carmine and surrounding area to watch the event and enjoy the music and stands selling sweets, toys, and food.

FESTA DI SAN GENNARO
Duomo di Napoli; Sat. before first Sun. in May, Sept. 19, Dec. 16

Every day of the year, San Gennaro is the beloved and revered patron saint of Naples, but there are a few very special days when all eyes are on the saint. This is when the reliquary vials holding the blood of the saint are said to miraculously liquefy during a special Mass in the Duomo di Napoli. Tradition says that when the miracle doesn't occur it's a bad omen for the city of Naples, and has in fact coincided with natural disasters and unfortunate events over the centuries. For the festival, the Duomo and surrounding area are crowded with people eager to see the miracle, celebrate the saint with processions, and enjoy the festive atmosphere with stands selling candy, food, and toys.

Shopping

The artisan tradition in Naples dates to ancient times when the Greek and later Roman craftsmen transformed coral into intricately carved treasures. However, it was in the 17th and 18th centuries that Naples became known for its fine shopping and craftsmanship, thanks to the patronage of the Bourbon kings and aristocracy of the time.

Many shops in Naples, especially the artisan boutiques and smaller shops, respect the local custom of closing for a lunch period from 1pm or 1:30pm to about 4pm. If you want to shop during the mid-afternoon, head to Via Toledo where some of the larger chain stores remain open. Many smaller shops will also

The Nativity Tradition in Naples

presepe for sale on Via San Gregorio Armeno

Of the many artistic traditions of Naples, one of the most unique is the **presepe,** which is Italian for nativity scene, or Christmas cribs. Dating back to Saint Francis of Assisi in the 13th century, the nativity is still an important part of Christmas celebrations throughout Italy. Starting in the mid-14th century, artists in Naples began creating both small and large-scale presepi for churches, private chapels for wealthy families, and eventually for displaying in homes during the Christmas season.

By the 1700s, the Neapolitan presepe was a work of art that extended far beyond the traditional manger scene. In addition to figures related to the birth of Jesus, the nativity grew to include an entire landscape that was representative of Neapolitan life in the 1700s. These figures, called **pastori,** include a host of characters, from peasants to farmers, animals, houses, and shops. A traditional Neapolitan nativity scene is a theatrical experience, full of passion and a spark of whimsy.

close on Sunday for the afternoon or entire day, and some take a break for a period in August surrounding the Ferragosto holiday on August 15.

CENTRO STORICO
Ceramics
COSMOS
Via San Gregorio Armeno 5; tel. 081/193-51165; www. cornocosmos.com; 10:30am-7:30pm Mon.-Sat., 10:30am-2:30pm Sun.

In Naples, horn-shaped items called corni are considered good luck charms and often take the shape of small, red hot peppers that look like the peperoncino used in many traditional Neapolitan recipes. Cosmos specializes in the production of handmade corni of all types, including customized requests.

Books
LIBRERIA COLONNESE
Via San Pietro a Majella, 32/33; tel. 081/459-858; www.libreriecolonnese.it; 10am-2pm and 3pm-7:30pm daily

Founded in 1965, this bookstore is a dream for bibliophiles with its floor-to-ceilings shelves of books, fine selection of rare books, antique maps and prints, and gifts with an Italian twist that are perfect for the writers and book enthusiasts in your life. Libreria Colonnese is also a publisher and has published over 450 books. Their second bookshop in the

The heart of the presepe tradition is **Via San Gregorio Armeno** in the historic center, where artisans have been handmaking nativities for centuries. Strolling down the street, you'll find one workshop after the next with elaborate displays of figures and elements for creating presepi of all sizes. Traditional figurines are made with terra-cotta or papier-mâché; the finest are delicately painted and feature handmade clothing. Leading up to the Christmas season the street becomes very crowded, but throughout the year you can stop by workshops to see artisans at work. Below are a few of the best:

FERRIGNO
Via San Gregorio Armeno 8; tel. 081/552-3148; www.arteferrigno.it; 9am-7:30pm daily
Along Via San Gregorio Armeno, this very special store is where brothers Giuseppe and Marco Ferrigno continue a family tradition of handmade figures for presepi, or nativity scenes. The figurines and nativities are created using the same materials as when the workshop was founded in 1836, including terra-cotta details and silk fabrics, and all are created by hand in the workshop on-site.

LA SCARABATTOLA
Via dei Tribunali 50; tel. 081/291-735; www.lascarabattola.it; 10:30am-2pm and 3:30pm-7:30pm Mon.-Fri., 10am-6pm Sat.
Created by three brothers, Salvatore, Emanuele, and Raffaele, this shop is a treasure of hand-carved and remarkably detailed figures for presepi as well as contemporary sculptures inspired by Neapolitan masked figure Pulcinella and Neapolitan traditions.

ARS NEAPOLITANA
Via dei Tribunali 303; tel. 081/193-30967; www.arsneapolitana.it; 10am-6:30pm Mon.-Sat., 10am-3pm Sun.
Combining family tradition and original talent, Guglielmo Muoio is a young, highly praised presepe artist. His wife, Laura Loinam, adds her tailoring and embroidery expertise to create inspired nativity pieces in the 18th-century traditional Neapolitan style.

historic center, **Colonnese libri & altro** (Via San Biagio dei Librai 100; tel. 081/420-1028; 10am-2pm and 3pm-7:30pm daily) is another great spot for book lovers located right on Spaccanapoli. The second location is more modern, with a great selection of books on Naples, foreign language books, and gifts.

SAN FERDINANDO
Specialty Items
MARIO TALARICO
Vico Due Porte a Toledo 4b; tel. 081/407-723; www.mariotalarico.it; 9am-8pm Mon.-Sat.
Umbrellas might not be at the top of your holiday shopping list, but that's because you haven't been to Talarico yet. Founded in 1860,

this small shop has been producing handmade umbrellas for five generations. Choose from a variety of styles and sizes to brighten up any rainy day with travel memories.

WATERFRONT
Clothing
E. MARINELLA
Via Riviera di Chiaia 287; tel. 081/764-3265; www.emarinella.com; 6:30am-1:30pm and 3pm-8pm daily
If there's one shop to visit to experience Naples's sartorial tradition, it's E. Marinella, a tiny boutique that is known worldwide for its handmade ties. The family-run company was founded in 1914 and all of its ties are hand-sewn in a workshop just a few doors

away using handprinted silk. Stepping inside is like being transported back in time with the original woodwork and handcrafted quality, yet the ties have a contemporary style that's fitting for one of the world's finest names in ties.

CILENTO 1780
Via Riviera di Chiaia 203-204; tel. 081/552-7465; www.cilento1780.it; 9am-1:30pm and 4pm-8pm Mon.-Sat., 9am-1:30pm Sun.
Leaders of Neapolitan fashion since 1780 when the family business was founded, today Ugo Cilento is the eighth generation of the family to guide Cilento 1780. Here you'll find

sartorial treasures, accessories, shoes, and shirts made to measure.

Accessories
FRANCESCO TRAMONTANO GIOIELLI
Via Vittorio Imbriani 44 bis; tel. 081/012-7855; www.tramontanogioielli.com; 10am-1:30pm and 4:30pm-8pm Mon.-Sat., closed last two weeks of Aug.
Young goldsmith and designer Francesco Tramontano comes from a long family line of Neapolitan artisans. His jewelry pieces are inspired by Mediterranean elements and are handcrafted in gold, silver, and brass; each one is a unique piece of art.

Food

It's not an exaggeration to say that food is a way of life in Naples. While you're in its birthplace, it's a must to try true Neapolitan pizza. Tradition reigns here, whether you're grabbing a quick pizza fritta (fried pizza) on the street or enjoying a hearty dish of pasta with a ragù sauce that has bubbled away for hours. Neapolitans have strong opinions on the best ragù (although it might be their grandma's), the best pizza, and the best place to get a warm sfogliatella pastry. With so many options, there are few better pastimes in Naples than trying out different places to find your favorites.

Pizza is an art form in Naples and is taken quite seriously, especially at the historic pizzerias where often you'll find pizza, and sometimes only pizza, on the menu. However, at many pizzerias you can expect to find delicious fried appetizers, and some restaurants serve full menus in addition to making an excellent pizza. Expect lines at the most popular pizzerias because they don't take reservations. As pizza only takes 60-90 seconds to cook in a very hot wood-fire oven, the line usually moves quite quickly. Compared to most restaurant settings in Italy where lingering over a meal is the norm, Naples's pizzerias are often

bustling places with simple decor and table settings, where it's all about the pizza.

Unlike in the coastal areas and on the islands, many restaurants in Naples close for a period in August. Some may close just for the Ferragosto holiday on August 15, while others will close for a 1-2 week holiday around Ferragosto or even for the entire month.

CENTRO STORICO
Regional Cuisine
MIMÌ ALLA FERROVIA
Via Alfonso D'Aragona 19/21; tel. 081/553-8525; www.mimiallaferrovia.it; noon-4pm and 7pm-midnight Mon.-Sat.; €7-16
A classic Naples address for beautiful dining, Mimì Alla Ferrovia is a favorite with locals and travelers alike. Start with the Passeggiata Napoletana, a series of classic Neapolitan appetizers, and try the delicately flavored ravioli with seabass and lemon. The grilled fish is done superbly. Reservations required for four or more people.

TANDEM RAGÙ
Via Giovanni Paladino 51; tel. 081/190-02468; www.tandemnapoli.it; 12:30pm-3:30pm and 7pm-11:30pm Mon.-Tues., 12:30pm-11:30pm Wed.-Sun.; €10-15

In Naples, ragù is essential. This is a tomato sauce simmered for hours upon hours and enriched with various types of meat and quite possibly a touch of magic. Tadem Ragù has a simple menu dedicated to only a handful of ragù-based dishes available daily along with a selection of vegetarian options and second courses. As the restaurant is quite small, reservations are a good idea. You'll also find two other locations in the historic center (Via Paladino 51 and Calata Trinità Maggiore 12) and one in Vomero (Via Bernini 74).

Pizzerias
SORBILLO
Via dei Tribunali 32; tel. 081/446-643; www.sorbillo. it; noon-3pm and 7pm-11pm Mon.-Sat., closed Aug. 12-25; €3-9

Coming from a big family of pizzaioli (pizza makers), Gino Sorbillo became an expert at a young age and has created one of the most notable pizzerias in Naples, as well as locations in major Italian cities, Miami, New York City, and Tokyo. The original location on Via dei Tribunali is always packed, but there's also a location at **Lievito Madre al Mare** (Via Partenope 1) as well as the **Antica Pizza Fritta da Zia Esterina Sorbillo** locations (Via dei Tribunali 35, Piazza Trieste e Trento 53, and Via Luca Giordano 33) dedicated to his fabulous pizze fritte (fried pizza).

L'ANTICA PIZZERIA DA MICHELE
Via Cesare Sersale 1; tel. 081/553-9204; www. damichele.net; 11am-11pm Mon.-Sat.; €5

This is easily the most iconic pizzeria in Naples, thanks not only to its divine pizza but also to Elizabeth Gilbert's book *Eat, Pray, Love*. L'Antica Pizzeria da Michele is certainly worthy of all the praise, which is why you can expect to find a good line here most days. Everything here is focused 100 percent on the pizza in its most traditional form. The menu only has two pizzas: the classic pizza Margherita and the marinara, topped with tomatoes, oregano, and garlic. Expect to wait a

bit to enjoy this classic Naples experience, as reservations are not accepted.

★ PIZZERIA DA ATTILIO
Via Pignaseca 17; tel. 081/552-0479; www. pizzeriadaattilio.com; noon-3:30pm and 7pm-midnight Mon.-Sat., closed Sun.; €4.50-10

Just off Via Toledo on the attractive and very typical Neapolitan street Via Pignasecca, this little restaurant is one of the top spots in Naples. Pizza maker Attilio Bachetti continues a long tradition of excellent pizza started by his grandfather (who was also called Attilio Bachetti) in 1938. From a young age Attilio has been making pizza, and the hard work has paid off as he is a true master of the craft.

Bakeries and Cafés
SCATURCHIO
Piazza San Domenico Maggiore 19; tel. 081/551-7031; www.scaturchio.it; 7am-10pm daily; €2-4

This coffee shop and bakery is a classic stop along Spaccanapoli at Piazza San Domenico Maggiore. Join the locals at the bar inside, which is the traditional way to have coffee in Italy. Listen to the Neapolitan dialect flow as you sip a strong coffee and try something sweet like their delicious rum-soaked babà or other tempting pastries.

SAN FERDINANDO
Regional Cuisine
DA DONATO DAL 1956
Via Silvio Spaventa 41; tel. 081/287-828; dadonato1956@gmail.com; 12:30pm-2:30pm and 7:30pm-10:30pm Tues.-Sun.; €7-15

Family-run for four generations, this trattoria and pizzeria is an excellent choice for a wide variety of homemade Neapolitan-style dishes like the traditional ragù or genovese pasta sauces that cook for 10-12 hours. The menu changes daily and the staff can guide your choice of a seafood or non-seafood menu, or you can order à la carte. Reservations are a good idea because it's a popular spot.

NAPLES AND THE RUINS
FOOD

☆ True Neapolitan Pizza

traditional Neapolitan pizza Margherita at Sorbillo

In 2017, the art of the Neapolitan Piazzaiuolo, or pizza maker, was added to UNESCO's list of Intangible Cultural Heritage of Humanity. It was a moment of great celebration in Naples, where the city's famous gastronomic delight is far more than just pizza: it's indelibly connected to Neapolitan identity.

The most classic of Neapolitan pizzas is the **pizza Margherita,** which dates to 1889 when Raffaele Esposito made pizzas for King Umberto I and Queen Margherita di Savoia during their visit to Naples. The queen most enjoyed the pizza topped with tomatoes, mozzarella, extra virgin olive oil, and basil—to represent the green, white, and red of the Italian flag—and so Raffaele named the pizza in her honor. You'll find pizza Margherita on every pizzeria menu, along with the **marinara pizza** topped with tomatoes, oregano, garlic, and extra virgin olive oil (no cheese). These two pizzas are considered the most traditional, with some pizzerias only serving those two varieties. However, in most pizzerias you will find a large selection of toppings on the menu.

Pizza in Naples is usually considered individual sized and is served about the size of a large plate. Your pizza will arrive whole and not presliced, so grab your knife and fork and dig in. There are no rules; you can eat it with knife and fork or slice your pizza into quarters and pick up a quarter, fold it in half, and enjoy! Naples is also famous for its **pizza fritta** (fried pizza): This is a pizza that's topped with a variety of different fillings, like ricotta and salami, and then folded in half and deep fried.

You don't have to go far in Naples to find an excellent pizzeria, and here are some suggestions to get you started.

- **L'Antica Pizzeria da Michele:** Try the classics here—Margherita and marinara are the only two options (page 65).

- **Sorbillo:** Among Sorbillo's multiple locations around the city are a restaurant in the centro storico and a seaside outpost with a view of the Castel dell'Ovo. Many of their branches specialize in pizza fritta (page 65).

- **Pizzaria La Notizia:** A bit off the beaten path, Pizzaria La Notizia serves the outstanding pizza created by Enzo Coccia (page 69).

- **50 Kalò:** This pizzeria is not far from the Mergellina harbor (page 67).

Pizzeria
PIZZERIA BRANDI
Salita S. Anna di Palazzo 1/2; tel. 081/416-928; www.pizzeriabrandi.com; 12:30pm-4pm and 7:30pm-midnight Tues.-Sun.; €2-22

Every pizzeria in Naples has a good story, but no story is so intimately tied to the origins of Neapolitan pizza as Brandi's. Pizza maker Raffaele Esposito and his wife, Maria Giovanna Brandi, made pizza in 1889 for King Umberto I and Queen Margherita di Savoia, who were visiting Naples. Of the three types of pizza, the queen was most pleased by the pizza with mozzarella and tomato, which Esposito then named in her honor. This is how the pizza Margherita, the most classic of all Neapolitan pizzas, was born. In addition to excellent pizza, the restaurant has a full menu.

International
KUKAI IKI RESTAURANT
Via Nardones 103-104; tel.081/186-39120; www.ikirestaurants.com; 12:30pm-3:30pm and 6:30pm-midnight daily; €15-28

Though Naples might be famous for its pizza, this is a great address if you're ready for something a little different. Created by Massimiliano Neri, the restaurant is a refreshing spot to enjoy sushi and Asian flavors, or simply stop in for a cocktail at the bar. The menu has many tempting creations like the hikari roll made with black rice, green peppers, and shrimp tempura.

Bakeries and Cafés
★ GRAN CAFFÈ GAMBRINUS
Via Chiaia 1/2; tel. 081/417-582; www.grancaffegambrinus.com; 7am-1am daily; €2-10

Gambrinus is in a class of its own when it comes to coffee and pastries in Naples. Founded in 1860, the café has beautiful art nouveau rooms; it has been a literary salon and meeting place for generations of Neapolitans. Sitting right between Piazza Trieste e Trento and Piazza del Plebiscito, the café couldn't be better situated for taking a break or just stopping in to try their famous coffee or deserts.

WATERFRONT
Regional Cuisine
UMBERTO
Via Alabardieri 30; tel. 081/418-555; www.umberto.it; 12:30pm-3:30pm and 7:15-midnight Tues.-Sun.; €10-20

Founded in 1916, this restaurant has been serving Neapolitan specialties for more than 100 years—and doing it exceedingly well. Here you can choose from a rich menu that changes seasonally to highlight locally sourced ingredients. Dishes include both seafood specialties like the paccheri "d' 'o treddeta" (large tube-shaped pasta served with tomatoes, baby octopus, black olives, and capers) or perfectly prepared baccalà (salted cod) and delicious non-seafood options like the incredible meatballs with ragù sauce. The pizza is also an excellent choice.

CARUSO ROOF GARDEN RESTAURANT
Grand Hotel Vesuvio, Via Partenope 45; www.vesuvio.it/caruso; 1pm-3pm and 8:30pm-11pm Tues.-Sun.; €24-30

Atop the Grand Hotel Vesuvio, with unbelievable panoramic views and a romantic setting, the Caruso Roof Garden Restaurant is named after the great tenor Enrico Caruso, who was Neapolitan through and through. Here you can even try a recipe created by Caruso, the bucatini alla Caruso, which is hollow spaghetti-shaped pasta served with a sauce made with San Marzano tomatoes, peppers, zucchini, and plenty of basil and oregano. A jacket is suggested for dinner, and reservations are recommended but can only be made a maximum of two weeks in advance.

Pizzerias
50 KALÒ
Piazza Sannazzaro 201/b; tel. 081/192-04667; www.50kalo.it; 12:30pm-4pm and 7pm-12:30am daily; €5-9.50

Not far from the Mergellina harbor and waterfront, this is a spot that pizza enthusiasts from around the world flock to, to taste the creations

In Search of the Best Sfogliatella

sfogliatelle in Naples

Naples has many traditional desserts, but nothing quite tops the shell-shaped sfogliatella. This pastry has a citrus-infused ricotta filling and comes in two varieties: The classic **sfogliatella riccia** has a crispy and flaky crust that makes an unavoidable mess as you bite into it, and the **frolla** variety has a soft short-crust pastry shell. The pastry originated on the Amalfi Coast in Conca dei Marini, but was modified at the end of the 1700s by Neapolitan pastry maker Pasquale Pintauro to the sweet treat enjoyed today. Now it is one of the desserts most commonly associated with Naples, and though it can also be enjoyed throughout the entire region, you've never tasted anything quite like the sfogliatelle made right in Naples. Locals hotly debate where to find the best sfogliatella in the city, but the tastiest way to find the answer is to throw your diet out the window and try them all. Here's where to start your sfogliatella tasting tour in Naples.

PINTAURO
Via Toledo 275; tel. 081/417-339; www.pintauro.it; 9am-8pm daily; €2
This small bakery on Via Toledo is the birthplace of the sfogliatella and a fine place to sample both the traditional sfogliatella riccia with its flaky crust as well as the frolla variety.

LA SFOGLIATELLA MARY
Via Toledo 66/Galleria Umberto I; tel. 081/402-218; 8am-8:30pm Tues.-Sun.; €1.80-2.50
Not far away, you'll find this popular bakery right off Via Toledo at the entrance of the Galleria Umberto I.

SFOGLIATELLE ATTANASIO
Vico Ferrovia 1-4; tel. 081/285-675; www.sfogliatelleattanasio.it; 6:30am-7:30pm Tues.-Sun.; €2
Often considered the top spot for sfogliatelle in the city, this tiny bakery is not far from the train station. Stop by to try them still warm from the oven.

of master pizza maker Ciro Salvo. Though it's relatively new (opened in 2014) compared to the iconic pizza establishments, 50 Kalò has quickly become a top choice for pizza in Naples.

★ PIZZARIA LA NOTIZIA
Via Michelangelo da Caravaggio 53; tel. 081/714-2155; www.pizzarialanotizia.com; 7:30pm-midnight Tues.-Sun.; €7-10
Born and raised in Naples and in the Neapolitan pizza tradition, Enzo Coccia opened his first pizzeria in 1994. With his dedicated attention to the highest-quality ingredients, as well as plenty of passion and hard work, Enzo has created not just one but two of the best pizza places in the city, both on the same street. The original pizzeria at Via Michelangelo da Caravaggio 53 is dedicated to tradition (think the best pizza Margherita of your life), while down the street at number 94 you'll find highly creative and delicious variations with other toppings.

Cafés
GRAN CAFFÈ LA CAFFETTIERA
Piazza dei Martiri 26; tel. 081/764-4243; www. grancaffelacaffettiera.com; 7am-10pm Mon.-Fri.,

7am-1am Sat., 7am-midnight Sun.; €3.50-7
This is a lovely spot in Chiaia to stop for coffee, tea, or drinks any time of the day, or late into the night. There's both indoor seating in a salon-style setting and outdoor seating on the elegant Piazza dei Martiri.

VOMERO
Regional Cuisine
BORBONIKA NAPULITAN RESTAURANT
Via Michele Kerbaker 112; tel. 081/1870-3243; www. borbonika.it; 7pm-11:30pm Mon., noon-3pm and 7pm-11:30pm Tues.-Sat., noon-4:30pm Sun.; €10-18
Just a couple of blocks from Piazza Vanvitelli in the Vomero, this welcoming restaurant has a menu dedicated to classic Neapolitan recipes. This is the place to try pasta with the traditional Naples genovese sauce made by slow cooking onions and beef. Or try the delicous pasta with potatoes, smoked provola cheese, and porcini mushrooms. You'll also find seafood options for first and second courses, including an excellent fried baccalà served with a pumpkin cream and ricotta cheese.

Bars and Nightlife

Naples is a vibrant city after dark with a lively and eclectic scene. Although it's a very large city, most of the nightlife spots are small clubs, literary cafés, or wine bars where you're more likely to rub elbows with locals than tourists. The city also has a rich musical heritage, and talented young musicians carry on the Neapolitan traditions. So whether your scene is more a glass of Campania wine, a formal concert, a good jazz club, or dancing until dawn, you'll find plenty of nightlife options, especially in the centro storico (historic center) area around **Piazza Dante** and **Piazza Bellini.**

CENTRO STORICO
Bars
ENNÒ
Via Vincenzo Bellini 43; tel. 392/658-8623; 7pm-1am daily
Located in a great nightlife area not far from Piazza Dante and Piazza Bellini, this club offers a large selection of artisan beers, wine, and cocktails along a dinner menu. The atmosphere is especially vibrant with live music on the weekends.

LIBRERIA BERISIO
Via Port'Alba 28-29; tel. 081/549-9090; berisio@ libero.it; 9:30am-1:30am Mon.-Thurs., 9:30am-1pm and 5:30pm-3:30am Fri.-Sat., 5:30pm-1:30am Sun.

Along Via Port'Alba lined with bookstores, Libreria Berisio opened its doors in 1956 and is now also a popular local wine and cocktail bar, especially late into the night. Check their schedule for live music events; this place often has a great jazz and blues vibe.

Clubs and Live Music
KESTÈ

Largo San Giovanni Maggiore Pignatelli 26/27; tel. 081/781-0034; www.keste.it; 2:30pm-2am Mon.-Thurs., 2:30pm-3am Fri.-Sat., 3:30pm-2am Sun.

Since 1997, Kestè has been a cornerstone in the music and nightlife scene in Naples. With a live music program throughout the year, as well as art, theater, stand-up comedy, and cultural events, it's a popular spot with locals, offering an artistic atmosphere on a little square in the historic center.

BOURBON STREET

Via Vincenzo Bellini 52/53; tel. 338/825-3756; www.bourbonstreetjazzclub.com; 8:30pm-2am Tues.-Sun.

Around the corner from Piazza Dante, Bourbon Street is one of the city's classic nightclubs, completely dedicated to jazz. The

setting is intimate, and live music is on the schedule regularly, along with jam sessions.

SUPERFLY SOULBAR

Via Cisterna dell'Olio 12; tel. 347/127-2178; gfiorito6704@yahoo.it; 7pm-1:30am Wed.-Thurs. and Sun.-Mon., 7pm-3am Fri.-Sat.

Superfly Soulbar is an iconic Naples nightlife spot with a good groove, just south of Piazza Dante in the centro storico. The cocktails are expertly mixed, and the setting is perfectly in tune with the jazz and soul music vibe.

VOMERO
Bars
SPRITZERÒ–APERITIVO ITALIANO

Via Enrico Alvino 50; tel. 081/1875-2947; www.spritzero.it; 4:30pm-1:30am Mon.-Thurs., 11:30am-2:30am Fri.-Sun.

The classic Aperol spritz cocktail has taken the world by storm, and this spot not far from Piazza Vanvitelli in the Vomero area is 100 percent dedicated to celebrating one of Italy's most popular drinks in a casual setting perfect for conversation and fun. You'll find another SPRITZERÒ located at Largo Antignano also in the Vomero neighborbood.

Accommodations

With accommodations ranging from friendly hostels to family-run B&Bs and historic palazzos transformed into modern hotels, Naples has a wide array of accommodations to suit every budget. If you want to be very close to the top sights, look in the San Ferdinando, Quartieri Spagnoli (Spanish Quarter), and centro storico (historic center) areas. The historic center is an especially good option if you're traveling to the Amalfi Coast via public transportation, because you'll be close to the Napoli Centrale train station. Unlike the Amalfi Coast and Capri, Naples offers plenty of accommodations that are open year-round, and breakfast is usually included in the price of the room.

CENTRO STORICO
Under €100
HOSTEL MANCINI

Via Pasquale Stanislao Mancini 33; tel. 081-200-800; www.hostelmancini.com; €15-22 per person for dorm, €35-55 per person for private room

Located near the Naples train station, this hostel offers comfortable and very cost-effective accommodations in the historic center of the city. Owned by husband-and-wife team Alfredo and Margherita, the hostel welcomes guests to enjoy the large common room and use the fully equipped kitchen for cooking and dining. Mixed-gender dorms and women-only dorm rooms with private bathrooms are available, in addition to private rooms with shared or en suite bathrooms. This hostel is an excellent choice for a friendly and budget-concious stay in Naples.

★ PALAZZO BEVILACQUA

Via Pietro Colletta 35; tel. 081/015-2412; www.palazzobevilacquanapoli.com; €79 d

A B&B with a lovely family story, the Palazzo Bevilacqua is located in an elegant building built in 1911 by Pasquale Bevilacqua for his family to live close together. Today the B&B is run by Luigi and Margherita, the fifth generation to live in the palazzo. With a touch of creativity and modern style, they have created an enchanting little B&B with three stylish and comfortable rooms, each with en suite bathroom. With some of the city's best pizzerias just steps away, as well as the top sights in the centro storico, it's a fine option for an authentic Neapolitan experience.

€100-200
HOTEL PIAZZA BELLINI

Via Santa Maria di Costantinopoli 101; tel. 081/451-732; www.hotelpiazzabellini.com; €130 d

Just a few steps from Piazza Bellini, this small hotel is full of modern style and comfort right in the historic center of Naples. The rooms are bright and modern, and the units with a private terrace are exceptional. Relax in the cozy library or the historic courtyard with a cocktail from the hotel's **Buvette Bar.** There are also eight fully remodeled apartments of various sizes all complete with kitchens at the same location for more independent stays.

★ PALAZZO CARACCIOLO NAPOLI

Via Carbonara 112; tel. 081/016-0111; www.palazzocaracciolo.com; €150 d

Walk through the imposing entrance and into the courtyard garden of the Palazzo Caracciolo, and you'll know you've arrived someplace special. Built in 1584, the palazzo was owned by the Caracciolo family, one of the most important noble families in Naples. The large historic complex has been beautifully remodeled with an air of timeless elegance, and it's now home to 146 finely appointed rooms.

Choose from superior rooms, deluxe rooms, or suites, some offering balconies. Dining options include the beautiful **Nel Chiostro** restaurant, set in a cloister from the 16th century.

SAN FERDINANDO
Under €100
HOSTEL OF THE SUN

Via Guglielmo Melisurgo 15; tel. 081/420-6393; www.hostelnapoli.com; €20 for dorm room, €72 private room

With a cheery atmosphere and a convenient location near the Castel Nuovo and ferry terminal, this hostel offers dorm-style shared rooms as well as private rooms for 2-4 people with private or shared bathroom. Wi-Fi access is fast and available throughout the hostel. The common spaces are welcoming and fun, and breakfast is included. The hostel can help organize excursions, or you can take advantage of the free walking tour of Naples offered by the hostel.

€100-200
★ LA CILIEGINA LIFESTYLE HOTEL

Via Paolo Emilio Imbriani 30; tel. 081/197-18800; www.cilieginahotel.it; €180 d

Well situated between Via Toledo and Castel Nuovo, this boutique hotel with 14 jewel-like rooms is an excellent choice for its refreshing Mediterraean style, location, and features. Every aspect of the hotel is beautifully detailed, from luxurious linen sheets to the stylish custom-designed furniture in the rooms to the panoramic rooftop terrace complete with Jacuzzi and sun beds. There's a friendly team dedicated to customer service, and each guest is sent a questionnaire before arrival so the concierge can prepare personalized suggestions and guidance.

WATERFRONT
Under €100
HOTEL REX

Via Palepoli 12; tel.081/764-9389; www.hotel-rex.it; €95 d

Just moments from the waterfront and set

in an art nouveau-style palazzo, this charming three-star hotel offers a very comfortable stay with excellent hospitality in one of the best areas of Santa Lucia. The 34 rooms are spacious and bright, and they are decorated in a clean modern style with unique artistic touches like the large paintings depicting Neapolitan scenes. Standard rooms include both doubles and triples, while the executive doubles with lateral sea views are worth the splurge.

€100-200
★ HOTEL PALAZZO ALABARDIERI
Via Alabardieri 38; tel. 081/415-278; www. palazzoalabardieri.it; €145 d
Only a few steps off of Piazza dei Martiri and surrounded by excellent shopping and dining options, this hotel captures the essence of Chiaia's style with its elegant and traditional decor. The classic and superior rooms are all comfortable, but for a splurge consider the

junior suite with a view overlooking Piazza dei Martiri.

Over €300
GRAND HOTEL VESUVIO
Via Partenope 45; tel. 081/764-0044; www.vesuvio. it; €300
The peak of elegance and refinement in Naples, the Grand Hotel Vesuvio is situated in a prized location along the waterfront overlooking the Borgo Marinari, Castel dell'Ovo, and the Gulf of Naples. Opened in 1882, the hotel maintains a gracious air of old-world charm mixed with modern comforts, including a fitness club with indoor pool, two restaurants with panoramic views, the Sky Lounge Solarium and Cocktail Bar on the 10th floor, and the top-quality service of a five-star hotel. The 160 rooms and suites are classically decorated and luxurious in every detail. This is a location where the sea view is well worth the splurge.

Information and Services

VISITOR INFORMATION
The city of Naples (www.comune.napoli.it) has Info Points located in Piazza Cavour near the Museo Archeologico Nazionale and one by the Porta Capuana not far from the Napoli Centrale train station. If you're in those areas, they can help with tourist information, city tours, and answer questions.

- **Azienda Autonoma di Soggiorno Cura e Turismo di Napoli:** Piazza del Gesù 7; tel. 081/551-2701; www.inaples.it; 9am-1pm daily

MEDICAL SERVICES
- **Antonio Cardarelli hospital:** Via Antonio Cardarelli 9; tel. 081/747-1111; emergency room (pronto soccorso) open 24 hours
- **Antica Farmacia Augusteo:** Piazzetta Duca D'Aosta 263; tel. 081/416-105; 8am-8:30pm Mon.-Fri., 10am-2pm and 4pm-8pm Sat.

MAIN POST OFFICE
- **Poste Italiane:** Piazza Giacomo Matteotti 2; tel. 081/428-9814; www.poste.it; 8:20am-7:05pm Mon.-Fri., 8:20am-12:35pm Sat.

Getting There

As Italy's third largest city, Naples is well connected to national and international transportation systems.

BY AIR

AEROPORTO INTERNAZIONALE DI NAPOLI

Viale F. Ruffo di Calabria; tel. 081/789-6259; www.aeroportodinapoli.it

The Aeroporto Internazionale di Napoli, also referred to as Capodichino, is located about 3.7 miles (6 km) northeast of the city center. Though it's not a large airport, it handles more than 10 million passengers a year. Direct flights to Naples arrive from destinations across Italy, including Palermo (1 hour; from €60 round-trip) and Catania (just over 1 hour; from €70 round-trip), as well as from 90-plus international cities. Direct flights from the United States are occasionally available during the peak travel season (May-Oct.), but you'll likely have to connect through a European hub. The airport has received many updates in recent years, including new dining and shopping options. Tourist information, car rentals, currency exchange, and public transportation options are available just outside the baggage claim in the Arrivals hall.

From the Airport

Alibus (ANM; tel. 800/639-525; www.anm.it; 7am-10pm daily; €5) offers a convenient bus line connecting the airport to three stops in the Naples city center: Piazza Garibaldi (15 minutes); Immacolatella/Porta di Massa; and Molo Angioino/Beverello (35 minutes). Tickets can be purchased onboard. Be sure to validate your ticket in the machine onboard and keep it with you for the entire journey. Buses leave the airport every 20 minutes or so, from just about 100 meters past the Arrivals hall.

You can also catch a taxi for the short, 15-minute ride from the airport into the center of Naples from the taxi stand, located right outside the Arrivals exit. Taxis are required to display a fixed-rate tariff card, usually about €18 to the centro storico and Napoli Stazione Centrale, €21 to the port and the San Ferdinando areas, and €25 to Mergellina, Chiaia, and Vomero. It's essential to tell the driver you would like to have the fixed-rate fare and agree on the price before departing the airport.

BY TRAIN

NAPOLI CENTRALE STAZIONE

Piazza Giuseppe Garibaldi; www.napolicentrale.it

Located in the heart of Naples at Piazza Garibaldi, the Napoli Centrale Stazione is the city's main train station; nearly 400 trains pass through daily. **Trenitalia** (www.trenitalia.com) operates on the Italian railway lines and runs regional, intercity, and high-speed trains from destinations across Italy. Journey times and prices vary, depending on the season, time of day, number of transfers, and speed of the train. **Frecciarossa** high-speed trains are fastest and most convenient, traveling from Rome to Naples in about 70 minutes (from €38.90), from Florence in about 3 hours (from €62.90), from Venice in about 5 hours 20 minutes (from €86.90), and from Milan in a little over 5 hours (from €82.90). There are cheaper options, but they take a lot longer and require transfers. For example, the journey from Rome on slower regional trains takes about 3 hours (from €12.65).

The private company **Italotreno** (www.italotreno.it) offers high-speed trains from Rome (1 hour 15 minutes; from €29.90), Florence (3 hours; from €55.90), Milan (5 hours; €74.90), Venice (6 hours; from €77.90), and many other smaller cities.

To reach Naples by train from the Amalfi Coast, you will first need to take the bus or ferry to the closest train station at Salerno or Sorrento. From Sorrento, you'll catch the

Circumvesuviana train (www.eavsrl.it; departures approximately every 30 minutes daily; 1-hour journey; €3.90), which also connects Naples with Pompeii and Herculaneum. The Circumvesuviana train platforms are connected to the Napoli Centrale station via an underground walkway. From Salerno, Trenitalia trains depart every 15-30 minutes for the Napoli Centrale Stazione, taking from 35 minutes-1 hour, depending on the type of train (from €4.70).

There are no direct trains from Puglia to Naples, but you can take a Trenitalia or Italotreno train to Caserta, northeast of Naples, from Bari (3-4 hours; €20-75 one-way), and then connect to Naples from there (30 minutes-1 hour depending on speed of train; from €3-10 one-way). From Sicily, it is possible to take the train to Naples from Palermo (9 hours 30 minutes; €40-60 one-way) or Catania Centrale (8 hours; €30-45 one-way). That said, this route involves loading the train onto a ferry from Messina (Sicily) to Villa San Giovanni (Calabria, in mainland Italy)—a unique journey that nevertheless takes a lot of time and creates frequent delays. Traveling by train may make sense, however, if you are able to catch an overnight train and save the cost of a night's sleep in a hotel.

BY BUS

Flixbus (www.flixbus.it) offers bus service to Naples from destinations across Italy for affordable rates. Buses can be booked to or from the Napoli Centrale train station and at the Aeroporto Internazionale di Napoli. **Curreri Viaggi** (www.curreriviaggi. it) offers 8-10 daily bus connections from Sorrento to Naples's airport (1 hour 30 minutes; €10). **SitaSud** (www.sitasudtrasporti. it) has limited bus lines connecting Salerno and the Amalfi Coast to Naples, with a stop at Varco Immacolatella near the ferry terminal. **Pintour** (www.pintourbus.com) operates a shuttle bus service from Amalfi and towns east on the Amalfi Coast (Atrani, Minori, Maiori, Erchie, Cetara, and Vietri sul Mare) to

the Aeroporto Internazionale di Napoli (from Apr.-Nov.; €20).

From Bari Centrale, SitaSud and Flixbus offer buses to Napoli Centrale that take approximately 3 hours (€15-25 one-way), probably the best option for getting to Naples from Puglia by public transportation. From Palermo Centrale, **Autoservizi Salemi** (https://autoservizisalemi.it) runs buses to Napoli Centrale that take approximately 11 hours 40 minutes (€35-60 one-way), stopping on the way in Catania (9 hours 15 minutes; €30-40 one-way).

BY BOAT
PORTO DI NAPOLI

Port of Naples; tel. 081/228-3257; www.porto.napoli. it

One of Italy's largest ports, the Porto di Napoli (Port of Naples) handles cruise ships, cargo transport, and ferries from the Gulf of Naples and around the country. Cruise ships usually dock near the **Stazione Marittima**, and the ferry terminal for arrivals from most destinations is nearby at the **Molo Beverello.** Both arrival areas are very near bus and metro options for public transportation at Piazza Municipio, or only a short walk from Castel Nuovo and Piazza Trieste e Trento. Continuing along the port to the left beyond Piazzale Immacolatella is the **Calata Porta di Massa,** where larger passenger and vehicle ferries depart for Capri. From Molo Beverello to the Calata Porta di Massa it's a 15-minute walk, or take a free shuttle bus that often circulates between the two.

A more adventurous option for getting to Naples from Sicily is the overnight ferry from Palermo's Molo Piave, offered daily by **Terrenia** (www.tirrenia.it) and **Grandi Nevi Veloci** (www.gnv.it), arriving in Porto di Napoli's Molo Beverello around 6:45am (10 hours 30 minutes; €20-60 one-way). Getting a good night's sleep depends in part on whether or not you get seasick, but ferries are generally modern and clean, and it's a novel way to save on the cost of a hotel while you arrive in Naples by sea.

Frequent, year-round ferry connections (fewer in the winter months), as well as high-speed jets and aliscafo (hydrofoil) ferries, make it easy to get around the Gulf of Naples to Sorrento and the island of Capri. Direct ferry service direct from Naples to the Amalfi Coast is not available, but you can take a ferry to Sorrento and Capri and connect from there in the summer (usually May-Oct.). Most ferry companies offer advance ticket purchase online, which is a good idea during the busy summer months. You can also purchase tickets from the ticket booths before boarding; just arrive with time to spare, in case there are lines at the ticket booths.

- **NLG** (tel. 081/552-0763; www.navlib.it; from €13.10 per person) operates jet routes to Capri and Sorrento.

- **Gescab** (tel. 081/428-5259; www.gescab.it; from €20.50) has jet routes from Naples to Capri and Sorrento.

- **SNAV** (tel. 081/428-5555; www.snav.it; from €17.70) operates lines to Capri.

- **Caremar** (tel. 081/189-66690; www.caremar.it; from €12.30 for passengers and €28.50 for vehicles) offers ferry service and can transport vehicles to Sorrento and Capri.

BY CAR

Naples is well connected to the autostrade (highways) that crisscross Italy. If you're traveling to Naples from points north, take the **A1** (Autostrada del Sole) and follow signs indicating Napoli Centro/Porto Marittima/Stazione Centrale to reach the city center. If you're arriving from **Salerno** and points south, take the **A3** and look for signs for Napoli Centro/Porto Marittima/Stazione Centrale. From **Bari,** it's about a 3-hour drive without stops (256 km/159 mi); from **Palermo,** the drive is 8 hours 30 minutes (720 km/447 mi), though make time for the 30-minute ferry crossing (€35) from Messina (Sicily) to Villa San Giovanni (Calabria, in mainland Italy).

Driving in Naples can be quite the adventure and is not the recommended means of transportation for exploring the city. Parking in Naples is also challenging. If you're staying in the city center, it's a good idea to contact your hotel in advance for guidance on arriving by car, navigating to the exact location, and parking.

Getting Around

Naples has a busy city center and some of the wildest traffic in Italy. Combined with parking challenges and the concentration of sights around the historic center and waterfront, navigating the city on foot and public transportation makes the most sense. There are plenty of bus lines, a metro system with modern stations, funicular train lines running up to Vomero, and regional trains. When you're out walking, be cautious at all times, even when crossing at crosswalks. Keep an eye out for scooters that zip through traffic and along narrow streets. Although pedestrians do technically have the right of way, it's not something you'll want to test in Naples.

PUBLIC TRANSPORTATION
Metro and Railway

Naples has a convenient metro and railway system. **ANM** (Azienda Napoletana Mobilità; tel. 800/639-525; www.anm.it) operates Line 1 and Line 6 of the metro system; **Line 1** is particularly convenient for tourists, as it connects Piazza Garibaldi at the Napoli Centrale train station to the historic center with stops at Municipio for the Piazza Municipio area, Toledo along the busy shopping street Via Toledo, Dante at Piazza Dante, Museo for the Museo Archeologico Nazionale, and Vanvitelli for the Vomero. **Line 6,** which is closed for a period of construction to extend the line, runs from Mergellina to the western suburbs of Naples. **Line 2** is a metro train line that's actually operated by **Trenitalia** (www. trenitalia.com; departures every 10 minutes; €1.30) and runs from Piazza Garibaldi as well, with stops at Cavour, Museo (to transfer to Line 1), Montesanto, Amedeo, Mergellina, and points west to Pozzuoli.

Bus and Tram

ANM (Azienda Napoletana Mobilità; tel. 800/639-525; www.anm.it) operates a large bus transit network that covers the city center day and night. From the Napoli Centrale train station, Line **R2** runs from Piazza Garibaldi to Piazza Trieste e Trento to reach the Galleria Umberto I, Piazza del Plebiscito, and Via Toledo area. Bus Line **151** connects Piazza Garibaldi with Piazza Vittoria in Chiaia, with stops for the port near Molo Beverello and Castel Nuovo. Line **V1** covers much of the Vomero area, including a convenient connection from near Piazza Vanvitelli and the Cimarosa and Morghen funicular train stations to reach the Castel Sant'Elmo and Certosa di San Martino. To reach the Museo di Capodimonte, catch the **178** bus at the Piazza Museo outside the Museo Archeologico Nazionale and get off at the Tondo di Capodimonte piazza or the Museo di Capodimonte.

A single ride ticket costs €1.10, or you can choose a 90-minute ticket for €1.60 that allows for transfers. Daily tickets for the ANM transit network (buses, funicular trains, trams, and metro lines 1 and 6) are €3.50, or weekly passes are available for €12.50. Buy your tickets at most tabacchi (tobacco shops), some newsstands, or at the ticket machines at some metro or train stations. Single-use or timed tickets must be validated at the machine when you board the bus or before boarding at the metro or train station. If you have a daily or weekly ticket, validate it the first time you use it and be sure to fill out the name and date information on the ticket. Be prepared to show ID if the ticket inspector asks. It is worth making sure you validate your tickets properly, or you may be fined.

Funicular

Naples has three funicular trains, called funicolari, operated by **ANM** (Azienda Napoletana Mobilità; tel. 800/639-525; www. anm.it), connecting the centro storico and Chiaia area with the Vomero. These train lines run up the mountainside, primarily used by locals, but a convenient and unique

Funicular trains connect Chiaia and the historic center to the Vomero neighborhood.

way to get around in the city. The **Funicolare Centrale** line starts in the Augusteo station just off Via Toledo opposite the Galleria Umberto I and arrives at the Fuga station in Piazza Ferdinando Fuga in the Vomero. The **Funicolare di Chiaia** starts at the Amedeo station in Piazza Amedeo and ends at the Cimarosa station just south of Piazza Vanvitelli in the Vomero. The **Funicolare di Montesanto** starts in the Quartieri Spagnoli and runs to the Morghen station not far from the Castel Sant'Elmo in Vomero. Each line makes several stops along the way, mostly connecting residential areas of Naples.

Funicular trains run in both directions on all the lines, about every 10 minutes, 7am-10pm. Ticketing is the same as for buses, and a single ride costs €1.10. Daily and weekly ANM tickets also include rides on the funicular lines.

Taxi

Taxis in Naples offer either metered or fixed-rate tariffs for each ride. Fixed-rate fares are available to and from the main transporation hubs like the airport, train station, and port. You must opt for a fixed-rate tariff at the beginning of a journey and tell the driver. Metered fares start at €3.50 Monday-Saturday and €6.50 on Sundays and holidays; the fare increases €.05 every 157 feet (48 m) and every 8 seconds stopped. There are extra fees for bags, more than four passengers, airport pickups or drop-offs, and more. All taxis must display the tariff card (in Italian and English) regulated by the city of Naples. Though you can flag a taxi down, it's much easier to go to the nearest taxi stand, located near transportation hubs and major landmarks and piazzas. Or

call ahead to **Consortaxi** (tel. 081/2222; www.consortaxi.it) or **Radio Taxi La Partenope** (tel. 081/0101; www.radiotaxilapartenope.it).

CAR AND SCOOTER RENTAL

Navigating Naples's famously chaotic traffic and maze of streets in the historic center by car is not a recommended way to get around. Outside Naples, however, having a car gives you more freedom to move around.

NAPOLI RENT

Calata Trinità Maggiore 28; tel. 081/1925-9711; www.napolirent.it; scooters from €26.10 per day, cars from €31.50 per day

Napoli Rent offers car and scooter rental options with different locations to pick up your rental in Naples, including the airport, Piazza Garibaldi at the Napoli Centrale train station, or near the Molo Beverello at the port.

BUS TOURS
CITY SIGHTSEEING

Info point at Largo Castello Piazza Municipio; tel. 335/780-3812; www.city-sightseeing.it/it/napoli; adults €23, children 5-15 €11.50, under 4 free

For a worry-free way to get around Naples, City Sightseeing offers easy-to-spot, bright red, double-decker buses with open seating on the top. With the company's convenient hop-on hop-off policy, you can for an entire day, getting on and off as many times as you wish. Line A makes a loop through the historic center and includes stops at all the top sights, including the Museo Archeologico Nazionale and Museo di Capodimonte. Line B runs along the waterfront to Mergellina and along Posillipo to Capo Posillipo.

Pompeii

With more than 3.8 million visitors annually, Pompeii is one of the most popular sights in all of Italy. The archaeological ruins offer visitors the virtually once-in-a-lifetime experience to step back in time. Before Mount Vesuvius erupted in AD 79, it was a large Roman city in Campania dating back to the sixth century BC, when the city was founded by the Oscans from central Italy. Over centuries, it passed from Etruscans to Greeks to Samnites, and eventually to the Romans.

In the first century AD, Pompeii sat much closer to the coastline than it does today, and the city was prized for its location near the sea and the Sarno river, which made it an important trading city. Of course, it was also not far from the base of Mount Vesuvius, which the ancient Romans didn't know to be a dangerous volcano. In AD 62, a violent earthquake caused significant damage to Pompeii, but that was only a prelude to what was coming. The hustle and bustle of daily life came to a dramatic end for the people of Pompeii on that fateful day in AD 79, when the explosive eruption of Mount Vesuvius covered the city with volcanic material, primarily pumice and ash, from the violent pyroclastic flows. Every part of life stopped in time and was preserved for centuries by the ash that covered the city. The city was abandoned and forgotten until it was accidentally rediscovered, first in 1599 and later in 1748, when official excavations began. Early archaeological treasures including statues, mosaics, and frescoes were uncovered and removed, and many are now on display in Naples's **Museo Archeologico Nazionale.**

ORIENTATION

The massive archaeological site of Pompeii covers roughly 163 acres (66 ha), of which about 109 acres (44 ha) have been excavated, enclosed by about 2 miles (3 km) of city walls. Seven city gates have been uncovered, as well as the main streets that crisscrossed the city. **The Forum,** located in the southwest area of Pompeii, was the heart of the city. Two main streets, the **Via dell'Abbondanza** and **Via di Nola,** run southwest to northeast and are crossed by the main street **Via Stabiana.** (A Roman from AD 79 wouldn't be able to get around with the street names we use today, modern conventions often based on important buildings and finds.) Archaeologists have also divided the site into nine areas (called regio); the map and booklet you'll receive at the ticket booth is divided into these areas with the main sites numbered.

Entrance to the archaeological site is through the ancient **Porta Marina** in southwestern Pompeii; **Piazza Porta Marina Inferiore** (Piazza Esedra), where after the ticket booth you can follow the **Viale delle Ginestre** and enter the site on the southern side near the Teatro Grande; and **Piazza Anfiteatro** on the eastern side (mostly used for school groups). You can exit Pompeii these gates or from the **Porta Ercolano** to the northwest (note that you cannot enter Pompeii via the Porta Ercolano). Porta Marina leads to Via Marina and the Forum, making it easy to delve into Pompeii's history at the Antiquarium museum before exploring the ruins.

VISITING POMPEII

Entrance to the **Parco Archeologico di Pompei** (tel. 081/857-5111; www.pompeiisites.org) includes access to all its sights, and the Antiquarium. It is open 9am-7pm (last entrance 6pm) April-October, and 9am-5pm (last entrance 3:30pm) November-March. The site is closed on Mondays and on January 1, May 1, and December 25.

Full-price admission to Pompeii is €16 per person. Kids under 18 are free, but be prepared to show identification for older kids. Italian COVID-19 restrictions require tickets to be purchased online in advance for Saturdays, Sundays, and holidays. Tickets for weekday visits can be purchased either online in advance or at the entrance ticket booths. Since this requirement may be eased or change over time, do check the Parco Archeologico di Pompei website in advance for the latest visiting information.

The **Campania Artecard** (www.campaniartecard.it) offers free and discounted entrance to many sights in Naples as well as both Pompeii and Herculaneum. The Campania Artecard is available in three-day (€32 adults, €25 youth age 18-25) and seven-day (€34 adults) versions. Entrance to Pompeii is free with the three-day Artecard if it is one of the first two sights where you present the card; you'll receive a 50 percent discount if it's the third or subsequent sight visited. For the seven-day pass, Pompeii is free if it's one of the first five sights visited, or you'll receive a 50 percent discount if it is the sixth or subsequent sight visited.

Keep in mind that your ticket to Pompeii is valid for only one entrance. Once you enter, you won't be able to exit the park and re-enter with the same ticket. There is a café for refreshments and there are restrooms located throughout the excavation site.

Please note that due to COVID-19, in 2020, two obligatory routes to visit Pompeii were established to allow for a safe and more socially distanced visit to the site. These two color-coded one-way itinerary options cover many of the main sights, including areas like the forum as well as private homes. Visiting restrictions will be removed once it is safe to do so. Check the Parco Archeologico di Pompei website (www.pompeiisites.org) for the latest information on visiting guidelines and restrictions.

Planning Your Time

With such a large footprint and so many archaeological treasures, Pompeii's ruins require at least 3-4 hours to see just the highlights, such as the Antiquarium, Forum area, thermal baths, the city's theaters and amphitheater, homes in the city center, and the Villa dei Misteri outside the city walls. Allow more time to see more homes and areas of the city, but prepare for a good deal of walking. Much of Pompeii requires walking on uneven stone roads, and there's limited shade on sunny days. Bring water, sunscreen, and a hat on hot days. Comfortable closed-toed walking shoes are the best option for the rough and dusty setting. Inclement weather can turn Pompeii muddy, so it's best to adjust your schedule if possible and avoid the site if it's raining hard.

Given Pompeii's popularity, expect crowds pretty much any time of day.

Audio Guides and Tours

An entrance ticket to Pompeii includes a map and a booklet with brief information on all the main sights. Audio guides (available only at the **Porta Marina entrance;** adults €8, €6.50 each for more than one person, children €5, €4.50 each for more than one child) and tours are available at an additional cost. Be prepared to leave a personal ID of some kind in order to rent the audio guide.

Hiring a **private guide** or joining a **tour** is one of the best ways to get the most out of a visit to Pompeii. Authorized guides for the region of Campania can be hired near all the ticket booths. You can join a group (usually 12-15 people) and enjoy a roughly 2-hour tour of the highlights for around €10-15 per person. Groups. You can also opt for a 2- or 3-hour private tour with a guide that will cost roughly €100-120. As Pompeii includes areas of active excavation as well as restoration to existing sights, it's not uncommon for some areas to be closed. Guides are up to date on the openings, and can save you a lot of time by showing you only the houses that are currently open. After seeing the highlights and learning about the history on a guided tour, you can always choose to stay in the archaeological site and continue exploring on your own.

Pompeii

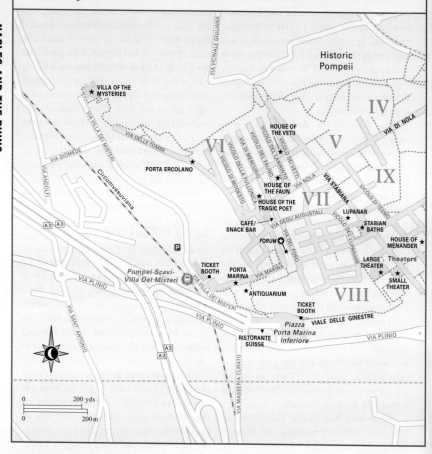

Historic
Pompeii

VILLA OF THE
MYSTERIES

VIA VICINALE GIULIANA

VIA VILLA DEI MISTERI

VIA DELLE TOMBE

VIA DIOMEDE

Circumvesuviana

VIA ANDOLFI

PORTA ERCOLANO

VI

VII

IV

V

IX

VIA DI NOLA

HOUSE OF
THE VETTII

VICOLO DI MERCURIO

VIA DEL FORO

VIA DEL LABIRINTO

VICOLO DEL FAUNO

VICOLO DEL LUPANARE

VICOLO STORTO

VICOLO BELVETTI

VIA NOLA

VIA STABIANA

VICOLO DI TESMO

HOUSE OF
THE FAUN

HOUSE OF THE
TRAGIC POET

CAFÉ/
SNACK BAR

FORUM

VIA DEGLI AUGUSTALI

LUPANAR

STABIAN
BATHS

HOUSE OF
MENANDER

VIA DELLA FULLONICA

P

Pompei Scavi-
Villa Dei Misteri

TICKET
BOOTH

PORTA
MARINA

VIA MARINA

VIA VILLA DEI MISTERI

LARGE
THEATER

Theaters

SMALL
THEATER

ANTIQUARIUM

VIII

VIA PLINIO

VIA SANT'ANTONIO

A3

A3

TICKET
BOOTH

VIALE DELLE GINESTRE

Piazza
Porta Marina
Inferiore

RISTORANTE
SUISSE

VIA PLINIO

VIA MASSERIA CURATO

A3

0   200 yds

0   200 m

WALKING TOUR OF POMPEII'S HIGHLIGHTS

The sights included here are the top highlights of Pompeii, but this only scratches the surface of all that Pompeii offers with its multitude of houses, civic and religious buildings, and public baths to explore at the site. Allow 3-4 hours to cover the sights included here, longer if you want to explore more of the buildings, temples, and sights you'll pass along the way.

Start: Antiquarium

Via Marina near Porta Marina entrance

Enter Pompeii through the Porta Marina gate and soon after the entrance you'll find the Antiquarium. This small museum is a great place to start your visit, as it offers an excellent introduction to Pompeii as well as a fine collection artefacts, artwork, and objects uncovered during excavations at Pompeii and other archaeological sites in the area.

★ Forum

Via Villa dei Misteri at Via Marina/Via dell'Abbondanza

From the Antiquarium, continue along Via

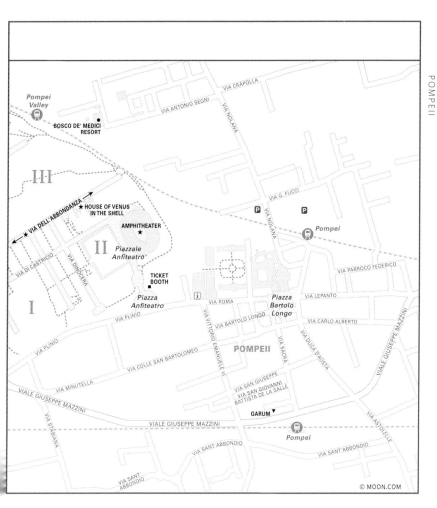

Marina until you reach the Forum, the heart of the ancient city. The large rectangular area is surrounded by temples dedicated to Jupiter, Apollo, Vespasian, and Venus. Looking toward the Temple of Jupiter on the northern side of the Forum you'll also find a perfectly framed view of **Mount Vesuvius** in the distance. On the south side, what is called the Basilica today was home to the law and commerce courts. The city's largest meat and fish market, called the Macellum, is located on the northeastern side of the Forum. Along the western side, stop to peer into the Forum Granary, which was once a large fruit and vegetable market, where you'll now see row after row of tall shelves lined with archaeological finds, including amphorae (large vases used for storage), pots and pans for cooking, statues, architectural details, and, most poignant, plaster casts of the bodies of victims of Pompeii that were created by archaeologists during the excavation process. Seeing the casts is a somber experience that can be unsettling to some visitors, especially young travelers. However, moments like this offer the chance to reflect on both the broad

Best Tours to Pompeii and Herculaneum

A guided tour is highly recommended for Pompeii and Herculaneum, and a group or private tour that includes transportation to the sites, or combines one or both of the cities with Vesuvius, can save you time and hassle.

RIMONTI TOURS

Via Monte di Dio 9, Naples; tel. 081/764-4934; www.rimontitours.com; group tours from €60 per person, private tours €300

If you're based in Naples, Rimonti Tours offers private and small-group excursions to Pompeii, Herculaneum, and Vesuvius, from fully private customized tours with a guide and transportation, to a small-group tour from Naples to Vesuvius, Herculaneum, and Pompeii. Group tours are often scheduled for set days of the week and require a minimum of eight people to run, so check in advance to see what is being offered during your visit. Bookings for daily excursions must be made in advance and can be done easily via the website.

ACAMPORA TRAVEL

Via del Mare 22, Sorrento; tel. 081/532-9711; www.acamporatravel.it; Apr.-Oct.; group tours from €38 per person

For daily group excursions to Pompeii, Herculaneum, and Vesuvius from Sorrento, Acampora Travel organizes a variety of half-day tours to individual locations, and full-day combo tours. Group tours include accommodation pickup and a guide, but not entrance fees. Different tours are scheduled for different set days of the week, so contact the company in advance to book.

SUNLAND

Corso Reginna 82, Maiori; tel. 089/877-455; www.sunland.it; Apr.-Oct.; group tours from €45 per person

From the Amalfi Coast, the Sunland travel agency offers many tour options, including private and group excursions to Pompeii and Vesuvius, Pompeii and Herculaneum, or half-day excursions to Pompeii. Tours include a guide and bus pickup from the Amalfi Coast. Tours of the archaeological sites take place on set days during the week and vary per tour, so check the schedule ahead of time. Advance bookings are required and can be made online.

CITY SIGHTSEEING

Info point at Largo Castello, Piazza Municipio, Naples; tel. 335/780-3812; www.city-sightseeing.it/it/napoli; from €15

The popular bus tour company offers a variety of transportation and tour options to make it easy to reach Pompeii, Herculaneum, and Vesuvius from Naples. All shuttle bus and tour options include an audio tour (available in English). With a variety of options to choose from, including a basic shuttle bus service, combined shuttle bus and priority entrance tickets or tours, or a combined Pompeii and Vesuvius or Herculaneum and Vesuvius shuttle bus option, this is a great choice if you're based in Naples and would like to explore the sights on your own without the hassle of public transportation.

historical significance of Pompeii and the tragic loss of individual lives.

Stabian Baths

Via dell'Abbondanza 15

From the Forum, follow Via dell'Abbondanza a few blocks east to see the Stabian baths, the oldest public baths in Pompeii dating back as early as the third century BC. The pristine state of the baths allows a rare glimpse into the splendid plumbing and heating systems that were used; the clever heating system is still quite intact. Public baths were a regular part of life in ancient

Rome, and as was the custom, the Stabian baths are divided into separate areas for men and women. You can walk through the changing rooms to another series of rooms, each one with a different water temperature. While the men's rooms are larger and more lavishly decorated with paintings, both the men's and women's areas offer a look at the multistep bathing process as well as the heating system with double floors and terra-cotta pipes in the walls where hot air was circulated throughout the structure from a furnace. There are two other interesting public baths in Pompeii, including the **Forum Baths** just north of the Forum and the **Central Baths** north of the Stabian Baths along Via Stabiana.

Lupanar

Vicolo del Lupanare at Vicolo del Balcone Pensile

Walk north a couple of blocks on Vicolo del Lupanare to visit the Lupanar, the largest brothel of the ancient city. The name of both the structure and the street come from the Latin word lupa, meaning prostitute. This two-level building has five rooms on the lower level, each one fitted with a built-in bed and that could be closed off with curtains. Along the main corridor are erotic-themed paintings that are thought to have encouraged clients or perhaps been used to communicate with clients speaking different languages. Let's just say they set the scene.

A visit to the Lupanar is included in most guided visits to Pompeii, but it can be skipped if it's not to a visitor's taste. However, it is interesting to note that erotic themes weren't particularly taboo in Roman culture. A large amount of art with erotic themes has been uncovered in Pompeii over the centuries, and much of it can be seen at the Gabinetto Segreto (Secret Cabinet) room at the **Museo Archeologico Nazionale** in Naples. It's also not uncommon to find erotic symbolism in the streets and houses of Pompeii, some of which are thought to have been a sort of porta fortuna (good luck symbol) for Romans.

Theaters

Near intersection of Via Stabiana and Via del Tempio d'Iside

From Lupanar, return down Vicolo del Lupanare, cross Via dell'Abbondanza to a beautiful part of Pompeii where the city's theaters are located. Here the **Large Theater** (Teatro Grande) is built into the hillside with steep seating and excellent acoustics. The theater was built around the second century BC and seated up to 5,000 people. Today it is still occasionally used as a particularly evocative setting for cultural and musical events. Next to the Large Theater, the Odeon or **Small Theater** (Teatro Piccolo) was originally a covered theater used for more intimate musical performances. Just south of the Large Theater, a large square—surrounded by 74 gray Doric columns—that was previously connected to the theater was transformed into a barracks for gladiators after the earthquake in AD 62.

House of Menander

Vicolo del Menandro between Vicolo del Citarista and Vicolo di Pasquius Proculus

From the theaters, go back the way you came, and take a right on Via dell'Abbondanza as it heads northeast into a residential area of the city, where you can walk through many fine Roman homes. One of Pompeii's most beautiful homes, House of Menander is located just off the main road and is worth a stop, if it's open, to see the frescoes depicting scenes from Homer's *Iliad* and *Odyssey.* (One thing to keep in mind is that, unlike the larger buildings, many of Pompeii's houses may be closed at any given time for restoration work.)

House of Venus in the Shell

Via dell'Abbondanza between Vicolo della Venere and Vicolo di Giulia Felice

Down farther on Via dell'Abbondanza, the House of Venus in the Shell is a very appealing house with detailed frescoes, including one of Venus reclining in a large shell. Via dell'Abbondanza, marked with deep grooves in the stone paving left by the wheels of countless carts rolling down the once busy street, is one of the main roads of Pompeii. On the way to the House of Venus in the Shell, don't miss the fine examples of thermopolia, which were somewhat like modern-day takeout or fast-food restaurants. You'll recognize them when you see their countertops with terra-cotta jars set into them, where ready-to-serve food was stored in the small restaurants, or dried goods were kept in the shops.

Amphitheater
Piazzale Anfiteatro

At the end of Via dell'Abbondanza, head south to visit the impressive Amphitheater built around 70 BC for gladiator fights. While smaller than more impressive amphitheaters like the Colosseum in Rome, Pompeii's oval Amphitheater is notable as the earliest known example of a large theater built primarily for gladiator combat. Built around 70 BC, it seated up to 20,000 people. With so many people coming and going, the Amphitheater was built on the outskirts to lessen the noise and crowding impact on daily life in Pompeii. Though there's no roar of the crowd today, the Anfiteatro is an impressive place to stand right in the center, gaze around, and imagine the scene.

House of the Vetii
Vicolo dei Vetti at Vicolo di Mercurio

Turn back toward the center of Pompeii along Via dell'Abbondanza and take a right on Via Stabiana and a left on Via della Fortuna. Stop to see the House of the Vetii, one of the richest and most finely decorated of all the houses excavated at Pompeii.

Café and Snack Bar

Back on Via della Fortuna, take a left on Via del Foro and stop for refreshments at the modern-day cafe and snack bar.

House of the Tragic Poet
Via della Fullonica between Via delle Terme and Vicolo di Mercurio

From Via del Foro, take a left and then an immediate right on Vicolo della Fullonica to see the a somewhat small house where glass covers the mosaic of a large and rather intimidating black dog with the words Cave Canem (Beware of the Dog) below.

House of the Faun
Vicolo di Mercurio between Vicolo del Fauno and Vicolo del Labrinto

Continue straight and take a right on Vicolo di Mercurio to see the House of the Faun, which is well worth the mini-detour. It is among the largest houses in Pompeii, whose name comes from the replica of a bronze statue of a faun in one of the atriums (the original is now at the Museo Archeologico Nazionale).

Villa of the Mysteries
Via Villa dei Misteri 2

Return back along Vicolo di Mercurio to Via Consolare and take a right. Keep walking as it passes through the ancient gate of Porta Ercolano and becomes Via delle Tombe, leading to the Villa dei Misteri (Villa of the Mysteries). Located outside the city walls northwest of Pompeii; this large villa is a fine example of a wealthy Roman agricultural estate. Built around large peristyle courtyard, the sprawling villa has many rooms you can explore on various levels. Because the villa received less damage during the eruption of Vesuvius than much of the rest of Pompeii, you can get an excellent sense of the original spaces with many ceilings and frescoes remarkably well intact. Its name comes from one series of captivating yet cryptic frescoes that have puzzled art historians, beautifully detailed with a striking red background, one of the largest and finest examples of painting from antiquity. A frieze depicts scenes of women performing various rituals along with a host of mythological figures, thought to be related to Dionysus, who appears in the center of the frieze.

1: remains of the House of the Faun 2: one of the rooms in the Stabian Baths 3: the Forum 4: fresco in the Villa of the Mysteries

End: Porta Marina Gate

You can exit the archaeological site near the Villa of the Mysteries or return along Via delle Tombe, Via Consolare, back through the Forum, and to Via Marina and the **Porta Marina gate.**

FOOD

Inside the archaeological site of Pompeii, a **café** located near the Forum offers a variety of snacks, sandwiches, and light meals as well as drinks. The restaurants below are located outside of the archaeological site.

GARUM

Viale Giuseppe Mazzini 63, Pompei; tel. 081/850-1178; www.ristorantegarumpompei.it; noon-4pm and 7pm-11:30pm Mon.-Tues. and Thurs.-Sat., noon-4pm Sun.; €8-16

Not far from the archaeological site near the modern-day city of Pompei, this restaurant specializes in traditional dishes and Campania wines. Special attention is given to ingredients like the antique garum fish sauce used in ancient Rome, which is featured in a variety of dishes, including a lovely spaghetti with tomatoes, pine nuts, raisins, and local anchovies.

RISTORANTE SUISSE

Piazza Porta Marina Inferiore 10/13, Pompei; tel. 081/862-2536; info@suissepompei.com; 8am-7pm daily Apr.-Oct., 8am-5pm daily Nov.-Mar.; €15-30

This popular restaurant is located in the piazza between the Porta Marina entrance and the entrance nearby off Piazza Porta Marina Inferiore. With a full restaurant, self-service bar for a quick meal, and pizzeria, there are plenty of options to choose from for the whole family. Stop for a coffee and something sweet in the morning before starting your tour, or have a snack or meal after a visit to the ruins.

ACCOMMODATIONS

BOSCO DE' MEDICI RESORT

Via Antonio Segni 43, Pompei; tel. 081/850-6463; www.pompeihotel.com/resort; €200

For a peaceful stay very near Pompeii, this resort is surrounded by citrus gardens and the Bosco de' Medici vineyard. After a day exploring the archaeological ruins, cool off and relax by the large pool while enjoying the view of Mount Vesuvius in the distance. There are 18 modern and comfortable rooms available with four suites that include a hot tub. All rooms have a private patio and entrance from the gardens surrounding the

Large Theater of Pompeii

resort. Free parking on site is a great feature if you're exploring the area by car.

GETTING THERE
By Train
Pompeii is easily reached by train from Naples (40 minutes; €2.80) and Sorrento (30 minutes; €2.40) with the **Circumvesuviana** train operated by **EAV** (www.eavsrl.it; departures every 30 minutes daily). Exit at the Pompeii Scavi-Villa dei Misteri stop, across the street from the Porta Marina entrance to Pompeii. Keep in mind that the Circumvesuviana is a commuter train for the area and can be quite crowded. However, it does provide an inexpensive way to reach Pompeii without the hassle of driving.

By Bus
Multiple bus lines connect Pompeii with surrounding cities. From Naples and Sorrento, the journey is much faster and more convenient by train. However, **City Sightseeing** (Info point at Largo Castello, Piazza Municipio, Naples; tel. 335/780-3812; www.city-sightseeing.it/it/napoli; adults €15, children 3-17 €8, children 2 and under free) offers a comfortable bus service from Naples to Pompeii. The easy-to-spot red buses depart from Molo Beverello port in Naples, from Piazza Garibaldi near the train station, and two other locations in the historic center. The price includes audio commentary in English. May-October there are four departures in the morning and four returns in the afternoon, while November-April there are two in the morning and two in the afternoon. A combined route including stops at Pompeii and Vesuvius is also available (from €25 per person).

From Salerno, **Busitalia Campania** (www.fsbusitaliacampania.it; €4) has two lines that connect the historic center of Salerno with Pompeii, stopping near Piazza Porta Marina Inferiore. Line 4 passes by the Salerno train station and takes about 1 hour 40 minutes; Line 50 also departs from Salerno's train station and takes about 1 hour 10 minutes.

To reach Pompeii from the Amalfi Coast, the easiest option is to first take the ferry or bus to Salerno and continue by bus, or first head to Sorrento and continue to Pompeii on the Circumvesuviana train.

By Car
Pompeii is located just off the **A3** autostrada (highway) connecting **Naples** (30 minutes) and **Salerno** (35-40 minutes). To reach Pompeii from **Sorrento** (45 minutes), follow the **SS145** east along the Sorrentine Peninsula to where it meets the A3. Whether you're coming from Naples, Salerno, or Sorrento, exit at Pompei Scavi, and in moments you'll arrive at the Porta Marina entrance. There are paid **parking** areas around the archaeological site, including one conveniently located near the Porta Marina entrance operated by Camping Zeus (tel. 081/861-5320; www.campingzeus.it; from €3 per hour).

Herculaneum

TOP EXPERIENCE

The same volcanic eruption that devastated Pompeii also destroyed the nearby city of Herculaneum, a Roman seaside resort. While Pompeii was covered with pumice and ash, Herculaneum's proximity to Vesuvius meant that it was buried below a very deep layer of mud combined with ash and volcanic materials, a horrendous end for the town's population that nevertheless preserved buildings, down to wooden structures like ceiling beams, upper floors, furniture, and doors.

The ruins of Herculaneum were rediscovered in 1709, before those of Pompeii, but the excavation of Herculaneum has always been a

Herculaneum

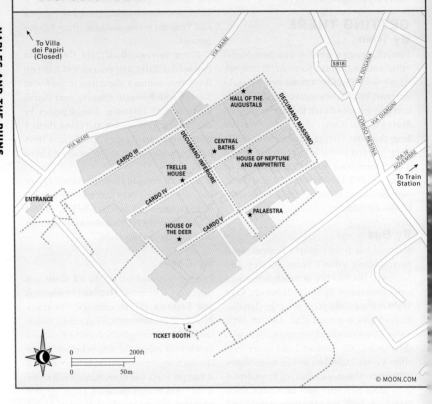

To Villa
dei Papiri
(Closed)

VIA MARE

VIA MARE

SB18

VIA DOGANA

CORSO RESINA

VIA GIARDINI

VIA IV NOVEMBRE

To Train
Station

HALL OF THE
AUGUSTALS ★

DECUMANO MASSIMO

CENTRAL
BATHS ★

DECUMANO INFERIORE

HOUSE OF NEPTUNE
AND AMPHITRITE ★

CARDO III

TRELLIS
HOUSE ★

CARDO IV

ENTRANCE

PALAESTRA ★

CARDO V

HOUSE OF
THE DEER ★

TICKET BOOTH ■

0   200ft
0   50m

© MOON.COM

challenge compared to Pompeii because the 52 feet (16 m) of volcanic mud covering the town turned into solid rock. And, unlike Pompeii, much of the ancient city of Herculaneum lies below the modern-day city of Ercolano. However, what has been uncovered so far of ancient Herculaneum has revealed true archaeological gems, and the site is certainly worth a visit.

ORIENTATION

The excavation site of Herculaneum is located well below street level and is accessed via a long, inclined walkway that offers a great view over the ruins before you even arrive. Much of the ancient city remains covered; only about 11 acres (4.5 ha) of the estimated 49 acres (20

ha) has been excavated. Based on the areas that have been brought to light, it's possible to get an idea of the city's original plan. As was traditional in Roman cities, Herculaneum is laid out in a grid, divided by at least three decumani, or main streets. Two of these have been uncovered, the **Decumano Inferiore** and the **Decumano Massimo,** running roughly southwest-northeast and crossed perpendicularly by five roads, called Cardo III, Cardo IV, and Cardo V on today's maps of Ercolano. The remaining two of the five crossroads lie in an unexcavated area northwest of the archaeological site. Since the Decumano Massimo is a noticeably larger street, researchers think it may mark where the Forum or center of the city started.

Before the eruption of AD 79, Herculaneum sat right at the edge of the sea. The volcanic material from the eruption moved the coastline much farther out to where we see it today. After you pass the ticket booth, look down to the right as you walk by the barrel-vaulted buildings below; these were originally boathouses opening to the beach. Herculaneum's most noted sight, the Villa of the Papyri, remains only partially excavated and is not open to the public. The ancient theater, which was the first sight at Herculaneum discovered in the early 18th century, is completely underground north of the archaeological area below modern-day Ercolano, and it is only rarely open to the public.

VISITING HERCULANEUM

The Herculaneum archaeological site is managed by the **Parco Archeologico di Ercolano** (Corso Resina, Ercolano; tel. 081/777-7008; www.ercolano.beniculturali.it) and is open 9:30am-7:30pm (last entrance 6pm) April-October, and 9:30am-5pm (last entrance 3:30pm) November-March. The site is open Thursday-Tuesday and is only closed on January 1 and December 25.

Full-price admission to Herculaneum is €13 per person. Kids under 18 get free admission, but bring identification, especially for older kids. Due to COVID-19 restrictions, tickets for entrance on Saturdays, Sundays, and holidays must be purchased online in advance, while weekday tickets can be purchased in person at the entrance. While this restriction may ease, it is best to check the Herculaneum website for the latest information and details on any possible restrictions or changes to opening hours.

If you purchase the **Campania Artecard** (www.campaniartecard.it), it includes many sights in Naples as well as free admission to both Herculaneum and Pompeii if the sites are the first two where you present the card; the card gives you a 50 percent discount if it's the third or subsequent site you visit. The

Campania Artecard is available in a three-day version (€32 adults, €25 youth age 18-25) and a seven-day version called the Campania Card (€34 adults).

Planning Your Time

Herculaneum doesn't receive the massive number of visitors that Pompeii gets, but you'll still find crowds here. The flow of visitors depends on the season and the number of cruise ships docked in nearby Naples and Sorrento, which means there's no one best time to plan a visit, though do try to explore the site in good weather. It takes 2-3 hours to see the site well. You'll do plenty of walking on uneven surfaces, although the inclined walkway and bridge down to access the site help to minimize the number of steps.

Audio Guides and Tours

Similar to a visit to Pompeii, admission to Herculaneum includes a **map** and **detailed booklet** with information on the most important sights. An **audio guide** is available for rent at an additional cost of €8 per person for adults, €6.50 each for more than one person, €5 per person for children, and €4.50 each for more than one child. You'll need to leave a form of ID for security in order to rent the audio guides. Smaller than Pompeii, Herculaneum is fairly easy for visitors to navigate with the booklet and audio guide combo. That said, the ruins really come to life with an **authorized tour guide,** available near the ticket booth for private and group tours.

SIGHTS

At Herculaneum, you'll find examples of many of the same types of buildings as at Pompeii, including public baths, shops, and eating establishments, and you'll enjoy the experience of walking down the streets of an ancient Roman town. The sights mentioned here are a selection of the top highlights, merely scratching the surface of what there is to see.

In the **Villa dei Papiri** (Villa of the

Papyri), one of the most sumptuous private houses in Herculaneum, more than 1,800 papyrus scrolls were discovered: a truly rare and precious find. As the villa is unfortunately closed to the public, the scrolls are now housed in the Biblioteca Nazionale di Napoli (National Library of Naples), where they are still undergoing intense study. Its famous sculptures are located in the Museo Archeologico Nazionale in Naples. The architectural design of the lavish villa was the inspiration for the J. Paul Getty Museum in Los Angeles, California.

Hall of the Augustals
Cardo III Superiore near Decumano Massimo
In this large building, a cult called the Augustals, dedicated to worshipping the Emperor Augustus, met and celebrated. Becoming a part of the Augustals was an important step for formerly enslaved people to move upward in Roman society. The rooms still retain traces of the original floors and wall decorations. Frescoes depict Hercules—the legendary founder of Herculaneum—in battle with the Etruscan god Achelous, and entering Olympus surrounded by a host of gods.

Central Baths
Cardo III Superiore and Cardo IV Superiore
The Central Baths, built in the second half of the first century BC, are divided into separate areas for men and women. The Men's Baths, accessed from Cardo III Superiore, include a dressing room where you can still see the niches where garments and personal items were stored. Beyond is a domed frigidarium for cold bathing and a tepidarium for warm bathing that includes a black and white mosaic of Triton, a sea god, surrounded by dolphins and a host of sea creatures. Beyond that is a caldarium, the hot room of the baths.
The Women's Baths are entered from Cardo IV Superiore and follow a similar progression of rooms, from the barrel-vaulted changing room to the tepidarium where shelves were located for personal items. This is followed by

the caldarium with a large vaulted ceiling, the furnace used to heat the rooms and water, and the well for the baths that drew water from a depth of about 27 feet (8.25 m). Adjacent to the baths is a large courtyard, surrounded by porticos, that was used as a palaestra, or gymnasium.

Houses of Herculaneum
Unlike its larger commercial neighbor, Herculaneum was a popular seaside resort town with luxurious homes and villas, meaning it has fine examples of houses, many with details that are even better preserved than at Pompeii. One of the loveliest houses, the **House of Neptune and Amphitrite** (Cardo IV Superiore) is noted for its remarkable wall mosaics, the most impressive of which depicts the god Neptune and his wife Amphitrite surrounded by decorative floral patterns and columns in brilliantly preserved shades of deep red, blue, yellow, and green. Nearby, easy to spot from the street with its wooden balcony supported by brick columns, the **Trellis House** (Cardo IV Inferiore) was originally a two-level boarding house with space for several families on the upper level; there's a separate entrance from the apartment on the lower level.
Another highlight, the elegant **House of the Deer** (Cardo V Inferiore) covers about 11,840 square feet (1,100 square m) and includes many rooms centered around a central garden. This is where archaeologists uncovered statues of deer being attacked by dogs, as well as statues of a Satyr and one of drunken Hercules, and round marble tables with ornately carved legs. Replicas of these statues and tables are located in the center of the garden.

Palaestra
Cardo V Superiore at Decumano Inferiore
The entrance to this building, between two

1: garden statue in the House of the Deer
2: mosaic in the House of Neptune and Amphitrite
3: the ruins of Herculaneum

large columns, leads into what was once a very large complex used for sporting activities. In the center there was originally a grand open space with a cross-shaped pool in the center, surrounded on three sides by arcades with columns and a corridor on the north side. The gymnasium complex included a variety of rooms, including a vast hall that was likely used for religious or cult ceremonies. Only a small area of the central garden and pool has been uncovered, but one of the finds includes a bronze fountain sculpture of the Lernaean Hydra, which was a frightening mythical monster with many snake heads.

FOOD
VIVA LO RE
Corso Resina 261, Ercolano; tel. 081/739-0207; www. vivalore.it; noon-4pm and 7pm-11pm Tues.-Sat., noon-4pm Sun.; €12-18

South of the archaeological park in Ercolano, this osteria and enoteca (wine bar) is a good spot to stop for a meal before or after visiting Herculaneum. Locally sourced ingredients are used beautifully to create traditional dishes with a twist, such as the lovely zuppa d'orzo con frutti di mare (barley soup with mixed seafood). The excellent wine list offers more than 1,500 labels.

GETTING THERE
By Train
The **Circumvesuviana** train run by EAV

(www.eavsrl.it; departures every 30 minutes daily; from Naples 20 minutes, €2.20, from Sorrento 40 minutes, €2.90) is the most comfortable public transportation option to reach Herculaneum. Exit at the Ercolano Scavi stop and head straight down Via Vittorio Veneto toward the sea and across the traffic circle to continue along Via IV Novembre for about 10 minutes. This will take you right to the entrance gate of the ruins.

By Bus
Shuttles buses from Naples to Herculaneum are run by **City Sightseeing** (Info point at Largo Castello, Piazza Municipio, Naples; tel. 335/780-3812; www.city-sightseeing.it/it/napoli; from €25), with a full-day route that includes stops at both Vesuvius and Herculaneum. It's a comfortable way to travel to both locations and includes an audio guide with information about the sights.

By Car
Herculaneum is located off the **A3** autostrada (highway) that connects Naples and Salerno. It's about a 30-minute drive from **Naples** and at least 45 minutes from **Salerno.** Exit at either the Ercolano or Portici/Ercolano exit and follow the signs indicating Scavi di Ercolano for a short distance to the archaeological site. There are paid **parking** lots southeast of the site (from €2 per hour).

Vesuvius

In ancient Roman times, the massive volcano Mount Vesuvius, called Vesuvio in Italian, was known as Monte Somma. The fertile land surrounding the mountain southeast of Naples was valued by the Romans, largely unaware that the lush green slopes of Vesuvius concealed a deadly, explosive volcano. Until the massive eruption in AD 79, only a few Roman scholars suspected the true nature of Monte Somma. Pliny the Elder studied the mountain,

and the geographer Strabo had written about stones on the mountain that looked as if they had been burned by fire. Yet the devastation of the eruption left no doubt of the fierce natural power below Vesuvius. Letters written by Pliny the Younger describe the events of that fateful day that killed his uncle Pliny the Elder as he tried to escape.

Vesuvius has erupted regularly over the centuries, though nowhere near as explosively as the AD 79 eruption. It is classified as a stratovolcano, made up of many layers of hardened lava, pumice, ash, and other materials and known for periodic and violent eruptions, similar to Mount St. Helens in the United States. Vesuvius is considered one of the most dangerous volcanoes in the world due to its unpredictable nature and the nearly three million people who live in the surrounding area. The last major eruption, in 1944 during World War II, was captured on film and video by the United States Air Force stationed near Naples at the time.

Today you can only occasionally catch a glimpse of wisps of steam coming out of the crater, but Vesuvius remains as much a threat as ever. It will come as no surprise that it's a heavily studied and constantly monitored volcano. Nevertheless, its gently curved slopes are an undeniable symbol of Naples. A climb to the top of the crater is a moving experience, both for the spectacular views and for the chance to be so close to such an incredible force of nature.

PARCO NAZIONALE DEL VESUVIO

Strada Provinciale Ercolano-Vesuvio; tel. 081/575-2524; www.parconazionaledelvesuvio.it; *hours to visit crater 9am-3pm daily Jan.-Feb. and Nov.-Dec., 9am-4pm daily Mar. and Oct., 9am-5pm daily Apr.-June and Sept., 9am-6pm daily July-Aug.; €10*

The Parco Nazionale del Vesuvio (Mount Vesuvius National Park) was created in 1995 to protect the area surrounding the volcano, along with its natural landscape, animal and plant species, and unique geological elements. The vast park covers 20,959 acres (8,482 ha), from the base of the volcano to the upper part around the cone. The fertile soil of the volcano has created a rich forest of pine and holm oak trees, along with maple, alder, chestnut, and oak trees. The park is especially rich in Mediterranean vegetation, with up to 23 types of orchids and several varieties of broom. Following the meandering road up the slopes of Vesuvius to the top leads through the natural landscape from the forested base up to the rugged, rocky area around the Gran Cono, the main cone of the volcano.

Even though the volcano is surrounded by a dense urban environment, the park is home to many different species of mammals, birds, and reptiles. Foxes, rabbits, and beech martens all call the slopes of the volcano home, along with more than 100 different species of birds, including migratory, wintering, and breeding

path on Mount Vesuvius

birds. It's a beautiful sight to catch a glimpse of a peregrine falcon gliding through the air along the slopes of the volcano.

★ Hiking to the Crater

Distance: 2.5 miles (4 km) round-trip
Time: 1-1.5 hours round-trip
Trailhead: Piazzale di quota 1,000 (parking area nearest the crater)
Information and Maps: Basic visiting information available at ticket stand and often at the top along the Gran Cono crater

By far the biggest draw at Vesuvius is the experience hiking around the crater, or Gran Cono, the highest point around the crater of the volcano. To hike to the crater, start with a drive or bus ride to the parking lot located at about 3,280 feet (1,000 m). First you'll need to purchase a ticket (€10 per person) at the ticket stand before the parking lot in order to access the pathway up to the crater. After buying your ticket, the steep and rocky pathway zigzags up to the edge of the crater. The path up to the crater is not shaded at all and rugged in parts, but there are plenty of spots to stop off and rest. Along the way, look over to the other peak on the other side of the volcano; it rises to 4,203 feet (1,281 m), and down to the valley of lava flow from the 1944 eruption.

Once you're at the top, the pathway levels out and opens to great views down into the crater, over the entire Naples area south to the Sorrentine Peninsula, and on a clear day to the islands of Capri, Ischia, and Procida in the Gulf of Naples. Along the crater you'll find an information and services booth where you can get more details on the volcano (available in English). A rocky pathway leading around a long section of the crater has wooden fences along either side and is a good vantage point to look down into the steep slopes of the crater. The hike up takes 20-30 minutes, depending on the number of photo stops or breaks you take. Plan to spend at least that long visiting the crater as well before doubling back on the same pathway for the 20-30-minute walk down. Mornings are the best time to visit the crater, as the view over the Gulf of Naples tends to be clearer and in the summer you can avoid the mid-day heat. To avoid having to rush, be sure to park in the lot area 1.5-2 hours before the park closes.

Keep in mind that the temperature at the summit can be quite cool, so it's a good idea to bring layers, even in the summer. Services are quite limited, though, so be sure to bring water and sunscreen. Comfortable footwear is highly recommended for the climb, but hiking boots are certainly not required. Note that the summit of Mount Vesuvius can be closed due to adverse weather conditions. To find out in advance if the crater is open, call the Parco Nazionale del Vesuvio for information (tel. 081/575-2524).

FOOD

KONA

Contrada Osservatorio, Ercolano; tel. 081/777-3968; ristorantekona@email.it; 11:30am-6pm daily and 7pm-11pm Fri.-Sun. (open for dinner daily May-Sept.); €8-15

Located along the road leading from the town of Ercolano up the slopes of Vesuvius, this restaurant is a convenient stop for a pizza or hearty lunch while you're driving to the crater of Vesuvius. There's a large dining area with indoor and outdoor seating and great views. The service is friendly and welcoming, and you can't go wrong with either the pizza or menu with traditional first- and second-course options. Set menus feature plenty of seafood and non-seafood choices.

GETTING THERE

Vesuvius is located about 6 miles (9.7 km) from Naples, 5 miles (8 km) from Pompeii, and 4.3 miles (7 km) from Herculaneum. The volcano is a popular day trip often combined with a visit to Pompeii or Herculaneum.

By Train

The **Circumvesuviana** train (www.eavsrl.it) stops at both the Pompeii and Herculaneum archaeological sites, where you can then connect to buses to reach the nearest point of the summit of Vesuvius before continuing on foot.

By Bus

From Pompeii, the public bus company **EAV** (www.eavsrl.it; departures every 50 minutes; approximately 1-hour journey; Apr.-Sept.; €2.70) operates a bus line during the tourist season connecting Pompeii with the Gran Cono of Vesuvius. Buses depart from the Piazza Anfiteatro with a stop at the Pompeii Scavi-Villa dei Misteri Circumvesuviana train station near the Porta Marina entrance. Tickets can be purchased onboard. Buses run 8am-3:30pm from Pompeii and return from Vesuvius to Pompeii 9am-5:40pm, and can be very crowded at times and may be standing-room-only during peak periods.

Busvia del Vesuvio (www.busvia delvesuvio.com; Apr.-Oct.; €10 round-trip) runs a line from Pompeii to Vesuvius, departing from the Pompeii-Villa dei Misteri Circumvesuviana train station near the Porta Marina entrance to Pompeii. Keep in mind that entrance to Vesuvius is not included in the price. Buses can be crowded and schedules might not be on the mark during peak season. From Ercolano, **Vesuvio Express**

(tel. 081/739-3666; www.vesuvioexpress.info; €10 round-trip, €20 including entrance to Vesuvius) operates a bus route departing from the Ercolano Circumvesuviana train station. Both Busvia del Vesuvio and Vesuvio Express services include the round-trip transfer and free time to hike to the crater of Vesuvius.

To visit Vesuvius from Naples, **City Sightseeing** (Info point at Largo Castello, Piazza Municipio, Naples; tel. 335/780-3812; www.city-sightseeing.it/it/napoli; from €20) offers shuttle buses with direct service to the volcano or combined routes with stops at Pompeii or Herculaneum. With audio guides included for the journey, it's the most comfortable way to get to Vesuvius from Naples.

By Car

From the **A3** autostrada connecting **Naples** (30 minutes) and **Salerno** (40 minutes), exit at Ercolano and follow signs for Parco Nazionale del Vesuvio. The road begins to climb up Via Vesuvio. The setting, landscape, and views improve as you continue to drive up. The road winds its way to a small parking area at an altitude of about 3,280 feet (1,000 m). You must park in the paid lot there before continuing on foot to the ticket booth. Expect to pay around €5 to park.

Sorrento, Capri, and the Amalfi Coast

Itinerary Ideas 104
Sorrento 105
Positano 120
Amalfi 141
Ravello 158
Salerno 167
Capri 180

With a beauty that has captivated travelers for ages, the UNESCO World Heritage protected Amalfi Coast's dramatic scenery, charming villages, rocky beaches, and famous views have made it one of Italy's most popular travel destinations. Positano, known as the Vertical City, is one of the biggest draws, with its pastel-hued buildings scattered down the mountainside to the beach. Amalfi is the namesake town and was the seat of a powerful maritime republic in the Middle Ages. High above Amalfi in the mountains, Ravello stretches out across a promontory with sweeping views of the coast.

Though not on the Amalfi Coast proper, sitting as it does on the north side of the Sorrentine Peninsula, Sorrento boasts a well-preserved historic center and a picturesque setting atop a rocky terrace.

Highlights

Look for ★ to find recommended sights, activities, dining, and lodging.

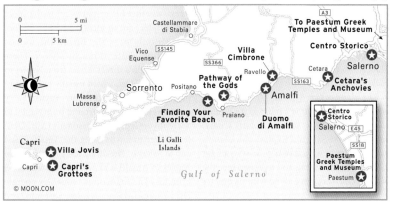

© MOON.COM

★ **Pathway of the Gods:** Hike the Pathway of the Gods to take in extraordinary views far away from the crowds (page 129).

★ **Finding Your Favorite Beach:** From the colorful umbrellas of Positano's stylish Spiaggia Grande to the quaint wooden fishing boats of Marina di Praia in Praiano, the Amalfi Coast's beaches rank among the best in the world (page 130).

★ **Duomo di Amalfi:** Step back in time to the splendor of Amalfi's medieval past at this impressive cathedral sitting atop a grand staircase in the town's main square (page 141).

★ **Villa Cimbrone, Ravello:** Gaze into endless beauty from the Terrace of Infinity in these finely landscaped gardens, where the sky and sea blend into one tantalizing view (page 160).

★ **Cetara's Anchovies:** With a fishing history dating back to Roman times, Cetara is known for its seafood. Anchovies are a specialty in local

dishes, and they're celebrated with a festival every July in this small town off the main tourist path (page 166).

★ **Centro Storico, Salerno:** Meander through the maze of narrow streets in Salerno's medieval historic center, with its lively atmosphere, excellent shopping options, and important historic landmarks (page 170).

★ **Paestum Greek Temples and Museum:** Marvel at the well-preserved Greek temples, and admire the archaeological treasures uncovered at the museum (page 177).

★ **Villa Jovis:** Hike to the top of Monte Tiberio on Capri to explore the ruins of the once palatial villa of Roman Emperor Tiberius. More stunning views are an added bonus (page 183)!

★ **Capri's Grottoes:** Enjoy a private or group boat tour around the island to see Capri's natural grottoes, including the Grotta Azzurra (Blue Grotto), up close (page 192).

To the east, the Amalfi Coast flows right into the large port city of Salerno. Though it's off the radar for many travelers, Salerno is a fascinating city with a wealth of history, and it is more tranquil than nearby Naples. Explore the medieval city center, stroll along the lungomare (waterfront), climb to the castle high above the city, and visit the impressive cathedral. With excellent train and ferry service, it's a good home base for travelers who enjoy a city vibe.

Beyond the tempting beaches and sparkling blue Mediterranean Sea, the not-to-be-missed archaeological site of Paestum is a short jaunt from Salerno. Its remarkable temples stand as testimony to the area's rich history. From these Greek temples to the medieval splendor of Amalfi, the history of the Amalfi Coast is a tapestry set against one of the most splendid backdrops in Italy.

The island of Capri has an allure known far and wide, and a visit is a must as it's located conveniently close to the Amalfi Coast, Sorrento, and Salerno. Explore the island's natural beauty on a day trip or stay longer for exceptional hiking and to experience the island's chic shopping along with its quieter side.

So pack a pair of comfortable shoes and explore the Amalfi Coast area with all its magnificent twists and turns, history, and beauty.

ORIENTATION

The Amalfi Coast lines the southern coast of the Sorrentine Peninsula, the finger of land between the Gulf of Naples and the Gulf of Salerno. The main towns of the Amalfi Coast, from west to east, are **Positano, Praiano, Amalfi,** and **Ravello** (which is not on the coast, but rather up in the hills northeast of Amalfi). **Salerno** is to the east of the Amalfi Coast and is a transit hub for getting to the Amalfi Coast towns. On the north coast of the Sorrentine Peninsula is **Sorrento,** which also serves as an important transit hub for those traveling to the Amalfi Coast. The lovely island of **Capri** is located just west of the Sorrentine Peninsula.

GETTING TO THE AMALFI COAST
Public Transportation

Naples is the main starting point for travelers to the Amalfi Coast, which can be reached via public transportation by ferry or a combination of train and ferry or train and bus. Getting to the Amalfi Coast by ferry (whether all or partway) is the most comfortable, not to mention scenic, option, but it's only possible during the tourist season from Easter through October. There are only limited direct ferries from Naples to the Amalfi Coast, which usually only run in the peak of summer from July-August. Ferry service is available year-round from Naples to Sorrento or Capri, and seasonally (Apr.-Oct.) from there to towns along the Amalfi Coast and to Salerno. The direct ferry journey from Naples to Amalfi is approximately 1 hour 45 minutes. The following companies operate ferry routes between Naples, Sorrento, and Capri:

- **NLG** (tel. 081/552-0763; www.navlib.it; from €13.10 per person) and **Gescab** (tel. 081/428-5259; www.gescab.it; from €20.50) operate jet routes between Naples, Capri, and Sorrento.

- **SNAV** (tel. 081/428-5555; www.snav.it; from €17.70) operates lines from Naples to Capri and from Sorrento to Capri.

- **Caremar** (tel. 081/189-66690; www.caremar.it; from €12.30 for passengers and €28.50 for vehicles) offers ferry service and can transport vehicles from Naples and Sorrento to Capri.

- **Alilauro** (tel. 081/878-1430; www.alilaurogruson.it; Apr.-Oct.; from €18.20

per person) connects Naples to Sorrento and Capri, with onward service to the Amalfi Coast.

Salerno is the closest major train station to the Amalfi Coast. Trenitalia (www.trenitalia.com) operates frequent train service between Naples and Salerno daily with travel times ranging from 40 minutes-1 hour 25 minutes, depending on the type of train. From the station you can catch SITA SUD buses to the Amalfi Coast or walk to the port nearby, to catch a ferry (seasonally, Apr.-Oct.) operated by Travelmar (tel. 089/872-950; www.travelmar.it; €3-14 per person) and Alicost (tel. 089/871-483 weekdays, 089/948-3671 weekends; www.alicost.it; €15-26.90 per person).

There is also a train station in Sorrento. The Circumvesuviana train line operated by EAV (www.eavsrl.it) connects Naples (from Piazza Garibaldi at the Napoli Centrale train station) with the archaeological sites of Pompeii and Herculaneum as well as Sorrento. The full journey from Naples to Sorrento takes about 60 minutes. Tickets can be purchased at the station. This regional commuter train runs frequently throughout the day and is an inexpensive way to travel between Naples and Sorrento, though there are many stops along the way. The train can get quite busy, so don't be surprised if you have to stand for part of the journey during peak hours in the morning and evening. From Sorrento, you can catch a SITA SUD bus right outside the train station, or in the summer season you can take a ferry.

To get to the Amalfi Coast from Puglia by public transport, you'll most likely need to travel to Naples first, though buses to Salerno also exist. Renting a car to explore Puglia, then driving the 3-plus hours to drop it off in Salerno—so you don't need to deal with the winding roads and crowded parking lots of the Amalfi Coast—may be your best option. From Sicily, though it's possible to travel to Salerno by train or bus, a quick flight from Palermo or Catania to Naples is probably the best bet.

GETTING AROUND THE AMALFI COAST

The landscape of the Amalfi Coast is rugged, with its famously twisty road weaving up and down, connecting towns situated both at sea level and dotted across the mountainsides. While it's certainly not the most straightforward area to explore, with a little preparation you'll be navigating the Amalfi Coast like a pro in no time.

By Car and Scooter

The Amalfi Coast Road (Strada Statale 163, also abbreviated as SS163) winds its way from Salerno west to Positano. The only road along the coastline, this very narrow and curvy route can become quite packed, especially during peak seasons, around Easter and from July-August. Driving the Amalfi Coast Road is not for the faint of heart. Be prepared for tight squeezes and the occasional traffic jam; if you're the driver, don't expect to enjoy those famous views, because it's hard to take your eyes off the road even for a moment. Locals know the route like the backs of their hands, and overtaking is very common. If the traffic behind you wants to move faster than you're comfortable, pull over when possible to let cars pass. Parking can be a challenge, especially during the summer, but there are paid parking lots or spaces in every town where you can pay hourly or daily.

To drive the Amalfi Coast Road with a bit less stress, consider renting a scooter. They make it easier to negotiate tight roads and allow you to zip around (or even through!) traffic jams. You can rent scooters in most of the towns on the Amalfi Coast. Many companies will even deliver a scooter right to your accommodation for a small fee. Bring an ID if you plan to rent a scooter. While parking a scooter is a bit easier, it can still be a challenge from July-August, even though paid parking areas for scooters are common.

By Bus

Buses are an inexpensive and relatively stress-free way to get around the Amalfi Coast. The

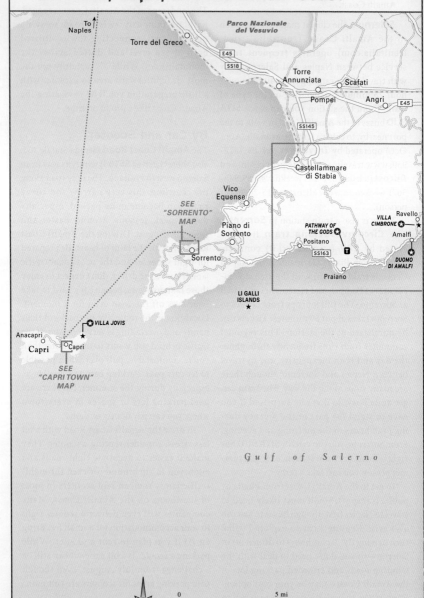

Sorrento, Capri, and the Amalfi Coast

To Naples

Torre del Greco

Parco Nazionale
del Vesuvio

E45

SS18

Torre
Annunziata

Scafati

Pompei

Angri

E45

SS145

Castellammare
di Stabia

Vico
Equense

SEE
"SORRENTO"
MAP

Piano di
Sorrento

Sorrento

VILLA
CIMBRONE ⊕ ★

Ravello

PATHWAY OF
THE GODS ⊕

Positano

SS163

T

Amalfi

DUOMO
DI AMALFI ★

Praiano

LI GALLI
ISLANDS ★

★ VILLA JOVIS

Anacapri

Capri

O Capri

SEE
"CAPRI TOWN"
MAP

Gulf   of   Salerno

0   5 mi

0   5 km

© MOON.COM

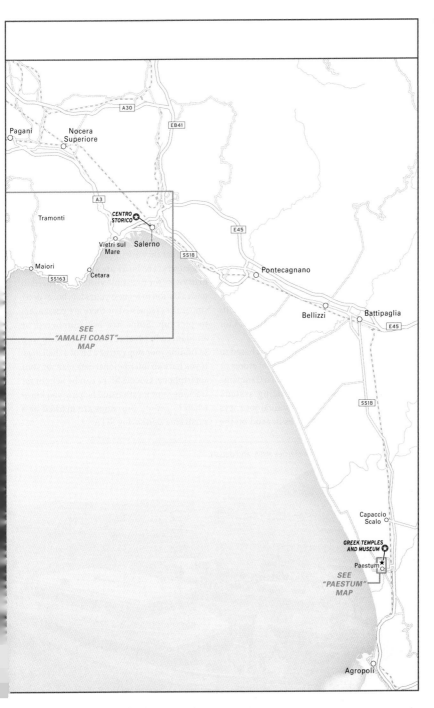

road, however, remains busy and tricky, which means that bus schedules rarely run precisely on time. If you're planning to travel by bus, be prepared to wait and to deal with crowds in the summer.

If you are traveling with luggage, you will need to take the SITA SUD bus, not the City Sightseeing bus, and it will need to be stored below the bus before boarding. Be sure to let the driver know you must retrieve luggage before getting off the bus.

SITA SUD PUBLIC BUSES

The Amalfi Coast towns are well connected with buses operated by **SITA SUD** (tel. 089/386-6701; www.sitasudtrasporti.it; from €1.30 per person) that run along the Amalfi Coast Road and to towns located higher in the mountains. **Amalfi** is a central bus hub along the Amalfi Coast Road, with the main bus lines running between Salerno and Amalfi and between Amalfi and Sorrento. Buses for Ravello depart from Amalfi, as well.

SITA SUD tickets need to be purchased in advance in local tabacchi (tobacco) stores or some bars. Tickets follow the Unico Campania (www.unicocampania.it) pricing system, where you can pay for individual journeys or daily passes. Ticket prices depend on the length of the journey and start at €1.30. Or opt for a **COSTIERASITA ticket** for €10 (€12 for one that also includes the internal bus lines for Positano) that covers all bus rides for 24 hours to and from most towns on the coast. Validate your ticket at the small machine located behind the driver only on the first bus you take, and be sure to write your name and birth date on the ticket where indicated. Ticket inspectors do circulate on the routes and will fine you if you haven't properly validated your ticket.

SITA SUD buses are popular with locals and travelers alike and can be absolutely jam-packed during peak season. Lines for getting the bus are chaotic, and buses can be so full that they are unable to stop to pick up passengers. The buses are also not the easiest to navigate for first-time visitors. You need to push a button to request your stop; buses don't stop unless requested or there are passengers to pick up. Stops are not numbered or announced in advance in any consistent way, so finding your stop can be a bit of a challenge. If you have an international data plan for your smartphone, Google Maps can be helpful for tracking your location and helping you know when to get off. Bus stops are marked by a small blue sign saying SITA.

Positano's cement pier, where ferries arrive and depart

CITY SIGHTSEEING

City Sightseeing (www.city-sightseeing.it; Apr.-Oct.; from €5 per person) has three bus lines on the Amalfi Coast, including one from Sorrento to Positano and Amalfi and one that connects Amalfi and Ravello. Buses are bright red and easy to spot; the Amalfi-Ravello line often has open-top buses with a view. These are a little more expensive than the public buses, but far more comfortable. Tickets are purchased onboard, and these buses only allow as many passengers as they have seats. Audio guides included with tickets. Unlike other City Sightseeing routes, this one is not hop-on hop-off. The first ticket costs €10, but if you get off at a midway point and get back on the same route you will need to pay again (€6 if you present your first full-price ticket).

By Ferry

Traveling by ferry is the most comfortable and least stressful way to navigate the Amalfi Coast, and it offers scenic views from the sea. Ferry service connects many towns on the Amalfi Coast, including Positano, Amalfi, and Salerno. Amalfi and Positano are the main ferry terminals along the coastline. Boat service to Salerno, Capri, and Sorrento is also available seasonally from the towns of Positano and Amalfi.

Travelmar (tel. 089/872-950; www.travelmar.it; €3-14 per person) and **Alicost** (tel. 089/871-483 weekdays, 089/948-3671 weekends; www.alicost.it; €15-26.90 per person) are the main ferry companies connecting Salerno, the Amalfi Coast, Capri, and Sorrento. Tickets can be purchased online in advance or at ticket booths near the ferry terminals. From Positano, **Positano Jet** (tel. 089/811-164; www.lucibello.it; €10-24.50 per person) offers ferry service connecting Positano, Amalfi, and Capri.

Keep in mind that ferry service is seasonal and only runs from about **Easter** through the beginning of **November.** Naturally, the service is also dependent on the weather and sea conditions. Even though rough seas rarely prohibit service in the summer, during the shoulder seasons of April-May and October, it's a good idea to have a backup plan for other transportation options.

By Taxi

Taxis are a comfortable but expensive way to get around the Amalfi Coast. Taxis between towns operate differently from city taxis insofar as the fares aren't usually based on time or distance but on the journey. A ride from one town to the next can cost €40 or more, even if it's a short drive, so be sure to negotiate and agree with the driver on a price before departing.

One time you may want to splurge on a taxi is arriving or departing from the Amalfi Coast, or anytime you need to be somewhere at a specific time, as buses can be delayed. Public transportation is not particularly easy to negotiate with luggage, so a private transfer to or from the airport or other point of arrival can help alleviate stress.

PLANNING YOUR TIME

Many travelers see the Amalfi Coast on a day excursion from a cruise ship, or from nearby Naples or Sorrento. Though spending a day is better than not visiting at all, a single day only gives you a small taste of what the coast has to offer. To explore more deeply, plan to spend at least three days to visit the three main towns on the coast—Amalfi, Positano, and Ravello—along with a bit of time to relax on the beach. With a week, there is plenty of time for hiking, enjoying water sports along the coastline, and adding day trips to nearby destinations, such as Capri or Sorrento.

Expect crowds, especially **June-August.** Visit during the shoulder seasons if you want a quieter visit.

For shorter visits, Amalfi makes an excellent home base, thanks to its central location and transportation connections. Although Positano is well connected to other towns by ferries, the public buses that pass by at the top of town are often very crowded.

Itinerary Ideas

ESSENTIAL AMALFI COAST

Make the most of a shorter stay on the Amalfi Coast by hitting the three most popular towns. Amalfi is a great starting point for delving deeper into the region's history, before heading up into the mountains to explore Ravello, famous for its fine views and peaceful gardens. And of course, a visit to the Amalfi Coast isn't complete without seeing Positano.

Day 1: Amalfi and Ravello

1 Start in the Piazza Duomo, where you'll find a striking view of the Duomo di Amalfi. Visit the historic bakery and coffee shop **Pasticceria Pansa** for the best espresso and cappuccino in town, and for one of their tempting sfogliatelle (shell-shaped pastries).

2 Climb the long staircase to visit the **Duomo di Amalfi,** taking time to savor the peacefulness of the Cloister of Paradise, admire the treasures in the museum, and see the crypt of Sant'Andrea, the town's patron saint.

3 Find out more about Amalfi's important role in the history of papermaking at the **Museo della Carta.**

4 Hop on a bus or taxi for the short drive up to Ravello. Savor lunch with a panoramic view from the **Ristorante Garden.**

5 Stroll through the charming Piazza Duomo and visit the **Duomo di Ravello** to see the mosaic-covered pulpit and ambon.

6 Enjoy a leisurely walk to the **Villa Cimbrone** to explore the famous garden and see the view from the Terrace of Infinity.

view of Amalfi from the sea

7 Return to Amalfi and watch the sunset over drinks at Gran Caffè, with a view of Marina Grande beach.

8 Enjoy a relaxed dinner overlooking the beach at Ristorante Marina Grande.

Day 2: Positano

1 If you're not based in Positano, the best way to arrive is by ferry to enjoy the spectacular view of the town from the sea. The ferry docks right at the Spiaggia Grande beach; walk along the beach and climb the steps to visit the Chiesa di Santa Maria Assunta. Step inside to see the town's prized Byzantine icon hanging above the altar.

2 Stroll along Via Positanesi d'America over to the Spiaggia di Fornillo beach and pick out a sun bed from Da Ferdinando for some relaxation in the sun. When it's time for lunch, enjoy a fresh meal just steps from the beach at their restaurant.

3 Spend the afternoon exploring all the little pathways lined with boutiques. Stroll along Viale Pasitea to find an excellent selection of some of Positano's popular fashion and homeware shops. Stop for a fresh juice from Casa e Bottega.

4 Shop for perfume at Profumi di Positano to take a little of the sweet scent of Positano home with you.

5 As the sun begins to set, enjoy a spritz at Franco's Bar before hopping on the ferry to wave arrivederci to Positano.

Sorrento

Sorrento, the land long associated with the mythical sirens, has been captivating travelers for centuries. On a long, flat terrace of craggy coastline, where the cliffs drop straight to the sea, the Greeks and later Romans built a fortified town protected by its inaccessible setting and thick stone walls, parts of which are still visible around the city today. Although much of the historic center's urban plan dates back to the ancient Roman city of Surrentum, the Sorrento we see today is a refined modern holiday destination.

This friendly place, noted for its hospitality and Mediterranean charm, became a popular spot for travelers in the 18th century during the Grand Tour. Weary after a long journey through Italy, travelers found in Sorrento a true respite where the sweet scent of citrus blossoms mingled with the salty breeze. Elegant hotels like the Grand Hotel Excelsior Vittoria are the bastions of Sorrento's old-world style and elegance with large gardens and captivating views, still savored by travelers from around the world today. Visiting the city's excellent museums reveals centuries of artwork inspired by Sorrento, including the city's important artisan craft of intarsia (inlaid woodwork). Tradition and hospitality combine beautifully in Sorrento; come discover for yourself the city's eternal allure.

ORIENTATION

Sorrento is a small city where all of the top sights and the charming historic center are easily explored on foot. Indeed, walking is a pleasure in Sorrento compared to much of the Amalfi Coast area, because it is quite flat. However, the town's two harbors, Marina Piccola and Marina Grande, are both located below the city center, which sits on a cliff. The names are pretty misleading: Marina Piccola (Small Harbor) is the largest port in town, where ferries arrive and depart for destinations in the Gulf of Naples, including Naples, Capri, and the Amalfi Coast. Marina

Itinerary Ideas

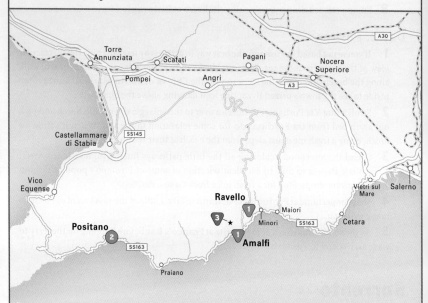

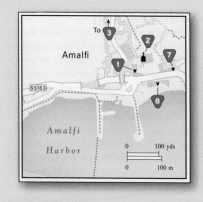

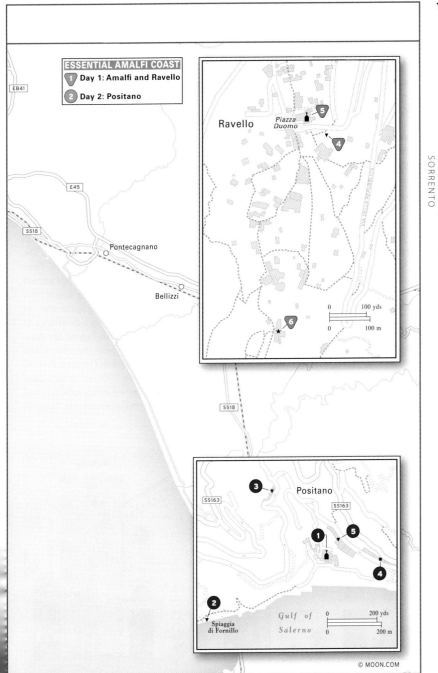

ESSENTIAL AMALFI COAST
1 Day 1: Amalfi and Ravello
2 Day 2: Positano

Ravello
Piazza Duomo
5
4

VIA DELLA REPUBBLICA

EB41

E45

SS18

Pontecagnano

Bellizzi

6

0   100 yds
0   100 m

SS18

3   Positano

SS163   SS163

1   5
4

2
Spiaggia
di Fornillo

Gulf of
Salerno

0   200 yds
0   200 m

© MOON.COM

Grande (Large Harbor) is a small port west of the historic center with a charming atmosphere that's perfect for a quiet swim or dining by the sea.

Piazza Tasso is the heart of Sorrento with the city's main thoroughfare, **Corso Italia,** running through it roughly east-west and parallel to the sea. Following Corso Italia east of Piazza Tasso leads to the **train station** at Piazza Giovanni Battista de Curtis. From Piazza Tasso heading west, Corso Italia is a lively spot for shopping and dining during the day and especially for the evening passeggiata (stroll). The **historic center** (centro storico) of Sorrento is north of Corso Italia, up to the steep cliffside overlooking the Gulf of Naples. It's a relatively small and highly walkable area stretching from Piazza Tasso on the east to Via Sopra le Mura on the west. An ancient urban plan dating back to the Romans, the historic center is a grid, where you'll find excellent shopping and dining options.

SIGHTS
Cattedrale di Sorrento

Via Santa Maria della Pietà 44; tel. 081/878-2248; www.cattedralesorrento.it; 8am-noon and 5pm-8pm daily Apr.-Oct., 8am-noon and 4pm-7pm daily Nov.-Mar.; free

Along Corso Italia not far from Piazza Tasso, Sorrento's Cathedral is dedicated to Saints Filippo and Giacomo. The first cathedral in Sorrento was founded as early as the 10th century, but it was completely rebuilt in the 16th century after being damaged during the Turkish invasions in 1558. The beautifully preserved baroque decorations inside the church date from an 18th-century restoration.

In fact, the cathedral's simple neo-Gothic façade from 1924 conceals a treasure trove of architectural design and remarkable examples of Sorrento's famed inlaid woodwork. The warm feel of the woodwork is enhanced by ornate golden ceiling decorations, deep orange marble panels on the columns down the nave, and terra-cotta-colored detail on the arches that perfectly complement the wood accents throughout the church. Look for the detailed intarsia work inside around the wooden entrance, depicting stories from the church's history, as well as the stations of the cross along the two side aisles and the incredible choir stalls behind the altar. In the central nave near the altar stand two interesting elements: On the left is the Cattedra, the Bishop's throne, which dates from 1573 and incorporates columns and pieces from ancient Roman temples. Opposite

Cattedrale di Sorrento

is a marble pulpit, also from the 16th century, with a bas-relief sculpture depicting the baptism of Christ. Back outside, you'll spot the bell tower, constructed around the 11th century in the Romanesque style, located not far from the church, with ancient columns at the base up to a clock with ceramic tiles near the top.

Centro Storico

Via San Cesareo north to Villa Comunale and Via Marina Grande between Via Luigi de Maio and Via Sopra le Mura

Sorrento sits on a foundation dating back to an ancient Greek settlement that later became an important urban center for the Romans, who called the town Surrentum. Their footprint is still evident in the grid of streets that make up the centro storico (historic center). Until the late 1800s, when Corso Italia was built, the main street of the historic center was Via San Cesareo, which corresponds to the ancient Greek decumano maggiore (most important street). **Piazza Tasso,** the bustling heart of Sorrento, sits at the eastern end of the centro storico. From the piazza, walk up **Viale Enrico Caruso** about a block and peer down at the **Vallone dei Mulini,** a deep valley that at one point extended all the way down to Marina Piccola, where you can spot the ruins of an abandoned old mill. Meander through the small historic center, which is now home to a host of shopping and dining spots, as well as churches and historic sights. Largely pedestrian-only, this area is ideal for popping in and out of shops or stopping for lunch or dinner at one of the many restaurants with outdoor seating.

Villa Comunale

Via San Francesco; 7:30am-8:30pm daily Jan.-Mar. and Nov.-Dec., 7:30am-11pm daily Apr. and Oct., 7:30am-midnight daily May, 7:30am-1am daily June-Sept.; free

Just beyond the Chiesa di San Francesco, this small square is a popular spot, primarily for the panoramic view it offers across the Gulf of Naples. With shady spots to sit beneath the trees, you can relax a moment and savor the view across to Naples and Mount Vesuvius. Walk right to the edge of the park and peer down the sheer cliff to Sorrento's beach area below. You can get down to the beach via a zigzag staircase or pay a small fee to take the available **elevator** (Sorrento Lift, Villa Comunale; tel. 081/807-2543; www.sorrentolift.it; hours same as Villa Comunale; €1 each way or €1.90 round-trip).

Museo Correale di Terranova

Via Correale 50; tel. 081/878-1846; www.museocorreale.it; 9:30am-1:30pm Tues.-Sun.; €8

Set in the historic residence of the noble Terranova family, this museum opened in 1924 through a donation from Alfredo and Pompeo Correale, counts of Terranova. On the ground level is a gallery dedicated to the Correale family, followed by a gallery showcasing the inlaid woodwork tradition of Sorrento. The final gallery on this floor displays fascinating archaeological finds, including Greek and Roman statues and two sculptures from Egypt which arrived in Sorrento during Roman times.

On the upper floors, paintings are displayed among fine examples of furniture, ceramics from China and Japan, and historic clocks, which periodically fill the galleries with their chimes. The Room of Mirrors is resplendent with its late 18th-century gold-embellished mirrors and consoles. There's an extensive collection of 18th- and 19th-century landscape paintings from the Posillipo School. On the upper level, the ceramics exhibits include majolica from Italy and France as well as porcelain dishes, vases, and figurines from significant European producers, such as Meissen and Sèvres, as well as Capodimonte pieces made by the Real Fabbrica di Napoli.

After visiting the museum, take time to explore the extensive gardens, an unexpected oasis right in the heart of Sorrento, including a citrus grove first planted in the 17th century and a pathway that leads to a large terrace with a fabulous view of the Gulf of Naples.

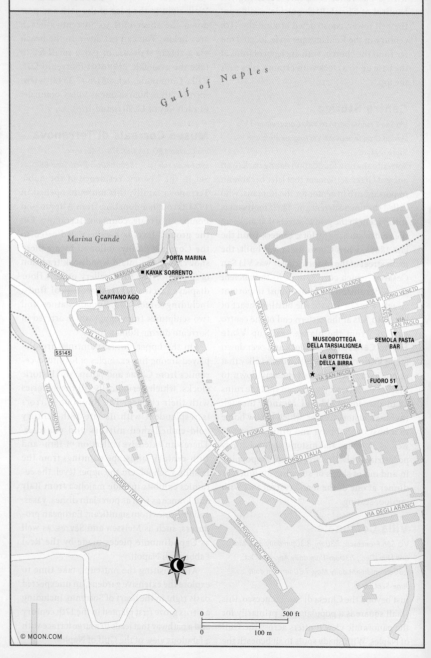

Gulf of Naples

Marina Grande

VIA MARINA GRANDE

PORTA MARINA

KAYAK SORRENTO

CAPITANO AGO

VIA MARINA GRANDE

VIA DEL MARE

SS145

VIA CAPODIMONTE

VIA DEL MARE/TUNNEL

VICO FUORO

VIA FUORO

CORSO ITALIA

VIA FUORO

VIA VITTORIO VENETO

VIA SAN PAOLO

MUSEOBOTTEGA
DELLA TARSIALIGNEA

LA BOTTEGA
DELLA BIRRA

VIA SAN NICOLA

VICO FUORO

VIA FUORO

CORSO ITALIA

SEMOLA PASTA
BAR

FUORO 51

VIA TASSO

VIA DEGLI ARANCI

VIA FUORO SANT'ANTONIO

0   500 ft
0   100 m

© MOON.COM

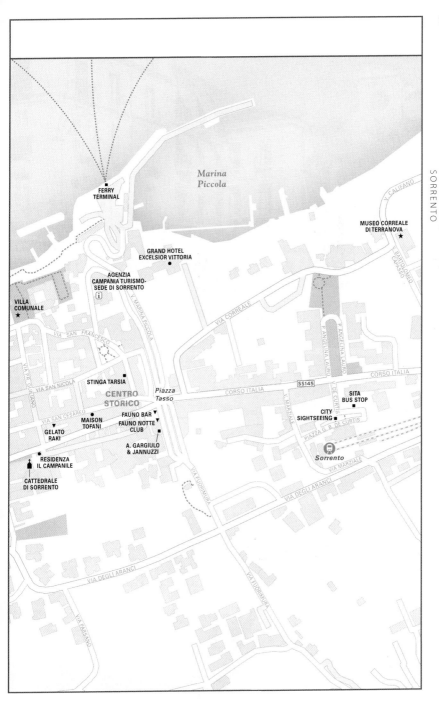

Marina Piccola

FERRY TERMINAL

MUSEO CORREALE DI TERRANOVA ★

GRAND HOTEL EXCELSIOR VITTORIA ●

AGENZIA CAMPANIA TURISMO- SEDE DI SORRENTO ⓘ

VILLA COMUNALE ★

VIA SAN FRANCESCO

VIA MARINA PICCOLA

VIA CORREALE

VIA PER GIULIANO

VIA SAN NICOLA

STINGA TARSIA ■

CENTRO STORICO

Piazza Tasso

CORSO ITALIA

SS145

CORSO ITALIA

VIA SAN CESAREO

MAISON TOFANI ▼

FAUNO BAR ▼

FAUNO NOTTE CLUB ■

GELATO RAKI ▼

A. GARGIULO & JANNUZZI ■

RESIDENZA IL CAMPANILE ●

CATTEDRALE DI SORRENTO ✝

SITA BUS STOP ■

CITY SIGHTSEEING ■

PIAZZA G. B. DE CURTIS

Sorrento

VIA MARZIALE

VIA FUORIMURA

VIA DEGLI ARANCI

VIA DEGLI ARANCI

VIA FUORIMURA

VIA PASSANO

V. CALIFANO

V. VERTIDOLOMEO CARASSO

P. ANGELINA LAURO

CORSO ITALIA

The Intarsia of Sorrento

Sorrento's tradition of intarsia (wood inlay or marquetry) dates back centuries and is kept alive today by the town's artisans. The craft has been associated with Sorrento since at least the 16th century and flourished in the 19th century; an intarsia school was even founded here in the 1880s. The labor-intensive process involves creating mosaic-type designs by inlaying thin slivers of wood into a base. Different types of wood provide different colors, and the tiny pieces are hand cut to create elaborate designs, from landscapes to ornate floral and geometric patterns. Today you can find intarsia on music boxes, decorative boxes and trays, frames, and tables. Classic motifs include lemons and images of Sorrento and its surrounding landscape. These pieces make lovely keepsakes from your visit. You'll find fine examples of intarisa thoroughout Sorrento, but here's a guide to the highlights around town.

MUSEOBOTTEGA DELLA TARSIALIGNEA

Via San Nicola 28; tel. 081/877-1942; www.museomuta.it; 10am-6:30pm daily Apr.-Oct., 10am-5pm daily Nov.-Mar.; €8, over 65 or 18 and younger €5

Dedicated to Sorrento's history of intarsia (inlaid woodwork or marquetry), this museum brings to life the traditional craft and houses a large collection of pieces by master craftsmen. It's set in the remarkable Palazzo Pomarici Santomasi, a five-floor building from the 1700s that was once surrounded by intarsia workshops. The building itself is beautifully restored and maintains many original features, the perfect backdrop to discovering the richness and creativity of Sorrento's intarsia artists over the centuries.

The museum's collection is displayed in three sections that span five floors. The first is dedicated to showing Sorrento in the 1800s with paintings, prints, and photographs of the town. The next section highlights intarsia in Italy from the 1400s to the 1800s, while the third area is the largest and highlights the intarsia work of Sorrento artisans in the especially rich period of the 19th century. Along with the remarkable pieces of art and furniture with inlaid designs, the museum does an excellent job demonstrating the process in displays of work tools and materials, discussions of technique, and explanations about design and innovation, with detailed information available in English.

OTHER PLACES TO SEE AND BUY INTARSIA

- **Cattedrale di Sorrento:** Look at the panels surrounding the portal on the inside of Sorrento's Cathedral, as well as the early-20th-century choir stalls and the stations of the cross (page 108).

- **Stinga Tarsia:** Brothers Franco and Roberto Stinga are third-generation woodworkers whose music boxes, frames, and furniture feature inlaid designs that range from delicate floral motifs to modern geometric patterns (page 114).

BEACHES

MARINA PICCOLA

Spiaggia San Francesco

Located just west of Marina Piccola and directly below the Villa Comunale, Sorrento's main beach area is not like most beaches in that there is a distinct lack of beach. While there is a small sandy area nearest the port

and shoreline, most sunbathing space consists of specially built beach club establishments (stabilimento balneare) that are constructed on a series of jetties. The platforms have sun bed loungers, umbrellas, facilities like changing rooms and showers, and access to the sea via steps. Located on the western side of the beach area, **Bagni Salvatore** (tel. 081/878-1214; www.bagnisalvatore.com; Apr. 25-mid Oct.; sun beds €13 and umbrellas €6) offers friendly service, tranquil water for

---

1: Piazza Tasso **2:** a green respite at the Villa Comunale garden

swimming, and a unique glimpse of Roman ruins as a backdrop. Marina Piccola can be reached via the port area directly, or from the Villa Comunale if you follow the zigzag staircase or take the elevator down.

MARINA GRANDE
Via Marina Grande

Only a short walk from the center of Sorrento, the Marina Grande harbor feels worlds away from the hustle and bustle of the city center. Here, you can stroll along the water's edge, enjoy a peaceful swim, or dine by the sea at a number of different restaurants. Fishing is still an important local activity as well, as the piles of nets, colorful fishing boats, and fishermen at work would attest. For swimmers, there's a small sandy beach area in the middle of the harbor, or opt for one of the sunbathing platforms built out into the harbor like **Ristorante Bagni Sant'Anna** (Via del Mare; tel. 081/807-4178; www. ristorantebagnisantanna.com; Mar.-Nov.; sun bed and umbrella €13), which offers sun beds, umbrellas, hot showers, and changing rooms. With sea access from the platform, you can swim with stunning views of the Gulf of Naples. You can reach the Marina Grande by car or bus along Via del Mare. However, if you opt to go on foot, a pleasant walk leads you down Via Marina Grande near Piazza della Vittoria. As you near the sea, you'll pass through a stone arch that dates to the third century BC and the Greek origins of the city.

WATER SPORTS
CAPITANO AGO
Via del Mare 92; tel. 081/188-62797; www. capitanoago.com; Mar. 15-Oct. 31; group tours from €65 per person, private tours from €350 for up to 12 people

See the Sorrento coastline up close, or see Capri or the Amalfi Coast by boat from Sorrento, with Capitano Ago's small-group (12 people maximum) and private boat excursions. Options include a Capri tour, an Amalfi Coast tour with stops ashore at Positano and Amalfi, and sunset or fishing

excursions. Private tours are available to the Amalfi Coast, Capri, Ischia, and Procida.

KAYAK SORRENTO
Via Marina Grande 90; tel. 328/702-1422; www. kayaksorrento.com; Mar.-Nov.; group tours from €40 per person, private tours from €70 per person

Spend time immersed in the natural beauty of the Sorrento coastline with a guided kayak excursion starting from Marina Grande. Guided 2-3-hour excursions are available following the coastline west past caves, beautiful coves, and historic sites. Learn about the landscape with its legends and history while gliding along the sea. Group tours are available daily, usually departing early afternoon, or you can take a sunrise or sunset tour starting 2 hours before sunrise or sunset. Group tours can accommodate up to 35 people, or you can opt for a private guided excursion.

SHOPPING
Woodwork and Artisan Crafts
A. GARGIULO & JANNUZZI
Viale Enrico Caruso 1; tel. 081/878-1041; www. gargiulo-jannuzzi.it; 9am-8pm daily

For six generations this store has been a source of artisan crafts right on Piazza Tasso in the heart of Sorrento. There's a fine and large selection of inlaid woodwork, including enchanting music boxes, gorgeous furniture, and even chess sets. You'll also find other local crafts, such as ceramics, hand-embroidered linens, and laces. Occupying three floors, this shop invites you to take time to browse, and you might just see artisans at work. Check the hours in advance, as the store may close later in the summer and slightly earlier in the winter.

STINGA TARSIA
Via Luigi de Maio 16; tel. 081/878-1165; www. stingatarsia.com; 9:30am-10pm daily Apr.-Oct., 9:30am-1:30pm and 4pm-8:30pm Nov.-Mar.

As third-generation woodworkers, brothers

1: Marina Piccola **2:** Marina Grande

1

2

3

Franco and Roberto Stinga are passionate about continuing the family tradition of creating handcrafted furniture, decorative items, and their particularly fine music boxes. Along with the intricate carved patterns in a style dating back to the 19th century, a selection of contemporary inlaid pieces with creative geometric designs bring a new look to Sorrento's traditional artisan craft.

FOOD
Seafood
PORTA MARINA

Via Marina Grande 25; tel. 349/975-4761; anna.
sorrento@alice.it; noon-3:30pm and 6pm-10:30pm
daily Apr.-Oct.; €15-25

Set right along the water's edge in Marina Grande, this small and casual seafood restaurant is run by six brothers who are fourth-generation fishermen dediated to bringing in the best daily catch. The menu is determined by what they've caught and is written up on a board. You might find fried calamari or grilled octopus, spaghetti with clams, or grilled fresh local fish. With a glass of crisp white Campania wine and the view of Marina Grande harbor, it just can't be beat.

Regional Cuisine
SEMOLA PASTA BAR

Via Torquato Tasso 53/55; tel. 081/1900-4857;
https://semola-pasta-bar.business.site;
noon-midnight daily Apr.-Jan.; €8-16

While pasta is a fixture on nearly every menu in Italy, Semola Pasta Bar focuses on handmade pasta served in a variety of traditional and creative dishes. Try the classic ravioli or the gnocchi alla sorrentina (potato and flour dumplings served with a tomato sauce enriched with mozzarella and basil). Or look for seasonal options like the pasta with pumpkin and shrimp. The restaurant is located on a quiet street in the historic center with nice outdoor seating. Takeaway service is also available.

FAUNO BAR

Piazza Tasso 13/15; tel. 081/878-1135; www.faunobar.
it; 7am-2am daily; €8-18

With a large terrace on Piazza Tasso, this bar and restaurant is right in the middle of it all. Open from early in the morning until late at night, it's a great spot to stop for cappuccino in the morning to watch the busy piazza scene. Later in the day, choose a light meal from their excellent selection of salads or full-menu dishes. Gluten free, vegetarian, and vegan menus are also available. With its central location, this is also a popular spot for aperitivo or after-dinner drinks.

Gelato
GELATO RAKI

Via San Cesareo 48; tel. 081/1896-3351; www.
rakisorrento.com; 11am-1am daily; €2.50-6

There's certainly no shortage of gelato options in the historic center, but Raki stands out because of the owners' focus on top-quality fresh and all-natural ingredients. The artisan gelato is made on-site, and the mouthwatering selection often includes a refreshing limone gelato made with Sorrento's lemons. Cash only.

NIGHTLIFE
Bars
FUORO51

Via Fuoro 51; tel. 081/878-3691; www.fuoro51winebar.
com; 11am-midnight daily Apr.-Oct., 11am-midnight
Tues.-Sun. Nov.-Dec. and Feb.-Mar.

For a relaxed setting and a selection of more than 800 wines, head to this enoteca (wine bar) in the historic center. There's an excellent choice of wines with a special focus on Italian producers, especially those of Campania. If you're interested in wine, this is a great place to try many Campanian wines that are challenging to find outside of the area. A selection of cured meats, salami, and cheese trays as well as a full menu of tempting dishes are available to enjoy along with your wine.

1: Fauno Bar on Piazza Tasso **2:** food with a view at Porta Marina **3:** Grand Hotel Excelsior Vittoria

LA BOTTEGA DELLA BIRRA

Via San Nicola 13; tel. 340/591-6221; labottegadellabirra-@libero.it; 5:30pm-1:30am daily Apr.-Oct., 6pm-1:30am Nov.-Mar.

Beer enthusiasts will enjoy this welcoming spot in the historic center, where Nunzio Manna cultivates his passion for the best beers. La Bottega della Birra offers a vast selection of Italian beers, as well as beers from Belgium, England, America, and more. A variety of local dishes, cheese and meat plates, and bruschette designed to pair well with beer are also available.

Clubs
FAUNO NOTTE CLUB

Piazza Torquato Tasso 13; tel. 081/878-1021; www. faunonotte.it; 11:30pm-3:45am daily Apr.-Oct.

For the nightclub scene in Sorrento, head to Fauno Notte Club right in Piazza Tasso. There's always something going on here after dark, as the club hosts visiting DJs, live music, and themed dance nights. During the week entrance is free and you pay only for drinks, which cost about €10. On Saturdays and for special events the cover charge goes up to €15-25.

ACCOMMODATIONS
€100-200
RESIDENZA IL CAMPANILE

Corso Italia 103; tel. 081/807-1886; www. ilcampanilesorrento.it; Mar.-Dec.; €100 d

It doesn't get more central or characteristic than this residence with six double rooms overlooking pedestrian only Corso Italia and the Cattedrale di Sorrento. The building dates to the 1800s, and the rooms are set on two levels. Breakfast is served on the rooftop terrace from April to September, and served in your room during colder months. Note that there is no elevator due to the historic nature of the building.

★ MAISON TOFANI

Via San Cesareo 34; tel. 081/878-4020; www. maisontofani.com; Feb. 13-Jan. 7; €189 d

Right in the historic center, not far from Piazza Tasso, this gorgeous hotel in an 18th-century building is full of historic charm. Each of the 10 rooms is different, with some featuring unique touches like exposed wood beams. Traditional terra-cotta floors with majolica tiles add a warm touch that's perfectly complemented by contemporary furnishings and colorful accents. Some rooms have balconies overlooking the town center. Breakfast is served in a beautiful room full of historic charm, with ornate doors and a frescoed ceiling.

Over €300
GRAND HOTEL EXCELSIOR VITTORIA

Piazza Tasso 34; tel. 081/877-7111; www.exvitt.it; Apr.-Jan. 7; €606 d

A bastion of Sorrento hospitality since its founding in 1834, the Grand Hotel Excelsior Vittoria commands prime real estate overlooking the sea above Marina Piccola, with a beautifully landscaped entrance from Piazza Tasso. Many notable guests have enjoyed this hotel, and the Neapolitan tenor Enrico Caruso's stay has been memorialized with the spectacular Caruso Suite, which includes the singer's piano. The hotel has retained old-world charm while offering all the modern comforts expected at a five-star hotel. The pool is set in landscaped gardens, and with the Michelin-starred **Terrazza Bosquet** restaurant for dining and a spa on-site, this could be your address for a luxurious escape right in the center of Sorrento.

INFORMATION AND SERVICES

In addition to its main office, the Sorrento tourist office has information points located at Piazza Tasso (10am-noon and 4pm-8pm daily Apr.-Dec.), as well as just outside the Circumvesuviana train station at Piazza Giovanni Battista de Curtis.

You'll find several **pharmacies** along Corso Italia and right in Piazza Tasso for non-emergency assistance.

- **Agenzia Campania Turismo – Sede di Sorrento:** Via Luigi de Maio 35; tel. 081/807-4033; www.agenziacampaniaturismo.it; 9am-7pm Mon.-Sat. and 9am-1pm Sun. Apr.-Oct., 9am-4pm Mon.-Fri. Nov.-Mar.

- **Sorrento Hospital (Ospedale):** Corso Italia 1; tel. 081/872-9111; emergency room (pronto soccorso)

GETTING THERE

By Car and Scooter

From **Naples,** follow the **A3** autostrada south and continue on the **Strada Statale della Penisola Sorrentina (SS145)** along the coastline to Sorrento. Drive time is about 1 hour 30 minutes, but expect longer when there's traffic during the summer months.

From the Amalfi Coast, follow **SS163** (the Amalfi Coast road) until it meets **SS145,** and continue straight into Sorrento from the east. Or take a left on SS145 and follow a route about 5 miles (8 km) longer via Sant'Agata sui Due Golfi to arrive in Sorrento from the west. Either way, the drive from **Amalfi** takes about 1 hour 30 minutes with no traffic, and about 45 minutes from **Positano.**

There are many paid **parking lots,** including at Marina Piccola harbor, near Piazza Tasso on Via Fuorimura, on Via Correale not far from the Museo Correale di Terranova, and on Via del Mare near Corso Italia. Expect to pay about €2 an hour or more.

By Bus

From Naples, **Curreri Service** (tel. 081/801-5420; www.curreriviaggi.it; €10) offers bus service from Capodichino Airport to Sorrento (every 1-1.5 hours 9am-7:30pm daily) with various stops along the way, including Pompeii, before arriving at the **Sorrento train station.** At the airport, tickets are available from an automatic vending machine just outside the Arrivals area and buses depart from the bus terminal outside the arrivals area near the P1 parking area. Advance booking and payment can be made online.

To reach Sorrento from the Amalfi Coast, **SITA SUD** (tel. 089/386-6701; www.

sitasudtrasporti.it, every hour 6:20am-9:20pm daily, fewer buses Sun. and holidays; from €1.30) has a bus line connecting Amalfi to Sorrento with stops along the coastline, including Positano. Travel time from Amalfi to Sorrento is about 1 hour 40 minutes; it's about 1 hour from Positano to Sorrento. Buses arrive in Sorrento at the **Piazza Giovanni Battista de Curtis** in front of the train station.

The **City Sightseeing** (081/1825-7088; www.city-sightseeing.it/it/sorrento; €10) Sorrento Coast to Coast buses run roughly every hour 8:50am-5:45pm daily, from Positano (40 minutes) and Amalfi (1 hour 25 minutes) to Sorrento's train station.

From Rome, **Autolinnee Marozzi** (tel. 080/579-0111; www.marozzivt.it; daily; €22) offers a 4-hour bus trip from outside the Roma Tiburtina train station to Sorrento, with a stop at Corso Italia 259b (near Piazza Giovanni Battista de Curtis, near the train station). Departures are once or twice daily, depending on the day of the week and season. Tickets can be booked in advance online, but the website is only available in Italian. You can purchase tickets onboard for a surcharge of €3.50 per ticket.

By Train

From Naples, you can take the **Circumvesuviana** train line operated by **EAV** (www.eavsrl.it; 60 minutes; €3.90) to **Sorrento's train station.** There are departures about every 30 minutes daily.

By Ferry

Ferries arrive at Sorrento's **Marina Piccola** from around the Gulf of Naples, including Naples (40 minutes), Capri (30 minutes), and, seasonally, Positano (40 minutes) and Amalfi (1 hour 15 minutes). There are many companies to choose from, from high-speed jet boats to aliscafo (hydrofoil) and slower traghetti (ferries) that transport passengers and vehicles. Gescab, Caremar, NLG, and SNAV all offer year-round service to Sorrento, but with a more limited schedule off-season from November-March.

- **Alilauro** (tel. 081/878-1430; www. alilaurogruson.it; Apr.-Oct.; from €18.20 per person) connects Sorrento to Naples, Capri, and the Amalfi Coast.

- **Gescab** (tel. 081/428-5259; www.gescab. it; from €18.20) offers many daily trips to Capri.

- **Caremar** (tel. 081/189-66690; www. caremar.it; from €16.40 for passengers and €28.50 for vehicles) offers passenger and car ferries to Capri.

- **NLG** (tel. 081/807-1812; www.navlib.it; from €13.10 per person) operates jet routes from Capri and Naples.

- **SNAV** (tel. 081/428-5555; www.snav.it; from €20.70) operates ferries to Capri.

- **Alicost** (tel. 089/871-483; www.alicost.it; Easter-Oct.; €15.00-16.50 per person) offers ferry service from Positano and Amalfi to Sorrento.

GETTING AROUND

Sorrento's historic center and main sights are quite easy to explore on foot. Local buses run through town and provide a good way to ride between the center of town and Marina Piccola or Marina Grande because they are located beneath the rest of Sorrento.

By Bus

EAV (www.eavsrl.it; departures every 20-30 minutes; from €1.30) offers four lines that cover the town with buses every 20 minutes. Bus schedules are not available online; the tourist office and info points are the best places to find the latest schedules and information. Linea A (Line A) runs from Sorrento to Capo di Sorrento 5:20am-1am daily (and 5:50am-12:20am the opposite direction). Linea B and Linea C run from Marina Piccola to Piazza Tasso and the train station 7am-11:30pm daily (7:30am-10:45pm in the opposite direction). Linea D and Linea E circulate around town with various stops including Marina Grande, Piazza Tasso, and the train station (7:10am-11:35pm daily). Tickets must be purchased before boarding at tabacchi (tobacco) shops and news agents.

Positano

With its romantic mosaic of pastel-hued buildings clinging to the cliffside, Positano has a seemingly impossible beauty that captures the heart. Set in a steep ravine, the town climbs from the beach to the mountains above. The Amalfi Coast Road winds its way through the top of Positano, leaving much of the town accessible only by a meandering smaller road or the town's famous steps. Whether you arrive by boat at sea level or by car or bus higher up, steps are everywhere in Positano. What did you expect in a town nicknamed the Vertical City? Fortunately, there are plenty of captivating views to stop and enjoy along the way.

Spiaggia Grande is the heart of town, and many of the main sights are within a short stroll—or climb—from the beach. With a relaxed yet chic atmosphere, Positano is a place for shopping, soaking up the sun, and perfecting la dolce vita, Amalfi Coast style.

Moving east from Positano, the coast juts out into the sea and Praiano spills down two sides of a mountain ridge that ends in a gently curved cape, Capo Sottile.

ORIENTATION

More than any other town along the Amalfi Coast, Positano is set into the steep mountainside, with buildings that seem to be stacked, one on top of the other. The center of town is near the Spiaggia Grande beach; **Via Marina**

1: the vertical buildings of Positano **2:** the Chiesa di Santa Maria Assunta **3:** beautiful view from Positano **4:** Positano from the sea

Amalfi Coast

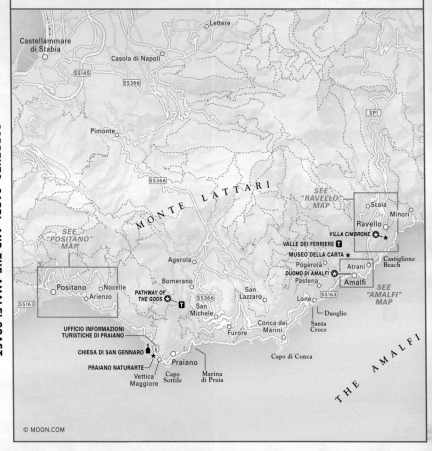

© MOON.COM

Grande runs along the beach, lined with restaurants and shops. Overlooking the beach, the Chiesa di Santa Maria Assunta sits right in the heart of Positano. Ferries arrive and depart from the large cement pier at the westernmost edge of Spiaggia Grande.

From the Chiesa di Santa Maria Assunta, **Via dei Mulini** is a bougainvillea-covered pedestrian-only walkway that leads up to **Piazza dei Mulini.** This is where you'll meet the **Viale Pasitea** (called Via Cristoforo Colombo east of Piazza dei Mulini), or the internal road, lined with shops and restaurants, that runs through Positano from two points along the Amalfi Coast Road (SS163; also called Via G. Marconi as it passes through Positano and Via Laurito to the east of the town's center). The Amalfi Coast Road (and the SITA SUD bus) winds through the higher parts of Positano, but most visitors on a short trip to Positano will focus on the lower area around Spiaggia Grande. By car or bus, the Piazza dei Mulini is the closest spot that you can reach to the Spiaggia Grande, and from there you will need to walk.

To the east of Positano along the coastline

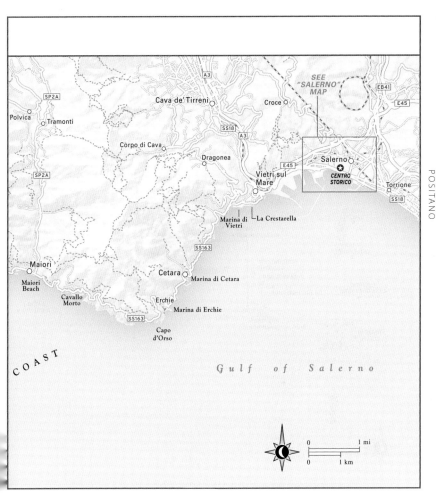

are several smaller beaches, the largest and easiest to reach being the **Arienzo beach,** accessible by a long staircase from the Amalfi Coast Road or by boat service from Positano's Spiaggia Grande. Farther east, in **Praiano,** charming **Marina di Praia** beach is set in a tiny cove and is a great place to set off with a kayak and explore the craggy shoreline.

SIGHTS
Chiesa di Santa Maria Assunta

Via Marina Grande; tel. 089/875-480; www.
chiesapositano.it; 8am-noon and 4pm-8pm daily;
free

Situated near the Spiaggia Grande beach right in the heart of the town, Positano's most important church is surrounded by colorful buildings climbing up the mountainside. The church is topped with a yellow, green, blue, and white ceramic-tiled dome.

Built over the ruins of a Roman villa, the church likely dates back to the second half of the 10th century, but what can be seen today was built much later. An open square in front of the church is decorated with artwork by the noted

Positano

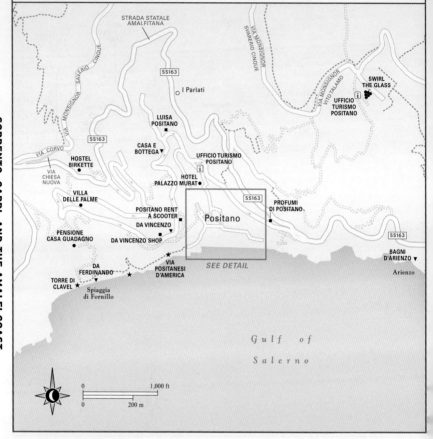

Italian artist Mimmo Paladino. Along one side, a four-level bell tower from 1707 stands separate from the church. Mounted to the bell tower is an ancient marble plaque depicting a pistrice, a mythological creature that's part dragon, part winged horse, and part sea monster.

Step inside the church to find a bright white neoclassical interior with gold decorative elements. Above the altar hangs the church's most treasured possession, a Byzantine icon of the Madonna from the 13th century. It is said that that the icon was aboard a ship sailing along the coastline, but when it reached Positano, the wind stopped and the boat was stranded. After trying everything, the sailors heard a voice calling out, "Posa, posa!" ("Put me down, put me down!") The captain took the icon ashore and suddenly the wind began blowing. This is also, according to local legend, how Positano came by its name.

Below the church are the ruins of an ancient Roman villa and later medieval crypts. The **Museo Archeological Romano Santa Maria Assunta** (Piazza Flavio Gioia 7; tel. 331/208-5821; www.marpositano.it; 9am-9pm daily Apr.-Oct., 10am-4pm daily Nov.-Mar.; €15, credit card only) offers 30-minute guided visits of the Roman villa (maximum

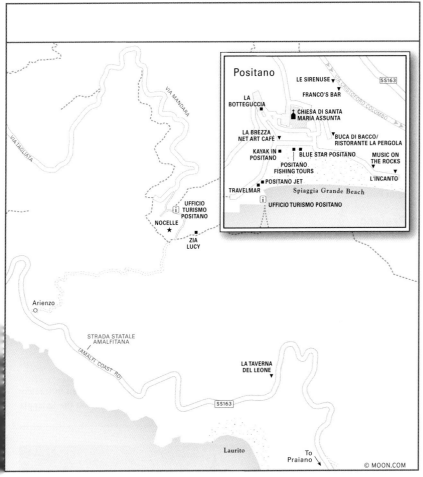

10 people). To preserve the site, it is kept at a cool temperature, so wear a jacket or layers. Book tickets in advance or purchase them at the ticket booth next to the bell tower.

Li Galli Islands

Sirenuse Islands, Positano

Just off the coast of Positano lie three small islands that have captivated travelers since ancient times. According to the ancient Greek historian and geographer Strabo, these islands were home to mythical siren creatures with human heads and bird-like bodies. Li Galli (The Roosters) refers to this half-bird

characteristic. According to myth, the sirens were not exactly hospitable: They lured sailors to their death with their beautiful music and songs. You may recall the story in Homer's *The Odyssey:* Odysseus filled his sailors' ears with wax and had them bind him to the mast of his ship as they sailed past the sirens, so he could hear their intoxicating song and live to tell the tale. When they failed to enchant Odysseus, the sirens, named Ligea, Leucosia, and Parthenope, died from humiliation, it is said, and were transformed into the three islands we see today.

In more recent times—the 14th century—a

watchtower was built on the ruins of an earlier Roman tower. Eventually, the islands were sold to private owners. In 1924, Russian choreographer and dancer Léonide Massine transformed the islands into a luxurious private villa with help from French architect Le Corbusier. Rudolf Nureyev, another famous Russian dancer, later added lavish decorative touches. Though the property is still privately owned today, it's possible to boat around and through the archipelago. You can swim in the beautiful waters around the islands if you rent a boat or go on a private or group boat tour from Positano.

Praiano

As the Amalfi Coast Road weaves through the Praiano, many travelers miss the chance to stop and explore this lovely little town, which means that for some time, it has been a hidden oasis for those who enjoy going off the beaten path. With its dreamy setting suspended between the mountains and sea, Praiano offers a quiet charm that is closely connected to nature. Though this town is certainly no longer off the radar, it is by no means as busy as its next-door neighbor Positano.

Driving on the Amalfi Coast Road, you'll see the colorful ceramic-tiled dome and bell tower of the **Chiesa di San Gennaro** (Piazza San Gennaro, Vettica Maggiore; tel. 089/874-799; piobozza@virgilio.it; 9am-noon and 4pm-8pm daily, until 10pm in summer) sitting just below the road. This large church dates back to 1589 and was constructed on the site of an older church, which was also dedicated to San Gennaro (St. Januarius), the patron saint of Naples. The baroque interior is richly decorated with an ornate ceramic floor, and the large piazza in front of the church is a lovely spot to admire the view of Positano in the distance. Praiano has also created more than 150 permanent art installations around town, known as **Praiano NaturArte,** and strung them together into eight suggested walks, each one leading to a collection of ceramic or stone artworks created by eight different artists. The works blend harmoniously with the landscape to create an outdoor museum, and pieces by local artists showcase the town's traditions, myths, and history. Visit the **Ufficio Informazioni Turistiche di Praiano** for a map of the NaturArte walks.

BEACHES

Life in Positano has always been intimately connected to the beach, from the Spiaggia

Chiesa di San Gennaro in Praiano

Grande in the heart of Positano to tiny beaches set in coves a short boat ride away. Three of the most popular beaches are also designated Blue Flag beaches, a special ranking that the Foundation for Environment Education gives to beaches with the finest water quality. Whether you like being in the center of activity or are looking for seclusion and romance, there's a beach for you in Positano.

Positano
SPIAGGIA GRANDE
Via Marina Grande

This picture postcard town of Positano wouldn't seem complete without the burst of color and activity of its main beach, with its perfect rows of umbrellas and chairs. Surrounded as it is by the cascade of buildings spilling down the mountainside right to the edge of the beach, it is an absolutely stunning setting. Standing on the beach, you get one of the best views of the vibrant Vertical City.

More than 1,000 feet (300 m) long, this Blue Flag beach is lined beach clubs. In the middle of the beach, **L'Incanto** (Marina Grande 4; tel. 089/811-177; www.lincantopositano.com; daily May-Oct.; from €22.50 for one bed and umbrella) is a good choice with sun beds, umbrellas, beach services, and drinks and snacks at the Blue Bar right on the beachfront. However, there is also a free section of the beach, where you can simply throw down a towel in any open space you can find. Expect crowds, especially during the summer, but that's an essential part of the scene. The safe swimming area is marked off by lines of buoys and is somewhat limited.

SPIAGGIA DI FORNILLO
Via Fornillo

Positano's second-largest beach is a wonderful option for a little less hustle and bustle, reached on foot by following the scenic **Via Positanesi d'America** west from near the pier at Spiaggia Grande. Pass the Torre Trasita watchtower and continue on the pathway through a tunnel and down to the beach level.

There are several beach clubs, such as **Da Ferdinando** (Spiaggia di Fornillo; tel. 089/875-365; daferdinando1953@gmail.com; 8am-8pm daily mid-May-mid-Oct.; €15-20 for sun bed and umbrella), which also has a great restaurant (€10-25) overlooking the beach. If you walk all the way to the end of the beach, there is a free beach near the **Torre di Clavel.** The water at this Blue Flag beach is clear and refreshing, particularly in the morning.

During beach season (Apr.-Oct.), the stabilimenti balneari at Fornillo also offer boat service from the corner of Positano's cement pier. The boat service is for clients, so when you hop off you'll be expected to rent a sun bed or dine at the beachside restaurant.

ARIENZO
Via Arienzo

In a ravine east of Positano's Spiaggia Grande, this picturesque little Blue Flag beach is accessible by 269 steps from the Amalfi Coast Road. It's one of the few rocky beaches near Positano that is reasonably accessible from the road, albeit after a pretty good hike down those steps (and back up at the end of the day). However, the **Bagni d'Arienzo** beach club (Via Arienzo 16; tel. 089/812-002; www.bagnidarienzo.com; 10am-6:30pm daily mid-May-mid-Oct.; €15 per person) offers free boat service from Positano's main pier for clients. With sun beds, umbrellas, showers, changing rooms, and an excellent restaurant and bar, it's a lovely escape from the busy beaches in Positano. Sun bed and restaurant reservations in advance are highly recommended.

Praiano
MARINA DI PRAIA
Via Marina di Praia

An important access point to the sea since ancient times, Marina di Praia is one of the coast's most captivating beaches. Set in a deep ravine with little houses and a tiny whitewashed church, this beach still has the atmosphere of a fishing village. Sunbathers vie for space with brightly painted wooden fishing boats. Besides the incredibly clear and

clean water, one of the most appealing features of Marina di Praia is the **walkway** cut into the cliffside that leads about 400 meters from the beach along the rugged coastline. Follow the scenic pathway past the medieval **Torre a Mare** watchtower all the way to the entrance of the iconic Africana Famous Club.

Marina di Praia is easy to access. A small road leads from the Amalfi Coast Road to a gentle slope of steps down to the beach. Like much of the coastline, the beach is pebbly. Sun beds are available for rental, or find a spot in the crowded free area among the fishing boats. There are also some cement platforms along the walkway where locals sunbathe and where rock jumping is popular. With steep cliffs on both sides, the sun hits Marina di Praia only during the middle hours of the day, but the location is just as enchanting in the evening or after dark, thanks to the beautiful walk along the sea and excellent restaurants.

SPORTS AND RECREATION

With its dramatic landscape, Positano is an ideal location to spend time outdoors. Get out on a kayak tour or boat to discover the hidden coves and tiny beaches nearby, and the mountain pathways above Positano are excellent for hiking.

Hiking

TOP EXPERIENCE

★ PATHWAY OF THE GODS
(Sentiero degli Dei)
Distance: *3.7 miles (6 km)*
Time: *3 hours one-way*
Trailhead: *Piazza Paolo Capasso, Bomerano*
Information and Maps: *www.carteguide.com; English and Italian versions available online; €5 each*
In a landscape famous for beautiful views, this trail is often considered the most breathtaking.

1: the Via Positanesi d'America with the Li Galli islands visible on the horizon **2:** Positano's Spiaggia Grande

The Pathway of the Gods is a rugged mountain trail stretching from **Bomerano,** an hour's drive to the northeast, to the small village of **Nocelle,** above Positano. Passing along the mountains high above the sea, the trail is dotted with Mediterranean vegetation and offers panoramic views of Praiano, Positano, and Capri.

The pathway can be hiked in both directions, but most people choose to start in Bomerano's Piazza Paolo Capasso. To reach Bomerano by public transportation, you'll need to take the SITA SUD bus on the line from Sorrento to Amalfi, which you can catch at one of the stops on Amalfi Coast Road in Positano, and then transfer to the bus from Amalfi to Agerola. Mention to the driver when boarding that you're hiking the Sentiero degli Dei, and they'll usually announce the stop in Bomerano. Look for the signs for the Sentiero degli Dei from the Piazza Paolo Capasso and follow the walkway out of town. Eventually, the road ends and a trail begins, passing by some lonely abandoned houses with sweeping views between mountains and the sea.

The hike isn't exceptionally hard, but the route is quite remote. It's partly on a mountain trail, so good walking shoes are recommended, and much of the hike is not shaded. The hike from Bomerano to Nocelle takes about three hours, depending on how much rest you take. From Nocelle, you can take a local bus or the steps down to Positano.

The pathway is more popular during the summer months from June-August, but is also at its hottest then. If you're hiking in the summer, get an early morning start and take plenty of water, which can be refilled at public fountains in Bomerano and Nocelle.

A local guide can help you to learn about the area's history and vegetation. Guides can also recommend the best hikes tailored your abilities and time available. For a private guided excursion, **Anna Naclerio** (tel. 335/731-5259; annanaclerioguida@gmail.com; 5-6-hour private hiking tour €200) loves sharing her passion for the landscape. **Zia Lucy** (Via Pizzillo 14; tel. 339/272-0971;

☆ Best of the Beaches

Marina Piccola and Capri's Faraglioni rocks in the distance

From the buzz of Positano's main beach, with its rows of brilliantly colored beach umbrellas, to hidden away rocky coves, the Amalfi Coast has many gorgeous beaches to discover. Here's a guide to help you find the right beach scene for your holiday.

- **Best for a Swim and a Snack:** Traditional fishing boats and restaurants perfect for relaxed dining by the sea line the harbor of **Marina Grande,** the smaller of Sorrento's two ports (page 114).

- **Best to See and Be Seen: Spiaggia Grande** is a large beach with colorful umbrellas and an iconic view of Positano in the background (page 127).

- **Best for Swimming and Water Sports:** On a rocky beach west of Amalfi, **Duoglio** is a popular local spot for windsurfing and kayaking (page 146).

- **Best Hidden Gem:** One of the prettiest and most secluded rocky beaches on the Amalfi Coast, **Santa Croce** is only accessible by boat (page 146).

- **Best Dramatic View:** In view of the impressive Faraglioni rock formations, **Marina Piccola** is a particularly picturesque spot for a swim on Capri (page 187).

www.en.zialucy.com; Mar.-Dec.; small group tours €55-60 per person) also offers private and small-group hiking excursions.

I Suoni degli Dei (The Sounds of the Gods; tel. 089/874-557; www.isuonideglidei. com; every Wed. in May, Sept., and Oct.; free) is an incredible concert series of classical and contemporary music that takes place on the portion of the Sentiero degli Dei pathway above Praiano and can only be accessed by hiking the trail. There are few more impressive settings for an open-air concert. For more details on reaching the concert locations from where you're staying, visit the website or tourist office for tips or to arrange a guide.

Water Sports
KAYAK IN POSITANO

Spiaggia Grande, Positano; tel. 333/614-5247; www. kayakinpositano.it; 8am-8pm daily Apr.-mid-Nov.; €40 for 4 hours

With a convenient location right on Spiaggia Grande, Kayak in Positano offers kayak rentals starting from as little as €15/hour; half-day and full-day rentals for longer excursions are also available. Want some expert guidance on finding hidden grottoes, caves, and the best beaches? A variety of excursions from Positano to Praiano and along the coastline are available from €45-120 per person.

POSITANO FISHING TOURS
Spiaggia Grande cement pier, Positano; tel. 334/980-674; www.positanofishingtours.com; Apr.-Nov.; from €400 per group

Founded by Alberto Russo and his father, two passionate fishermen, this family-run company offers half-day, full-day, sunset, night, or even giant squid fishing options. It's not often you can learn traditional fishing techniques to catch giant squid from the depths of the Mediterranean. All fishing excursions are private and customized to your interests and schedule.

WINDSURF & KAYAK PRAIANO
Marina di Praia, Praiano; tel. 339/483-5115; www.windsurfpraiano.it; 9:30am-7pm daily May-Oct.; kayak rental from €10 per hour

Set off from the beach and explore the coastline kayaking or stand-up paddleboarding around Praiano. It's the best way to enjoy the area's natural beauty while getting a bit of exercise in as well. In addition to kayak and paddleboard rentals, Windsurf & Kayak Praiano offers windsurfing lessons for all skill levels (from €100), as well as kayak excursions (€40-95 per person) along the coastline.

LA BOA CHARTER & DIVING
Marina di Praia, Praiano; tel. 089/813-3034; www.laboa.com; 8am-9pm daily May-Oct.; from €90 per person

Discover the underwater beauty of the Amalfi Coast on a diving excursion from Praiano. La Boa Charter & Diving has two diving centers on the Sorrentine Peninsula; the one in Marina di Praia is the starting point for dives along the Amalfi Coast. All immersions include an instructor and equipment. There are many types of dives possible, ranging in experience level from easy immersions below Vettica Maggiore to challenging dives around the Li Galli islands. Both group and private boat excursions along the Amalfi Coast and to Capri are also available (small group excursions from €90 per person and private tour with captain from €600 per group).

Boat Tours
BLUE STAR POSITANO
Via Del Brigantino 1; tel. 334/235-4122; www.bluestarpositano.it; Easter-early Nov.; small group tours from €65 per person, private from €400 per group

Seeing the Amalfi Coast from the sea is a must, and Blue Star offers small-group or private boat excursions. With a team dedicated to customer service, offering excellent assistance in English and many other langues, Blue Star is a popular choice. Join a small group tour with a maximum of 12 people for a day-trip along the Amalfi Coast, or book a private tour for a fully customized experience. Book in advance online or simply head to the booth right on the Spiaggia Grande.

Wine Tours
SWIRL THE GLASS
Via Pestella 70; tel. 366/123-1358; www.swirltheglass.com; flexible schedule available daily Apr.-Oct.; tastings from €70 per person, tours from €190 per person

Discover the wines of Campania and the Amalfi Coast with true wine experts. Tours are led by professional sommelier and Positano native Cristian Fusco, and his wife, Jenny Konopasek, a wine specialist. Let them guide you on a wine tour where you'll have a wonderfully authentic experience visiting a local vineyard to learn more about the unique Amalfi Coast winemaking process, from the vine to the bottle. Wine tours include transportation, a vineyard and winery tour, lunch, and wine tasting.

Hiking on the Amalfi Coast

vew on the Valle delle Ferriere hike

With spectacular views and rich natural beauty, the mountainous landscape of the Amalfi Coast and Capri is truly ideal for hiking. The towns and tiny villages dotting the coastline are inteconnected by pathways that were the only way to get around before the Amalfi Coast Road was built during the 19th century. What this means for hikers today is that getting from town to town on foot is quite easy—just be ready for a lot of steps!

Trail	Starting Point	Hiking Time	Description
Pathway of the Gods (page 129)	Bomerano (in Agerola) or Nocelle (near Positano)	3 hours	Mountain trail with panoramic views of Praiano, Positano, and Capri.
Valle delle Ferriere (page 147)	Amalfi	2.5 hours	Hike in the valley above Amalfi, passing old paper mills and waterfalls.
Arco Naturale to Belvedere di Tragara Walk (page 188)	Capri town	2.5 hours	Walk to a few of Capri's most scenic spots to escape the crowds.
Belvedere della Migliera Walk (page 189)	Anacapri	30 minutes	A short, scenic walk through grapevines and gardens to Capri's coastline.

ENTERTAINMENT AND EVENTS

If you enjoy local experiences and cultural events, time your visit for one of Positano's annual festivals.

FERRAGOSTO

Spiaggia Grande and various locations; Aug. 14-15

Although Ferragosto is a public holiday celebrated in August throughout Italy, it takes on special meaning in Positano. Roman emperor Augustus declared Ferragosto a holiday in 18 BC to celebrate the summer harvests. The holiday also falls on the Catholic day honoring the Assumption of the Virgin Mary. Because Positano's main church is dedicated to the Santa Maria Assunta, or the Assumption of the Virgin, Ferragosto is the town's largest religious celebration of the year. Festivities start on August 14 with a re-creation of the arrival of the icon of the Virgin Mary and continue through August 15, capped off by an incredible fireworks display over the sea. With a wonderful blend of religious meaning and tradition, and a few pirates thrown in, Ferragosto in Positano is a festive experience. Check with the tourist office for the schedule of events.

FESTA DEL PESCE

Spiaggia di Fornillo; www.festadelpesce.net; last Sat. in Sept.

With Positano's deep connection to the sea and fishing tradition, it's no surprise that this town puts on a festival dedicated to seafood. The Festa del Pesce (Fish Festival) takes over the Spiaggia di Fornillo beach on the last Saturday in September for an extravagant evening of fresh seafood, music, and fun, a celebration of Positano's community pride as much as its wonderful cuisine.

SHOPPING

Shopping in Positano has been all about fashion since the 1960s, when the seaside town became a favorite of stylish vacationers, and there are still shops that create their designs right in Positano. The perfect complement to your summer wardrobe is a pair of custom-made leather sandals, another local tradition still going strong in Positano.

The main shopping area centers around the Chiesa di Santa Maria Assunta and follows **Via dei Mulini** up to where it meets the internal road **Viale Pasitea** that winds through Positano at **Piazza dei Mulini.** Follow Viale Pasitea west to find some of Positano's most traditional fashion and houseware shops. In the other direction, follow **Via Cristoforo Colombo** east uphill toward Sponda, at the intersection with the Amalfi Coast Road for a treasure trove of shops to browse along the way.

La Moda Positano

Don't miss the boutiques with colorful displays of clothing in Positano's own unique style, perfect for a seaside town. The local look includes flowing linen in Mediterranean hues, lace, and relaxed chic beachwear. In the 1950s and 1960s, when the jet-set travelers arrived in Positano, they began wearing colorful, local style, and the rest of the world became aware of La Moda Positano.

LUISA POSITANO

Via Pasitea 78; tel. 089/875-549; www.luisapositano.it; 9am-9pm daily

Full of beautifully patterned fabrics, classic linen, and summery styles, this boutique was founded by Luigia Pollio, known as Luisa, a model during the glamorous '60s in Positano. Her children have continued the family enterprise, and all of their very Positano designs are handmade in the workshop located right below the boutique.

LA BOTTEGUCCIA

Via Regina Giovanna 19; tel. 089/811-824; www.labottegucciapositano.it; 9am-10pm daily Mar.-Oct.

This tiny shop has been a Positano fixture since the early 1960s. Inside, you'll find Dino, son of the shop's founder, pounding away at work, creating handmade sandals. Stop by and have your measurements taken, and he'll create a custom pair while you wait.

Ceramics and Home Goods
DA VINCENZO SHOP

Via Pasitea 200; tel. 089/875-128; shop@davincenzo. it; 9:30am-9:30pm daily, closes 10:30pm in summer

A tempting and well-curated selection of ceramics, custom linen designs, tableware, and locally sourced products are on display in this inviting shop. A highlight is the La Selva natural soap and skincare line, all handmade in the mountains above Positano.

Perfume
PROFUMI DI POSITANO

Via Cristoforo Colombo 175; tel. 089/875-057; www. profumidipositano.it; 10am-10pm daily

Since the 1920s, the Barba family have produced soaps and perfumes right in Positano. Take home the sweet scents of Positano with their locally made products featuring classic Mediterranean scents, such as lemon, jasmine, wisteria, citrus, and almond blossoms.

FOOD

Positano's diverse landscape, stretching from the sea deep into the mountain forests high above town, is reflected in the local cuisine, from freshly caught seafood to grilled meat and locally grown vegetables. Reservations are a good idea for much of the season.

Seafood
LA TAVERNA DEL LEONE

Via Laurito 43; tel. 089/811-302; www. latavernadelleone.com; 1pm-3pm and 7pm-10:30pm Wed.-Mon. mid-Feb.-July and Sept.-Dec., 1pm-3pm and 7pm-10:30pm daily Aug.; €12-26

Since 1965 this restaurant has been a popular choice with locals and travelers alike. Located between Positano and Praiano, La Taverna del Leone is excellent for seafood. Try the tortelli (stuffed pasta) filled with lobster and a delicate and creamy lemon-infused buffalo milk cheese, or the pasta with fresh-caught local fish like scorfano (red scorpionfish). The restaurant is best reached from the center of Positano or Praiano by car or taxi, but a bus stop on the SITA SUD line connecting Positano and Amalfi is located just west of the restaurant.

BUCA DI BACCO

Via Rampa Teglia 4; tel. 089/875-699; www. bucadibacco.it; noon-3pm and 7pm-10:30pm daily Apr.-Oct.; €14-25

Overlooking a lush green pergola and Spiaggia Grande, this restaurant a household name since the 1950s. There are excellent appetizers as well as classic pasta dishes with clams, lobster, or baccalà (cod). For the main course,

typical Positano shops

try grilled octopus or the fried mixed seafood platter. There are plenty of non-seafood options on the menu, too; the Black Angus sirloin is especially good.

★ DA VINCENZO
Via Pasitea 172; tel. 089/875-128; www.davincenzo. it; noon-2:45pm and 6:15pm-10:45pm daily Mar.-mid-Nov.; €25-50

An excellent spot for traditional Positano cooking in a friendly setting. The indoor dining area spills out onto the sidewalk during nice weather. While you'll find a varied menu, seafood is a specialty here and is nicely prepared. The pasta is handmade, and when it's paired with fresh seafood like mussels or prawns, it is a sure win. Reservations are a must, especially for dinner.

Regional Cuisine
★ CASA E BOTTEGA
Viale Pasitea 100; tel. 089/875-225; casaebottegapositano@gmail.com; 8:30am-4:30pm daily Apr.-Oct.; €12-18

When you're ready for a break from pizza and pasta, this is your place. The menu highlights delicious organic fare and features plenty of healthy salads, smoothie bowls, and juices. Try the zucchini spaghetti with pesto and mozzarella di bufala; the chicken, avocado, and tomato salad; or the lovely orzo with grilled zucchini, avocado, and orange-infused shrimp. A buffet displaying freshly made sweets is tempting for dessert. The restaurant includes a shop with a well-curated selection of ceramics, linens, and housewares.

RISTORANTE LA PERGOLA
Via del Brigantino 35; tel. 089/811-461; www. bucadibaccolapergola.com; 8:30am-11pm daily Mar.-mid-Nov.; €20-50

This restaurant is just steps from the Spiaggia Grande beach. Set under a broad pergola, it is a lovely choice for breakfast or morning coffee, lunch, an aperitivo at sunset, or a romantic dinner. The menu features a little of everything, with excellent scialatielli ai frutti di mare (handmade local pasta with

seafood), grilled fish, a variety of hearty salads, and pizza. The house pizza with cherry tomatoes, fresh arugula, mozzarella di bufala, and parmesan is a wonderful choice. Save room for something sweet since everything, from the cornetti for breakfast to the selection of gelato and pastries, is made directly on site.

Cafés
LA BREZZA NET ART CAFÉ
Via del Brigantino 1; tel. 089/875-811; www. labrezzapositano.it; 10:30am-midnight daily Easter-Nov.; €12-30

With a scenic setting right at the corner of Positano's Spiaggia Grande, this will quickly become your go-to bar for any time of the day, thanks to its convenient location and great menu. La Brezza Net Art Café offers fresh local seafood based lunch and dinner options as well as excellent cocktails. Free Wi-Fi is available. Just below the café, check out their takeaway option for sandwiches and drinks to go.

NIGHTLIFE
Though the Positano isn't known for lively nightlife, it is one of the finest spots to enjoy a sunset on the Amalfi Coast. Grab a table at a bar or beachside restaurant and enjoy cocktails as the sun sinks behind the mountains. Compared to the hustle and bustle of Positano during the day, when ferries bring in crowds of day-trippers, the evening delivers a much more relaxed atmosphere.

For a memorable evening, consider dinner with a sea view followed by drinks or dancing at the town's one notable nightclub. Or enjoy a moonlit stroll along the sea and after-dinner drinks by the water's edge.

Positano
MUSIC ON THE ROCKS
Via del Brigantino 19; tel. 089/875-874; www. musicontherocks.it; 10:30pm-4am daily Apr.-Oct.

The one vibrant exception to Positano's otherwise sedate nightlife scene is Music on the Rocks. This nightclub is literally

on the rocks, in a cave carved out of the mountainside just steps from the sea. For more than 40 years, this has been a hot spot on the Amalfi Coast, and it still attracts national and international DJs and musicians. There is a cover charge that varies depending on the event.

FRANCO'S BAR

Via Cristoforo Colombo 30; tel. 089/875-066; www. francosbar.com; 12:30pm-12:30am daily May-Oct.

Next door to the stylish Le Sirenuse hotel and named after one of its founders, Franco's Bar is one of the most chic spots in Positano. As the sun sets and Positano turns all rosy-hued, a spritz never looked so good. The warm ambiance lingers on well into the night, making this a great choice for after-dinner drinks. Do note there is a minimum spend of €20 required.

Praiano
AFRICANA FAMOUS CLUB

Via Terramare 2; tel. 089/874-858; www. africanafamousclub.com; 9pm-4am Sat. May, daily June-Sept.; cover charge varies

This unique nightclub has been a music and entertainment hot spot since the 1960s. In a cave carved into the mountainside, just 32 feet (10 m) above the sea level, this unique space features a large dance floor, DJ station, VIP area with private tables, and terrace overlooking the sea. Music genres include lounge and disco, and there are often themed nights in the summer. There's a dress code, so opt for evening club attire. It's a good idea to call in advance to verify opening hours and dates because the club is a popular spot for private events and can sometimes be closed to the public. Arrive on foot via the pathway from Marina di Praia, come via the nightclub's boat service from Positano and Amalfi, or arrange a shuttle bus service in advance, available for the entire Amalfi Coast.

1: organic salad at Casa e Bottega **2:** the offerings at Ristorante La Pergola

ACCOMMODATIONS

Positano is a great place to consider splurging on accommodations. With hotels that are regularly voted among the best in all of Italy by travelers, Positano knows how to do luxury and service without losing the laid-back style and local, family-run feel of the Amalfi Coast. There are also affordable options that are still centrally located and provide the same views for which Positano is so famous.

Whatever your budget, one key to enjoying your stay in Positano is booking well in advance. Positano is one of the most popular destinations on the Amalfi Coast, and accommodations of all sizes fill up very early, despite the large number of options in town. If you have your heart set on a particular hotel or budget range, book as early as possible.

When it comes to your arrival and departure, ask your accommodation if they offer assistance with luggage. Sometimes available for an extra charge, in Positano this is well worth it, especially if you're staying near the beach or lower part of Positano and arriving by car or bus. Nothing puts a damper on a holiday faster than hauling a suitcase up and down the cobblestone walkways and steps!

Under €100
HOSTEL BRIKETTE

Via G. Marconi 358; tel. 334/904-8692; www. hostel-positano.com; Easter-Oct.; from €35 shared room

The Amalfi Coast doesn't have many hostels, but this one makes up for the shortage, offering gorgeous views at a very good rate. The super-clean, cheery rooms all have air-conditioning, a nice plus during the summer months. The shared dorms sleep 4-10 people, and all but two offer en suite bathrooms, sea views, and terraces. A private room with double bed and en suite bathroom is also available. There are plenty of breakfast options, and the staff are friendly and ready to help with local information and tips. The hostel is located at the top of Positano just 100 meters (300 ft) west of the Chiesa Nuova bus stop.

€100-200
VILLA DELLE PALME

Viale Pasitea 252; tel. 089/875-162; www.inpositano.com; Mar.-mid-Nov.; €160 d

Family-run since 1959, this charming small hotel near the top of Positano really has a knack for making guests feel at home. The family is always on hand to help with recommendations, getting around, and anything needed for a pleasant stay. With panoramic views over town and decor in classic Amalfi Coast shades of turquoise and blue, all nine rooms include a private terrace or balcony. Breakfast is served on the shared terrace or on your own private terrace, which is a lovely way to start your day in Positano.

€200-300
PENSIONE CASA GUADAGNO

Via Fornillo 34/36; tel. 089/875-042; www.pensionecasaguadagno.it; mid-Mar.-early Nov.; $220 d

Situated above Fornillo beach, this small pensione with seven rooms offers a comfortable stay in a quieter area of Positano. The sea-view rooms are worth the extra splurge and feature private terraces. Fornillo beach is accessible via steps, or walk along Viale Pasitea, or hop on an internal bus nearby to reach the center of Positano quickly. Rates are much more affordable outside of high season.

Over €300
★ PALAZZO MURAT

Via dei Mulini 23; tel. 089/875-177; www.palazzomurat.it; Apr.-early Nov.; €400 d

Situated in the heart of Positano, next to the Chiesa di Santa Maria Assunta, this historic 19th-century home was once the preferred summer residence of Gioacchino Murat, the King of Naples and brother-in-law of Napoleon. The 32 rooms have a timeless feel, with elegant historical details, antique decor, and unforgettable views of Positano. The courtyard garden is dotted with lemon trees and flowers that add a sweet scent around the restaurant and pool area. This is the place for a peaceful stay in the center of Positano.

★ LE SIRENUSE

Via Cristoforo Colombo 30; tel. 089/875-066; www.sirenuse.it; late Mar.-Oct.; €2,200 d

Since 1951, the Sersale family have specialized in personalized luxury and unforgettable stays in a setting that exudes modern elegance while still retaining the air of a family home. Le Sirenuse's 58 rooms and suites embody classic Positano style with traditional ceramic floors, a medley of antique and modern design, and private balconies or terraces with sea views in most rooms. You'll feel like a movie star as you lounge by the outdoor heated pool or enjoy dining at one of the many restaurants, from fine dining at La Sponda Restaurant to the Poolside Bar and Restaurant, Aldo's Cocktail Bar & Seafood Grill, or chic Franco's Bar.

INFORMATION AND SERVICES

- **Ufficio Turismo Positano:** Info Point booths located near ferry terminal, Piazza dei Mulini, and Nocelle; tel. 334/911-8563; turismo@comune.positano.sa.it; June-Sept.

- **Ufficio Informazioni Turistiche di Praiano:** Via Gennaro Capriglione 116b, Vettica Maggiore; tel. 089/874-557; www.praiano.org; 9am-1pm Mon.-Sat. and 5pm-9pm daily June-Sept., 9am-1pm and 4:30pm-8:30pm daily Oct.-May

- **Post office:** Poste Italiane; Via Guglielmo Marconi 318; tel. 089/875-142; www.poste.it; 8:20am-1:45pm Mon.-Fri., 8:20am-12:45pm Sat.

- **Laundry:** Lavenderia L'Arcobaleno; Viale Pasitea 249; tel. 089/811-552; 8:30am-1pm and 4pm-8pm Mon.-Sat. Apr.-Oct., closes 7pm Nov.-Mar.; from €6 per wash

GETTING THERE
By Car and Scooter

Positano is situated toward the western end of the Amalfi Coast, 11 miles (18 km) west of **Amalfi** (50 minutes) and 27 miles (43.5 km) west of **Salerno** (2 hours) on the **Amalfi Coast Road (SS163).** From **Ravello** (15.5 mi/25 km; 45 minutes), take the **SS373** road down the mountain to connect with the Amalfi Coast Road (SS163) and continue west to Positano. From **Sorrento** (9 miles/15 km; 45 minutes), follow **SS145** south over the mountains of the Sorrentine Peninsula until it merges with the Amalfi Coast Road (SS163) and head east to reach Positano. From **Naples** (37 mi/60 km; 2 hours without traffic), drive south along the **A3** autostrada until Castellammare di Stabia, where the SS145 road begins. Follow that west along the coastline to Sorrento and then continue on to reach the Amalfi Coast Road (SS163) for Positano.

Though the distances don't seem far, that the roads along the Sorrentine Peninsula are very twisty and narrow. During the tourist season, Easter-October, expect longer drive times.

Parking in Positano can be expensive, from €3-5 per hour or €20-30 per day. You'll find parking options along Viale Pasitea, especially around Piazza dei Mulini. If you're staying in Positano, ask your accommodation about the best parking options.

The **Amalfi Coast Road (SS163)** runs right through Praiano, making it easy to reach from nearby **Positano,** which is only about a 20-minute drive. The main sights in Praiano are located along or very near the Amalfi Coast Road. Driving on the Amalfi Coast Road east from Praiano, look for the sharp turnoff to the right with a narrow road, Via Marina di Praia, that leads down to Marina di Praia. **Parking** is available in paid areas along the side of the road, or in paid parking lots (€2.50-3 per hour).

By Ferry

Ferry service on the Amalfi Coast runs seasonally, from around Easter to the beginning of November. Ferries arrive at, and depart from, the large cement pier on the western end of Spiaggia Grande. Positano is the closest ferry port for Praiano. Tickets can be purchased at the ticket booths along the pier. Because the pier is open to the sea, ferry service to Positano depends on good weather and sea conditions, with a stronger possibility of rough seas in early spring or October. So if you're traveling by ferry, it's good to have alternative transportation options in mind.

Ferry service to Positano from Amalfi (25 minutes) and Salerno (70 minutes) is operated by **Travelmar** (tel. 089/872-950; www.travelmar.it; 9:30am-6pm; €9-14 per person), every 1-2 hours. For some routes, you may need to transfer boats in Amalfi to reach Positano. It's a good idea to purchase your tickets in advance online or via the Travelmar app, especially from June-September.

Alicost (tel. 089/811-986; www.alicost. it; €15-21.30 per person) connects Positano to **Capri** (45 minutes; daily, more available June-Sept.) and **Sorrento** (50 minutes; two daily), with service from Amalfi and Salerno as well. Tickets can be purchased online in advance. Another option is **Positano Jet** (tel. 089/811-164; www.lucibello.it; €9-21 per person), which runs three trips to **Capri** and 2-3 trips to **Amalfi** each day.

By Bus

The public bus line connecting Positano to Sorrento, the rest of the towns on the Amalfi Coast, and Salerno is operated by **SITA SUD** (tel. 089/386-6701; www.sitasudtrasporti. it; from €1.30). Buses make two main stops along Amalfi Coast Road in Positano at Chiesa Nuova and Sponda, along with stops available throughout the town center (look for the blue and white SITA signs). The **Sponda bus stop,** located at the intersection where Via Cristoforo Colombo meets Amalfi Coast Road, is the best choice for the center of Positano near the beach. The bus ride from Sorrento to Positano takes about 1 hour, and from Amalfi the journey is a little less.

City Sightseeing (www.city-sightseeing. it; Apr.-Oct.; from €10 per person) offers a more comfortable way to travel to Positano from Sorrento and Amalfi. They stop at the Sponda stop. Tickets are purchased onboard, and audio guides for the journey are included in the price. This is not a hop-on, hop-off bus; you buy a ticket for each ride. However, after the first ticket, subsequent tickets on the same day are €6 instead of €10. Note that if you are traveling with luggage, you will need to take the SITA SUD bus.

Public buses operated by **SITA SUD** (tel. 089/386-6701; www.sitasudtrasporti.it; from €1.30) pass through Praiano on the Amalfi Coast Road, but they can be very crowded, so it's best to be patient. Buses can be so full before arriving in Praiano that they are unable to stop to pick up passengers. Stops are located throughout Praiano and Vettica Maggiore, including near the Chiesa di San Gennaro, intersections with Praiano's internal road, and above Marina di Praia.

To reach Praiano by bus from Positano (25 minutes), catch the bus heading to Amalfi from one of the stops in Positano. From Amalfi (25 minutes), take the bus heading to Sorrento. To travel to Praiano from Ravello and Salerno you must first take a bus to Amalfi and then transfer to the bus to Sorrento.

You can also get to Praiano from Positano and get around Praiano by a local bus service, **Mobility Amalfi Coast** (tel. 089/813-077; info@mobilityamalficoast.com; €1.30-1.80). These smaller buses stop throughout Praiano, including at the Chiesa di San Gennaro and Marina di Praia, roughly every hour. Tickets available in local tabacchi and some shops, or onboard for a slightly higher price.

By Taxi

To get to Positano by taxi, it's best to book in advance. **Positano Drivers** (tel. 338/888-6572 and 339/886-9182; www.positanodrivers.com; from €100) offers transfers from Naples, Sorrento, and other destinations along the Amalfi Coast.

GETTING AROUND
By Car and Scooter

There's a one-way internal road through

Positano, Viale Pasitea, that starts on the western edge of town high up in Positano. To access the lower part of Positano, follow Viale Pasitea, which winds through Positano down to Piazza dei Mulini and then changes its name to Via Cristoforo Colombo as it climbs out of town to rejoin the Amalfi Coast Road at Sponda, the intersection with the Amalfi Coast Road.

With the narrow roads of the Amalfi Coast, a small rental car is a good idea. **Positano Car Service** (Via Cristoforo Colombo 2; tel. 089/875-867; www.positanocarservice.com; from €110 per day) offers pint-sized Smart cars. Or, **Positano Rent a Scooter** (Via Pasitea 99; tel. 089/812-2077; www.positanorentascooter.it; from €70 per day) offers a variety of scooter options.

By Bus

Mobility Amalfi Coast (tel. 089/813-077; info@mobilityamalficoast.com; €1.30-1.80) provides bus service along Positano's internal road. Buses pass about every half hour for the internal route 9am-midnight. Tickets can be purchased in tabacchi or onboard.

By Taxi

Taxis in Positano are independently owned, high-quality vehicles, and they charge flat fees based on destination. As a result, prices are high. You can generally find a taxi at Piazza dei Mulini from April-October, but you'll need to budget €20 or more just to move around town.

Taxis in Praiano can usually be found at the beginning of Via Giuglielmo Marconi, just off the Amalfi Coast Road east of the Chiesa di San Gennaro, and at the crossroads of the Amalfi Coast Road and Via Umberto I. Look for the orange Taxi sign for more information. The town of Praiano has set taxi fares to most locations on the Amalfi Coast, starting from €15 within Praiano town limits and €40 to Positano. The tourist office in Praiano can offer the latest rates and help with any questions.

On Foot

Positano isn't called the Vertical City for nothing. Getting around town means navigating a lot of steps and inclines. From Piazza dei Mulini down to the beach, you'll walk on a cobblestone path mixed with steps, a bit of an expedition if you have a lot of luggage. If you're staying near the beach, it's worth asking in advance if your accommodation offers a luggage service; there may be an additional fee, but it's worth it. Opt for comfortable shoes and sandals, and a nice pair of flats rather than heels for evenings out.

Amalfi

It only takes one glimpse of Amalfi to understand why the Amalfi Coast's namesake town is one of its most popular spots. Nestled in a valley with pastel-hued buildings climbing up both sides of the mountain, interspersed with terraces of lemon groves, the bell tower of the town's impressive cathedral marks the center of Amalfi, the beautiful Piazza Duomo. A powerful sea republic in the Middle Ages, Amalfi has a fascinating history of dukes and duchesses, wars and wealth, innovation, and exploration.

With a seeming maze of streets and staircases, Amalfi is best explored on foot. While Piazza Duomo and the main street are home to most of the activity, shops, and restaurants, do spend some time wandering and exploring the quieter side streets, where you'll find arched passageways, hidden gardens overflowing with lemons, and tiny piazzas.

Amalfi has one of the most picturesque harbors along the coastline. A scenic passeggiata (stroll) leads from the Marina Grande beach along the sea all the way to the end of the Molo Foraneo, the largest pier in Amalfi, with its red port marker. From the walkway along the pier, enjoy a stunning view looking across the harbor, captivating during the day, but especially after dark with the lights of Amalfi stretching out across the water and the salty sea breeze filling the air.

ORIENTATION

In Amalfi's harbor, the ferry terminal is located at the central **Molo Pennello** pier. Nearby, a large traffic circle around **Piazza Flavio Gioia** is the main hub for buses and taxis. The town of Amalfi spreads north from these two main transportation hubs, with many shops and restaurants clustered on the streets closest to the harbor. Marina Grande beach is just east of Piazza Flavio Gioia.

Two small roads lead from Piazza Flavio Gioia to the **Piazza Duomo,** the heart of Amalfi, where you'll find the Duomo di Amalfi. Amalfi has one main street called **Via Lorenzo d'Amalfi** (changing names to Via Pietro Capuano, Via Cardinal Marino del Giudice, and Via delle Cartiere) starting from Piazza Duomo and leading far into the valley above town. The Amalfi Coast Road (SS163) runs along the waterfront and through Piazza Flavio Gioia.

The waterfront, Piazza Duomo, and main street of Amalfi leading into the valley are all relatively flat by Amalfi Coast standards, but on quieter side streets, you can expect to find plenty of steps.

SIGHTS
★ Duomo di Amalfi

Piazza Duomo; tel. 089/871-324; www. museodiocesanoamalfi.it; 9:30am-5:15pm daily Mar., 9am-6:45pm daily Apr.-June and Oct., 9am-7:45pm daily July-Sept., 10am-3:15pm daily Nov.-Dec., closed Dec. 25 and Jan. 7-Feb. 28; €3

Sitting atop a grand staircase and overlooking Piazza Duomo, Amalfi's cathedral is dedicated to the town's beloved patron Sant'Andrea Apostolo (St. Andrew the Apostle). Most often simply referred to as the Duomo, meaning the most important church, it is a monumental

complex of incredible beauty and interest, and the religious heart of the city.

Before climbing the Duomo's 57 steps, take a moment to admire the **Fontana di Sant'Andrea** in the Piazza Duomo, with an 18th-century central marble statue of Sant'Andrea in front of the X-shaped cross (one of the saint's symbols), surrounded by angels, a siren, and mythical creatures. Stop along the way up the stairs to gaze at the bell tower, built between 1180-1276, featuring interlacing arches and geometric patterns created with yellow and green ceramic tiles. Looking up to the facade of the church, you'll see black and white striped details, mosaics glimmering in the sun, and prominent arches with white tracery opening to the entrance portico. Despite being full of medieval architectural elements, the facade was not completed until 1891, designed by Neapolitan architects Errico Alvino and Guglielmo Raimondi after the earlier baroque facade collapsed during an earthquake in 1861. The current design, inspired by details of the 13th-century original, was implemented in a distinctly colorful 19th-century revival fashion.

At the top of the steps, you'll find a set of large bronze doors that date from 1065. In the center are four bronze panels depicting Sant'Andrea, San Pietro, the Virgin Mary, and Christ. To the left is the entrance to the **Complesso Monumentale di Sant'Andrea,** which includes the **Cloister of Paradise, Museo Diocesano, Crypt of Sant'Andrea,** and the **Duomo.** The aptly named Cloister of Paradise, built between 1266-1268, is surrounded by 120 columns and intertwined arches, once the cemetery for Amalfi's nobility.

From the cloister, you'll enter the **Basilica of the Crucifix,** the oldest part of the cathedral, dating back to the sixth century. It now houses the **Museo Diocesano,** which displays the most impressive treasures of the Duomo di Amalfi, including reliquaries,

chalices, religious paintings and sculptures, and a precious 13th-century miter made of gold, silver, and gems, covered in tiny pearls. Follow the steps down to the **Crypt** where the relics of Sant'Andrea are held below the altar, topped with a large bronze statue of the saint. The final stop on the visit to the complex is the grand **nave** of the cathedral, decorated in a baroque style dating from the early 18th century. The elegant gold-paneled ceiling has four large paintings inset into it depicting scenes of the life of Sant'Andrea.

If you visit when the Complesso Monumentale di Sant'Andrea is closed in January and February, you can still enter the Duomo, as it is open and free to the public 7:30am-11:30am and 4pm-6:30pm daily.

Museo della Carta

Via delle Cartiere 23; tel. 089/830-4561; www. museodellacarta.it; 10am-6:30pm Tues.-Sun. Mar.-Oct., 10am-4pm Tues.-Sun. Nov.-Jan.; from €4.50

Discover Amalfi's long tradition of papermaking in the town's paper museum, which is located in a 13th-century mill near the top of town. The working mill offers a rare look at how paper was made in Amalfi before industrialization. Even older papermaking equipment is on display inside the mill, and during the guided tour included in the price, you'll learn about ancient and more modern methods of papermaking and get a chance to try your hand at making traditional Amalfi paper. It's fascinating to go inside one of the town's historic mills and learn how Amalfi's famous paper was made for centuries.

BEACHES

Amalfi's harbor has several beaches, ranging from the popular Marina Grande beach with its rows of candy-colored umbrellas to beaches tucked away in nearly hidden spots. There are even more options for a more secluded beach day if you head west down the coastline to the small beaches located in rocky coves a short boat ride away.

1: Duomo di Amalfi **2:** town of Amalfi
3: a captivating view of Amalfi from the sea

Amalfi

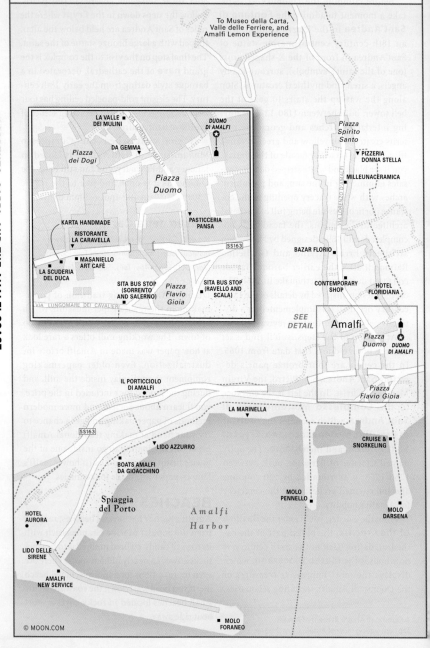

To Museo della Carta,
Valle delle Ferriere, and
Amalfi Lemon Experience

LA VALLE
DEI MULINI

DA GEMMA

Piazza
dei Dogi

DUOMO
DI AMALFI

Piazza
Duomo

Piazza
Spirito
Santo

PIZZERIA
DONNA STELLA

MILLEUNACERAMICA

KARTA HANDMADE

RISTORANTE
LA CARAVELLA

PASTICCERIA
PANSA

SS163

BAZAR FLORIO

MASANIELLO
ART CAFÉ

LA SCUDERIA
DEL DUCA

SITA BUS STOP
(SORRENTO
AND SALERNO)

Piazza
Flavio
Gioia

SITA BUS STOP
(RAVELLO AND
SCALA)

VIA LUNGOMARE DEI CAVALIERI

CONTEMPORARY
SHOP

HOTEL
FLORIDIANA

SEE
DETAIL

Amalfi

Piazza
Duomo

DUOMO
DI AMALFI

IL PORTICCIOLO
DI AMALFI

Piazza
Flavio Gioia

LA MARINELLA

SS163

LIDO AZZURRO

CRUISE &
SNORKELING

BOATS AMALFI
DA GIOACCHINO

Spiaggia
del Porto

Amalfi
Harbor

MOLO
PENNELLO

MOLO
DARSENA

HOTEL
AURORA

LIDO DELLE
SIRENE

AMALFI
NEW SERVICE

MOLO
FORANEO

© MOON.COM

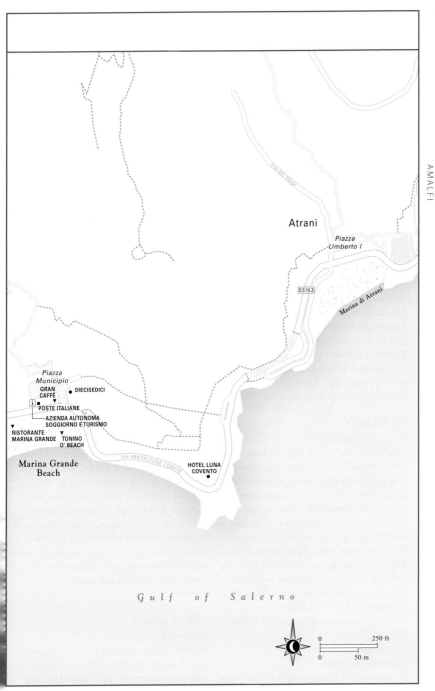

Atrani

Piazza
Umberto I

VIA DEI DOG?

SS163

Marina di Atrani

Piazza
Municipio

GRAN
CAFFÈ   DIECISEDICI

i   POSTE ITALIANE

AZIENDA AUTONOMA
SOGGIORNO E TURISMO

RISTORANTE   TONINO
MARINA GRANDE   O' BEACH

VIA PANTALEONE COMITE

HOTEL LUNA
COVENTO

Marina Grande
Beach

Gulf   of   Salerno

0   250 ft

0   50 m

MARINA GRANDE BEACH
Via Marina Grande

Historic photos show fishing boats lined up along Amalfi's largest beach, just east of Piazza Flavio Gioia and the Molo Darsena. Today the scene is a little different, with the beach's buzz of energy and colorful umbrellas and sun beds. Much of the beach is lined with restaurants that also offer sun bed and umbrella rental, along with shower and changing room facilities. For a small fee, you can pick out a sun bed and an umbrella in your favorite color and enjoy a comfortable day at the beach.

Tonino O' Beach (Via Marina Grande; tel. 089/873-364; www.toninobeach.com; Apr.-Oct.; from €10 for sun bed and umbrella) is located on the eastern side of the beach, the best swimming area, and offers sun bed and umbrella rentals, changing rooms, showers, bathrooms, and boat rentals. The beach also has two free areas, located at either end of the beach. The eastern end is most popular with locals; look for the arches supporting the Amalfi Coast Road as it winds its way out of town. Though the free beach is quite busy in the summer, the water is gorgeous on this rocky side, especially in the morning and if you swim out a bit.

LA MARINELLA
Via Lungomare dei Cavalieri

Stroll along the harbor and just west of the Molo Pennello, you'll spot this minuscule beach with transparent water. Only accessible via **La Marinella** stabilimente balneare (tel. 089/871-043; www.lamarinella.net; Apr.-Oct.; €10 per person), a platform for sunbathing is constructed during the summer months. There are steps down from the platform to the sea, a good spot for families with young children because the beach has small pebbles and easy access to calm water. West of La Marinella is the local beach (meaning no beach club services) **Spiaggia del Porto.**

LE SIRENE
Piazzale dei Protontini 4

Located on the western edge of Amalfi just outside the port, this is a beautiful, rocky beach with clear water for swimming and nice light well into the afternoon. The beach is accessible only via the **Lido delle Sirene** restaurant and beach club (tel. 089/871-756; daily Apr.-Oct.; €25 for beach entrance, two sun beds, and umbrella) where you can rent sun beds and umbrellas, and use the shower and changing facilities. Only a short stroll from the busy center of Amalfi, this is a good option for a quieter day at the beach.

DUOGLIO
Spiaggia Duoglio

Along the rocky coastline west of Amalfi is this small beach with restaurants and stabilimenti balneari that are built during the summer season, leaving two small areas on either end of the beach for free swimming. The beach is accessible via 400 steps down from the Amalfi Coast Road, starting from a small stone gate just east of the intersection for SS363. (The gate is usually open 8am-7pm during the summer season, but not always.) However, the best way to reach the beach is by boat service.

For a small fee, a boat to Duoglio run by **Gruppo Battellieri Costa d'Amalfi** (www.gruppobattellieriamalfi.com; June-Sept.; about every 30 minutes 9am-5:30pm; €4 round-trip per person) departs from the Molo Pennello. Or, if you're planning to visit one of the restaurants with sun bed and umbrella rental (the best option at this rocky beach), you can take a free boat shuttle from Molo Darsena. **Lido degli Artisti** (tel. 331/996-5635; www.lidodegliartisti.it; daily May-Oct.; €25) runs boats every 30 minutes from 9am-sunset; reservations for the boat service and beach are recommended. Round-trip boat service plus umbrella and sun bed is €15 per person.

SANTA CROCE
Spiaggia di Santa Croce

West of Duoglio is one of the Amalfi Coast's most beautiful beaches, with stunning water beneath a sheer cliff surrounded by large rocks. Because a storm damaged the steps leading to the beach in 2011, the only way to get here is by boat. Two stabilimente balneare offer free boat service for clients from the Molo Darsena. Look for small boats marked **Da Teresa** (www.ristorantedateresa.com; late Apr.-Oct.; sun bed and umbrella rental €25 per person) or **Santa Croce** (www.ristorantesantacroce.it; Apr.-Oct.). Good swimmers can swim a short distance to a natural arch called the Lover's Arch.

SPORTS AND RECREATION
Hiking
VALLE DELLE FERRIERE
Distance: 3 miles (5 km)
Time: 2.5 hours round-trip
Trailhead: Via Paradiso (follow to top of valley)
Information and Maps: Cart&guide maps and www.lavalledelleferriere.com

To immerse yourself in the natural beauty of the Amalfi Coast, hike into the valley above Amalfi, where you'll find ruins of old mills covered in natural growth, a cool mountain stream, and a surprisingly tropical landscape with waterfalls, wild orchids and cyclamen, and even a rare prehistoric fern called *Woodwardia radicans*. This area is sometimes called the Valle delle Ferriere and sometimes the Valle dei Mulini, referring to the ironwork factories and paper mills that once lined the valley, powered by the Canneto stream.

At the top of Amalfi past the Museo della Carta, look for signs for Valle delle Ferriere and continue on Via Paradiso past terraces of lemons until it turns into a dirt path. The walk follows the Canneto, with some impressive waterfalls near the top. The uppermost area is a nature reserve and requires advance booking and a small fee to enter (tel. 338/560-5550; www.lavalledelleferriere.com; €5).

There are nice areas to stop for a picnic alongside the mountain stream. Or take a break at **Agricola Fore Porta** (Via Paradiso 22; tel. 339/243-6450; www.agriturismoamalfi.it; 10am-6pm daily Easter-Nov., sometimes closed Tues. or Thurs., advance booking recommended), an agriturismo nestled into the valley along the hiking pathway about 25 minutes from Amalfi. Set in a rustic farm building, they offer freshly made drinks and traditional dishes made with organic ingredients from their gardens.

Water Sports
LIDO DEGLI ARTISTI BEACH CLUB
Spiaggia Duoglio; tel. 331/996-5635; www.lidodegliartisti.it; May-Oct.; windsurfing rentals €18 per hour, €45 per day

Head to the tiny and very rocky Duoglio beach west of Amalfi to find the Lido degli Artisti Beach Club, which offers a windsurf school, stand-up paddleboard rentals, water skiing, wakeboarding, and more. Windsurfing lessons are available for all ages, with a 4-day course (1 hour 30 minutes each day) from €180 per person. Contact to book lessons in advance. The stabilimento balneare also offers sun bed rentals and a restaurant for a comfortable full day at the beach.

Boat and Kayak Tours
AMALFI KAYAK
Spiaggia Duoglio, Via Mauro Comite 41; tel. 338/362-9520; www.amalfikayak.com; Apr.-Oct.; from €49 per person

For active travelers, a kayak tour is one of the best ways to experience the natural beauty of the Amalfi Coast. Amalfi Kayak offers multiple half-day and full-day excursions, where expert local guides show you the best spots along the coast. The most popular is the half-day tour from Amalfi to the Runghetiello Grotto.

During the summer months (June-Sept.), excursions depart from the Spiaggia Duoglio beach, and during the shoulder season (Apr.-May and Oct.), excursions depart from the Le Sirene beach in Amalfi. All equipment is included in the price.

BOATS AMALFI DA GIOACCHINO
Via Lungomare dei Cavalieri 286; tel. 338/264-0895; www.boatsamalfi.it; Apr.-Oct.; from €150

Started by Amalfi local Giacchino Esposito, who left his career as a chef to be closer to the sea, this friendly family-run operation offers boat rentals and excursions with and without a captain. For independent travelers, rent a traditional wooden boat or small motor boat (no need for a nautical license) and spend a day exploring the coastline. Larger boats and yachts with captain are also available for private tours along the Amalfi Coast or to Capri. Though the main season is April-October, Gioacchino usually has boats in the water year-round. You never know when a beautiful winter day might call you out to the sea.

CRUISE & SNORKELING

Darsena Pier, Amalfi; tel. 338/362-9520; www.cruiseamalfi.com; Apr.-Oct.; from €69 per person

For a more adventurous cruise experience on the Amalfi Coast or to Capri, join a small group boat excursion from Amalfi with a local captain at the helm. The Amalfi Coast Highlights excursion is a half-day tour spent exploring the coastline, stopping in the best spots to snorkel in incredible clear water and to explore caves and grottoes. The Capri Island tour is a full-day experience that offers the chance to snorkel in Capri's most beautiful spots. Maximum 8 people.

Local Tours
AMALFI LEMON EXPERIENCE

Via delle Cartiere; tel. 089/873-211; www.amalfilemonexperience.it; 10am and 3pm daily Mar.-Oct.; from €25 per person

The lemon and Amalfi are inextricably connected, and there's no better way to experience this firsthand than to walk among Amalfi's historic lemon groves as you learn about the cultivation of this very special product. Since 1825, six generations of the Aceto family have been growing lemons on the steep slopes of the Amalfi Coast. The family is passionate about maintaining

traditional techniques, from the dry stone wall construction that creates the garden terraces to the details of running an organic farm. A daily group tour offers the chance to meander through the Aceto family's lemon gardens, enjoy a taste of their lemon products, and visit the family's **Museum of Rural Life Arts and Crafts,** a fascinating collection of historic pieces from Amalfi's past. The final touch is a visit to the production lab, where the Acetos transform their lemons into limoncello and other traditional products. Book your spot for the lemon tour in advance; private tours and experiences can also be arranged, such as a sweet Honey Lemon Experience and Tour that showcases the honey made in the lemon grove. There are also wine tastings and cooking classes that, of course, highlight the lemon!

ENTERTAINMENT AND EVENTS

Amalfi's scenic setting and the beautiful Piazza Duomo make for a stellar backdrop for concerts, fashion shows, and festivals. Events take place throughout the year, so stop in the tourist office in Amalfi to find out about upcoming programs.

You can count on Amalfi coming to life during several annual religious festivals, when the town becomes the setting for elaborate processions and spectacular fireworks displays. Capodanno (New Year's Eve) is capped off by the biggest fireworks show of the year, which makes Amalfi the most popular location on the coast to celebrate.

EASTER IN AMALFI

Piazza Duomo and various locations; Holy Week and Easter Sunday

Easter is one of Italy's biggest holidays, with events taking place throughout the week leading up to Easter Sunday. Many towns on the coast have Good Friday and Via Crucis (Stations of the Cross) processions, and Amalfi's are among the most impressive. The Via Crucis often on Holy Thursday, retells the story of Christ's crucifixion. The procession

1: the Lido delle Sirene **2:** produce at agriturismo Agricola Fore Porta **3:** Santa Croce beach **4:** hiking around the top of the Valle delle Ferriere

on Good Friday, representing Christ's funeral and burial, is extremely moving; after dark, the lights are turned off in Piazza Duomo, and a candlelit procession starting from the Duomo moves down the steps and through the town. Accompanied by haunting choral music, masked figures carry the statue of Christ after being taken down from the cross, followed by a statue of the Madonna Addolorata (Virgin Mary in mourning).

Easter Sunday is a joyous day in Amalfi and is followed by Pasquetta (little Easter), traditionally spent outdoors with family and friends. The Easter is the unofficial start of the tourist season on the Amalfi Coast, so book your accommodation well in advance.

HISTORICAL REGATTA OF THE ANCIENT MARITIME REPUBLICS
Hosted in Amalfi every four years; first Sunday in June

Amalfi celebrates its rich heritage and the medieval splendor of the Duchy of Amalfi each year at the Regatta of the Ancient Maritime Republics (Regata delle Antiche Repubbliche Marinare). This festival brings together the four powerful maritime republics of Italy from the Middle Ages—Amalfi, Pisa, Genoa, and Venice—in a rowing contest and historical parade. The first event was held in 1955, and has been held annually since. Each city takes turns holding the regatta, which arrives in Amalfi every four years, usually taking place on the first Sunday in June. If your visit coincides with the regatta in Amalfi, you are in for a very special experience.

FESTIVAL OF SANT'ANDREA
Piazza Duomo and various locations; June 27 and Nov. 30

Twice a year Amalfi honors its patron Sant'Andrea (St. Andrew) with a grand religious festival that is one of the biggest and most popular of the year on the Amalfi Coast. Celebrations take place June 27 to remember the time Sant'Andrea is said to have heeded the prayers of the town's faithful in 1544,

and protected Amalfi from a pirate attack by bringing on a sea storm so intense that it destroyed the invading ships. The November 30 celebration marks the traditional festival day honoring Sant'Andrea.

The festivals center around the Duomo di Amalfi. It does get very crowded, so arrive early in Piazza Duomo to get a good view. After a special Mass, a large 18th-century silver-and-gold statue of Sant'Andrea is taken down the long staircase of the Duomo and carried through town, even down to the beach where boats gather in the harbor for a blessing. The grand finale has to be seen to be believed: The large group of men carrying the statue pause at the bottom of the Duomo's 57 steps before running the statue back to the top. Once they reach the top, the piazza packed full of people bursts into applause as Sant'Andrea returns safely home.

The festive atmosphere continues with music in Piazza Duomo and a spectacular fireworks display over the harbor after dark. The two events honoring St. Andrew are similar, though the summer festival usually comes with excellent weather. In June, the procession begins after evening Mass, and in November it starts after a mid-morning Mass. Since these are the biggest celebrations of the year in Amalfi, do book your accommodation well in advance, especialy for the June 27 festival.

BYZANTINE NEW YEAR
Piazza Duomo and various locations; Aug. 31–Sept. 1

During the Middle Ages, the September 1 was the start of the legal and fiscal new year, according to the calendar of the Byzantine Empire. Given Amalfi's strong ties to that part of the world, that date was used to appoint their elected officials with an elaborate ceremony. This cultural event is celebrated today with a historical procession including more than 100 people dressed in costumes of the former Republic of Amalfi. The event includes selecting a local Amalfitan or important figure to represent the Magister di Civiltà Amalfitana in a ceremony at the

Chiesa di San Salvatore de Birecto in Atrani, followed by a procession to the Duomo in Amalfi. It's a fascinating event, even more elaborate than the historical parade during the Regatta of the Ancient Maritime Republics.

SHOPPING

Amalfi has a wonderful array of shops, mostly centered around Piazza Duomo and the main street leading from the piazza up into the valley and through the center of town. You'll find plenty of opportunities to discover the Amalfi Coast's traditional crafts and products, such as handmade paper, limoncello and lemon-themed items, ceramics, and clothing. Shops in Amalfi rarely close for lunch between Easter-October, but during the winter, especially January-February, some shops close midday for a break, on select days during the week, or for an extended holiday. Most of the shops below are open year-round, with exceptions noted.

Clothing and Accessories
CONTEMPORARY SHOP
Via Pietro Capuano 2; tel. 335/121-9319; www. contemporary-shop.com; 10am-9:30pm daily

A beautifully curated selection of clothing, jewelry, accessories, and ceramics are on display in this tiny shop tucked away in an arched passageway just off Amalfi's main street. There's also a nice selection of books and detailed hiking maps for the area.

BAZAR FLORIO
Via Pietro Capuano 5-7; tel. 089/871-980; www. amalfibazar.com; 8:30am-10pm daily

This is the place to find a large selection of beautiful Italian leather bags and accessories of all shapes, sizes, and colors. The owners stock their own production line of bags as well as notable brands from around Italy. Need a purse to match those sandals you had custom-made in Positano or Capri? Stop in here and you'll find something tempting to bring home.

Paper
LA SCUDERIA DEL DUCA
Largo Cesareo Console 9; tel. 089/872-976; www. carta-amalfi.com; 10am-7pm daily Apr.-Oct., 10am-6pm Mon.-Sat. Nov.-Mar.

Situated near the ancient arsenals where Amalfi's ships were built in the Middle Ages, this treasure trove of a shop offers an incredible selection of paper products, stationery, and prints, all created with paper handmade in Amalfi. They also have an intriguing selection of artwork, ceramics, and antiques. Look for two additional locations in Amalfi's main square (Piazza Duomo 31 and 41) as well as at **Dalla Carta alla Cartolina** (Via Cardinale Marino del Giudice 82), located in a historic paper mill.

KARTA HANDMADE
Largo Cesareo Console 9; tel. 338/289-8170; paoladelucakarta@gmail.com; 10am-7pm daily

A unique and artistic spot in Amalfi, here you'll find a lovely selection of handmade journals and artwork along with vintage clothing, books, and ceramics. The journals especially are one-of-a-kind souvenirs. Each one is handcrafted and stitched using Amalfi-made paper and featuring artistic covers created by shop owner and artist Paola De Luca. The collage of designs on the covers tell a story, and the joy is finding one that speaks to you where you can capture your own stories.

Ceramics
MILLEUNACERAMICA
Via Pietro Capuano 36; tel. 089/872-670; www. milleunaceramica.com; 9am-9pm daily Apr.-May, 9am-11pm daily June-Sept., 9am-8pm daily Oct., winter months open with limited hours

A love for the Amalfi Coast's ceramic traditions shines through in the handpicked collections on display in this colorful ceramic shop. Owner and ceramics enthusiast Maria Anastasio works only with local artists in the Amalfi Coast area, and many pieces are custom-made for Milleunaceramica. This is a unique opportunity to support artists, mostly quite young, who are keeping alive the important ceramic-making tradition on the Amalfi Coast.

Specialty Foods
LA VALLE DEI MULINI

Via Lorenzo d'Amalfi 11; tel. 089/872-603; www. amalfilemon.it; 9:30am-10pm daily, closed Jan. 10-31

Stepping into this shop feels like you've arrived in lemon heaven. All of the limoncello and liqueurs are made in Amalfi in the family's laboratory at the top of the town in the Valle dei Mulini. The lemons are grown on the family's organic farm, so it doesn't get more local than this. They also have a lovely selection of local products, candies, and food specialties.

FOOD

Dining along the waterfront in Amalfi, with its beautiful harbor setting, is a memorable experience. However, don't forget to explore the side streets and little piazzas in the heart of town for other unique dining choices. You'll find plenty of eateries around Piazza Duomo for a quick break or aperitivo with a view. Reservations are recommended, especially at the seaside restaurants.

Seafood
LIDO AZZURRO

Via Lungomare dei Cavalieri 5; tel. 089/871-384; www.ristorantelidoazzurro.it; 12:30pm-3pm and 7pm-10:30pm daily, closed Jan. 10-end of Feb.; €15-28

With a beautiful little terrace right on the harbor, this is a picturesque spot for lunch or dinner. The menu is local, with seafood a natural specialty. Yet there's something for all tastes, with tempting risotto and pasta dishes. Reservations are recommended, especially for one of the coveted tables right around the edge of the terrace by the sea.

DA GEMMA

Via Fra Gerardo Sasso 11; tel. 089/871-345; www. trattoriadagemma.com; noon-3pm and 7pm-11pm daily, closed Wed. mid-Nov.-mid-Mar.; €16-28

Dating back to 1872, this is one of Amalfi's historic restaurants, and it's a popular choice. The dining area also includes a terrace with views overlooking the Piazza Duomo nearby. Seafood is served brilliantly here, and the risotto with red prawns and the zuppa di pesce (fish soup) are excellent choices. Tasting menus are also available. Reservations are recommended.

Regional Cuisine
★ RISTORANTE MARINA GRANDE

Viale della Regione 4; tel. 089/871-129; www. ristorantemarinagrande.com; noon-3pm and 6:30-10pm Wed.-Mon. mid-Apr.-mid-Nov.; €14-38

Enjoy the view overlooking Amalfi's main beach while dining at Marina Grande. The menu changes seasonally throughout the year and highlights regional specialties served with a creative flair, and is well balanced with seafood and meat choices. Locally sourced ingredients take pride of place, including freshly caught seafood and Gentile pasta produced in Gragnano in the hills above Sorrento. This casually elegant restaurant also offers beach service with comfortable lounge chairs just steps from the sea.

RISTORANTE LA CARAVELLA

Via Matteo Camera 12; tel. 089/871-029; www. ristorantelacaravella.it; noon-2:30pm and 7pm-11pm Wed.-Mon., closed mid-Nov.-Christmas and Jan. 10-Feb. 10; lunch tasting menu €60 per person (minimum two people), dinner tasting menu €100-150 per person

This gem of a restaurant was the first in southern Italy to earn a a Michelin star. Amalfi born and raised, chef Antonio Dipino is a proud custodian of tradition. The restaurant is situated in a building dating to the 1100s that

---

1: lemons growing around Amalfi **2:** Festival of Sant'Andrea **3:** outdoor seating of the Gran Caffè

once belonged to the Piccolomini Family, early Dukes of Amalfi. Only one of 10 restaurants in Italy to be classified as a Ristorante – Museo, the restaurant and nearby art gallery house the finest collection of ceramics on the Amalfi Coast. Tasting menus change seasonally, but the Tubettoni di Gragnano con ragù di pesce (Pasta from Gragnano with a ragout of fish) is an exceptional first course followed by locally caught pezzogna fish stewed with Greco di Tufo wine, fennel, sun dried tomatoes, and fresh mint. Il Sole nel Piatto (The Sun in the Dish), the restaurant's lemon soufflè, deserves special mention. For wine enthusiasts, there's a remarkable selection. Reservations highly recommended.

Pizzeria
PIZZERIA DONNA STELLA
Via Salita d'Ancora 4; tel. 338-358-8483; donna. stella@alice.it; noon-3:30pm and 6pm-10:30pm daily June-Sept., noon-3:30pm and 6pm-10:30pm Wed.-Mon. Apr.-May and Oct., dinner only Nov.-Mar.; €7-14

If eating delicous pizza under a lemon tree pergola sounds just right, then you'll enjoy this pizzeria, with lots of fresh toppings to try. The specialty is Pizza Annabella, prepared with mozzarella and ricotta di bufala, black olives, and arugula. Appetizers, seasonal vegetables, and pasta and main course dishes are also available. There's a small indoor dining area for inclement weather.

Bakeries and Cafés
★ PASTICCERIA PANSA
Piazza Duomo 40; tel. 089/871-065; www. pasticceriapansa.it; 7:30am-11pm daily, until 1am June-Sept., closed Jan. 7-Feb. 3; pastries from €2-3.50

Since 1830, this bakery has been a fixture of Amalfi's Piazza Duomo. The fifth generation of the Pansa family proudly runs the family bakery, and they have made it one of the most popular in the area for pastries, traditional Christmas and Easter desserts, and chocolates. The candied lemon and citrus peels start in the family's property above Amalfi and are

transformed into delicious sweets. Try the sfogliatelle (shell-shaped pastry), delizia al limone (lemon cake), or any of the sweets on display. You truly can't go wrong!

GRAN CAFFÈ
Corso delle Repubbliche Marinare 37/38; tel. 089/871-047; www.bargrancaffeamalfi.it; 7:30am-1am Tues.-Sun. Oct.-Jan. and Mar.-July, daily Aug.-Sept.; €5-10

Open all day with an outdoor dining area overlooking Marina Grande, this is a popular spot with locals and travelers for everything from a morning espresso or cappuccino to a light lunch or a sunset aperitivo. During the summer the atmosphere is lively until late. The bruschetta and salads are particularly good and fresh, but they also offer pizzas and daily specials for something more substantial. There's an extensive drink menu, but you can't go wrong with a classic spritz or their unique version with limoncello.

NIGHTLIFE
MASANIELLO ART CAFÈ
Largo Cesareo Console 7; tel. 339/471-0752; www. masanielloartcafe.it; 9am-3am daily, closed Mon. for lunch Feb.-Mar.; €8-12

If you're looking nightlife in Amalfi, this is the place. Popular during the day for drinks and for the best hamburger (yes, you read that right) in town, the Masaniello Art Café really comes to life after dark. The cocktails are on point; if you're a gin fan, don't miss their house-made version. Locally produced beers are also on the menu. Live music and events are scheduled throughout the year. This is the go-to spot for the younger crowd in Amalfi, and in a town that can feel somewhat touristy, it's refreshingly local.

ACCOMMODATIONS
Amalfi offers a large range of accomodations, from small B&Bs to extraordinary five-star hotels with that family-run touch that is a inviting characteristic of luxury on the Amalfi Coast. If you're looking for a unique experience, consider a stay in one of Amalfi's

two former monasteries that have been transformed into lovely hotels with incredible views overlooking the harbor.

€100-200
IL PORTICCIOLO DI AMALFI

Via Annuziatella 38; tel. 089/873-096; www. amalfiporticciolo.it; mid-Mar.-mid-Nov.; €120 d

In the upper part of town with a sweeping view of the harbor, this welcoming B&B offers an authentic stay in its five simply decorated, comfortable rooms. Breakfast can be served on the large terrace with panoramic views or delivered to your room. The terrace is also a lovely spot for evening cocktails. The B&B is only accessible via a long and steep staircase from the center of Amalfi, or an inclined, 10-minute walk along the road, followed by steps, but you are rewarded with a peaceful setting on arrival.

HOTEL FLORIDIANA

Salita Brancia 1; tel. 089/873-6373; www. hotelfloridiana.it; Apr.-Oct.; €150 d

Situated right in the center of Amalfi, this hotel is a wonderful choice for easy access and beautiful rooms. The 12th-century palazzo includes beautiful features like a salon from the 1700s with lavish I and a sumptuously frescoed ceiling. The 13 rooms vary in style from standard rooms to junior suites with Jacuzzi tubs. Parking is available at no extra charge.

€200-300
HOTEL AURORA

Piazzale dei Protontini 7; tel. 089/871-209; www. aurora-hotel.it; Apr.-Oct.; €219 d

Well situated in a quiet spot overlooking a rocky beach and Amalfi's harbor, this family-run hotel has 28 spacious rooms with sea views, some with large terraces that are perfect for sunbathing. You can also take advantage of the hotel's private beach access nearby. Service is very friendly, and breakfast is served on a bougainvillea-covered terrace with fine views. Three fully equipped apartment rentals are also available in the center

of Amalfi and start at €180 per day (3-night minimum).

DIECISEDICI

Piazza Municipio 13; tel. 089/872-737; www. diecisedici.com; early Mar.-early Nov. and New Year's Eve; €290 d

This B&B on a quiet piazza behind the Duomo has easy access to Marina Grande and six rooms, four with beautiful sleeping loft areas and two situated on an upper level with a glimpse of the sea. The decor is modern, with striking ceramic floors. Minimum stay requirements vary, depending on the season. There's no elevator, but the views from the second or third floors are worth the climb.

Over €300
HOTEL LUNA CONVENTO

Via Pantaleone Comite 33; tel. 089/871-002; www. lunahotel.it; Mar.-Dec.; €340 d

One of Amalfi's most romantic spots, the Hotel Luna Convento is situated in a former monastery that dates back to 1200s near the seaside watchtower at the eastern edge of town. Inside, a peaceful cloister transports you back in time. All of the rooms have sea views, each with its own unique style thanks to the historic nature of the building. The hotel also owns the **Torre Saracena** restaurant across the street, offering the chance to dine with incredible views. Below the watchtower, down a meandering staircase of about 80 steps, you'll find a saltwater pool and sunbathing terrace with access to the sea and splendid views of Atrani.

INFORMATION AND SERVICES

- **Tourist information:** Agenzia Regionale Campania Turismo; Corso delle Repubbliche Marinare 11; tel. 089/871-107; www.amalfitouristoffice.it; 9am-1pm and 2:30pm-6pm daily May-Oct., 9am-1pm daily Nov.-Apr.

- **Hospital:** Ospedale Costa d'Amalfi; Via Civita 12; www.aslsalerno.it

- **Post office:** Poste Italiane; Corso delle Repubbliche Marinare 31; tel. 089/830-4831; www.poste.it; 8:20am-1:35pm Mon.-Fri., 8:20am-12:35pm Sat.
- **Luggage storage:** Divina Costiera; Piazza Flavio Gioia 3; tel. 089/871-181; www.divinacostierainteragency.com
- **Laundry:** Self-Laundry; Via Cardinal Marino del Giudice, 2B; tel. 335/718-4127; 8am-10pm daily; from €6 per wash

GETTING THERE

With its larger harbor and convenient central location, Amalfi is a transportation hub along the coastline for buses and ferries. This makes it a popular base for exploring the area by public transportation.

By Car and Scooter

Amalfi is centrally located along the Amalfi Coast, about 1 hour (15.5 mi/25 km) west of **Salerno** and 45 minutes-1 hour (10 mi/16 km) east of **Positano.** The **Amalfi Coast Road (SS163)** runs through Amalfi at sea level. From **Ravello** (20 minutes), follow the **SS373** down to where it intersects the Amalfi Coast Road at Castiglione and take a right to continue to Amalfi. From **Naples** (1 hour 30 minutes-1 hour 45 minutes) follow the **A3** highway south out of Naples, exit at Castellammare di Stabia and follow the **SS145** to the intersection with the **SS366** that leads up the mountains, through Agerola, and down to the Amalfi Coast on the other side. It ends at the Amalfi Coast Road (SS163), where you'll bear left and shortly arrive in Amalfi. You can also stay on the A3 highway until Vietri sul Mare and then take the Amalfi Coast Road west to Amalfi to see more of the coastline.

Amalfi has several paid **parking lots** (€1-5 per hour), including limited parking right along the waterfront near Piazza Flavio Gioia, behind the Molo Foraneo, and the **Luna Rossa** parking garage (www.amalfimobilita.com), carved out of the mountain. During peak periods, all parking may be full. Call ahead to your accommodation to reserve a spot, as many offer parking at an additional cost.

By Ferry

Ferries to Amalfi arrive and depart from **Molo Pennello,** in the center of Amalfi's harbor. Along the pier's western side, you'll find smaller boats to and from nearby beaches. Larger ferries from Salerno, Positano, Capri, and Sorrento dock at the end of the pier. Tickets can be purchased at booths on the pier, or in advance from many operators, a good idea during from June-September.

The most frequent ferry service to Amalfi is operated by **Travelmar** (tel. 089/872-950; www.travelmar.it; €3-9 per person). During the ferry season from April to early November, there are regular arrivals—6-11 daily, depending on departure point—throughout the day from Positano (25 minutes) and Salerno (35 minutes).

Alicost (tel. 089/811-986; www.alicost.it; €20.80-23.30 per person) offers daily ferry service to Amalfi from Capri (1 hour 20 minutes), Sorrento (1 hour), Positano, and Salerno. There are usually 1-4 daily departures from Capri to Amalfi (more during the peak summer period June-Sept.), and 1-2 daily departures to Sorrento. Exact times can vary seasonally, so check the schedule in advance. Many of the ferries from Capri and Sorrento also stop in Positano.

By Bus

Amalfi's **Piazza Flavio Gioia** traffic circle is the central hub along the coastline for the public **SITA SUD** buses (tel. 089/386-6701; www.sitasudtrasporti.it; from €1.30) with service from all of the most popular spots in the area: Salerno (1 hour 15 minutes), Sorrento (1 hour 40 minutes), Positano (40 minutes), and Ravello (25 minutes). Two main bus lines run along the Amalfi Coast Road and meet in Amalfi: One starts in Salerno and travels west along the Amalfi Coast, and the other departs from Sorrento and passes through Positano, among other towns, before arriving in Amalfi from the east.

Buses for **Salerno** and **Sorrento** arrive and depart from **Via Lungomare dei Cavalieri** at the western edge of Piazza Flavio Gioia. The signage for each route is not very clear, but the final destination is listed on the top front of each bus. Buses to **Ravello** arrive and depart from the eastern side of Piazza Flavio Gioia near the beach (there's a sun-protective awning that is marked for Ravello).

The red **City Sightseeing** buses (www. city-sightseeing.it; Apr.-Oct.; from €5 per person) are more comfortable. There are multiple lines to Amalfi, from Sorrento (1 hour 25 minutes), Positano (50 minutes), and Amalfi (30 minutes). The buses from Ravello are open-top, enjoyable on a sunny day. The stop in Amalfi is at the Ravello SITA stop on the eastern side of Piazza Flavio Gioia. Audio guides for the journey are included in the price, and tickets can be purchased onboard or from the assistant before boarding.

Pintour (tel. 081/879-2645; www. pintourbus.com; Apr.-early Nov.; 1 hour 55 minutes; €20 adults, €10 children up to 12 years) offers a convenient, affordable bus to Amalfi from the Naples airport (Aeroporto Internazionale di Napoli at Capodichino). Buses depart from the bus terminal outside the arrivals hall at the airport. The bus stops at Pompeii and every town along the Amalfi Coast from Vietri sul Mare to Amalfi, where it stops right in Piazza Flavio Gioia. Tickets can be booked in advance online (a good idea). There are usually about five departures daily, but check times in advance, as they can change from season to season.

By Taxi

Amalfi Turcoop (tel. 081/873-1522; www. amalfiturcoop.it; from €110) offers transfers to Amalfi from any area point of arrival.

GETTING AROUND

Amalfi is very walkable from end to end. The main sights and most of its land-accessible beaches can be reached on foot from the ferry terminal and Piazza Flavio Gioia bus circle.

By Bus

Amalfi has a small mini bus service, **Amalfi Mobilita** (tel. 089/873-518; www. amalfimobilita.com; €0.50), that runs from the western end of the port to near the top of the town at the Valle dei Mulini stop, passing through Piazza Flavio Gioia and Piazza Duomo. Service runs about every half hour 8am-8pm. Tickets can be purchased onboard.

By Car and Scooter

Amalfi New Service (Piazzale dei Protontini; tel. 089/871-087; www.amalfinewservice.it; 8:30am-8pm daily) offers scooters and a variety of car rentals, including new and vintage options. Car rental rates start at €70 per day, while scooters are €60 for the first day and €40 for each additional day. Scooters are available to rent from March-November, and car rentals are available all year.

By Taxi

You'll find taxis in Amalfi year-round at the taxi stand located on the eastern side of Piazza Flavio Gioia. Set fares are clearly marked on the sign near the taxi stand or on the Comune di Amalfi website (www.amalfi.gov.it/taxi). A ride around Amalfi to hotels in the area (convenient if you have luggage) begins at €10-25. There are also set fares from Amalfi to Ravello of €40-50, from Amalfi to Positano (€70-85), and most of the towns on the Amalfi Coast. All other journeys are based on the taxi meter, starting from €6.

Ravello

Along with Positano and Amalfi, Ravello is one of the Amalfi Coast's most visited towns, a completely different experience from the seaside. It sits at 1,200 feet (365 m) above sea level, on a long, flat promontory jutting out of the mountains.

Ravello's history is tied closely to Amalfi, as Ravello was a part of the Republic of Amalfi in the Middle Ages. Its grand villas and palazzos, many now home to luxury hotels, were once the residences of wealthy merchants who built the remarkable churches that dot the town. Today the grounds of two of the largest estates, Villa Rufolo and Villa Cimbrone, offer visitors the chance to explore their beautifully landscaped gardens and take in their famous views.

A place of inspired beauty, Ravello has been a haven for artists for centuries. Known as the City of Music, the town produces a rich and varied calendar of performances throughout the year, including the annual summer Ravello Festival.

While Ravello is popular with travelers, the town remains tranquil even during the busy summer months. Charming pedestrian-only areas, including Piazza Duomo, feel far away from traffic. Summer evenings are especially enchanting when the day-trippers have moved on and music is in the air during the Ravello Festival. If you can't get enough of the famous Amalfi Coast views, be sure to plan time to explore Ravello's beautiful gardens and enjoy one of the most relaxing towns on the coast.

ORIENTATION

The heart of Ravello is **Piazza Duomo,** right in the center of town, where you'll find the town's largest church, great shopping and dining options, and the entrance to **Villa Rufolo,** one of the two noted gardens in town. The **Villa Cimbrone** is located at the tip of the promontory and is well worth the 15-minute walk to reach it.

SIGHTS
Duomo di Ravello

Piazza Duomo; tel. 089/858-029; www.chiesaravello. it; 9am-noon and 5:30pm-7:30pm daily; free

Founded in the 11th century, Ravello's most important church has gone through many renovations, with the latest restoring many of the medieval features and preserved later baroque additions. At the top of a small flight of steps, the entrance is through a pair of bronze doors that were created in 1179 by Barisano da Trani, whose bronze work can also be seen on the Monreale Cathedral in Sicily and the Trani Cathedral in Puglia. The doors feature 80 panels of bas-relief designs depicting religious figures and scenes.

The columns that line the nave are topped with antique capitals, taken from ancient sites in the area. On the left side of the nave is a 12th-century ambon with mosaics depicting the story of Jonah and the whale. The winged monster devouring Jonah is a pistrice, a mythical sea creature with a long snake-like tail and wings. Just opposite, a pulpit from the 13th is covered with intricate mosaics.

To the left of the altar is an ornate chapel that is dedicated to San Pantaleone (St. Pantaleon), the town's patron saint. Behind the 17th-century chapel altar is a reliquary containing the blood of the saint. It is said that every year on July 27, the saint's festival day, the blood liquefies in the reliquary: a religious miracle that just can't be explained!

MUSEO DELL'OPERA DEL DUOMO

Piazza Duomo 7; tel. 089/858-029; www. museoduomoravello.com; 10am-6pm daily May-Oct., 11:30am-5:30pm daily May, with advance reservation Nov.-Mar.; €3

More historical treasures are on display in the crypt of the church, which houses the Museo dell'Opera del Duomo. Among the pieces on display are reliquaries, paintings, and architectural pieces like the remains of

Ravello

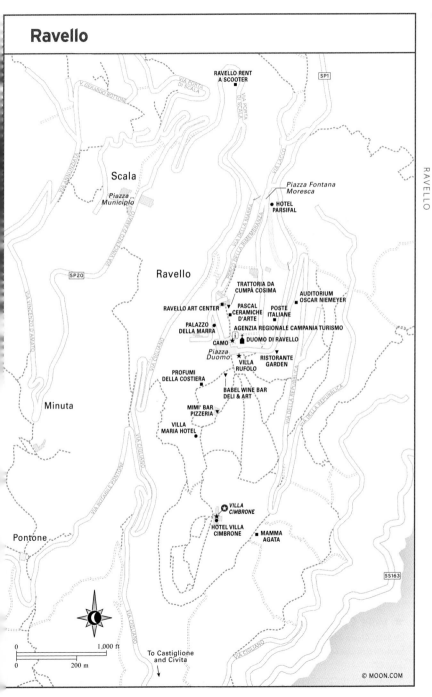

Scala

Piazza Municipio

SP20

Ravello

Piazza Fontana Moresca

HOTEL PARSIFAL

TRATTORIA DA CUMPÀ COSIMA

AUDITORIUM OSCAR NIEMEYER

RAVELLO ART CENTER

PASCAL CERAMICHE D'ARTE

POSTE ITALIANE

PALAZZO DELLA MARRA

AGENZIA REGIONALE CAMPANIA TURISMO

CAMO

DUOMO DI RAVELLO

Piazza Duomo

VILLA RUFOLO

RISTORANTE GARDEN

PROFUMI DELLA COSTIERA

Minuta

BABEL WINE BAR DELI & ART

MIMI' BAR PIZZERIA

VILLA MARIA HOTEL

VILLA CIMBRONE

HOTEL VILLA CIMBRONE

MAMMA AGATA

Pontone

SS163

0   1,000 ft

0   200 m

To Castiglione and Civita

© MOON.COM

an impressive tabernacle from 1279 that was donated by Matteo Rufolo. When the church doors are closed, you can still visit the church by paying a small fee to visit the museum.

Villa Rufolo

Piazza Duomo; tel. 089/857-621; www.villarufolo. com; 9am-sunset daily; €7

Take a walk back in time in the gardens of the Villa Rufolo. This sprawling estate belonged to the wealthy Rufolo family during the Middle Ages. Climb to the top of **Torre Museo,** a 13th-century tower that has been transformed into a museum, to learn the fascinating history of the villa through historic photos, videos, and archaeological finds. As a bonus, you get an incredible bird's-eye view over Ravello from the top. While exploring the villa, you'll spot traces of the unique architectural style of the Amalfi Coast, blending Arabic, Sicilian, and Norman influences. Don't miss the cloister with its delicate twin columns supporting intricate interlocking foliate arches.

The terraced gardens are dotted with wisteria-covered pergolas that frame the incredible view, fountains, and romantic nooks. Floral beds are planted seasonally with colorful flowers to complement the beautiful bougainvillea vines, hydrangeas, roses, and cypress and pine trees, along with Mediterranean herbs and plants. There's an air of enchantment in the gardens, which inspired the scenography for Richard Wagner's opera *Parsifal* after a memorable visit he made in 1880. Today the musical tradition continues as the Villa Rufolo hosts the celebrated **Ravello Festival** every year from June-August. While the gardens are at their best from early spring through the fall, the views and Torre Museo make a visit to Villa Rufolo worthwhile throughout the year.

★ Villa Cimbrone

Via Santa Chiara 26; tel. 089/857-459; www. hotelvillacimbrone.com/villa-cimbrone; 9am-sunset daily; €7

At the tip of the promontory where Ravello sits, this lush green estate is now a five-star hotel, its beautiful gardens open to visit. The peaceful gardens and stunning views make this one of the highlights of the entire Amalfi Coast. The estate has been in this coveted location in Ravello since ancient Roman times, when it was called Cimbronium, and was home to noble Ravello families during the Middle Ages. Ernest William Beckett, Lord Grimthorpe, an English banker and politician, purchased it in 1904. He revived the gardens with the help of local and notable English garden designers and architects. The result blended original Renaissance features, like a long central avenue, with English elements, such as the temples, grottoes, tearoom, and rose garden.

As you enter the gardens, visit the serene **Gothic cloister** with its pointed arches and spiral columns, a blend of Arab, Sicilian, and Norman architecture. Continue down the aptly named **Avenue of Immensity** to the **Terrace of Infinity,** covered with wisteria vines and rimmed with 18th-century marble busts. This spot offers a breathtaking view over the water—one of the best on the Amalfi Coast. From the Avenue of Immensity, wander off and explore the beautifully landscaped gardens. You'll see the **Rose Terrace,** with its geometric flower beds of roses that bloom from May-October. Nearby, the open pavilion tearoom is where Lord Grimthorpe often gathered with members of the Bloomsbury Group, an association of English writers, philosophers, and artists, including Virginia Woolf. There's still an artistic air, as if you might just happen across an artist at an easel or a writer scribbling away in a notebook.

Other lovely spots include Eve's Grotto, home to a marble statue of Eve by Bolognese artist Adamo Tadolini (1788-1868), and a temple dedicated to Bacchus where Lord Grimthorpe's ashes were interred, so he could rest forever in the gardens he loved.

To reach Villa Cimbrone, head down **Via**

1: Ravello town square **2:** a picturesque street in Ravello **3:** the entrance to Villa Rufolo

dei Rufolo from Piazza Duomo and follow signs that lead up a series of staircases and meandering pedestrian-only walkways to the entrance of the gardens, a 15-minute walk.

COOKING CLASS
MAMMA AGATA
Piazza San Cosma 9; tel. 089/857-845; www. mammaagata.com; classes offered Mon., Tues., Thurs., Fri. Apr.-Oct., closed Aug. 11-28; from €200 pp

Located in a tranquil spot in Ravello, Mamma Agata is a little culinary haven where cooking is a passion and truly a family affair. Mamma Agata, who began cooking on the Amalfi Coast at a very early age, was the inspiration for this cooking school created by her daughter Chiara Lima. In cooking classes, Mamma Agata and Chiara's husband, Gennaro—also a talented chef and sommelier—share their traditional family recipes, home-cooking style, locally produced and organic products, and a wealth of cooking secrets. After the cooking class, an exquisite lunch is served on the terrace with panoramic views over their gardens and the Amalfi Coast.

ENTERTAINMENT AND EVENTS

Known as the City of Music, Ravello offers no shortage of concerts and musical events throughout the year.

Concerts
RAVELLO CONCERT SOCIETY
Annunziata Historic Building, Via della Annunziata; tel. 089/842-4082; www.ravelloarts.org; concerts usually held 8pm Mon., Wed., and Fri.-Sat. during summer, 6pm Mon., Wed., and Fri.-Sat. in spring and autumn; €27.50

The Ravello Concert Society has been presenting concerts since 1933 in historic locations throughout Ravello. Because the season runs most of the year, it's a wonderful opportunity to enjoy a concert in the City of Music, no matter when you visit. Classical and contemporary concerts take place in the **Annunziata Historic Building** (a beautiful

setting in a former 13th-century church), as well as in the **Ravello Art Center,** which is located near the Chiesa di Santa Maria a Gradillo. Note that the entrance to the Annunziata Historic Building is at the top of about 90 steps, so concertgoers with mobility issues should select a concert at the Ravello Art Center. Concerts do often sell out, so it's a good idea to purchase in advance.

AUDITORIUM OSCAR NIEMEYER
Via della Repubblica 12; tel. 089/857-096; www. ravellotime.com; contact tourist office for visiting information

Since 1997, the Amalfi Coast has been a UNESCO World Heritage Site, which tells you there has been very little new construction in the area. One distinctive exception is the Auditorium Oscar Niemeyer, which takes its name from its designer, Brazilian architect Oscar Niemeyer. With Ravello's music and art tradition, a state-of-the-art concert hall for year-round performances was needed, and this venue was inaugurated in 2010. The sweeping curved roofline of the bright white building is a striking addition to Ravello's cityscape. A variety of shows are staged here throughout the year, from concerts during the Ravello Festival to movies during the winter months. The large terrace in front of the auditorium is often used for art installations during the Ravello Festival.

Festivals and Events
RAVELLO FESTIVAL
Villa Rufolo and various locations; tel. 089/858-422; www.ravellofestival.com; July-Sept.; €25-70

Inspired by Ravello's visitor in 1880, Richard Wagner, the Ravello Festival began in the 1930s and became a yearly event in the 1950s. While exploring the Villa Rufolo gardens, Wagner was inspired to create the scenography for the magical garden of Klingsor in his opera *Parsifal*. The town transformed that musical moment into a tradition of performances and events. At first, the festival was dedicated primarily to Wagner's music, but over time it has expanded classical, opera, jazz, and contemporary performances, as well as ballet, dance, theater, and cultural events. The majority of the performances take place on a specially constructed stage in the Villa Rufolo gardens, with the Amalfi Coast serving as a one-of-a-kind backdrop. Other events are held in the Auditorium Oscar Niemeyer and at various locations in Ravello. Concerts take place throughout over a weekl the schedule is usually announced around May each year, with tickets available online shortly thereafter. Tickets frequently sell out, so book early to avoid disappointment.

FESTIVAL OF SAN PANTALEONE
Duomo di Ravello and various locations; July 27, contact tourist office for program of events
Ravello celebrates its patron San Pantaleone (St. Pantaleon) with a religious festival that starts in the Duomo and takes over the entire town. The festivities take place on July 27, the date San Pantaleone was martyred in AD 305, and the date that it's said the blood of the saint miraculously liquifies. After a special Mass, a procession following a statue of the saint meanders through the narrow streets, accompanied by the town's faithful. Concerts take place in the piazza, and after dark a huge fireworks display is set off above Ravello.

SHOPPING
With a fine selection of boutiques, ceramic stores, and local products, you'll find most of Ravello's shops around Piazza Duomo and the two streets that branch off from the square: **Via San Francesco,** toward Villa Cimbrone, and **Via Roma** in the opposite direction.

Clothing and Accessories
CAMO
Piazza Duomo 9; tel. 089/857-461; www. museodelcorallo.com; 8:30am-8pm daily May-Oct., 8:30am-4pm Tues.-Sat. Nov.-Apr.
The late master cameo and coral carver Giorgio Filocamo created one of Ravello's most remarkable shops, which is set right below the Duomo. While the shop looks tiny from the outside, step inside to find a treasure-house of jewelry. The museum at the back of the shop showcases Camo's prized collection of coral carving masterpieces.

Ceramics
PASCAL CERAMICHE D'ARTE
Via Roma 22; tel. 089/858-576; www. ceramichedarte.com; 9am-10pm daily Mar.-Oct., 9am-5pm daily Nov.-Feb.
A fine selection of ceramics is on display at this large shop in the center of Ravello. The

Ravello Festival stage and performance in the Villa Rufolo

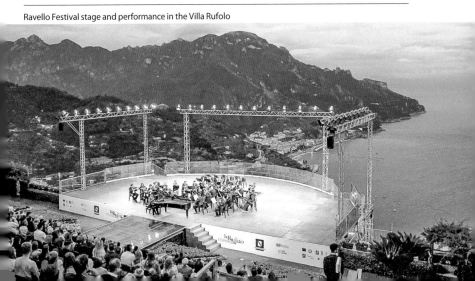

pieces are curated by Pasquale Sorrentino, who is passionate about handpicking and creating beautiful designs. You'll find a tempting choice of dishes as well as garden furniture, tables, and vases in the courtyard and in an additional shop located just around the corner.

Specialty Foods
PROFUMI DELLA COSTIERA

Via Trinità 37; tel. 089/858-167; www. profumidellacostiera.it; 8:30am-7pm daily May-Oct., 8:30am-5pm daily Nov.-Apr.

Stop in here to find a large selection of locally made liqueurs, including the iconic limoncello (lemon liqueur) made with Amalfi Coast lemons. For something a little different, don't miss the liqueur with finocchietto selvatico (wild fennel).

FOOD

With a setting suspended between land and sea, Ravello offers traditional cuisine that reflects both the mountains and the ocean, from freshly caught seafood to hearty meat dishes or crespolini, a local dish of rich and creamy stuffed crepes that are baked in the oven.

Regional Cuisine
RISTORANTE GARDEN

Via Boccaccio 4; tel. 089/857-226; www. gardenravello.com; noon-3pm and 7:30pm-10pm Wed.-Mon. Easter-mid.Nov.; €16-25

With a large terrace and sweeping views, this is a great choice for dining with a view. The restaurant offers excellent choices, even if you aren't into seafood; but if you are, it is very delicately prepared here, including spaghetti con le vongole (with clams) that is top-notch.

TRATTORIA DA CUMPÀ COSIMA

Via Roma 44; tel. 089/857-156; noon-4pm and 6pm-11pm daily Mar.-Dec., noon-4pm and 6pm-11pm Tues.-Sun. Jan.-Feb.; €15-40

Tucked away on a small street, this trattoria is the real deal. Netta Bottone, with her apron neatly tied around her waist, serves up local, hearty specialties. Can't choose just one

pasta from the menu? Try the sample platter that combines some of the restaurant's daily choices, or go for the crespolini—Netta's take on this local dish of baked stuffed crepes is out of this world.

Pizzeria
MIMI' BAR PIZZERIA

Via San Francesco 12; tel. 089/857-134; www. mimiravello.com; 12:30pm-3pm and 7pm-10pm daily May-Sept., contact for hours Oct.-Apr.; €8-25 and pizzas €7-12

With indoor seating and a pretty outdoor garden terrace, as well as outdoor seating on a charming street, this restaurant specializes in pizza and does it exceptionally well. Top quality ingredients and a tempting selection of pizzas makes this a tasty spot for lunch or dinner. The menu also features an excellent selection of first and second courses, and their Spaghetti di Mezzanotte with garlic, chili peppers, olive oil, and Pecorino cheese foam is a house specialty.

Wine Bar
BABEL WINE BAR DELI & ART

Via Santissima Trinità 13; tel. 089/858-6215; www. babelravello.com; 11:30am-3:30pm and 7pm-10pm daily mid Mar.-mid Nov., €6-15

For a light lunch, dinner, or drinks, head to this wine bar, just a short jaunt from Piazza Duomo. Try one of the excellent salads for a refreshingly healthy option with a local twist, like the fabulous buffalo bresaola (air-dried salted meat) and fig salad with white truffle honey. There are also creative bruschette topped with lovely combinations like goat cheese and caramelized onion, or creamy burrata cheese with pesto and tomato confit. Choose from local beer and wines in an artistic setting.

ACCOMMODATIONS

Ravello is noted for its five-star hotels, but there are also cute B&Bs set in historic buildings and seaside villas. It's a very good idea to book well in advance, especially because it's a popular location for destination weddings.

If relaxing by the sea or pool is key for your holiday, keep in mind that there aren't any beaches in Ravello near the center of the town. You can compensate by picking a hotel with a lovely pool, or choose one with direct sea access or a private beach club.

Under €100
PALAZZO DELLA MARRA

Via della Marra 3; tel. 089/858-302; www. palazzodellamarra.it; closed Jan.; €80 d

Just a few steps from Piazza Duomo, this B&B is set in a historic palazzo once belonging to the Della Marra family, who were important nobles in 13th-century Ravello. The four rooms have views over the Piazza Duomo or across the valley. The family also offers an apartment rental right in the center of Ravello. This B&B offers a central location and excellent service.

€100-200
HOTEL PARSIFAL

Viale Gioacchino d'Anna 5; tel. 089/857-144; www. hotelparsifal.it; €175 d

Taking its name from Wagner's opera inspired by Ravello, this hotel certainly has an enchanting setting. Sitting high atop Ravello, it was founded as a convent in 1288, converted into a hotel in 1948. The tranquil hotel's lovely terraces, central cloister, and 17 rooms have a family feel and offer the kind of gorgeous Amalfi Coast views that you'd find at the five-star hotels nearby, yet at a much more affordable price point. It's also open year round, which means you can enjoy Ravello's charms off season, too.

€200-300
VILLA MARIA HOTEL

Via Santa Chiara; tel. 089/857-255; www.villamaria. it; €230 d

Near the entrance to the Villa Cimbrone gardens you'll find this hotel through a small garden courtyard, beautifully decorated and with the air of a noble residence. The spacious rooms are full of light from the large windows, and there are terraces with excellent views of the tranquil valley and the sea. With handpainted majolica tiled floors and antique furnishings, the rooms boast historic elements as well as all the modern comforts. The hotel restaurant is set below a wisteria-covered pergola in the courtyard and is a top choice in Ravello. The hotel is open year-round, but the restaurant is open seasonally, from Palm Sunday-early November.

Over €300
HOTEL VILLA CIMBRONE

Via Santa Chiara 26; tel. 089/857-459; www. hotelvillacimbrone.com; Apr.-Oct.; €572 d

Nestled in beautiful gardens, stunning Villa Cimbrone offers the rare chance to stay on a 12th-century estate. The hotel and its rooms are full of historic details like frescoed ceilings, marble fireplaces, and handpainted ceramic floors. The pool and private garden area for guests are perfectly manicured. The hotel isn't accessible by car, but it's a pleasant 10-minute walk from Piazza Duomo.

INFORMATION AND SERVICES

- **Tourist information:** Agenzia Regionale Campania Turismo; Viale Richard Wagner 4; tel. 089/857-096; www.ravellotime.com; 9am-8pm daily June-Sept., 9am-3pm daily Oct.-May

- **Hospital:** Ospedale Costa d'Amalfi; Via Civita 12; tel. 089/935-8180; www. aslsalerno.it

- **Post office:** Poste Italiane; Via Giovanni Boccaccio 21; tel. 089/858-6631; www. poste.it; 8:20am-1:35pm Mon.-Fri., 8:20am-12:35pm Sat.

GETTING THERE
By Car and Scooter

Ravello, at 1,200 feet (365 m) above sea level along the Amalfi Coast, is about 4 miles (6.7 km) from **Amalfi,** a 20-minute drive. It is not located along the Amalfi Coast Road

☆ Little Fish with a Big Flavor: Cetara's Anchovies

Heading east toward Salerno, in a relatively isolated valley along the coastline, Cetara is beautifully preserved, with historic buildings along the seafront, a beach with fishing boats, and maze-like streets and piazzas where locals chat and children play. Cetara's long fishing tradition is embedded in the town's name, thought to come from Latin or even ancient Greek words all having to do with fishing. Cetara's fishing fleet is still very active, and you'll spot both larger fishing boats and the colorful little wooden rowboats bobbing in the port. The specialties are tuna caught in the deeper waters of the Mediterranean, and anchovies (alici). Rich in omega-3, iron, and other nutrients, anchovies have long been a key part of the local diet.

Even if you think you're not keen on anchovies, give them a chance in Cetara. You'll find alici prepared in many ways in Cetara's restaurants; the tiny fish can be marinated in vinegar or lemon, breaded and fried, used in a variety of pasta dishes, baked in the oven, or used as a pizza topping.

COLATURA DI ALICI

The most prized production is colatura di alici, a deep amber-colored oil made from pressing anchovies. This intensely flavored oil is thought to be the descendent of the ancient Roman garum, a creamy fish sauce created by salting and preserving fish, which was produced in Pompeii.

The process to create colatura di alici is passed down through generations of fishermen in Cetara, and many families have their own secret recipes. It starts with freshly caught anchovies placed in wooden barrels, called terzigni, and covered with salt. The fish are usually caught from March-July so that the heat of the summer can help advance the maturation process. The barrels are weighted down and the anchovies are slowly pressed inside. Months later, a small hole is punctured in the bottom of the barrel to release the precious liquid, which has a super-concentrated fish and salt flavor.

The colatura di alici is traditionally ready at the beginning of December, but colatura di alici is used year-round, to add extra flavor to everything from antipasti to pasta dishes and fresh vegetables. Join in the celebration and try local recipes during the **Notte delle Lampare** festival in July that is dedicated to Cetara's anchovy fishing tradition.

GETTING THERE

Located about 6 miles (10 km) west of Salerno, a 25-minute drive, Cetara offers a more secluded feel while still well connected via ferry and bus to Salerno and other towns along the Amalfi Coast. From Positano (1 hour 25 minutes) and Amalfi (1 hour 25 minutes), follow the Amalfi Coast Road east to Cetara. Once you're in Cetara, hourly paid parking is available in a large lot next to the port.

Travelmar (tel. 089/872-950; www.travelmar.it; €6-14 per person) operates ferry services from Salerno (15 minutes), Amalfi (40 minutes), and Positano. The **SITA SUD** (tel. 089/386-6701; www.sitasudtrasporti.it; from €1.30) bus line from Amalfi (45 minutes) to Salerno (30 minutes) arrives about every hour depending on the time of year. The main stop in town is right in the center where Corso Garibaldi meets the Amalfi Coast Road.

(SS163), but can be reached by following **SS373** from the crossroads at Castiglione, a frazione (hamlet) of Ravello. Along the drive from Castiglione up to Ravello, you will pass through Civita, another frazione. Keep following the road straight past the well-marked turnoff on the left to Pontone, and at the Scala crossroad bear right to reach Ravello's town center. The road to Ravello is among the trickiest on the coast, as one section is very narrow. During the tourist season from Easter-October, there is a traffic light limiting traffic to one-way during the day. If you're driving this road, go slowly and be prepared to back up if needed. From **Positano,** the drive is about 1 hour (15 mi/25 km) along the Amalfi Coast Road east to SS373 and then up to Ravello. To reach Ravello from **Salerno,** this drive is about 1 hour (20 mi/30 km) along the Amalfi Coast Road west to SS373.

A well-marked paid **parking lot** below Piazza Duomo is accessed by following Via della Marra below the Chiesa di Santa Maria a Gradillo. A small parking lot is available below the Auditorium Oscar Niemeyer, and paid parking is also available along the roads surrounding Ravello. Expect to pay about €3 per hour for parking. Scooter parking (€1.50 an hour or €8 for the day) is available near the Chiesa di Santa Maria a Gradillo and on Via della Repubblica leading down to the Auditorium Oscar Niemeyer.

By Bus

The local public bus company **SITA SUD** (tel. 089/386-6701; www.sitasudtrasporti.it; from €1.30) has a bus line connecting Ravello with Amalfi (25 minutes). Buses arrive every 30-60 minutes throughout the day, depending on the time of year. There are two bus stops in Ravello. The **Galleria Nuova stop** is located on Via Giovanni Boccaccio near the entrance to the tunnel that leads to Piazza Duomo. The **Gradillo stop** is just below the Chiesa di Santa Maria a Gradillo. To reach Ravello by bus from Salerno, Positano, and other locations on the Amalfi Coast, you will first need to arrive in Amalfi and transfer from there,

The easy-to-spot, bright red **City Sightseeing** (tel. 081/877-4707; www.city-sightseeing.it; Apr.-Oct.; from €5 per person) buses are a more comfortable option for traveling from Amalfi to Ravello. These open-top buses arrive in Ravello at the Galleria Nuova area just like the SITA SUD buses. Yet, because they only admit as many passengers as they have seats, they are never as overcrowded as a SITA SUD bus might be. Tickets are purchased onboard and include an audio guide in many languages.

GETTING AROUND

Ravello is best explored on foot, but **Ravello Rent A Scooter** (Via Porta di Scala 1; tel. 366/951-5631; www.ravellorentascooter.com; mid-Mar.-mid-Nov.; from €65) will deliver scooters to your accommodation in Ravello for free, or to other locations for a small fee.

Salerno

The vibrant city of Salerno stretches out along a large gulf set between two of the most beautiful coastlines in Italy—the Amalfi Coast to the west and the Cilento Coast to the south. Despite its scenic setting and proximity to the Amalfi Coast, Salerno has an off-the-beaten-path atmosphere that appeals to many travelers. You can explore the medieval historic center, catch a show at the elegant Teatro Giuseppe Verdi, stroll along the waterfront, or visit the Castello di Arechi for a bird's-eye view over Salerno.

Salerno has a rich heritage dating back to the early Middle Ages, when it was a flourishing Lombard principality noted for its culture and learning. This Schola Medica Salernitana was the first medical school in the west. Not far from Salerno you can uncover even more of the area's ancient origins while visiting the ruins of Paestum, where you'll find some of the best-preserved Greek temples in the world.

For travelers who enjoy a city vibe, a stay in Salerno is a great alternative to Naples. With a train station and port right in the center of the city, you'll have easy access to day trips to the Amalfi Coast, Paestum, Capri, and also to Pompeii and Naples. There's a wealth of history to uncover, and all the top spots in the area are just a train or ferry ride away.

ORIENTATION

Though Salerno is a large city, the top sights are walkable, primarily located in the **centro storico** (historic center) or along the waterfront **lungomare**. An important shipping center, Salerno's large **port** on the western side of the city is where cruise ships dock. Ferry service for the Amalfi Coast and Capri departs from the Molo Manfredi at the **Stazione Marittima di Salerno.** From the port, **Villa Comunale,** and **Teatro Giuseppe Verdi** to the west, the lungomare is a pleasant path east along the sea to **Piazza Concordia,** where you'll find another touristic port, which offers more frequent ferry service to the Amalfi Coast.

Salerno's **train station** is located about two blocks north of Piazza Concordia. Roughly parallel to the lungomare, the **Corso Vittorio Emanuele** starts at the train station and continues west through the city to the **Piazza Sedile di Portanova.** From there, Via Mercanti leads into the medieval **centro storico** (historic center) of Salerno. The city's museums, most intriguing churches, and excellent shopping are all located along Corso Vittorio Emanuele and the historic center.

SIGHTS
Centro Storico

Between Piazza Sedile di Portanova and Piazza Matteo Luciani, and between Via Roma and Via Torquato Tasso

The centro storico (historic center) of Salerno has origins dating back to Roman times, around 197 BC, when the city was known as Salernum. A few remains of the ancient city can be seen at the ruins of the Tempio di Pomona, next to the Duomo, often the setting for art exhibits throughout the year. The centro storico as it appears today is largely medieval, with the main artery, the **Via Mercanti** (Merchant's Street), running from Piazza Sedile di Portanova past Via Duomo, which leads up to the cathedral, and continuing along until it disperses into a seeming labyrinth of even narrower streets. With its cobblestone streets and historic buildings, the centro storico is a lovely area to walk and explore, as many of the streets are lined with shops, cafés, and little restaurants.

Cattedrale di Salerno

Piazza Alfano I; tel. 089/231-287; www. cattedraledisalerno.it; 8:30am-8pm Mon.-Sat., 8:30am-1pm and 4pm-8pm Sun.; free

One of the architectural gems of Campania, the Cattedrale di Salerno, also called the Cathedral of San Matteo or the Duomo, was consecrated in 1085; it houses the **relics of San Matteo** (St. Matthew). Behind the neoclassical facade lies a masterpiece of Norman architecture. Climb the steps and enter through the Porta dei Leone that leads into a grand atrium. Look up on the right to see the 12th-century bell tower, an impressive sight with its sturdy square levels and rounded top decorated with interlacing arches.

Step inside to find a soaring nave with baroque decor and two 12th-century ambons covered in intricate mosaics. While many of the original decorations have been lost over time, in the transept the three apses have beautiful 13th-century Byzantine mosaics. The apse to the right of the altar is the **Cappella dei Crociati** (Chapel of the Crusaders), where crusaders would receive a blessing before sailing for the Holy Land. This is also the final resting place for Pope Gregorio VII, who died in exile in Salerno in 1085. In the apse to the left of the altar is the grand 15th-century monument to Margherita di Durazzo, Queen of Naples and Hungary. Follow the steps on the left down to the baroque crypt, complete with polychromatic marble designs and shimmering golden elements. Here is where the relics of St. Matthew are held, below the two central bronze statues of the saint by Michelangelo Naccherino from 1622.

Museo Archeologico Provinciale

Via San Benedetto 28; tel. 089/231-135; www. museoarcheologicosalerno.it; 9am-7:30pm Tues.-Sun.; €4

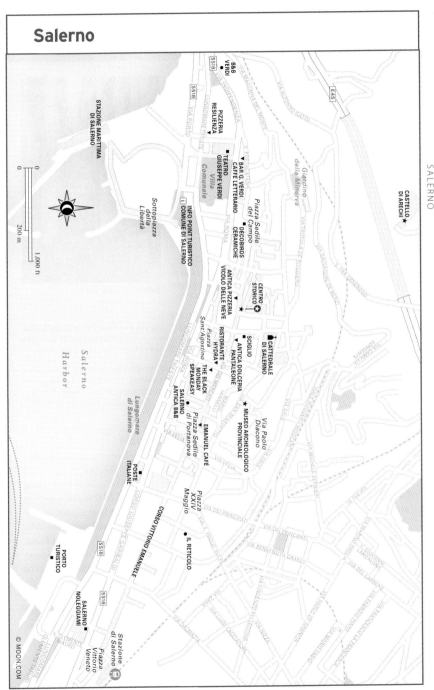

Salerno

© MOON.COM

☆ Walking Tour of Salerno's Centro Storico

While on first impact Salerno can feel like a larger city, especially compared to the towns along the Amalfi Coast, the centro storico is easily walkable and its narrow streets lined with shops and restaurants have a pleasant historic atmosphere.

Salerno's Centro Storico

- Begin in **Piazza Sedile di Portanova,** a broad square that opens to the Corso Vittorio Emanuele to the east, and to the west the much narrower entrance to Via Mercanti.

- Follow **Via Mercanti** into the heart of Salerno's old town and what was historically the center of commerce. The street is still lined with elegant buildings and small shops to explore, with many fine jewelry and clothing stores.

- Just beyond the Pinacoteca Provinciale di Salerno, take a right on Via Duomo follow about two blocks to reach the **Cattedrale di Salerno.** Climb the steps and enter to see the courtyard and visit the cathedral.

- Return down Via Duomo and take a right on Via Mercanti. Continue along straight as the road changes names to Via Dogana Vecchia and follow to reach **Piazza Sedile del Campo,** a small piazza surrounded by historic palazzi. Elements of the fountain date back to the 1600s; two metal sculptures of dolphins were added later.

- From here you can continue to explore the many small streets that crisscross through the centro storico. Or continue along Via Portacatena until it reaches Piazza Matteo Luciani. Cross the street to visit the **Villa Comunale** gardens and relax on a bench for a peaceful break.

Salerno's Archaeological Museum has a fine collection of finds that were uncovered in sites across the province of Salerno. Housed in the former abbey of San Benedetto dating from the 11th century, the museum offers an evocative setting for visitors to admire the collection, including ceramics, bronze vases, jewelry, and objects from daily life that date from prehistoric antiquities to Roman times. A large part of the collection documents the Etruscan-Campano settlement of Fratte in the northern part of modern-day Salerno, where a large part of the museum's collection was uncovered. A special room is dedicated to the museum's important bronze statue of the Head of Apollo dating from the first century BC. A detailed map and information are available in English.

Villa Comunale

Via Roma and Via Lungomare Trieste; 8am-midnight Apr.-Oct., 8am-8pm Nov.-Mar.; free

Just next to the Teatro Giuseppe Verdi along the waterfront, you'll find this public garden, which was created in 1874 as a quiet retreat. The garden was constructed around an 18th-century fountain called the Fontana del Tullio, and statues of political and military figures are dotted throughout the garden. During the Luci d'Artista Christmas light festival from November to January, the Villa Comunale is transformed into a magical garden with light installations, tunnels, and plenty of whimsy.

Castello di Arechi

Via Croce; tel. 089/227-237; www.ilcastellodiarechi. it; 9am-5pm Tues.-Sat., 9am-3:30pm Sun.; €4

Situated in the mountains about 980 feet (300 m) above Salerno, this castle dating back to the 8th century is named after the Lombard duke Arechi II, who transferred his kingdom from Benevento to Salerno. The castle was part of the Lombard defensive system and was added to over the centuries, with each new invasion and change of power in Salerno. The on-site **Museo Medievale** (Medieval Museum) houses historical finds uncovered during various restoration projects on the castle, including collections of ceramics, glass vessels, iron and bronze objects from daily life, as well as weapons. Besides the fine views overlooking the city and Gulf of Salerno, the castle's rugged walls are an evocative setting to delve deeper into Salerno's history. The castle can be reached from the center of Salerno on the Busitalia Campania (www.fsbusitaliacampania.it; from €1.10) line 19 that departs from the Via Vinciprova bus hub (about 15 minutes' walk east of the train station) and runs through the center of Salerno along Corso Giuseppe Garibaldi. Take the bus to the end of the line at Croce, which is at the entrance to the Castello di Arechi.

SPORTS AND RECREATION

LUNGOMARE

Lungomare Trieste

Stretching out nearly 1 mile (1.5 km), the lungomare (waterfront) of Salerno is a pedestrian-only garden lined with trees overlooking the Gulf of Salerno and Amalfi Coast. It leads from near the Villa Comunale gardens to Piazza Concordia and is a popular spot to enjoy a passeggiata (stroll) with a lovely view with the ports of Salerno nearby and the beginning of the Amalfi coastline to the west.

ENTERTAINMENT AND EVENTS

Salerno has a lively entertainment scene. Even in winter when the Amalfi Coast is sleepy, Salerno's **Luci d'Artista** Christmas light

festival attracts large numbers of visitors during the holiday season.

Performing Arts

TEATRO GIUSEPPE VERDI

Piazza Matteo Luciani; tel. 089/662-141; www. teatroverdisalerno.it; season May-Dec.; tickets from €15 for concerts and €30 for operas

Inaugurated in 1872, Salerno's Teatro Giuseppe Verdi is an impressive venue for a concert or show. Inspired by the grand Teatro di San Carlo in Naples, the architects created a smaller version that was then decorated by celebrated Neapolitan artists. The stunning interior of the theater, one of the few remaining original wooden 19th-century theaters in Italy, has been beautifully restored with its brilliant red seats, four tiers of boxes, shimmering gold details, and a ceiling mural depicting Gioachino Rossini surrounded by muses. The lyric, concert, and ballet season runs from May to December, but there are often concerts and performances throughout the year.

Festivals and Events

FESTIVAL OF SAN MATTEO

Cattedrale di Salerno and various locations; Sept. 21

On the traditional day honoring San Matteo, September 21, Salerno celebrates its patron saint with a religious festival that is fittingly grand for an apostle and evangelist. The evening procession leads through the streets of the centro storico with statues of San Matteo, San Giuseppe, San Gregorio VII, and the saints Gaio, Ante, and Fortunato, accompanied by marching bands. As the procession makes its way through the narrow streets, balconies are packed with onlookers and the streets are lined with people leaving just enough room for the procession to squeeze through. For a moment, city activity pauses and time seems to stand still during this annual event that has taken place for centuries. After the procession a Mass is given in the crypt of the Duomo, followed by concerts in Piazza Alfano I, Piazza Cavour, and Piazza

Amendola. The finishing touch is a huge fire-works display after dark.

LUCI D'ARTISTA
Villa Comunale and the historic center; lucidartista. comune.salerno.it; early Nov.-mid-Jan.

There are holiday lights, and then there's the Luci d'Artista, which takes Christmas lights to a whole new level. Starting in November, the entire city is decorated with elaborate light displays that transform an evening stroll through the city into a dreamlike experience. A soaring Christmas tree graces Piazza Sedile di Portanova and the Villa Comunale is always decked out with an abundance of light displays, often shaped like animals and whimsical floral designs, to create an enchanted garden setting.

SHOPPING

Salerno's centro storico is a fun destination for shopping for a variety of Italian brands as well as locally owned shops. In Salerno, most shops will close for lunch from around 1:30pm-4:30pm and many are also closed Monday morning, especially in the winter.

Corso Vittorio Emanuele is the main shopping street in Salerno and runs from the train station at **Piazza Vittorio Veneto** to **Piazza Sedile di Portanova**. Lined with shops, cafés, and restaurants, this tree-lined street has limited traffic and makes a pleasant place to stroll. Along the way, you'll find larger department stores as well as Italian and international brand clothing, jewelry, and shoe shops.

Cross Piazza Sedile di Portanova and look for the narrow entrance to **Via Mercanti,** the original merchant area of medieval Salerno. This is the entrance into the oldest part of the city, where you'll find smaller artisan shops mostly selling clothing and jewelry. The maze of little streets that cross Via Mercanti are also fun to explore.

1: Castello di Arechi in the mountains above Salerno 2: strolling on Corso Vittorio Emanuele 3: boats at Porto Turistico 4: Cattedrale di Salerno

LA BOTTEGUCCIA AL DUOMO
Via Duomo 43; tel. 089/222-687; vm@viamercanti. sa.it; 9:30am-1:30pm and 4pm-8:30pm Tues.-Sat., 10am-1:30pm Sun., 4pm-8:30pm Mon.

Located across from the Cattedrale di Salerno, this lovely artisan leather workshop has handmade bags, shoes, and accessories.

SCIGLIO
Via Duomo 46; tel. 089/296-1785; www. scigliovintage.com; 10am-1pm and 5pm-8:30pm Tues.-Sat., 5pm-8:30pm Sun.-Mon.

Stop in Sciglio for a beautifully curated selection of vintage clothing as well as illustrations, ceramics, jewelry, accessories, and artwork all created by a group of young and talented local artists.

DECOBIRDS CERAMICHE
Via Portacatena 21/23; tel. 347/480-5208; 10am-1pm and 3pm-8pm Tues.-Sat., 10am-1pm Sun.

At the western end of the centro storico is DecoBirds Ceramiche, where owner Donatello Ciao is often at work hand-painting the cheerful ceramics on display; many pieces feature birds, which is his unique personal touch.

FOOD

Much larger than the towns along the Amalfi Coast, Salerno has a thriving restaurant scene. There's excellent pizza, influenced by nearby Naples, as well as trattorias to enjoy local specialties, and even a variety of international options. You don't have to walk far in the centro storico to find a host of restaurants; there are also plenty of choices along the lungomare and near the Villa Comunale.

Regional Cuisine
RISTORANTE HYDRA
Via Antonio Mazza 30; tel. 089/ 995-8437; www. ristorantehydra.com; noon-3pm and 6pm-midnight daily; €15-50

Just off of Via Mercanti, this is a fine spot for lunch or dinner. With a beautiful minimalist decor, the restaurant offers the opportunity to dine inside or outside in their garden setting, right in the historic center. The menu is creative and highlights both seafood and meat; their grilled menu is a highlight as is the wine list with over 500 labels.

Pizzerias
PIZZERIA RESILIENZA

Via Santa Teresa 1; tel. 347/607-3735; www.resilienza.pizza; 12:30pm-3pm and 7:30pm-midnight Mon.-Sat., 7:30pm-midnight Sun.; €3.50-10

Located near the Villa Comunale gardens and with a pleasant outdoor dining area, this pizzeria was created in 2013 by Gennaro Coppeta with a focus on locally sourced and organic ingredients. Very popular with locals, you'll find a delicious selection of pizzas to choose from as well as traditional dishes on the menu. The classic pizza Margherita with organic tomatoes is perfection, or try their namesake pizza, Resilienza, with a parsley pesto, anchovies from Cetara, and fior di latte mozzarella cheese.

ANTICA PIZZERIA VICOLO DELLA NEVE

Vicolo Della Neve 24; tel. 089/225-705; www.vicolodellaneve.it; 7pm-11:30pm Mon.-Tues. and Thurs.-Sat., 12:30pm-4pm Sun.; €7-15

Located down a tiny side street off Via Mercanti, this small restaurant is an iconic spot for pizza and hearty home cooking, all from the traditional wood-fired pizza oven. Try the pasta e fagioli (pasta with beans) or the baccalà con patate (cod with potatoes).

Bakery
ANTICA DOLCERIA PANTALEONE

Via Dei Mercanti 75; tel. 089/227-825; www.dolceriapantaleone.it; 8:30am-2pm and 4:30pm-8:30pm Mon. and Wed.-Sat., 8:30am-2pm Sun.; €2-18

Right in the historic center, this bakery was founded in 1868 and is still the spot to try classic Campania desserts as well as Salerno specialties. You'll catch the sweet scent even before you arrive at the entrance to what was once a church. For something very local, try the scazzetta, a brilliant red-hued cake with

chantilly cream, wild strawberries, and a strawberry glaze. Or try the dolce della strega (dessert of the witch) flavored with Strega liqueur made in Benevento, a city inland in Campania.

NIGHTLIFE

Salerno's nightlife scene keeps the centro storico and lungomare buzzing well after dark. On Via Roma from Via Antica Corte to the Villa Comunale, you'll find about every type of bar and restaurant.

BAR G. VERDI CAFFÈ LETTERARIO

Piazza Matteo Luciani 28; tel. 320/897-2096; barverdi1910@yahoo.it; 6:30am-1am Tues.-Fri., 6:30am-11pm Mon., 6:30am-2pm and 5pm-1am Sat.-Sun., closed two weeks mid-Aug.; €3-6

Located across the street from the Teatro Giuseppe Verdi, this café has been a hub of creativity since it opened in 1910. Inside, you'll find photos of the artists who have visited, which is a tradition that continues today during the theater season. The eclectic decor and quirky style are the perfect setting for a literary café that also hosts weekly events that range from music and theater to book presentations and children's programs. There's even a small independent bookstore inside. They roast their own beans, so this is the place for coffee lovers. You'll also find organic teas, fresh juices, and homemade desserts, as well as wine and cocktails.

THE BLACK MONDAY SPEAKEASY

Via Mazza 26; tel. 348/263-7594; 8pm-3am daily Oct.-Apr.; €8-20

This unique speakeasy, open only autumn through spring, offers creative and sophisticated drinks, a vintage vibe, a friendly local crowd, and frequent live music. It's the perfect spot to warm up with a drink after seeing the holiday Luci d'Artista lights.

EMANUEL CAFE

Corso Vittorio Emanuele 234; tel. 089/221-112; midnight-2am daily; €6-15

Set on one of Salerno's most vibrant and

busy pedestrian-only streets, this café is a popular spot for an aperitivo or after-dinner drink thanks to its fine selection of cocktails and drinks. You'll also be tempted by a menu that changes monthly with a choice of sandwiches and salads for a light lunch or first and second courses for something more substantial.

ACCOMMODATIONS
Under €100
IL RETICOLO
Via Giovan Angelo Papio 14; tel. 089/995-8585; www.ilreticolobebsalerno.it; €75 d

Located in the historic center about a 10-minute walk from the train station, this B&B offers four bright rooms, each one named after a town in the area that is featured in a panoramic photo in the room. The building has an elevator and two wheelchair-accessible rooms. Private parking is also available for a daily fee.

SALERNO ANTICA B&B
Via Masuccio Salernitano 8; tel. 328/331-1881; www.salernoantica.com; €80 d

With an ideal location just off of Piazza Sedile di Portanova, this lovely B&B is set in a historic palazzo dating back to the 1400s. The building has been remodeled and has an elevator. The three large rooms are all beautifully appointed, and owner Daniele Abbondanza is on hand to help with information and suggestions. A wonderful find right in the heart of Salerno's historic center.

€100-200
B&B VERDI
Via Indipendenza 5; tel. 345/341-6372; www.bbverdi.it; €100 d

This friendly B&B not far from the Teatro Giuseppe Verdi and the Villa Comunale has three comfortable rooms, all with private bathrooms. The breakfast is abundant, and both sweet and savory options are offered. Note that if you're arriving by train or ferry, the B&B is located on the other side of town

and you'll need to catch a bus or taxi from the terminals.

INFORMATION AND SERVICES
- **Visitor information:** Info Point Turistico Comune di Salerno; Corso Vittorio Emanuele 193; tel. 089/662-951; www.comune.salerno.it; 9am-1pm and 5pm-8pm Mon.-Fri., 9am-1pm Sat.
- **Hospital:** Ospedale San Leonardo; Via San Leonardo; tel. 089/671-111; www.sangiovannieruggi.it
- **Post office:** Poste Italiane; Corso Giuseppe Garibaldi 203; tel. 089/275-9749; www.poste.it; 8:20am-7:05pm Mon.-Fri., 8:20am-12:35pm Sat.

GETTING THERE
By Car
Salerno is located east of the Amalfi Coast and is quite easy to reach from all towns along the coastline. From **Positano** (1 hour 45 minutes) and **Amalfi** (1 hour), head east on the **Amalfi Coast Road (SS163)** and Salerno is located just beyond Vietri sul Mare. From **Ravello** (1 hour 15 minutes), first follow the **SS373** road down to where it intersects the Amalfi Coast Road and take a left to continue east until you reach Salerno. From **Naples** (1 hour) follow the **A3** highway south to the Salerno exit.

By Train
Salerno's train station, the **Stazione di Salerno** (Piazza Vittorio Veneto), is conveniently located in the city center and is served by Italy's national train line, **Trenitalia** (www.trenitalia.com), as well as **Italo** (www.italotreno.it). The piazza in front of the station is also a bus hub, and it's a short walk to Porto Turistico near Piazza Concordia for ferries. There are local, regional, and high-speed trains to Salerno from cities across Italy, with trains arriving direct to Salerno or by transfering in large cities like Naples and Rome.

From Naples, trains depart every 15-30

minutes (or even more frequently, depending on the time of day) from about 5:30am-10:30pm. The length of the journey ranges from 40 minutes-1 hour 25 minutes, depending on the type of train; prices start at €4.70.

From Rome, trains run every 10-30 minutes from 5:30am-11pm daily. The journey time varies depending on the type of train and number of transfers; the fastest and most convenient trains are the Frecciarossa high-speed trains that travel from Rome to Salerno in about 2 hours. Fares also vary, depending on the train type and season, but start around €30.

It is possible to reach Palermo (9 hours; €30-55) and Catania (7 hour 15 minutes; €30-45) by train, though it's a full day's journey and delays are common. To get to Puglia by train, you'll need to depart from Caserta, a 30-minute train ride from Naples.

By Bus

SITA SUD (tel. 089/386-6701; www.sitasudtrasporti.it; from €1.30) runs a bus line from Amalfi to Salerno (1 hour 15 minutes). Buses run 5:15am-9pm roughly every hour. The bus passes through Castiglione (Ravello) before arriving in Salerno. To reach Salerno from Ravello and points west of Amalfi, such as Positano, requires transferring in Amalfi. Buses from the Amalfi Coast pass along the waterfront in Salerno, where there are multiple stops before the bus arrives at the Via Vinciprova bus hub, about 15 minutes' walk east of the train station. For the center of Salerno, you'll want to get off along the waterfront or Piazza Concordia.

From Naples, buses for Salerno depart from near the Piazza Immacolatella along the port about every 30 minutes 6am-9pm, and the journey takes about 1 hour 15 minutes. Note that the bus arrives at the bus hub at Via Vinciprova.

FlixBus (www.flixbus.it; from €2) offers 136 routes to Salerno from destinations all across Italy, including Bari (about 4 hours; €12-35), Matera (3 hours 10 minutes; €12-20), Lecce (5 hours; €20-40), and Catania (8 hours

10 minutes; €30-35). The most central of the four stops in Salerno is the stop at **Piazza Concordia.**

By Boat

Salerno's large port is divided the city's commerical port on the western side, where large cruise ships often dock, and Porto Turistico on the eastern side, not far from the train station, where ferries arrive from the Amalfi Coast. In the center is the Stazione Marittima di Salerno (Maritime Station), or Molo Manfredi, where ferries arrive from the Amalfi Coast, Capri, and the surrounding area.

PORTO TURISTICO
Piazza Concordia

Salerno's main port for ferries is the Porto Turistico, also called the Marina Masuccio Salernitano, located at Piazza Concordia. **Travelmar** (tel. 089/872-950; www.travelmar.it; €6-14) ferries arrive at the end of the pier from Amalfi (35 minutes) and Positano (1 hour 10 minutes). Ferry service runs from April to early November. Departures are every 1-2 hours, 9am-7pm.

STAZIONE MARITTIMA
DI SALERNO
Molo Manfredi; tel. 800/115-110; www.salernostazionemarittima.it

Salerno's maritime station at Molo Manfredi is located on the western side of the port. Architect Zaha Hadid designed the Stazione Marittima di Salerno with its sleek lines and sweeping roofline. **Alicost** (tel. 089/871-483; www.alicost.it; from €25.40 per person) ferries from Capri (2 hours) arrive at this port, often stopping at Positano and Amalfi. Ferry service is available seasonally from April-October, but exact start and end dates vary each year. From Capri there are usually one or two ferry services in the evening.

GETTING AROUND

Salerno's historic center is not that large, and the best way to get around is on foot. The majority of the city's main sights are very walkable. However, there are local buses that run along the town's main thoroughfares to speed up crossing the city.

By Car and Scooter

If you want to rent a car or scooter, many of the internationally known names like Hertz and Avis have offices near the Stazione di Salerno train station. Though traffic in Salerno is tame compared to nearby Naples, keep in mind that it is still a good-sized city and you should be cautious, especially when navigating traffic on a scooter. Located just across the street from the train station, **Salerno Noleggiami** (Corso Giuseppe Garibaldi 63; tel. 089/252-579; www.salernonoleggiami.it; from €45 per day for a scooter and €39 per day for cars) offers daily and longer rentals of scooters and cars.

By Bus

Salerno's local buses are run by **Busitalia Campania** (www.fsbusitaliacampania. it; from €1.10), with many lines crisscrossing the city, running frequently from about 6am-11pm daily. Many bus lines run along the waterfront of Salerno, from west to east on Lungomare Trieste and from east to west on Corso Giuseppe Garibaldi. Main stops along the waterfront and the centro storico are near the Villa Comunale. There are also several stops along Lungomare Trieste and Corso Giuseppe Garibaldi, along with Piazza Concordia near the tourist port. Buses 4, 5, and 6 run frequently throughout the day, but if you're just moving around the center of Salerno to see the sights, nearly every bus that runs along the Lungomare Trieste and Corso Giuseppe Garibaldi will get you from one side of the centro storico to the other. Tickets need to be purchased before boarding and can be found in most tabacchi (tobacco shops), as well as some coffee shops and bars. Validate your ticket after boarding using the machine usually located near the driver.

To reach the Amalfi Coast by bus, the **SITA SUD** (tel. 089/386-6701; www.

sitasudtrasporti.it; from €1.30) bus line from Salerno to Amalfi departs from Via Vinciprova, with a stop in Piazza Vittorio Veneto in front of the train station as well as on Via Roma on the western edge of town, across from the Teatro Giuseppe Verdi.

★ DAY TRIP TO ANCIENT PAESTUM

Not far south of Salerno is one of Italy's most remarkable archaeological treasures, the ruins of the city of Paestum with its incredibly well-preserved Greek temples. The site makes an excellent day trip from Salerno and the Amalfi Coast.

Parco Archeologico di Paestum

Via Magna Grecia 919; tel. 082/811-023; www. museopaestum.beniculturali.it; 9am-7:30pm daily (museum closed Mon.), closed Jan. 1 and Dec. 25; €12 for archaeological site and museum, free for children under 18

The ancient city of Paestum was founded by Greek colonists around 600 BC as Poseidonia, a defensive outpost of Magna Graecia. Once surrounded by an impressive wall over 23 feet (7 m) tall with towers and four entry gates, parts of the original wall still exist, although not at the original height. Named after Poseidon, the Greek god of the sea, the colony was later conquered by the Lucanians, an Italic tribe of people on Italy's mainland, at the end of the fifth century BC. Excavations on the site have revealed how the Greek and Italic cultures blended and then later continued to transform when, in 273 BC, the city became a Roman colony called Paestum.

While visiting the archaeological site, you'll see both Greek and Roman ruins, all worth exploring in detail. A modern-day road called **Via Magna Grecia** cuts through the center of the ancient city with the archaeological area on the west side and a museum on the east side. Enter through one of the two gates along the pedestrian-only section of Via

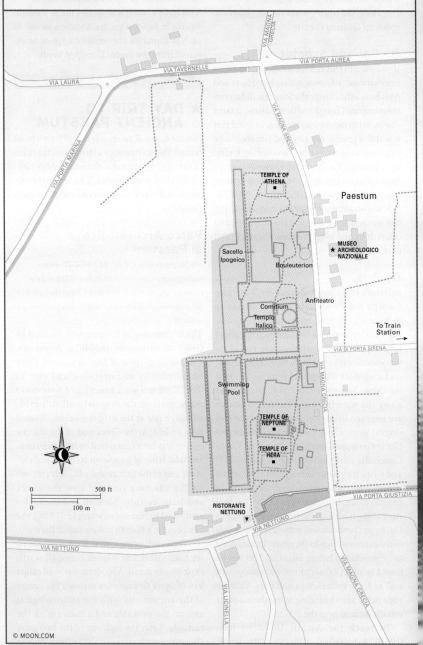

© MOON.COM

Magna Grecia and the ancient city spreads out in front of you. What captures the most attention, however, are the three incredible Greek temples.

TEMPLES

The oldest on the site is the **Temple of Hera,** also referred to as the Basilica, located near the southern side of the city. Dating from around 560 BC, it's the finest and best-preserved example anywhere of early Greek temple architecture. Just to the north is the **Temple of Neptune,** the largest in Paestum, which was built in the mid-fifth century BC. It's an essential example of a Doric-style temple, and although its name refers to Neptune, the later Roman name of the god of the sea, archaeological evidence has revealed it was likely dedicated to Hera or perhaps even Zeus. On the northern side of the site is the **Temple of Athena,** dating from around 500 BC; this is the only temple in Paestum where excavations have revealed with certainty that the temple was originally dedicated to Athena. Along with the temples, you can see the ruins of the agora—later transformed into the Roman forum, which was the heart of the city—as well as part of an amphitheater, thermal baths, and more.

MUSEO ARCHEOLOGICO NAZIONALE

Opposite the archaeological area across Via Magna Grecia, the Museo Archeologico Nazionale is a must during your visit to Paestum. The museum houses artifacts uncovered at Paestum, and rarely is it possible to see such a detailed portrait of an ancient city and how it changed over the centuries. Inside you'll find areas dedicated to the prehistory and protohistory of Paestum, the largest area dedicated to the Greek and Lucanian city, and a section on the Roman period.

Don't miss the extensive collection of ancient vases produced in local workshops, the room dedicated to the carved stone metopes from temples in the area, and the many incredible tombs. The most famous is the Tomb of the Diver, the only known example of a Greek burial tomb with painted figures. Captivating in their simplicity and elegance, the painted scenes date from 470 BC and show figures taking part in a symposium as well as the namesake scene depicting a man diving.

The museum is closed on Mondays. During winter (Dec.-Feb.) the entrance to the archaeological site and museum is reduced to €6. The archaeological area is open until 7:30pm (last tickets at 6:45pm) year-round and is

the ancient ruins of Paestum

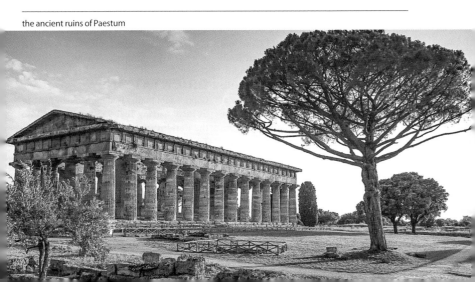

illuminated after dark. Seeing the temples at night is a special experience, but keep in mind that you'll need to stick to the illuminated trail if you visit after sunset.

Food

RISTORANTE NETTUNO

Via Nettuno 2; tel. 082/881-1028; www. ristorantenettuno.com; noon-3:30pm Tues.-Sun. Mar.-Apr. and Oct., noon-3:30pm and 7:45pm-11pm Tues.-Sat., noon-3:30pm Sun. June-Sept.; €10-18

Located right at the southern Porta Giustizia entrance to Paestum, this is a lovely restaurant to stop for lunch or dinner during your visit. Steps from Paestum, there are views of the temples and archaeological site from the indoor and outdoor dining areas. The menu is broad with both seafood and meat-based specialties. This is an excellent spot to sample locally made buffalo mozzarella cheese.

Getting There

From Salerno, the easiest way to reach Paestum is to catch a local train operated by **Trenitalia** (www.trenitalia.com; departures daily every 30-60 minutes 6am-9pm; journey about 30 minutes; from €2.90) and get off at the Paestum stop. Just across the street from the station is the Porta Sirena entrance to the archaeological area. It's a 15-minute walk through the park to reach Via Magna Grecia with the museum to the right and the archaeological area directly ahead.

By car, the **SP175** highway runs south from Salerno and along the coastline and leads to the site after a 50-minute drive.

Capri

With a natural beauty that's famous around the world, the island of Capri is one of Italy's most popular travel destinations. What this small island lacks in size it easily makes up for with its mesmerizing blue sea, soaring cliffs, and Mediterranean charm. In this place of stunning scenery, there is so much to discover beyond the breathtaking views... but you won't want to miss those views!

Split between two towns called Capri and Anacapri, the island's sights spread from rocky beaches to mountain peaks, with historic sights and shopping to enjoy along the way. Visit La Piazzetta, a bustling square at the heart of Capri; enjoy iconic views of the famous Faraglioni rock formations that jut straight out of the water off the coastline. Then, get away from it all by exploring the island's quieter side. Hike to incredible overlooks, ride a chairlift to the top of Monte Solaro, and meander down pedestrian-only pathways past bougainvillea-draped villas. Once you've enjoyed the top sights on land, get out on the water to take in the landscape from the sea, explore the island's grottoes, and find tiny coves where you can dive into the sea for a swim.

While its popularity means plenty of crowds during the busy season, Capri should still be on every traveler's list. Whether you're planning a day trip or staying longer, there are plenty of ways to enjoy Capri, from popular spots to tranquil corners of the island immersed in nature. Find those quiet moments, and Capri will surely capture your heart just as it has so many travelers for ages.

ORIENTATION

Capri is mountainous, dominated by **Monte Solaro** soaring to 1,932 feet (589 m) on the western side of the island, and **Monte Tiberio** rising to 1,095 feet (334 m) on the northeastern side. The island's largest town, also called **Capri,** is situated along the dip between the two mountains just east of the middle of the island, while **Anacapri** spreads out around the base of Monte Solaro on western side. Capri has two harbors, with the main ferry harbor and transportation hub of **Marina Grande** on the northern coast and

Capri Town

Marina Piccola on the southern side of the island.

PLANNING YOUR TIME

Capri's main sights are centered around the island's two towns, Capri and Anacapri; plan to divide your time between them. Day-trippers will likely spend a bit more time in Capri town and a little less time in Anacapri. If you're staying longer, after seeing the main sights in the center of Capri and Anacapri, such as **Giardini di Augusto** and the **Villa San**

Michele, consider walking farther afield, to sights like **Villa Jovis** or the **Arco Naturale.**

SIGHTS
Capri Town

Capri's iconic Torre dell'Orologio clock tower is the first welcoming sight when arriving by bus, taxi, or funicular train. Here you'll find the buzzing **Piazzetta** (officially named Piazza Umberto I), the heart of Capri and the crossroads of town. As Capri's transportation hub, with buses and taxis nearby and the funicular to Marina Grande, all life seems to pass through the Piazzetta. Stop at a local café to watch the vibrant scene play out. Capri's international allure has created a welcoming atmosphere where daily life for the locals blends seamlessly with visitors from around the world, and there's no place better to take it all in than the Piazzetta.

Beyond the Piazzetta and through the arch to **Via Longano** and **Via le Botteghe** is the **medieval quarter** of the city, with its maze of little streets and courtyards. This is an intriguing area to explore, home to lovely little boutiques and restaurants. Or follow the elegant **Via Vittorio Emanuele,** which turns into the Via Federico Serena, on a slightly downhill stroll past Via Camerelle, the island's most exclusive shopping address, to reach the beautiful Giardini di Augusto for the best views of the Faraglioni rocks.

CHIESA DI SANTO STEFANO
Piazza Umberto I; tel. 081/837-0072; 8am-1pm and 4pm-9pm daily Apr.-Oct., 8am-1pm and 4pm-7pm Nov.-Mar.; free

Located at the top of a small flight of steps from the Piazzetta, the facade of Capri's largest church feels squeezed into an impossibly narrow passageway. The luminous white baroque interior is filled with light from the windows and domes along the nave and the large dome over the crossing. The church was built in the late 17th century on the site of an earlier church and is dedicated to Santo Stefano (St. Stephen). However, there's also a special reverence here for San Costanzo (St. Constantius), Capri's patron saint. The church holds an important silver bust reliquary statue of the saint from 1715, and that statue is carried during the procession for the saint's festival on May 14. Don't forget to look down when exploring the church, for in the main altar area you'll find a multicolored marble floor that was uncovered at the Villa Jovis, and in the side chapel to the left of the altar there's another Roman-era marble floor, likely from ruins near Punta Tragara.

GIARDINI DI AUGUSTO
Via Matteotti 2; tel. 081/837-0686 (tourist office); www.cittadicapri.it; 9am-7:30pm daily Apr.-Sept., 9am-4pm in winter; €1

The beautiful Giardini di Augusto (Gardens of Augustus) were created on land purchased in the late 1800s by German Industrialist Friedrich Alfred Krupp. While there is a strong connection between Capri and ancient Rome, the gardens didn't receive their name

Via Camerelle

in honor of Augustus until after World War I. Spread across several terraces, the lush gardens are full of seasonal flowers as well as plant and flower species that are typical of Capri, like ginestra (broom), bougainvillea, cacti, and bird of paradise. The terraced garden offers shaded spots with ceramic-tiled benches, giving you a relaxing spot to sit and rest. However, the main draw here is the sweeping view from the edge of the garden of the Faraglioni rocks in one direction, and the bay of Marina Piccola in the other.

Look down from the highest terrace of the garden to see the famous **Via Krupp,** a zigzagging pathway down the mountain connecting Capri with Marina Piccola below. Excavated out of the mountainside, this remarkable pathway was created at Krupp's expense by the engineer Emilio Mayer. Unfortunately, the scenic pathway has been closed for some time due to the danger of falling rocks. Yet, the view looking down on Via Krupp with the bright turquoise sea just beyond is not to be missed.

I FARAGLIONI

Punta Tragara

Perhaps Capri's most iconic symbol, the Faraglioni are three large rocks located just off the Punta Tragara. With sheer cliffs and a scattering of vegetation on top, the three Faraglioni are majestic to behold. The rock closest to the land is connected to the island and rises to 358 feet (109 m), while the center rock with the hole in the middle rises to 266 feet (81 m), and the farthest one out is 341 feet (104 m) high. On the outer rock and the nearby rock formation called Monacone lives a rare type of lizard called the lucertola azzurra (blue lizard), which has an incredible blue tint, the color of the deep sea surrounding the Faraglioni. The rocks can be admired from many vantage points around the island, including the Giardini di Augusto, Belvedere di Tragara, and the top of Monte Solaro. You can also see the Faraglioni close up from the sea; small boats

can cruise right through the opening in the center rock.

ARCO NATURALE

Via Arco Naturale

To immerse yourself in Capri's natural beauty, take a walk to the Arco Naturale (Natural Arch) from the Piazzetta. Set about 656 feet (200 m) above sea level, the craggy natural arch is about 66 feet (20 m) tall and 39 feet (12 m) wide. Located in a peaceful landscape surrounded by pine trees, the outside part of the arch is thick and massive and tapers to only a narrow connection on the side closest to the island, creating a naturally framed view of the sea. The walk to the arch through Capri town becomes quieter and more secluded as you go, and leads to a set of steps down to a series of small overlooks where you can admire the arch from a variety of different viewpoints. In the distance, you'll spot the **Sorrentine Peninsula** and beyond to the right the **Li Galli islands** off Positano. The setting is nearly untouched nature, where you can listen to the wind blowing through pine trees and catch the scent of the sea far below as boats pass by. You can also spot the Arco Naturale from the sea on a boat tour around the island.

★ VILLA JOVIS

Via Tiberio; tel. 081/837-0381; www.musei.campania.
beniculturali.it; 10am-7pm daily June-Sept.,
10am-6pm Oct. and Apr.-May, 10am-4pm Nov.-Dec.
and Mar.; €6

Sitting atop the highest point of Monte Tiberio on the northeastern point of Capri are the ruins of a lavish villa built for Emperor Tiberius. From this perch, Tiberius ruled the Roman Empire from AD 27 to 37. The largest of Tiberius's villas on the island, Villa Jovis was a massive estate that functioned as a fortress yet included all the modern comforts of a Roman imperial residence.

Though it's hard to imagine the original design from the state of the ruins, the Villa Jovis was once a splendid example of Roman architecture, and visiting offers a chance to imagine the ancient Roman lifestyle on Capri.

Given the limited surface area near the top of Monte Tiberio, the villa occupied many levels rather than following the more traditional sprawling layout of Roman imperial villas. Exploring the site's multiple levels, you can see parts of the imperial residence as well as the servant's quarters, baths, and the ingenious series of large cisterns that held the villa's water supply, fundamental because Capri has no natural water sources.

The villa's setting is dramatic, overlooking a sheer cliff dropping straight to the sea; this is sometimes called Tiberius's Leap, where it's said people the emperor wasn't pleased with were shown the exit. Adjacent to the ruins you'll find a small **church** with a plain gray facade and arched entrance. It is dedicated to Santa Maria del Soccorso and dates from around the 16th century, but it's most popular for the large terrace in front with panoramic views over the ruins, the island, and the Gulf of Naples and Gulf of Salerno.

Located at the extreme northeastern tip of the island at the highest point of Monte Tiberio, the 45-minute walk to reach Villa Jovis is almost entirely uphill from the center of Capri. Starting from La Piazzetta, look for the signs to Villa Jovis and follow Via Longono, Via Sopramonte, and Via Tiberio. Comfortable shoes are recommended, and during the summer months don't forget to bring water as there are limited opportunities to purchase refreshments as you near Monte Tiberio. Walking is the only way to reach Villa Jovis.

Anacapri

Spread out around the base of Monte Solaro, the island's highest peak, the town of Anacapri is quieter than Capri town. **Piazza Vittoria** is the main transport hub and also the location of the chairlift to reach the top of Monte Solaro.

___

1: the ruins of the palace where Roman Emperor Tiberius once lived at Villa Jovis **2:** view of I Faraglioni from the Giardini di Augusto **3:** the Arco Naturale

GROTTA AZZURRA

Grotta Azzurra; tel. 081/837-5646; www.musei. campania.beniculturali.it; 9am-5pm daily Apr.-Oct., 9am-2pm daily Nov.-Mar., weather permitting; €14

Synonymous with Capri, the Grotta Azzurra (Blue Grotto) is one of the island's most popular sights. This natural cavern is about 197 feet (60 m) long and 82 feet (25 m) wide, but the entrance to the grotto is very small and can only be accessed by rowboats that hold up to four people. You must lie nearly flat as your skipper carefully pulls the boat into the grotto. Inside, you'll see deep, electric blue water that shimmers with a silvery glow thanks to the refraction of light from an opening below sea level.

Given its popularity and limited access, the Grotta Azzurra can be a bit challenging to visit, especially in the busy summer season. Be prepared for a long wait, which can seem disproportionate to the limited amount of time you actually get to stay inside (about 10 minutes). However, if seeing the Grotta Azzurra is on your bucket list, it's a unique experience and the colors don't disappoint.

The entrance to the Grotta Azzurra can be reached by land or sea, but you can only enter the grotto by boat. Several boat companies, including **Motoscafisti Capri** (Marina Grande; tel. 081/837-5646; www. motoscafisticapri.com; from €17 per person) and **Laser Capri** (Via Cristoforo Colombo 69; Marina Grande; tel. 081/837-5208; www. lasercapri.com; from €15 per person) offer group boat service from Marina Grande to the Grotta Azzurra, with the option to add a boat tour around the island for an additional fee. Do note that the fee for the boat transfer is separate from the €14 entrance fee paid to access the grotto. By land, get to the grotto, located in the ruggedly beautiful northwestern area of the island, by taxi or the local Capri bus to the Grotta Azzurra. You'll walk down some steps to the entrance, where you board the rowboats to enter.

Plan to visit the grotto in the morning, as occasionally wind or weather changes can require the grotto to close in the afternoons. A visit is not guaranteed; even on days when the weather seems nice, the sea conditions near the grotto can be unsafe. The Grotta Azzurra is often closed during the winter from November-March, but it may occasionally be open if the weather and sea conditions are appropriate. If the Motoscafisti Capri ticket booths are open in Marina Grande, that means the grotto is open.

VILLA SAN MICHELE

Viale Axel Munthe 34; tel. 081/837-1401; http://villasanmichele.eu; 9am-4:30pm daily Mar., 9am-5pm daily Apr. and Oct., 9am-6pm daily May-Sept., 9am-3:30pm daily Nov.-Feb.; €8

Reached by following Via Capodimonte from Piazza Vittoria, Villa San Michele was the home of noted Swedish doctor and writer Axel Munthe (1857-1949), largely known today for his autobiographical work *The Story of San Michele* (1929). Admission includes a visit to his home, transformed into a museum, and the chance to explore the gorgeous garden dotted with statues. Stroll along the pergola-covered walkway to the very end to find a loggia with an Egyptian sphinx and you will enjoy an extraordinary view overlooking Marina Grande below and the Gulf of Naples.

MONTE SOLARO

Chairlift: Via Caposcuro 10; tel. 081/837-1438; www.capriseggiovia.it; 9:30am-4pm daily Mar.-Apr., 9:30am-5pm daily May-Oct., 9:30am-3:30pm daily Nov.-Feb.; €12

At 1,932 feet (589 m), Monte Solaro is Capri's highest point and offers a splendid bird's-eye view overlooking the island. From here you'll also enjoy an excellent vantage point to take in the entire area from the Sorrentine Peninsula to the islands of Ischia and Procida and Mount Vesuvius, all located across the Gulf of Naples. With the sound of the wind blowing through ragged pine trees, the sunbaked Mediterranean vegetation, and the call of seagulls in the air, this is one of Capri's most majestic spots and simply must be experienced.

Getting to the top of Monte Solaro is an experience in itself, thanks to the **Seggiovia Monte Solaro,** a chairlift that runs from Piazza Vittoria to the summit. Simply hop on one of the 156 single seats that run continuously and enjoy the 13-minute ride to the top. On the way down, there's an excellent view from the chairlift across the gulf, especially on a clear day.

It's also possible to hike up or down Monte Solaro (1.4 mi/2.2 km one-way; 1 hour). From Anacapri's central **Piazza Vittoria,** head down Via Capodimonte and after a few minutes' walk, look for signs indicating Monte Solaro and a staircase leading up on the right. Follow Via Monte Solaro as it climbs up the mountainside; you'll traverse stone steps as well as concrete and dirt pathways. To ride the chairlift up and hike down (or vice-versa), there are one-way tickets (€9) available.

CHIESA MONUMENTALE DI SAN MICHELE

Piazza San Nicola; tel. 081/837-2396; www.chiesa-san-michele.com; 10am-2pm daily Mar., 9am-7pm daily Apr.-Oct., 10am-3pm daily Nov.-Jan.; €2

This baroque 17th-century church dedicated to San Michele Arcangelo features an 18th-century floor covered with marvelous hand-painted majolica tiles depicting Adam and Eve in the Garden of Eden. Created by master majolica artist Leonardo Chiaiese in 1761, the floor is a remarkable work of art and can be examined from a narrow platform along the edge. Climb the spiral staircase to the upper level near the organ for an even better view. From Piazza Vittoria, follow Via Giuseppe Orlandi through a charming shopping area to reach the church.

BEACHES

With gorgeous colors ranging from deep cobalt blue to shockingly bright turquoise, the sea around Capri just beckons for a swim. However, be prepared for higher prices compared to other towns in the area. For private beach clubs, there's usually a set price per person that includes a chair and access to a shower and changing rooms; there's often an additional cost to rent umbrellas. Given that the beaches are very rocky, it is generally worth the splurge for a comfortable beach experience.

Capri
MARINA GRANDE

Just steps west of the Marina Grande is a long, narrow stretch of beach, a good spot for a quick swim. **Le Ondine Beach Club** (Via Marina Grande; tel. 081/277-9056; www.dagemma.com; 9:30am-6:30pm daily mid-Apr.-mid-Oct.; beach chair €10, sun bed €15, and unbrella €7) offers sun bed and umbrella rentals along with changing rooms and showers. Head to the westernmost side of the beach for the free area. The water is clear and pleasant for swimming, with the western side offering finer pebbles and gentler slope into the sea. It's a popular and busy beach with tourists, but you'll find the western side has a more local scene.

Small boats depart from the eastern side of the beach for the nearby **Bagni di Tiberio** (Via Palazzo a Mare 41; tel. 081/837-0703; www.bagnitiberio.com; May 1-Sept. 30; €12 entrance per person plus additional for sun beds and umbrellas), a beach club to the west. With incredible water and set in an area rich with Roman history, Bagni di Tiberio offers a more secluded experience. The beach can also be reached on foot after a 25-minute walk from Marina Grande, following Via Marina Grande to Via Palazzo a Mare.

FARAGLIONI
Punta Tragara

One of Capri's most dramatic and exclusive beach experiences is right at the foot of the Faraglioni rocks. Two notable beach clubs are located on the rocky stretch connecting the island with the first Faraglioni, with platforms and ladders for sea access: **Da Luigi ai Faraglioni** (Via Faraglioni 5; tel. 081/837-0591; www.luigiaifaraglioni.com; late Apr.-Oct. 1; from €25 per person for entrance and deck chair) and **La Fontelina** (Località Faraglioni; tel. 081/837-0845; www.

fontelina-capri.com; late Apr.-mid-Oct.; from €30 per person for entrance and seating), a popular spot with VIP travelers. Both beach clubs have excellent restaurants steps from the sea (restaurant reservations are required for beach access).

To reach the Faraglioni beach clubs, follow the step pathway from the **Belvedere di Tragara.** The beach clubs also offer boat shuttles from Marina Piccola (complimentary for Da Luigi ai Faraglioni clients, from €25 for up to four La Fontelina clients).

MARINA PICCOLA

On Capri's southern side is the island's very charming Marina Piccola. It's a buzzing seaside spot during the summer months thanks to the beautiful, albeit rocky, beaches and restaurants, popular with locals and tourists alike. The marina is split in two by a small, rocky promontory that juts out into the bright turquoise sea, with swimming areas, beach clubs, and small free beaches on both sides.

For sunbed rentals, try **Bagni Internazionali** (Via Marina Piccola 95; tel. 081/837-0264; www.bagninternazionali.com; May-Oct. daily), or **La Canzone del Mare** (Via Marina Piccola 93; tel. 081/837-0104; www.lacanzonedelmare.com; end of Apr.-Oct.1; €60 per person includes entrance, sun bed, pool access, and €25 food credit), founded by English actress and singer Gracie Fields.

Beyond Marina Piccola, in a tiny cove, the water at the **Torre Saracena** beach is an impossibly bright shade of turquoise. It's a secluded spot accessed via the **Torre Saracena Beach Club** (Via Marina Piccola; tel. 081/837-0646; www.torresaracenacapri.com; May-Oct. daily). They offer clients complimentary boat service from Marina Piccola to the Torre Saracena Beach Club. You can also walk there by taking Via Krupp off of Via Marina Piccola and following the signs to Spiaggia Torre Saracena.

Marina Piccola can be reached by bus or taxi from all the main points on the island.

You can also enjoy a pleasant, 25-minute, downhill walk down from Capri town by following Via Roma from the Piazzetta to the roundabout where the road splits to go up to Anacapri or down to Marina Grande. Continue along Via Mulo, which leads through the quiet residential area of Marina Piccola. It's a more direct and enjoyable walk compared to following the zigzagging road connecting Marina Piccola and Capri town.

Anacapri
PUNTA CARENA
Str. Faro di Carena

The pink and white striped lighthouse that sits on the Punta Carena is one of the prettiest sights on Capri. This spot marks the southwesternmost point on the island and is surrounded by impressive craggy mountains. Easily spotted from the sea on a boat trip around the island, the **Lido del Faro** (Str. Faro di Carena; tel. 081/837-1798; www. lidofaro.com; 9:30am-sunset daily June-Sept.; €30 per person for entrance, sun bed, and sea access) beach makes this a popular area for swimming in the summer months. This area is about as rugged as swimming gets on Capri, so be prepared for rocky entrances to the sea and a higher price tag in the peak of summer,

due to the isolated and exclusive setting. From Anacapri, local buses on the Anacapri-Faro route run back and forth about every 30 minutes and provide a convenient way to reach the beach.

SPORTS AND RECREATION
With its remarkably varied landscape from rugged mountains to sea grottoes, Capri is a fun destination for active travelers.

Walks
Exploring Capri on foot is one of the best ways to enjoy the island's natural beauty, and get away from the crowds. You won't have to wander very far off the beaten path to find quiet spots, residential streets lined with beautiful villas, and incredible views.

ARCO NATURALE TO BELVEDERE DI TRAGARA WALK
Distance: *2.2 miles (3.6 km) round-trip*
Time: *2.5 hours round-trip*
Trailhead: *Piazzetta, Capri*
Information and Maps: *Local tourist offices or the Cart&guide Island of Capri map (www. carteguide.com; English version available; €5)*
Explore Capri's quieter side on this enjoyable,

traditional wooden fishing boats in Marina Grande

well-marked walk that leads from the busy Piazzetta through peaceful side streets to a large natural arch and scenic overlook above the Faraglioni rocks. Start off in the Piazzetta opposite the **Chiesa di Santo Stefano** and look for an arched walkway and signs pointing to the Arco Naturale. The walk leads through the narrow streets and begins to head east out of the center of town along Via Matermania. As you approach the natural arch, there's a series of terraces and steps you can follow down to enjoy various viewpoints of the arch and the turquoise sea.

Walk back up the steps from the Arco Naturale and look for the signs for the **Grotta di Matermania.** From there a steep staircase called Via del Pizzolungo leads down the forested mountainside past the Grotta di Matermania, a large cavern that the Romans once used as a luxurious nymphaeum (a monument dedicated to nymphs). Continue along Via del Pizzolungo, which becomes a more level and well-maintained walkway hugging the cliffside. Along the way you'll pass above the **Villa Malaparte,** a striking red villa that stands out against the natural setting, created by Italian writer Curzio Malaparte. Soon after, the captivating Faraglioni rocks come into view. When you reach the **Belvedere di Tragara,** you'll find a shady spot with an incredible view overlooking the Faraglioni rocks. From here, continue along Via Tragara, which leads to Via Camerelle and takes you back into the Piazzetta.

If stairs are an issue, consider either doing the first part leading to the Arco Naturale and then turning back, or starting on the Via Camerelle, walking to the Belvedere di Tragara, and returning without doing the entire loop. To walk the entire loop takes about 2 hours, depending on the number of times you stop to take photos, of course.

BELVEDERE DELLA MIGLIERA WALK

Distance: *1.4 miles (2.2 km) one-way*
Time: *30 minutes one-way*
Trailhead: *Piazza Vittoria, Anacapri*

Information and Maps: *Local tourist offices or the Cart&guide Island of Capri map (www. carteguide.com; English version available; €5)*

One of Capri's most peaceful and easy walks leads to a remarkable view at the **Belvedere della Migliera** (Via Migliera, Anacapri), where you can see all the way from the Faraglioni to the tip of the Punta Carena with its pink and white lighthouse. Starting in Piazza Vittoria, look for the chairlift to Monte Solaro. To the left of the chairlift, follow **Via Caposcuro** until it bends to the left and becomes **Via Migliera.** Continue along this road to the viewpoint at the very end. The relatively level walkway leads you through a rural landscape with terraces of grape vines, gardens, and a view in the distance across the Gulf of Naples to Ischia.

Hiking

Capri is excellent for hiking: The island's small size and public transportation routes make hikes relatively accessible. If you're looking to explore the natural landscape of Capri away from the crowds, there are plenty of options, along rugged dirt trails and beautiful cliffs, and they offer spectacular views. Hiking to **Monte Solaro** is a popular choice. There will be plenty of steps and altitude changes during hikes, so sturdy, comfortable walking shoes are recommended. Because much of the landscape is exposed to the strong Mediterranean sunshine, bring a hat, sunscreen, and plenty of water. Trails are generally well marked with signs throughout the island.

CAPRI TRAILS

tel. 347/368-1699; www.capritrails.com; year-round; from €140 for 3-hour private hike

Experience Capri's most beautiful hikes with Luigi Esposito, a local Capri hiking guide, who is passionate about sharing the island's natural treasures and scenic spots. Luigi can organize private guided hikes around Capri based on your experience and schedule, from shorter 3-hour hikes to full-day (6-8 hours)

hikes. Contact him in advance to decide which hikes is the best one for you.

Boat Tours and Rentals

Seeing Capri from the water is one of the best ways to enjoy the island's natural beauty up close. There are a number of different options readily available, from group boat tours that depart regularly from Marina Grande to private boat excursions. Marina Grande offers the most options for last-minute booking of group tours, which can be purchased right before boarding. But if you're traveling during the summer season, especially in July and August, it's a good idea to book a private boat excursion in advance.

GROUP TOURS

- **Laser Capri:** Via Cristoforo Colombo 69, Marina Grande; tel. 081/837-5208; www.lasercapri.com; 9am-4:30pm daily; €15-18 per person
- **Motoscafisti Capri:** Private pier at dock number 0, Marina Grande; tel. 081/837-5646; www.motoscafisticapri.com; 9am-5pm daily; from €16 per person

PRIVATE EXCURSIONS AND BOAT RENTALS

- **Capri Excursions:** Marina Grande; tel. 366/317-0573; www.capriexcursions.com; Apr.-Oct.; from €150
- **Capri Blue Boats:** Via Mulo 72, Marina Piccola; tel. 339/619-2151; www.capriblueboats.com; Apr.-Oct.; from €80

Cooking Classes
GIARDINO DI CAPRI

Via Vecchia Grotta Azzurra, Anacapri; tel. 347/334-6696; www.giardinodicapri.com; cooking classes and experiences vary by season; from €175 per person with advance booking required

1: Giardini di Augusto **2:** the chairlift to Monte Solaro **3:** view of the Faraglioni rocks from the top of Monte Solaro

Cooking classes, tastings, experiences such as olive harvests, and yoga at Giardino di Capri take place directly on the garden terraces surrounded by nature with the sound of the sea as your backdrop. Learn how to cook authentic Caprese dishes or enjoy a sunset aperitivo with all-natural produce and a spectacular view overlooking the Gulf of Naples. Advance booking is required.

FESTIVALS AND EVENTS

Capri has a vibrant cultural scene with festivals and concerts throughout the summer season, with Capri's beauty as a stunning backdrop. The Villa San Michele in Anacapri and the Villa Lysis in Capri also host concerts and events throughout the season.

Capri
ROLEX CAPRI SAILING WEEK

www.rolexcaprisailingweek.com, info@rolexcaprisailingweek.com; early to mid-May

For a week every year in May, Capri is a top sailing hub of the Mediterranean. The Rolex Capri Sailing Week includes a variety of races and the celebrated sailing Regata dei Tre Golfi that starts dramatically at midnight in Naples and ends in Capri.

FESTA DI SAN COSTANZO

Piazzetta and Marina Grande; May 14

Celebrations for Capri's patron San Costanzo include a grand procession from the Chiesa di Santo Stefano in the Piazzetta and down to the Chiesa di San Costanzo along the road to Marina Grande. The heart of the procession is a large and very precious silver reliquary of the saint dating from 1715, carried on a flower-covered platform and accompanied by music and the town's faithful.

Anacapri
FESTA DI SANT'ANTONIO

Chiesa di Santa Sofia; June 13

Anacapri honors Sant'Antonio every year on June 13 with a colorful summer festival. Every neighborhood along the procession

☆ Cruising Around Capri's Sea Grottoes

Grotta Azzurra

Though the Grotta Azzurra, the Blue Grotto, gets most of the attention, Capri has many beautiful, colorful grottoes, and the best way to see them is on a boat tour around the island. Pack a picnic for the day, and remember to bring your swimsuit and plenty of sunscreen! While there are many small grottoes, the following self-guided tour takes in the largest and most impressive ones to visit around the island. There are tons of options for boat tours or rentals from Marina Grande. If you decide to rent your own boat, small boats can be rented without a boat license. Plan for at least 2 hours just to cruise around, but a half day is the better option to give you time to stop and swim.

route is adorned with elaborate altars and designs created with flower petals on the ground. Balconies are draped with flowers and brightly colored blankets, and onlookers shower the statue of the saint with flowers as the procession passes. The procession begins at the Chiesa di Santa Sofia in Anacapri and leads through the streets of town before returning to the church.

SHOPPING

Famous around the world for fashion, Capri truly is a dream for shoppers, whether you're picking out a perfume made with flowers on the island, enjoying the iconic Capri experience of having sandals custom made, or splurging at a big-name designer boutique.

Even if you're not big on shopping, it's still quite fun to browse the shop windows while strolling through Capri town or Anacapri.

Capri

Capri town is known for fine shopping, and you'll see why as you stroll the shopping areas immediately surrounding the Piazzetta, **Via Vittorio Emanuele** and elegant **Via Camerelle.** This is where you'll find boutiques from top Italian and worldwide fashion designers, like Dolce & Gabbana, Salvatore Ferragamo, Valentino, Dior, and Chanel. The shops selected below represent Capri's artistic heritage, traditions, and style. Many are also smaller spots you might miss if you don't know where to look.

- Head out from Marina Piccola west toward the **Grotta Verde** (Green Grotto), noted for its intensely green water. It's a popular spot to stop and swim through little caves and a natural arch in the water.

- Continue along the coastline to the westernmost tip of the island, **Punta Carena,** which is marked by a pink and white lighthouse.

- Cruise along the rugged western coastline of the island past old **watchtowers** and **forts** perched at the edge of the cliffs.

- On the northwestern side of the island you'll find the famous **Grotta Azzurra** (Blue Grotto). Stop for a visit inside to see the light shimmering across the electric blue water. Here, you'll have to pay an entrance fee and transfer aboard a rowboat to be taken inside the grotto.

- Enjoy the views of Marina Grande while continuing east past the port. On the northeast corner of the island, look up high to catch a glimpse of the ruins of **Villa Jovis.**

- Cruising along the eastern coastline, stop to see the **Grotta Bianca** (White Grotto), a large cave that gets its name from the white hue of the calcareous material on the cliffside. Most impressive when seen from the sea, peering deeper inside reveals the Grotta Meravigliosa (Marvelous Grotto) high above.

- Not far from the White Grotto, keep gazing up to the mountain to look for the **Arco Naturale,** a large natural arch located high above the sea. This is a beautiful area to drop anchor for a swim, with soaring cliffs of unspoiled natural beauty and incredible turquoise water.

- Soon you'll see the striking red **Villa Malaparte,** a modern villa nestled right on top of the Punta Massullo promontory.

- End the day with a spectacular cruise right through the hole in the middle **Faraglioni** rock before returning to Marina Piccola.

CARTHUSIA

Factory: Viale Matteotti 2d; tel. 081/837-5393; www.carthusia.it; 9am-8pm daily May-Sept., 9am-4:30pm daily Oct.-Apr.

Legend has it that the first Carthusia perfume dates back to 1380, when the father prior of a Carthusian monastery noticed that the water from a special floral bouquet he made for a visit by Queen Joanna I of Anjou had been infused with a captivating scent. Carthusia produces perfumes, soaps, lotions, and home products inspired by the flowers of Capri, such as geranium, lily of the valley, and citrus blossoms. Every step of the production is done by hand and with great care. You can watch fragrances being produced in Carthusia's factory and main store on Viale Matteotti, and find their products at several outlets on Capri and around the region.

CANFORA

Via Camerelle 3; tel. 081/837-0487; www.canfora.com; 9:30am-11pm daily Apr.-Oct., 10:30am-5pm daily Nov.-Mar.

One of Capri's historic sandal boutiques, Canfora helped make handmade sandals synonymous with the jet-set life on Capri. In 1946, Amedeo Canfora decided to open a sandal shop across from the elegant Grand Hotel Quisisana. Before long, word spread about the exquisite sandals created there, and famous clients, including Princess Margaret, Grace Kelly, Maria Callas, and Jacqueline Kennedy, came to have custom-fitted sandals made.

Whether you're looking for something classic or glam, you'll find it here. For a unique piece of Capri history you can wear and enjoy, have a pair of sandals custom made to fit while you wait.

ECO CAPRI

Via Fuorlovado 14; tel. 081/837-4510; www.ecocapri. com; 10am-8pm daily Apr.-Oct.

Tucked away on one of Capri's most charming shopping streets in the historic medieval center, this remarkable boutique captures the style and beauty of Capri with custom clothing, accessories, and home decor made by the Cerio family. Federico Alvarez de Toledo, the grandson of artist Laetizia Cerio, has created a shop that is imbued with the spirit of Capri. Look for stunning scarves, clothing, and decorative objects made with authentic prints and designs from the 1940s and '50s, reimagined in a modern resort style.

LA CONCHIGLIA

Via Le Botteghe 12; tel. 081/837-6577; www. edizionilaconchiglia.it; 9am-9pm daily Apr.-Sept., 9:30am-1pm and 3:30-7:30 Mon-Sat. Oct.-Mar.

Brimming with books and art, this bookstore will catch the eye of any book lover. Inside you'll find an excellent selection of books on local Capri history, culture, and landscape. Many of the works are published by their own publishing house Edizioni La Conchiglia, with versions available in English of popular titles. You'll also find a bookshop in **Anacapri** (Via Giuseppe Orlandi 205).

Anacapri

Though you won't find as many high-fashion designer names in Anacapri as in Capri town, Anacapri has many wonderful small boutiques, local artisans, and a quieter pace. The best shopping area centers around the busy **Piazza Vittoria, Via Giuseppe Orlandi,** and **Via Capodimonte,** where you'll find shops selling ceramics, linen clothing, sandals, and jewelry.

NINO & FRIENDS

Via Axel Munthe 16; tel. 081/837-3967; www. ninoandfriends.it; 10am-5pm daily Apr.-Oct.

The delicious scent from this large shop will lure you in to try chocolates, limoncello, coffee, and candies. The owners share a firm belief that you must sample their products to savor the flavors. You'll find Capri-inspired perfumes and elegant sandals as well. There's also a location in **Capri** (Piazza Ignazio Cerio 4) just off the Piazzetta near the Chiesa di Santo Stefano.

SALVATORE FEDERICO

Via Capodimonte 58; tel. 081/837-3061; fabio@capri. it; 10am-7pm daily Apr.-Oct.

An Anacapri native with a grand passion for painting and music, Salvatore Federico has been capturing the ever-changing beauty of the island in his paintings and drawings since he was seven years old. Along the walkway to Villa San Michele, you'll find his gallery full of captivating pieces, from large oil paintings down to delicate watercolors and charcoal sketches. Whatever your budget or space allows, you'll find a unique view of Capri by Salvatore to help you remember your visit.

FOOD
Marina Grande
BAR IL GABBIANO

Via Cristoforo Colombo 76, Capri; tel. 081/837-6531; bargabbiano@gmail.com; 7am-8pm daily Mar.-Nov.; €3-10

Whether you need a strong espresso after getting off the ferry or a spritz and a rest at the end of a day of sightseeing before leaving Capri, this friendly family-run bar along the harbor is a good choice. Just steps from where the ferries arrive and depart, choose from a great selection of cocktails, local wine, and freshly made juices and a menu with sandwiches, bruschette, and light lunch

1: shopping along the elegant Via Camerelle
2: Buonocore Gelateria **3:** Carthusia **4:** Canfora sandal boutique on Via Camerelle

options that can also be prepared for take-away if you're planning a boat trip around the island.

RISTORANTE DA GEMMA

Via Cristoforo Colombo, Capri; tel. 081/277-9056; www.dagemma.com; 9:30am-6:30pm daily (lunch served noon-3:30pm) mid-Apr.-mid-Oct., also open 8pm-11pm Fri.-Sun. July-Aug.; €12-15

Just beyond the harbor at Marina Grande, this restaurant has a seafront terrace, a lounge bar, and **Le Ondine** beach club. Family-run for more than 80 years, this iconic Capri restaurant moved to its current location in 2017. With its setting overlooking the sea, the natural choice here is seafood. Each dish is as beautiful as it is delicious, focusing on freshness and tradition, from an appetizer with raw tuna, watermelon, and mint to the pasta with zucchini flowers, you'll find new and interesting flavors to tempt your palate.

Capri
PESCHERIA LE BOTTEGHE

Via le Botteghe 19; tel. 081/837-6942; www. pescherialebotteghe.it; 1pm-3pm and 7pm-11pm daily Apr.-Oct.; €5-20

Tucked away on a narrow street near the Piazzetta, this local fish shop transforms into an excellent seafood diner for a casual lunch or dinner. You'll enjoy the freshest fish, oysters, crudo di pesce (raw seafood), and outstanding fried calamari and alici (anchovies).

PULALLI

Piazza Umberto I, 4; tel. 081/837-4108; pulallicapri@ gmail.com; noon-3pm and 7pm-midnight Wed.-Mon. Apr.-mid Nov.; €14-26

Dine right in the Piazzetta but above the crowds at this charming restaurant and wine bar next to the bell tower, with great views in all directions from its panoramic terrace The lemon risotto is light and fresh, or opt for classics like the traditional ravioli Caprese. Wine enthusiasts will enjoy the extensive list with over 250 wines.

★ IL GERANIO

Viale Giacomo Matteotti 8; tel. 081/837-0616; www. geraniocapri.com; noon-3pm and 7pm-11pm daily Apr.-Oct.; €14-30

Situated above the Giardini di Augusto, with the same gorgeous view overlooking the Faraglioni, this is one of Capri's most romantic dining spots. Whether you're looking for lunch with a view or a peaceful candlelit dinner under the pine trees, this is a great choice. Try the pappardelle (thick noodles) with fresh prawns followed by the grilled seafood platter. There's an excellent wine selection, and great desserts to finish off a delicious meal in an unforgettable setting.

BUONOCORE GELATERIA

Via Vittorio Emanuele 35; tel. 081/837-7826; buonocore.capri@libero.it; 8am-10pm daily Apr.-May, 8am-midnight daily June-Oct.; €3.50-6

Stroll down Via Vittorio Emanuele from the Piazzetta to Via Camerelle, and the divine scent of this gelateria and bakery will stop you in your tracks. It's a popular spot offering excellent quality. There's a selection of gelato you can buy at the window right off the street, but go inside to find baked goods like their caprilù (lemon and almond cookies).

Anacapri
★ DA GELSOMINA

Via Migliara 72; tel. 081/837-1499; www.dagelsomina. com; 12:30pm-3:30pm and 7pm-11pm daily mid-Apr.-mid-Oct.; €12-26

Escape from the crowds at this restaurant near the beautiful Belvedere Migliera overlook, a pleasant walk from the center of Anacapri. (The restaurant also offers a complimentary shuttle service from the center of town if you call ahead.) This family-run restaurant has a welcoming atmosphere and serves up local favorites like ravioli filled with caciotta cheese, as well as traditional chicken and rabbit dishes. If you're looking for a quiet escape, the restaurant also has a small B&B (rooms from €180) and a large pool nearby.

LA ZAGARA

Via Giuseppe Orlandi 180; tel. 081/837-2923; www. casamariantonia.com; noon-3pm and 7pm-11pm daily Apr.-Oct.; €16-34

Located at the serene Casa Mariantonia right in the center of Anacapri, this lovely restaurant is set among the villa's lemon grove where citrus scents blend perfectly with the Mediterranean flavors and creations of chef Flavio Astarita. The menu options are well balanced between seafood specialties like spaghetti with sea urchins or fresh seared tuna and the excellent grilled beef tenderloin.

RESTAURANT IL RICCIO

Via Gradola 4; tel. 081-837-1380; www.capripalace. com; 12:30pm-3:30pm Mon.-Wed., 12:30pm-3:30pm and 7:30pm-11pm Thurs.-Sun. mid Apr.-mid Oct.; €30-60

Capri's most exclusive seaside dining address is on the rugged northwest tip of the island near the Blue Grotto. Boasting a Michelin star, this is the spot for seafood dining overlooking the sea. Start with their divine plateau royal with assorted raw fish, and then try the spaghetti with sea urchins: a local specialty.

NIGHTLIFE

If you enjoy a night out, stay in Capri town, the center of the island's chic nightlife. Capri town offers a variety of lively spots to sip cocktails, relax with a prosecco at a rooftop bar, or dance until the early hours of the morning in one of the island's hottest nightclubs.

Capri
TAVERNA ANEMA E CORE

Via Sella Orta 1; tel. 081/837-6461; www.anemaecore. com; 10:30pm-3am Thurs.-Sun. Apr.-May and Oct., 10:30pm-3am daily June-Sept.; entrance starts at €40 per person

A Capri nightlife institution in the best possible way, Guido Lembo is the heart and soul of Taverna Anema e Core. Born and raised on Capri, Guido has a passion for music and an engaging style of performing that brings the audience into the experience and has made his nightclub one of the most famous in the world. This is the spot where you might catch sight of international movie stars, musicians, athletes, and VIP visitors to Capri. This is a truly unique Capri hot spot that stands apart from other clubs. Entrance is €40 per person, and for a table prices start at €100. Reservations for tables are highly recommended July-August.

CAPRI ROOFTOP

Via Matteotti 7; tel. 081/837-8147; www. caprirooftop.com; 10am-2am daily mid-May-mid-Sept., 9am-midnight daily mid-Apr.-mid-May and mid-Sept.-Nov.

If your idea of evening entertainment is a cocktail and gorgeous view, head to Capri Rooftop. Set above the Hotel Luna next to the Giardini di Augusto, this rooftop bar affords spectacular views of the Faraglioni in the distance. Choose from a tempting selection of classic cocktails and signature creations like the Luna Caprese made with limoncello, vodka, citrus, and soda.

Anacapri
MALIBLU SUNSET

Faro Punta Carena; tel. 081/837-2560; www. maliblusunset.com; 11am-sunset daily Apr.-Oct.; €10-12

With a gorgeous setting on Punta Carena at the southwest tip of Capri, this beach club is popular for sunbathers during the day, and the fun kicks up a notch as the sun begins to set. Summer events include sunset parties with DJs and live music.

ACCOMMODATIONS

Although not a very large island, Capri has an abundance of accommodations. Yet, because it's one of the most popular destinations in the Campania region, it's not unusual for hotels to be fully booked for much of the season. It's always a good idea to book in advance for Capri, especially if you have a certain hotel or experience in mind. Capri isn't exactly cheap when it comes to accommodations, so that gives you even more reason to book an affordable room well in advance.

Capri

Capri town is very much the island's hub and a good base, especially if you enjoy shopping, nightlife, and easy access to the beach.

HOTEL 4 STAGIONE

Via Marina Piccola 1; tel. 081/837-0041; 4stagionicapri@gmail.com; €85 d

This small hotel is located right at the roundabout that is the hub for buses connecting to all parts of the island. You can hop on a bus, follow the scenic Via Mulo down to Marina Piccola, or walk about 10 minutes to the Piazzetta nearby. The 13 rooms range from double to quadruple occupancy, and many have sea views. For relaxation, the hotel also includes a sun terrace and garden.

★ HOTEL CANASTA

Via Campo di Teste 6; tel. 081/837-0561; www. hotelcanastacapri.it; closed Dec. 9-Feb. 28; €180 d

Set in a tranquil spot, this boutique hotel is a little Capri gem. Inside you'll find only 15 rooms, but all are nicely appointed and very welcoming. Standard rooms have a patio with internal view, while Medium rooms offer a terrace with garden view. For a sea view, try to score one of the two superior double rooms with a terrace. There's also a top-notch restaurant, **Villa Margherita** (tel. 081/837-7532; www.ristorantevillamargheritacapri.com; noon-2:30pm and 7pm-midnight daily Apr.-Oct.; €20-35). Recently remodeled and offering a swimming pool with lovely outdoor lounge areas, this is a place you will love to call home on Capri.

HOTEL LUNA

Viale Giacomo Matteotti 3; tel. 081/837-0433; www. lunahotel.com; May-Oct.; €330 d

With a dream location by the Giardini di Augusto, this hotel boasts stellar views of the Faraglioni as well as a large pool, gym with sea view, small spa, and beautifully landscaped grounds. The rooms are all classically furnished with Mediterranean accents. Rooms range from Standard to Imperial, but go for one of the 20 Camera Deluxe, two Imperial,

or four Suites to have a private terrace with a view of the sea. Dining well is right at your fingertips with two restaurants and two bars on-site, including the Capri Rooftop bar.

Anacapri

Anacapri's setting, higher on the island than Capri town, lends it a sense of calm that makes it a quieter spot for a holiday stay.

VILLA CESELLE

Via Monticello 1/D; tel. 081-838-2236; www. villaceselle.com; Apr.-Nov.; €150 d

This boutique hotel is set in a garden in a residential area of Anacapri that has been a retreat for artists, writers, and travelers since the early 1900s. It includes 10 rooms, two suites, and an independent annex, along with a relaxing garden area and hot tub. Owned by the same family as Da Gelsomina, the hotel also offers a large pool with panoramic views near the Belvedere della Migliera. The walk to the pool is beautiful, or there is also a transfer service available.

★ CASA MARIANTONIA

Via Giuseppe Orlandi 180; tel. 081/837-2923; www. casamariantonia.com; end of Mar.-early Nov.; €300 d

One of the prettiest spots on the island, this boutique hotel is set in a lemon grove and offers a peaceful escape right in the center of Anacapri. Named after the grandmother of the current hosts, the hotel has a welcoming family feel and the service is as warm and inviting as the nine rooms and relaxing pool. Dine under lemon trees at the hotel's restaurant **La Zagara** or enjoy an evening aperitivo at the well-stocked wine bar Vinoteca della Zagara.

HOTEL CAESAR AUGUSTUS

Via Giuseppe Orlandi 4; tel. 081/837-3395; www. caesar-augustus.com; mid-Apr.-Oct; €490 d

Perched on the edge of a cliff boasting a breathtaking view of Mount Vesuvius, Ischia, and the entire sweep of the Gulf of Naples, this remarkable property began as a private home two centuries ago. It later became an exclusive retreat for artists and intellectuals from around the world, and today it's a popular spot for travelers looking for a luxurious and calm oasis on Capri. The double infinity pool is a place of dreams, and just beyond is a 2-acre (0.8-ha) garden where the majority of produce used in the onsite restaurant is grown. There are 49 finely appointed rooms and six exclusive suites, each one more beautiful than the last. This is where you definitely want to splurge on a sea view cliffside room.

INFORMATION AND SERVICES

In adddition to the main info point in Piazza Umberto I, upon arrival at Marina Grande, you'll find one at the western end of the port across from the ferry and bus ticket booths (tel. 081/837-0634) and one in Anacapri at Piazza Vittoria 5 (tel. 081/837-0424).

- **Agenzia Regionale Campania Turismo:** Piazza Umberto I, Capri; tel. 081/837-0686; www.capritourism.com; 8:30am-8:15pm daily June-Sept., 8:30am-4:15pm Mon.-Fri. Nov.-May
- **Hospital:** Ospedale Capilupi; Piazzale Anacapri 3, Capri; tel. 081/838-1227

TRANSPORTATION

Capri is reachable by boat year-round from Naples and Sorrento, and seasonally from the Amalfi Coast. Transportation options, including taxis, buses, and the funicular train to Capri town, are readily available near where ferries dock.

Getting There

All ferries to Capri arrive at **Marina Grande,** also the island's **Porto Turistico** (www.portoturisticodicapri.com); cruise ships drop anchor off of Marina Grande and tender passengers in to the port. Prices and speed vary depending on the type of ferry, but all are comfortable. Tickets from most companies can be purchased online in advance or at ticket booths at the departure port. For peak summer travel, buying tickets in advance is a good idea, if only to avoid long ticket queues.

FROM NAPLES

To reach Capri from Naples, head to the Molo Beverello in the Naples port where the majority of the passenger ferries depart and arrive. If you're looking for speed, opt for a jet or aliscafo (hydrofoil) from **NLG** (tel. 081/552-0763; www.navlib.it; from €23 per person), **Gescab** (tel. 081/704-1911; www.gescab.it; from €23), or **SNAV** (tel. 081/428-5555; www.snav.it; from €22.70). If you're transporting a car, you'll need to book on a traghetto or motonave (ferries) operated by **Caremar** (tel. 081/189-66690; www.caremar.it; from €14.80-20.30 for passengers and €37.20 for vehicles). Crossing to Capri takes about 1 hour.

FROM SORRENTO

Ferries for Capri depart from Sorrento's Marina Piccola harbor and offer regular connections throughout the year with more departures from April-October. The companies **NLG** (tel. 081/807-1812; www.navlib.it; from €13.10 per person), **Alilauro** (tel. 081/878-1430; www.alilaurogruson.it; from €18.20 per person), and **Gescab** (tel. 081/428-5259; www.gescab.it; from €18.20) offer frequent service from Sorrento to Capri. **Caremar** (tel. 081/189-66690; www.caremar.it; from €16.90 for passengers and €28.50 for vehicles) also offers passenger and car ferries from Sorrento to Capri. It is a quick 30-minute ferry ride from Sorrento to Capri.

FROM THE AMALFI COAST

While ferry service to Capri runs year-round from Naples and Sorrento, ferries from the Amalfi Coast only run from about Easter through early November. **Alicost** (tel. 089/871-483; www.alicost.it; from €21.30 per person) offers regular ferry service from Salerno (2 hours), Amalfi (1 hour 20 minutes), and Positano (45 minutes). Depending on the point of origin, there 1-4 daily departures, usually in the morning. From Positano, **Lucibello** (tel. 089/875-032; www.lucibello.

it; €22 per person) also offers a ferry service to Capri.

CAR RESTRICTIONS

Due to its small size and narrow roads, Capri limits the number of cars on the island during the high season; from March until the end of October and December 20-January 7, non-residents are not permitted to bring a car to Capri. So, if you're traveling around Italy by car, you'll need to leave your car in a garage in Naples or Sorrento before continuing on to Capri via ferry. If you're visiting outside of those dates, you can bring your car on one of the larger ferries, usually called a traghetto. However, even off-season, a car isn't recommended, as parking is extremely limited and the island is quite small and fairly easy to navigate by public transportation.

Getting Around

With the island's incredibly narrow and twisty roads and extremely limited parking, the best way to get around Capri is via public transportation or taxi. With plenty of transportation options and the island's small size, Capri is easy to navigate—in theory. The challenge comes when the island gets crowded, especially during peak summer season. Be prepared for lines and allow extra time to get around on public transportation. The good news is that, although it can be busy, Capri is full of inexpensive ways to get around.

BY BUS

Capri's public buses are pint-sized to match the island and connect all the main points on Capri, including Marina Grande, Capri town, Anacapri, Marina Piccola, Punta Carena, and the Grotta Azzurra. Buses are operated by A.T.C. (tel. 081/837-0420; 6am-midnight; tickets €2 per ride, €2.50 if purchased on board). Buses run every 15-30 minutes but can be very crowded in the summer.

In Marina Grande, the bus terminal is located on the western side of the port next to the ticket booths. In Capri town, the main bus terminal is on Via Roma very near the Piazzetta. In Anacapri, buses pick up in Piazza Vittoria and the nearby terminal at Viale T. De Tommaso 22. Given the high demand, there are usually points indicating where to wait for each bus line.

BY FUNICULAR

Capri's **Funicolare** (Servizio Funicolare S.I.P.P.I.C.; Piazza Umberto I, Capri; tel. 081/837-0420; www.funicolaredicapri.it;

The funicular train connects Marina Grande port with Capri town.

6:30am-8:30pm or 9pm daily; €2 each way) is a train line connecting Marina Grande with Capri town at the Piazzetta. The cable car train runs diagonally up the side of the mountain and offers an inexpensive and relatively quick way to travel between the port and Capri town. Tickets can be purchased before boarding in the office at the entrance in the Piazzetta or across the street from the large entrance marked Funicolare in Marina Grande. During the busy season, there can be long lines at Marina Grande in the morning to go up to Capri town as well as to return to the port later in the day. Plan accordingly to avoid stress or rushing, especially if you are going down to Marina Grande to catch a ferry. The funicular runs about every 15 minutes.

BY TAXI

The most comfortable way to get around Capri is by taxi, especially one of the classic open-top ones. You'll find them in Marina Grande near where the ferries arrive and depart, in Capri town at Piazza Martiri d'Ungheria near the Piazzetta, and in Piazza Vittoria in Anacapri. Rates are higher than in some other locations, with a minimum rate of €9 and set rates starting at €17 for the short jaunt between Marina Grande and Capri town, going up to €40 for a trip from Marina Grande to the Grotta Azzurra. **Cooperative Taxi Capri** (tel. 081/837-6464; www.capritaxi. it) offers round-the-clock service.

BY SCOOTER

If you'd like more freedom to move about the island and have a sense of adventure, renting a scooter on Capri could be a good choice. Keep in mind that the roads are very narrow and twisty, and busy with traffic during the season from early spring through October. Parking is difficult to find, too, which can make things a little tricky. However, a scooter does offer the chance to explore the entire island relatively quickly and at your own pace. There are multiple options to rent one on the island, but **Oasi Motor** (Via Cristoforo Colombo 47; tel. 081/837-7138; www.oasimotorcapri.it; 9am-8pm daily Mar.-Oct., 9am-1:30pm and 3pm-6:30pm Mon.-Sat. Nov.-Feb.; starting at €25) is conveniently located right in Marina Grande.

Puglia and the Best of the South

Itinerary Ideas 207
Bari....................210
Around Bari...........220
The Salento...........240
Matera.................259
Highlights of Calabria
   and Basilicata 267

At the southeastern heel of Italy's boot, Puglia

is a top destination for travelers seeking a real, authentic Italian experience. Its long coastline, 540 miles (860 km) of glamorous beaches and secret coves, is just a fraction of what this region has to offer—you'll also find experiences ranging from history and gastronomy to slow living and relaxation. Even those just passing through understand pretty quickly what the Pugliesi mean by la bella vita—the beautiful life.

Still less visited than similarly beautiful areas like Tuscany and the Amalfi Coast, Puglia offers an authentic culinary and cultural vacation without breaking the bank. Here, simple seasonal eating is the rule of thumb; cucina povera, roughly translated as poor cooking

Highlights

Look for ★ to find recommended sights, activities, dining, and lodging.

★ **Handmade Pasta in Bari:** Weave your way through the back alleys of the Bari Vecchia neighborhood to watch the local ladies making traditional handmade orecchiette right on their doorsteps (page 215).

★ **Castel del Monte:** This 13th-century hilltop castle is full of unique architectural features that still mystify visitors today (page 227).

★ **Spiaggia di Lama Monachile:** Travel to the tiny coastal town of Polignano a Mare to see one of Puglia's most picture-perfect beaches (page 229).

★ **Grotte di Castellana:** These 90-million-year-old caves are a labyrinth of amazing stalactites, stalagmites, fossils, and canyons, hidden 200 feet (60 m) below the surface (page 235).

★ **The Trulli of Alberobello:** Alberobello's unforgettable landscape is characterized by these quintessentially Apulian, conical dry-stone houses (page 236).

★ **Lecce's Centro Storico:** In Puglia's cultural capital, an unearthed Roman Amphitheatre dating to the second century AD sits in view of one of the best collections of Baroque architecture in the world (page 242).

★ **Beaches and Coves in the Salento:** At the southernmost tip of Puglia, the Salentine peninsula offers over 155 miles (250 km) of sand beaches and rocky coasts along the Adriatic and Ionian seas (page 254).

★ **Matera's Sasso Caveoso:** There's truly nothing like wandering the narrow streets of Matera's picturesque old town, lined by ancient cave dwellings inhabited for at least 8,000 years (page 260).

Puglia and the Best of the South

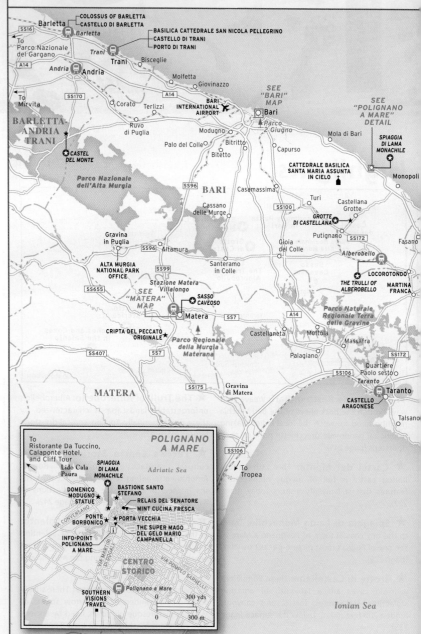

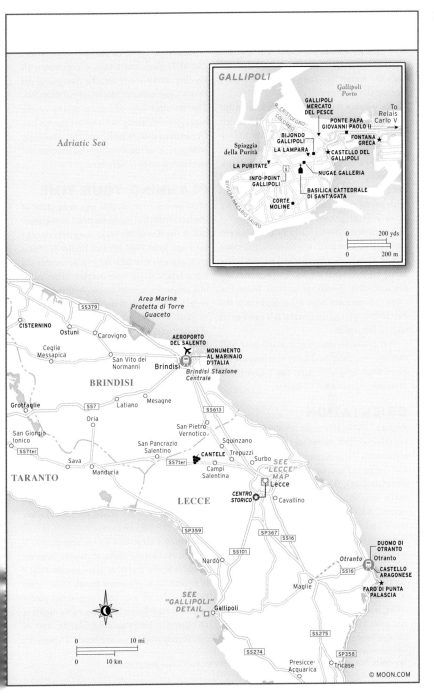

GALLIPOLI

Gallipoli Porto

GALLIPOLI MERCATO DEL PESCE

PONTE PAPA GIOVANNI PAOLO II

To Relais Carlo V

R. CRISTOFORO COLOMBO

Spiaggia della Purità

BIJONDO GALLIPOLI

LA LAMPARA

FONTANA GRECA

CASTELLO DEL GALLIPOLI

LA PURITATE

NUGAE GALLERIA

INFO-POINT GALLIPOLI

BASILICA CATTEDRALE DI SANT'AGATA

CORTE MOLINE

RIVIERA NAZARIO SAURO

0   200 yds
0   200 m

Adriatic Sea

Area Marina Protetta di Torre Guaceto

SS379

CISTERNINO

Ostuni   Carovigno

Ceglie Messapica

San Vito dei Normanni

AEROPORTO DEL SALENTO

MONUMENTO AL MARINAIO D'ITALIA

Brindisi

Brindisi Stazione Centrale

BRINDISI

Grottaglie   SS7   Latiano   Mesagne

Oria

San Giorgio Ionico

SS7ter

Sava   Manduria

San Pietro Vernotico

SS613

San Pancrazio Salentino

SS7ter

CANTELE   Trepuzzi

Squinzano

Surbo

SEE "LECCE" MAP

TARANTO

Campi Salentina

Lecce

LECCE

CENTRO STORICO

Cavallino

SP359

SP367   SS16

SS101

Nardò

DUOMO DI OTRANTO

Otranto

Otranto

CASTELLO ARAGONESE

SS16

Maglie

FARO DI PUNTA PALASCIA

SEE "GALLIPOLI" DETAIL

Gallipoli

SS275

0   10 mi
0   10 km

SS274

Presicce-Acquarica

SP358

Tricase

© MOON.COM

or peasant food, originated out of necessity when cheese, eggs, and meat were luxuries only used for special occasions. Extra virgin olive oil is usually a main ingredient in every dish; the region has some of the oldest olive trees in all of Europe.

Yes, among foodies, Puglia is known for its cultivation of grapes and olives, but this region has even more to offer, from hilltop villages and coastal towns to 90-million-year-old caves and peaceful national parks. Picturesque destinations like whitewashed Ostuni or the village of Alberobello, dotted with memorable conical dry-stone houses known as trulli, shape the landscape.

To the west, technically in the adjacent province of Basilicata, the famous limestone city of Matera can be reached in just a few hours from central Puglia. Its breathtaking ancient cave dwellings carved from the river canyon have been inhabited since the Paleolithic period and make it a can't-miss stop in the region.

Get ready to discover a place that will capture your heart and leave you longing for more. One thing is for sure: You'll have travel memories to relive for a lifetime.

ORIENTATION

Puglia's 7,500 square miles (19,500 square km) are relatively flat, except for the mountainous areas in the Parco Nazionale dell'Alta Murgia and Gargano Promontory. The region's most populated city, **Bari,** also home to Puglia's main airport, is centrally located on the eastern, Adriatic coast. In the province of Bari, you'll find some of Puglia's most famous sites, including the tiny coastal town of **Polignano a Mare, Alberobello** with its conical stone houses, and the **Grotte di Castellana** caves. To the north, the province of **Barletta-Andria-Trani,** named for its three main cities, boast some of Puglia's best vineyards and olive oil groves; farther north still is the off-the-beaten path **Parco Nazionale del Gargano** and the tiny outlying **Tremiti Islands.**

Heading south is the province of **Salento,** one of Puglia's most visited regions, with another, smaller airport, the Aeroporto del Salento, just outside the port city of **Brindisi.** The Baroque city of **Lecce** is one of the highlights, as along with resort towns like **Otranto** and **Gallipoli,** and the seemingly endless miles of mostly unspoiled beaches and swimming coves in between.

PLANNING YOUR TIME

Most people arrive in this region by plane at the **Bari International Airport** (sometimes called the **Karol Wojtyla Airport,** named for Pope John Paul II), but Puglia is also a great place to visit by road trip, accessible via a few hours' drive from Naples, other parts of Campania, or even Rome. Visiting Puglia requires three days at the very least, but with so much to explore, you may want to stay for at least a week to give yourself enough time to lounge on the beach, dine out, and uncover the region's many beautiful towns. Though many simply pass through **Bari,** Puglia's capital city, on the way from the airport, it offers enough sights, restaurant, and nightlife for at least a half-day's exploring, and its amenities and location make it a great base for visits to smaller towns like Alberobello and Polignano a Mare. In the Salento, **Lecce** is another great base. If you want to tack on a (highly recommend) visit to **Matera** in the nearby province of Basilicata, the 2019 European Capital of Culture, you should allow at least a full weekend.

In such a large and scenic region, you'll have to make some difficult choices in terms of where to stay and what to see and do. Puglia is a place for experiential travel, rather than ticking sights off your list; give yourself plenty of time for unplanned detours, extra nights at an especially lovely accommodation, and, of course, relaxing days at the beach. Though the

Previous: Polignano a Mare; trulli houses of Alberobello; traditional food of Puglia.

northern province of **Foggia** and its **Parco Nazionale del Gargano** are famous for their pure, undeveloped beauty, these areas often don't make it onto the itinerary for a first trip to Puglia. On the other hand, hidden treasures like the Salento's **Grotta della Poesia** and **Cala dell'Acquaviva** swimming holes are worth going out of your way to visit.

There are train and bus services in place, but especially if you've never been to Puglia before, the best way to travel here is on a **road trip,** in order to discover the authentic restaurants and luxury farmhouses outside the city centers. It's easier to drive here than in other parts of Italy, since the terrain is generally flat and roads and parking areas less crowded, but do give yourself extra time to drive, as many small regional roads are not well paved. Central Puglia is a good place to start, with two well-serviced airports in Bari and Brindisi, and plenty of car rental agencies based there as well. Rental car prices stay fairly reasonable year-round (€85/day in summer and as low as €15/day in winter). Having your own vehicle allows you to stop by highly celebrated towns like Polignano a Mare and Alberobello, but then escape the crowds on your way to the next stop. In between, Puglia's famous luxury farmhouse accommodations, known as **masserie,** are so dreamy that they may tempt away from the road for longer than you originally planned.

In a pinch, if you don't want to drive yourself during your time in Puglia, hotels will often provide shuttle services from the airport; check with your accommodations for recommendations on how to best reach them.

Although Puglia is best explored in warm weather months, the larger towns can be enjoyed all year round. In the winter and shoulder seasons, when the crowds empty out, you can visit monuments, parks, churches, and historic city centers at a tranquil pace. One of the joys of this region in general is that it runs on a slower pace than the rest of the country.

Itinerary Ideas

TWO DAYS IN PUGLIA

Day 1: Bari and Central Puglia

1 Start your day in Bari with a walk through the **Bari Vecchia** neighborhood, where you'll see the Apulian nonne (grandmothers) making fresh orecchiette in the streets.

2 Hop in your rental car and drive 40 minutes south to **Spiaggia di Lama Monachile** cove in the seaside town of Polignano a Mare.

3 Next, drive 30 minutes southwest to Alberobello, where you can start your visit with a very special farm-to-table lunch at **Trattoria Terra Madre.**

4 Wander through the **Zona Trulli Rione Monti** district, past Alberobello's famous stone trulli houses.

5 Head back 30 minutes toward the coast to your luxurious accommodation for the night, **Borgo Egnazia,** where you'll have your choice of in-house restaurants in a setting straight out of an Italian fairy tale.

Day 2: Lecce

1 From Borgo Egnazia, head 1 hour south to Lecce, the geographical and cultural heart of

Two Days in Puglia

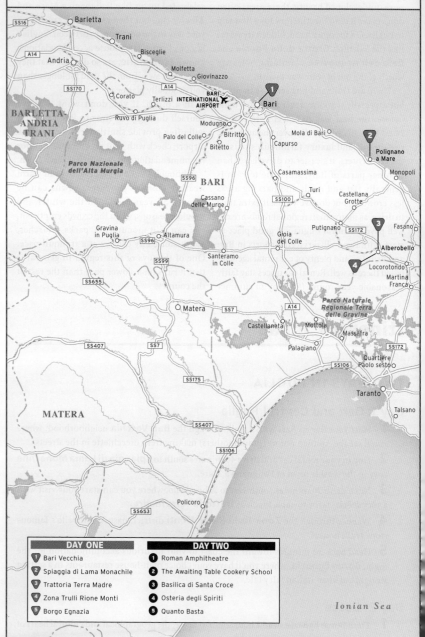

SS16

Barletta

Trani

Bisceglie

A14

Andria

Molfetta

Giovinazzo

SS170

Corato

Terlizzi

BARI INTERNATIONAL AIRPORT

Bari

1

Ruvo di Puglia

A14

Modugno

BARLETTA-ANDRIA-TRANI

Palo del Colle

Bitritto

Capurso

Mola di Bari

2

Polignano a Mare

Parco Nazionale dell'Alta Murgia

Bitetto

Monopoli

SS96

BARI

Casamassima

Cassano delle Murge

Turi

Castellana Grotte

SS100

Gravina in Puglia

Altamura

SS96

Gioia del Colle

Putignano

SS172

Fasano

3

Alberobello

SS99

Santeramo in Colle

Locorotondo

4

Martina Franca

SS655

Matera

SS7

A14

Parco Naturale Regionale Terra delle Gravine

Castellaneta

Mottola

Massafra

SS407

SS7

Palagiano

SS172

MATERA

SS175

Quartiere Paolo sesto

SS106

Taranto

Talsano

SS407

SS106

Ionian Sea

Policoro

SS653

DAY ONE

1. Bari Vecchia
2. Spiaggia di Lama Monachile
3. Trattoria Terra Madre
4. Zona Trulli Rione Monti
5. Borgo Egnazia

DAY TWO

1. Roman Amphitheatre
2. The Awaiting Table Cookery School
3. Basilica di Santa Croce
4. Osteria degli Spiriti
5. Quanto Basta

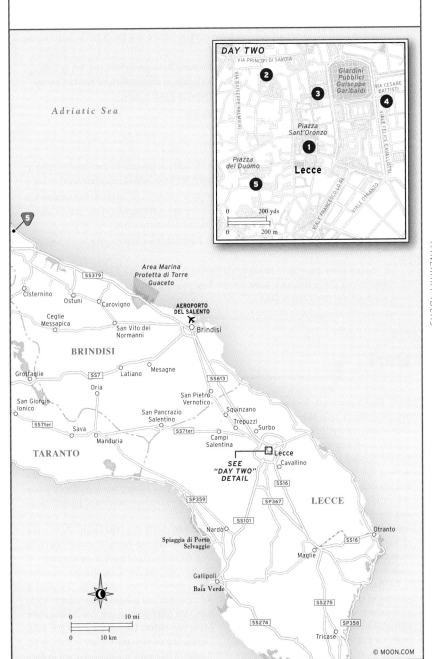

DAY TWO

VIA PRINCIPI DI SAVOIA

2

3

*Giardini
Pubblici
Guiseppe
Garibaldi*

VIA CESARE
BATTISTI

4

*Piazza
Sant'Oronzo*

1

*Piazza
del Duomo*

Lecce

5

0   200 yds

0   200 m

Adriatic Sea

5

SS379

*Area Marina
Protetta di Torre
Guaceto*

**AEROPORTO
DEL SALENTO** ✈

Cisternino

Ostuni

Carovigno

Ceglie
Messapica

San Vito dei
Normanni

Brindisi

BRINDISI

Grottaglie

SS7

Latiano

Mesagne

SS613

Oria

San Pietro
Vernotico

San Giorgio
Ionico

San Pancrazio
Salentino

Squinzano

SS7ter

Trepuzzi

Surbo

Sava

SS7ter

Manduria

Campi
Salentina

TARANTO

*SEE
"DAY TWO"
DETAIL*

Lecce

Cavallino

SS16

SP359

SP367

LECCE

SS101

Nardò

Otranto

*Spiaggia di Porto
Selvaggio*

SS16

Maglie

Gallipoli

Baia Verde

SS275

SP358

SS274

Tricase

0   10 mi

0   10 km

© MOON.COM

Puglia's Salento peninsula. Start your visit at the second-century **Roman Amphitheatre,** smack-dab in the middle of one of Italy's prettiest Baroque piazzas.

2 In the afternoon, meet up with Silvestro Silvestori, founder of **The Awaiting Table Cookery School,** for a half-day hands-on cooking lesson and lunch in the heart of the historic center.

3 Take a stroll through the city of Lecce for some Baroque sightseeing, being sure not to miss the fever-dream ornamentation of the facade of the **Basilica di Santa Croce.**

4 Enjoy a traditional Salentine dinner at **Osteria degli Spiriti.**

5 Treat yourself to a cocktail at **Quanto Basta.**

ONE DAY IN MATERA

Before your day in Matera, book a guided tour with **Sassi di Matera** (www.sassidimatera.it) so you can wander the ancient city's mazelike streets with the help of an expert local guide.

1 Meet your previously reserved certified tour guide from **Sassi di Matera** at Via Lucana 185 to enjoy an introduction to Matera during a walking tour of the Sasso Caveoso district, typical ancient cave dwellings, and frescoed rock churches.

2 After your tour, grab a creative lunch at **Agriristories Ristorante,** with beautiful wine and aperitivo pairings available as well.

3 Spend some time in Matera's most important church, the **Cattedrale di Maria Santissima della Bruna e Sant'Eustachio,** pausing to admire the view of the sassi cave dwellings from Piazza Duomo.

4 For dinner, sample authentic local cuisine at top-notch **Stano.**

Bari

Bari, Puglia's capital, is a great jumping off point for a trip through the region, conveniently located just 20 minutes from the region's main airport. Originally founded by the Greeks and a significant trading center during the third century BC, this lively metropolitan city can be split into two parts: the bustling modern city, known as Murat; and the neighboring San Nicola district, the heart of the historic town center also known as Bari Vecchia. Both are walking distance from the main harbor, which dates back to as early as 181 BC.

In Bari, many visitors get their first glimpse of the distinct Apulian Romanesque architecture, which developed in the 11th-13th centuries when the region was a jumping-off point for pilgrims heading to the Holy Land, similar to other Romanesque architecture of the time but combined with Byzantine and Arab elements. Get lost along winding alleys in the old town center, Bari Vecchia, where you can watch the local women making orecchiette pasta by hand near the 12th-century Castello Normanno-Svevo, or take a walk along the Lungomare di Bari with a slice of the city's famous tomato and olive focaccia barese.

When walking through Bari, the monumental, red-brick Teatro Petruzzelli is good central landmark to orient yourself in the city center; Castello Normanno-Svevo plays the same role in Bari Vecchia. A lovely waterfront promenade connects Molo San Vito ferry port in the west to the older Molo San Nicolà fishing docks to the west. Depending on your travel time and interests, it might make sense to situate yourself in Bari,

Bari

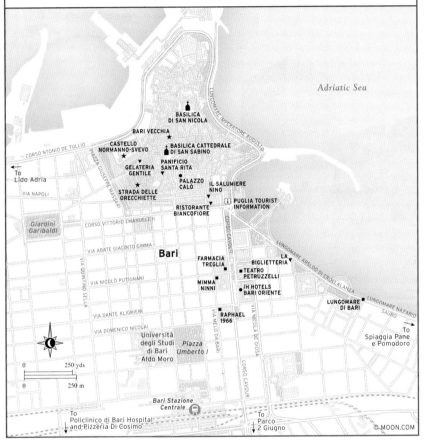

enjoying the amenities of a larger town while taking short day trips to nearby destinations like Polignano a Mare and Alberobello.

SIGHTS
Bari Vecchia

The San Nicola district of Bari, also known as Bari Vecchia, is the historic heart of the city, located on a small peninsula jutting out into the Adriatic. One of the first things you'll notice upon arrival in Bari, especially if you're arriving by train in the more modern city center, is that walking toward the old town is

like taking a trip back in time, where winding streets are lined with freshly laundered clothes hanging to dry, kids playing football in courtyards, and families barbecuing on their front stoops. Bari Vecchia's quiet, narrow alleyways are bordered by ancient city walls, dating back to the fourth century BC, and lead to the Castello Normanno-Svevo and the Romanesque Basilica di San Nicola. This also where you'll find the Strada delle Orecchiette, where you can watch women making pasta by hand on small tables in the street.

BASILICA DI SAN NICOLA

Largo Abate Elia, 13; tel. 080/573-7111; www.
basilicasannicola.it; 7:15am-8:30pm daily; free

Built in 1197, when Puglia was ruled by the Normans, this basilica is a masterpiece of Romanesque Apulian architecture, notable for its impressive height and vaulted ceilings, detailed interior mosaics, and Byzantine-inspired details like pointed arches. Framed by two large towers, the Torre del Catapano and the Torre delle Milizie, the light-colored stone facade features a central embellished doorway surrounded with intricate Arabian, Byzantine, and classical style carvings of foliage and fantastical beasts. Inside, the basilica is adorned with marble columns topped with Romanesque capitals, high arches above the nave, gilded 17th-century wooden ceilings, and a marble throne.

The crypt houses a gold and silver alter and the remains of San Nicola—known as the Miracle Worker and one of the most revered Orthodox saints—and is accessible via a staircase. There is also a small museum, Museo Nicolaiano, which contains other relics related to the saint and basilica.

BASILICA CATTEDRALE
DI SAN SABINO

Piazza dell'Odegitria; tel. 080/521-0605; www.
arcidiocesibaribitonto.it/luoghi-di-culto/cattedrale;
10am-1pm Mon.-Thurs., 10am-1pm and 5pm-8pm Sat.,
10am-2pm Sun.; free

Though not as famous as the Basilica di San Nicola, this Apulian Romanesque-style cathedral in Bari Vecchia is the seat of the Archbishop of Bari-Bitonto and Bari's most important church. It was constructed during the 12th-late 13th centuries over the existing ruins of a Byzantine cathedral. Behind the relatively simple, pleasingly symmetrical facade with a central rose-shaped stained glass window, the cathedral's interior is decorated with mosaic flooring and relatively plain stone

walls. A subterranean crypt contains the ancient relics of Saint Sabinus, worshipped for building churches throughout Puglia in the fourth century.

CASTELLO NORMANNO-SVEVO

Via Pier l'Eremita, 25/b; tel. 080/528-5000;
8:30am-6:30pm Wed.-Mon.; €9

Traveling throughout Puglia, you'll begin to notice most towns, especially the ones on the coast, have two main features: the central church, and the castle. Many of the region's fortified castles were first built by the Normans, who dominated the region around the 12th century. The castle in Bari Vecchia, built on former Byzantine fortifications, is a symbol not only of Norman power, wealth, and greatness, but also of the impact of Frederick II of Swabia on the region. This influential Germanic king of Sicily and holy roman emperor saw numerous castles built and improved under his rule (from 1220-1250 AD). Bari's towering castle covers a huge area on the west side of Bari Vecchia, complete with a stone bridge, walls rebuilt under Aragonese rule, and a courtyard added in the 16th century.

Today, the castle houses a regional museum and other rotating exhibitions. The Aragonese Room has a permanent photo exhibition of the history of the fortress, while other areas feature collections of pottery, stones, and jewelry, as well as an interesting collection of plaster copies of sculptures in the Gipsoteca Room. The museum can be reached by crossing the entrance bridge over the grass-covered lawn on the south side of the castle, where the moat used to be.

SPORTS AND RECREATION
Parks
PARCO 2 GIUGNO

Via della Resistenza, 155; tel. 080/523-8335; www.
comune.bari.it; 8:30am-11pm daily; free

In a city with limited green spaces, Bari's 20-acre (8-ha) urban park is located in the

---

1: the exterior of Bari's impressive Norman castle, Castello Normanno-Svevo **2:** alleyways in Bari Vecchia **3:** Bari's seafront

Carrassi district, a 30-minute walk south of the historic center along the Viale della Repubblica boulevard. It's a peaceful place with picnic areas, a bocce court, recreational playgrounds, and a pond.

LUNGOMARE DI BARI

Lungomare Araldo di Crollalanza, Lungomare Nazario Sauro, and Lungomare Armando Perott; open 24 hours; free

These connected waterfront promenade areas along the Adriatic Sea are the perfect spot to walk off the slices of focaccia barese and heaps of orecchiette pasta you'll certainly be consuming on your trip. The walkable coastline runs from the Molo San Nicola pier to the Spiaggia Pane e Pomodoro beachfront (1.6 mi /2.5 km). Take a seat on one of the park benches along the lungomare to relax and people-watch at sunset, stop for a cold refreshment at the small bars situated on the Molo di San Nicolà docks near the port, or continue on with a 30-minute stroll to the beach.

Beaches

With Bari as a base for a few days, guests can enjoy the convenient access to the nearby sand beaches at both the north and south outskirts of the city. Lido San Francesco is among the most popular but can become overcrowded in summertime, especially in the free public beach section.

LIDO SAN FRANCESCO

Via Umberto Giordano, 2-6; open 24 hours; free

The free beach portion of Lido San Francesco is located on the southern end of the shore, closer to the city center of Bari. Guests can arrive by car in 15 minutes from the port of Bari and enjoy the sandy beachfront and optional restaurants, bars and lounge chairs, and umbrella rentals from **Lido San Francesco Alla Rena** (Via Giuseppe Verdi, 59; tel. 080/534-1542; www.facebook.com/sanfrancesco.allarena; 8:30am-7pm Mon.-Sat., 9am-7pm Sun.; umbrella and two chairs €25).

LIDO ADRIA

Lungomare IX Maggio, 1; open 24 hours; free

The free public beach and private **La Capannina** (tel. 351/226-1088; www.baribeachclub.it) lido club are accessible with a 20-minute drive north of the city center. La Capannina offers beach chair and umbrella rentals, seasonal cabana changing room huts, restaurant services, aperitivo specials, live music, and DJ sets in summertime.

SPIAGGIA PANE E POMODORO

Corso Trieste; open 24 hours; free

This city beach is within 30 minutes walking distance from the city center of Bari, popular with the native Barese who have the opportunity to take a quick dip without traveling too far. The free sand beach is equipped with a parking facility, bar, and pizzeria. The calm shore is suitable for families and small children protected from waves by the surrounding rocks.

FESTIVALS AND EVENTS

FESTA DI SAN NICOLA

Basilica San Nicola, Largo Abate Elia, 13; tel. 080/573-7111; www.basilicasannicola.it; Dec. 3-6 and May 7-9; free

Both regular churchgoers and more secular Barese faithfully celebrate their patron saint and protector, Saint Nicholas, twice each year. Festivities include music, heartfelt processions, a grand parade, fireworks, and a red, white, and green colored smoke display by the Italian Air Force. San Nicola, often associated with Santa Claus, is also a connection between Eastern and Western Christianity, with strong followings in Greece, Turkey, Southern Italy, and Venice.

December traditions include feast day foods such as pettole (deep-fried dough), marzipan almond sweets, carteddate (halo-shaped cakes), torrone nougats, and, of course, lots of hot chocolate. The inaugural tree-lighting ceremony in the Piazza San Nicola takes place at dusk on December 3, but the main celebration is on December 6, with

★ The Handmade Pasta of Bari

handmade orecchiette

Just across from the Castello Normanno-Svevo, under the quiet arched backstreets of the Bari Vecchia neighborhood, Bari celebrates the age-old tradition of making fresh pasta. These pastai, or pasta experts, are not professional chefs; they are local women who sit together in front of their houses and make pasta all day long while chatting with each other, and they are happy to introduce tourists to Puglia's local specialty, **orecchiette.**

This "little ear"-shaped pasta is perfect for scooping up tomato salsa and is often paired with cima di rapa turnip greens, broccoli rabe, or chicory. They vary in size, from teeny ones that barely fit on the tip of your finger, to large ones that require more than one bite. The recipe is simple, using only flour from local hard durum wheat and boiling hot water. Often you'll see a gray or dark brown version, made with grano arso, a burnt wheat. In the era of cucina povera, people even found a way to make use of grains that were left on the ground after fields were burnt to replenish the soil after the harvest.

MAKING ORECCHIETTE

The only tools needed for preparing fresh orecchiette are a wooden table and a simple ridged butter knife. The dough is mixed and kneaded by hand, then rolled out into a log shape and cut into small dumpling pieces. With precision and years of practice, the pastai drag the small pieces of dough across the table with the kitchen knife to create the little ear shapes. The ridges of the knife help create the rough texture, which helps in catching the sauce. Once shaped, the pasta is dried on screens, with an oscillating fan pointed toward them to help speed up the process.

HOW TO BUY IT

The "Orecchiette Ladies" of Bari Vecchia can be found along the **Strada delle Orecchiette,** from Arco Basso to Strada Barone. There's a sort of agreement between the women in Bari Vecchia to keep the standard price at €5 per kilo of fresh pasta. The warmest and most welcoming to foreign tourists is Signora **Nunzia Caputo,** who can be found 365 days a year at a small wooden table in front of Arco Basso, 11.

To help support the pasta grannies, make sure to purchase something in addition to spending time taking photos and asking questions. Be aware that some of the women are not as open to guests just stopping by without shopping. Often there will be local items such as sun-dried tomatoes or Apulian taralli crackers available for sale as well, if you're looking for something easier to transport in your suitcase.

holy mass celebrated every hour at the Basilica San Nicola, a sculpture of the saint paraded through the city, and fireworks display over the Molo Sant'Antonio docks.

In May, the rituals begin with a procession carrying a picture of the saint, followed by a holy mass and parade. On May 8, the statue of San Nicola is carried from the Basilica San Nicola, through the streets of Bari Vecchia, and toward the sea, where the harbor fills up with fishermen paying tribute from their boats, finally concluding with a momentous communion service. The final day of the spring festival begins and ends with a firework display; the saint's statue is sent out from the San Nicola Pier to bless the sea before returning by candlelight back to the Basilica.

The May festival is the most popular time to visit Bari, meaning the city can become quite crowded; plan accordingly if you plan to travel during this time.

THE ARTS
TEATRO PETRUZZELLI

Corso Cavour, 12; tel. 080/975-2810; www.
fondazionepetruzzelli.it; ticket office 11am-7pm
Mon.-Sat.; free entrance

Teatro Petruzzelli is Bari's main opera house and the fourth largest in all of Italy.

It was built between 1898-1903 by the Petruzzelli brothers, well-known traders and shipbuilders from Trieste, when the smaller Teatro Piccini (Corso Vittorio Emanuele, 84; tel. 080/577-2465), closer to Bari Vecchia, was deemed too small for the city's growing art-loving population. Built in the Umbertino style, popular at the time, it originally accommodated 2,200, but after being destroyed by a devastating arson attack in 1991, it was rebuilt and now houses only 1,500 due to modern safety regulations. This highly celebrated theater remains an important cultural landmark and has hosted numerous distinguished performers over the years, including Luciano Pavarotti, Plácido Domingo, Ray Charles, Frank Sinatra, and Liza Minnelli. The theater now stages seasonal operas, concerts, and ballets.

SHOPPING

Strolling through Bari, you'll notice there's a refined local style, ranging from streetwear to high-end fashion. If you want to dress like the locals or maybe just window-shop, head to the shopping district in the **Murat quarter,** located on the main streets Via Sparano, Corso Cavour, and Via Manzoni, where you'll find a plethora of boutiques and designer stores

Teatro Petruzzelli

including **Prada** (Via Sparano da Bari, 136; tel. 080/220-6066; www.prada.com; 10am-8pm Mon.-Sat., 11am-8pm Sun.), **Gucci** (Via Sparano da Bari, 75-77-79; tel. 080/522-7020; www.gucci.com; 10am-8pm daily), and **Louis Vuitton** (Via Sparano da Bari, 113; tel. 02/0066-08888; it.louisvuitton.com; 10am-8pm Mon.-Sat., 11am-8pm Sun.).

RAPHAEL 1966

Via Dante Alighieri, 24; tel. 080/521-6351; www. raphael1966.com; 9:30am-1pm and 5pm-8:30pm Mon.-Sat., 10:30am-1pm and 5:30pm-8:30pm Sun.

Opened in 1966 as a boutique by Raffaele Pisciotta, a local tailor and industrial manufacturer, Raphael 1966 has evolved into an upscale men's clothing store with a selection of blazers, outerwear, dress shirts, footwear, and sunglasses. Check out their other shop with same name only two blocks away (Via Principe Amedeo, 41; tel. 080/521-0631; 10am-1pm and 4:30pm-8:30pm Mon.-Sat.) for cutting-edge streetwear, cult-classic sneakers, unisex clothing, and travel accessories including backpacks and duffle bags.

MIMMA NINNI

Via Nicolò Putignani, 32; tel. 080/352-9580; www. mimmaninnishop.com; 5pm-8pm Mon., 10am-1pm and 5pm-8pm Tues.-Sat.

This 2,700-square-foot (250-square-m) concept store is an offshoot of the Mimma Ninni menswear (Via Melo da Bari, 91B; tel. 080/5216103) and womenswear (Via Nicolò Putignani, 26; tel. 080/5282921) shops established at this very street corner over 30 years ago. There's a selection of the hottest trends in clothing, footwear, technology, and lifestyle with a range of high-end Italian and international brands.

FOOD

Although there are options for fine dining in Bari, the truly local dishes will be sold at bakeries, pizza shops, and small street food kiosks, making this a great place to eat well on a budget. Definitely make sure to try **focaccia**

barese, a thick-crust pizza made with riced potato in the dough, topped with tomatoes, unpitted olives, and extra virgin olive oil, and then baked in a very hot oven to crisp up the bottom. It's usually sliced into quarters and eaten by hand (a cold beer and a handful of napkins are highly recommended).

Restaurants
★ RISTORANTE BIANCOFIORE

Corso Vittorio Emanuele, 13; tel. 080/523-5446; www.ristorantebiancofiore.it; noon-3pm and 7pm-11pm daily; raw fish antipasti €20, mains €16-18

At the eastern edge of Bari Vecchia, just a stone's throw from the Molo San Nicolà docks, Biancofiore is Bari's top place for fresh seafood, paired with extremely friendly service and an all-star wine list. Owner Diego Biancofiore radiates warm hospitality and pride for his land. The young local chef, Giacinto Fanelli, puts a new spin on typical dishes found around Puglia, such as spaghetti with mussels, fava beans, and pecorino, or squid stuffed with sun-dried tomatoes and olives. The elegant white-and-blue-tiled dining room seats around 40 guests; reservations are recommended. Check out their brand-new wine bar, Mostofiore (Via Roberto da Bari, 128; tel. 080/865-1616; www. mostofiore.net).

Bakery
PANIFICIO SANTA RITA

Str. dei Dottula, 8; tel. 346/616-9152; www.facebook. com/PanificioSantaRitaBari; 8am-2pm and 6:30pm-9:15pm Mon.-Wed. and Fri., 8am-2pm Thurs., 8am-2pm and 6:30pm-10:30pm Sat.; €2

When a city has its own specialty recipe, you'll see eateries everywhere trying to replicate it, but only a few will make it at its very best. On a search for the best slice of warm toasty focaccia barese, look no further than the Panificio Santa Rita, within the walls of Bari Vecchia. Patrons typically line up outside the bakery each day the moment the focaccia comes fresh out of the oven. When Bari celebrates its patron saint, San Nicola, on December 6, the forno runs all night long.

Cafés and Light Bites

IL SALUMIERE NINO

Strada S. Benedetto; tel. 080/521-9851;
7:30am-3:15pm and 5pm-10:30pm daily; €3

From capocollo to mortadella, caciocavallo, prosciutto, and scamorza, this family-run salumeria is the place to fill up for a day of sightseeing. Nino, the family patriarch and head salumiere, makes the best sandwiches in town, stuffed with all the cured meats and cheeses you can think of. If you ask for his recommendation, you'll get something better than you can dream up yourself. Stock up on traditional taralli olive oil crackers, or ask them to vacuum seal ("sotto vuoto") your deli selections to take home with you.

GELATERIA GENTILE

Piazza Federico II di Svevia, 33; tel. 080/528-2779;
www.gelateriagentile.com; 11am-12:30am Sun.-Thurs.,
11am-1am Fri.-Sat.; €3

Since 1880, the art of homemade gelato has been handed down for generations at Gelateria Gentile in Bari Vecchia. Try non-traditional flavors like marasca (cherry), percoca (peach), strawberry cream, kiwi, or Slow Food Presidio Toritto almond.

LA BIGLIETTERIA

Largo Adua, 3; tel. 080/222-7704; www.facebook.
com/LaBiglietteriaBari; 7am-2am daily; cocktails
€7-12

The abandoned ticket office of the historic 1920's Kursall Theater was renovated to create this very special restaurant, café, and American-style cocktail bar. The "new deco" style space designed by the Italian studio SMALL transformed the foyer of this theater-turned-cinema into a cozy chic place to stop for a top-quality libation or bottle of champagne. The dramatic vaulted ceilings and bardiglio marble floors might make you feel like you're in a novel by F. Scott Fitzgerald.

Pizzeria

PIZZERIA DI COSIMO

Via Giovanni Modugno, 1; tel. 080/504-1513; www.
facebook.com/pizzeriadicosim; 6pm-midnight
Mon.-Tues. and Thurs.-Sat., 6:30pm-midnight Sun.;
panzerotti €1.50, pizzas €5-7

Prepare yourself for a wait to try Di Cosimo's famous panzerotti, a traditional Apulian deep-fried pizza dough pocket most commonly stuffed with tomato sauce and mozzarella. Do as the locals do and bite off the corner first to let the steam out before diving in. It's located a 10-minute drive south of the city center.

ACCOMMODATIONS

Despite being a large provincial capital, there are not many hotel options in Bari, making Airbnb an extremely popular option. Staying in a small apartment in Bari Vecchia is a great option for exploring local restaurants, bars, and city sights on foot.

IH HOTELS BARI ORIENTE

Corso Cavour, 32; tel. 080/525-5100; www.ih-hotels.
com; from €80

This Liberty-style four-star hotel is located on five floors of the elegant Palazzo Marroccoli in the Murat district, right near the Lungomare seaside promenade and the Teatro Petruzzelli. The hotel has 75 simply designed rooms, as well as a penthouse garden terrace with one of the best views in town offering cocktail service from May-September. Amenities include air-conditioning, security safe, Wi-Fi and television service, and bathroom necessities including hair dryers, robes, slippers, and bath products.

PALAZZO CALÒ

Strada Lamberti, 8; tel. 080/527-5448; www.
palazzocalo.com; from €130

The 12 rooms of Palazzo Calò, conveniently located right on the winding streets of Bari Vecchia, are all bright, clean, and modern, with conveniences like small kitchens and complimentary Wi-Fi. The rooftop terrace and garden has a great view of Bari's cathedral.

INFORMATION AND SERVICES

Pharmacies are conveniently located throughout Bari, as well as supermarkets, groceries, tabacco shops, and newsstands where you can pick up any necessities you may have forgotten.

- **Puglia Tourist Information:** Piazza del Ferrarese, 29; tel. 080/524-2244; www.viaggiareinpuglia.it; 9am-7:30pm daily

- **Info-Point Bari Airport:** Bari International Airport, Arrivals Gate; tel. 080/5800200; www.viaggiareinpuglia.it

- **Policlinico di Bari Hospital:** Piazza Giulio Cesare, 11; tel. 080/559-1111; www.sanita.puglia.it/web/ospedalegiovannixxiii; open 24 hours

- **Police station** (Polizia di Stato – Questura): Via Gioacchino Murat, 4; tel. 080/529-1111; www.questure.poliziadistato.it/Bari; open 24 hours

- **Ufficio Postale Poste Italiane:** Piazza Umberto I, 33/A; tel. 080/525-0150; www.poste.it; 8:20am-7pm Mon.-Fri., 8:20am-12:30pm Sat.

- **Farmacia Treglia:** Corso Cavour, 77; tel. 080/521-9326; 8:30am-1pm and 4:30pm-8pm Mon.-Fri., 8:30am-8pm Sat.

GETTING THERE AND AROUND

Visitors generally arrive in Bari by car from other parts of Southern Italy, or on a flight into Bari International Airport. It is possible to reach Bari by train and bus, but travel on public transportation is generally slower than self-driving; that said, once arrived, the city of Bari is fairly well connected to the rest of Puglia by public transport. Bari can also be reached by ferries from international destinations including Albania, Montenegro, Croatia, and Greece. Ferries arrive at the **Molo San Vito** pier (Porto Bari; tel. 080/521-1726; www.guardiacostiera.gov.it/bari).

Though Bari does have a bus system, the city center is walkable enough that travelers will not have a need for public transportation.

By Air
BARI INTERNATIONAL AIRPORT
Viale Enzo Ferrari, Bari; tel. 080/580-0200; www.aeroportidipuglia.it

Officially named for Pope John Paul II, **Aeroporto Karol Wojtyla** (BRI) is one of the two main airports in the region of Puglia. It's located just 20 minutes north of Bari's city center along the SS16 state road. Extremely affordable flights connect Bari with cities throughout Europe as well as Italian cities, including **Rome Fiumicino** (Ryanair; 1 hour; €5), **Milan Bergamo** (Ryanair; 1 hour 25 minutes; €31), **Palermo** (Volotea, 1 hour 10 minutes; €19), and **Catania** (Volotea, 1 hour 10 minutes; €33).

There are a few ways to reach Bari from the airport. A one-way fixed-tariff **taxi** (provided by Apulia Taxi; tel. 080/534-6666; www.baritaxi.it) to Murat, San Nicola, or Bari's Stazione Centrale costs approximately €23 and will take about 20 mintues. Alternatively, the **train** (Ferrovie Nord Barese; tel. 080/5299111; www.ferrovienordbarese.it; €5) from the airport runs 6am-midnight and takes 20 minutes. Tempesta Auto Servizi also offers a 30-minute **bus transfer** between the Bari airport and the city center (tel. 080/521-9172; www.autoservizitempesta.it; €4). Rental cars are available for pickup at the airport with reservations in advance from **Goldcar** (tel. 06/4520-9634; www.goldcar.es) and **Sixt** (tel. 02/9475-7979; www.sixt.it).

The **Puglia Airbus** (tel. 080/5790211; www.aeroportidipuglia.it) shuttle bus line regularly connects the Bari airport with scheduled services to Matera, Vieste on the Gargano Promontory, and Taranto, as well as the Brindisi and Foggia airports.

By Car
Bari is located in the central portion of the

east coast of Puglia, on the Adriatic Sea. From **Naples** or the **Amalfi Coast,** take the **A16/E842** east to the **A14** Autostrada Adriatica (155 mi/260 km; 3 hours); the shortest route will lead you past the city of Andria, north of Bari, and then south along the coast (165 mi/266 km; 3 hours 20 minutes). Driving to Bari from **Palermo** (415 mi/668 km) will take about 8.5 hours with the required ferry crossing between Sicily and Calabria.

Street **parking** in Bari follows Italy's color-coded zone policy, with blue striped spaces indicating paid parking with a ticket from a nearby meter from 8:30am-8:30pm Monday-Saturday. Yellow spaces are for residents or reserved for drivers with disability permits, and white parking spaces are free of charge. In the Murat district, paid parking will cost €2/hour; in Bari Vecchia, €1/hour. The most centrally located parking garages are the 24-hour **Garage Tiemme** (Via Raffaele de Cesare, 10; tel. 080/523-7791; €20/day) in the new part of town or the **Parcheggio Saba Porto** (Corso Vittorio Veneto, 5, tel. 080/558-0492; www.sabait.it; 6am-midnight) near the Molo Pizzoli pier. When driving in the city center, pay attention for signs labeled Zona Traffico Limitato (ZTL), indicating limited traffic zones, where rental cars are not permitted. Driving in these areas can result in fines of €60-150.

By Train
BARI STAZIONE CENTRALE
Bari Centrale, Piazza A. Moro, 50/B; www.trenitlia.com

Bari's central station is in Piazza Aldo Moro, a 10-minute walk from the Murat district and 20 minutes to the Molo San Nicola pier or Bari Vecchia neighborhood. Train service provided by Trenitalia runs between Bari and other nearby Apulian cities quite frequently, including Polignano a Mare (30 minutes; €3), Trani (30 minutes; €2.60), Barletta (50 minutes; €4.50), Andria (1 hour 35 minutes; €5.60), Monopoli (25 minutes, €4), Lecce (1 hour 40 minutes; €12), and Matera Centrale (2 hours; €10). Tickets can be purchased inside the station or online and must be time stamped at the station before boarding.

It is possible to take the train from Napoli Centrale to Bari Centrale with a transfer in Caserta (www.trenitalia.it; 4 hours; €47), or from Salerno to Bari with a transfer in Benevento (www.trenitalia.it; 5 hours 25 minutes; €39).

Around Bari

North of Bari, the triangle of cities formed by Barletta, Andria, and Trani are between 20-30 minutes apart from one another, with Barletta and Trani on the Adriatic Sea and Andria 8 miles (13 km) inland. Grouped together, they form one of Puglia's six provinces. The countryside here is focused on agriculture, mainly olives and wine, while the coastal cities host a thriving fishing industry. Dine on fresh fish in the coastal cities and rustic hearty dishes in the countryside, including the culinary specialty, burrata cheese. The main highlight of this area is the 13th-century Castel del Monte, an octagonal fortress built on the top of a hill south of Andria. It rules over the mountainous 262-square-miles (679-square-m) of Parco Nazionale dell'Alta Murgia. Though the cities in this region are accessible by car or train from Bari, a rental car is necessary to properly discover the countryside.

Driving south of Bari along the Adriatic, the true wonders of Puglia begin to reveal themselves: a seemingly endless shoreline punctuated by paradisiacal rocky inlets filled with clear turquoise water, each more tempting than the next. Visit the jewel box town of Polignano a Mare and its famous Lama

Monachile swimming cove—and ask locals where they go for a swim without the crowds if you get the chance. Inland, you'll find one of the most distinctive sights in all of Puglia, the trulli houses of Alberobello, dry-stone, conical houses that have become one of the biggest tourist draws in the region. Along the way, the scattered towns in the Valle d'Itria in central Puglia are among the most charming villages to visit in Puglia, remaining fairly untouched by tourism.

TRANI

The beautiful coastal city of Trani, with its distinctive, bright white Romanesque cathedral, is often overlooked by tourists, which is a shame. Though Trani's history bears similarities to many of the towns on Puglia's Adriatic coast—a conveniently positioned port that gained prominence in the 1200s as a commercial center and jumping-off point for the Crusades—it was also uniquely home to one of the largest Jewish populations in the region, meaning it boasts a few precious synagogues, many of which were converted to churches during waves of antisemitism throughout the Middle Ages.

Trani's picturesque harbor, the **Porto di Trani** (Via Statuti Marittimi), also feels more bustling and used than some of the other port cities in this region, filled with colorful fishing boats and with locals gathering at seaside bars and restaurants, especially in the warmer months. It's a great place for a couple hours' wandering as a day trip from Bari, or as a jumping-off point to the closely connected cities of Barletta and Andria; come here to wander 11th-century streets, take in the view from the Swabian Castello di Trani, and get lost in the greenery of the Villa Comunale city park.

Sights
BASILICA CATTEDRALE SAN NICOLA PELLEGRINO
Piazza Duomo; tel. 088/3500293; www.cattedraletrani.it; 9am-12:30pm and 3:30pm-7pm Mon.-Sat., 9am-12:30pm and 4pm-7pm Sun.; free

Trani's Apulian-Romanesque style Roman Catholic cathedral, located at the water's edge, was originally constructed in 1099, but the monumental bell tower with its large archway, completed in the 14th-century, remains its most iconic feature. Its dramatic location, set apart from the rest of the town against the deep blue sea, makes the pinkish white of its locally quarried tuff stone stand out all the more. A unique double staircase leads to an arched bronze doorway surrounded by intricate carvings, underneath a small rose window. The interior is dramatic and stark, for the most part unornamented; visit the crypts below the basilica for a view the remains of San Nicola Pellegrino, or climb the campanile (bell tower) for €5.

CASTELLO DI TRANI
Piazza Re Manfredi, 16; tel. 0883/506603; www.castelloditrani.beniculturali.it; 9am-1pm Wed. and Fri., 3pm-7pm Thurs.; free

Castello di Trani is a landmark Swabian castle built in 1233 by Emperor Federick II, just a short walk from the Port of Trani and the main cathedral. Constructed as a fortress and built on the banks of the Adriatic Sea, the stone castle went through renovations while under the Angevins and then Charles V, eventually becoming a prison in the 19th century. It has been overseen by the Ministry of Cultural Heritage and open to the public since 2014.

Parks
VILLA COMUNALE
Piazza Plebiscito, 14; tel. 0883/481105; daily 7am-10pm Oct.-Mar., 7am-9pm Apr.-June, 7am-midnight July-Aug., 7am-11pm Sept.; free

This elevated seaside park garden near the harbor is lined by the white stone city walls of Trani. It includes views of the cathedral, 12th-century Church of Sant'Antonio, and the Adriatic Sea. The spacious shaded areas are equipped with walking paths and park benches, perfect for stretching your legs after a long drive or a day of sightseeing.

Synagogues of Trani

Trani once had one of the largest Jewish communities in Apulia, dating back to the Roman times and flourishing up until the early 1540s, by which time hundreds of Jews were forced to convert to Christianity. Scholars believe Jews may have originally come to Trani, a well-connected maritime port, fleeing persecution in Spain and France. Over the years, Trani's Jewish community was treated with varying degrees of tolerance as power changed hands in this part of Italy; it was Holy Roman Emperor Charles V who ordered that the practice of Judaism in Southern Italy come to an end in the 16th century.

Set between Trani's harbor and the cathedral, the former Giudecca, or Jewish quarter, was eventually renamed for San Donato, but it retains street names commemorating its Jewish past—Via La Giudea, Via Sinagoga. The legacy of Jewish wealth and influence can be seen in three former, and one current, synagogues throughout the city—these were also forcibly converted into Christian churches at various times throughout Trani's history. As recently as 2005, the 13th-century **Sinagoga de Scolanova** (Piazzetta Scola Nova; tel. 347/107-7486; www.comune.trani.bt.it) was returned to the Jewish community of Trani. You can also visit the **Synagogue Museum of Sant'Anna** (Ex Sinagoga e Chiesa di Sant'Anna, Via la Giudea, 24; tel. 0883/582470; www.fondazioneseca.it; 9:30am-1:30pm and 3:30pm-6:30pm Mon.-Fri.), which houses a collection of Jewish artifacts.

Food

★ IL VECCHIO E IL MARE

Via Tiepolo, Sottoportico Fornino; tel. 0883/197-0320; www.vecchioeilmare.it; 11:30am-midnight Tues.-Sun.; à la carte dishes €9-18

The Pugliese take aperitivo time quite seriously, and there's no better place in Trani to enjoy it than at this restaurant, whose name translates to "the old man and the sea." Dine al fresco on the terrace, situated on the southern side of the Porto di Trani. It's a chic beach restaurant with an energetic ambiance, string lights, nautical décor, cozy lounge areas, and coastal views, perfect for a casual meal of fried seafood or drinks at sunset. For lighter fare and takeaway food, order from their on-site outpost, La Piazzetta, which offers sandwiches, salads, fish tacos, hamburgers, and fast casual raw and fried seafood dishes from €8-14.

RISTORANTE CORTEINFIORE

Via Ognissanti, 18; tel. 0883/508402; www.corteinfiore.it; 12:30pm-2:15pm and 8pm-10:30pm Tues.-Sat., 12:30pm-2:15pm Sun.; €13-22

This exceptional fish restaurant is tucked away inside the former Palazzo Pignatelli-Filangeri near the tourist port and what was once Trani's Jewish quarter. Open since 2000, this small informal restaurant was built inside of the palace's stone-walled courtyard garden, a place where pomegranate, citrus fruit, and apricot trees spontaneously grow between the tables. Chef Massimiliano Quacquarelli's dishes feature unique ingredients such as finger limes, bergamot, langoustines, local cardoncelli mushrooms, sea urchin, mullet bottarga, and cicala mantis shellfish. They also have simply appointed rooms and suites available for overnight stays.

Information and Services

- **Info-point Trani:** Piazza Trieste, 8, Trani; tel. 375/557-5405; www.prolocotrani.it; 10:30am-1pm and 5pm-8pm daily

Getting There

From **Bari** or the airport, Trani is about a 30-minute (24-mi/38-km) drive north, following the **SS16** state road. Paid street **parking,** marked with the blue lines, is available in the city center, and metered parking lots are located at the Piazza Castello in front of the castle and Molo Santa Lucia in the port. **Trani** is 20 minutes (8 mi/13 km) south of **Barletta** by car, and 25 minutes east of **Andria** (9 mi/14 km).

TRANI TRAIN STATION
Piazza XX Settembre; www.trenitalia.com
Perhaps even easier than driving is taking the train from **Bari Centrale** (40 minutes; €3.40), which leaves every 30 minutes or so. Trani is also well-connected to **Barletta** (8 minutes; €1.10) and **Polignano a Mare** (1 hour 12 minutes; €6). It's only a 10-minute walk from the train station to the harbor.

Andria is unfortunately not as well connected to Trani, but it is possible to take the N579 bus run by **Flixbus** (tel. 080/975-2672; www.stpspa.it; 30 minutes; from €1).

BARLETTA
The name of the seaside town of Barletta makes it into the history books for the famous Disfida, or Challenge, of Barletta, in which Italian and French soldiers became embroiled in a duel after one of the French knights insulted the Italians. The Italian knights prevailed, and the fight was immortalized in a 19th-century book, *La disfida di Barletta.* Today, the city maintains a connection to this heritage with the nickname La Città della Disfida (City of the Challenge).

With a population of 94,000, Barletta is the largest of the Barletta-Andria-Trani provincial capital cities, and like its neighbor Trani to the south, it maintains its off-the-beaten-tourist-path vibe, albeit with a slightly bigger-city feel. Soft golden-sand beaches flank both sides of the town port to the north and south coasts, accessible on foot from the city center. Recognized as the Apulian City of Art in 2005, this charming town merits a visit, especially if traveling between Bari and Gargano to the north.

Sights
CASTELLO DI BARLETTA
Piazza Castello; tel. 0883/578621; www. barlettamusei.it; 10am-8pm daily; €6
Barletta's Norman castle is located within an urban garden area, which replaced the fortress's original moat. Though its slightly outside of the walled historic town, it's accessible on foot from the harbor or train station. It's one of the largest medieval castles in Italy. Most of the castle you see today was built around 1200 by the Swabians on an existing Norman fortification; the building is now home to the Barletta Museum and Art Gallery, housing masterpieces by the native 19th-century painter Giuseppe de Nittis.

COLOSSUS OF BARLETTA
Corso Vittorio Emanuele II, 20; www. ilcolossodibarletta.it; open 24 hours; free
This 16-foot-tall (5-m-tall) bronze statue, nearly three times larger than life, is located on Barletta's main avenue was discovered during excavations in 1231, though a legend also says that it washed up on the shore after a shipwreck. Dating from the late fourth or fifth century AD, it represents an armored Roman emperor, assumed to be Heraclius I, with his arm raised holding a cross that was added in the 15th century to make this classical figure more acceptable to the Christian leaders of the time.

Food
PASTICCERIA MOSÈ
Via Isidoro Alvisi, 68; tel. 0883/332545; www. pasticceriamose.net; 6am-9pm Thurs.-Tues.; €5
This historic family-run pastry shop and coffee bar has been open since 1968 and in the same location since 1993, known for its amazing black cherry panettone Christmas bread, which uses a mother-yeast starter that has been in the family for 25 years.

RISTORANTE BACCO
Piazza Marina, 30; tel. 0883/334616; www. ristorantebacco.it; 8:30pm-11pm Tues., 1pm-3pm and 8:30pm-11pm Wed.-Sat.; tasting menus €80 per person, à la carte dishes €18-30
This cozy, romantic restaurant in the historic center of the city of Barletta was awarded its first Michelin star in 2020. Refined dishes celebrate Apulian ingredients and feature Mediterranean flavors from the land and

sea including local pink shrimp, octopus, burrata, samphire sea beans, prickly pears, spiny lobster, and truffles.

Information and Services

- **Info-point BARLETTA:** Corso Giuseppe Garibaldi, 204; tel. 0883/331-331; www. viaggiareinpuglia.it; 8am-2pm Mon., 8am-2pm and 4pm-7pm Tues.-Fri.
- **Monsignor Raffaele Dimiccioli Hospital:** Viale Ippocrate, 15; tel. 0883/577111; www.aslbat.it; open 24 hours

Getting There

From **Trani,** Barletta is less than 20 minutes north (8 mi/14 km); driving from **Bari,** head north on the coastal **SS116** road for 50 minutes (40 mi/65 km) to reach the town center. From **Andria,** the 12-mile (20-km) drive takes 25 minutes.

Parking is readily available along the waterfront Lungomare Pietro Paolo Mennea, near the harbor and one block from the front of the entrance to the Castello di Barletta (Via Cavour, 83; open 24 hours).

BARLETTA TRAIN STATION

Piazza Francesco Conteduca; www.trenitalia.com
The city of Barletta can be reached with frequent service every 15 minutes from Bari Centrale (50 minutes; €4.50) and Trani (8 minutes; €1.10). Taxi services are available at the train station when you arrive in Barletta, but the walk to the port only takes about 20 minutes.

ANDRIA

The fertile farmland surrounding Andria, just 9 or so miles (15 km) inland from coastal Barletta and Trani, is dominated by the production of olive oil, with groves of olive trees stretching as far as the eye can see. It's also home to the country's famous,

gluttony-inducing burrata cheese. You can spend a beautiful afternoon here just driving through the countryside, perhaps finding an agriturismo, or farm stay, where you can stay the night. This area is also a great jumping-off point for the spectacular Castel del Monte, a 13th-century citadel perched on the green hills of Parco Nazionale dell'Alta Murgia.

Vineyard Visits and Wine Tasting

Vineyards in this region grow predominantly Nero di Troia, Primitivo, and Negroamaro grapes, and often offer food pairings along with wine tastings (or even a full lunch upon request). Many of the larger winemakers in the area also have their own masseria (farmhouse), with accommodations for guests set right among the vineyards. Reservations are highly recommended.

VIGNUOLO

Via Sosta S. Riccardo, 1, Andria; tel. 0883/542912; www.vignuolo.it; 8am-1pm and 3pm-6pm Mon.-Fri., 8am-1pm Sat.
This cantina is located in the city center of Andria, a 25-minute drive from Barletta or 20-minute drive from Trani, but the Vignuolo vineyards span across 500 acres (200 ha) near Castel del Monte. It was founded in 1959 and is known as "La Cantina di Andria," and winemakers here strive to promote the use of organically grown local grapes.

MIRVITA

Minervino Murge; tel. 334/563-1352; www.mirvita.eu; 9am-8pm daily
Founded in 1990, MIRVITA Opificium Arte Vino produces around 150,000 bottles per year in Minervino Murge, a 40-minute drive between Barletta or Andria. They take an avant-garde approach, combining wine, art, and the natural landscape on a 27-acre (11-ha) property. They have implemented programs to save water, naturally power their property, and ecologically treat wastewater on site, all to protect the biodiversity and preserve the terroir of their land.

1: Trani's port **2:** quiet street in Trani **3:** Biomasseria Lama di Luna, outside Andria **4:** Polignano a Mare's Spiaggia di Lama Monachile

Andria Olive Oil

As you drive through the central Puglia, endless rows of sage-colored olive trees are the common element of the landscape. The extra virgin olive oil that is pressed and extracted from the fruit is used abundantly in the cooking all throughout Southern Italy. The olive trees around Andria are mostly native Coratina olives, known for their robust vegetal flavor, with fruit-forward, freshly cut grass, and bitter almond notes. They are also very high in antioxidants, making them a healthy part of the Mediterranean diet.

Though many of the olive oil production facilities in the area aren't open to the public, you'll get opportunities to try Andria olive oil in shops, restaurants, and farm stays all over Puglia. Look for new-harvest extra virgin olive oil, which has been picked and pressed within the last year. The best way to taste it is in its raw state, without heating it up or using it for cooking; try it in a salad dressing, as a finishing touch to pasta and meat dishes, or drizzled over warm bread and focaccia.

The region around Andria is known for its olive groves.

FRANTOIO MURAGLIA
Via S. Candido, 83; tel. 0883/195-0959; www.frantoiomuraglia.it; showroom hours 9am-1:30pm and 3pm-6:30pm Mon.-Fri., 9am-noon Sat.
Frantoio Muraglia is a fifth-generation family-run olive oil producer with groves spanning across 100 acres (40 ha) in the uplands of the Murgia plateau. With a modern facility in the heart of Andria's town center, this is a great stop for those looking to learn more about extra virgin olive oil, purchase bottles to take home, or enjoy organized **tastings** (available for minimum 2 guests, Mon.-Fri. with reservation; 1-hour tastings €5, 90-minute visit with small food pairings €18, 2-hour visit with tastings and trip to artisanal ceramics workshop €25 per person).

Food
The famous **Burrata di Andria** is perhaps Puglia's most famous culinary export. This delectable I.G.P. stretched cow's milk cheese is stuffed with strands of more cheese and cream.

CASEIFICIO OLANDA
Via Santa Maria dei Miracoli, 150, Andria; tel. 0883/551810; www.caseificioolanda.it; 7am-2pm and 5:30pm-8:30pm Mon.-Wed. and Fri.-Sat., 7am-2pm Thurs.
Stop by this family-run cheese shop in the center of Andria to indulge in Puglia's most precious culinary treasure, Burrata di Andria.

IL TURACCIOLO
Piazza Vittorio Emanuele II, 4, Andria; tel. 388/199-8889; www.facebook.com/ilturacciolo; 8:45pm-11pm Mon.-Sat.; €6-12
Pop into Luciano Matera's Il Turacciolo, in the heart of Andria, for a glass of wine and a sampling of their innovative small plates. This charming wine bar was built in the former stables of a historic mansion in the town center. It features a local wine list and a limited menu of specialty cheese boards, cured meats, and seasonal dishes. Reservations are recommended, especially in the high season and on weekends.

★ ANTICHI SAPORI

Piazza Sant'Isodoro, 10, Montegrosso; tel.
0883/569529; www.pietrozito.it; 1pm-3pm Mon.,
1pm-3pm and 8pm-10:30pm Tues.-Fri., 1pm-2:30pm
Sat.; €30-45

Pietro Zito, a celebrated local restaurateur, farmer, and chef, shares Apulian flavors in his hometown village of Montegrosso, a 20-minute drive southwest of Andria. Antichi Sapori is a welcoming, upscale, farm-style trattoria focusing on authentic dishes, sourcing the region's best raw materials, housemade pastas, and seasonal produce harvested directly from the restaurant's biodynamic garden or from nearby farms. Zito wants his guests to feel at home and welcomes them to enter the kitchen and visit the garden. Reservations are highly recommended.

Accommodations
★ BIOMASSERIA LAMA DI LUNA

Contrada Lama di Luna, Località Montegrosso,
Andria; tel. 0883/569505; www.lamadiluna.com;
from €150

Time stands still here in the heart of olive oil country, particularly on this organically certified, 520-acre (210-ha) countryside property. The owner, local Pietro Petroni, purchased and began to restore the 18th-century masseria in 1991. Today, his self-sustaining estate is filled with 10,000 olive trees, almond groves, cherries, vineyards, and grain fields. The gorgeous, eco-friendly, warm earth-toned rooms are powered by solar panels and have been carefully appointed with vintage furniture, natural mattresses, and raw cotton sheets and towels. The farmhouse sits at 1,000 feet (300 m) above sea level, with panoramic views out over the olive groves from the outdoor pool or masseria restaurant, where you'll be treated to hearty home-cooked meals using organic vegetables grown on the grounds. Relax under the olive trees, browse through the private library, or cuddle up with a classic Italian movie in the cinema.

Information and Services

- **Info-point ANDRIA:** Piazza Vittorio Emanuele II, 16, Andria; tel. 088/329-0231; www.viaggiareinpuglia.it; 8:30am-1:30pm Mon.-Wed. and Fri., 8:30am-1:30pm and 3pm-6pm Thurs.

Getting There

The 7-mile (12-km) drive inland from Barletta to Andria takes around 25 minutes, or just over 20 minutes (8/13 km) from Trani. The drive north from Bari to Andria takes 45 minutes (27 mi/59 km).

There are no direct train connections between Andria and Bari or Trani, making a car a more sensible option. You can take the bus from Barletta Centrale (www.stpspa.it; 18 minutes; €1.10) or Trani (20 minutes; €1.20). The train station Piazza Bersaglieri d'Italia; www.trenitalia.com) is located a 15-minute walk from the city center.

★ CASTEL DEL MONTE

SS170; tel. 327/980-5551; www.facebook.com/
CastelDelMonte.PoloMusealePuglia; 9am-5pm
daily; €7, ages 18-25 €2, 45-minute guided tours
available in Italian for an additional €5, private
English-speaking group tours can be organized with
advanced notice for groups of 1-25 people for €95

Another castle constructed under the Holy Roman Emperor and King of Sicily Frederick II of Swabia, the 13th-century Castel del Monte is stunning and unique, with several features that set it apart from its numerous Swabian cousins lining Puglia's coast. Built in 1240, this castle towers over the olive grove-lined Alta Murgia National Park, a 30-minute drive from Andria's city center. Its distinct octagonal shape emerges abruptly from an 1,800-foot-high (540-m-high) green hill, one of the most recognizable castles in Italy, as it's featured on the European €0.01 coin. Also unique among castles constructed at the time, the Castle del Monte has no moat, leading some historians to think it was built as an imperial hunting lodge rather than for

PUGLIA AND THE BEST OF THE SOUTH

AROUND BARI

defensive purposes; it's also widely believed that Frederick II had a very prominent role in the design, now considered a masterpiece of medieval military architecture. Its 82-foot-high (25-m-high) walls and eight 85-foot-high (26-m-high) towers borrow elements from Roman, Norman, Arab, and Gothic architecture.

A visit to the castle will allow you to explore its marble-columned inner rooms, many of them trapezoidal; what may have been Europe's first flushing toilets; and panoramic views from the top of the fortress. Invest in the audio guide to get the most out of your visit. This UNESCO World Heritage Site is the most visited monument in Puglia, bringing in over 250,000 visitors per year. Reservations to visit the castle are highly recommended during spring and summer and can be set up via email or over the phone. Public parking is available at the Parcheggio Castel del Monte, 560 feet (170 m) from the castle.

From Andria, the 25-minute drive (11 mi/18 km) through the countryside follows SS170 southwest and on to Via Castel del Monte. From Trani, the 35-minute drive (20 mi/32 km) will follow SP238 to SP103 and on to SP234 in Andria. Continue with directions from Andria along SS170 following signs for Castel del Monte. From Barletta, take the SS170 toward Andria and continue on to the Castel del Monte (45 minutes; 22 mi/35 km). From Bari, take SP231 to SP63 in Ruvo di Puglia, exit toward Minervino and Castel del Monte, and continue on to the castle (1 hour; 35 mi/56 km).

The Castel del Monte rules over the vast **Parco Nazionale dell'Alta Murgia** (tel. 080/326-2268; www.parcoaltamurgia.gov.it), spread across a territory of 168,000 acres (68,000 ha). Located within the provinces of Bari and Barletta-Andria-Trani, the park protects ancient Roman roads, archaeological areas, golden limestone plateaus, and endless rolling hills popular for trekking and outdoor adventures, as well as celebrated honey and DOP olive oil producers. Visit the park website, or local visitor centers, for more information on choosing a hike and other points of interest in the park. The official **Alta Murgia National Park office** (Ufficio Parco Nazionale Alta Murgia; Via Firenze, 10) is located in Gravina in Puglia, on the western side of the park, an hour drive west of Bari (37 mi/60 km), or 30 minutes northwest of the city of Matera in Basilicata (19 mi/30 km).

Castel del Monte

POLIGNANO A MARE

The small, delightful town of Polignano a Mare, a little over 30 minutes south from the Apulian capital of Bari by car, is often referred to as the "pearl of the Adriatic Sea." The village dates back to the fourth century BC, when it was founded by the tyrant of Syracuse, Dionysius II, who originally named it Neapolis.

Almost as soon as you arrive in Polignano a Mare, you'll immediately spot one of the most recognizable beaches in all of Italy. The enticing Lama Monachile pebble beach cove and its 65-foot-high (20-m-high) limestone cliffs are located just below Piazza Giuseppe Verdi and the stone arched **Ponte Borbonico** bridge, within walking distance from the town's historic center. Set time aside to take a boat tour to the natural marine caves that characterize the coast of this region, walk through the winding streets of the old town, or enjoy a relaxing afternoon at the less crowded beach in the village of San Vito, just 10 minutes north.

Located in the center of Puglia's eastern coast, Polignano a Mare is easily to reach from the both the Bari International Airport and the Aeroporto del Salento in Brindisi, each being less than an hour's drive along the coastal highway, and it's not far from other Apulian highlights like Alberobello and Ostuni, making this an extremely popular destination. The town of less than 1,000 inhabitants depends mainly on tourism during the summer months. To avoid the rush, visit in spring or autumn, on the cusp of the busy season.

Sights
CENTRO STORICO

The charming backstreets of the historic center in Polignano a Mare are lined with whitewashed residences inhabited by locals and vacation rentals, cafés, shops, and lovely churches. The white cobblestone streets begin at the 16th-century **Porta Vecchia** city gate, also known as the Arco Marchesale, on Piazza Giuseppe Verdi, and wind toward the sea to the scenic lookout point from the stone cliffside known as **Bastinone Santo Stefano** (Via Porto, 83), where you can get a view of the Lama Monachile beach and crystal blue waters below.

DOMENICO MODUGNO STATUE
(Monumento a Domenico Modugno)
Lungomare Domenico Modugno; open 24 hours; free
If you find yourself blasting "Volare" from your Italian holiday playlist as you drive through olive groves en route to Puglia's best beaches, stop by the Domenico Modugno statue, a 3-minute walk north of the Lama Monachile, and pay your respects to the singer-songwriter of the hit song, "Nel blu dipinto di blu," in his hometown of Polignano a Mare.

Beaches
★ SPIAGGIA DI LAMA MONACHILE
Via S. Vito; tel. 080/425-2336; open 24 hours; free
By far the most popular and crowded beach along the Adriatic, possibly in all of Puglia, spectacular Lama Monachile still should not be missed, even if you're only checking it out from above from Ponte Borbonico bridge or the Bastione Santo Stefano. Lama Monachile and the nearby Grotta Piana, a flat, rectangular-shaped stone marine cave accessible from the water, make up what is easily the most recognizable beach in Puglia. Its pristine, turquoise waters are protected by dramatic limestone cliffs and golden-hued pebble shores.

Travelers with small children should plan on bringing water shoes, since access to the cove is not via a sandy beach, but via a shore covered with small stones and shells. You'll also need to climb down a stone staircase from the Ponte Borbonico to reach the beach. The beach itself is small, with more room in the water than there is to lay out a beach towel, and has no amenities, so you should bring everything you need for your day at the beach with you. That said, because of lack of shade and amenities, and the immense crowds July-August, Lama Monachile may be a better

Puglia's Wild North

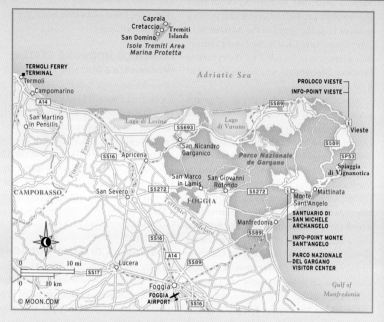

Most of the main sights in Puglia's northernmost province of Foggia are packed into the Gargano Promontory, protected by the expansive **Parco Nazionale del Gargano** (www.parcogargano.it), a 300,00-acre (120,000-ha) paradise of wetlands, beaches, forests, and coastal caves, including the marine protected area of the Tremiti Islands archipelago. This hikers paradise, complete with beach resort towns and breathtaking mountaintop villages, make the lesser-known Gargano Promontory the place local Pugliese go for an outdoor escape. Most travelers to Puglia find themselves tempted by charms farther south, but if you're contemplating a visit to this northern province, here are some of the highlights.

SANTUARIO DI SAN MICHELE ARCHANGELO

Via Reale Basilica, 127, Monte Sant'Angelo; tel. 0884/561150; www.santuariosanmichele.it; 7:30am-12:30pm and 2:30pm-7pm Mon.-Thurs., 7am-1pm and 2:30pm-8pm Sat.-Sun.

In addition to the panoramic views from the highest point of Gargano National Park, the main draw to the lovely hilltop town of Monte Sant'Angelo, an hour's drive east of the city of Foggia, is the Santuario di San Michele Arcangelo Roman Catholic sanctuary. This UNESCO World Heritage Site is known worldwide for the saints, emperors, popes, and kings who have made pilgrimages to pray at the cave altar of Archangel Michael since the Middle Ages.

SPIAGGIA DI VIGNANOTICA

Strada Provinciale 53, Vignanotica; tel. 088/4708806; open 24 hours; free

This dreamy and uncontaminated beach is set under the steep white limestone cliffs on the southern coast of the Gargano Promontory, about an hour's drive east of the city of Foggia. The Spiaggia di Vignanotica has options for free public beach access, as well as refreshment stands, restrooms, and umbrella rentals including the **Vignanotica Beach club** (tel. 0884/554005; 8am-7pm daily). The pebble beach is accessible only via the Sentiero Natura Mergoli-Vignanotica, a 2-mile (3-km) winding unpaved trail from the paid parking lot, Parcheggio Libertà (Località Vignanotica).

VIESTE

The town of Vieste is set on the easternmost part of the Gargano promontory, with a well-preserved medieval historic center and more than 20 beaches spread across 20 miles (30 km) of coastline. At the heart of the old town is the Romanesque **Cattedrale Basilica Santa Maria Assunta in Cielo** (Via Vescovado; www.turismovieste.it). It's also a departure point to the Tremiti Islands to the north. It's a 1.5-hour drive east of the city of Foggia.

TREMITI ISLANDS

www.isoletremiti.it

The Tremiti Islands archipelago, located 29 miles (46 km) from the northern coast of Puglia's Gargano Promontory, are composed of five precious islands: San Nicola, San Domino, Capraia, Cretaccio, and Pianosa, which look more Caribbean than Italian. The main reasons to visit these isolated gems are the secluded swimming spots, the wonderful snorkeling and diving opportunities, and the sense of almost complete solitude.

Reaching these islands is an adventure in itself. Most visitors opt for a **ferry** from Termoli (Molo Nord Est, Porto di Termoli; www.traghettilines.it), which is an hour-long drive from the city of Foggia (57 mi/91 km) or just under 2 hours from Vieste (80 mi/129 km), though ferries only run during the tourist season. Termoli can also be reached by train (www.trenitalia.it) from Foggia (45 minutes; €20.90). That said, flying in via **helicopter** from Foggia is exciting and surprisingly affordable (Alidaunia; tel. 0881/619696; www.alidaunia.it; Jan.-June and Sept.-Dec. €30/adult, €15/child age 2-11, €3/infant, June-Sept. €59/adult, €30/child age 2-11, €6/infant). You can also take off from Vieste (30 minutes) and Peschici (25 minutes). Once on the islands, there are no automobiles are allowed, but they're small enough to explore on foot.

LEARN MORE

There are information points and tourist visitor centers scattered throughout the Gargano Promontory and Gargano National Park; below is a select list. To let someone else do the planning for you, try a guided tour with **Garganonatour** (tel. 393/175-3151; www.garganonatour.it), who organizes unexpected adventures including walks in the woods, cave explorations, mountain biking, and night trekking programs.

- **Parco Nazionale del Gargano Visitor Center:** Via Sant'Antonio Abate, 121, Monte Sant'Angelo; tel. 0884/568911; www.parcogargano.it

- **Info-Point Monte Sant'Angelo:** Castello Monte Sant'Angelo; tel. 088/4562062; www.viaggiareinpuglia.it

- **Proloco Vieste:** Viale XXIV Maggio, 78; tel. 334/978-8871; www.prolocovieste.it; 6pm-8pm Mon.-Wed., 6pm-8pm Fri.-Sat.

- **Info-Point Vieste:** Piazza Kennedy, 13; tel. 088/4708806; www.viaggiareinpuglia.it

GETTING THERE

The province's capital, also named Foggia, is not a top destination in Puglia, but it does have its own airport, **Foggia Airport** (Viale degli Aviatori, 1; tel. 080/580-0200; www.aeroportidipuglia.it) for people who want to get to the Gargano as quickly as possible. If you're driving from elsewhere in Puglia (recommended), from Barletta to Foggia, the drive is about 1 hour (47 mi/75 km), and from Bari it's 1 hour 30 minutes (83 mi/134 km). In addition, the convenient Puglia Airbus shuttle service runs May-October from the airport in Bari to the center of Vieste.

place for a quick dip or to take in the view than for a full beach day—consider some of the other, less crowded nearby beach options if you want to spend a few hours lounging on the sand. Or, come at dawn to watch the sun rise over the Adriatic Sea, when you're likely to find the beach much less crowed.

LIDO CALA PAURA

Via S. Vito; tel. 330/508-963; open 24 hours; free
Take a 10-minute walk north along Via S. Vito away from the crowds of Lama Monachile to Cala Paura beach. This local destination has a free beach section as well as beach clubs (lidos) where you can rent umbrellas, lounge chairs (€6 each), and paddleboats. The smooth pebble beach has two coves and a small dock for fishing boats. Cala Paura has been recognized with the Blue Flag and 4 Sails awards for Italy's most beautiful and clean beaches.

SPIAGGIA SAN VITO

Via S. Vito; open 24 hours; free
This popular rocky beach is located in the port of San Vito, accessible by car with a 7-minute, 2-mile (3-km) drive north of Polignano a Mare's city center. What makes the beach truly spectacular is the presence of the monumental 10th-century **Abbazia di San Vito Martire** (tel. 080/425-2336) abbey just behind it, today inhabited by the religious order of the Marquises la Greca. At the pristine white umbrella-lined **Cala San Giovanni** beach club (Contrada S. Giovanni, 214/A; www.calasangiovanni.it), you can rent chairs and umbrellas on sandy beaches that are more accessible than the many pebble beaches on this coast. Along the Via S. Giovanni beach path, the **Spiaggia di Torre San Vito** offers an even more secluded beach and swimming area.

Tours
SOUTHERN VISIONS TRAVEL

Via Gandhi, 5; tel. 338/131-8026; www. southernvisionstravel.com; office hours 9am-7pm Mon.-Sat.; programs from €170 per person

When it comes to designing a culinary or cultural experience in Puglia, the friendly and resourceful travel experts at Southern Visions Travel are your golden ticket. Based in Polignano a Mare, founder Antonello Losito and his team can organize anything from cooking with locals in a country farmhouse to cheesemaker visits, active cycling food tours, private olive grove lunches, or luxurious villa rentals. Their thoughtful customer care and unique programming are sure to make for an unforgettable and truly authentic Apulian adventure. You won't find anyone more excited to share Puglia with you than Antonello and the Southern Visions crew.

CLIFF TOUR

Via S. Vito, 342; tel. 327/241-3669; www.clifftour. com; Apr.-Oct., office hours 9am-7pm daily; €29 per person, children 3-6 €20, children under 3 free
The 10-mile (16-km) coastline of Polignano a Mare is covered with nearly 40 hidden coves and caves, many of which are only accessible by boat. The bewitching rocky caves were naturally created through erosion by the powerful emerald sea over thousands of years. Ninety-minute excursions with Cliff Tour depart from the San Vito Marina, and can be scheduled between 10am-6pm. Their boat tours include cave excursions, a chance to stop and swim, and a light aperitivo onboard. Visiting Lama Monachile by boat is also a great opportunity to see the famous cove from a different angle.

Food
MINT CUCINA FRESCA

Via S. Benedetto, 32; tel. 080/424-1373; www. mintcucinafresca.com; 7pm-10pm Mon.-Wed., 12:30pm-2:30pm and 7pm-10pm Thurs.-Sat., 12:30pm-2:30pm Sun.; €16-27
Mint Cucina Fresca is a casual bistro in the heart of Polignano a Mare's historic town center with a warm, vibrant atmosphere and inviting energy. The menu includes beautifully plated seasonal dishes such as octopus with mountain herbs and black olive

Snacking by the Sea, Apulian-Style

On the border of the province of Bari and the Salentine peninsula, the coastal section of Savelletri (SP90 Strada Provinciale Torre Canne) offers a shoreline speckled with traditional seafood restaurants and beach bars serving up the typical shellfish specialty of the region, sea urchin. Savelletri can be reached with a 25-minute (15-mi/24-km) drive south of Polingano a Mare along the main SP90 state road.

This rocky coast is known for ricci di mare (hedgehogs of the sea, or sea urchin), shucked to order and available September-April, though it is better to eat them in moderation May-April, to give them time to reproduce. The Mediterranean sea urchin ranges in color from a deep orange to beige, carefully harvested before being opened with a knife or small scissor, served raw inside its shell, and then eaten with a small spoon or picked out with a piece of bread. There are at least 10 different bars and restaurants to choose from in Savelletri; here are some of the best places to grab a beachside snack:

- **Ristorante Albachiara** (tel. 339/536-5659; www.facebook.com/ristorantealbachiarasavelletri; 9am-11pm daily; sea urchin €0.80-1 each): A no frills, off-the-beaten-path stop for a glass of wine and as many ricci di mare (fresh-shucked sea urchin) as you can handle. There's an indoor dining space frequently used for celebratory family lunches such as christenings or anniversaries, and an outdoor area at the edge of the shore, equipped with plastic tables and chairs under palm frond tiki umbrellas.

- **Lido La Rotonda** (tel. 347/560-3024; 8am-midnight daily; sea urchin €0.80 each): For a mid-range alternative, also decked out with plastic tables and chairs, try La Rotonda for a tasting of specialties such as cozze ripiene e fritte (fried mussels served in their shells), local raw shellfish including sea urchin, pasta dishes, and grilled fish entrees. This beach club and swimming area checks all the boxes for a simple meal overlooking azure blue waters, with beach beds/umbrellas available to rent in summertime (€21).

- **La Locanda del Riccio** (tel. 389/025-8995; www.ricciodisavelletri.it; 9am-4pm Mon.-Tues. and Thurs., 10am-4pm and 7pm-11pm Fri.-Sun.; mains €12-20, sea urchin €0.80): At this moderately priced waterfront seafood restaurant, guests can enjoy a slow lunch sampling raw shellfish dishes featuring purple shrimp from Gallipoli, langoustines, sea truffles, furry local mussels, and sea urchin. The nautical indoor-outdoor dining space is a bit more upscale than the other restaurants in Savelletri.

or Apulian gazpacho made with tomatoes, burrata, anchovies, and locally made bread. Don't miss out on their vegan, vegetarian, and gluten-free options and creative libations. Mint's South Tyrolean and Brazilian owners truly bring this hidden corner of the old town to life.

THE SUPER MAGO DEL GELO MARIO CAMPANELLA

Piazza Giuseppe Garibaldi, 22; tel. 0804/240025; www.mariocampanellailsupermagodelgelo.it; 5:30am-1:30am Sun.-Fri., 5:30am-3am Sat.; €2
This legendary bar was founded in 1935 by Cavaliere Giuseppe Campanella, an almond distributor who started selling flavored shaved ice from a small carriage in town. His son Mario learned the secrets of gelato-making when he was only 7 years old, and took over the family business, transforming it to the coffee bar and ice cream parlor it is today. They are famous for their "caffe speciale," a specialty espresso drink made with fresh whipped cream, amaretto liquor, and the zest of a lemon for only €1.80. Just steps away from the beach, Super Mago del Gelo is a classic stop for an espresso or mulberry slushed ice granita in an atmosphere that the Italian food writer Katie Parla says "looks like it was designed by Scarface's interior decorator."

RISTORANTE DA TUCCINO

Contrada Santa Caterina, 69/F; tel. 080/424-1560; www.tuccino.it; 12:30pm-3:30pm and 8pm-11pm Tues.-Sun.; antipasti €8-25, pasta dishes €20, tasting menus €80-110 per person

Here you'll find generations of family history and fresh seafood in the classiest establishment around. The family patriarch and founder, Vito "Tuccino" Centrone, began selling mussels from a wooden shack at the beach in the 1960s and with his wife Tonetta's guidance turned it into a small restaurant serving grilled fish and pasta dishes. Years later, Ristorante Da Tuccino maintains the family legacy and has blossomed into a highly acclaimed upscale beachfront restaurant serving up some of Puglia's best seafood.

Accommodations

CALAPONTE HOTEL

Via S. Vito; tel. 080/424-0747; www.calapontehotel. com; from €82

Located near the Cala Ponte bay and the seaside hamlet of San Vito, a 10-minute drive north of Polignano a Mare town center, this four-star hotel is a great option for those looking for a more peaceful coastal refuge that's still accessibly to one of Puglia's most popular towns. Lovers of minimalistic design will appreciate their 58 spacious rooms, spa center, and beautiful garden pool.

RELAIS DEL SENATORE

Vico San Benedetto, 33; tel. 320/532-7250; www. relaisdelsenatore.it; from €89

In the heart of Polignano a Mare, just minutes from the famous Lama Monachile beach, this charming three-story bed-and-breakfast was built in a medieval tower, now equipped with an elevator and a stunning panoramic terrace overlooking the sea. Start and end your day with sea views and the calming sound of waves through your window in a stone-walled room updated with all the modern conveniences, including air-conditioning and heat, a mini bar with a refrigerator, television, and Wi-Fi.

BORGO EGNAZIA

Strada Comunale Egnazia, Savelletri; tel. 080/225-5000; www.borgoegnazia.com; from €392

Transport yourself into a Pugliese fairy tale, just outside the seaside village of Savelletri. Constructed in the traditional white and beige tuff stone of the area, Borgo Egnazia is a five-star hotel featuring 92 rooms, suites, and private houses dispersed throughout their own dreamy holiday village. Elegant whitewashed accommodations are equipped with stone bathtubs, comfortable sitting areas, chic Apulian décor, a security safe, Wi-Fi service, and minibar. Enjoy their six restaurants, Mediterranean-style gardens, indoor and outdoor pools, tennis courts, kids club, wellness center, and spa.

Information and Services

- **Info-Point turistico Polignano a Mare:** Via Martiri di Dogali, 2; tel. 080/425-2336; www.facebook.com/infopointpolignano; 9:30am-1:30pm and 3:30pm-8pm Tues.-Wed., 9am-8pm Thurs.-Mon.

Getting There and Around

Polignano a Mare is located 32 miles (51 km) south of the **Bari International Airport** and 44 miles (71 km) north from the **Aeroporto del Salento** in Brindisi. From **Bari,** take **SS16** south to the Polignano a Mare Sud exit, a 40-minute drive. From **Brindisi** (55 minutes), take **SS379** north and continue on.

A **taxi** from Bari would cost approximately €50-60. It's also possible to take a bus operated by **Flixbus** (tel. 807/1239-9123; www.flixbus.com) from Bari (35 minutes; from €5) or Brindisi (1 hour; from €7). Visitors arriving with their own boat or by yacht will dock in the **Cala Ponte** marina (Contrada Cala Ponte; tel. 080/424-78691; www.calaponte.com), located 1.7 miles (2.7 km) north of the town center.

Parking in the city center is restricted, meaning it's best to leave your car in a parking lot, in a paid metered parking spot marked with blue stripes, or, if you're staying overnight, check with your accommodation for recommendations on where to park. There is a large parking lot near the train station.

Tiny Polignano a Mare is best explored on foot, though you'll want your own car to explore the area around the town at your own pace.

POLIGNANO A MARE TRAIN STATION

Viale Trieste; www.trenitalia.com

Polignano a Mare's train station is an 8-minute walk (0.4 mi/0.6 km) south of the historic town center. From Bari, the ride is about 40 minutes (from €2); from Brindisi, 50 minutes (from €5).

★ GROTTE DI CASTELLANA

Piazza Franco Anelli, Castellana Grotte; tel. 080/499-8221; www.grottedicastellana.it; 9:30am-5pm Sun.-Fri., 9:30am-6pm Sat., closed Christmas and New Year's Day; €15

Just over 30 minutes inland from Monopoli, you'll find the Grotte di Castellana, one of Italy's natural wonders, the country's longest cave system and one of the most visited attractions in Puglia. Extending for almost 2 miles (3 km) and up to 400 feet (120 m) deep, the caves are estimated to be some 90-100 million years old. Mostly made of limestone, the caves are left behind from a time when Italy was mostly underwater, and the light-colored stone gives some caverns an eerie, almost bright white glow. Throughout the caves, the limestone has also been carved into spectacular formations, from icicle-thin stalactites to stalagmites that look almost like waterfalls, tinted by minerals to all the different colors of the rainbow.

There are two paths through the caves; one shorter, 0.6-mile (1-km) itinerary, and another 2-mile (3-km) itinerary that covers most of the caves' known area. The first cave is accessible for guests with wheelchairs using the elevator service, and with a reservation of at least 48 hours in advance a representative can assist guests with disabilities to discover the entire path. The only way to visit the caves is by booking a tour, which must be reserved in advance. It tends to be chilly in the caves, so remember to bring layers.

To reach the Grotte di Castellana from Monopoli, drive 25 minutes west on SP237, an 11-mile (18-km) drive. From Bari, it's a 28-mile (45-km), 40-minute drive southeast on the SS100, SS172, and SP32. Parking is available on site. Bus service through Ferrovie del Sud Est (www.fseonline.it) connects the nearby towns to the Via Grotte stop in front of the caves, departing from the bus terminal at Bari Centrale (1 hour 20 minutes; €2.90), Viale Europa in Martina Franca (55 minutes; €2.20), Via Alberobello in Locorotondo (45 minutes; €1.80), and Via Bari 15 in Alberobello (30 minutes; €1.40).

ALBEROBELLO

Arriving in Alberobello, the town best known for trulli, the quintessential Apulian agricultural huts, a sea of white and gray conical limestone houses is stacked up the sides of the old town's hills, like something out of a fairy tale. The just over 10,500 people who live here do not all actually live in trulli, but they have restored them to be used as souvenir shops, boutiques, guest accommodations, and even restaurants. Dating as far back as the mid-14th century (though the technique used to make them is even older, dating to prehistoric times), these unique stone huts shape the landscape of the town, just as much as the landscape shaped their development and construction.

These curious, conical stone huts are completely unique to this region, and this cultural legacy comes at a cost: Alberobello is on the itinerary of almost every visitor who passes through Puglia, meaning that the town is has become extremely touristy, and some trulli are now occupied by cheesy souvenir shops. That said, there are small, less visited treasures to discover, like the historic Trullo Church or farm-to-table restaurants. Try walking through the Rione Monti district, where the majority of the trulli are concentrated, at sunset, once the shops have closed and the streets quiet down, or early in the morning, before the tour buses arrive—the parking lots are usually full by 11am. The town can be explored in a half day, but a handful of exceptional restaurants and an overnight stay in a trulli house might make you want to spend at least one night here.

Sights
★ ZONA TRULLI RIONE MONTI
Via Monte Cucco; open 24 hours; free

The Zona Trulli, also called Rione Monti, covers a 37-acre (15-ha) area at the top of a hill, and is where the bulk of Alberobello's trulli—1,000 of the town's total of 1,500 stone huts—are concentrated. The conical, whitewashed trulli houses of Puglia's Itria Valley have become some of the most memorable and iconic sights in Southern Italy, and Alberobello boasts the highest concentration; its "trulli zone" has been recognized as a UNESCO World Heritage Site since 1996. Although the typical domed roof, internal alcove, neighboring garden, and space for collecting rainwater bear some similarities to other building designs around the Mediterranean, from ancient burial tombs in Greece to the dammusi houses of

the Sicilian island of Pantelleria, Alberobello is the only place in the world where so many houses still exist and have actually become a livable village.

The trulli were built in the mid-14th century using a prehistoric Mediterranean technique, which used dry stones without any mortar or cement. Oddly enough, this old method of construction was resurrected in this region as an attempt to avoid taxation—the technique's simplicity allowed builders to claim they were unstable and temporary structures and therefore didn't need to be taxed. This makes it all the more impressive that so many trulli are solid and intact today. You'll notice the limestone structures often have symbolic, esoteric markings painted on the rooftops, such as sunbursts or soaring eagles; it's unclear whether these markings were pagan or Christian emblems, or whether they were used to simply identify the houses, or as a kind of visible prayer.

Originally, the trulli were used as field huts, animal shelters, storage sheds, and housing for peasants and farmers. Today, they have been renovated to house shops, restaurants, and bed-and-breakfasts, evidence of how dependent this little village is on tourism. The best way to experience these

trulli houses of Alberobello

magical streets and alleys is just to wander, preferably early in the morning or late in the day to escape the crowds. The main streets of the Zona Trulli, running northeast-southwest off the larger, more modern Largo Martoletta, include Via Monte San Michele, Via Monte Nero, and Via Monte Pasubio. Off Via Monte Nero, keep an eye out for the double-domed house nicknamed **Trullo Siamese.** At the southern end of the historic area, you'll find the **Trullo Church,** or Chiesa a Trullo Parrocchia Sant'Antonio di Padova (Piazza Antonio Lippolis Canonico, 16; tel. 080/432-4416; www.santantonioalberobello. it; 7:30am-11pm daily; free), the only one of its kind, constructed in 1927 in accordance with the traditional whitewashed exterior and visible conical roof of the houses of the area. You might also consider a guided trulli tour, such as the Alberobello Express tour offered by **Charming Trulli** (Piazza Sacramento, 8; tel. 080/432-3829; www.charmingtrulli.com; €320 for 2 guests).

RIONE AIA PICCOLA

Cross north over the Largo Martoletta main road from Rione Monti into this quieter, far less visited trulli district, offering the same charming, hut-lined streets, albeit much more residential, just a quick walk away from the crowds. Here, you'll also find the **Belvedere Santa Lucia** (Via Contessa; open 24 hours; free), which offers a panoramic view of Rione Monti.

TRULLO SOVRANO

Piazza Sacramento, 10; tel. 080/432-6030; www. trullosovrano.eu; 10am-12:45pm and 3:30pm-6:30pm daily; €2

The only multi-story trullo in Alberobello, Trullo Sovrano was built in the 17th century and now houses a unique museum, dedicated to bringing to life how people would have lived in trulli before they became world-renowned tourist attractions. You'll see rooms authentically decorated as a bedroom and a kitchen with period furniture, plus an enjoyable souvenir shop.

Food

L'ARATRO

Via Monte S. Michele, 27; tel. 080/432-2789; www. ristorantearatro.it; noon-3pm and 7:30pm-10:30pm daily; mains €10-16

This traditional homestyle trattoria is built with passion and respect for the land in a renovated trullo from the 1400s. Multitasking chef-owner-sommelier Domenico Laera focuses on L'Arato's wine list and fills the menu with exceptional cured meats, regional cheeses, and local produce grown in the Alberobello area. Their strictly regional Apulian menu can be enjoyed in the rustic dining room or in the terrace room tucked between the brick conical rooftops of the neighboring trulli.

EVO RISTORANTE

Trullo Sovrano, Via Giovanni XXIII, 1; tel. 320/848-1230; www.evoristorante.com; 7pm-9pm Mon. and Thurs.-Fri., noon-2:30pm and 7pm-8:30pm Sat., noon-1:30pm Sun.; antipasti €6-12, mains €15, tasting menus available

Evo Ristorante was opened in 2015 by a group of young friends who aimed to bring together Apulian flavors and old-world hospitality, transforming peasant dishes with a modern approach. The restaurant is located in the Trullo Sovrano museum and often hosts temporary art exhibitions that change every season with the menu. Their ingredients come from their own organic vegetable garden and small local producers, and they offer exclusively Pugliese wines to pair with chef Gianvito Matarrese's seasonal modern fare. Dine indoors or outdoors in the gazebo, shaded by billowing white linens. Reservations are highly recommended.

★ TRATTORIA TERRA MADRE

Piazza Sacramento, 17; tel. 080/432-4326; www.trattoriaterramadre.it; 1pm-2:45pm and 7:15pm-9:45pm Tues.-Sun.; tasting menu €35

The simply prepared, mostly vegetarian dishes at Trattoria Terra Madre are made with love with ingredients from their restaurant garden and local farm property.

The Most Beautiful Villages of the Valle D'Itria

Ostuni, the White City

Puglia's olive grove and vineyard-lined Itria Valley spans across the provinces of Bari, Brindisi, and Taranto, from the mysterious Grotte di Castellana caves to Alberobello's clusters of trulli houses. Though these are some of the valley's best-known attractions, one of the joys of this region is discovering tiny, lost-in-time villages that are off the beaten path; below are a few of the prettiest.

For an excellent resource on the places named the Most Beautiful Villages in Italy, or Borghi piu belli d'Italia, visit www.borghipiubelliditalia.it. The best way to get to these more remote villages is in your own rental car, but that said, bus service between many of the cities and towns in this region of Puglia is provided by companies like **Flixbus** (www.flixbus.com) and **Ferrovie del Sud Est** (www.fseonline.it).

LOCOROTONDO

Whitewashed Locorotondo, set between Alberobello and Ostuni, is recognized as one of the most beautiful villages in Italy. Perched at the top of a hill, Locorotondo gets its name, "round place," from the circular layout of the walled historic center. The main sights here are the **Chiesa Madre di San Giorgio** (Piazza Fra Giuseppe Andrea Rodio; tel. 080/431-1236; 6:30am-12:30pm and 4pm-8pm daily; free), with a Renaissance facade built between 1769-1821, and the 1870 **Palazzo Morelli** (Via Morelli, 30; tel. 080/444-1100; free), notable for its traditional Baroque-style wrought iron balconies and lavishly ornamental entrance. This is also a winemaking area, featuring exclusively white grape varietals including Verdeca, Bianco d'Alessano, and Fiano, and is the only DOP in Puglia with a superiore designation for a white wine. To get here, it's an hour-long, 40-mile (70-km) drive south from Bari, and an hour-long, 40-mile (70-km) drive north from Brindisi.

Everything is made by hand, and each ingredient is treated like precious caviar, from the black chickpeas to the flowering broccoli, purple cabbages, and perfectly balanced hearty fava puree with bitter chicory greens.

Upon entering, there are two small indoor dining rooms, and down the stairs past the kitchen there is another indoor area overlooking the garden, where additional tables are placed in the summertime.

MARTINA FRANCA

Just a 10-minute, 4-mile (7-km) drive south of Locorotondo, Martina Franca is among the most charming villages of the Valle d'Itria, a bit larger and more vibrant than the other peaceful, white stone towns nearby. Martina Franca's masterpiece is the **Basilica di San Martino,** built from 1747-1785 on the site of a 10th-century Romanesque church with rococo and Baroque features. Stone walls and four city gates surround the centro storico, filled with restaurants, bars and cafés, spectacular piazzas, and Baroque architecture around each corner.

While here, make sure to try Capocollo di Martina Franca (referred to in the local dialect as "chépecùedde"), the local culinary delicacy, a cured and spiced pork salami smoked with local oak wood and aged for six months. Martina Franca is located just over an hour (45 mi/75 km) south of Bari, and one hour (40 mi/65 km) north of Brindisi.

CISTERNINO

Located between the sea and the stunning white stone towns of Locorotondo and Ostuni, this small town of 11,000 residents seems untouched by the centuries. Rightfully named one of Italy's most beautiful villages, Cisternino's highlights include the 12th-century **Torre Normanno Sveva** (Via San Quirico, 1; open 24 hours; free) and the **Chiesa di San Nicola di Patara** (Piazza Giuseppe Garibaldi; tel. 080/444-8026; 7am-8pm daily; free), the town's main church, built in the 14th century with impressive Roman ruins and frescoed interiors.

The town of Cisternino is also famous for braceria, a kind of barbecue where you first select the meat you want from the butcher's display case before your selected tray of goodies is grilled or cooked over a spit and brought out to the table. Check out **Zio Pietro** (Via Duca D'Aosta, 3; tel. 080/444-8300; www.ziopietro.it; 7:30pm-11pm Fri.-Sat., 12:30pm-3pm and 7:30pm-11pm Sun.; €20-30) for the town's most highly regarded braceria experience. Cisternino is located an hour (45 mi/75 km) from Bari and a 50-minute (35-mi/60-km) drive from Brindisi.

OSTUNI

The picturesque city of Ostuni was built on three limestone hills rising up to 755 feet (230 m) above sea level, completely surrounded by olive orchards. Inhabited since the Stone Age and rebuilt by the Greeks in the fourth century BC, Ostuni is known as the White City and is one of Puglia's most popular destinations. Be sure to walk all the way up the winding streets of the medieval center to the **Duomo** (Piazza Beato Giovanni Paolo II; tel. 0831/301177; 9am-noon and 3:30pm-7pm daily; free), enjoy a meal in town, and rest for a while in one of the city's charming piazzas.

Ostuni is easily reached by car from other towns in the Valle d'Itria including Martina Franca (30 minutes; 16 mi/25 km), Locorotondo (35 minutes, 16 mi/27 km), and Alberobello (45 minutes, 22 mi/36 km), as well as Bari (1 hour 10 minutes; 60 mi/100 km) and Brindisi (40 minutes; 25 mi/41 km). Parking is available outside the historic center (Via Salvatore Tommasi, 10). Ostuni can also be reached by train, but the station (Via Stazione in the Zona Sisri) is a 10-minute taxi ride (€20) from the city center. Direct train service to Ostuni is provided from Brindisi (25 minutes; €3), Bari Centrale (45 minutes; €6), and Lecce (1 hour; €6).

Accommodations
CHARMING TRULLI

Piazza Sacramento, 8; tel. 080/432-3829; www. charmingtrulli.com

Want to spend the night in a traditional trullo house? Charming Trulli is your connection to find the best guest houses, bed-and-breakfasts, or luxury renovated trulli and villas in the area. From a romantic getaway to a family trip, the trulli houses available both in the historic city center and in the surrounding countryside offer a range of amenities including a private villa with swimming pool and a charming house for two in the heart of Alberobello. Trulli rentals are equipped with vintage furnishings and come with bed linens, bath towels, an amenity set with soap, shampoo, and body wash. Select properties also include Wi-Fi service, heating, air-conditioning, television, and kitchen space. Two-night stays in the historic center, with a welcome dinner and breakfasts included, start at €320/couple.

LE ALCOVE

Piazza Re Ferdinando IV di Borbone, 7; tel. 080/432-3754; www.lealcove.it; €250

This five-star hotel is made up of individual trulli houses located next to one another in the historic center of Alberobello. As the name indicates, the beds are placed within the traditional alcove arch of the simply furnished trulli, making guests feel at home in a unique and authentic private house within a 10-minute walk to the Trullo Church. Amenities include daily breakfast, non-smoking rooms suitable for families or guests with disabilities, and Wi-Fi access, as well as spa services and airport transfers upon request.

Information and Services

- **Alberobello Tourist Info Office:** Via Monte Nero, 3; tel. 080/432-2060

Getting There and Around

From **Bari,** Alberobello can be reached within 1 hour by car (34 mi/55 km); from **Polignano a Mare,** Alberobello is 30 minutes (18 mi/29 km) away. From **Ostuni,** take the SS172 through Locorotondo to reach Alberobello in 40 minutes (22 mi/35 km). From **Brindisi** and the Airport of the Salento, drive north for 1 hour (48 mi/78 km).

Cars can be left in paid **parking** areas near the Zona Trulli or the Alberobello transit station; from the Parcheggio Alberobello Centro Storico lot (Via Monte S. Gabriele, 105), it's a 10-minute walk. Do note that the parking lots tend to fill up, especially during high season, and it's advised to arrive in Alberobello as early as possible. Expect to pay around €6 per day for parking. Once parked, it's easy to discover relatively compact Zona Trulli on foot.

Flixbus (www.flixbus.com) and **Ferrovie del Sud Est** (www.fseonline.it) offer bus service to Alberobello from Bari (1 hour 5 minutes; from €3).

ALBEROBELLO TRAIN STATION

Viale Margherita and Via Giuseppe Mazzini; www.trenitalia.com

Direct train service is provided between Alberobello and Locorotondo (13 minutes; €1.10) or service with transfers are available from Bari Centrale (1 hour 50 minutes; €5.10) and Brindisi (3 hours 35 minutes; €8.60). The 10-minute walk from the Alberobello train station to the Zona Trulli follows Via Giuseppe Garibaldi toward the town center (0.5 mi/800 m).

The Salento

The southern heel of Italy's boot is known as the Salento, an unspoiled region famous for its olive oil production, peaceful shores, lingering Greek history, and vibrant gastronomic appeal. No matter where you are on this long peninsula, you're never far from the beach, which lures travelers from around the world.

Breathtaking cities like Lecce, known as the "Florence of the South," and Gallipoli, Greek for "beautiful city," are considered among the loveliest places in Italy and remind us of the romantic side of travel in Puglia. But slowing down and traveling a bit off the beaten path can often lead to new

Brindisi and Salento's Airport

AEROPORTO DEL SALENTO
Contrada Baroncino; tel. 831/411-7406; www.aeroportidipuglia.it

Originally established as a military base in the 1920s, the Brindisi airport, also known as Aeroporto del Salento, is located 4 miles (6 km) from the provincial capital city of the same name. It's a good departure point for visitors who want to explore the southernmost part of Puglia; frequent flights include Rome Fiumicino (1 hour 10 minutes; €44), Palermo (1 hour 15 minutes; €25), and Milan Linate (1 hour 40 minutes; €31) as well as international connections to London (2 hours 50 minutes; from €34) and Paris Orly (2 hours 30 minutes; €34).

STOPOVER IN BRINDISI

Most visitors to the Aeroporto del Salento simply pick up their rental cars and head farther south, as Brindisi is more modern port town than tourist destination. But there are a few attractions to keep you occupied for a few hours. The boat-rudder-shaped, 177-foot (54-m) concrete **Monumento al Marinaio d'Italia** (Via Duce degli Abruzzi, Brindisi; tel. 0831523072; open 24 hours; free), dedicated to the fallen Italian sailors during World War I and II, has a panoramic view of the harbor from its marble observation deck, accessible via a 259-step interior spiral staircase. The **Chiesa di San Giovanni al Sepolcro** (Via S. Giovanni al Sepolcro, 5; www.comune.brindisi.it; 8am-9pm Fri.-Wed.; €3), a circular carparo-stone temple from the 10th century featuring Roman ruins and frescoed interiors, is hidden away on a small alleyway off Via Piertommaso Santabarbara.

Train service with Trenitalia (www.trenitalia.com) connects Brindisi's central station on Corso Umberto I with Ostuni (22 minutes; €3), Lecce (32 minutes; €3), and Bari Centrale (1 hour 15 minutes; €9). The historic center is reachable on foot from the station with a 10-minute walk (0.5 mi/800 m). Brindisi is also an embarkation point for guests traveling to Corfu (Grimaldi Lines; www.grimaldi-lines.com; 8 hours 30 minutes; €40) and Igoumenitsa, Greece (Grimaldi Lines; www.grimaldi-lines.com; 9 hours; €45), and Vlorë, Albania (Red Star Ferries; www.directferries.com; 7 hours 30 minutes; €42), via **ferry service,** departing from the ferry terminal in the Porto di Brindisi (E90, Pedagne), a 15-minute (4-mi/6-km) drive from the city center.

surprises and unforgettable experiences, from the breathtakingly beautiful Grotta della Poesia swimming hole to the narrow inlet of Acquaviva and the natural pools of Marina Serra. Every nook and cranny along the Adriatic Sea to the east and the Ionian Sea to the west has a hidden cove or secluded beach to explore.

The Salento is best enjoyed on a road trip, especially to explore the 200 miles (300 km) of coastline. Not only does this allow you to find beaches tucked out of the way into the boot's craggy shoreline, but for every well-known southern city, there are small towns not covered in the guidebooks where you might just find your own little slice of Italian paradise.

TOP EXPERIENCE

LECCE

Often referred to as the "Florence of the South," with art and architecture around every corner, the university town of Lecce is filled with precious monuments, 22 stunning churches, and wonderful restaurants. Founded by the Messapians, a tribe indigenous to the Salento, and conquered by the Romans in the third century BC, Lecce's layered history and thriving historic city center make it one of Puglia's most interesting and visited cities. After the fall of the Roman Empire, the city, like most of Southern Italy, was successively conquered by Norman, Byzantine, and Spanish regimes; it was the

Lecce

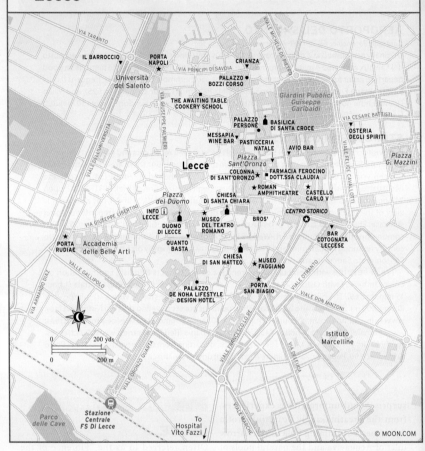

Spanish who left behind a treasure trove of 17th-century Baroque architecture so unique, it's been given its own name: Barocco Leccese, or Lecce Baroque. It's thought the unique golden "Lecce stone" commonly found in the area, singularly easy to work with, led to the extremely ornamented churches and public squares seen throughout the city.

You can count on a vibrant late-night vibe in Lecce, with a youthful population and a plethora of great pubs, wine bars, dance clubs, and music venues. The lively city streets and piazzas are often filled with people enjoying drinks until the sun comes up.

Any visitor to the Salento should spend at least one to two days in Lecce, exploring its second-century Roman amphitheater, Baroque cathedral, and celebrated pastry and coffee shops. Lecce is a great home base on a trip to the Salento, within a few hours of most of its major attractions. There's a great selection of hotels, restaurants, bars, and shopping, all within the historic center.

Sights
★ CENTRO STORICO

The white, Lecce stone streets of the historic center are lined with restaurants, stunning town squares, and plenty of churches to explore. The city was fortified with walls by order of Charles V, king of Spain and Holy Roman emperor, starting in the 16th century, including four monumental city gates, three of which border the historic city center. **Porta Rudiae,** a 6-minute walk east of the Piazza del Duomo, was built in the 1400s and reconstructed in 1708 with a statue of the patron Saint Oronzo on the top. Baroque **Porta San Biagio,** near the Chiesa di San Matteo and the Museo Faggiano, was built in the 18th-century, and the most impressive **Porto di Napoli** or Arco di Trionfo (a 10-minute walk from the Roman Amphitheatre and Piazza Saint Oronzo) was built in 1548. For a perfect day in Lecce, start in the main square, **Piazza Sant'Oronzo,** in view of the ancient Roman Amphitheatre, pick a direction, and start wandering. The centro storico is relatively compact, only a few square kilometers in size, but packed with impressive buildings, making it the perfect base for travelers who enjoy a daily stroll.

The **LeccEcclesiae** (www.chieselecce.it; €9) combination ticket gets you into to many main sights, including the Duomo, Chiesa di San Matteo, Chiesa di Santa Chiara, and the Basilica di Santa Croce. Tickets can be purchased online, through the LeccEcclesiae mobile app, or in person at ticket offices located in Piazza Duomo, at the Basilica di Santa Croce, or the Chiesa di San Matteo. Most of the sites have an individual entrance fee of €6, making the ticket a steal for those looking to deep dive into the centro storico.

MUSEO FAGGIANO

Via Ascanio Grandi, 56; tel. 0832/300528; www. museofaggiano.it; 9:30am-8pm daily; €5, ages 8-16 €3, children under 8 free

In 2001, Luciano Faggiano was renovating his private home, thinking of turning it into a trattoria, when he happened upon 2,000-year-old artifacts including pottery, coins, an emerald and gold bishop's ring, clay toys for children, and underground chambers used as a granary, burial site, and cisterns. Digging deeper, his family unearthed a series of medieval stones, a Messapian tomb, a Roman granary, and remnants of a Franciscan chapel with etchings of the Templar Knights. Since 2008, the Faggianos' family home—a former palace—has been transformed into Lecce's only independent museum. It's a unique chance to see so much of Lecce's history squeezed into one compact place.

CHIESA DI SAN MATTEO

Via dei Perroni, 29; tel. 0832/245035; www. sanmatteolecce.it; 9am-9pm daily; €6

Built between 1667-1700 under Luigi Pappacoda, the Catholic bishop of Lecce, this Baroque church of was designed by Achille Larducci di Salò but finished by Giuseppe Zimbalo, the architectural mastermind behind many of Lecce's most famous buildings. The rounded facade is a mixture of concave and convex Lecce stone, while the most notable aspects of the interior are likely its many marble altars, each more elaborate than the next.

CASTELLO CARLO V

Viale Felice Cavallotti; tel. 0832/246517; www. castellocarlov.it; 9am-9pm Mon.-Fri., 9:30am-9pm Sat.-Sun.; €5

In the 16th century, Holy Roman Emperor Charles V ordered the existing 12th-century Norman fortress in Lecce to be added onto and fortified, in response to continual attacks on this part of Italy from the Ottoman Empire. Today, the trapezoidal castle is the largest in Puglia. It houses a green central courtyard—a great place to stroll around to see the still-visible defensive battlements, arrow slits, and bastions—as well as Lecce's cultural center, making it the site of rotating exhibitions and events. Several halls, complete with stained glass and decorations fit for royalty, are open to visitors who pay a fee, as well as the castle's appropriately gloomy and dank basement level.

PIAZZA SANT'ORONZO

The principal square of Lecce, named for Saint Orontius, the venerated patron saint of the city, is an ideal meeting point and important historical landmark in the heart of the town center. Although the town celebrates this Roman Catholic saint's feast day on August 26, it might be one of the very few times during the year when tourists should steer clear, opting to avoid the crowds and beat the heat. The square features buildings ranging from the Middle Ages through the 19th century, lined with cafés and shops, all surrounding the partially excavated, sunken Roman Amphitheatre. Another sight that will surely catch your eye is the 95-foot-high (29-m-high) **Colonna di Sant'Oronzo,** a resurrected Roman column rebuilt in 1666 topped with a statue of the piazza's namesake saint on the southern side of the square. Mostly, Lecce's busiest square is a great place to get a drink overlooking Lecce's Roman Amphitheatre, contemplating Lecce's layered history.

ROMAN AMPHITHEATRE

Via XXV Luglio, 51; tel. 0805/285210; https://musei. puglia.beniculturali.it/musei/anfiteatro-romano-lecce/; open 24 hours; free

About one-third of Lecce's sunken Roman Amphitheatre is visible from the Piazza Sant'Oronzo. It was only discovered in 1929, when nearby buildings were being excavated in anticipation of new construction. The white limestone, Augustan-period amphitheater was once capable of hosting an audience of over 25,000 spectators for tragedy and comedy theater performances as well as brutal gladiatorial battles. Although it is not often open to the public, the Roman Amphitheatre can be viewed from above. Theatrical performances, concerts, and Christmas nativity scenes all take place right here in the ancient Roman Amphitheatre. Check out the nearby **Museo del Teatro Romano** (Via degli Ammirati;

tel. 0832/279196; 9:30am-1pm Mon.-Sat. by reservation only) for a different look into the city's Roman history, along with centuries-old archeological findings.

CHIESA DI SANTA CHIARA

Piazza Vittorio Emanuele II; 9am-9pm daily; €6

Just behind the Piazza Sant'Oronzo, this Baroque-style Catholic church dedicated to Santa Chiara of Assisi is one of Lecce's most beloved, with a unique convex facade and ornate altar. Built between 1429-1438 and then almost completely rebuilt in 1687 by the architect Giuseppe Cino, it is known for its octagonal, 3,200-square-foot (300-square-m) interior "false ceiling," constructed with papier-mâché made to look like wood.

DUOMO DI LECCE

Piazza del Duomo; tel. 0832/308557; www. cattedraledilecce.it; 9am-9pm daily; €6

The jewel of **Piazza del Duomo** (which in itself is a Baroque masterpiece), the most important of Lecce's many churches is also known as the Cattedrale Maria Santissima Assunta. Erected in 1144 in the traditional soft white-and-pink Lecce stone of the area, it has undergone major renovations three times over the centuries, most dramatically in the mid-17th century, when the striking 233-foot (71-m) bell tower was added and the facade got a facelift, both engineered by the mastermind architect responsible for many of Lecce's finest buildings, Guiseppe Zimbalo.

One of the cathedral's most distinct features is visible from the outside: It actually has two facades, one facing west and one facing north—both covered in fine Baroque stonework, with statues of saints, massive columns, and fanciful floral motifs, all in Lecce stone white. Inside, the ornateness continues: checkerboard marble floors, solid-looking marble-arched columns, and a patterned dark wooden ceiling decorated with carved, gilded crosses and flowers.

The location of Lecce's Duomo makes it all the more dramatic, with the almost closed

---

1: Lecce's Piazza del Duomo 2: a Pride flag on a Baroque facade in Lecce 3: the ornate facade of the Basilica di Santa Croce 4: Lecce's Baroque Duomo off **Piazza del Duomo** accessible only via a narrow entrance on its northern side, with the towering cathedral to the south, and the bell tower, bishops' palace, and seminary on either side. The homogeneity of the golden Baroque architecture, all made out of Lecce stone, makes it one of the most impressive piazzas in Italy. Climb to the top of the bell tower for views of the entire city, as well as the Adriatic coast.

BASILICA DI SANTA CROCE
Via Umberto I, 1; tel. 0832/241957; www. basilicasantacrocelecce.it; 9am-9pm daily; €6

If you thought Lecce's Duomo was ornate—just wait. The seemingly endless details of the stunning facade of the Basilica di Santa Croce look like something out of a Hieronymus Bosch painting. Lecce's architectural maestro Guiseppe Zimbalo was involved in the design of this basilica, though the building took longer than one lifetime to build, with construction starting in the mid-1500s and not complete until 1695. Though the interior is slightly more staid, it's still worth a look: tall marble columns topped with capitals carved into wedding-cake-like swirls and patterns, and a wide and airy central nave bathed in light.

With its its ornamental abundance and exuberant carvings of dancing cherubs, flowers, fruit, and fantastical animals—each a symbol it would take a history book to unravel—the basilica has become a landmark of Lecce's magnificent Baroque architecture.

Parks
GIARDINI PUBBLICI GIUSEPPE GARIBALDI
Via XXV Luglio, 42; tel. 0832/682111, 9am-10:30pm daily; free

Also known as Villa Comunale, this entirely fenced-in urban park and Italian garden, dedicated to Giuseppe Garibaldi, covers 366,000 square feet (34,000 square m) with tree-lined walking paths, park benches, the neoclassical La Flora pavilion, and various stone busts made by local artists. A perfect spot to relax in the shade during a long day of touring the city.

Cooking Classes
THE AWAITING TABLE COOKERY SCHOOL
Via Idomeneo, 41, Lecce; tel. 334/767-6970; www. awaitingtable.com; 10am-3pm and 6pm-10pm Mon.-Fri.; from €145 per person

The Awaiting Table Cookery School offers half-day, full-day, and weeklong courses at its kitchen in the historic city center of Lecce and educational hands-on wine, cooking, olive oil, and tomato sauce workshops at a castle near the town of Castro, just 2 miles (4 km) from the Adriatic Sea. Silvestro Silvestori, an Italian American AIS-trained sommelier and local culinary instructor, opened the doors of his cooking school in 2003 and has hosted students from nearly 60 different countries around the world. This highly acclaimed school focuses on the unique cultural and regional culinary traditions of the Salento by educating guests with in-depth discussions on foraging, agriculture, and the history and importance of winemaking in the south.

Vineyard Visits and Wine Tasting
CANTELE
SP365, Km 1, Guagnano; tel. 0832/705010; www. cantele.it; 9:30am-12:30pm and 3pm-5:30pm Mon.-Fri.

Founded by Giovanni Battista Cantele, this third-generation, sustainable family winery is nestled on a 120-acre (50-ha) property in the fertile Salice Salentino winemaking region, 30 minutes northwest of Lecce. The wines they produce are made from local grape varietals featuring Negroamaro, Primitivo, Susumaniello, and Fiano del Salento, with the addition of chardonnay. After a guided visit of the winery, guests are welcomed into **iSensi,** the Cantele family's state-of-the-art test kitchen and elegant tasting room, where they offer cooking classes and culinary demonstrations, olive oil tastings, and private dining including brunch, lunch, and dinner. Guests can choose between a tasting of the whole line of wines at the wine bar, a tasting of four wines enjoyed on the terrace with a classic Pugliese charcuterie board, or a traditional lunch paired with select wines. Reservations can be set up online in advance.

Food
AVIO BAR
Via XXV Luglio, 16; tel. 0832/304150; www.facebook.com/AvioBar; 7am-10pm daily

Avio is a classic stop in Lecce for a coffee break or breakfast. Try the town's specialty, caffè in ghiaccio. Also known as a caffè salentina or caffè leccese, this iced espresso served with a hefty glug of almond syrup is the perfect summer pick-me-up.

BAR COTOGNATA LECCESE
Via G. Marconi, 51; tel. 0832/302800; www.cotognataleccese.com; 6am-9:30pm daily; pastries €4

Located just down the street from the Castello Carlo V, this pastry shop and bar is known for its cotognata leccese, quince paste sweets. Stop by for a quick snack or pick something from the pastry-filled display case.

PASTICCERIA NATALE
Via Salvatore Trinchese, 7; tel. 0832/256060; www.natalepasticceria.it; 10am-12:30am daily; gelato €5

Fernando Natale and his wife Michelina's Pasticceria Natale is a historic gelateria and pastry shop, open since 1978. Throughout the year, they produce up to 50 flavors of gelato with special additions including fiorone made from the first figs of the summer, strawberry, stracciatella, almond, and dark chocolate with peperoncino.

CRIANZA
Via Principi di Savoia, 64; tel. 0832/091705; www.facebook.com/crianza.lecce; 12:15pm-3pm and 6:30pm-2am Thurs.-Tues.; €6-18

Just around the corner from the Palazzo Bozzi Corso hotel, Crianza is an indoor/outdoor wine bar serving up a spin on street food classics from the region along with juicy burgers, salads, bruschette, and taglieri charcuterie platters. Their rustic and cozy dining room decorated with wooden furniture and hanging Edison bulbs for optimal mood lighting makes you feel right at home. A great stop for a bottle of wine with friends, a casual night out, or quick lunch.

OSTERIA DEGLI SPIRITI
Via Cesare Battisti, 4; tel. 0832/246274; www.osteriadeglispiriti.it; 8pm-11:30pm Mon., 1pm-3:30pm and 8pm-11:30pm Tues.-Sat., 1pm-3:30pm Sun.; €25-45

At Osteria degli Spiriti, owners Tiziana and Piero focus on serving up traditional Salentine cuisine paired with Puglia's best wine and craft beer. The air-conditioned dining room with stone vaulted ceilings is elegant yet inviting. It's a great place to try simply prepared regional dishes such as orecchiette pasta or fava puree with chicory greens for an authentic dining experience in Lecce.

BROS'
Via degli Acaja, 2; tel. 0832/092601; www.brosrestaurant.it; noon-1pm and 8pm-9pm Wed.-Sat., noon-1pm Sun.; 8-course tasting menu €130 per person, 13 courses €200

For those looking for something more upscale than Puglia's traditional, homestyle restaurants, Michelin-starred BROS' is worth the splurge. Led by two young, up-and-coming chefs, Isabella Potì and Floriano Pellegrino, BROS' creative tasting menus and interesting wine list. Celebrating the local ingredients and special flavors of the region, satisfying dishes include head-spinning combinations like sea urchin with fermented ricotta or chilled soup with alphabet gummies for dessert. This intimate and casual restaurant is run by impeccably trained multilingual waitstaff, who devote their utmost attention to every guest.

Bars and Nightlife
★ QUANTO BASTA
Via Marco Basseo, 29; tel. 347/008-3176; www.facebook.com/quantobastalecce; 6pm-2am daily; €8

There's nothing wrong with a daily late-afternoon Aperol spritz in the piazza, but when it's time to treat yourself with a real-deal cocktail bar experience, head to Quanto Basta. The drinks are creative, the music is classic, and the place is always packed. Known as one of the best cocktail bars in the region, Quanto Basta went on to open a second location, **Cubi** (Via S. Giuseppe, 12, Maglie), just 35 minutes south of Lecce. A perfect stop to add to your southern Salento road-trip map.

MESSAPIA WINE BAR

Via Giacomo Matteotti, 6; tel. 328/656-2966; 11am-midnight daily

Located near the Basilica di Santa Croce, this wine bar offers indoor and outdoor tables with full-service dining as well as charcuterie platters of cured meats and cheeses to pair with their extensive wine list and craft beer selection. Stop in to enjoy a spritz aperitivo under an umbrella outside while people-watching and settle into a vacation-induced dolce vita.

IL BARROCCIO

Via Egidio Reale; www.barroccio.com; 6pm-2am daily; €10

Stop by this no-frills student haunt right across the road from the Porta Napoli city gates and the Università del Salento. Snag one of the very few seats inside near the bar or relax outside with a glass of wine and classic Apulian bar snacks like olives and taralli. Expect live music, cheap drinks, and a vibrant dive-bar ambiance. Start your night off just behind Il Barroccio with a pizza and some craft beer from La Succursale (Viale dell'Università, 15; tel. 391/497-7749; 6:30pm-10:30pm Tues.-Sun.).

Accommodations
PALAZZO DE NOHA
LIFESTYLE DESIGN HOTEL

Via Guglielmo Paladini, 47; tel. 0832/241466; www. palazzodenoha.it; from €110

This four-star design hotel features nine minimalistic rooms with high vaulted ceilings, friendly service, bougainvillea flowered gardens, and a rooftop pool. Located in the historic center of Lecce, between the Duomo cathedral and the central train station, an overnight at Palazzo de Noha can offer the convenience and comfort of exploring this magnificent city while still saving time to relax and catch some rays on the terrace.

PALAZZO PERSONÈ

Via Umberto I, 5; tel. 0832/279968; www. palazzopersone.it; from €182

In the heart of Lecce's historic city center, this former 15th-century synagogue has been transformed into an elegant six-room hotel. Named for Diego Personè, a local musician from the 17th century, the spacious nonsmoking rooms at Palazzo Personè feature vaulted wooden ceilings, stonework, and modern furnishings, each one equipped with air-conditioning and Wi-Fi.

PALAZZO BOZZI CORSO

Via Umberto I, 38; tel. 0832/156-0335; www. palazzobozzicorso.com; €440

This renovated 18th-century Baroque mansion features 10 luxurious, stylishly decorated rooms just a short walk from the Duomo. Their elegant accommodations feature high ceilings, extra-large beds, stucco walls, marble bathtubs, and parquet flooring. Amenities include Wi-Fi, complimentary minibar, and a smart television, and the Blue Room has its own in-suite sauna.

Information and Services

- **Info Lecce:** Piazza del Duomo, 2; tel. 0832/521877; www.infolecce.com

- **Poste Italiane:** Piazza Giuseppe Libertini, 5; tel. 0832/274221; www.poste.it; 8:20am-7:00pm Mon.-Fri., 8:20am-1:30pm Sat.

- **Ospedale Vito Fazzi:** Piazza Filippo Muratore, 1; tel. 0832/661111; open 24 hours

- **Farmacia Ferocino Dott.Ssa Claudia:**

Piazza Sant'Oronzo, 31; tel. 0832/309181; 8:30am-9pm daily

Getting There and Around
From the Salento Airport in **Brindisi,** Lecce can be reached with a 40-minute drive (31 mi/50 km), heading south on the main Brindisi-Lecce route, the **SS613.** From **Bari,** the 94-mile (151-km) route through Brindisi will take about 1 hour 30 minutes, heading south along the **SS379** to **SS16** and SS613. Paid **parking** lots are situated outside the historic center; convenient Oberdan Parking (Via G. Oberdan, 43; tel. 0832/454601; www.oberdanparking.it; €2/hour) is a 12-minute walk from the Carlo V Castle.

Using the Piazza Sant'Oronzo square as a central point, the city center of Lecce is an extremely walkable city. Most of the museums, restaurants, and city sites can be reached easily on foot within a span of 20 minutes.

STAZIONE CENTRALE FS DI LECCE
Piazzale Oronzo Massari; tel. 0832/303403; www. ferroviedellostato.it
The main train station is located just south of the city center, making it easily accessible for travelers without their own car. **Trenitalia** (www.trenitalia.it) services Lecce with regularly scheduled routes from Bari Centrale (1 hour 45 minutes; €12), Brindisi (30 minutes; €3), and Ostuni (1 hour; €6). Piazza Sant'Oronzo central square is within a 15-minute (0.6-mi/1-km) walk.

OTRANTO
This coastal city is in fact Italy's easternmost town, located on the strait where the Adriatic and Ionian seas meet. Once thought of as the Porta d'Oriente, or Gateway to the East, Otranto was originally founded as Hydrus by the Greeks and went on to become a thriving and integral Roman port. Due to its prime location, it was sought after by the Byzantines and the Normans, who also made their mark on the city's history. The historic center of Otranto features a landmark cathedral built in the 11th century and Frederick II's medieval Aragonese castle, which inspired Horace Walpole's 1764 Gothic novel *The Castle of Otranto.*

Note that Otranto does get overrun with tourists in the summertime, drawn to its convenient location and crystal, clear, Carribbean-style waters. Visit in the off-season, or escape the crowds at the 19th-century Punto Palascìa lighthouse at the eastern edge of the cape of Otranto for a sunrise view over the Adriatic.

Sights
CASTELLO ARAGONESE
Piazza Castello; tel. 0836/210094; www.comune.otranto.le.it; 10am-midnight daily; €12
Do make time to stop inside Otranto's Castello Aragonese, a 15th-century fortress and defensive stronghold whose chambers, frescoed chapel, halls, and tunnels are open to the public. Accessed by stairs leading to the drawbridge, Emperor Frederick II's reconstructed castle was designed with a pentagonal plan, surrounded by a moat and four main towers overlooking the sea. The castle hosts cultural and art exhibitions for the town.

DUOMO DI OTRANTO
Piazza Basilica, 1; tel. 0836/802720; www. terredotranto.it/cattedrale.php; 8am-noon and 3pm-7:45pm daily; free
The Cattedrale di Santa Maria Annunziata, commonly referred to as the Duomo of Otranto, is the city's main Romanesque cathedral, famous for its elaborate 12th-century floor mosaics stretching for 52 feet (16 m) from the entrance through the altar. This intricate, colorful mosaic carpet, executed by artists led by the monk Pantaleon, features depictions of the Tree of Life, circular designs signifying the 12 months of the year, and biblical stories of the Old Testament such as Noah's ark, Adam and Eve, the Tower of Babel, and Solomon and the Queen of Sheba. Commissioned by Count Roger I and consecrated in 1088, it was built on the

remains of a Messapian village, a Roman house, and Christian temple. Its stone facade is reminiscent of the cathedral of Bari with its Gothic-style rose cutout window above the main door and 12th-century bell tower. During the Ottoman siege of Otranto, when the cathedral was turned into a mosque, many ancient frescoes were destroyed, but thankfully the mosaics remained untouched.

FARO DI PUNTA PALASCIA

SP87; open 24 hours; free

Built in 1867, the white stone lighthouse on Otranto's Punta Palascia cape is the easternmost point on Italy's peninsula. The simple, white lighthouse also marks the point where the Ionian and Adriatic seas meet. It's a dramatic, windy, and popular local destination to view the first sunrise on New Year's Day. From the center of Otranto, the 3.6-mi (5.8-km), 15-minute drive along SP87 will lead you to an 8-minute walking path, where you can admire the 105-foot-high (32-m-high) lighthouse from the outside, along with the spectacular view.

Beaches

SPIAGGIA DEI GRADONI

Via Lungomare Kennedy

Just to the north of Otranto's centro storico, this beach is where you're likely to find the majority of the crowds in the summertime. Luckily, the beach is fairly large, with both private areas with umbrellas to rent and free public areas. The water itself is shallow, calm, and clear, making this a perfect place for a leisurely beach day.

Food

Compared to the rest of Puglia, Otranto's restaurants tend to be touristy and overpriced; either opt for a quick sandwich or traditional bite with an aperitivo, or try one of the highly recommended restaurants at your accommodation if you choose to stay in the area.

POSTOFISSO PUCCERIA AGRICOLA

Via Costantino, 15; tel. 083/680-2976; https:// postofisso.business.site; 11am-11pm daily; sandwiches €6

Stop by this adorable, tiny sandwich shop in the centro storico to try the local specialty puccia sandwich, a delectable concoction of pizza dough-style flatbread stuffed with anything from meatballs to local sardines.

L'ORTALE

Via Cenobio Basiliano, 14; tel. 0836/307-413; lortale. com; 10am-2am daily; small plates €3-15

This delightful wine bar and takeaway shop with a lovely terrace is the perfect place to sip an aperitivo with some traditional Apulian snacks, from a locally made cheese plate to bruschetta or local vegetables marinated in olive oil.

Accommodations

For those who want to spend the night or make Otranto a base for a few days of exploring, there are a few great hotels, plus luxury farm stay options available just outside of town.

HOTEL OTRANTO ALBERGO SAN GIUSEPPE

Via Ottocento Martiri, 60; tel. 0836/802298; www. hotelsangiuseppeotranto.it; €90

Located near the city center of Otranto, via a 5-minute walk along Via Nicola d'Otranto and Via Ottocento Martiri, the four-star Hotel San Giuseppe provides affordable stays year-round in a renovated 16th-century stone farmhouse featuring a wellness center, gym, indoor pool, steam room, and spa, with charming terraces and parking on-site. Simple rooms include amenities such as television and Wi-Fi, air-conditioning and heating, security safe, and a minibar.

1: dining on Otranto's city walls **2:** Otranto's Castello Aragonese **3:** Otranto's beach waterfront

HOTEL PALAZZO PAPALEO

Via Rondachi, 1; tel. 0836/802108; www.
hotelpalazzopapaleo.com; €111

Right in the center of Otranto's old town, steps away from the waterfront and a 3-minute walk from Castello Aragonese, the contemporary five-star Hotel Palazzo Papaleo offers spacious and bright rooms designed with marble and mosaics. Basic and Classic guest rooms include free Wi-Fi, flat-screen televisions, air-conditioning, and minibars. Guests of the hotel can dine on traditional Salentine cuisine on the terrace of the Papaleo Restaurant.

MASSERIA MONTELAURO

SP358, 14; tel. 0836/806203; www.
masseriamontelauro.it; from €145

A 5-minute drive out of town, the four-star Masseria Montelauro is a peaceful, restored 19th-century farmhouse offering in-house dining, a relaxing atmosphere, and countryside pool. The 29 guest rooms, ranging from classic to superior and junior suites, are built from local Lecce stone and equipped with air-conditioning, minibars, security safes, and televisions. Wi-Fi is available only in the common areas.

Information and Services

- **Info-Point Otranto Porto:** Via del Porto, Piazza dell'Umanità Migrante; tel. 083/6801436; www.viaggiareinpuglia.it

Getting There

The small historic center of Otranto is nestled around the harbor, following the waterfront promenade of Lungomare degli Eroi on to Via Corso Garibaldi and Via del Porto in the seaport.

Otranto is best reached by car, with a 1-hour drive (59 mi/95 km) south from the Aeroporto del Salento in **Brindisi.** From the city center of Lecce, the 35-minute drive (28 mi/45 km) follows along **SS16** north to Otranto. Visitors can park in the **Parcheggio**

Sant'Antonio (Via Papa Giovanni Paolo II, 21; €1.50/hour), a 7-minute walk to the Castello Aragonese.

OTRANTO TRAIN STATION

The Otranto transit station is located on Via Stazione, a 5-minute drive or 15-minute walk to the city center, with limited train and bus transfers provided by **Ferrovie del Sud Est** (www.fseonline.it). If you are traveling by public transit, you may find more bus options provided by **Flixbus** (tel. 807/1239-9123; www.flixbus.com) and **SAIS** (tel. 091/704-1211; https://saistrasporti.it) One of the more convenient bus routes runs from Via Don Bosco near the central train station in Lecce to Otranto (45 minutes; €2.90).

GALLIPOLI

Gallipoli is a historic port on Puglia's western coast whose Greek name, Kallípolis, translates to "beautiful city." A 16th-century bridge connects the modern part of the city to the old town center, surrounded by 14th-century limestone walls. Destroyed by the Vandals and the Goths, then rebuilt during the Byzantine era, it was once a thriving commercial center for Puglia's booming wine and olive oil commerce, making it closely connected to its Mediterranean neighbors—it is one of a few Apulian towns where Griko, and Italian-Greek dialect, is still spoken.

Though no longer quite the thriving port it once was, fishing boats here still unload regional specialties like Gallipoli's famous red shrimp in the early morning, and the fish market stalls gleam with farmed mussels, local oysters, ricci di mare (sea urchin), and hand-dug clams. Men sit on the docks mending their fishing nets near the port and hand-weave "nassa" fishing traps in small garages along the walled coast. In recent years, Gallipoli has become a popular destination for LGBT travelers and has been rated one of the top five Italian cities preferred by gay tourists, especially in summertime when crowds flock to beaches like nearby Baia Verde.

If you're looking for sandy beaches, good shopping, and lively restaurants and cafés, Gallipoli is a great destination in the Salento.

Sights
CASTELLO DEL GALLIPOLI
Rampa Castello; www.gallipolinelsalento.it; 4pm-10pm Tues.-Sun.; €7

This towering 14th-century castle is Gallipoli's most recognizable sight, standing guard over the entrance to the old town, just over the 16th-century **Ponte Papa Giovanni Paolo II** (also known as the Ponte Seicentesco). Its thick walls and five robust, circular towers attest to how often Gallipoli was sacked over the years, and ancient catapults and cannons used to defend the city are still visible on the castle's ramparts. The fifth, circular tower, known as **Il Rivellino,** juts out into the harbor, separate from the rest of the castle. It was built later, in the 16th century, a half-moon shape that made it possible to defend the city from attacking ships on all sides. Today, like many of the castles defending seaside towns throughout Puglia, the Castello it used as a cultural center to showcase art exhibitions and performances. Even when no performances are taking place, the view from the castle is wonderful.

BASILICA CATTEDRALE DI SANT'AGATA
Via Duomo, 1; tel. 0833/261987; www. cattedralegallipoli.it; free

The main duomo cathedral of Gallipoli was built in the 17th century, in the Byzantine and Renaissance styles. It's known for its unique and moving portrait of the martyrdom of Sant'Agata, its collection of frescoes, and intricate, golden-stone Baroque facade designed by Giuseppe Zimbalo, the architect behind many of Lecce's most beloved Baroque buildings.

FONTANA GRECA
Corso Roma; open 24 hours; free

The Fontana Greca is the oldest fountain in Italy, located near the bridge that connects the old town and urban city center. Thought to date back to the third century BC, the 16-foot-high (5-m-high) stone fountain situated in what is now known as the Piazza Fontana Greca is made up of two facades, with bas-reliefs including Latin inscriptions, depictions of the metamorphoses of Greek mythological figures, the insignia of Carlo III, and the Gallipoli coat of arms.

Beaches
SPIAGGIA DELLA PURITÀ
Riviera Sauro; open 24 hours; free

Within the historic center of Gallipoli, this free public beach on the northwestern side of the centro storico is a convenient stop for a dip. Though there are no amenities available on the beach itself, all the restaurants, coffee bars, and shops of Gallipoli Vecchia are right nearby. To get here, you'll have to park outside the historic center, on the other side of the Ponte Papa Giovanni Paolo II.

BAIA VERDE
Lungomare G. Galilei; Baia Verde; tel. 0833/262529; open 24 hours; free

The shallow sea at this 2-mile (3-km) stretch of beach surrounded by sand dunes is one of the Salento's top beaches, recognized by the Legambiente environmental association with their "3 Sail" award. The shore is lined with restaurants, bars, and night clubs, with both public beach space and lidos for renting umbrellas and lounge chairs for the day. In summertime, as well as during several scheduled events throughout the year, the wild club-style beach party **Samsara Beach** (Lungomare G. Galilei; Baia Verde; tel. 0833/261799; www. samsarabeach.it) hosts well-known DJs on these golden, sandy shores. Only a 10-minute (2-mi/4-km) drive south of Gallipoli's centro storico, Baia Verde is reachable in 6 minutes via bus 108 (Autoservizi Chiffi; tel. 347/3787870; www.chiffibus.it; every two hours 8:30am-8pm daily; €1 tickets available

☆ The Salento's Best Beaches and Swimming Holes

The 4-meter-deep (13-ft-deep) Grotta della Poesia is a great place for a dip.

Although a trip to the Salento can be enjoyed any time of the year, it truly comes alive during beach season. With hidden swimming holes, natural caves, and scattered soft sand beaches, any beach lover can easily find their ideal place along southern Puglia's 155-mile-long (250-km-long), varied coastline, looping around the heel of Italy's boot from the Adriatic Sea, which tends to be sandier, to the Ionian, with more rock and pebble beaches.

GROTTA DELLA POESIA

Strada Statale San Cataldo-Otranto; tel. 0832/832111; open 24 hours; free

The Cave of Poetry, whose name is actually derived from the Greek "posià," indicating fresh, potable water, is located 25 minutes north of Otranto. Part of the Roca Vecchia archaeological site (SP368; guided tours managed by VivArch; www.facebook.com/ReteVivArch; 4pm-8pm Sat.-Sun. June and Sept., 4pm-10pm Tues., Thurs., and Sat.-Sun. July-Aug.; €2), a 74-acre (30-ha) Bronze Age settlement, there is evidence this 13-foot-feep (4-m-deep) swimming hole and series of natural sea caves were used for cult practices as far back as the eighth century BC. Today, a swim in the breathtaking Grotta della Poesia is accessible for those brave enough to climb down the steep rocks to the pool. Even if you don't want to swim, it's worth a visit to admire the rocky coast. Parking is located on the opposite side of the SP368. Swimming is only recommended for adults without mobility issues. No amenities are available on site.

SPIAGGIA DI TORRE DELL'ORSO

SP366, Melendugno; open 24 hours; free

Torre dell'Orso is a popular destination for kayaking and stand-up paddle activities. It's a mix of

on the bus), which departs from Gallipoli's transit station in Piazza Giacomo Matteotti and arrives in Baia Verde at the Lido San Giovanni stop. Parking is available on Gran Viale al Mare, 40, near Baia Verde.

Shopping
BIJONDO GALLIPOLI

Via XXIV Maggio, 23/25; tel. 0833/183-4385; www. bijondo.com; 10am-2pm, and 5pm-midnight daily

Shop with a purpose. In this chic boutique,

free public beach space and private beach clubs providing all the amenities needed for a full beach day. Parking is available at the Parcheggio Mare Torre dell'Orso (Via Lenin, 68). Torre dell'Orso beach is located 25 minutes (10 mi/16 km) north of Otranto along SP366 and 35 minutes (17 mi/27 km) southeast of Lecce via SP1 and SP297.

SPIAGGIA DI PORTO BADISCO

Porto Badisco, Otranto; tel. 0836/801436; open 24 hours; free

Surrounded by prickly pears and fragrant myrtle bushes, the mixed sand and rocky beach of Porto Badisco is in a natural bay nestled between two rocky ridges, located 15 minutes (6 mi/10 km) south of Otranto. Paid parking is available at the Parcheggio Privato di Porto Badisco (SP87; 8am-8pm daily). There are restaurants and bars on SP87, along the 7-minute (1,800-ft/550-m) walk from the parking lot to the beach cove.

CALA DELL'ACQUAVIVA

Via Litoranea, Marina di Marittima; tel. 0833/777237; open 24 hours; free

A 30-minute drive (14 mi/22 km) south of Otranto along SP358, this small cove has a natural spring water source that keeps the water cool, even in summertime. There is no sand beach, only wild rocky terrain to climb onto and bask in the Apulian sunshine. Follow the short path down from the parking area, and pack everything you'll need for a beach day; there are no amenities available at the Cala dell'Acquaviva, apart from a tiny beach shack kiosk.

SPIAGGIA E PISCINA NATURALE DI MARINA SERRA

Via Carlo Mirabello, Tricase; tel. 0833/777237; open 24 hours; free

At this peaceful natural swimming pool surrounded by sea caves and rocky cliffs, the sea level is low and easy to reach, making it a good beach for small children. Pack your water shoes and plan on bringing plenty of water and a picnic lunch since there are no amenities available at the rocky pools, except for a pizzeria and restaurant near the parking lot. From Otranto, drive 45 minutes (28 mi/45 km) south along the coast; street parking along Via Carlo Mirabella fills up quickly in summer, so arrive early to get a spot or head 5 minutes south to the Parcheggio Marina Serra (Via Grotta Matrona) for more free parking.

SPIAGGIA DI PORTO SELVAGGIO

Parco Naturale Regionale Porto Selvaggio e Palude del Capitano, Loc. Porto Selvaggio, Nardò; tel. 0833/836928; open 24 hours; free

The 23-mile (37-km) sand beach in Porto Selvaggio is located 30 minutes (12 mi/20 km) from Gallipoli. Loved by naturalists and the LGBTQ community, the nature reserve is a top destination for its private surroundings, wild landscape, and nude beach portion near the Grotta del Cavallo cave on the northern side of the shore. The beach is accessible via a 20-minute walking path through the pine forest from the Parcheggio Porto Selvaggio (SP286; open 24 hours; free) public parking area. Visitors traveling by car from Lecce can arrive at Porta Selvaggio in 45 minutes (23 mi/37 km) via SS101.

you'll not only find beautiful handmade jewelry, summer caftans, and must-have rattan bags, but products made according to Verena and Luigi's principles of eco-sustainability.

NUGAE GALLERIA

Via Antonietta de Pace, 56; tel. 0833/263285; www.nugae.gallery; 10:30am-5:30pm Tues. and Thurs.-Sat., 10:30am-3:30pm Wed.

Hidden in the courtyard of a centuries-old

palace, owners Giulia and Vittoria pay homage to the Latin poet Gaius Valerius Catullus, with their own spin on his signature concept of nugae, which means "rubbish" or "stuff." Their small gallery-shop features handmade jewelry from a curated selection of artisans.

Food

GALLIPOLI MERCATO DEL PESCE

Riviera Cristoforo Colombo, 28; 7am-midnight daily; €5-20

At the gates of the old town, Gallipoli's outdoor fish market not only sells the fresh catch of the day from fishmonger stalls but also turns into a place to dine on Puglia's best local seafood in the evenings. At aperitivo time in early evening, stop by one of the stalls to taste mussels, clams, shellfish, oysters, and sea urchin with an aperitif cocktail or glass of wine.

LA PURITATE

Via Sant'Elia, 18; tel. 0833/264205; www. trattorialapuritate.it; 12:30pm-3pm and 7:45pm-11:30pm daily; mains €15-30

Come here for classic Italian hospitality in a well-maintained old-school seafood trattoria. Treat yourself to a long leisurely lunch or request a seat by the window for sunset views during an early dinner. Make sure to try the mixed antipasto starter including a bounty of oysters, fresh Mediterranean tuna, shrimp tartare, octopus, palamita fish cakes with celery, small totani squid, and breaded mussels. The staff is extremely efficient and friendly; the décor has most likely been left unchanged since they opened.

LA LAMPARA

Via Incrociata, 10/12; tel. 0833/261939; www. lalamparagallipoli.it; 11am-3:30pm and 7pm-11:30pm Thurs.-Tue.; €16-25

This fourth-generation family business runs a seafood restaurant as well as a stall in Gallipoli's historic fish market. Fishermen since the 1950s, this family knows fresh fish and wants to share their love of the sea with you, offering freshly cooked pasta and main-course dishes featuring ingredients from the fish market. The simply decorated white and blue indoor and outdoor dining spaces feature a hint of nautical style that will automatically put you in the mood for a seafood feast. Pay attention to fish that is priced by weight and ask your waiter for an estimate price before being surprised when the bill turns up after your plate has been wiped clean.

Accommodations

RELAIS CARLO V

Via Moline, 20; tel. 347/379-0631; https:// cortemoline.com; from €100

Relais Carlo V is located inside a 19th-century building in the newer part of Gallipoli, across the bridge from the centro storico. In the lobby, many of the historic details are intact, from the wooden shuttered windows to frescoes on the ceiling, but the rooms are warmly modern, painted in Mediterranean tones of orange and burnt umber. Accommodations are squeaky clean, many with unique layouts that include a lofted sleeping or living area and whirlpool tubs.

CORTE MOLINE

Via Moline, 20; tel. 347/379-0631; https:// cortemoline.com; from €120

Right in Gallipoli's old town, the five rooms of Corte Moline are decked out in minimalist yet still cozy and rustic décor, in shades of white and warm brown and gray. All guests receive access to a rooftop deck with views of the centro storico and the sea, and room rates include breakfast, air-conditioning, TV, and Wi-Fi.

Information and Services

- **Info-Point Gallipoli:** Via Antonietta De Pace, 86; tel. 083/3262529; www. viaggiareinpuglia.it

---

1: fresh-as-can-be seafood in Gallipoli's fish market
2: seafood pasta in Gallipoli's La Puritate
3: Gallipoli's castle

Museo Archeologico Nazionale di Taranto

Via Cavour, 10; tel. 099/453-2112; https://museotaranto.beniculturali.it; 8:30am-7:30pm Tues.-Sat., 9am-1pm and 3:30-7:30pm Sun.; €8

The port city of Taranto is one of the largest on the Ionian side of the Salento peninsula, with a long history as an important naval port—for the Greeks and Romans, and continuing even today, as Taranto now plays host to one of the outposts of the Italian navy. Mostly due to its status as a modern, industrial port city, Taranto is not thought of as a required stop for travelers to Puglia. But for archaeology buffs, one sight here definitely merits a visit: the excellent Museo Archeologico Nazionale di Taranto, or MARTA, the best of its kind in Puglia.

THE COLLECTIONS

With precious artifacts ranging from prehistory to the Middle Ages, this museum attests especially to Taranto's importance to Magna Graecia, the part of the Greek empire that covered much of Southern Italy and Sicily. The museum's extensive, modern rooms are chronologically organized, telling a compelling story about the region's history with important highlights including the terra cotta collection and the Ori di Taranto, a bedazzling collection of gold jewelry and art from the Hellenic era. History lovers who want to learn more about the archaeological underpinnings of this beautiful region of Puglia may find Taranto a worthwhile stop when heading back north from the beaches of the south.

OTHER SIGHTS

If you decide to make a stop in Taranto, there are plenty of other sights to stop by on your way to the archaeological museum. Like Gallipoli, Taranto is divided into two very distinct parts: the old city, clustered on a tiny island and guarded by a solid **castle** (Piazza Castello, 4; tel. 099/775-3438; www.castelloaragonesetaranto.com; 9am-2am daily; free), connected to the modern city by two bridges: the 19th-century stone **Ponte de Piedra,** and the 20th-century **Ponte Girevole** swing bridge.

GETTING THERE

Taranto is a 55-minute (44-mi/71-km) drive from Brindisi, 1-hour 15-minute (68-mi/110-km) drive from Lecce, and 1-hour 10-minute (53-mi/85-km) drive from Bari. Trains from **Taranto Train Station** (www.trenitalia.com), located 0.6 miles (1 km) north of Taranto's old town, arrive from and depart for destinations including Bari (1 hour 15 minutes; €8) and Brindisi (1 hour; €5).

Getting There and Around

From the **Brindisi** airport, Gallipoli is a 1-hour (53-mi/86-km) drive southwest; from **Lecce** it's a 35-minute (22-mi/39-km) drive. Gallipoli's centro storico is closed off to car traffic, but visitors can pay for street **parking** or leave their car in a lot in the modern part of the city near the bridge (approximately €1/hour), a 5-minute walk from the old town.

GALLIPOLI TRAIN STATION

Piazza Giacomo Matteotti; www.trenitalia.com

The Gallipoli train station is located in the new part of town, a 12-minute walk along Corso Roma to the bridge to the historic center. Train service connects Gallipoli with Lecce (1 hour 40 minutes; €4.30) and Brindisi (2 hours 50 minutes; €20.30), both departing every two hours.

Matera

In the heartland of the often-overlooked region of Basilicata just west of Puglia, the provincial capital city of Matera is one of the most fascinating cities in all of Italy, one of the oldest inhabited areas in the world, and a tourist destination on the rise. The area's natural limestone caves are what first drew Neolithic inhabitants more than 7,000 years ago, and over the millennia inhabitants expanded upon these subterranean dwellings—some little more than single-room caverns, others fully realized churches, adorned with precious ancient frescoes. In 1993, the city's cave dwellings and churches were named a UNESCO World Heritage site, bringing much-deserved attention to Matera, which only grew when the city was named the 2019 European Capital of Culture.

This is a huge turnaround given the state Matera was in less than a century ago. As recently as the 1950s, this was one of the poorest areas in Italy, with people living in the cave dwellings in squalid conditions. The residents of Matera were moved to newer dwellings, and today, the caves host shops and boutique accommodations. It's just an hour drive from Bari and 2 hours from Brindisi, and as a growing number of tourists have begun to discover Matera, they often couple it with a holiday tour through Puglia, or include it as a road-trip destination from Naples or the Amalfi Coast, a 3-hour drive away. This ancient city deserves at least two full days, giving you a chance to fall in love with Matera's labyrinthine alleyways and intoxicating history.

ORIENTATION AND PLANNING

It's useful to break the historic center of Matera down into two main districts, here called sassi, each one offering panoramic views of the other on the edge of a dramatic, limestone ravine, the **Gravina di Matera,** and divided by a drainage canal that once flowed into the ravine. In the **Sasso Caveoso,** to the south, you can see cave dwellings much as they were some 70 years ago, along with highlights such as Casa Noha, a highly recommend museum on the history of the city; and Casa Grotta, a recreation of a typical 19th-century cave dwelling. To the north, in the older part of town, the cave dwellings of **Sasso Barisano** have been much more redeveloped; this is where you will find most of the hotels, shops, restaurants, and bars. In between is the Apulian-Romanesque Cattedrale di Maria Santissima and its Piazza Duomo, a useful landmark in the often hard to navigate, steep, and winding streets of this cliffside city. You'll find a much more modern side of Matera to the west, across main thoroughfare **Via Lucana** (though this area still boasts the 16th-century Castello Tramontano). And farther east, across the ravine, the **Parco Regionale della Murgia Materana** awaits, with 15,150 acres (6,128 hectares) of greenery in addition to some of the best-preserved cave churches.

Walking Tours

The twisty, windy streets of Matera can be hard to navigate, and are so full of history that one of the best ways to experience them is to book a tour with an experienced local guide. The companies mentioned below offer a range of experiences, from walking tours to guided bike rides, most of which last 2-3 hours. You can also choose excursions to the nearby Parco Regionale della Murgia Materana or other parks and sights around Matera.

- **Martuilli Viaggi:** Via Lucana, 15; tel. 0835/334543; www.martulliviaggi.com; from €15 per person
- **Materavventura:** tel. 328/4599470; http://materavventura.it; reservations required; from €25 per person
- **Sassi di Matera:** tel. 328/2908464; www.sassidimatera.it; €30 per person, children under 9 free

Matera

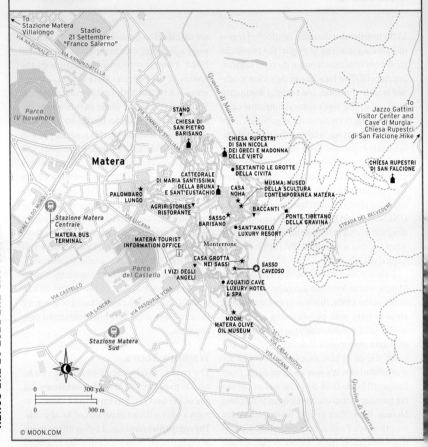

To Stazione Matera Villalongo
Stadio 21 Settembre-"Franco Salerno"
VIA NAZIONALE
VIA ANNUNZIATELLA

Parco IV Novembre

VIA TOMMASO STIGLIANI

Matera

STANO
CHIESA DI SAN PIETRO BARISANO

CHIESA RUPESTRI DI SAN NICOLA DEI GRECI E MADONNA DELLE VIRTÙ

To Jazzo Gattini Visitor Center and Cave di Murgia-Chiesa Rupestri di San Falcione Hike

CHIESA RUPESTRI DI SAN FALCIONE

SEXTANTIO LE GROTTE DELLA CIVITA

CATTEDRALE DI MARIA SANTISSIMA DELLA BRUNA E SANT'EUSTACHIO

CASA NOHA

MUSMA: MUSEO DELLA SCULTURA CONTEMPORANEA MATERA

PALOMBARO LUNGO

VIALE ALDO MORO

AGRIRISTORIES RISTORANTE

BACCANTI

PONTE TIBETANO DELLA GRAVINA

STRADA DEL BELVEDERE

SASSO BARISANO

VIA LUCANA

Stazione Matera Centrale

MATERA BUS TERMINAL

SANT'ANGELO LUXURY RESORT

MATERA TOURIST INFORMATION OFFICE

Monterrone

CASA GROTTA NEI SASSI

SASSO CAVEOSO

VIA CASTELLO

Parco del Castello

I VIZI DEGLI ANGELI

VIA LANERA

VIA PASQUALE VENA

AQUATIO CAVE LUXURY HOTEL & SPA

Gravina di Matera

VIA CASALNUOVO

VIA LUCANA

MOOM: MATERA OLIVE OIL MUSEUM

Stazione Matera Sud

0   300 yds
0   300 m

© MOON.COM

SIGHTS

TOP EXPERIENCE

★ Sasso Caveoso

Matera is one of those towns, like Venice, where nearly every single street is worthy of a photo-op, rewarding aimless wandering. A good place to start your Sasso Caveoso stroll is in Piazza Duomo, which offers a beautiful view of the cave dwelling district across the ravine. You'll descend into the Sasso Caveoso via stairs and steep, narrow streets, finding layer after layer of cave dwellings stacked up on one another; sometimes, you'll find the road you're walking on is in fact the roof of a cave dwelling below. Many of the sassi are no longer inhabited and are open to visitors to enter in freely, peek around, and imagine what life may have been like for inhabitants of Matera centuries ago.

CASA NOHA

Recinto Cavone, 9; tel. 0835/335452; www.
fondoambiente.it/luoghi/casa-noha; 10am-5pm
Thurs.-Mon.; €6, FAI members free

Casa Noha is a great place for travelers to Matera to start their visit, giving essential context on the history of this ancient city, from prehistoric times up to the current day with an immersive video experience. Itself set in a carefully restored and preserved tuff stone cave dwelling, donated to the Fondo Ambiente Italiano national trust in 2004, the information this museum provides, especially on the difficult living conditions in 20th-century Matera, will illuminate your journey through the city's sassi neighborhoods.

MUSMA: MUSEO DELLA SCULTURA CONTEMPORANEA MATERA

Via S. Giacomo, Sasso Caveoso; tel. 366/935-7768; www.musma.it; 10am-6pm Tues.-Sun. Oct.-Mar., 10am-8pm Tues.-Sun. Apr.-Sept.; €7

Take a break from walking through the hillside, sassi-lined streets and spend a few hours wandering through Matera's Museum of Contemporary Sculpture, one of the only museums of its kind set in a cave. Covering three floors of the 17th-century Palazzo Pomarici, MUSMA displays a plentiful collection of sculptures as well as ceramics, jewels, monographs, and photographs.

CASA GROTTA NEI SASSI

Vico Solitario, 11; tel. 0835/310118; www.casagrotta.it; 9:30am-8pm daily; €3

Carve out a half hour during your trip to Matera to visit the Casa Grotta, a preserved cave home in the Sasso Caveoso district, for a glimpse into how inhabitants of the Sassi lived up until 1956. In this particular house, a family of 11 people lived together, without drinking water or toilets. The cave dwelling is equipped with period furniture, giving amazing insight into the family's daily life in the 20th century. The visit is enhanced by multilingual audio guides providing additional context.

MOOM: MATERA OLIVE OIL MUSEUM

Vico I Casalnuovo, 3; tel. 380/701-5042; www.moom.bio; 10am-1pm and 4pm-6pm Sun. with reservation; €5, ages 6-17 €4, children under 6 free

The MOOM olive oil museum is inside an ancient underground mill in the Sasso Caveoso district, where a 30-minute guided tour includes a full explanation of the oil production and winemaking systems. Open to visitors only with a reservation.

Sasso Barisano
CATTEDRALE DI MARIA SANTISSIMA DELLA BRUNA E SANT'EUSTACHIO

Piazza Duomo; tel. 0835/332908; www.chiesacattolica.it; 10am-7pm daily; €1, €2 audio guide rental

The principal cathedral in Matera is located at the highest point of the city, which divides the two Sassi districts and offers spectacular views from the Piazza Duomo square. Dedicated to Matera's patroness saint, the Madonna della Bruna, as well as Saint Eustace, this Roman Catholic cathedral was built in the 13th century in the Apulian Romanesque style. Its main features include the rose window on the western facade, the Porta di Suso archway through the medieval walls, ancient frescoed crypts visible from above, Baroque interiors from the 17th and 18th centuries, a 16th-century nativity scene, frescoes, and gilded stuccoes.

PALOMBARO LUNGO

Piazza Vittorio Veneto, 34; tel. 339/363-8332; www.diocesimaterairsina.it; 10am-1pm and 3pm-6pm daily; €3 entrance fee

This subterranean, 3,000-year-old water reservoir is the largest cistern in the city of Matera. Hidden beneath the piazzas, this natural spring and rainwater collection system was the main water source for the area. The Palombaro Lungo was only rediscovered in 1991 during renovations of the square; it is now a popular tourist attraction and considered part of Matera's UNESCO World Heritage Site. The underground cistern is best explored with a reservation that includes 20-minute guided tours in English, offered periodically throughout the day.

Matera's Chiese Rupestri

Another reason (of many) that Matera was given UNESCO World Heritage status is its many cave churches, or chiese rupestri, ancient places of worship built on or even carved right into the limestone walls of Matera's hills and ravine. They're often decorated with spectacular, peeling frescoes and evocative, crumbling columns. As many as 150 cave churches can be found throughout the city, scattered in the sassi districts and on the slopes of the Parco Regionale della Murgia Materana. A great way to be guided to some of the best of these churches is via a walking tour, which will provide more context on these centuries-old churches, but below are some of the most notable to seek out while wandering Matera.

CHIESA DI SAN PIETRO BARISANO

Via S. Pietro Barisano; www.sassidimatera.net; 10am-7pm daily; €3.50

The largest rupestrian rock church in the city of Matera is located in the Sasso Barisano district, a 10-minute walk from the Duomo. Through excavations, it has been discovered that the foundation dates back to the 12th century, but it has undergone renovations as recently as the 18th century. The tuff stone exterior has three portals, a unique four-lobed rose window, and freestanding bell tower. Inside are ancient frescoes, sculptures of saints, six altars, an excavated ossuary filled with bones, and the underground tombs where important religious figures were laid to rest.

CHIESA RUPESTRI DI SAN NICOLA DEI GRECI E MADONNA DELLE VIRTÙ

Via Madonna delle Virtù; tel. 377/444-8885; www.caveheritage.it; 10am-7pm daily; €3.50

This ancient rock church and its adjacent crypt, digging into the limestone rock cliffs between the two Sassi districts, were built in the 10th and 11th centuries, later decorated with frescoes in the 14th century. Today, the crypt houses archaeological findings from the Iron Age.

CHIESA RUPESTRI DI SAN FALCIONE

Contrada Murgia Timone; tel. 0835/332262; www.ceamatera.it; open 24 hours; €1 guided tours are organized by CEA with a reservation

The abandoned site of this rock church dates to the 9th-10th centuries, attributed to the first Italian-Greek monastic community that settled in this area. It includes burial sites, tombs, a chapel, and two frescoes depicting San Nicola. Outside are the recognizable walls of what was once a sheep pen; there's also evidence that the church was once used as an apiary to produce honey and wax for candles, a common tradition in the area.

Vicinity of Matera
CRIPTA DEL PECCATO ORIGINALE

Contrada Pietrapenta; tel. 320/334-5323; www.criptadelpeccatooriginale.it; 9:30am-6:30pm Tues.-Sun.; €10

Discovered only in 1963, the Crypt of the Original Sin is home to one of the region's most impressive collections of 8th-9th-century frescoes. This rock church commonly referred to as the "Sistine Chapel of Rupestrian Art" was a cult site of a nearby Benedictine monastery during the Lombard period, and the monks decorated it with colorful frescoes of flowers, the Archangels, the Virgin Mary, the Apostles, and depictions of creation and the original sin. Guided tours and pre-reserved admission are offered several times a day, except in December.

SPORTS AND RECREATION
Hiking

The **Parco Regionale della Murgia**

1: the landscape around Matera 2: the city of Matera, a UNESCO World Heritage Site

Materana (tel. 0835/336166; www. parcomurgia.it; open 24 hours; free), covering an area of over 15,000 acres (6,000 ha), lies in the hills east of Matera, across the ravine where many of Matera's cave dwellings are perched. Here, you'll find prehistoric sites, dramatic cliffs and caves, lush green valleys, chiese rupestri (rock churches), and farming villages dating back to the Neolithic, Bronze, and Iron ages. Hike up to the **Chiesa Rupestri di San Falcione,** which offers a stunning view of Matera below, or join a guided trekking experience with Cosimo Santeramo (tel. 329/7917056; www.visitaisassidimatera.it; private tours from €130 for 2 hours 30 minutes covering approximately 3 mi/5 km, group rates from €20 per person) on foot, by donkey, or on horseback.

The **Centro Visite Jazzo Gattini** (Contrada Murgia Timone; tel. 0835/332262; www.ceamatera.it; 9:30am-4:30pm daily Nov.-Mar., 9:30am-6:30pm daily Apr.-June and Sept.-Oct., 9:30am-11:30pm daily July-Aug.) offers additional tourist information, exhibitions, and a small bookstore. It can be reached by car from Matera in 5 minutes along the SS7 state road at kilometer 583, following the signs toward the CEA/Visitor Center, or on foot, by crossing the **Ponte Tibetano della Gravina** pedestrian bridge (Via Madonna delle Virtù, 27), about a mile and a half walk. Or check out Matera's visitor center for more information on the park.

Note that Matera does become very hot in the summer, and it's not recommended to venture out into the park in the middle of the day. Regardless of when you go, be sure to bring sunscreen, a hat, and plenty of water.

CAVE DI MURGIA - CHIESA RUPESTRI DI SAN FALCIONE HIKE
Distance: *2.6 mi (4.2 km) loop*
Time: *1 hour 30 minutes*
Trailhead: *Jazzo Gattini visitor center (Contrada Murgia Timone; tel. 0835/332262)*
Information and Maps: *Matera Tourist Information Center*

This moderate hiking trail, with an elevation gain of 305 feet (93 m), includes suggestive views of Matera heading toward the rock church chapel of San Falcione. From the trailhead, guests can stop into the visitor center at the renovated 19th-century Jazzo Gattini sheepfold and enjoy the panoramic lookout point at Contrada Murgia Timone. The rugged terrain leads guests through fields, fortified farms, and unique rock formations, offering a wide range of flora and fauna native to the park.

FESTIVALS AND EVENTS
FESTA DELLA BRUNA
www.festadellabruna.it; July 2; free
The Madonna della Bruna is the patroness saint and protector of the city of Matera. Some say "della Bruna" derives from the early medieval term brùnja meaning armor, while others believe it refers to the olive skin tone of the Byzantine-style fresco depicting the *Madonna della Bruna and Child,* located inside the Duomo. Celebrated annually on July 2 since at least 1389, festivities in her honor include the Procession of the Shepherds, a parade of marching bands and armored knights, flower-covered horses, and the procession carrying the statue of the Madonna from the Church of Saint Francis of Assisi (Piazza S. Francesco; 10am-8pm daily) to the Parish of Piccianello (Via G. Marconi, 103; tel. 0835/385667). At night, a papier-mâché "Triumphal Chariot" arrives carrying the statue as the streets burst into celebration, finishing up with a firework display over the Gravina di Matera.

MATERA FILM FESTIVAL
Via del Capricorno, 6; www.materafilmfestival.it; Sept./Oct.
Perhaps not surprising giving its dramatic location and arresting beauty, over 40 films have been made here in Matera. Italy's finest directors including Pier Paolo Pasolini, Roberto Rossellini, and Giuseppe Tornatore

have used this magnificent town as their backdrop, as have international box office sensations such as the James Bond film *No Time to Die* (filmed here in 2019), *The Passion of the Christ* with Mel Gibson, *Wonder Woman,* and *Ben-Hur.* Honoring the history of filmmaking in Matera since 2020, this annual three-day film festival takes place either in September or October, and includes international competitions, exhibitions, art performances, and master classes. All events are open to the public.

SASSI DI MATERA LIVING NATIVITY SCENE

tel. 0835/339401; weekends in Dec.; €10, children under 10 free

Matera covered in snow is the stuff dreams are made of. For the Christmas holidays, various indoor and outdoor locations around the city put on a Living Nativity performance, each year with a different theme. Throughout the Sasso Caveoso and Sasso Barisano districts, performances of eight scenes are played out, including the Annunciation, a market, the Court of Herod, a Roman camp, the Shepherds and Peasants, and finally the Nativity with the Three Kings. Also at Christmastime, the **Villagio di Babbo Natale** (Santa's Village) is set up in the ex-convent of Santa Lucia e Agata (Via del Corso).

FOOD AND DRINKS

The cuisine of Basilicata is based on peasant cooking, using cheap ingredients to create a hearty and satisfying meal, often featuring local produce such as sun-dried sweet peppers, chickpeas, beans, and wild greens, and based more on meat than fish.

I VIZI DEGLI ANGELI

Via Domenico Ridola, 36; tel. 0835/310637; www.ivizidegliangeli.it; 11:30am-1:30pm and 4:30pm-7:30pm daily; under €5

Situated near Matera's tourism office, this artisanal gelateria features an impressive range of naturally flavored gelati including unique combinations such as grapefruit and

black pepper, mallow and thyme, ginger pineapple, seasonal prickly pear or strawberry granita, and of course the traditional favorites guaranteed to please any ice cream lover.

AGRIRISTORIES RISTORANTE

Via Sette Dolori, 62; tel. 0835/256632; www. agriristories.com; 11am-10pm Fri.-Sun.; tastings from €10

Head down the stairs and enter a world of flavors in this softly lit, white limestone, underground bistro. Agriristories offers genuine hospitality and a casual environment with affordable choices for lunch, aperitivo, and dinnertime. For travelers looking for traditional fare, the menu features dishes such as legume soups, regional caciocavallo and pecorino cheeses, or bruschetta with cardoncelli mushrooms, all made with ingredients sourced from the Matera area, including the wine and craft beer.

★ STANO

Via Santa Cesarea, 67/69; tel. 0835/344101; www.stanoristorazione.it; 12:30pm-2:30pm and 7:30pm-11pm Tues.-Thurs., 12:30pm-3pm and 7:30pm-11pm Fri., 12:30pm-6pm and 7:30pm-11pm Sat.-Sun.; €12-35

This is hands down the best place to dine in Matera. Stano is not a restaurant built into an ancient cave or a fine-dining destination, but the traditional cuisine, simple modern indoor dining room, and friendly service cannot be beat. Be sure to try Franco and Maria's house specialty, La Pignata, a lamb, chicory, and potato stew slowly cooked and served inside a terracotta pot.

BACCANTI

Via Sant'Angelo, 58/61; tel. 0835/333704; www.baccantiristorante.it; 12:30pm-3pm Sun., 12:30pm-3pm and 7:30pm-11pm Tues.-Sat.; €14-30

A 5-minute walk from the Casa Noha museum, Baccanti offers affordable upscale dining specializing in the authentic flavors of the territory and an excellent wine list.

The panoramic stone terrace offers outdoor dining with views of the whole district while the indoor cave complex features an intimate dining area carved directly from the ancient rocks. The menu celebrates the land, sea, and mountains of Basilicata with thoughtful dishes pairing flavors such as the salted cod ravioli with figs and ricotta, a rabbit terrine with black olive powder, or glazed sweetbreads with hazelnuts and black truffle. Reservations are recommended.

ACCOMMODATIONS
Sasso Caveoso
SANT'ANGELO LUXURY RESORT
Piazza S. Pietro Caveoso; tel. 0835/314010; www. santangeloresort.it; from €159

Since 1999, this family-run hotel and ancient courtyard have become one of the most popular places to stay the night in Matera. The rooms are spacious and bright, and an upgrade from the Deluxe to their Junior or Superior suites provide additional amenities, such as balconies and lounge areas. Guests can dine on upscale Lucanian food and wine at the Regia Corte restaurant, or have a panoramic aperitivo on the Lounge Terrace.

★ SEXTANTIO LE GROTTE DELLA CIVITA
Via Civita, 28; tel. 0835/332744; www.sextantio.it/ legrottedellacivita/matera; from €195

In the world of hotels, the Sextantio name is synonymous with beautiful designs that honor their natural surroundings and top-notch service. This location in the oldest part of Matera is what's known as an "albergo diffuso," offering various "scattered" residences throughout the hotel property. With spectacular views of white tuff stone cliffs, it's worth splurging on an overnight stay in one of these comfortable, stunning stone cave residences. You'll arrive to a candlelit room, get a bountiful, locally sourced breakfast, and concierge services can organize unforgettable experiences including city tours, hot air balloon rides, and wellness treatments.

AQUATIO CAVE LUXURY HOTEL & SPA
Via Conche, 12; tel. 0835/189-1014; www. aquatiohotel.com; from €220

Located a 5-minute walk from the MOOM underground olive oil museum and MUSMA contemporary sculpture museum, this five-star luxury hotel and spa offers 35 rooms and suites built into the tuff stone with its own restaurant, hammam (Turkish bath), wellness center, and heated indoor pool. Their air-conditioned, nonsmoking, modern stone guest rooms and suites come with a sweet and savory breakfast plus Wi-Fi service.

INFORMATION AND SERVICES
- **Matera Tourist Information:** Via Alessandro Volta, 3/5; tel. 0835/334543; www.visiteguidatematera.com; 9am-9pm daily

GETTING THERE
By Car
Matera can be reached in approximately 1 hour (41 mi/66 km) by car from **Bari's** city center. From **Brindisi,** the 85-mile (136-km) drive takes 1 hour 45 minutes. From **Naples,** the 155-mile (250-km) trip takes approximately 3 hours.

The central Sassi area is not accessible by car, except with special permits or within limited hours during the day. Fairly convenient **parking** areas are located on the edge of the city center at Piazza Cesare Firrao (www.accessibilitacentristorici.it), Parcheggio Nicoletti Michele (Via Vincenzo Cappelluti, 1; tel. 0835/330896; www.welcomematera.it; open 24 hours), and the Parcheggio – Stazione Centrale/Tribunale (Viale Aldo Moro) near the train station, each costing approximately €1/hour. It's worth calling ahead to your accommodation to arrange transport upon arrival, so as to avoid walking through steep, cobblestone streets with a roller bag.

By Train
The city of Matera has three train stations:

Matera Villa Longo (Via Nazionale), the main station in the urban city center, **Matera Centrale** (Piazza Giacomo Matteotti; tel. 080/572-5670), and **Matera Sud** (Via Lanera), closest to the old town. Trenitalia (www.trenitalia.com) offers regular services to Matera from Bari Centrale (2 hours, with a transfer in Altamura; from €4), with an additional route from Bari Centrale provided by Ferrovie Appulo Lucane (www.ferrovieappulolucane.it; 1 hour 40 minutes; €27).

By Bus

Bus Miccolis (www.miccolis-spa.it) offers service to the Matera Villa Longo station (Via Nazionale) from the Bari Airport (55 minutes; €13), Bari Centrale train station (65 minutes; €11), Taranto (2 hours 15 minutes; €21), Lecce (3 hours 45 minutes; €30), Brindisi (3 hours 10 minutes; €29), and Naples (4 hours; €25).

Flixbus (global.flixbus.com) offers service from the Bari airport to Via Don Luigi Sturzo (Chiesa S. Paolo) in Matera (1 hour 35 minutes; €14).

GETTING AROUND

The historic center of the Sasso Caveoso and Sasso Barisano districts are restricted as pedestrian zones, which means those driving to Matera must leave their car in a paid parking lot on the outskirts of the old town. Given Matera's hilly and narrow streets, it's really best to avoid having a car at all during a stay in Matera if possible; one of the highlights of a visit here is exploring the city on foot. Consult your accommodations for the best recommendation on private drivers and taxi services in Matera for airport transfers or assistance with luggage. To be prepared for stairs and steep roads, be sure to wear comfortable shoes.

Highlights of Calabria and Basilicata

From the delights of Neapolitan pizza to the sobering ruins of Pompeii and Herculaneum, to the paradisiacal beaches of Capri and the Amalfi Coast, to the vibrant streets to Palermo, to the impressive slopes of Mount Etna—Southern Italy is a densely packed region that would require a lifetime to fully explore. It's no wonder, then, that full parts of Italy's "boot" get left off most travelers' itineraries, including the "toe" regions of Basilicata, just west of Puglia, and Calabria, stretching toward Sicily.

With so much to see and do, it's understandable many visitors to Southern Italy fly between the regions of the Naples and the Amalfi Coast, Puglia, and Sicily to make the most out of their valuable time in these stunning destinations, each unique in their own way. But if you're driving between any of these regions, or simply want to beat the crowds and get off the beaten path, here are some of the best places to go in off-the-tourist-map Calabria and Basilicata.

REGGIO CALABRIA

Reggio is mostly known for being the largest town in Calabria and for its excellent **Museo Nazionale di Reggio Calabria** (Piazza da Nava 26; tel. 0965/812-255; http://sabap-rec.beniculturali.it; 9am-8pm Tues.-Sun.; €8), which houses artifacts from Neolithic times all the way up to the Romans, with the focus being on the Hellenistic objects left behind from when this area was part of Magna Graecia, the Italian part of the Greek colonies.

Here you can arrive by plane at the tiny **Aeroporto di Reggio Calabria** (Via Ravagnese, 11; tel. 965/64-0517; reggiocalabriaairport.it), with flights to Rome (1 hour 10 minutes; from €45) and Milan (1 hour 40 minutes; from €50); by **train**—frequent departures from Rome (5 hours; from €35) and

Naples (5 hours 30 minutes; from €26)—and by **bus** from all around Italy. It's also a departure point for **ferries** to Messina in Sicily (30 minutes; from €4), and a short, 15-minute drive from Villa San Giovanni, which offers more departures for the island. It's a 4-hour 30-minute drive from Matera to the north.

ASPROMONTE NATIONAL PARK

parcoaspormonte.gov.it

Farther south, covering much of the toe of the Italian peninsula, Parco Nazionale dell'Aspromonte is much larger even than Sila to the north, at 250 square miles (640 square km). The landscape is rugged and dramatic, with nearly abandoned villages perched on peaks reaching up to 6,600 feet (2,000 m), and opportunities for hiking, visiting lakes and waterfalls, and even skiing, depending on the season.

The gateway town is **Gambarie,** where you'll find the national park office (Via Aurora 1; tel. 0965/743-060), as well as the most amenities and best roads for self-driven adventures in the area. It's a 4.5-hour drive from Matera and 1 hour from Reggio Calabria.

TROPEA

This stunning, cliffside coastal town was named the most beautiful in Italy in 2021. Its beaches, which have a mix of free public and paid private areas, make it popular among Italian sun seekers, but it's still more or less unknown by international tourists. **Spiaggia della Rotonda** (Via Lungomare), right at the foot of the old town and the mountaintop Byzantine **Santuario di Santa Maria dell'Isola di Tropea** (Via Lungomare; 9am-9pm daily), is a sea of beach umbrellas in July and August. Visit **Spiaggia Michelino** to the north for something a bit less crowded.

Beyond the beaches, Tropea's centro storico is an enchanting maze of cobblestone streets, with a 12th-century Norman **cathedral** (Largo Duomo 12; 7am-noon and 4pm-8pm daily). Visit the tourist office (Piazza Ercole; tel. 347/531-8989; www.prolocotropea.eu; 9am-1pm and 4pm-8pm daily) for more information on this charming town, which is a 1-hour 30-minute drive or 1-hour 45-minute train ride from Reggio Calabria (from €6), or a 4-hour drive from Matera.

PARCO NAZIONALE DELLA SILA

www.parcosila.it

Situated in Calabria in what would be the ball of Italy's foot, evenly situated a 3-hour drive from Matera and a roughly 3-hour drive from Reggio Calabria, Parco Nazionale della Sila is 50 square miles (130 square km) of hills, forests, lakes, and mountains reaching up to 6,600 feet (2,000 m). Its huge footprint means that it's usually divided up into three areas: Sila Grande, so named because it's home to the park's highest mountains, which are tall enough to ski in the wintertime; Sila Greca, named for its Greek-Albanian heritage; and Sila Piccola, whose tree-covered hills are some of the best places in the park to look for mushrooms in the fall.

The largest town in the region is **San Giovanni in Fiore,** named for the lovely 12th-century Abbazia di San Giovanni in Fiore, but you'll find more tourist information in **Camigliatello Silano,** also the winter sports center for the park, where you can stop by the Pro Loco tourist office (Via Roma; tel. 0984/578-159; www.prolococamigliatello.it).

Palermo and Western Sicily

From the capital city of Palermo down to the

13-square-kilometer (8-sq-mi) archaeological park of the Valle dei Templi in Agrigento, Sicily's extraordinary western coast offers an enormous amount to explore, even enough to occupy an entire trip.

No trip to Sicily is complete without a few days in the fascinating city of Palermo, a nucleus of art, culture, and gastronomy. Most travelers get their first taste of what makes Sicily unique wandering the streets of Palermo's historic city center, snacking their way through its outdoor markets, and enjoying the rowdy nightlife. You'll know right away that this is not Rome, Venice, or Milan: Palermo has its own lively flavor and old-world charm, thanks to the buskers in the piazzas, slow early evening passeggiata walks, spontaneous bursts of music from cars

Itinerary Ideas 275
Sights 277
Sports and Recreation. .285
Entertainment
    and Events..........288
Shopping..............291
Food 292
Bars and Nightlife......300
Accommodations 302
Information
    and Services.........303
Getting There..........304
Getting Around 305
Vicinity of Palermo 306
Trapani and the
    West Coast 314
Agrigento and the
    Southern Coast 322

Highlights

Look for ★ to find recommended sights, activities, dining, and lodging.

★ Palazzo dei Normanni: This monumental palace is a stunning hodgepodge of architectural styles emblematic of centuries of conquerors and cultures (page 282).

★ Palermitan Street Food: Test out traditional Palermitan snacks, like panelle chickpea fritters, crocchè fried potato dumplings, or sfincione, a fluffy focaccia-style pizza, many of them only made here in Palermo (page 296).

★ Mondello's Beaches: Hit the beach like the Palermitani in this charming beach town just north of the capital (page 307).

★ Saline di Trapani e Paceco: Watch sea salt being extracted using traditional methods. Wide seawater ponds and tall mountains of white salt line the WWF-protected coastal road from Trapani down to Marsala (page 316).

★ Tasting Marsala: Experience the resurgence of one of Italy's unique winemaking styles, honed and perfected in the city of Marsala since the 1770s (page 322).

★ Valle dei Templi: Take a trip back in time to ancient Greece at the well-preserved remains of seven Doric-style temples, dating all the way back to the sixth century BC in Agrigento (page 322).

★ Aegadian Islands: At this tropical paradise just 9 miles (15 km) off the coast of Trapani and Marsala, you can swim through clean crystal blue waters, discover ancient caves dating back to the Neolithic Age, and explore sleepy fishing villages on three tiny isles (page 326).

passing by, and cute old grannies providing an unofficial "neighborhood watch" from their balconies above.

Originally settled by Phoenicians in 734 BC, Palermo has always been an important city, located in the center of the Mediterranean and right along the Afro-European trade routes. When the Greeks conquered Palermo between the eighth and seventh centuries BC, they renamed the city Panormos, meaning "all port." Through Roman, Byzantine, and Arab rule over the centuries, the city developed its distinctive layers of cultural and architectural history, visible in its churches, palaces, and monuments. The Palazzo dei Normanni is a perfect example, dating to the eighth century BC and with Arab, Norman, and Spanish architectural elements.

Outside Palermo are bustling smaller cities like Trapani, charming beach towns, and the Aegadian Islands to explore. To look deeper into the island's history, save time for half-day trips to the archaeological sites of Valle dei Templi, Selinunte, and Segesta.

Food and wine lovers will quickly settle into la dolce vita here. Treat yourself to affordable street food, gourmet restaurants, and bountiful homemade meals on vineyard visits. Sicily is a true melting pot of flavors. Each dish tells the history of the island, with ingredients brought here by way of Greece, Northern Africa, and Spain. Keep an eye out for can't-miss regional dishes that can't be found anywhere else, like couscous with fish in Trapani and panelle (chickpea fritters) or sfincione (focaccia-style pizza) in Palermo.

This is a warm region in every sense: the kindness of its people, the strong Sicilian sunshine, and the sense of joy that's instantly felt by visitors. Walking through vineyard-lined countryside or floating in a salty crystal blue sea, there is a magnetic energy here that will keep you wanting more.

ORIENTATION

In Palermo, the **Quattro Canti** ("four corners") crossroads at **Via Maqueda** (running northwest-southeast) and **Corso Vittorio Emanuele** (running southwest-northeast) should be the central point on your mental map, dividing the **centro storico** into four main neighborhoods. Starting in the northeast and moving clockwise, they are La Loggia, Kalsa, Albergheria, and Capo.

La Loggia, also known as Castellammare, is home to Palermo's port and the Mercato Vuccira. To the south, **Kalsa** is home to some of the city's best green spaces: the extensive, historic Orto Botanico dell'Università di Palermo gardens, Villa Giulia park, and the Foro Italico seaside promenade. West of Kalsa, **Albergheria** is one of the city's oldest sections, home to many of Palermo's North African, Sri Lankan, and Bangladeshi residents. Its main highlights are the Mercato di Ballarò, Palermo's oldest and largest market, and the ancient Palazzo dei Normanni. North of Albergheria, **Capo** also has its own outdoor market, along with the Cattedrale di Palermo and the famous Teatro Massimo.

Palermo Centrale train station sits south of the Quattro Canti, wedged between Albergheria and Kalsa.

Only a few main sights lay outside the city center: the **Giardino Inglese,** north of the city; and the 12th-century, Islamic-inspired **Castello della Zisa** and the **Catacombe dei Cappuccini,** both in the northwestern neighborhood of **La Zisa.** It's worth noting that though Palermo boasts some lovely waterfront areas; the city's main beach is in **Mondello,** half an hour's drive northwest.

Outside Palermo, you'll find more beaches, including the picture-perfect strand of **Cefalù** an hour east of the city, and several less developed ones heading south along the coast.

PALERMO AND WESTERN SICILY

Previous: University of Palermo's Botanical Garden; Palazzo dei Normanni; panelle chickpea fritters.

Palermo and Western Sicily

MEDITERRANEAN SEA

Spiaggia
di San Vito lo Capo

*Riserva Naturale
Orientata dello
Zingaro*

LA TONNARA
DI SCOPELLO · Cala Mosca
Guidaloca

CASTELLO ARABO · Cala Petrolo
NORMANNO

Castellammare
del Golfo

*SEE
"TRAPANI"
MAP*

Erice · Valderice

Trapani

Casa Santa

Paceco

Alcamo

SS187

A29dir

SALINE
DI TRAPANI E PACECO

GROTTA DEL
GENOVESE · Levanzo

Spiaggia
di Cala Dogana

TEMPIO
DI SEGESTA

Marettimo

IL PIRATA
RISTORANTE

*AEGADIAN
ISLANDS*

La Praia
dei Nacchi

Favignana

FORMICA

*Riserva Naturale
Marina Isole Egadi*

Scogliera
di Cala Rossa

*Riserva Isole
dello Stagnone
di Marsala*

TRAPANI

Salemi

A29

CANTINE
PELLEGRINO · Marsala

CANTINE FLORIO
DI MARSALA

Partanna

SS624

MARCO
DE BARTOLI

Castelvetrano

Mazara del Vallo

Campobello
di Mazara

SS115

Menfi

PARCO
ARCHEOLOGICO
DI SELINUNTE

CEFALÙ

LA ROCCA
HIKE

BASTIONE &
COSTANZA · Piazza del Duomo

CEFALÙ
MEDIEVAL
LAUNDRY

MUSEO
MANDRALISCA

DUOMO DI CEFALÙ

TAVERNA TINCHITÈ

ENOTECA
LE PETIT
TONNEAU

CORTILE PEPE

VISIT
CEFALÙ

TEMPIO DI DIANA

Spiaggia di Cefalù

Cefalù

La Rocca

To
Hotel le
Calette

To
Lido Eolo

Cefalù Train
Station

0   600 yds

0   600 m

0   6 mi

0   6 km

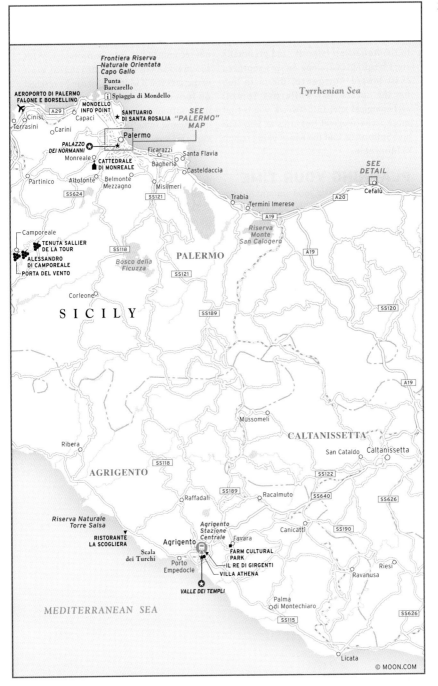

© MOON.COM

Western Sicily

Continuing southwest, you'll find the larger towns of **Trapani** and **Marsala,** gateways to the **Aegadian Islands**, and eventually start heading east along Sicily's southern coast toward **Agrigento,** the main hub for the spectacular **Valle dei Templi** archeological site. In between, you'll find more archaeological treasures at **Segesta** and **Selinunte,** and the winemaking region of **Monreale.**

PLANNING YOUR TIME

Three to five days is a good amount of time to spend in Western Sicily; an overview of **Palermo** requires at least two days. Sicily's capital is likely your best base for the region; from here, it's easy to take day trips to most of the highlights of the area by bus, train, or rental car. That said, if you prefer a quieter, more pastoral setting for your vacation, there are lovely accommodations throughout the southern coastal region, or you could opt to stay the night in a seaside town like Cefalù. Trapani is a great base for exploring the Aegadian Islands, while visitors who are interested in history should consider staying closer to the Valle dei Templi in Agrigento.

Falcone Borsellino (PMO) airport, formerly known as Punta Raisi, is the main hub for flights arriving in Sicily, located 19 miles (30 km) west of Palermo city center on Sicily's northwestern coast. In Palermo proper, having your own car is not recommended or truly necessary. With accommodations in the centro storico, most of the sites you'll want to visit can be reached **on foot** or with a quick taxi ride. However, in the surrounding region's smaller towns, it's helpful and sometimes necessary to **rent a car** to get around. **Trains** and **buses** connect Palermo to most of the main towns and cities in the region, but service can be infrequent or delayed, and having your own rental car can offer more flexibility.

Sicily's subtropical Mediterranean climate, with **mild winters** and **hot dry summers,** makes it an ideal destination all year round, with the exception of a few weeks in August when the island becomes crowded with tourists on their summer holidays.

Safety

Overall, Palermo is a safe place to travel, but you should be smart about not flashing valuable jewelry or cameras and always keep an eye on your bags and backpacks while moving through more crowded areas. Main squares remain crowded and safe well into the evenings, but visiting the areas around the **Ballarò** and **Capo Markets** in the late evening is not recommended.

Itinerary Ideas

THREE DAYS IN WESTERN SICILY

These three days in the western part of Sicily will introduce you to the island's varied layers of Greek, Byzantine, and Norman history. Arriving in the capital city of Palermo, head south through the DOC winemaking region of Monreale toward the Valle dei Templi, enjoying a mix of walking tours, traditional meals, vineyard visits, and sightseeing.

Guided tours, vineyard visits, accommodations, and **car rentals** should be reserved in advance to avoid disappointment, and **restaurant reservations** are recommended.

Day 1: Palermo

1 Start your day with an espresso on the panoramic rooftop bar of the **Rinascente** luxury department store on Via Roma.

2 At 10am, meet up with your guide from Palermo Street Food at the **Teatro Massimo** for a walking tour of Palermo's historic outdoor food markets: Vucciria, Capo, and Ballarò. Enjoy a grazing street food lunch and samples of Sicilian specialties as you move through the labyrinth of greengrocers, mountains of fresh produce, and boisterous vendors.

3 Walk 15 minutes south along Via Porta di Castro to spend a few hours inside Europe's oldest royal residence, the **Palazzo dei Normanni.** Save time to admire the Byzantine mosaics inside the nearby Cappella Palatina chapel.

4 When it's just about that time for a classic Sicilian midday nap, head back to the convenience of your luxury apartment at **Palazzo Sovrana,** a 20-minute walk northeast via Via Vittoria Emanuele and Via Maqueda.

5 Refreshed, stop for an aperitivo at **Enoteca Picone** wine bar, just a few blocks off of the high-end shopping area of Via della Libertà. It's a 15-minute walk northwest on Via Messina.

6 Just across the street, enjoy a seafood-centric dinner at **Corona Trattoria.** Soak in the Sicilian hospitality of the cheerful Corona family in their modern trattoria, before returning to your apartment for a peaceful rest after all that walking.

Day 2: Palermo and DOC Monreale Wine Country

1 Start with breakfast at Palermo's oldest family-run coffee roaster, **Casa Stagnitta,** on Discesa dei Giudici in Piazza Bellini.

2 Around the corner at the **Fontana Pretoria,** meet up with the best guide in town to discover Palermo's noble palaces on a tour with native Palermitana Marcella Amato. She's your hookup for a private glimpse into the city's luxurious aristocratic past that a typical tourist would never get to see on their own.

3 After your tour, just across Via Maqueda from Piazza Pretoria, enjoy a light Sicilian lunch at **Bisso Bistrot** before checking out of your room at Palazzo Sovrana.

4 Pick up your rental car to say goodbye to Palermo. Spend the late afternoon in the

Itinerary Ideas

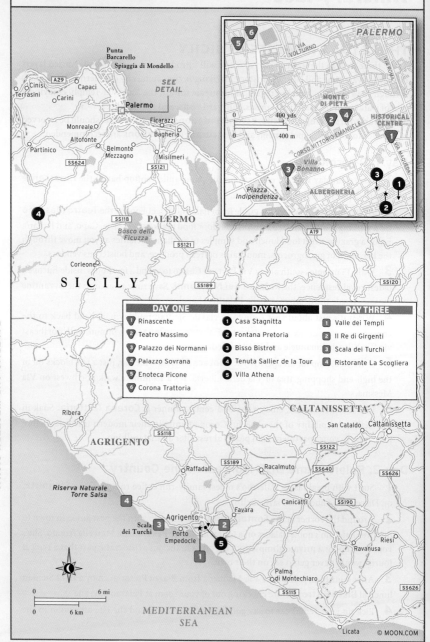

DAY ONE
1. Rinascente
2. Teatro Massimo
3. Palazzo dei Normanni
4. Palazzo Sovrana
5. Enoteca Picone
6. Corona Trattoria

DAY TWO
1. Casa Stagnitta
2. Fontana Pretoria
3. Bisso Bistrot
4. Tenuta Sallier de la Tour
5. Villa Athena

DAY THREE
1. Valle dei Templi
2. Il Re di Girgenti
3. Scala dei Turchi
4. Ristorante La Scogliera

© MOON.COM

vineyards with Costanza Chirivino at **Tenuta Sallier de La Tour** for a wine tasting in Camporeale, a 45-minute drive south on SS624 into the DOC Monreale region.

5 Continue driving south on SS624 for another 2 hours to **Villa Athena,** your luxury accommodation at the foot of the Valle dei Templi, which you'll be visiting the next day. Treat yourself to dinner at the Michelin-starred hotel restaurant after a long day of driving.

Day 3: Agrigento and the Valle dei Templi

1 In the morning, head just up the road from the hotel to the **Valle dei Templi** before the day gets too hot. You'll need the morning to get the most out of a visit to this 8-square-mile (20-sq-km) site, dotted with ancient Greek temples and surrounded by olive and almond groves.

2 After taking in all that history, it's time for a well-deserved lunch at **Il Re di Girgenti,** still in view of the archaeological site.

3 After a 20-minute drive to the west, you'll arrive at the stunning **Scala dei Turchi;** bring everything you need for a beach day to this dramatic rock formation, and spend the day lounging on the cool limestone.

4 Finish your day with the freshest seafood dinner at beachfront **Ristorante La Scogliera,** a 15-minute drive up the coast.

Sights

QUATTRO CANTI

Via Maqueda and Corso Vittorio Emanuele; open 24 hours; free

The historic "Four Corners" landmark splits the city of Palermo into its main neighborhood quarters, or quartieri. Built in the classic Sicilian baroque style developed in the 1600s, this early example of city planning lies at the cross streets of Via Maqueda and the Corso Vittorio Emanuele. At each corner, beautiful, nearly identical curved facades feature a quartet of fountains portraying the rivers that once flowed through the city, sculptures representing the four seasons, the Spanish kings of Sicily, and the main patron saints of the Palermo: Ninfa, Oliva di Palermo, Agata, and Christina.

KALSA

Kalsa's main pedestrian square, **Piazza Bellini,** is located around the corner from the Quattro Canti and the Piazza Pretoria. In Piazza Bellini, you'll find two of Palermo's Arab-Norman style UNESCO World Heritage Sites: the Church of Santa Maria dell'Ammiraglio, also known as **La Martorana,** and its adjoining domed **Chiesa di San Cataldo.** On the corner of Piazza Pretoria and Piazza Bellini, the garden and rooftop views from **Chiesa di Santa Caterina d'Alessandria** (Piazza Bellini, 2; tel. 091/271-3837; www.monasterosantacaterina.com; 10am-6pm daily; free), famed for the pastry shop inside, are also a highlight.

This popular meeting point is used for tour groups, as well as those who are meeting for a coffee at the landmark torrefazione (coffee roaster) **Casa Stagnitta.** Here, you can also access the city's free Wi-Fi or stop by the **Tourist Information Point** (Via Maqueda; www.visitpalermo.it; 9am-8pm Mon.-Sat.). On summer evenings, the square is filled with groups who organize meetups for dancing, friends meeting for an aperitivo, or, if you're lucky, a street busking accordion player.

Palermo

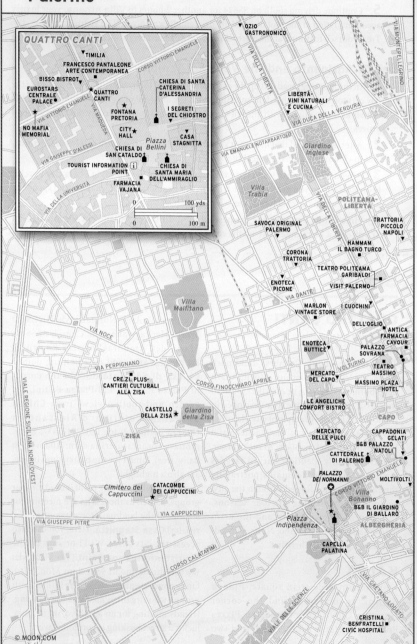

QUATTRO CANTI

TIMILIA

FRANCESCO PANTALEONE
ARTE CONTEMPORANEA

BISSO BISTROT

EUROSTARS
CENTRALE
PALACE

QUATTRO
CANTI

CHIESA DI SANTA
CATERINA
D'ALESSANDRIA

FONTANA
PRETORIA

I SEGRETI
DEL CHIOSTRO

NO MAFIA
MEMORIAL

CITY
HALL

Piazza
Bellini

CASA
STAGNITTA

CHIESA DI
SAN CATALDO

CHIESA DI
SANTA MARIA
DELL'AMMIRAGLIO

TOURIST INFORMATION
POINT

FARMACIA
VAJANA

CORSO VITTORIO EMANUELE

VIA VITTORIO EMANUELE

VIA MAQUEDA

VIA GIUSEPPE D'ALESSI

VIA DELLA UNIVERSITÀ

0   100 yds

0   100 m

OZIO
GASTRONOMICO

VIA DELLA LIBERTÀ

VIA MONTEPELLEGRINO

LIBERTÀ-
VINI NATURALI
E CUCINA

VIA DUCA DELLA VERDURA

VIA EMANUELE NOTARBARTOLO

Giardino
Inglese

Villa
Trabia

POLITEAMA-
LIBERTA

VIA DELLA LIBERTÀ

SAVOCA ORIGINAL
PALERMO

TRATTORIA
PICCOLO
NAPOLI

CORONA
TRATTORIA

HAMMAM
IL BAGNO TURCO

TEATRO POLITEAMA
GARIBALDI

ENOTECA
PICONE

VISIT PALERMO

VIA DANTE

Villa
Malfitano

MARLON
VINTAGE STORE

I CUOCHINI

DELL'OGLIO

VIA NOCE

ANTICA
FARMACIA
CAVOUR

ENOTECA
BUTTICE

PALAZZO
SOVRANA

VIA PERPIGNANO

VIA VOLTURNO

MERCATO
DEL CAPO

TEATRO
MASSIMO

CORSO FINOCCHIARO APRILE

MASSIMO PLAZA
HOTEL

VIALE REGIONE SICILIANA NORD OVEST

CRE.ZI. PLUS-
CANTIERI CULTURALI
ALLA ZISA

LE ANGELICHE
COMFORT BISTRO

CAPO

CASTELLO
DELLA ZISA

Giardino
della Zisa

MERCATO
DELLE PULCI

CAPPADONIA
GELATI

ZISA

B&B PALAZZO
NATOLI

CATTEDRALE
DI PALERMO

Cimitero dei
Cappuccini

CATACOMBE
DEI CAPPUCCINI

PALAZZO
DEI NORMANNI

MOLTIVOLTI

Villa
Bonanno

VIA GIUSEPPE PITRÈ

VIA CAPPUCCINI

CORSO VITTORIO EMANUELE

B&B IL GIARDINO
DI BALLARÒ

Piazza
Indipendenza

ALBERGHERIA

CORSO CALATAFIMI

CAPELLA
PALATINA

VIALE DELLE SCIENZE

VIA GAETANO LODATO

CRISTINA
BENFRATELLI
CIVIC HOSPITAL

© MOON.COM

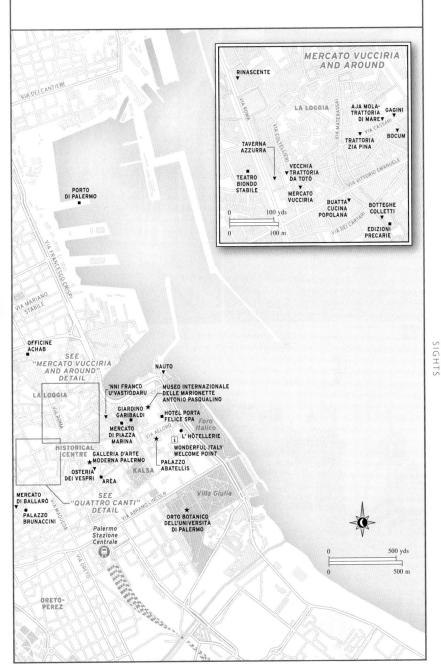

MERCATO VUCCIRIA AND AROUND

RINASCENTE ▼

VIA ROMA

LA LOGGIA

VIA MATERASSAI

VIA COLTELLIERI

AJA MOLA-
TRATTORIA
DI MARE ▼   GAGINI ▼

VIA CASSARI

BOCUM ▼

TRATTORIA
ZIA PINA ▼

TAVERNA
AZZURRA

VECCHIA
TRATTORIA
DA TOTÒ ▼

VIA VITTORIO EMANUELE

TEATRO
BIONDO
STABILE ■

MERCATO
VUCCIRIA

BUATTA ▼
CUCINA
POPOLANA

BOTTEGHE
COLLETTI ▼

0   100 yds
0   100 m

VIA DEI CARTARI

EDIZIONI
PRECARIE ▼

VIA DEI CANTIERI

PORTO
DI PALERMO ■

VIA FRANCESCO CRISPI

VIA MARIANO
STABILE

OFFICINE
ACHAB ■

SEE
"MERCATO VUCCIRIA
AND AROUND"
DETAIL

LA LOGGIA

VIA ROMA

NAUTO ▼

'NNI FRANCO
U'VASTIDDARU ▼

MUSEO INTERNAZIONALE
DELLE MARIONETTE
ANTONIO PASQUALINO ▼

GIARDINO ★
GARIBALDI ■

HOTEL PORTA
FELICE SPA ▼

MERCATO
DI PIAZZA
MARINA ■

Foro
Italico

VIA ALLORO

ℹ L' HÒTELLERIE ●

HISTORICAL
CENTRE

GALLERIA D'ARTE
★ MODERNA PALERMO

WONDERFUL ITALY
WELCOME POINT

OSTERIA ▼
DEI VESPRI

ARÈA ●

PALAZZO
ABATELLIS ■

KALSA

Villa Giulia

MERCATO
DI BALLARÒ ▼

SEE
"QUATTRO CANTI"
DETAIL

VIA ABRAMO LINCOLN

PALAZZO
BRUNACCINI ▼

VIA MAQUEDA

Palermo
Stazione
Centrale 🚉

ORTO BOTANICO ★
DELL'UNIVERSITÀ
DI PALERMO

VIA ORETO

ORETO-
PEREZ

0   500 yds
0   500 m

Fontana Pretoria

Piazza Pretoria; open 24 hours; free

Especially given its location just across the street from a church, the 16th-century citizens of Palermo were shocked by the 48 nude statues that adorn this fountain, representing the 12 Olympians of Greek mythology among other figures. The citizens referred to it as "the fountain of shame." With the fountain located right in front of the **City Hall** (Palazzo Pretorio, Piazza Pretoria, 1; tel. 091/326056; www.comune.palermo.it), the nickname also applies to the unsavory corruption of Palermitan government throughout the 18th and 19th centuries.

What has become one of the city's most recognizable landmarks was not originally designed for this location. The Praetoria Fountain was built in 1554 by Francesco Camilliani, a Tuscan Renaissance sculptor, to be placed in the Florentine garden of Luigi de Toledo. Twenty years later, after de Toledo passed away, his son decided to sell the masterpiece to the Senate of Palermo. The fountain had to be dismantled into over 600 pieces and moved down to Sicily by ship, and the surrounding buildings had to be torn down to create a space for this massive structure.

La Martorana
(Chiesa di Santa Maria dell'Ammiraglio)

Piazza Bellini, 3; tel. 345/828-8231; www.arcidiocesi. palermo.it; 8:30am-1pm and 3:30pm-7pm Mon.-Sat.; €2 entrance fee

The Chiesa di Santa Maria dell'Ammiraglio, better known as La Martorana, was built in 1143 and underwent extensive modification between the 16th and 18th centuries. Although only a handful of the original iconographic mosaics remain, this church is characterized by its overlapping ornate baroque decorations, Islamic inscriptions, Byzantine dome, and Norman columns. It was

given to a Benedictine monastery and became known as La Chiesa della Martorana for its noble founder, Eloise Martorana. Following along with Sicily's history of pastry making, the nuns of this convent were famous for their sculpted marzipan fruit and vegetable-shaped sweets known as frutta di Martorana, which they say originated right here.

This church is the seat of the Greek Orthodox parish of San Nicolò dei Greci as well as the Italo-Albanian Catholic community. Since 2015, it has been included in the Arab-Norman UNESCO World Heritage Sites of Palermo. Adjoining Santa Maria dell'Ammiraglio is the Catholic **Chiesa di San Cataldo** (Piazza Bellini, 1), another prime example of Arab-Norman architecture easily recognizable by three red domes on the roof.

Galleria d'Arte Moderna Palermo

Via Sant'Anna, 21; tel. 091/843-1605; www. gampalermo.it; 9:30am-6:30pm Tues.-Sun.; general admission €7

Located on a pedestrian street just off Via Roma, Palermo's GAM, or Gallery of Modern Art, is housed in an 15th-century palazzo and Franciscan convent. The museum includes over 200 works of art including paintings by Giuseppe Sciuti, Francesco Lojacono, Giovanni Boldini, and Ettore de Maria Bergler. Sicilian art buffs will recognize pieces by Renato Guttuso, a 20th-century expressionist and social realist painter from Bagheria, and Antonio Leto, a top impressionistic style landscape painter from Monreale. Even if these names don't ring a bell, guests will enjoy browsing through their extensive works featuring Sicilian landscapes. Entrance to tour the permanent collection is free on the first Sunday of the month, and guided tours of the repositories of art hidden behind the scenes are available on the second Sunday of each month.

1: Piazza Bellini **2:** a street in Palermo **3:** Quattro Canti

Museo Internazionale delle Marionette Antonio Pasqualino

Piazza Antonio Pasqualino, 5; tel. 091/328060; www. museodellemarionette.it; 10am-2pm Sun.-Mon., 10am-6pm Tues.-Sat.; general admission €5, students and children €3, performances €12

Up until the introduction of the television, puppet shows were a traditional form of entertainment here in Sicily. Located on a small street in the Kalsa quarter, just one block from the sea, Antonio Pasqualino's International Marionette Museum is an incredible collection of handmade theater puppets and home to the theater for the Sicilian puppeteering troupe Fratelli Napoli.

Palazzo Abatellis

Via Alloro, 4; tel. 091/6230011; www.regione. sicilia.it/beniculturali/palazzoabatellis/home.htm; 9am-6:30pm Tues.-Fri., 9am-1pm Sat.-Sun. and holidays; general admission €8, reduced rates €4, free first Sun. of each month

A masterpiece of Catalan-Gothic architecture, dating back to the 15th century, this palace was originally built as the residence of Francesco Abatellis, the port master of the Kingdom of Sicily. It has since acted as an ancient noble home, a cloistered monastery for nuns, and now as the location of the Regional Gallery of Sicily, restored by the Venetian architect Carlo Scarpa to exhibit the largest collection of Sicilian works from the Romanesque to baroque periods. Highlights of the museum include 12th-century wooden artifacts, 14th- and 15th-century sculptures, and tiles from the 14th-17th centuries. The gallery also features Francesco Laurana's 15th-century bust of Eleanor of Aragon and the 15th-century *Virgin Annunciate* painting by Antonello da Messina. **Guided tours** available upon request.

Orto Botanico dell'Università di Palermo

Via Lincoln, 2; tel. 91 23891236; www.ortobotanico. unipa.it; 9am-6pm daily Mar. and Oct., 9am-7pm daily Apr. and Sept., 9am-8pm daily May-Aug., 9am-5pm daily Nov.-Feb.; general admission €5, children ages 6-17 and seniors €3, less abled guests and their companions and children under 5 free, family ticket (two adults, two children) €10

This enormous outdoor museum has been around for nearly 200 years. The Herbarium Mediterraneum was founded at the beginning of the 19th century and hosts a collection of Sicilian plants, ferns, mosses, mushrooms, a diverse selection of preserved and dried fruit, and seeds dating back to the early 20th century, as well as thousands of exotic plant species. Palermo's favorable climate has allowed many exotic tropical plants to thrive here, making this an important point of reference for other large botanical gardens around Europe. During the summer season, the garden staff collects plants and seeds throughout Sicily that will be identified and stored in the botanical garden's seed bank. It's a great place to spend an afternoon, especially during the spring and fall **Zagara Festival,** a market exhibition dedicated to biodiversity and rare collectible plants.

ALBERGHERIA
★ Palazzo dei Normanni

Piazza Indipendenza, 1; tel. 091/6262833; www.ars. sicilia.it/visita-il-palazzo-reale; 8:15am-5:40pm Mon.-Sat., 8:15am-1pm Sun. and holidays; Royal Palace, special exhibition, Royal Apartments, and Palatine Chapel combination ticket €14.50, additional access to the Royal Gardens €2, reduced rates available for seniors, children, and students, children under 13 accompanied by an adult free

Discover the complex beauty of Sicily's history in the Palazzo dei Normanni, where layers of architectural styles are piled on top of one another, one for each of Sicily's rulers over time. The palace was originally constructed on what was the highest point of the ancient city; the remains of eighth-century BC Punic construction can still be found in the basement. When Arabs conquered Sicily in the ninth century AD, the first portion of the current complex was built as a military fortress. In 1072, when the Normans arrived in Palermo, the castle was expanded into a royal palace, then known as Palazzo Reale. In turn, the Spanish Bourbons renovated and beautified their kings' home with additions that include a room of frescoes dedicated to the Greek god Hercules.

Entrance to the palace includes access to the sumptuous, richly furnished Royal Apartments, decorated with murals of angels and mythological allegories; lovely gardens designed in the 17th century; appropriately austere dungeons; a tower built as an astronomical observatory in the 18th century; and rooms still used by legislators of the Sicilian government, including the Salone d'Ercole, with its frescoes of Hercules painted by Velazquez. Because parts of the palace are still in use by the Sicilian parliament, it's important to note that the Royal Apartments are closed to the public Tuesday-Thursday.

But perhaps the most important stop on your visit is the famous **Cappella Palatina,** the royal chapel added by King Roger II in 1132. This precious chapel is completely covered from top to bottom in golden Byzantine mosaics depicting Christ and biblical scenes including Adam and Eve, as well as wooden ceilings masterfully carved by Egyptian artisans. In the chapel, Norman and Northern African Fatimid architecture styles, Byzantine domes, Arabic arches, and eight-pointed stars are mixed with Christian crosses in a structure that could only exist in a place like Sicily.

CAPO

NO Mafia Memorial

Via Vittorio Emanuele, 353; tel. 347/9673896; www.nomafiamemorial.org; 11am-6pm daily; free entrance or a requested donation

This narrative museum and exhibition area recounts how the history of Palermo is intertwined with the mafia. Supported by Mayor Leoluca Orlando, the NO Mafia Memorial is a journey through important stories, often untold or misinterpreted. The museum strives to be a space to explore and understand the reality of organized crime and the anti-mafia movements here in Sicily.

Cattedrale di Palermo

Corso Vittorio Emanuele; tel. 091/334373; www.cattedrale.palermo.it; 7am-7pm Mon.-Sat., 8am-1pm and 4pm-7pm Sun.; entrance fees €5-10, reduced rates available for children and seniors

The city's main cathedral, located on Corso Vittorio Emanuele west of the Quattro Canti and dedicated to the Virgin Mary, was reconstructed several times between 1185-1801, but it was originally built on the site of Roman and Carthaginian temples dating back to 400 BC. The temples became a Byzantine basilica, then a mosque, and finally the current Christian cathedral. The cathedral you see today is a real masterpiece, covered in countless columns, arches, and elaborate geometrical carvings. The interior, though massive, it perhaps a bit less impressive, almost completely white marble, though it's worth a trip inside to visit the tombs, treasury, and the panoramic rooftop for an extra €8.

OUTSIDE CITY CENTER

Catacombe dei Cappuccini

Piazza Cappuccini, 1; tel. 091/652-7389; www.catacombepalermo.it; 9am-1pm and 3pm-6pm daily, closed Sun. afternoons Oct.-Mar.; general admission €3

The remarkably creepy Capuchin Catacombs display thousands of mummified remains of Palermitani from the 17th-19th centuries. Originally used as a burial ground for the monks of the Capuchin monastery, the catacombs were eventually expanded to include the remains of secular citizens, as it became a status symbol to be buried here. This mysterious museum of the dead is certainly not for the faint of heart: The walls are covered with skeletons, some of which are extremely well-preserved, mummified fully dressed and even retaining some of their hair. The catacombs can be reached on a 20-minute (1.8-km/1.1-mi) walk from the Cattedrale di Palermo along Via Cappuccini, located outside of the historic center of Palermo in the western neighborhood of La Zisa.

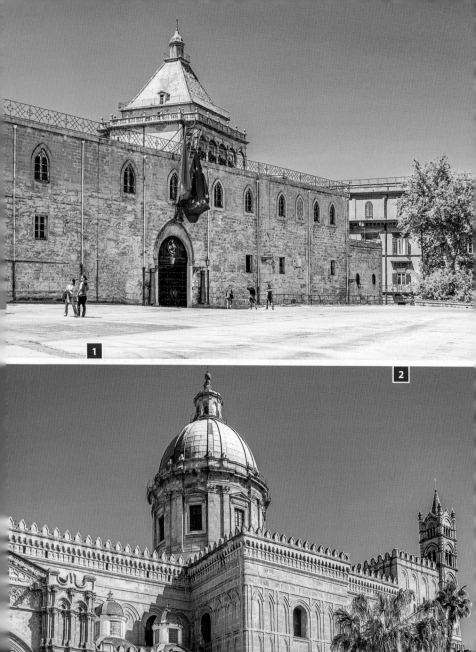

Castello della Zisa

Piazza Zisa; tel. 091/652-0269; www.
arabonormannaunesco.it; 9am-6:30pm Mon.-Sat.,
9am-1pm Sun. and holidays; €6, reduced rates €3,
under 18 free

Located near the Capuchin Catacombs, the Zisa castle is recognized as a UNESCO World Heritage Site for its unique Arab-Norman heritage. Built in the 12th century as the summer home and hunting lodge of King William I of Sicily, it was ultimately finished by his son, William II. Norman rule of the Kingdom of Sicily was characterized by what was, for the time, a remarkable level of respect for the Muslim, Roman, and Byzantine people who lived there, visible in the obvious influence of North African royal residences on Castello della Zisa's architecture. Arab craftsmen were employed to build the castle's typically Arab courtyard cooled by a fountain, mosaics, and muqarnas, or vaulted, ornamented ceilings.

Though it was used from 1808-1950 as a private residence of the Princess Notarbartolo di Sciara, the castle stood abandoned for some time until restoration of the castle began in 1991. Today, a visit to the Castello della Zisa is an important journey through the influence of Islamic art and artifacts on the city of Palermo.

Sports and Recreation

PARKS

VILLA GIULIA

Via Lincoln; tel. 091/7404028; 8am-sunset daily; free

This tranquil, square 18th-century city garden was built in 1777 for the Viceroy's wife, Giulia d'Avalos. Located right next to the University of Palermo Botanical Gardens and across the street from the sea, this park is a perfect place to peacefully read a book or take a stroll. Highlights within the park include the neoclassical entrance, the central 12-sided sundial clock, and various marble sculptures including the Fontana del Genio, a fountain depicting "The Genius," a protective spirit and symbolic patron of Palermo.

FORO ITALICO

Foro Italico Umberto I, 1; tel. 091/7401111; open 24 hours; free

The panoramic promenade here was commissioned in 1582 by the viceroy Marco Antonio Colonna. Now, this popular park is open to runners, sunbathers, athletes, and all city dwellers who need a little bit of space to stretch out. The open lawn spans from Via Cala to Piazza Vincenzo Tumminello along a 1-kilometer (0.6-mi) coastal **walking trail and bike path.** The newly constructed wellness area, known as **Il Parco della Salute,** includes a multipurpose sports pitch for soccer and basketball, a children's play area, and a landscaped garden filled with native Mediterranean tree species.

GIARDINO INGLESE

Via della Libertà, 63; tel. 091/740-6790; daily 8am-8pm; free

This 60,000-square-meter (650,000-sq-ft) historic garden was built in 1850 by G. B. Filippo Basile, one of the most famous Sicilian architects of the 19th century. The geometric green garden includes the central fountain, walking paths lined with exotic plants, a skating rink, children's amusement park, and numerous statues of famous personalities of the period. The entire garden spans various hills and valleys that now host seasonal concerts, festivals, and sports events. The gardens can be reached on foot with a straight shot up Via Maqueda, which turns into Via Ruggero Settimo and then Via della Libertà, a 30-minute (2.5-km/1.5-mi) walk.

1: Palazzo dei Normanni **2:** Cattedrale di Palermo

WALKING TOURS
PALERMO STREET FOOD

www.palermostreetfood.com; group tours available daily; €30-45 plus the cost of tastings

Palermo Street Food just might be the very first tour organization dedicated to street food in Palermo. This little company was founded in 2012 by Salvatore Agusta and Danielle Aquino Roithmayr. Tours are managed by Giorgio Flaccavento, one of their best and most knowledgeable guides.

Don't expect a watered-down, G-rated street food experience here. All the tours are hosted by licensed local Palermitani. They know the city like the backs of their hands and have grown up with these foods. Some of the city's most typical street foods will be tasted on this tour, including panelle, crocchè, arancine, and cannoli. While respecting the guests' special tastes and food restrictions, the selection of street food samples will vary depending on the season and even the day of the week. What makes the folks at Palermo Street Food special is their passion for authenticity and their pure excitement in sharing their city with you.

Walking tours last from 2.5-4 hours and can be offered in Italian, English, Spanish, or French. Expect around 6-8 stops to sample street food while walking through the historic center of town and deep into the **Mercato Vucciria.** Your guide will also point out art and architecture, and describe the history behind each snack. Make sure to bring coins and small bills; food is not included in the cost of the tour, and the vendors will appreciate the correct change. Email for reservations and availability.

PALERMO MARKET TOURS

Mercato di Ballarò; tel. 338/426-9041; www.lindasarris.com; 10am Tue.-Sat.

The best way to understand a culture is to dive deep into its food, and the quickest way is to head straight into the market. This walking tour introduces food lovers to two of Palermo's oldest outdoor markets: **Mercato del Capo** and **Ballarò.** Guests have the opportunity to chat with trusted purveyors while wandering through a labyrinth of hollering vendors, vibrant seasonal colors, and the delicious aromas of fried Sicilian snacks. The classic samples usually include sfincione, panelle, baked ricotta, and Sicilian almonds. Depending on the season and the gumption of the guests, the tour can swing more toward desserts or to more extreme snacks like babbalucci snails, the famous spleen sandwich, or charcoal-grilled stigghiole. This private, two-hour, chef-led experience includes street food tastings along the way. Email for reservations, pricing, and availability.

MARCELLA AMATO: UNIQUE LUXURY EXPERIENCES

tel. 347/480-9632; www.marcellaamato.it; by appointment only

Palermo native Marcella Amato has been working in the tourism industry since 1996 and has become the go-to reputable guide for luxury experiences, from meeting small artisans to discovering noble palaces and magnificent, often-overlooked city sights. She offers private guided tours of the city in English, Spanish, or Italian, always with an extremely kind and knowledgeable approach.

Cooking Classes
A DAY COOKING WITH THE DUCHESS

Via Butera, 28; tel. 333/3165432; www.butera28.it/palermo-cooking-classes-sicily; 8:30am-3:30pm daily by reservation; group lessons €160 per person

Spend a day with the duchess for a true authentic Sicilian experience and a glimpse into Palermo's noble history. In the former home of Prince Giuseppe Tomasi di Lampedusa (author of the novel *The Leopard*), Nicoletta, the Duchess of Palma, begins by escorting guests through the vibrant **Mercato del Capo** to select seasonal ingredients before heading back to the beautiful 18th-century

PALERMO AND WESTERN SICILY
SPORTS AND RECREATION

1: a snack in Palermo **2:** shopping in Mercato Vucciria **3:** street food in Palermo with various seafood

palazzo by the sea for a hands-on cooking lesson. She highlights typical Sicilian dishes like perfectly fried panelle or a summer gelo di melone watermelon pudding decorated with fresh jasmine flowers from the garden, and many of her own family specialties. Working around her blue and white majolica ceramic-tiled kitchen, guests roll up their sleeves and get cooking to prepare a full meal to be shared in the formal dining room or on the lush garden terrace. A truly memorable experience not to be missed.

GARAJO TAILOR-MADE CHEF

Various locations around the city depending on the number of guests; tel. 320/559-3008; www. gabriellagarajo.it; cooking lessons for 2-6 guests €135-180 per person

For the simplicity of traditional and genuine cooking with a pinch of personality, take a cooking lesson with Palermitan chef Gabriella Garajo in a relaxing, convivial, and friendly environment. Her classic recipes are often drawn from her nonna's cookbooks, revisited in a modern way. Gabriella offers a "home restaurant," where guests are welcomed with an aperitivo or a traditional meal, various options for hands-on cooking lessons in select locations around the city, or a special lesson and meal for groups of 12 or more in Palazzo Francavilla, in front of Teatro Massimo. Email for reservations, pricing options, and availability.

Spas and Relaxation
HAMMAM IL BAGNO TURCO

Via Torrearsa, 17/d; tel. 091/320-783; hours for women 3pm-8pm Mon.-Wed., 11:30am-8pm Fri., hours for men 4pm-8pm Tues., mixed hours 3pm-8pm Thurs., 11:30am-8pm Sat.; Turkish bath from €40, massages from €30

In the heart of the busy city center, discover a place of relaxation at Palermo's Turkish bath hammam. This spa offers massages, body scrubs, nourishing masks, facials, and traditional Turkish bath treatments. Treat yourself and cleanse your body from impurities in an atmosphere of pure tranquil luxury.

HOTEL PORTA FELICE SPA

Via Butera, 45; tel. 091/617-5678; www. hotelportafelice.it; 1pm-9pm daily with reservations only; foot massage €41, hot stone massage €62, mini facials €35, body waxing from €8

Find a little oasis in the middle of the city. The wellness center at the Hotel Porta Felice features a steam bath, sauna, and jacuzzi. Personalized anti-stress, deep tissue, and stone massages or body scrubs can be organized for guests of the hotel and others who wish to rejuvenate and beautify their body in the midst of a busy travel schedule. Their base package (€31) includes access to the sauna, steam bath with aromatic essences, showers, jacuzzi, and complimentary herbal tea.

Entertainment and Events

PERFORMING ARTS

Palermo has always been the cultural hub of Sicily, especially for the aristocratic upper-class. It was recognized as the 2018 Italian Capital of Culture, which stimulated a positive insurgence of cultural events, performances, and art exhibitions within the city. The **Museo Internazionale delle Marionette Antonio Pasqualino** is another great place to check out an artform truly unique to Sicily, with frequent puppet shows.

La Loggia
TEATRO POLITEAMA GARIBALDI

Via Filippo Turati, 2; tel. 091/6072532; www. orchestrasinfonicasiciliana.it; ticket office 9:30am-4:30pm Mon.-Sat., 9:30am-1:30pm Sun.; tickets €6-35

One of Palermo's main opera houses and home of the Sicilian symphony orchestra (the Orchestra Sinfonic Siciliana), the Politeama Garibaldi was built in 1865 to satisfy the needs of aristocratic society while the Teatro

Massimo was still under construction. Check the website for the schedule of regular seasonal concerts from November-June.

Capo
TEATRO BIONDO STABILE
Via Roma, 258; tel. 091/7434302; www.teatrobiondo. it; ticket office 9am-1pm and 4pm-7pm Tues.-Sat., 9am-noon and 4pm-7pm Sun.; from €45

Located on Via Roma just across from the Vuccuria Market, Teatro Biondo is one of Palermo's main theaters. It was built in the early 1900s and is recognized by the Ministry of Cultural Heritage and Tourism as "a theater of significant cultural interest." Teatro Biondi houses theatrical and dance performances as well as a concert hall for mainstream Sicilian performing artists.

TEATRO MASSIMO
Piazza Verdi; tel. 091/6053580; www.teatromassimo. it; guided visits every hour 9:30am-6pm Tues.-Sun.; performance tickets €25-125

Teatro Massimo is one of Palermo's most iconic landmarks, Europe's third largest after Paris and Vienna. The theater was built at the end of the 19th century, its facade an homage to classic Greek temples. Following the passing of its original architect, Giovani Battista Basile, the construction was completed by his son Ernesto in the neoclassical style. Opened in 1897, it was dedicated to King Victor Emanuel II. You might recognize it from Francis Ford Coppola's 1990 film *The Godfather Part III.* The acoustically perfect, horseshoe-shaped auditorium can host up 1,250 guests in gallery seating along with its five floors of box seats. Seasonal opera, ballet, concerts, and recital performances run consistently September-June; visit the theater's website for more details.

Although not otherwise open to the public outside performances, 30-minute **guided visits** (www.ticketone.it; from €8) allow visitors to admire the theater's graceful stuccoes, baroque-style deep garnet velvet and gold seating areas, wooden and glass decorations, and the intricate flower-wheel ceiling, created by Palermitan painter Rocco Lentini, featuring petals that open up to control the temperature of the theater.

ART GALLERIES
La Loggia
FRANCESCO PANTALEONE ARTE CONTEMPORANEA
Via Vittorio Emanuele, 303; tel. 091/332-482; www. fpac.it; 10am-1pm and 4pm-7pm Tues.-Sun.; free

The Francesco Pantaleone Arte

Teatro Massimo

Contemporanea, or FPAC, was founded in 2013 in the Vucciria Market area before moving to a new space at the corner of Palermo's Quattro Canti. Curator Francesco Pantaleone continues his original goal of representing established contemporary artists as well as opening up his space to emerging local talent. Each carefully curated exhibition features a story of the artist's home territory and a deep personal connection to their natural landscapes.

Outside City Center
CRE.ZI. PLUS - CANTIERI CULTURALI ALLA ZISA

Via Paolo Gili, 4, Cantieri Culturali alla Zisa 10/11; tel. 334/1520175; www.creziplus.it; 8:30am-9:30pm Mon.-Thurs., 8:30am-midnight Fri.-Sat.; free

Within the Cantieri Culturali alla Zisa complex, in a formerly industrial area behind the Castello della Zisa, this art center is a recent addition to the city's cultural footprint. Cre. Zi. Plus's creative projects intersect culture with social innovation, with co-working and special event spaces. The innovative Social Kitchen project brings people together to share ideas and values through food. Check out their **bistro** or their ongoing schedule of community programs, art exhibitions, food and wine festivals, and special events.

FESTIVALS AND EVENTS

Palermo is a warm and vivacious city, where any given day can turn into a celebration, from busking street performers to the songs of fishmongers promoting goods from their market stalls. There isn't a "festival season" per se, but when the weather is nice (which is nearly all year long), people gather in the streets with any reason possible to celebrate la dolce vita.

ZAGARA FESTIVAL

Orto Botanico dell'Università di Palermo, Via Lincoln, 2; tel. 091/23891236; www.ortobotanico.unipa.it/zagara.html; 9am-7pm, spring festival in Mar., fall festival in Oct.; €6 entrance free

This three-day, semi-annual festival of the zagara citrus flower has been running for the last 20 years at the University of Palermo's Botanical Garden. The festival was created by botanical experts to highlight plant nurseries from all around Italy and educate attendees on gardening, ecology, and horticulture. The paths through the botanic gardens are filled with educational programs, tented booths, and an extensive offering of plants, flowers, bulbs, seeds, and trees for sale. The festival highlights include special guided tours of the garden, themed exhibitions, gardening workshops, and children's programs.

FESTA DI SANTA ROSALIA

Cattedrale di Palermo; tel. 338/4954084; www.facebook.com/FestinoDiSantaRosaliaPalermo; July 10-14; free

This annual five-day celebration for the patron saint of Palermo has been going on for nearly 400 years. The multiday festival, known in the Sicilian dialect as "u fistìnu," includes a traditional historical procession, a mix of folklore and religion, that culminates with a firework display over the Foro Italico seaside park. The great procession on July 14 includes a solemn parade for Santa Rosalia's triumphant chariot, carrying her relics through the city streets to celebrate Palermo's liberation from the plague of 1624.

This event attracts tens of thousands of tourists to the city every year. Traditional culinary specialties are served in honor of the patroness, including pasta con le sarde, garlic babbalucci snails, and fresh wedges of summer watermelon. It's a great time to visit Palermo and see the town at its liveliest.

BALLARÒ BUSKERS

Mercato di Ballarò; www.ballarobuskers.it; late Oct.; free

During this annual international celebration, artists, bands, clowns, acrobats, jugglers, and dancers take to the streets of the Ballarò neighborhood, whose main feature is its vivacious outdoor food market. The festival aims to create a sense of community with colorful festivities including circus arts, music, parades, performances, and workshops for children throughout the neighborhoods.

Le Vie dei Tesori

Via E. Amari, 38; tel. 091/774-5575; www.leviedeitesori.com; weekends late Sept.-Nov. and around Christmas; €12 for 10 visits, €6 for 4 visits, €2.50 for single entrance
Le Vie dei Tesori is an islandwide cultural heritage festival, transforming each participating city into an open-air museum. Discover hidden secrets with guided visits to palaces, terraces, monasteries, churches, and gardens that are usually closed off to the public. In the city of Palermo, visitors can obtain access to private locations such as **Villa Pottino** and **Palazzo Ajutamicristo,** both sumptuous private residences, the former built in the early 20th century in the art nouveau style, the latter built for a 15th-century merchant to display his newfound wealth. As part of the holiday festivities, **Christmas concerts** are scheduled annually at the end of December in Palermo, Catania, Marsala, Ragusa, and Naro/Agrigento.

Outside Palermo, additional participating cities include:

- **Western Sicily:** Trapani, Marsala, Sambuca di Sicilia, Naro, Sciacca, and Caltanissetta

- **Eastern Sicily:** Acireale, Catania, and Messina

- **Southeastern Sicily:** Modica, Noto, Ragusa, Scicli, and Syracuse

Shopping

Palermo is a great place to shop for Sicilian souvenirs, antiques, food, and home goods. Prominent shopping areas are concentrated in the historic city center around the three main outdoor food markets (Capo, Ballarò, and Vuccria), or along **Via della Libertà** and **Via Ruggero Settimo.**

LA LOGGIA
Clothing and Accessories
OFFICINE ACHAB
Via Roma, 340; tel. 091/616-1849; www.facebook.com/OfficineAchab; 4pm-7:30pm Mon., 9am-1pm and 4pm-7:30pm Tues.-Wed., 9am-1pm Thurs., 9am-1pm and 4pm-7:30pm Fri.-Sat.
This boutique concept store offers quality clothing, artisan jewelry, children's toys, and books from select artists and designers.

KALSA
Markets
MERCATO DI PIAZZA MARINA
Piazza Marina, 22; 9am-1pm Sat.-Sun.

Stroll down to Piazza Marina, located in the Kalsa district, for the weekend flea market. Search through 20th-century memorabilia, old vinyl and cassettes, wooden toys, books, paintings, and art prints. A perfect place to track down hard-to-find-items like antique kitchen utensils, antiques, jewelry, watches, and Sicilian puppets. While you're there, check out **Giardino Garibaldi,** the piazza's small public park, to see the famous *Ficus macrophylla* tree; it's the largest in all of Europe!

Souvenirs
EDIZIONI PRECARIE
Via Alessandro Paternostro, 75; tel. 320/0141065; www.edizioniprecarie.it; 10:30am-2:30pm and 4:30pm-8:30pm Mon.-Sat.
This printmaking workshop and paper store sells handmade screenprinted art pieces, precious ceramics, and unique notebooks made from the traditional papers used in butcher shops and vegetable stands.

ARÈA

Piazza Rivoluzione, 1; tel. 338/888-7303; www. facebook.com/areapiazzarivoluzione; 5pm-midnight daily

This art gallery offers a public exhibition of local artisan works along with the option to purchase pieces made here in Palermo. From paintings to hand-carved wooden tableware, limited-edition prints, and pottery, Arèa is a great stop for those looking to take an original piece of artwork home with them.

CAPO
Markets
MERCATO DELLE PULCI

Piazza Domenico Peranni, 2; www.antiquariatoantico. it; morning-sunset daily, including holidays

Bring a little piece of Sicily home with you. Interior designers, decorators, art collectors, and tourists alike flock to this street market located between Piazza Peranni and Piazza del Papireto behind Palermo's main cathedral. The garage-style kiosks are filled with all kinds of antiques, treasures, vintage and up-cycled goods, and period furniture. This flea market opened immediately after World War II, playing an important role in the economic revitalization of the city. Today, it has become a crossroads of past and present filled with bargain deals on colorful ceramics as well as paintings and silverware.

Clothing and Accessories
MARLON VINTAGE STORE

Via Paolo Paternostro, 41A/41B; tel. 335/458-025; www.marlonvintagestore.business.site; 10:30am-1pm and 4pm-8pm Mon.-Sat.

Just a short walk from the Mercato del Capo and the Teatro Massimo opera house, Marlon offers unique vintage clothing, accessories, footwear, handbags, and vinyl records.

DELL'OGLIO

Via Ruggero Settimo, 26b; tel. 091/320238; www. dellogliostore.com; 4pm-8pm Mon., 10am-1:30pm and 4pm-8pm Tues.-Fri., 10am-1:30pm and 4:30pm-8pm Sat.

Tap into Palermo's rich aristocratic past with a few finely tailored pieces from Dell'Oglio. This boutique family-run clothing store offers mens and womenswear right on the main shopping avenue in Palermo. Dress to the nines with top-notch garments and live your best dolce vita, dressed like a real Italian.

Food

The culinary scene in Palermo accommodates all kinds of food lovers, with dishes from affordable and filling street food snacks to fresh seafood, fine dining, simply prepared and abundant plates of pasta, and decadent sweets. Compared to other major cities in Italy and Europe, the cost of food here is extremely inexpensive, and there is a huge variety of dishes: You'll find French-influenced, aristocratic family recipes drenched with bechamel and luscious flavors that date back to the Normans, who came to the Kingdom of Sicily with their own in-house family chefs; as well as **cucina povera,** the art of making delicious food with cheap ingredients. The layers of Sicily's cultural heritage shine through in the sweet-and-sour flavorings known as agrodolce, thought to be influenced by Arab cuisine, and over-the-top decorated desserts, remnants of the decadent baroque era. No matter what you're eating, dried citrus and candied fruit, as well as locally grown almonds and pistachios, are ubiquitous.

LA LOGGIA

Pizzeria
TIMILIA
Via Maqueda 221; tel. 091/784-6088; www.
pizzatimilia.it; 11:30am-12:30am daily; slices €2-5

A rarity on this major pedestrian street, where most of the souvenir shops, bars, and restaurants are not worth your while, this is a great option for a slice of pizza on the go. The selection changes daily, the pizzas are always made with top-quality flour, and the prices are extremely affordable. There are a few high-top tables out front where you can sit with a cold beer and slice of pizza to people-watch while the locals enjoy an evening passeggiata walk.

Markets
MERCATO VUCCIRIA
Via dei Frangiai, 50; market hours 8am-1pm
Mon.-Sat., nightlife center and street food after 9pm
Mon.-Sat.

Once one of the most important food markets in the city, nowadays La Vucciria has dwindled down to just a handful of fishmongers and street food vendors. It can be a nice stop on an early morning walk, but is more frequented in the evenings, when the square and its surrounding alleyways become completely packed with young people standing outside drinking, dancing, and snacking on Palermo's famous street food like sfincione, boiled octopus, and panelle.

Trattorie
VECCHIA TRATTORIA DA TOTÒ
Via Coltellieri, 6; tel. 333/315-7558; 9am-midnight
daily; €10-18

Perfect for a hearty plate of pasta and a half-liter of house wine, in the heart of the Vucciria, this simple trattoria is the real deal, with affordable prices and authentic fare. Try the fried sarde allinguate appetizer or a portion of fried calamari before diving into their pasta dishes. It's a great spot for sharing plates since the portions are bountiful. For two or three people, start with an appetizer and a carafe of white wine and then split one or two plates of pasta and one secondo piatto of grilled or fried fish.

★ AJA MOLA - TRATTORIA DI MARE
Via dei Cassari, 39; tel. 091/729-6599; www.
ajamolapalermo.it; 12:30pm-2:30pm and
7:45pm-11pm Tues.-Sun.; €12-24

The freshest seafood in town, located on a back street between the Vucciria square and La Cala port. The restaurant is named for an old Sicilian song from the centuries-old tradition of tuna fishing. Peruvian Chef Diego Recarte transforms local ingredients with a fresh and finely tuned flair. The front-of-house staff confidently pairs meals with their long list of Italian natural wines. The raw seafood dishes, such as tuna tartare with zucchini blossoms and sesame or the thinly sliced sashimi with burnt milk and almonds, are just as delightful to taste as they are to look at. Like most smart seafood restaurants, Aja Mola is closed on Mondays to mirror the fish market schedules.

TRATTORIA PICCOLO NAPOLI
Piazzetta Mulino a Vento, 4; tel. 091/320-431; www.
trattoriapiccolonapoli.it; 12:30pm-3:30pm and
7:30pm-11pm Mon.-Sat.; €14-25

This long-running family trattoria, specializing in seafood and typical Sicilian cuisine, is located not far from the port of Palermo. Friendly hospitality in a very casual setting, perfect for an intro to the home cooking of Sicily. Fresh local fish comes in daily, and dishes feature classics like fried panelle and artichokes, pasta con le sarde, local marinated raw white or red shrimp, and typical desserts like cannoli, biancomangiare, and cassata.

TRATTORIA ZIA PINA
Via dei Cassari, 69; tel. 327/086-2709; noon-3pm
Mon., noon-3pm and 7pm-1am Tues.-Sat.,
7pm-midnight Sun.; €20-25

Always a favorite for freshly grilled seafood and simple pasta dishes, Trattoria Zia Pina is not a fancy restaurant; think paper tablecloths and plastic water glasses. There is no set menu and they will bring you a handwritten check at the end of the meal. The two brother-in-law owners put out a large daily buffet of self-serve hot and cold antipasti, and guests can select their own seafood to order fried, grilled, or tossed with pasta. Just point to what you want, from swordfish steaks, big prawns, fresh calamari, whole sardines, and bite-sized anchovies. Get a table outside to enjoy the full experience. Zia Pina is best enjoyed at lunchtime. The staff is very friendly but for the most part nobody speaks English here, so get ready to gesture and smile your way through it.

Cafés and Light Bites
RINASCENTE
Via Roma, 289; tel. 391/377-1774; www.rinascente.it; 11am-3:30pm and 6pm-11:30pm daily
The rooftop of this high-end department store is a perfect place to sip your afternoon coffee with a panoramic view of the city. Stop by just to snap a few photos or enjoy an evening al fresco at aperitivo time.

Fine Dining
GAGINI
Via dei Cassari, 35; tel. 091/589-918; www.gaginirestaurant.com; 12:30pm-3pm and 7:30pm-11:30pm daily; tasting menus €45-85
Named for Antonello Gagini, an Italian Renaissance sculptor from Palermo, Gagini is a luxurious culinary experience highlighting top-quality products with the creative touch of one of the city's top chefs. Their series of four-, six-, or eight-course tasting menus combine seasonal produce with Sicily's best "materie prime" natural raw ingredients like almonds and pistachios, lumache snails, Slow Food Presidio garlic, sesame seeds, and capers. Their exceptionally curated wine list includes international, Italian, and Sicilian labels made with classic, organic, and natural practices.

KALSA
Cafés and Light Bites
★ I SEGRETI DEL CHIOSTRO
Chiesa di Santa Caterina, Piazza Bellini, 33; tel. 327/588-2302; www.isegretidelchiostro.com; 10am-6pm daily; €5
I Segreti del Chiostro (Secrets of the Cloister) is a pastry shop hidden away inside the **Chiesa di Santa Caterina** near the famous Fontana Pretoria between Piazza Pretoria and Piazza Bellini. Look for a small sign and an attendant outside, who will direct you upstairs to a small indoor garden and this very special shop, where long-lost Sicilian pastries pastry recipes have been preserved from many of the city's monasteries. Pick up a few almond biscotti, frutta di martorana marzipan fruits, or a pack of cannoli to take home with you—if you can resist eating them all on the spot.

CASA STAGNITTA
Discesa dei Giudici, 46; tel. 091/617-2819; www.casastagnitta.it; 6:30am-7pm Mon.-Sat.; under €5
Ideal Caffè Stagnitta has been around since 1928 and is the oldest torrefazione (coffee roaster) in the city still in its original location. Overseen by fourth-generation brothers, Massimo and Gianfranco Marchese, they produce coffee for many restaurants and bars in town and also sell directly at the store and online. Casa Stagnitta opened next door to the roasting shop when the street became a pedestrian zone, of course serving their own coffee, but also preparing gelato and typical pastries. It's a special little place in the historic center of Palermo, tucked away next to Piazza Bellini and around the corner from the famous fountain of Piazza Pretoria.

Fine Dining
OSTERIA DEI VESPRI
Piazza Croce dei Vespri, 6; tel. 091/617-1631; www.osteriadeivespri.it; 12:30pm-2:30pm and 7:30pm-10:30pm Mon.-Sat.; tasting menus €35-95

Chef Alberto Rizzo's innovative and modern way of working with Sicilian ingredients is one of the dining highlights of Palermo. By transforming traditional flavor combinations, he brings a fresh outlook to Sicilian cuisine. Authentic Palermitan dishes like pasta con tenerumi are revisited with the addition of ginger and house-smoked mackerel. The seasonal menu is surprising and always satisfying. A connoisseur of fine wines, chef Alberto's carte dei vini (wine list) is extensive and carefully curated. The small dining room is comfortable and cozy with a knowledgeable front-of-house team. Tables are moved outside into the quiet piazza in summertime.

Bistros
BUATTA CUCINA POPOLANA
Via Vittorio Emanuele, 176; tel. 091/322-378; www.buattapalermo.it; 12:30pm-2:30pm and 7:30pm-10:30pm daily; €23-36
This perfect small bistro highlights top-quality ingredients and typical Sicilian fare. It's one of the only places in town with an exceptional natural wine list. Daily rotating specials are usually the highlight of a meal here. The chef's personal recipe for Palermitan sfincione pizza rivals the best street food stalls around town. With a rounded menu of vegetarian, fish, and meat dishes, there's something for everyone at Buatta. Awarded with Michelin's "Bib Gourmand" award. Reservations recommended.

Street Food
'NNI FRANCO U'VASTIDDARU
Via Vittorio Emanuele, 102; tel. 091/325-987; 9am-1am daily; €2-8
A classic stop on a late-night street food tasting tour of the city, Franco's small fast-food corner is best known for its plates of fried chickpea panelle and arancine rice balls, as well as the most popular panino con la milza sandwich, made with slow-cooked slices of spleen and lungs topped with caciocavallo or ricotta cheese.

ALBERGHERIA
International
MOLTIVOLTI
Via Giuseppe Mario Puglia 21; tel. 091/271-0285; www.moltivolti.org; 9am-11pm Sun.-Thurs., 9am-midnight Fri.-Sat.; entrées €7-14
Moltivolti is a melting pot of a bistro and co-working space in the Ballarò neighborhood. Still unfortunately rare in Palermo, this special kitchen staff is led by chefs of multiple nationalities from Italy, Greece, Senegal, Gambia, and Afghanistan working in harmony together. Their trademark phrase "La mia terra è dove poggio i miei piedi" ("My land is where I rest my feet") clearly conveys their core mission of inclusivity. The menu ranges from dishes like pasta alla norma, lasagne, and Sicilian couscous, to moussaka, Tunisian brik, and mafè, a Senegalese beef stew with peanut sauce. Everyone is welcome to work, drink, and eat here.

Markets
★ MERCATO DI BALLARÒ
Via Ballarò, 1; 8am-5pm daily
This 1,000-year-old market in the historic Ballarò neighborhood is the largest and oldest open-air food market in the city. Locals and tourists alike weave through the winding labyrinth of stalls to purchase fresh fruit, vegetables, cheese, fish, meat, and local street food. Prices are truly up for debate here, with vendors singing and shouting out deals. All purchases must be made in cash, and the products found here are among the cheapest of all of the markets. Ballarò is one of the only places in the city where you'll see Palermo's Sri Lankan, North African, Bangaladeshi, and Italian purveyors selling specialties side by side.

CAPO
Bistros
BISSO BISTROT
Via Maqueda, 172A; tel. 328/131-4595; www.bissobistrot.it; 9am-11pm Mon.-Sat.; €12-20
Located on the corner of Palermo's Quattro Canti in the former premises of a bookstore,

☆ Street Food in Palermo

stigghiole

As Anthony Bourdain said, "In Palermo, street food is deadly serious." Although street food has become internationally trendy, the original place to try it is truly in the streets of Palermo, from vendors who have been making these items for their entire lives.

The best way to experience Palermo's street food scene is with a trusted guide. There are several options for food market tours and tastings that include street food samples, but the most authentic experience will be with a local culinary expert from **Palermo Street Food.**

Make sure to sample some of these can't-miss Palermitan street foods.

ARANCINE

It's debated whether to call these breaded and fried rice balls arancine (feminine) or arancini (masculine), but here in Palermo, they are always referred to as arancine (derived from the name of a small orange). These deep-fried treats are typically filled with bright yellow saffron risotto, tomato-based meat ragù, and green peas. Extremely large "arancine bombe" are served at **Touring Cafè** (Via Roma, 248; 6:30am-9pm daily), not far from Mercato Vucciria, and more creative fillings like pumpkin with pork sausage or sweet pistachio pesto are sold from street food kiosks like **Ke Palle** (Via Maqueda, 270; tel. 091/611-2009; 10:30am-midnight daily) in Mercato del Capo. For the real deal, head over to **Pasticceria Porta Sant'Agata di Trentacoste** (Via Porta Sant'Agata, 10; tel. 091/652-6778; www.pasticceriaportasantagata.it; 6:45am-9pm daily) in Ballarò.

BABBALUCCI

Small land snails sautéed with olive oil, whole cloves of garlic, parsley, and black pepper. Typically served for the **Festa di Santa Rosalia,** they can be found through most of the summer. The trick to eating them is to pick up one at a time with your fingers and suck the snail out from the shell. They are often served with toothpicks to help get the trickly little guy out of there. The very best are sold in Piazza della Kalsa, not far from Palazzo Abatellis.

CROCCHÈ

Sometimes referred to as cazzilli, these deep-fried potato dumplings are made with onion and parsley, often served in a panino along with panelle and a squeeze of fresh lemon juice. Find them in the Mercato di Ballarò during the day and in Mercato Vucciria at night.

FRITTOLA

Walking through the ancient markets of the Capo and Ballarò, you'll find frittola vendors carrying baskets filled with steaming pieces of fried meat, seasoned with bay leaf and lots of black pepper. Originally a way to use up the leftovers that the butchers could not sell in their shops, these crispy, chewy, and tender bites—when served on a sesame bun with a heavy dose of salt, black pepper, and fresh lemon juice—are completely divine.

PANELLE

Naturally gluten-free Sicilian chickpea crisps, deep-fried and seasoned simply with fresh parsley and a squeeze of lemon. A typical afternoon snack for school children or workers before or after a long day. The pane e panelle is a sandwich roll stuffed with panelle and a few crocchè potato croquettes.

PANI CÀ MEUSA

Also known as a panino con la milza, this hard-core street food sandwich is filled with thinly sliced cuts of spleen and lung, boiled and then slowly cooked in lard, and served on a traditional "vastedda" sesame seed bun. You get to decide if you want it schietta (single—only with lemon and salt) or maritata (married—with shredded caciocavallo cheese or fresh ricotta). Try it at Rocky Basile (Via Vittorio Emanuele, 211; 11:30am-4am daily) near Vucciria, or Nino U' Ballerino (Corso Camillo Finocchiaro Aprile, 76/78; open 24 hours) near Mercato del Capo.

SFINCIONE

A fluffy focaccia-style Sicilian "pizza" topped with tomato sauce, breadcrumbs, onion, and anchovies. Traditionally served as street food and only found in the city of Palermo. Most of food carts selling sfincione pick up it up from the same late-night bakery, so the quality will only vary depending on how fresh they are. Ask the "sfinciunaru" vendor to toast it inside their hidden griddle and enjoy it warm.

STIGGHIOLE

With roots from the Latin word "extilia," meaning intestines, this dish actually has Greek origins, and you'll even find something very similar in Turkey. Stigghiole are made with lamb, veal, and sometimes goat intestines that have been wrapped around green spring onion and a few sprigs of fresh parsley. It's the perfect balance of fat, salt, and freshness. Find them in the Vucciria Market at night or in the Ballarò Market in the morning.

FOOD

PALERMO AND WESTERN SICILY

this is a favorite spot for a quick lunch, with heaping portions of pasta or simple Sicilian soups like macco di fava or minestra di tenne-rumi for under €7. At night, Bisso becomes very busy, so it's best to put your name down on the waiting list and grab a glass of wine while you wait outside.

★ LE ANGELICHE COMFORT BISTRÒ

Vicolo Abbadia, 10, Mercato del Capo; tel. 091/615-7095; www.leangeliche.it; noon-7pm Mon., 9am-7pm Tues.-Thurs., 9am-11pm Fri.-Sat.; granita and gelato €6-8, main dishes €16

This spot is a joyful success story of a group of four young entrepreneurs, Floriana, Veronica, Chiara, and Barbara, who came together to build this dreamy Sicilian bistro-café and backyard garden patio with lounge chairs and hammocks. Hidden on a side street within the Capo Market, the restaurant focuses on specialized pastries and the old recipes of great-grandmothers that have nearly been forgotten. In summertime, the girls rotate a daily list of granita made from seasonal fruit, from kiwi to strawberries and prickly pears, that pair perfectly with fresh-from-the-oven almond or orange brioche buns. While sporadically open for breakfast time, the bistro is mainly open for lunch, dinner, and special events featuring local natural winemakers. The main goal here is to make customers feel at home.

Cafés and Light Bites
CAPPADONIA GELATI

Via Vittorio Emanuele, 401; tel. 392/568-9784; www.cappadonia.it; noon-6pm Mon.-Fri., noon-8pm Sat.-Sun.; €5

Since July 14, 2018 (the day of the Santa Rosalia Festival in Palermo), master ice cream maker Antonio Cappadonia has maintained his prices as well as unparalleled quality in his precious gelato shop. The fruit-based

flavors change according to the seasons. Each batch uses the same recipe, with the addition of flavors like strawberry, lemon, coffee, and Slow Food Presidium Trapani sea salt caramel. This incredible gelateria has a second location near the Teatro Politeama Garibaldi (Piazzetta Francesco Bagnasco, 29).

Markets
MERCATO DEL CAPO

Via Cappuccinelle; 8am-1pm Mon.-Sat.

Situated behind the Teatro Massimo, the Capo Market is part of the heart and soul of the city, a place for grocery shopping, local food tastings, and sampling typical products like capers, tomato paste, Sicilian oregano, vacuum-sealed sun-dried tomatoes, olives, pistachios, and pasta to take home in your suitcase. As market tourism has become more popular in the last decade, the vendors and restaurants have adapted to offer ready-to-eat options for guests who might not be purchasing ingredients to cook for themselves. Small kiosks provide fresh-squeezed orange and pomegranate juices, fried street food treats, and even simple traditional plates of sarde a beccafico, parmigiana di melanzane, stuffed artichokes, caponata, and even a glass of wine or a sparkling spritz cocktail.

Street Food
SAVOCA ORIGINAL PALERMO

Via Sammartino, 103; tel. 091/341-228; 5pm-10:30pm daily; €0.80/piece

This typical Sicilian rosticceria take-out counter offers hot snacks like pizzette, arancine, timballi, baked calzone, and roast chickens. Perfect for a quick stop before a night out. Taste your way through the city's specialties with their fast-casual buffet of savory bites.

I CUOCHINI

Via Ruggero Settimo, 68; tel. 091/581-158; www.icuochini.com; 8:30am-2:30pm Mon.-Fri., 8:30am-2:30pm and 4:30pm-7:30pm Sat.; €5

I Cuochini is the ultimate antica rosticceria in Palermo, tucked away, but not forgotten, for nearly 200 years! In Sicily, a rosticceria is

---

1: vew from the Rinascente department store's rooftop lounge **2:** strolling through Mercato di Ballarò **3:** fresh produce in Mercato di Ballarò

a place to buy hot food to be quickly eaten on the spot at the banco counter or taken away. This hidden gem is located in a small courtyard a bit north of the city center, not far from Teatro Politeama Garibaldi. Still in its original location, I Cuochini is a savory bakery that has been serving small pezzi (bites) in classic Palermo-style since 1826. Don't expect sit-down service or even proper plates and cutlery; most of their bites are served in a napkin or on a plastic plate. It's cheap, high quality, and the kitchen is spotless. Wash it all down with a cold Partannina citrus soda. It's a simple, quick stop for a savory breakfast or lunchtime snack.

Trattoria
★ CORONA TRATTORIA

Via Guglielmo Marconi 9; tel. 091/335-139; www. coronatrattoria.it; 12:30pm-3pm and 8pm-11pm Tues.-Sat., 12:30pm-3pm Sun.; €20-30

The Corona family brings a cheerful, loving vibe to their chic trattoria. Daily offerings feature local seafood and traditional Sicilian specialties like spaghetti with squid ink and bottarga, sweet-and-sour caponata, a raw plate of local gamberi rossi, or fried calamaretti.

Top-notch service and exceptional high-quality ingredients make this place shine. The extensive wine list, curated by Orazio Corona, features hard-to-find natural and traditional wines from all around Sicily. Get a reservation because this small trattoria books up fast.

OUTSIDE CITY CENTER
Pizzeria
★ OZIO GASTRONOMICO

Via di Blasi Francesco Paolo, 2; tel. 091/346-306; www.oziogastronomico.com; 1pm-3pm and 6:30pm-midnight daily; €18-30

Although it's a long walk north of city center (1.9 mi/3 km; 40 minutes via Via Maqueda/ Via della Libertà), pizza lovers flock to Ozio Gastronomico for the best pie in town. Friendly and knowledgeable owner Dario Genova is a Palermitan who brought real Neapolitan pizza to his hometown. Working with small food producers and the highest quality ingredients possible, this upscale pizzeria is definitely worth the trek. Enjoy the greatest hits like a pizza margherita or test out some of Dario's original creations like his version of sfincione topped with slow-cooked red onions, citron zest, and grated tuna bottarga.

Bars and Nightlife

If you're ready to take the city by storm, the nightlife in Palermo has a lot to offer, from small casual bars to chic cocktail spots, and of course lots of delicious street food for a late-night bite.

LA LOGGIA
TAVERNA AZZURRA

Via Maccherronai, 15; tel. 091/304-107; 9am-5am Mon.-Sat.

Stay out all night with the locals at Taverna Azzurra in the vivacious La Vucciria Market. This no-fuss pub is the meeting point for young locals looking for a cheap night out

with great music. Mixed drinks are served in plastic cups to take outside into the street, the beers are cheap, and the atmosphere is perfectly Palermitan.

BOCUM

Via dei Cassari, 6; tel. 091/332-009; www.facebook. com/bocumpalermo; 6pm-2am Wed.-Mon.

From the Good Company restaurant group (Buatta, Aja Mola, Gagini Social Club, Libertà), Bocum was Palermo's first "mixology" bar. A great place to cuddle up on date night and enjoy elaborate cocktails and natural wines.

NAUTO

Piazzetta Capitaneria di Porto; tel. 366/540-9382;
www.facebook.com/nautoscopioarte; 9am-2am daily
June-Sept.

Created as Nautoscopio Arte for an installation by Giuseppe Amato, this summer beach bar near the port of Palermo has developed into a casual setting for art, music, and theater performances. Although Palermo is not technically a beach town, Nauto brings a seaside vibe to the city. Enjoy a cocktail overlooking the sea at sunset or cozy up on their upcycled wooden pallet couches into the evening. Follow their calendar for special events and parties throughout the high season.

KALSA

BOTTEGHE COLLETTI

Via Alessandro Paternostro, 79; tel. 091/781-5000;
6:30pm-2am daily

A truly fantastic cocktail bar with talented top-notch bartenders just off of Corso Vittorio Emanuele. Colletti is a tiny vintage spot decked out with antique furniture, deep green walls, exposed wood ceilings, and sexy mood lighting. Pop in for one of their famous smoked negroni and enjoy the small bites like crostini, salads, and mini sandwiches from their daily aperitivo buffet.

CAPO

ENOTECA BUTTICÈ

Piazza S. Francesco di Paola, 12; tel. 091/251-5394;
www.enotecabuttice.it; 12:30pm-3pm and
5pm-11:30pm Mon.-Sat.

Originally opened in 1936 by Giuseppe Butticè as a salumeria deli and wine shop just behind Teatro Massimo, Enoteca Butticè is now known as one of the best wine bars in the city. Stop by for a glass of wine and their plentiful aperitivo platters from 5pm-8:30pm, or make a reservation for dinner in their small dining room. Their wine list includes over 700 Sicilian, Italian, and international labels.

ENOTECA PICONE

Via Guglielmo Marconi, 36; tel. 091/331-300;
www.enotecapicone.com; 9:30am-1:30pm and
5pm-11:30pm daily

After a day of touring the city, it's time to treat yourself. Meet up for aperitivo time at Enoteca Picone, a historic wine bar open since 1946. Picone's whip-smart sommelier, Vera Bonanno, is one of the top wine experts in the city. Their selection of over 7,000 international, Italian, and Sicilian wines can be served with a mixed meat-and-cheese platter or enjoyed with a basket of fresh bread and electric-green extra virgin olive oil. Sit outside for an hour or two with a bottle of wine or sip on a cognac, whisky, or grappa.

OUTSIDE CITY CENTER

LIBERTÀ - VINI NATURALI E CUCINA

Via della Libertà, 93d; tel. 091/910-2341; 10am-3pm
and 6pm-11pm Tues.-Sun.

This newly opened natural wine bar is located in Palermo's upper-class neighborhood on Via della Libertà, north of the city center. Restaurateurs Stefania Milano and Franco Virga created a chic local haunt for wine lovers. Their young chefs, Alessandro Fanara and Francesco Mango, pair contemporary Sicilian dishes with top-quality bottles from hard-to-find producers.

Accommodations

When looking for accommodations in Palermo, the most convenient will be located within walking distance from the **Quattro Canti.** Additional apartment rentals are available through websites such as Airbnb, but as Palermo is relatively affordable, basing yourself in a hotel or resort can be a great choice to ensure you have the additional service and guidance of a hotel concierge.

LA LOGGIA
€100-200
MASSIMO PLAZA HOTEL
Via Maqueda, 437; tel. 091/325-657; www. massimoplazahotel.com; from €118

Right in front of the Teatro Massimo, the four-star Massimo Plaza Hotel is in the middle of all the action. Family-owned since 1921, this 11-room hotel offers simple and convenient accommodations with the centro storico of Palermo right at your fingertips.

★ PALAZZO SOVRANA
Via Bara All'Olivella, 78; tel. 351/561-5444; www. palazzosovrana.it; €150-300

Make yourself at home in the historic city center of Palermo. The luxury apartment rentals at Palazzo Sovrana, located right in front of the Teatro Massimo, have the best view in town. This historic palace was recently renovated and each of the spacious and modern apartments are at least 430-750 square feet (40-70 square m), to ensure peace and quiet in the comfort of your home away from home. Each apartment has two or three balconies, a queen-size bed, television, and private bathroom. Enjoy top-tier Sicilian hospitality from a friendly English-speaking concierge staff who can organize stress-free airport transfers, offer free parking, and arrange guided itineraries around Palermo.

KALSA
€100-200
L' HÔTELLERIE
Foro Italico Umberto I, 13; tel. 339/589-8058; www. lhotellerie.it; €155

Located near the botanical gardens and the city's waterfront promenade, L'Hôtellerie is one of the very few design hotels in Palermo. This 16th-century palace has rooftop views of the city along with stylish rooms equipped with Wi-Fi service, flat-screen televisions, coffee machines, private bathrooms with bidets and complimentary toiletries, and on-site breakfast service. Pets are welcome and airport transfers can be organized (both with advanced notice).

ALBERGHERIA
Under €100
PALAZZO BRUNACCINI
Piazzetta Lucrezia Brunaccini, 9; tel. 091/586-904; www.palazzobrunaccini.it; from €88

In the heart of the lively Ballarò neighborhood just steps away from the outdoor food market, this boutique four-star hotel offers charming yet sometimes noisy sun-lit rooms and suites overlooking a stone courtyard. The hotel restaurant, **Da Carlo a Palazzo Brunaccini,** celebrates authentic Sicilian cuisine highlighting fresh fish dishes inspired by the seasonality of the market.

€100-200
B&B IL GIARDINO DI BALLARÒ
Via Porta di Castro, 75/77; tel. 091/212215; www. ilgiardinodiballaro.it; from €100

Located in a restored 18th-century palazzo on a residential street connecting the Ballarò outdoor food market and the Norman Palace, this quaint family-run bed-and-breakfast offers understated rooms, a beautiful hidden garden, rooftop courtyard, guest kitchen, and outdoor hot tub.

B&B PALAZZO NATOLI
*Via Santissimo Salvatore, 6; tel. 091/7780666; www.
palazzonatoli.com; €190*
Perfectly situated just off the main avenue of
Corso Vittorio Emanuele near the picturesque
Quattro Canti intersection, Palazzo Natoli of-
fers bright and modern four-star accommoda-
tions along with 24-hour front desk service,
Wi-Fi connection, air-conditioning, and op-
tional room service.

CAPO
Under €100
EUROSTARS CENTRALE PALACE
*Via Vittorio Emanuele, 325; tel. 091/8539; www.
eurostarshotelcompany.com; from €65*
A four-star hotel centrally located in the
heart of Palermo's historic center right next
to the Quattro Canti, the Palermo branch
of the Eurostars hotel group features bright

air-conditioned rooms, a private terrace with
views of the city, and a grand continental
breakfast.

€200-300
CASA NOSTRA BOUTIQUE HOTEL
*Via Sant'Agostino, 134; tel. 091/327003; www.
casanostrapalermo.com/boutique-hotel; €210*
This Boutique Hotel is located in the heart
of Palermo's city center, near the Teatro
Massimo theater and the Mercato del Capo
outdoor food market. Built in a historic palace, the 12 carefully renovated rooms and
suites are equipped with Wi-Fi service, smart
televisions, coffee machines, and minibars.
The common spaces also include a fitness
center, small bistro, garden, outdoor courtyard, and jacuzzi pool. For a budget-friendly
option, try their bed-and-breakfast on Vicolo
Maestro Cristofaro, 2.

Information and Services

TOURIST INFORMATION
Visit Palermo (www.visitpalermo.it) information desks can be found at the harbor, Piazza
Bellini, and the Teatro Politeama Garibaldi. In
addition to distributing information and tourist materials, the Wonderful Italy Welcome
Point (Via Torremuzza, 15; tel. 02/8088-9702;
www.visitpalermo.it; 10am-1pm and 5pm-7pm
Mon.-Sat., 10am-2pm Sun.) can help tourists
with printing boarding passes and booking
tour guides, taxis, excursions, wine tastings,
tours, and restaurant reservations.

OTHER SERVICES
- **Poste Italiane:** Via Roma, 320; tel.
091/753-5392; www.poste.it; 8:20am-7pm
Mon.-Fri., 8:20am-12:30pm Sat.
- **Antica Pharmacy Cavour:** Via Camillo

Benso Conte di Cavour, 96; tel. 091/611-
9419; open 24 hours
- **Pharmacy Vajana:** Via Maqueda, 189; tel.
091/616-2769; 8:30am-1:15pm and 4pm-
8pm Mon.-Fri.
- **State Police:** Polizia di Stato/Questura
Palermo, Piazza della Vittoria, 8; tel.
091/210111; www.questure.poliziadistato.it
- **Cristina Benfratelli Civic Hospital:**
Ospedali Civico Di Cristina Benfratelli, Via
Ernesto Tricomi; tel. 091/666-1111; www.
arnascivico.it; open 24 hours
- **United States Consulate:** Conosolato
Stati Uniti D'America, Via Giovan Battista
Vaccarini, 1; tel. 091/30-5857; www.
it.usembassy.gov/embassy-consulates/
naples/consular-agency-palermo; 9am-
12:30pm Mon.-Fri.

Getting There

Most international visitors arrive to Palermo with a connecting flight via a larger Italian city, like Rome or Milan. Palermo can also be reached on an overnight ferry from Naples. Though it is possible to drive to Sicily from Puglia or Naples and the Amalfi Coast, it will take the better part of a day and is not recommended. To make the best use of your time, take advantage of quick flights on budget airlines.

BY AIR

AEROPORTO DI PALERMO FALONCE E BORSELLINO

Località Punta Raisi, Cinisi; tel. 800/541-880; www. aeroportodipalermo.it

Still often referred to by its original name, **Punta Raisi,** the airport in Palermo was renamed to commemorate two Italian judges who were assassinated in 1992 for their efforts to take down the Sicilian mafia. The airport is located in the seaside town of Cinisi, 19 miles (31 km) west of Palermo city center, with a runway that seems to head straight into the deep blue sea. Two currency exchange desks are available for international travelers (Check-in Area A and in the Departures Hall). Free Wi-Fi is accessible in the terminal. Wheelchair-accessible elevators, restrooms, and the Sala Amica Lounge are available for guests who require additional assistance. Shops, cafés, a post office, and pharmacy are conveniently located throughout the airport.

Several major airlines offer daily/weekly service to several top Italian and European destinations, including **Rome** (1 hour 15 minutes; €25), **Naples** (1 hour 5 minutes; €50), and **Bari** (1 hour 15 minutes; €100).

Rental cars can be picked up at the Palermo airport from **Avis** (tel. 091/591684; www.avisautonoleggio.it), **Budget** (tel. 06/6501-0678; www.budgetautonoleggio.it), **GoldCar** (tel. 06/4520-9634; www.goldcar.es/it), and **Sicily by Car** (tel. 091/591250; www.

sicilybycar.it). Additional small autonoleggio providers are available with a navetta shuttle bus service off-site. It's a 30-minute (19 mi/31 km) drive to Palermo's historic center from the airport, mostly on the **E90** coastal highway.

Shuttle bus service from the airport to Palermo's city center is provided by **Prestia e Comandè** (www.prestiaecomande.it; €6 one-way). Tickets can be purchased in advance online, at the arrivals gate inside the airport, or on-site directly from the bus driver. Buses from the city run 4am-11pm every 30 minutes; buses from the airport run from 5am-midnight. Departing from the bus terminal in the central station, along Via Roma, and Via Libertà, the bus ride takes approximately 45 minutes to 1 hour.

Train service from the airport to the Palermo Centrale station is provided by **TrenItalia** (www.trenitalia.it; €5.90 one-way). Tickets can be purchased in advance online or from an automated kiosk in the basement level of the airport. This trip takes 50 minutes, making several stops in various residential areas of the city before arriving at the main station, Palermo Centrale. Tickets must be time stamped at the station before boarding. Bathrooms are available on the train.

Taxis are available outside the arrivals gate at the airport. The ride to downtown Palermo will take about 30 minutes and cost around €45. Shared taxi vans can be utilized when guests are headed to main locations in the city, such as Palermo Centrale train station. Shared taxis are located just to the right of the main exit near the shuttle buses and cost €7 per person.

BY TRAIN

PALERMO STAZIONE CENTRALE

Piazza Giulio Cesare; www.trenitalia.com

The main train station in the historic center is Palermo Stazione Centrale, located at

Via Roma and Via Lincoln. Tickets can be purchased in advance online or from an automated kiosk at the train station entrance. Tickets must be time stamped at the station before boarding the train. Palermo is well-connected by train to **Agrigento** (2 hours; from €9), **Cefalù** (1 hour; from €4), and **Milazzo** (2 hours 30 minutes; from €12), gateway to the Aeolian Islands. From **Catania** (2 hours 30 minutes; from €11), you can connect to various points on Sicily's eastern coast. If traveling all the way to the Italian mainland, there are trains available to **Napoli Centrale** (9 hours 30 minutes; from €35), but this is by no means the fastest way to travel, and is often not even the cheapest.

BY FERRY

PORTO DI PALERMO

Molo Santa Lucia; www.adsppalermo.it
Ferries and cruise ships arrive in the ferry terminal in the port of Palermo. Guests traveling from the Amalfi Coast to Sicily can take advantage of the year-round, overnight ferry from Napoli to Palermo, organized by **Traghetti Lines** (www.traghettilines.it; seats €31, cabins €67, car transport €14-30). Tickets for the 11-hour trip can be reserved in advance online or in the Massa port of Naples ticket counter. This can be a good option for some, as it saves the cost of a hotel for the night.

In summer (June-Sept.), it's also possible to travel from Palermo to the Aeolian Islands via hydrofoils operated by **Liberty Lines** (tel. 0923/873-813; www.libertylines.it).

Palermo is also a port of call for cruise lines visiting the Mediterranean, including itineraries from **Norwegian Cruise Line** (www.ncl.com), **Royal Caribbean** (www. royalcaribbean.com/cruise-to/sicily-palermo-italy), **Costa Cruises** (www.costacruises. com), and **MSC Cruises** (www.msccruises. com).

BY CAR

Palermo's infamous reputation for bad traffic proceeds it—this is probably not a place you'll want to be navigating with your own car, so if you're traveling Sicily on a road trip, it may be best to find a way to drop your car off before you get to the capital city. That said, Palermo is a fairly easy drive from **Catania** (2.5 hours; 120 mi/200 km) and points on the eastern coast through the island's mountainous interior (though do be prepared for construction and detours), and is no more than 2 hours from any of the highlights on the western coast.

Getting Around

Palermo's centro storico is very walkable, making cars, motorbikes, and public transportation in many cases unnecessary for tourists.

BY BUS

The **AMAT** (www.amat.pa.it) bus system within the city of Palermo is truly a local's public transportation system, mostly utilized by commuters, but it can be useful for travelers who want to save time walking. Timetables are posted at each bus stop, but make sure you plan for extra travel time, as buses often run on "Sicilian time." **Bus 101** runs from Stazione Centrale to the Teatro Politeama Garibaldi and Giardino Inglese. **Bus 806** (leaving from Piazza Francesco Crispi at the western end of the Giardino Inglese) connects to the beach town of Mondello. A single ride ticket costs €1.40 and can be purchased ahead of time at any tabacchi shop, newsstand, or AMAT bus office. Bus tickets should be time stamped with a small machine near the driver upon boarding. City buses are often patrolled by the municipal police, and you risk a €54 fine if you do not have a ticket, or if it has not been properly time stamped.

BY TAXI

For a few important city sights that are a bit farther from the centro storico, such as the Catacombe dei Cappuccini and Castello della Zisa, it can be helpful to take a taxi, which are usually fairly reasonably priced. A one-way taxi to the Castello della Zisa, for example, costs €15, while a lift up to the Sanctuary of Santa Rosalia is €30. Local taxi services are provided by **Radio Taxi Trinacria** (tel. 091/6878) and **Autoradio Taxi** (tel. 091/8481). Taxi stands are located in Piazza Giuseppe Verdi by the Teatro Massimo, Piazza Castelnuovo near the Teatro Politeama Garibaldi, in front of the Stazione Centrale train station, and on Corso Vittorio Emanuele by the Fontana Pretoria.

BY CAR OR PRIVATE DRIVER

Driving a car around Palermo is not generally recommended. Tricky ZTL restrictions in the historic center (regulations to limit traffic), limited secure places to park, and undeniably fearless Sicilian drivers are best avoided if at all possible. To drive in the centro historico, daily **ZTL passes** must be purchased at a tabacchi shop, or you'll risk a fine of at least €150. Renting a car when you plan to leave Palermo and venture off to other parts of the island can be a great option, but a car for your days in Palermo is not necessary. Rental agencies in Palermo include **Hertz** (Via Messina, 7E) and **Sicily By Car** (Via Mariano Stabile, 6A). If you choose to park a car in Palermo, expect guarded parking lots to cost between €12-20/day, or inquire with your hotel about parking.

Vicinity of Palermo

Within the province of Palermo, hit the road to relax on the sandy beaches of Mondello or Cefalù. If you're looking for the best quality accommodations, restaurants, and nightlife, plan to stay in the city of Palermo and take quick day trips outside town with your own rental car or the train when possible. Be sure to explore the peaceful Sicilian countryside with a vineyard visit and wine-tasting experience in Camporeale, and pencil in a few hours to see the Cattedrale di Monreale, a UNESCO World Heritage Site and extraordinary example of Norman-Arab-Byzantine architecture.

MONDELLO

A 20-minute bus ride from the center of Palermo is the seaside village of Mondello, where you can enjoy a gelato on the beach, or relax under an umbrella at a lido, or beach club. Once only a swampy hunting reserve plagued by malaria, Mondello has become one of the busiest beaches in Sicily. Its close location to the capital city makes it a popular location for second homes for Palermo's

upper class. In the late 19th century, the art deco style villas that were built here began the town's transformation into the quaint seaside village it is today. Mondello has become the heart of Palermo's summer beach scene from June through September. The village becomes a ghost town in winter, except for the residents who live here year-round and the active locals who enjoy exercising along the lungomare.

Sights
SANTUARIO DI SANTA ROSALIA

Via Bonanno Pietro; tel. 091/540-326; www. santuariosantarosalia.it; 7:30am-1pm and 1:30pm-6:30pm daily, 7am-1pm and 3pm-6:30pm Easter and Christmas; free

Located between the city of Palermo and Mondello, the Sanctuary of Santa Rosalia sits at the top of Monte Pellegrino overlooking the bay of Palermo. If you can't make it during the annual July 14 **Festa di Santa Rosalia,** simply drive up to the Sanctuary of Santa Rosalia to pay respect to Palermo's patron saint at her sacred cave at the top of

Monte Pellegrino. It's a unique chance to see a lovely church built deep into a cave. According to tradition, she belonged to the 12th-century noble Sinibaldi family from the province of Agrigento. After retiring to her cave to live as a hermit, she appeared to a hunter in a dream in 1624, nearly 500 years after her death, indicating where he could find her remains, which she told him should be carried in a procession through the city in order to save it from the plague.

Nestled at the top of the mountain, the church and the cave sanctuary are traditionally visited by local families praying for the health of their loved ones. During the COVID pandemic, Palermitans looked to Santa Rosalia to help overcome the virus and protect their citizens. The 7-mile (11-km) drive from the port of Palermo via SS113 will take about 25 minutes. The Sanctuary is located 25 minutes from the beach in Mondello, following Via Monte Ercta northwest to the Viale Margherita di Savoia. The number 812 AMAT city bus (www.amat. pa.it; 35 minutes; €2) to Montepellegrino departs every two hours from the Liberta' - Archimede bus stop on Via Libertà and Via Archimede, in front of the Hermès store; guests should get off at the Santuario stop (number 1904) right in front of the entrance to the shrine of Santa Rosalia. For those driving up to Monte Pellegrino, parking is available at the Stele Croce di Via al Santuario Santa Rosalia (Via Santuario Monte Pellegrino), a 4-minute walk from the entrance. A taxi ride will cost €30 each way, however, the local drivers offer a package for €70 that includes a round-trip ride including the time they will wait while you tour the sanctuary.

★ Beaches

Mondello's mile-long (1.5-km) sandy stretch of golden beach, the closest beach to the city of Palermo, gets busy quick when summer hits. More isolated and rocky, the **Riserva Naturale di Capo Gallo** (www.

riservacapogallo.it) begins at the northwestern end of town, a good option to avoid the summer crowds in Mondello or a quiet place to explore on foot any time of year.

SPIAGGIA DI MONDELLO

Viale Regina Elena, Mondello; open 24 hours; free
Just 20 minutes northwest of Palermo's city center, the Spiaggia di Mondello is a long, golden-sand beach frequented by travelers, local beachgoers, and surfers. Sections of the beach are free and open to the public while other areas, like **Italo-Belga** (Viale Regina Elena, 59a; www.mondelloitalobelga. it) and **Lido Onde** (Viale Regina Elena, 53; tel. 091/450436; €16-25) are accessible only to those who pay the daily beach club fee, which conveniently includes bathrooms and outdoor showers. Beach beds and umbrellas can be rented daily at the ticket booths on the Viale Regina Elena beachfront or reserved in advance online (www.mondello. marcomedia.it; €11-20). The beachfront runs along the Viale Regina Elena road and is easily reached by car, taxi, or city bus. This main road is filled with bars, cafés, and ice cream shops. For those using the free beach areas, there are unfortunately no public restrooms available except at the cafés and bars that offer these services to paying customers only.

PUNTA BARCARELLO

Capo Gallo Natural Reserve, Via Barcarello, 31; www. parks.it/riserva.capo.gallo
Located at the west end of Mondello in the Capo Gallo Nature Reserve, this secluded rocky beach coast is a great place to escape the crowds at the Spiaggia di Mondello. There are no amenities or beach services here, just a wild natural place to enjoy a walk or a relaxing swim. The current can be rougher than the protected bay in Mondello, and accessing the water requires climbing over large rocks. Make sure to bring along your own towels, umbrellas, and water shoes to make the most of your day.

Water Sports

ALBARIA CLUB

*Viale Regina Elena 89/a; tel. 091/453-595; www.
albaria.org; 9am-6pm daily; windsurfing rentals €25/
hour, SUP rentals €16/hour*

For those looking to soak up the sun while
getting in their exercise, Albaria offers
walk-in rentals for stand-up paddleboards
(SUP), wind surfboards, and canoes. Albaria
also offers private and group **lessons** for SUP,
windsurfing, and sailing.

BOAT SERVICE MONDELLO

*Via Piano di Gallo; tel. 327/561-8175; www.
boatservicemondello.it; 8am-7pm daily; rentals
from €80*

Boat Service Mondello offers half- and full-
day gommone and motor boat rentals for up
to six people (from €80). A nautical license
is not required. If you would prefer to have
a skipper on board, this can be added to your
reservation (additional €40 half day, €70
full day). They also offer a guided half-day
boat excursion, also for a maximum of six,
leaving at 9am from the Mondello tourist
marina (€220 fee includes 3-hour 30 minute-
excursion, boat rental, skipper, snorkeling kit,
and fuel).

Food

BARETTO

*Viale Regina Elena, 83, Mondello; tel. 335/677-4759;
www.barettomondello.it; 8am-8pm daily Apr.-Oct.;
€5*

The Schillaci family has been serving gelato
from this tiny green beach shack since
1957. Seasonal specialties include mulberry,
strawberry, prickly pear, and lemon as well as
classic Italian flavors like hazelnut, pistachio
and stracciatella. Try their famous coffee-
flavored caffè gelato; ask for it "con panna
sotto" to have freshly whipped cream added
to the bottom of your cone. Make sure to stop
by to enjoy a treat at the end of a beach day
before heading back to Palermo.

Information and Services

- **Mondello Info Point:** Piazza Mondello,
  2; www.visitpalermo.it; 8am-2:30pm and
  3:30pm-7pm daily

Getting There

From central **Palermo,** Mondello is a
15-minute drive: pass the Stadio Renzo
Barbera on Viale Diana, which becomes
Viale Margherita di Savoia. This will take

Spiaggia di Mondello

you directly to Viale Regina Elena/SS113 for Mondello. Paid parking spots (€1/hour) are marked with a blue stripe and will need to be paid with a ticket from a nearby blue kiosk machine. There are a few private parking lots (from €2/hour) near the beach, but make sure to check their closing times so your car does not get locked in the gate for the night. A taxi ride from Palermo to Mondello will cost approximately €25.

The number **806 bus** (www.amat.pa.it) is scheduled to run approximately every 20 minutes from Palermo's centro storico, but be prepared for the wait time to be longer than expected. Check the signs posted at the bus stop and confirm with the driver for daily timetables and when the last return bus will depart. The 806 bus leaves from the Piazza Francesco Crispi square at the western end of the Giardino Inglese and takes about 25 minutes to arrive in Mondello. A one-way ticket costs €1.40 and can be purchased ahead of time at any tabacchi shop, newsstand, or AMAT bus office.

CATTEDRALE DI MONREALE

Piazza Guglielmo II, 1; tel. 091/640-4413; www. monrealeduomo.it; 9:30am-12:30pm and 3pm-4:30pm Mon.-Fri., 8:30am-9:30am and 3pm-4:30pm Sat.-Sun. and holidays, open only for personal prayers during Easter season (Mar.-Apr.); free, €4 for treasury and roof access

In the small hillside town of Monreale, overlooking Palermo, is the astonishing Cattedrale di Monreale, one of Sicily's treasured UNESCO World Heritage Sites. Thought of as one of the best existing examples of Norman architecture, this 12th-century masterpiece is one of the island's most-visited attractions.

The history of the cathedral dates back to the 12th century, when the Normans seized Palermo and its surrounding area from Arab rule. Despite the conflict, the Norman ruler at the time, William II or William the Good, was famed for being open-minded and tolerant, and when he set about building a new church (in competition with the Palermo Cathedral down the hill), he incorporated many North African and Middle Eastern artistic and architectural influences. Construction, blessed by the Pope, began in 1174 and was finished in an impressive 11 years. William II lived just long enough to see it completed and was buried within, alongside his father William I.

The duomo is stunning even before you

inside the Cattedrale di Monreale

walk through its bronze doors, green with age and decorated with biblical scenes, griffins, and floral motifs. The interior is covered in spectacular gilded mosaics, with a Middle Eastern-style triple-apsed choir and a layout that's part-Roman Catholic, part-Orthodox—another complex depiction of Sicily's layered history. The geometric marble flooring, baroque chapels, Byzantine stained glass, and intricate woodworked rooftops will take your breath away. Don't neglect to visit the adjacent cloister, with its marble column and arched Arabic arcade containing a lush, contemplative garden. For an additional fee, you can visit the treasury and get access to the panoramic rooftop terrace.

Getting There

From the center of Palermo, the Monreale Cathedral can be reached in 25 minutes with a straight route from the Cattedrale di Palermo along Corso A. Amedeo. The road will veer right then become Corso Calatafimi. Continue on SP69 and drive to Via Arcivescovada in Monreale. There are parking lots near the Cattedrale di Monreale where you can leave the car while touring the church. A taxi will cost around €30 each way. It's also possible to take AMAT **bus 389** (35 minutes; €1.40), which runs about every hour from Piazza Indipendenza near Palazzo dei Normanni.

CAMPOREALE

In the town of Camporeale, a 45-minute drive from Palermo in Sicily's Monreale DOC winemaking region, the local economy is very closely linked to agriculture and the production of its main products: grapes, wheat, and olives. The hills of Camporeale are famous for their exceptional production of syrah. The medieval town was founded in 1452, with a charming historic center. For three days at the beginning of October, the town celebrates **Camporeale Day,** a festival of food, wine, and music that highlights ancient crafts such as pottery and textile embroidery. During the festival, the town

organizes shuttle bus services to take guests to the nearby vineyards. A half-day vineyard visit and wine tasting in Camporeale can be an easy break during your Palermo-based travels.

Vineyard Visits and Wine Tasting

Many of the vineyards here in Monreale are around 1,600 ft (500 m) above sea level, with a sandy soil that cannot retain too much water, keeping winemakers extremely busy all year long. Most of the cantinas you'll see in this part of Sicily will be housed in renovated country homes nestled among the rolling hills, rows of vineyards, olive orchards, or wheat fields.

ALESSANDRO DI CAMPOREALE

Contrada Mandranova, Camporeale; tel. 0924/37038; www.alessandrodicamporeale. it; by appointment only, 10:30am, 12:30pm, 3pm Mon.-Fri.,10:30am Sat.

Winery tours, tastings, and lunch options are available at this family winery in the town of Camporeale. Options range from 90-minute basic wine tastings (€12 per person) to 2-hour food-and-wine tastings, including samples of five wines (€25 per person). A full lunch following your winery tour and tasting can also be organized for €40 per person. Call ahead to schedule a visit. Alessandro di Camporeale can be reached via a 45-minute drive from Palermo, exiting at the Camporeale – San Cipirello turnoff from SS624.

TENUTA SALLIER DE LA TOUR

Viadotto Pernice, Camporeale; tel. 091/645-9711; www.tascadalmerita.it/tenuta/sallier-de-la-tour; by appointment only; €40 per person for a tour and tasting of 3 wines

Within the Monreale DOC winemaking region, with vineyards spread across rolling hills, this wine estate is one of five properties under the umbrella of Tasca d'Almerita, one of the top winemaking families in Sicily. Since the 1950s, they have been cultivating mainly syrah grapes, an international varietal that grows extremely well in the Camporeale area, as well as Grillo, Inzolia, and Nero d'Avola. Call ahead to schedule a visit or tasting. Sallier de La Tour can be reached with a 40-minute drive from Palermo, exiting at the Camporeale – San Cipirello turnoff from SS624.

PORTA DEL VENTO

Contrada Valdibella, Camporeale; tel. 335/6692875; www.portadelvento.it; by appointment only; €15 per person

The certified biodynamic and organic property of Marco Sferlazzo spans 44 acres (18 ha) in the DOC Alcamo and DOC Monreale winemaking regions alongside Camporeale. The vines are trained with an albarello system, meaning they are pruned to grow freestanding like a small tree, and most of them are over 50 years old. Ninety-minute vineyard visits and wine tastings can be scheduled for groups of 4-20 people. Smaller tastings can be organized for a minimum of €60. Call to schedule an appointment. Porta del Vento can be reached with a 50-minute drive from Palermo, exiting at the Camporeale – San Cipirello turnoff from SS624.

Getting There

From central **Palermo,** Camporeale is a 45-minute drive on the **SS624** toward Sciacca. The town of Camporeale does not have many sightseeing options and most visits to this area will be focused on visiting wineries. For winery visits outside of Palermo, guests will have to provide their own transportation or hire a private driver.

CEFALÙ

If you've seen promotional photos of sandy beaches in Sicily, more often than not they have been taken in the picturesque town of Cefalù, located east of Palermo. Situated at the foot of a dramatic promontory, today known as La Rocca, this has been a desirable site of strategic importance and for trade since even before Greek settlement. Like Palermo, Cefalù was ruled in turn by Byzantines and then the Normans, who left their mark on the city with the Norman-style Duomo di Cefalù in the main **Piazza del Duomo** square. An ancient Greek temple and what was once a Norman castle dominate the towering La Rocca cliffs, offering breathtaking views. Mosey along the gorgeous beachfront and old port; the golden shoreline includes a large stretches of free public beaches as well as private lido clubs, where you can spend the day relaxing under an umbrella.

This is definitely one of the most popular destinations for a summer beach day, but it's equally enjoyable in winter, when you can enjoy the city sights and stroll along the serene beach without the usual crowds. It makes for a great break from the hustle and bustle of Palermo over an ice cream or aperitivo cocktail.

Sights
DUOMO DI CEFALÙ

Piazza del Duomo; tel. 092/192-2021; www. cattedraledicefalu.com; 8:30am-daily, closing times vary by season; general entrance €3, reduced rates for groups of 10 and guests over 65 €2, students €1

The landmark Roman Catholic basilica in the heart of Cefalù's Piazza del Duomo is a UNESCO World Heritage Site. Sitting just below the La Rocca mountain, the 12th-century cathedral features the mixture of Norman, Arab, and Byzantine styles of architecture typical to the area. A popular location for grand Sicilian weddings and film shoots, it's a perfect place for people-watching.

MUSEO MANDRALISCA

Via Mandralisca, 13; tel. 0921/421547; www. fondazionemandralisca.it; 9am-7pm daily Sept-July, 9am-11pm daily Aug.; adults €6, students €2

The Mandraliscas were a noble Sicilian family well-connected with the Italian government during the early 1800s. The Mandralisca museum art gallery is located on the street where the family once lived. Their personal collection includes archaeological treasures, ancient furniture, and most importantly the petite, smirking *Portrait of an Unknown Sailor* by

Antonello da Messina, one of Sicily's foremost Renaissance painters.

CEFALÙ MEDIEVAL LAUNDRY
(Lavatoio Medievale Fiume Cefalino)
Via Vittorio Emanuele; open 24 hours; free
Tucked away in a small courtyard in the center of Cefalù, lava stone steps lead down to the centuries-old site of the public laundry. Built in the Middle Ages, it was a place for women to meet, wash their clothes, and bathe in the health-giving, ice-cold water.

TEMPLE OF DIANA
Via Passafiume, Salita Saraceni; open 24 hours; €5 entrance fee to the La Rocca Park
The ancient temple of this fourth-century BC megalithic stone landmark were built in dedication to the Greek goddess Artemis, or Diana to the Romans. Sacredly linked to the worship of water, the ruins of small chapels and barracks here were probably originally intended for the cult of pagan divinities, but were later replaced with a Christian church dedicated to Santa Venera. Visit the temple on a hike along the La Rocca cliffs for panoramic views of Cefalù.

Hiking
LA ROCCA HIKE
Distance: *2 miles (3.2 km) round-trip*
Time: *1 hour round-trip*
Trailhead: *End of Corso Ruggero and Via Carlo Ortolani di Bordonaro, near the lungomare beach promenade*
Information and Maps: *Local tourism office*
A 1-hour hike leads up to La Rocca, where the ruins of its former Norman castle and surrounding medieval walls dramatically overlook the beach below. On the west side of La Rocca, you'll find the remains of the Temple of Diana, dating back to the fourth century BC. This hike can be extremely hot in summertime; bring along a hat and a few bottles of water.

1: countryside outside Palermo **2:** Duomo di Cefalù
3: view of Cefalù

Beaches
SPIAGGIA DI CEFALÙ
Lungomare Giuseppe Giardina; open 2 hours; free
The golden sands of Cefalù's public beach in Cefalù are one of Sicily's top destinations in summer. Free showers are available along the coastline, and the warm, still waters of this beach are perfectly suited for families and small children.

An affordable option for visitors who want the amenities of a beach club is **Lido Eolo** (Lungomare Giuseppe Giardina, 11; tel. 338/523-7623; www.lidoeolo.business.site; 9am-7pm daily; €15/day). Daily umbrella and beach bed rentals are available in summer. A restaurant, bathrooms, and bar service can be used by guests of the club.

Food and Bars
CORTILE PEPE
Via Nicola Botta, 15; tel. 0921/421630; www. cortilepepe.it; 7:30pm-11pm Thurs., 12:30pm-2:30pm and 7:30pm-11pm Fri.-Tues.; four-course tasting menu €39, six-course chef's tasting menu €65, entrées €16-20
Dine under the stars at Cortile Pepe's beautiful outdoor space in the center of town. Restaurateur Toti Fiduccia and chef Giovanni Lullo have created a space that combines modern dining with traditional top-quality local ingredients. Lullo's fresh pasta spaghettone with pressed swiss chard, red shrimp, sea urchin, and tuna bottarga is a complex and satisfying dish to follow a long day at the sea.

ENOTECA LE PETIT TONNEAU
Via Vittorio Emanuele, 49; tel. 0921/421447; www.lepetittonneau.it; 9:30am-1am Sun.-Thurs., 9:30am-1:30am Fri.-Sat.; €25
The most romantic enoteca with private tables for two overlooking the sea from your own little stone cave balcony. The wine list features traditional and natural wines from all around Sicily. Reservations required.

BASTIONE & COSTANZA
Piazza Francesco Crispi, 13; tel. 0921/571222; www.bastionecefalu.com/bastione-costanza;

10:30am-3pm and 6pm-midnight Tues.-Sun.; pizzas €6-12

This restaurant serves up fresh fish and top-quality pizza using a natural lievito madre yeast starter and only the best local ingredients.

TINCHITE' TAVERNA & PUTIA

Via XXV Novembre, 37; tel. 0921/421164; www. tavernatinchite.com; 12:30pm-3pm and 7pm-11:30pm daily; entrées €10-20

This small bar and restaurant is located just one block from the beach. It's a perfect spot for a quick lunch featuring antipasti, octopus salad, fried salt cod fritters, pasta, and main dishes, as well as great craft Sicilian beers.

Accommodations
HOTEL LE CALETTE

Via Cavallaro, 12; tel. 0921/424144; www.lecalette. it; from €198

In the center of the gulf of Cefalù, this five-star hotel can be a great place to spend the night after a long beach day. The luxurious gardens lined with flowers, dining options, spa services, private lido deck, and the pool overlooking the sea are among the many perks of this gorgeous resort.

Information and Services

• **Visit Cefalù:** Corso Ruggero, 77; www. visitcefalu.com

Getting There

From **Palermo,** you can drive the 47 miles (75 km) to Cefalù in under 1 hour via the **E90** highway. Street **parking** in Cefalù is available, but keep a close eye on the signage and parking grid colors. Parking spaces marked with a blue outline on the street will require paid hourly (€1/hour) tickets purchased from a nearby parking kiosk. White parking spaces are free, but make sure to check all nearby signs before leaving your car. Yellow spots are restricted and generally used only by town residents. There is a parking lot at the train station, paid parking spaces along the beachfront, or at the 24-hour **Parcheggio Coco** parking lot (Lungomare Giuseppe Giardina). Once guests arrive in Cefalù by car, train, or private driver, the city is small enough to explore on foot in a half or full day.

CEFALÚ TRAIN STATION

Via Passafiume, 40; www.trenitalia.com

The train station in Cefalù is just a 10-minute walk from the beach. Tickets can be purchased in advance online or from an automated kiosk at the train station entrance. The train from Palermo Centrale to Cefalù takes 1 hour and costs €6.20. Tickets must be time stamped at the station before boarding the train.

Trapani and the West Coast

According to Greek mythology, the sickle of the goddess Demeter fell into the sea to form the crescent-shaped city that is now known as Trapani. Located on Sicily's western coast, it's the sixth largest port in Italy, important for salt production and tuna fishing and known for its sea salt flats, fresh seafood, and excellent white wines. Many people arrive here to embark on the ferry to the Aegadian Islands, off the coast. Trapani's beautiful, walkable city center

has well-preserved architecture dating back to the 14th century, including palaces and churches with Gothic and baroque influences. Just east of Trapani is its sister town of Erice, perched on its eponymous mountain. Take the funicular to the summit for a beautiful view of the city.

Around Trapani are more treasures to explore. The province is filled with small swimming coves, especially along the coast from Trapani to San Vito lo Capo, as well

Trapani

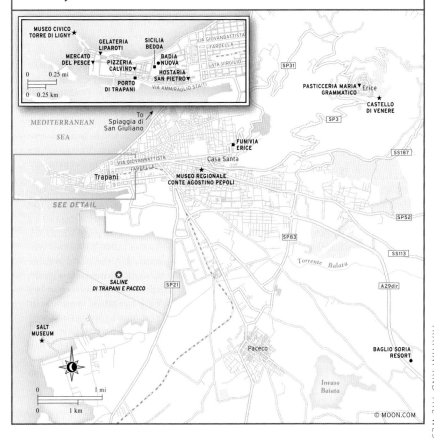

as unparalleled glimpses into Sicily's ancient Greek past. To the east, you'll find the Lo Zingaro Nature Reserve, a protected coastal paradise that was the first of its kind in Sicily, and the Temple of Segesta, a spectacularly well-preserved Doric temple from the fifth century BC. Twenty miles (30 km) of Trapani, plan a day in the beautiful city of Marsala to explore its famous vineyards and rediscover the long-lost history of marsala wine; continue southeast along the coast to the ancient ruins of the Greek settlement of Selinunte, the largest archaeological site in all of Europe.

SIGHTS

The historic center of Trapani is concentrated on a slender peninsula protruding west into the sea, with the port of Trapani in a sheltered cove to the south, and the Torre di Ligny tower and museum at the peninsula's western tip. Main road Corso Vittorio Emanuele runs from the tower through the center, with pedestrian areas that have myriad options for dining and drinking.

Museo Civico Torre di Ligny

Via Torre di Ligny, 37; tel. 333/808-1462; 10am-1pm Mon.-Sat.; €2

This 17th-century tower, used as a watchtower and garrison to protect Trapani from the sea, sits at the very tip of a pier jutting off from the city's historic center. Today it houses an archeological museum devoted to the history of Trapani, but the real highlight is the view you get from the top of the tower—especially at sunset.

Museo Regionale Conte Agostino Pepoli

Via Conte Agostino Pepoli, 180; tel. 0923/553269; 9am-5pm Tues.-Sat., 9am-noon Sun.; €6

Check out the Museo Regionale Conte Agostino Pepoli to see the private collection of jewels, sculptures, paintings, coral, silver, and metalwork donated by the Pepoli, Fardella, and Hernandez noble families of Trapani and Erice. The museum also features historical exhibitions and archaeological findings discovered onsite, inside the convent of Padri Carmelitani, a structure that dates back to the early 1300s and today houses the museum.

★ Saline di Trapani e Paceco

Via Libica; tel. 092/3867700; www. wwfsalineditrapani.it; open 24 hours; free

Trapani is an ideal place for the extraction of sea salt. At the Saline di Trapani e Paceco, or Sea Salt Pans of Trapani and Paceco, the long, hot Sicilian summers, strong, dry winds coming off Northern Africa, humidity, and the high salinity of the Mediterranean Sea are perfect for a love affair between sun, wind, and sea water. People have been producing sea salt in this area for centuries—the first written record dates back to the year 1,000. Artisanal Sicilian sea salt is world-renowned for being untreated, unrefined, and naturally rich in magnesium and potassium. Most gift shops and even grocery stores in Trapani and Marsala will sell local sea salt.

South of the port of Trapani, leaving the city by the S21, also known as the **Via del Sale** or Salt Road, the shores are lined with a patchwork of wide sea salt pans. Since 1995, almost 2,500 acres (1,000 ha) of this area have been protected by the World Wildlife Fund Italia through a partnership with the region of Sicily. This special terrain is a living, breathing ecosystem, continuously changing all year round, playing host to migrating birds like grey parrots, flamingoes, wild ducks, and herons. You can simply pull off on the side of the road to take a look at the salt pans, colored in shades varying from

Saline di Trapani e Paceco

white to lilac and pastel blue. Or, spend some time at the **Salt Museum** (Museo di Sale; Via Chiusa, Nubia; www.museodelsale.it; tel. 0923/867061; 9:30am-7pm daily; €2.50), housed in the former home of a salt worker built in the 16th century, where you'll learn about salt production and see traditional and modern tools used in the process. The entire landscape is dotted with some 50 medieval windmills, historically used to pump water through the salt pans and grind up the salt.

Erice

The medieval village of Erice, at the top of eponymous Monte Erice (2,500 ft/750 m), overlooks the city Trapani, with views of the Aegadian Islands and San Vito lo Capo, a rocky cap protruding into the sea, to the west. Its labyrinthine layout of narrow, cobbled alleyways was actually built to slow down and trap invaders, but today it's a great place to get lost on purpose on a leisurely stroll. Erice has around 27,000 residents and extraordinarily includes over 60 churches. The village is accessible via a scenic 10-minute **cable car** ride (Funivia Erice, Via Capua, 4; tel. 0923/569306; www.funiviaerice.it; €5.50 one-way, €9 round-trip). The valley station in Trapani is located on SP31 heading toward Erice on the corner of Via Capua, while the mountaintop station, Erice Vetta, is located on Via delle Pinete. Most tourists start their visit at the **Porto di Trapani** village gate (Piazza Porta Trapani; www.comune.erice.tp.it), an impressive, arched entry into a tall stone wall.

CASTELLO DI VENERE

Largo Castello; tel. 3297/823035; 10am-6:30pm daily; €4

The Castello di Venere was built by the Normans in the 12th century, allegedly on the site of the ancient Temple of Venus, from which it gets its name. For a small fee, visitors can access an interior courtyard with a green lawn, with panoramic views (often through defensive arrowslits) of Trapani and the coast of Western Sicily below.

BEACHES

SPIAGGIA DI SAN GIULIANO

Lungomare Dante Alighieri; www.trovaspiagge.it/san-giuliano

On the northern outskirts of Trapani is the city beach, Spiaggia di San Giuliano. This 1-mile (2-km) stretch of fine golden sand is equipped with lido beach clubs where you can rent umbrellas and lounge chairs, and there is also free public beach access. It's a popular and convenient destination for local Trapanese residents and surfers in summertime.

SHOPPING

SICILIA BEDDA

Via Torrearsa, 66; tel. 923/27509; https://sicilia-bedda.it; 9:30am-midnight Mon.-Sat., 10am-midnight Sun.

This hole-in-the-wall shop in Trapani's Old Town is positively packed with made-in-Sicily crafts and gourmet gifts, including world-famous Trapani sea salt. Grab some hand-painted ceramics or bring a taste of Trapani home with you in carry-on-friendly packages.

FOOD AND BARS

Trapani's local specialty is **fish couscous,** a steaming dish of couscous served with a side dish of fish and seafood broth. Commonly eaten in countries around North Africa, this dish was brought to Sicily by the Arabs and has kept its place in Trapani cuisine. You won't find couscous in any other part of Italy, so take advantage while you're here! A **pane cunzatu** sandwich packed with anchovies, olive oil, oregano, tomato, cheese, and olives is a simple local snack to pack with you for a beach day, available in most bakeries and bars. The traditional pasta to order here is the **busiate con pesto trapanese,** a twirled corkscrew-shaped noodle with a red pesto made from almonds, garlic, chili pepper, basil, and fresh tomato.

Trapani

MERCATO DEL PESCE

Via Cristoforo Colombo, 3; 6am-2pm daily

Trapani does not have a central outdoor food

West Coast Beach Road Trip

Castellammare del Golfo

Though the quickest route between Palermo and Trapani takes you inland, traveling along the coast of the Gulf of Castellammare will take you past some of Western Sicily's best beaches, some quirky cultural attractions, and unspoiled nature to boot. The best way to take this coastal tour is to rent a car.

CASTELLAMMARE DEL GOLFO

Castellammare del Golfo is a great place to stop on a drive between Palermo and Trapani. The scenic overlook of the **Belvedere Castellammare del Golfo** (Località Belvedere, 53; open 24 hours), off the SP187, offers a bird's-eye view of the seaside town, its beaches, and the **Castello Arabo Normanno** (Piazza Castello; 924/592-555; 9am-1pm and 3pm-7pm daily), the medieval castle standing guard over it all. The sand beach at **Cala Petròlo** (9am-5pm daily) is conveniently situated close to the town's traditional restaurants, bars, gelaterias, and pizzerias.

Castellammare del Golfo is an hour-long drive (40 mi/70 km) west from Palermo and 40 minutes (25 mi/40 km) from Trapani. For extended travel in this area, reach out to **Authentic Italy** (www.authenticitaly.com) to help with your holiday planning. Founder Gary Portuesi creates tailor-made travel experiences in his hometown of Castellammare del Golfo and beyond.

SCOPELLO

The enchanting beach town of Scopello's main attraction is its old tuna fishery, **La Tonnara di**

market like the other large Sicilian cities. Instead, there are vendors on most corners selling fruit and vegetables. The main event is the fish market, located near the port. Vendors sell just-caught Mediterranean fish like sardines, red tuna, mackerel, swordfish, and small red mullet. Squid, cuttlefish, and sea urchin come and go with the seasons, but you'll find that everything is extremely fresh.

HOSTARIA SAN PIETRO

Largo Porta Galli; tel. 337/960902; www.facebook.com/hostaria.sanpietro; 1pm-3pm and 8pm-11pm Thurs.-Tues.; €12-20

Hostaria San Pietro is the perfect place to try Trapani's specialty, fish couscous. (Try it with a 10-year Marsala Superiore Secco Riserva!) This cozy and casual tavern offers a real authentic Trapanese experience for travelers and locals.

Scopello (Largo Tonnara; tel. 388/829-9472; www.latonnaradiscopello.it; 9am-7pm daily; €8). Dating back to the 13th century, the tonnara sits on the edge of an emerald cove and beautiful natural scenery. The facility is made up of two medieval watchtowers, fishing village housing units, and an old courtyard. Nowadays, the tonnara has been transformed into a museum and event space, popular for photoshoots and weddings. The main swimming areas around Scopello include Cala Mosca (open 24 hours; free) and, closer to Castellammare del Golfo, Guidaloca (Contrada Ciauli; tel. 0924/592506; open 24 hours; free).

From Palermo, Scopello can be reached in about an hour (45 mi/75 km); from Trapani, it's a 45-minute drive (20 mi/35 km). It's 15 minutes (7mi/11 km) from Castellammare del Golfo.

RISERVA NATURALE ORIENTATA DELLO ZINGARO

Via Salvo D'Acquisto, 1; tel. 0924/35108; www.riservazingaro.it; 7am-7pm daily Apr.-Sept., 8am-4pm daily Oct.-Mar.; €5 entrance fee (includes trail map)

Practically around the corner from Castellammare del Golfo, this stunning coastal nature reserve includes several miles of hiking paths, including a 4-mile (7-km) coastal path that passes the reserve's seven swimming coves. Unfortunately, in summer 2020, the nature reserve was severely damaged by a fire, but it reopened the following year and continues to thrive and grow back to the lush nature preserve it once was. Since the beaches here take a little extra work to get to, they're often less crowded. For a beach day, make sure to pack water for the whole day, a picnic, sun protection, and sturdy shoes for walking.

The Lo Zingaro Nature Reserve is located 45 minutes (25 mi/40 km) northeast of Trapani, between Scopello and San Vito lo Capo. There are two main entrances to access the reserve. The north entrance can be reached along the state road SS187 heading toward San Vito lo Capo, following signs for Villaggio Calampiso. The southern entrance is accessible from the A29 Palermo-Mazara del Vallo highway, exiting at Castellammare del Golfo and then following SS187 toward Trapani, passing Scopello and leaving your car in the parking lot near Cala Mazzo di Sciacca. Keep in mind the only public bathrooms are located at the two entrances.

SPIAGGIA DI SAN VITO LO CAPO

Via Litoranea Lungomare, San Vito lo Capo; open 24 hours; free

The soft white-sand beach in San Vito lo Capo makes it one of the most beautiful and popular summer destinations in Sicily. This seaside town is known for its history of tuna fishing and its annual weeklong Cous Cous Fest (www.couscousfest.it), which takes place every September. The waterfront is lined with small restaurants, bars, and shops, perfect for a full beach day and long summer night. The crystal-clear blue water, framed by mountains, is reminiscent of the Caribbean, and you might just forget you're in Italy for a little while. San Vito lo Capo is a 45-minute drive from Trapani (25 mi/40 km) and a 1.5-hour drive from Palermo (70 mi/110 km).

PIZZERIA CALVINO

Via Nunzio Nasi, 71, Trapani; tel. 0923/21464; 7pm-midnight Wed.-Thurs. and Sat.-Sun., 7pm-11pm Fri.; pizzas €6.50-13

Locals and tourists gather every night outside this brothel-turned-pizzeria waiting for a pie. You can peek into the kitchen to watch the pizzaioli quickly throwing dough while you wait. Tables are set in tiny alcove rooms, and the pizza arrives already cut into tiny squares for easy eating. The classic local pizza is the rianata, made with sliced cherry tomatoes (instead of tomato sauce), preserved anchovy, Sicilian pecorino cheese, and the namesake dried oregano. Expect casual pizzeria service and order a few beers for the table while you enjoy a delicious pizza for a low-key night.

★ GELATERIA LIPAROTI

Viale delle Sirene, 21, Trapani; tel. 389/299-8096;
4pm-midnight Tues.-Sat., noon-2pm and
4pm-midnight Sun.; cones €1.50, cups €1.50-3.50,
gelato with brioche €3.50

This artisanal gelato shop has unique flavors, like fig and walnut, peanut butter, ginger pear, licorice, watermelon, Sicilian mango, and mulberry.

Erice
PASTICCERIA MARIA GRAMMATICO

Via Vittorio Emanuele, 14, Erice; tel. 0923/869390;
www.mariagrammatico.it; 9am-9pm Tues.-Sun.
Nov.-Apr., 9am-midnight daily May-Oct.; under €5

The pièce de résistance of a visit to Erice is Pasticceria Maria Grammatico, where you can taste the handmade delicacies from the "pastry queen of Sicily." Maria Grammatico's incredible life story includes growing up in a Sicilian convent, where she "stole" secret recipes by watching the nuns through a crack in the floor above the kitchen. At Pasticceria Maria Grammatico, stock up on almond pastries like belli e brutti, lingua di suocera, bocconcini, perfectly sculpted marzipan fruit, bucellati cookies stuffed with dried figs, and perhaps best of all, warm genovese, big, round, baked short-crust pastries filled with yellow pastry cream.

ACCOMMODATIONS
BADIA NUOVA

Via Badia Nuova, 33; www.badianuova.it; tel.
0923/24054; from €75

The Badia Nuova hotel is centrally located in the pedestrian area of the city of Trapani, just 150 feet (50 m) from the beach. It has a beautiful rooftop bar and tastefully furnished suites and apartments with balconies and private terraces.

BAGLIO SORIA RESORT

Contrada Soria; tel. 0923/861679; www.firriato-baglio-soria-trapani.it; €160

Located on the Firriato winery estate, only 20 minutes outside the city of Trapani, Baglio Soria is a charming 17th-century courtyard surrounded by vineyards and olive orchards overlooking the sea. Chef Andrea Macca's dishes are exquisitely plated, bringing together the natural flavors of the island in the resort's fine-dining restaurant. Wine tastings and cooking lessons are available upon request. Guests of the elegant resort can enjoy afternoons relaxing at the panoramic pool or in the wellness center.

GETTING THERE

There is no direct train from Palermo to Trapani; to get here, you'll have to either have your own rental car, or take a bus. Once arrived, Trapani can easily be explored on foot. To get to the mountaintop village of Erice, you'll want to take the **Funivia Erice** funicular, with stations located on SP31 and Via Capua in Trapani and Via delle Pinete in Erice.

By Car

From **Palermo,** it's a 1-hour 15-minute drive to Trapani (about 60 mi/100 km), via E90 and A29dir/E933. Parking in Trapani is available in the Piazza Vittorio Emanuele, near the beach on the northern coast of the city, and within walking distance from the historic center of town. Paid parking spots (€1/hour) are marked with a blue stripe and will need to be purchased with a ticket from a nearby blue kiosk machine.

By Bus

The **Segesta Autolinee** (Via Fazello; www.segesta.it; tel. 06164160) bus line has multiple daily services from Palermo to Trapani (2 hours; €9.60). Tickets can be purchased ahead of time online or at the Segesta ticket office in the Palermo bus station. Enter the Palermo Centrale train station and follow signs through the back of the station and exit on the right side of the building to find the newly renovated bus terminal. The final stop on the bus line from Palermo to Trapani will leave you at the port of Trapani, exactly where you need to be for those catching a ferry to the nearby Aegadian Islands.

TEMPLE OF SEGESTA
(Tempio di Segesta)

Contrada Barbaro, Calatafimi; tel. 0924/952356;
www.parcodisegesta.com; 9am-6:30pm daily; €6
entrance fee

The Temple of Segesta is a magnificent site: an unusually intact and expansive Doric temple, perfectly situated on 1,300-foot-high (400-m-high) Monte Barbaro, a 40-minute drive southeast of Trapani. This 85-foot-wide (26-m-wide) ruin, with its dozens of solid Doric columns, is a complete masterpiece, known to have been built around 420 BC. Though the Hellenistic influence of ancient Greece here is unmistakable, archaeologists believe it was built by an indigenous population known as the Elymians, though Greek colonists likely participated in the construction. There's also evidence that this extremely well-preserved temple was never finished; its columns lacks the usual ornamentation, and the ruins have no roof. Still, the view from this monumental and statuesque temple is breathtaking, and promotes meditative contemplation.

Higher up Monte Barbaro are the remains of a Greek theater, thought to have been built in the third century BC, with similarly sweeping views of the Gulf of Castellammare and surrounding windswept countryside. It's just over half a mile (1 km) up from the site's parking lot to tour both the temple and the theater; for those who would rather avoid a steep walk, a shuttle runs past both sites from the parking lot every 30 minutes (€1.50).

Getting There

A trip to the Temple of Segesta is a great break from the nearby beaches; pack a picnic lunch and spend a few hours at this picturesque ruin set amid the tranquil countryside. On the main road between Palermo and Trapani, it's a 40-minute drive from Trapani (19 mi/30 km) and an hour-long drive from Palermo (80 mi/50 km). To explore these areas without having to worry about your own transportation, consider hiring a private driver such as **Sunny Sicily** (sunnysicily.com; €62 per person).

SELINUNTE ARCHAEOLOGICAL PARK
(Parco Archeologico di Selinunte)

Via Selinunte, Castelvetrano; tel. 0924/46277; www.
selinunte.gov.it; 9am-7pm daily; €6

Located in the town of Castelvetrano, along the southwest coast of Sicily, Selinunte is one of the largest archaeological sites in Europe. The remnants of this Greek settlement, dating back to 628 BC, sit on a plain high above the golden-sand coastline below. Left abandoned for over 2,500 years, Selinunte was originally one of the most powerful cities in Magna Graecia, or the Greek colonies of Southern Italy, once thought to have had as many as 30,000 inhabitants. Little else is known about Selinunte's history, besides evidence that the city ultimately fell to a powerful alliance between the nearby Segestans, Carthaginians, and Athenians.

The extensive ruins of Selinunte include several temples, the largest of which is known as Temple E, and will be one of the first things you see upon entering the park. Visitors can also explore the remains of a port; an acropolis, or public gathering space; several necropolises; and the skeleton of the city's streetscape, including what would have been residential and commercial buildings. The widespread archaeological park (657 ac/270 ha) is walkable, but golf cart transportation can be organized upon request, and there's also a tiny tourist train that can take you on a set tour of the sites (€6). To do the site justice, devote 3-4 hours.

Getting There

From **Trapani** (1 hour; 90km/55mi), take the autostrada **A29/E90** highway to Via Caduti di Nassirya in Castelvetrano and follow the **SS115** state road to Selinunte. From **Palermo,** the drive is 1.5 hours (75 mi/120 km); from **Agrigento,** it's also a 1.5-hour drive (62 mi/100 km). Once you arrive in Castelvetrano, there are two entrances to the archeological park: one in the village of Marinella di Selinunte on Selinunte Street, the other in the village of Triscina di Selinunte on Mediterraneo Avenue.

☆ Tasting Marsala Wine

One of Italy's most specialized winemaking styles is having a resurgence. Chefs, sommeliers, and wine lovers are once again singing the praises of marsala, a fortified wine made here in the charming city of Marsala on the west coast of Sicily since the 1770s. John Woodhouse, a British wine merchant, started out distributing other fortified wines like sherry, port, and madeira before arriving in Marsala. He found the location ideal for growing grapes and strategic for shipping wine, with its very hot and windy summers with mild and fairly dry winters, and he developed marsala as another high-alcohol beverage that could withstand long voyages by sea from Sicily to England.

Ranging from amber to toasted golden brown to ruby red in color, marsala's incredible range is its most unique characteristic. In different bottles, you'll recognize notes of bitter almonds, burnt honey, vanilla, and spices, or the essence of dried figs, carobs, balsamic, or dried fruits. Although marsala is commonly paired with desserts or dark chocolates, it can also be served with aged cheeses and marmalade, fresh oysters, smoked fish, or Sicily's famous tuna roe bottarga. The lively city of Marsala is filled with small bed-and-breakfasts, restaurants, and bars, perfect for exploring on a trip to western Sicily or an adventure to the nearby Aegadian Islands.

Check out some of these amazing winemakers to rediscover marsala in Marsala!

CANTINE PELLEGRINO

Via del Fante, 39; tel. 0923/719911; www.carlopellegrino.it; tastings available by reservation only Mon.-Sat.
The Pellegrino family is one of the only three original 19th-century founders of the marsala trade still in existence, handing vineyards down from father to son for seven generations. Cantine Pellegrino is located in the northern part of the town of Marsala, and winery tours include a tasting of five marsala wines accompanied by five typical Sicilian dishes (2.5 hours; €50 per person, minimum 4 participants). Walk-in tastings are available at the Ouverture wine shop (Lungomare Battaglia delle Egadi, 10; tel. 0923/719970; 9:30am-1pm Mon.-Sat.; €9-14).

CANTINE FLORIO DI MARSALA

Via Vincenzo Florio, 1; tel. 0923/781111; www.duca.it/florio; available appointment only 9am-1pm and 3:30pm-6pm Mon.-Fri., 9:30am-1:30pm Sat.; tours from €15

Agrigento and the Southern Coast

Archaeology buffs should make a point of checking out this part of the southwestern coast of Sicily. The Valle dei Templi, outside the city of Agrigento, contains some of the best-preserved Greek ruins in the world. Founded in 581 BC, Agrigento was a prime center of commerce on the trade routes from Africa to Europe. Though the modern city is not one of Sicily's most beautiful towns, the golden limestone ruins of the Valle dei Templi should not be missed, and nearby you can still find some pristine sand beaches, beautiful nature reserves, and wonderful restaurants. Past seemingly endless almond and olive groves, the landscapes change drastically as you travel toward the WWF-protected beachfront at Torre Salsa and Scala dei Turchi's terraced limestone beach.

SIGHTS

TOP EXPERIENCE

★ Valle dei Templi

On the coastal state road SP4 in Agrigento; tel. 0922/1839996; www.parcovalledeitempli.it; 9am-7pm daily; adults €12, reduced rates €7, combined ticket to temples and Giardino della Kolymbetra €17, concessions €11, free first Sun. of the month.

Cantine Florio has been in continuous operation since 1862, owned by one of Sicily's most prominent families, famous in the worlds of winemaking, tuna fishing, and motor racing. Besides their line of internationally recognized aged marsalas, Cantine Florio is also known as a quality producer of amaro liqueurs. Their winery is located right in the town of Marsala, near the marina.

MARCO DE BARTOLI

Contrada Fornara Samperi, 292; tel. 0923/962093; www. marcodebartoli.com; 9am-1pm and 3pm-6pm Mon.-Fri.
In 1978, Marco De Bartoli, an agronomist and racing car connoisseur, took over the 200-year-old Samperi estate and built a name for himself in the marsala winemaking world. Their soleras method uses mainly native Grillo grapes to carefully mix small portions of older vintages with new vintages to create outstanding marsala wines. Vineyard visits and wine tastings can be organized by reservation. The Samperi estate is located 20 minutes southeast of the center of Marsala. Check out their web-

a glass of marsala wine

site to confirm driving directions, as this location is a bit difficult to find.

GETTING THERE

Marsala can be reached by car from Trapani in 35 minutes along the SS115 state road. The main marsala producers have facilities right here in the center of town, while small artisan producers will be located outside of town and require a car to reach them. It's also possible to get here from Trapani by train (40 minutes; from €2), bus (30 minutes; €2.50), and ferry (1 hour 15 minutes; from €12).

Sicily's most-visited historical attraction is the Valley of the Temples, which showcases well-preserved and restored Greek ruins that easily stand toe-to-toe with those in Greece. The massive Archaeological and Landscape Park of the Valley of the Temples is one of the largest archaeological sites in the world, extending for over 3,000 acres (1,200 ha), with forests of almond and olive groves, grapevines, myrtles, carob trees, and dwarf palms.

Known as Akragas in ancient times, this splendid Greek colony competed with the cities of Segesta and Selinunte at its peak. The long archaeological park—walkable if you've got the stamina—is split in to into two sections, the eastern zone and western zone, with car parks and ticket offices in the northeastern and southwestern corner. It's speckled with eight ancient temples from 510-430 BC: the temples of Hera, Concordia, Heracles, Zeus, Castor and Pollux, Hephaestos, Demeter, and Asclepius. The best-known temples are in the eastern zone, including the **Temple of Concordia.** Built approximately 2,500 years ago, it's the largest Greek ruin in Sicily and one of the best-preserved temples in the world. It's easily recognizable with tall, fluted Doric columns and a rectangular shape that closely resembles the Parthenon in Athens.

From July-mid-September, evening tours are offered through **Luci in Valle** (Lights in the Valley). Call ahead for reservations or book online (€10 plus the entrance fee, children under 12 free). The tour meets at the tree-lined area of the Temple of Juno.

Plan to spend at least 2-3 hours on a walking tour of the temples. Audio guides are available in Italian, English, French, Spanish, German, and Chinese for €5, with a deposit of identification card or driver's license. Private certified guides are highly recommended to best enjoy your visit. **Michele Gallo** (tel. 360/397930) is one of the top guides recommended by the park. It's also possible to be shuttled around both of the archaeological park's zones on small electric **shuttles** that run from both ticket offices. Summer visits are extremely hot and can be overcrowded. February and March, while the almond trees are in bloom, are the most beautiful times to visit, but if you want to escape the crowds, you'll have the archaeological park all to yourself in autumn or winter.

GIARDINO DELLA KOLYMBETRA

Via Panoramica de Templi, Agrigento; tel.335 1229042; www.fondoambiente.it/luoghi/giardino-della-kolymbethra; 10am-11pm daily; adults €17, European residents €11, students €11, 17 and under free

Combine your trip to the Valle dei Templi with a walk through the Kolymbetra Gardens, accompanied by their ancient aqueduct. This hidden paradise consists of centuries-old olive groves, citrus trees, and wild gardens, now overseen by FAI (Fondo Ambiente Italiano), a nonprofit organization that helps protect and preserve Italy's cultural heritage. Guided tours are available upon request.

MUSEO ARCHEOLOGICO

Contrada San Nicola, 12, Agrigento; tel. 092/240-1565; www.coopculture.it; 9am-7:30pm Mon.-Sat., 9am-1:30pm Sun.; adults €8, reduced rates €4, joint ticket with Valle dei Templi €13.50

This archaeological museum, on the site of a former convent, features a collection of Phoenician, Greek, Etruscan, Carthaginian, and Roman artifacts, including sculptures from the surrounding area of the Valle dei Templi and Agrigento as well as Selinunte. Guided tours should be booked in advance.

BEACHES
SCALA DEI TURCHI

SP68 in Realmonte; open 24 hours; free

Save time to visit the smooth white terraced marl stone cliffs of the Scala dei Turchi, one of Sicily's most seductive beach sites. Just outside the city of Agrigento, near the town of Porto Empedocle, this bright limestone rock formation appears out of nowhere, cascading like a whitewashed staircase leading right down to the sea. This breathtakingly wild beachfront has no amenities and can be difficult for travelers with mobility issues. Pack a lunch and plenty of refreshments to spend the day laying out on the cool white stone, or visit in the off-season for a more tranquil sightseeing experience.

RISERVA NATURALE ORIENTATA TORRE SALSA

SP75 in Siculiana; tel. 0922/818220; www.wwftorresalsa.com; open 24 hours; free

The Torre Salsa nature reserve is a 4-mile (6-km) stretch of sandy beaches and 1,880 acres (760 ha) of limestone cliffs, juniper fields, wetlands, and rolling hills along the southern coast of Sicily near the town of Siculiana, about 30 minutes west of the provincial capital of Agrigento. There is a beautiful orchid garden on the WWF property, just down a dirt road from the **visitor center.** Guided visits can be organized through the nature reserve's office on Monday, Wednesday, and Friday year-round. From Agrigento, take SS115 west and exit at Montallegro – Torre Salsa. Follow signs for the nature reserve on SP87. The Pantano entrance and visitor center is located 2.1 miles (3.3 km) after you bear left off the main road.

TOURS
ESSENCE OF SICILY

tel. 0922/605810; www.essenceofsicily.com

Agrigento-based agency Essence of Sicily

1: the beautiful countryside around Agrigento **2:** Giardino della Kolymbetra **3:** the limestone terrace of Scala dei Turchi **4:** the ruins at Valle dei Templi

☆ The Aegadian Islands

Levanzo is the smallest of the three Aegadian Islands.

The Aegadian Islands (Isole Egadi in Italian) archipelago, just 6 miles (10 km) off the west coast of Trapani, are Sicily's low-key alternative to Capri in the Gulf of Naples. With three main islands—Favignana, Marettimo, and Levanzo—these popular summer destinations turn back into sleepy fishing villages in the off-season (Nov.-Mar.), and are still relatively off international tourists' radars. If you have the time and need a vacation from your get-up-and-go Sicily vacation, a day trip to the Aegadian Islands is a great bet.

CHOOSE YOUR ISLAND

- **Favignana:** The butterfly-shaped island of Favignana is the largest and most popular of the Aegadian Islands, since it is the closest to mainland Sicily and offers the most **nightlife and restaurant options.**

- **Marettimo:** Though not the smallest of the three main islands, Marittimo is the least developed, with **hiking trails** crisscrossing its mountainous and rocky landscape, and cats roaming free in search of a quick seaside snack

- **Levanzo:** The smallest island, Levanzo has great **pebble beaches** with small fishing boats packed into the harbors. It's also known for prehistoric cave paintings discovered at the **Grotta del Genovese** cave.

organizes an authentic series of cultural, culinary, and sightseeing experiences. Their single-day excursions can be set up to explore Agrigento as well as Taormina, Catania, Ragusa, Syracuse, Palermo, and Trapani. Contact them directly for pricing and reservations for a Sicilian family lunch, hands-on cooking lesson, winery visit, or guided Sicilian heritage tour.

SHOPPING
FARM CULTURAL PARK
Cortile Bentivegna - Sette Cortili, Favara; tel. 0922/34534; www.farmculturalpark.com;

BEST BEACHES

The best beaches on the Aegadian Islands are mainly accessible by boat, and they vary from untouched deep-blue swimming holes to pebbled and rocky coasts to sandy shorelines. The islands are also a hot spot for sailing and other water sports; **Marettimo Giro dell'isola con Pippo** (Via Umberto, 44; tel. 327/768-8194; www.marettimoconpippo.com; 9:30am-4:30pm daily) offers boat excursions, private boat trips, sunset aperitivo at sea, and beach taxi services on the island of Marettimo.

- **Scogliera di Cala Rossa, Favignana:** A picturesque rocky beach with clear turquoise water on the easternmost part of the north coast, Favignana is the only Aegadian Island with sand beaches. It's perfect for travelers of all ages.

- **La Praia dei Nacchi, Marettimo** (tel. 368/343-8107): For those looking for a more secluded and natural area, this pebbled beach at the southern tip of the island is a good option.

- **Spiaggia di Cala Dogana, Levanzo:** On the sleepy fishing island of Levanzo, all the beaches you'll find will be wild, rocky, and secluded. Try the emerald waters of the Spiaggia di Cala Dogana for the most convenient beach near the village port

BEST RESTAURANTS

The cuisine here is almost completely based on fresh seafood and fish, with local specialties including Trapanese couscous, sardine dishes, pasta with sea urchin or patella sea snails, and anything and everything made from Mediterranean tuna.

- **Formica, Favignana** (Via Roma, 52; tel. 340/212-6169; www.formicaosteria.com; open for dinner 7:30pm daily; €15-24): At Formica, Federica and Taka use their combined respect for the sea to create a range of blended dishes playing with Mediterranean and Asian flavors.

- **Il Pirata Ristorante, Marettimo** (tel. 0923/923027; noon-2pm and 5pm-11pm daily; €25-50): Make sure to call ahead to book a table at this waterfront restaurant, known for its zuppa di aragosta, a tomato-based stew made with butterflied spiny lobsters and broken spaghetti.

GETTING THERE AND AROUND

Liberty Lines (tel. 0923/873813; www.libertylines.it) offers multiple crossings per day to the Egadi Islands from **Trapani** (Port of Trapani, Viale Regina Elena) and **Marsala** (Porto di Lylibeo, Lungomare Mediterraneo, 3). The most frequent crossings run to and from Favignana (30 minutes; €11-12), but you can also find transfers to the ferry terminal on Levanzo (25 minutes; €11) and Marettimo (1 hour 15 minutes; €18). One-way ferry service connects Favignana with Levanzo (10 minutes; €5.50) and Marettimo (45 minutes; €10.50), and Levanzo and Marettimo (30 minutes; €9.80).

On the island of Favignana, you can rent a scooter or bicycle with **Noleggio Isidoro** (Via Giuseppe Mazzini, 40; tel. 347/323-3058; www.noleggioisidoro.it; 8am-7pm daily). Levanzo and Marettimo are best explored **on foot.**

10am-10pm Tues.-Thurs., 10am-midnight Fri.-Sun.; gallery €5

This cultural center and contemporary art gallery, open since 2010, is located in a series of courtyards within the historic center of Favara, 12 miles (20 km) west of Agrigento. Founders Andrea Bartoli and Florinda Saieva purchased the property in this abandoned town center and completely transformed the area to include a test kitchen, a garden cocktail bar, and artisan shops. It has been a fresh resurgence of creativity and energy for the town of Favara, with its art exhibitions, dynamic outdoor murals, street art, workshops, and educational events.

FOOD

IL RE DI GIRGENTI

Via Panoramica Valle dei Templi, 51, Agrigento; tel. 0922/401-388; www.ilredigirgenti.it; 12:30pm-2:30pm and 7:30pm-10:30pm Wed.-Mon.; antipasti €10, entrées €12-18

Slip deeply into an Arabian dream at the stunning Il Re di Girgenti restaurant overlooking the Valle dei Templi in the heart of Agrigento. Taste your way through a menu of carefully thought-out and surprisingly affordable dishes, from grilled octopus with fava beans and carob dust to fresh ravioli with John Dory fish and sea urchin sauce. Pair your meal with regional wines and enjoy sourdough breads baked daily in-house.

OSTERIA EX PANIFICIO

Piazza Giuseppe Sinatra, 16, Agrigento; tel. 0922/595-399; www.osteriaexpanificio. it; 12:30pm-2:30pm and 7:30pm-11pm daily; entrées €15-46

This renovated rustic osteria has been recognized with the "Bib Gourmand" award from the Michelin dining guide. Set in the historic city center of Agrigento, near Teatro Pirandello in a former World War I-era bread bakery, Osteria Ex Panificio features regional meat and seafood options from a rotating seasonal menu while paying homage to their flour-dusted roots, with unforgettable homemade bread and warm Sicilian hospitality.

RISTORANTE LA SCOGLIERA

Via San Pietro, 54, Siciliana Marina; tel. 0922/817532; www.facebook.com/ lascoglierasiciliana; 7pm-11pm Mon., 11:30am-3:30pm and 7pm-11pm Tues.-Sun.; €35-50

This beachfront treasure features fresh seafood, nestled between the Torre Salsa nature reserve and the city of Agrigento. La Scogliera is a family-run restaurant with indoor and outdoor dining areas overlooking the cliffs and marina of the small village of Siciliana. Treat yourself to a seaside feast of raw langoustines, oysters and raw fish carpaccio, spiny lobster in tomato sauce, pasta with nero di seppia squid ink, or grilled mix plates of the catch of the day.

ACCOMMODATIONS

★ VILLA ATHENA

Via Passeggiata Archeologica, 33; tel. 0922/596288; www.hotelvillaathena.it; from €120

If you're planning on staying right in the city of Agrigento, Villa Athena is the best choice. This luxurious 18th-century villa hotel has an extraordinary view of the Temple of Concordia, and if you request a temple view, you'll be able to see it lit up at night from your window, balcony, or terrace. The prime location, beautifully manicured garden property, Michelin-mentioned Terrazza degli Dei hotel restaurant, and Villa Athena Spa center built around an ancient Greek cistern can be just what you need to relax after a long drive or full day of sightseeing.

DORIC BOUTIQUE HOTEL

Strada E.S.A. Mosé - San Biagio, 20; tel. 0922/180-8509; www.doric.it; from €167

This 22-room boutique eco-hotel offers unique sea views also overlooking the Temple of Juno in the Valle dei Templi. The resort also features an in-house restaurant, spa and wellness center, jacuzzi, and infinity pool. The air-conditioned accommodations are minimally decorated with panoramic photo murals of the nearby Scala dei Turchi white stone beach, but the real pièce de résistance is the deluxe suites that even include their own private swimming pools and mini patios overlooking the property's vegetable and herb gardens.

GETTING THERE

Though Agrigento has a train station that connects to Palermo, the southwestern coast of Sicily is best explored with your own car. The beaches, archaeological sites, and top dining options are not very accessible with public transportation.

By Car

The drive from **Palermo** to Agrigento (2 hours 15 minutes; 80 mi/130 km) cuts south through the center of the island on a series of winding country roads. Plan for some extra time along the winding coastal roads, especially in summertime when the surrounding area becomes extremely busy. From **Trapani,** the drive is 2 hours (110 mi/180 km). From **Catania,** it's also a 2-hour drive (100 mi/160 km).

By Train

AGRIGENTO CENTRALE STATION

Piazza Guglielmo Marconi; www.trenitalia.com

Train service to Agrigento is provided by **TrenItalia** (www.trenitalia.it). Tickets can be purchased in advance online or from an automated kiosk at the station and must be time stamped before boarding the train. Bathrooms are available on the train. Daily service runs every hour from **Palermo Centrale** (2 hours; €10 one-way).

By Bus

AGRIGENTO STAZIONE AUTOBUS

Piazzale Fratelli Rosselli

SAIS Trasporti (tel. 091/617-1141; https://saistrasporti.it) operates buses from Catania Fontanarossa Airport (2 hours 40 minutes; from €11). It's also possible to travel from Palermo by bus with **Camilleri Argento & Lattuca** (tel. 0922/471-886; www.camilleriargentoelattuca.it; 2 hours; from €9).

Catania, Northeastern Sicily, and the Aeolian Islands

Itinerary Ideas 334
Catania 336
Taormina 354
Mount Etna............362
The Aeolian Islands 375

Under the shadow of Mother Etna, on this compelling, action-packed coast of Sicily, you can enjoy luxurious resorts in Taormina, hike the volcano and taste wine grown on its slopes, and savor Catania's vibrant nightlife, all within an hour's drive. In summertime, for the ultimate in beachside relaxation, tack on a few extra days in the Aeolian Islands, off Sicily's northern tip.

The history of the intricate black rock city of Catania, the province's largest city and home to Sicily's biggest airport, is one of destruction and renewal. The Baroque city you see today was literally reborn from the ashes after repeated, devastating volcanic eruptions and earthquakes. Smaller and not as brash as Palermo, but more vivacious than timeless Syracuse to the south, Catania's spirited, youthful

Highlights

Look for ★ to find recommended sights, activities, dining, and lodging.

★ **Catania's Piazza del Duomo:** Catania's main square is home to its Baroque cathedral and an elephant statue beloved by the city (page 337).

★ **Pescheria di Catania:** Catania's exuberant fish market is an open-air culinary theater (page 341).

★ **Festa di Sant'Agata:** The multi-day procession and religious festival attracts nearly one million people every February (page 346).

★ **Teatro Antico di Taormina:** This picturesque ancient Greek theater is nestled on the cliffs of Taormina overlooking the Ionian Sea (page 355).

★ **Climbing Mount Etna:** It's a rite of passage to summit Europe's highest volcano (page 364).

★ **Tasting Volcanic Wines:** The wines that come from the high-altitude, lava-stone-lined vineyards climbing Mount Etna are complex, mineral-rich, and utterly unique (page 368).

★ **Salina:** Head to lush, green Salina for wine tastings, luxury accommodations, and fine dining in the volcanic Aeolian archipelago (page 386).

energy can be seen in its lively fish market and piazzas frequented by the city's large student population.

Just a short drive north, dramatically situated on cliffs overlooking the Ionian Sea, Taormina is the most visited destination on Sicily's east coast, its ancient Greek heritage drawing tourists since the 19th century. The postcard-perfect scenery comes at a cost, as Taormina becomes very crowded in the high season. It's a place to splurge if you're looking for luxury and sea views, with a wide selection of lavish five-star hotels and award-winning fine-dining locales.

For a more off-the-grid alternative, take the ferry to the spectacular Aeolian Islands, located between mainland Sicily and the toe of mainland Italy's boot, where you'll find some of the best swimming, natural landscapes, and fresh seafood in Sicily.

ORIENTATION

The northeastern coast is yet another Sicilian region that offers something for everyone, from archeological sites to bustling cities, outdoor adventures, gorgeous beaches, and island excursions. The **A18** eastern highway connecting **Messina,** almost in Sicily's northernmost tip, to **Catania** makes coastal travel from the **Catania Fontanarossa Airport** to the cliffside town of **Taormina** extremely accessible. Traveling inland to **Mount Etna** to hike or sample wine can be a bit slower; the steep slopes of the 25-mile-wide (40-km-wide) volcano require some time and patience to navigate; seasoned visitors often divide the area up into slopes and concentrate on one specific area. The seven-island **Aeolian archipelago** is about 35 miles (56 km) off Sicily's northern coast.

PLANNING YOUR TIME

Flying into the Catania Fontanarossa Airport is the most efficient way to arrive on the eastern side of Sicily; traversing the rural roads of the island from the airport in Palermo takes at least 2-3 hours, depending on your destination. Though major cities like Catania and Taormina are connected by train, most travelers to this part of Sicily rent a car, the most convenient way to move from town to town and practically essential for visiting Mount Etna unless you're traveling with a tour.

This region deserves at least a 5-7-day trip; for the **Aeolian Islands,** add on a few extra days, or dedicate an entire week to relax, swim, and island-hop. **Catania, Taormina,** or even **Syracuse** to the south are ideal bases, from which you can take day trips to nearby attractions. Taormina can be visited in one day, although once you see the views, you'll want to stay much longer (if your budget allows). Catania offers cheaper accommodations and is worth day or two of exploring, with some of the best nightlife on the island.

The slopes of **Mount Etna** also require a few days in themselves, in order to pack in wine tastings (nearly all of which must be reserved in advance), agriturismo farm stays, amazing restaurants, and some trekking or even skiing. Booking a **private driver** for wine-tasting trips is highly recommended and driving after dark on the mountain roads should be avoided when possible; one of the best ways to hike to the summit is on a private tour. Be sure to bring good hiking boots and warm layers for any trip up Mount Etna, whose high elevation (11,000 ft/3,300 m) means cool temperatures are possible year-round and can even drop down to -12°C (10°F).

This region can be visited any time of year; **July** and **August** are generally busiest in any part of southern Italy, and prices increase drastically during this period. To make the most of your trip, try quieter alternatives, like a springtime Mount Etna wine-tasting trip, skiing in March, seeing the ancient Greek theater of Taormina in the quiet of winter, or visiting the Aeolian Islands in late summer.

Previous: vineyards in the shadow of Mount Etna; Catania's Piazza del Duomo; climbing Mount Etna.

Catania, Northeastern Sicily, and the Aeolian Islands

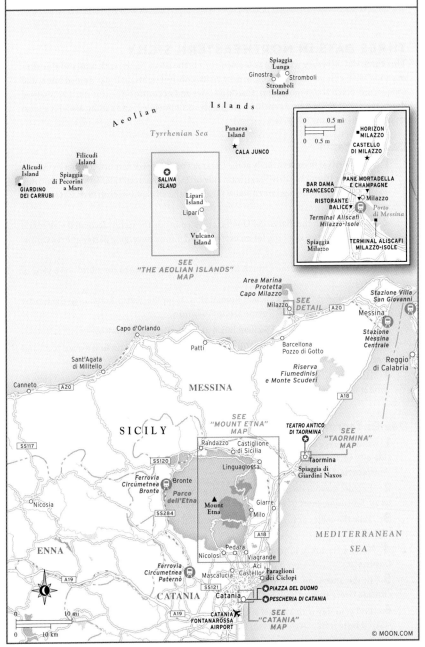

Spiaggia Lunga
Ginostra ○ ○ Stromboli
Stromboli Island

Aeolian Islands

Tyrrhenian Sea

Panarea Island
★ **CALA JUNCO**

0   0.5 mi
0   0.5 m

■ **HORIZON MILAZZO**

CASTELLO DI MILAZZO ★

Alicudi Island
Filicudi Island
Spiaggia di Pecorini a Mare
GIARDINO DEI CARRUBI

⊗ **SALINA ISLAND**

Lipari Island
Lipari ○
Vulcano Island

SEE "THE AEOLIAN ISLANDS" MAP

PANE MORTADELLA E CHAMPAGNE ▼
BAR DAMA FRANCESCO ▼
Milazzo ○
RISTORANTE BALICE ▼
Terminal Aliscafi Milazzo-Isole
Porto di Messina
Spiaggia Milazzo
TERMINAL ALISCAFI MILAZZO-ISOLE ■

Area Marina Protetta Capo Milazzo
Milazzo ○ *SEE DETAIL* A20

Stazione Villa San Giovanni
Messina

Capo d'Orlando ○
Patti ○
Barcellona Pozzo di Gotto ○
Stazione Messina Centrale

Sant'Agata di Militello ○
Riserva Fiumedinisi e Monte Scuderi
Reggio di Calabria ○

Canneto ○
A20
MESSINA
A18

SICILY
SS117
SEE "MOUNT ETNA" MAP
TEATRO ANTICO DI TAORMINA ★
SEE "TAORMINA" MAP

Randazzo ○
Castiglione di Sicilia ○
SS120
Linguaglossa ○
Taormina ○
Spiaggia di Giardini Naxos

Ferrovia Circumetnea Bronte
Bronte ○
Parco dell'Etna

Nicosia ○
SS284
▲ Mount Etna
Giarre ○
Milo ○

MEDITERRANEAN SEA

ENNA
A18

Pedara ○
Nicolosi ○
Viagrande ○

Ferrovia Circumetnea Paternò
Mascalucia ○
Castello ○
Aci
Faraglioni dei Ciclopi

A19
SS121
CATANIA
Catania ○
● **PIAZZA DEL DUOMO**
● **PESCHERIA DI CATANIA**

A19
✈ **CATANIA FONTANAROSSA AIRPORT**
SEE "CATANIA" MAP

0   10 mi
0   10 km

© MOON.COM

Itinerary Ideas

THREE DAYS IN NORTHEASTERN SICILY

This three-day itinerary will give you a taste of northeastern Sicily, with a mix of fine dining and casual culinary experiences, winery visits, cultural sights, half-day guided tours, and unique, top-notch accommodations. **Guided tours** and **accommodations** must be reserved in advance, **restaurant reservations** are highly recommended, and calling ahead is a must if you want to visit any **wineries.**

Day 1: Catania

1 Upon arrival in eastern Sicily at the Catania Fontanarossa Airport, transfer to the city center with a 10-minute drive/taxi/train ride or 25-minute train ride. Spend the morning watching the famous open-air culinary theater of the vibrant **Pescheria di Catania** fish market.

2 Stroll through the Piazza del Duomo and step inside the richly decorated Cattedrale di Sant'Agata before stopping for an espresso and minna di vergine pastry at **Prestipino Duomo.**

3 Climb to the top of the **Chiesa della Badia di Sant'Agata** for a bird's-eye view of the city.

4 Tour some of Catania's ancient Roman sites, from the Teatro Romano to the nearby remains of thermal baths at **Terme Della Rotonda.**

5 Take a break with a light Sicilian lunch at **Uzeta Bistro Siciliano.**

6 You'll end up at the peaceful **Villa Bellini** park, where you can find a place to sit and snack on a baked good from nearby Pasticceria Savia.

7 Head back down Via Etnea toward Piazza del Duomo for a casual dinner and glass of wine at **Razmataz.**

Day 2: Taormina

1 Today, make a luxurious day trip (by train, private driver, or rental car) to the cliffside city of Taormina. Start your morning with a traditional Sicilian breakfast at **Bar Pasticceria Etna dal 1963.**

2 Explore on your own to visit shops such as Majolica and Feliciotto in the historic center of Taormina, most of which are on or just off the main road of **Corso Umberto.**

3 Take the cable car to **Isola Bella,** a tiny island nature preserve floating in Taormina's bay.

4 Take a leisurely lunchtime break over a relaxing meal at Michelin-starred **La Capinera.**

5 In the afternoon, visit the **Teatro Antico di Taormina,** a well-preserved, ancient cliffside Greek theater built in the third century BC.

6 End your day with a sunset aperitivo on the picturesque terrace of another Michelin-starred restaurant, **Otto Geleng,** before the hour-long drive or train back to Catania.

Itinerary Ideas

DAY ONE	DAY TWO	DAY THREE
1 Pescheria di Catania	1 Bar Pasticceria Etna dal 1963	1 Perivancu
2 Prestipino Duomo	2 Corso Umberto	2 Etna Sud
3 Chiesa della Badia di Sant'Agata	3 Isola Bella	3 Silvestri Craters
4 Terme Della Rotonda	4 La Capinera	4 Barone di Villagrande
5 Uzeta Bistro Siciliano	5 Teatro Antico di Taormina	5 Ristorante Ramo d'Aria
6 Villa Bellini	6 Otto Geleng	
7 Razmataz		

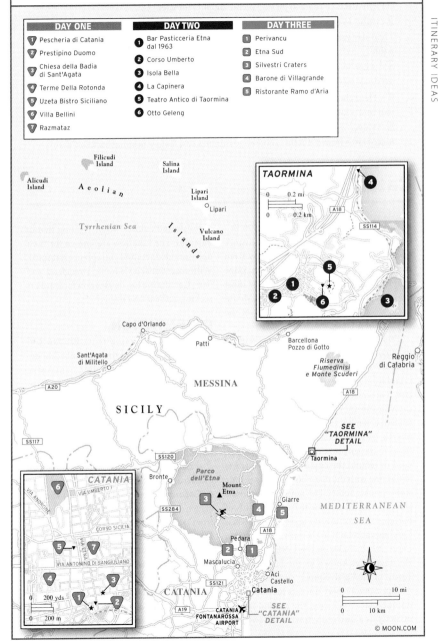

Day 3: Mount Etna

1 After an early breakfast at your hotel, drive one hour north to Mount Etna, stopping at **Perivancu** en route to pick up picnic supplies for later.

2 Head to **Etna Sud** station, where you'll meet up with your guide from Go Etna for a half-day tour of Mount Etna's steaming craters, all the way up to the volcano's highest point.

3 After an adventurous morning, enjoy a picnic made up of locally grown ingredients overlooking the lunar landscapes of the nearby **Silvestri Craters.**

4 Head about 40 minutes east to the **Barone di Villagrande** winery for a pre-scheduled tour and wine tasting.

5 You've earned a quiet evening sipping volcanic wines during a special dinner at **Ristorante Ramo d'Aria,** another 20 minutes east, before heading back to Catania.

Catania

Founded by the Greeks as Katané in 729 BC, Catania experienced much the same history of successive regimes as the rest of Sicily, from the Romans, to the Vandals, to the Byzantine Empire, to the Normans. Perhaps the most dramatic shaper of Catania's history is Mount Etna, a constant presence looming over the city's red rooftops.

Etna's largest recorded eruption occurred in 1669, followed by a devastating earthquake in 1693, which wiped out two-thirds of the population and nearly destroyed the entire city. This makes Catania's relationship with the volcano they call "Mamma Etna" conflicted: a symbol of destruction, but also of rebirth. The earthquake broke apart old lava flows in the surrounding area that were then used to rebuild the city and pave the streets of Catania with the distinctive black volcanic stone you see today. The repeated eruptions are also responsible for the city's wealth of Baroque architecture, the style in vogue when Catania was rebuilt in the early 18th century; Catania is included in the UNESCO World Heritage Sites known as the Late Baroque Towns of the Val di Noto.

A prosperous port since its founding, this unique black rock city, the second largest in Sicily, is a university town with a vibrant nightlife and cultural scene rivaling that of Palermo. The Catanese are known for their open-mindedness and entrepreneurial spirit. With exceptional restaurants, street food, and bars, Catania is a top destination for travelers seeking authentic Sicily.

ORIENTATION

The center of Catania is its **Piazza del Duomo,** where you'll find the cathedral devoted to the city's patron saint, Sant'Agata. The vivacious morning fish market is located just off this main piazza. Most of the restaurants, hotels, and bars are located over the kilometer or so between the **Cattedrale di Sant'Agata** and **Villa Bellini** park to the north, along major avenue **Via Etnea.**

Catania is a busy commercial port, with most cruise ships and ferries docking at **Porto di Catania**'s Cruise Port, south of the city center. This means much of Catania's waterfront isn't exactly scenic, but it is convenient for people arriving by boat. Heading northeast up the coast on the **SS114** road, you'll pass the **Stazione Catania Centrale,** about 1 mile (1.5 km) from Piazza del Duomo, and after another 2 miles (3 km) or so, hit a more picturesque part of Catania's waterfront, lined by the **Lungomare Franco Battiato.**

SIGHTS
★ Piazza del Duomo

The history and legends of Catania are all condensed into its principal square, surrounded by historic palazzos housing lively cafés, all built in the city's trademark black lava stone. Most of the buildings visible today were built at the turn of the 18th century, after the earthquake that devastated much of the region, on the site of Roman baths dating to the second century AD. This is the central meeting point of the city, where the massive Festa di Sant'Agata celebration takes place every February. The pièce de résistance, of course, is the cathedral dedicated to the patroness saint of Catania, Sant'Agata, dominating the cathedral's eastern side.

The piazza's principal entrance is from the south, through **Porta Uzeda,** a four-story-high Baroque portal built in the late 17th century. Cross the square north and you'll find yourself on Via Etnea, Catania's bustling main thoroughfare. Via Giuseppe Garibaldi, another main street, also crosses Piazza del Duomo from the west; walk about a kilometer down this street and you'll reach another major gate to the city, 18th-century, black-and-white striped **Porta Garibaldi.**

There are a few other landmarks of note in the square, the most eye-catching of which is definitely the basalt elephant statue, topped by an obelisk, perched on the 18th century **Fontana dell'Elefante,** right in the center of the piazza. This bemused looking pachyderm is said to date to Roman times and has become a symbol of Catania; locals look to it for good luck and protection from temperamental Mount Etna. The Catanese refer to the elephant as "u Liotru," a name said to derive from that of an eighth-century magician, Eliodoro, who is said to have rode the elephant through the city, mystifying the locals with his tricks. Near the entrance to Catania's outdoor fish market, southwest of Piazza del Duomo, the 19th-century marble waterfall **Fontana dell'Amenano** is named for the Amenano River, which flows underneath the city, toward the sea port.

Cattedrale di Sant'Agata

Piazza del Duomo; www.cattedralecatania.it; tel. 095/320044; 10:30am-noon and 4pm-5:30pm Mon.-Sat.; free

The Cattedrale di Sant'Agata, commonly referred to simply as **the Duomo,** was originally built in 1078, but has been destroyed and rebuilt several times after disastrous earthquakes and eruptions of Mount Etna. The current cathedral was built in Norman and Baroque styles using dark gray and black lava stones salvaged from imperial Roman structures, a typically Catanese architectural style that you'll see throughout the city. The distinctive, towering facade features a bell tower, granite Corinthian columns, and marble statues of Saint Agatha, Saint Euplius, and Saint Birillus, while the interior has a typical Latin cross layout, complete with an original 12th-century apse, medieval windows, several 17th-century paintings, and tombs including the final resting places of Catania's patroness herself, Saint Agatha, as well as favored son Vincenzo Bellini, best known for composing the opera *Norma.*

Consider a visit to the cathedral's **Museo Diocesano** (tel. 095/281-635; www.museodiocesanocatania.com; 9am-2pm Mon.-Fri., 3pm-6pm Tues. and Thurs., 9am-1pm Sat.; €13 for access to museum, Roman baths, and panoramic terraces) to view sacred treasures collected by the cathedral over the centuries, as well as the Terme Achilleane, the remarkably well-preserved second-century Roman baths beneath the cathedral that were only discovered during excavations in the 18th century. You'll also get access to panoramic terraces on the cathedral's upper levels, which require stairs to reach and are not accessible to visitors with mobility issues.

The church is famous for housing an important silver reliquary of Saint Agatha, as well as the saint's relics, in one of its chapels, but they are not always open for public view. This makes the saint's appearance at the Festa di Sant'Agata all the more exciting.

Catania

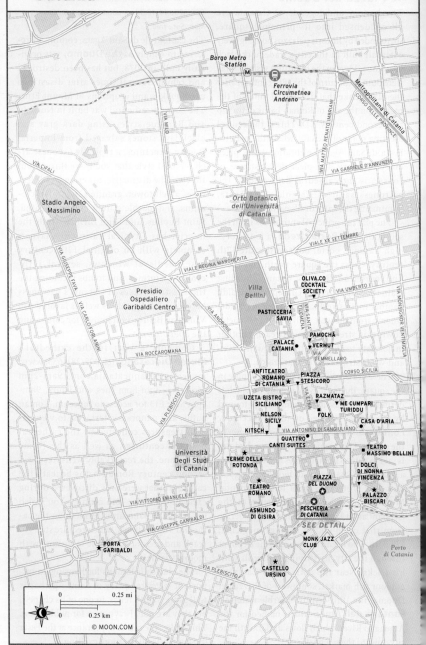

Borgo Metro Station

Ferrovia Circumetnea Andrano

Metropolitana di Catania

CORSO DELLE PROINCE

VIA MATTEO RENATO IMBRIANI

VIA GABRIELE D'ANNUNZIO

VIA CIFALI

VIA MILO

Stadio Angelo Massimino

Orto Botanico dell'Università di Catania

VIA GIUSEPPE FAVA

VIALE XX SETTEMBRE

VIALE REGINA MARGHERITA

Villa Bellini

Presidio Ospedaliero Garibaldi Centro

VIA CARLO FORLANINI

VIA ANDRONE

OLIVA.CO COCKTAIL SOCIETY

VIA UMBERTO I

VIA MONSIGNOR VENTIMIGLIA

PASTICCERIA SAVIA

VIA SANTA FILOMENA

PAMOCHÀ

VERMUT

VIA GEMMELLARO

VIA ROCCAROMANA

PALACE CATANIA

CORSO SICILIA

ANFITEATRO ROMANO DI CATANIA

PIAZZA STESICORO

VIA PLEBISCITO

UZETA BISTRO SICILIANO

RAZMATAZ

VIA ETNA

ME CUMPARI TURIDDU

NELSON SICILY

FOLK

CASA D'ARIA

KITSCH

VIA ANTONINO DI SANGIULIANO

QUATTRO CANTI SUITES

TEATRO MASSIMO BELLINI

Università Degli Studi di Catania

TERME DELLA ROTONDA

I DOLCI DI NONNA VINCENZA

PIAZZA DEL DUOMO

TEATRO ROMANO

PALAZZO BISCARI

VIA VITTORIO EMANUELE II

ASMUNDO DI GISIRA

PESCHERIA DI CATANIA

VIA GIUSEPPE GARIBALDI

SEE DETAIL

Porto di Catania

PORTA GARIBALDI

MONK JAZZ CLUB

VIA PLEBISCITO

CASTELLO URSINO

0   0.25 mi

0   0.25 km

© MOON.COM

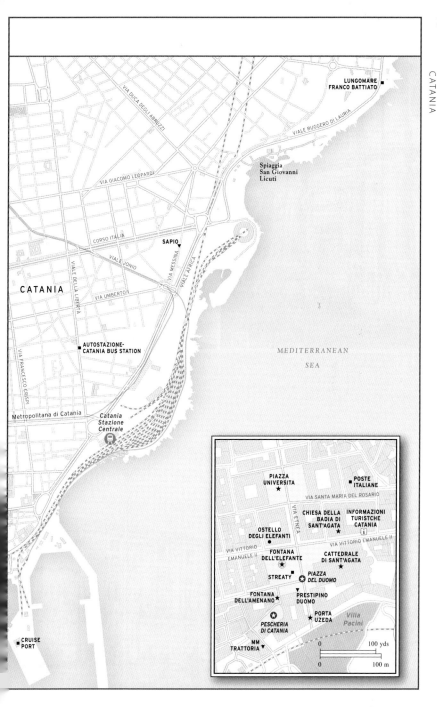

LUNGOMARE FRANCO BATTIATO

VIA DUCA DEGLI ABRUZZI

VIALE RUGGERO DI LAURIA

VIA GIACOMO LEOPARDI

Spiaggia San Giovanni Licuti

CORSO ITALIA

SAPIO

VIALE JONIO

VIA MESSINA

VIALE AFRICA

CATANIA

VIALE DELLA LIBERTÀ

VIA UMBERTO I

AUTOSTAZIONE-CATANIA BUS STATION

VIA FRANCESCO CRISPI

MEDITERRANEAN SEA

Metropolitana di Catania

Catania Stazione Centrale

CRUISE PORT

PIAZZA UNIVERSITA

POSTE ITALIANE

VIA SANTA MARIA DEL ROSARIO

VIA ETNEA

CHIESA DELLA BADIA DI SANT'AGATA

INFORMAZIONI TURISTCHE CATANIA

OSTELLO DEGLI ELEFANTI

VIA VITTORIO EMANUELE II

VIA VITTORIO EMANUELE II

FONTANA DELL'ELEFANTE

CATTEDRALE DI SANT'AGATA

STREATY

PIAZZA DEL DUOMO

FONTANA DELL'AMENANO

PRESTIPINO DUOMO

PORTA UZEDA

Villa Pacini

PESCHERIA DI CATANIA

MM TRATTORIA

0   100 yds

0   100 m

1

2

3

Chiesa della Badia di Sant'Agata

Via Vittorio Emanuele II, 182; tel. 340/4238663;
www.badiasantagata.wordpress.com;
9:30am-12:30pm Tues., 9:30am-12:30pm and
4:30pm-7:30pm Wed.-Sat., 9:30am-12:30pm and
7pm-8:30pm Sun.; €3

Located just around the corner from the Cattedrale di Sant'Agata, this Baroque church was built in the 1700s. Though its larger and more famous neighbor steals the spotlight, its solid white marble facade and octagonal dome are distinctive, and its interior boasts an impressive marble floor. But perhaps the most exceptional thing about this church is its rooftop (if you're willing to trek up several narrow staircases). From here, you'll see the Duomo from a different perspective, as well as the entire city center, much of the coast, and even Mount Etna. There is unfortunately no elevator to the rooftop, and the church itself is accessible only via a 12-step staircase.

Palazzo Biscari

Via Museo Biscari, 10; tel. 095/328-7201; www.
palazzobiscari.it; 9am-12:30pm and 5pm-6:30pm
Mon.-Tues., 9am-12:30pm and 5pm-6:30pm
Thurs.-Fri., 9am-12:30pm Sat., 10:30am-12:30pm and
5pm-6:30pm Sun.; guided tours €5-10

Built for Prince Ignazio V in the 18th century, this Baroque palace located behind the Cattedrale di Sant'Agata is one of the most distinctive palaces in Catania. You'll admire opulent salons, the mirrored, rococo-style "feast hall," the stucco-covered ballroom, and a wealth of precious frescoes covering the ceilings. Thirty-minute guided tours in Italian and English are available upon request.

★ Pescheria di Catania

Piazza Alonzo di Benedetto; 7am-2pm Mon.-Sat.; free

Most Italian cities have street markets lined with seasonal fruit and vegetable stands, but Catania's open-air seafood market, known as **A' Piscaria** in Sicilian, is truly unique.

Located not far from the harbor, through an arched opening in the old city walls, the seafood—including tuna, swordfish, red mullet, shrimp, sardines, silver scabbardfish, and mackerel—is as fresh as it gets, sometimes still alive. Vendors spread their haul out on trays, stone work tables, and fishing buckets with the goal of selling everything out by lunchtime (which begs the question: Why isn't there any ice?).

Catania's fish market is not for the faint of heart: It's noisy, crowded, and sometimes bloody, but that's what makes it such an authentic spectacle, one that stimulates all your senses. This market is not generally as friendly as others you might find in Sicily, since fresh fish is not something most tourists are often compelled to purchase. The local fishermen and vendors in the A' Piscaria market are there to work and sell to the local Catanese. As such, this rowdy open-air theater is best viewed from the street above, so you can avoid having to tip-toe around puddles of seawater and can respectfully stay out of the way of the fishermen wheeling and dealing about that day's catch. If you don't have a gourmet kitchen at your disposal to cook it, you're in luck: The market is surrounded by seafood restaurants, and chances are if you order fish almost anywhere in Catania, this is where it came from.

Castello Ursino

Piazza Federico II di Svevia; tel. 095/345830; www.
comune.catania.it/la-citta/culture/monumenti-
e-siti-archeologici/musei/museo-civico-castello-
ursino; 9am-7pm daily; adults €6, reduced rate €3,
students €2

Half a kilometer southwest of the pescheria, this imposing 13th-century castle with thick, 100-foot-high (30-m-high) stone walls has been used as the royal residence of the rulers of Sicily, from the Aragonese to the Spanish Viceroys, as well as the seat of the Sicilian Parliament, and as a prison. When it was finally acquired and restored by the city of Catania in 1932, the castle transformed once again to showcase art collections, regional

---

1: Cattedrale di Sant'Agata 2: Pescheria di Catania
3: Piazza del Duomo

artifacts, temporary exhibitions, and civil union ceremonies. It's worthwhile to just walk around the classically square castle's solid lava stone walls and round towers, in the middle of park-like Piazza Federico II di Svevia, which has plenty of benches where you can sit and contemplate the impregnable-looking fortress. Inside, you'll find the exhibits of the **Museo Civico,** including a decent collection of Greek and Roman sculptures and mosaics, which require about an hour to visit.

Piazza Universita

Bordered by buildings belonging to the University of Catania and the main Via Etnea, this central town square in the heart of Catania's historic city center is the site of public events, outdoor dining, art exhibitions, and protests. Though no longer the modern center of the university, which moved a few kilometers away decades ago, this square is still a popular meeting point for students as well as a prime spot for watching the processions of the Festa di Sant'Agata in February. Notable features of the piazza include its four bronze candelabra street lamps, added in 1957, each one symbolic of a protagonist from Catanese folklore.

Teatro Romano

Via Vittorio Emanuele II, 266; tel. 095/7150508; 9am-5pm Mon.-Sat., 9am-1pm Sun.; €3-6, first Sun. of month free

Catania is host to several notable classical sites, including not one, but two, ancient places of entertainment. Smaller, but closer to Piazza del Duomo, and with more regular opening hours, Catania's Teatro Romano is sometimes still referred to by locals as the "tiatru grecu," as archaeologists believe that this Roman theater expanded on a preexisting Greek one, during a period when Roman Catania was undergoing rapid expansion in the second century AD. Built of sandstone and basalt, it was large enough to host up to 7,000 spectators in its heyday, but today it is partially covered by the encroaching residential neighborhood surrounding it. You'll

only need about an hour to visit this theater, its nearby odeon (a classical indoor theater), and other associated structures, which may have served as snack stands for visitors back in the day.

Terme Della Rotonda

Via Rotonda; tel. 095/7150951; 9am-1pm Mon.-Sat.; €6

Just a 5-minute walk from the nearby Roman Theater and Roman Amphitheatre, the domed Roman baths of Terme Della Rotonda is one of the several thermal complexes and saunas that remain from the Roman era in Catania. Skillfully built between the first-second centuries, the Terma Rotonda and its treasured medieval and Baroque frescoes survived the earthquake of 1693, and this structure was even used as a model for the Pantheon in Rome.

Anfiteatro Romano di Catania

Piazza Stesicoro; tel. 095/7472268; www.regione. sicilia.it; 9am-12:40pm and 3pm-5:40pm Tues.-Sat, 9am-1pm Sun.; free

Today, what's left of Catania's other second-century theater, the Anfiteatro Romano, is just a small section of the original, once one of the largest in the Roman world and the largest in Sicily, designed to host up to 15,000 spectators. After the decline of the Roman empire and the amphitheater's abandonment, many of its stones were used in the construction of the Cattedrale di Sant'Agata. The site's opening hours tend to be unreliable, but there's still a good view from the Piazza Stesicoro if you find it closed to visitors.

SPORTS AND RECREATION
Parks
VILLA BELLINI

Viale Regina Margherita, 6; tel. 095/320761; 6am-10pm daily; free

In 1864, the public gardens of Villa Bellini, on the northern end of the city center, were adapted from the botanical mazes built by the Prince of Biscari and his noble Sicilian family.

Named for the local Catanese composer and town hero, Vincenzo Bellini, the landscaped lawns, gazebos, and fountains of the property make up the oldest urban park in Catania, located along the main avenue of Via Etnea. It's a perfect place to rest your feet and snack on the arancino you just picked up across the street at Pasticceria Savia.

ORTO BOTANICO DELL'UNIVERSITÀ DI CATANIA

Via Etnea, 397; tel. 095/7102767; www. attivitaortobotanico.unict.it; 9am-7pm Mon.-Fri., 9am-1pm Sat. Apr.-Sept., 9am-5pm Mon.-Fri., 9am-1pm Sat. Oct.-Mar.

Just north of the Villa Bellini gardens, Catania's botanical gardens host a collection of 50 species of palms, over 2,000 varieties of succulents, and rare Sicilian trees. Built in 1858 by Francesco Tornabene, a prominent botanist of the time, this 4-acre (16,000-square-m) garden is currently used as a natural escape and educational center for the city's residents. It hosts outdoor concerts in the spring and summer, along with other performances in its neoclassical freestanding colonnade.

Beaches

Despite being a coastal city intimately connected to the sea (as the Pescheria di Catania attests), Catania can feel quite separated from its waterfront, especially around the historic center. The nearby port is very commercial and mostly inaccessible to casual visitors, separated from the old town by the coastal SS114 road and train tracks leading to Catania's central train station. That said, there are a few nearby beaches where locals indulge in that very Sicilian summer pastime of stretching out on the sand. Still, for some of the best beaches Sicily has to offer, you'll want to travel farther from the city, whether you're visiting the luxury resorts around Taormina or the more secluded beaches of the island's southeastern coast.

SPIAGGIA SAN GIOVANNI LICUTI

Via S. Giovanni Li Cuti; open 24 hours; free

About 2.5 miles (4 km) northeast of Piazza del Duomo, this is a small, rocky free beach with pristine water, which gets deep quickly, making for good swimming. There is a patch of black sand, making it more comfortable to just throw down a towel, but access to the water is either via the rocks or a small, wooden platform.

Spiaggia San Giovanni Licuti is near the beginning of the **Lungomare Franco Battiato,** Catania's 1-mile-long (1.6-km-long) paved seaside walkway, lined with more rocky beaches and various seafront cafés, restaurants, and bars. A pleasant round-trip walk up and down the promenade takes less than 45 minutes. To get here, you can take Bus 935 (www.amt.ct.it; €1) toward Pezzano Est from Piazza Stesicoro and get off at Messina Picanello FS, about a 30-minute trip, or it's a 10-minute taxi ride (approximately €10).

ACI TREZZA

Via Lungomare dei Ciclopi, Aci Trezza; open 24 hours; free

Farther north of the city center (about 7 mi/12 km), on the 7-mile long (12-km-long) stretch of coast known as the **Riviera dei Ciclopi,** is another Catanese beach destination, with the added bonus of being associated with Homer's *Odyssey.* Off the coast of the charming fishing village of Aci Trezza, the **Faraglioni dei Ciclopi** (Via Lungomare Dei Ciclopi, 119, Aci Trezza) are an arresting set of craggy stone islets emerging from the Ionian Sea. The most common legend describes the faraglioni as stones that the blinded man-eating giant, the Cyclops Polyphemus, threw into the sea in a rage to attack Ulysses's ships as they were sailing away.

Like most of the beaches on this part of the coast, it's not a true beach per se, but a rocky coastline where you can either throw down a towel, or pay to access one of the beach clubs with amenities like lounge chairs and waterfront restaurants. Try **Ghenea Beach Club** (Via Lungomare Dei Ciclopi, beach club access €6 per person, sunbeds from €10).

The faraglioni rock formations are best observed at sunrise from the beach in Aci Trezza, or, for an up close and personal experience, rent a stand up paddleboard through **Acitrezza SUP** (Lungomare dei Ciclopi; www.facebook.com/acitrezzasup; 9am-7pm daily; €10/hour), or take a boat tour with **Sailing Tour Ciclopi** (tel. 349/890-8190; www.facebook.com/sailingtourciclopi). Getting here with a rental car is a fairly easy 30-minute drive north of Catania, with cheap, rarely full parking in lots and garages along the coast. Or take Bus 534 (www.amt.ct.it; tickets €1 valid for 90 minutes, available at local tabacchi, or purchase onboard with cash) from Piazza Borsellino, just south of Piazza del Duomo, to Terminal Aci Trezza, a ride of just over an hour.

Cooking Classes and Food Tours
COTUMÈ

Piazza del Duomo meeting point; tel. 328/1495832; www.cotume.it; cooking lessons with minimum of 4 participants Mon.-Sat. year-round; from €110 per person

Discover the layered cuisine of Sicily with a seasonal cooking lesson in the heart of Catania. Four-hour cooking lesson experiences include a walk through the Pescheria di Catania to gather ingredients, hands-on cooking instruction, and a communal lunch. Your instructor, Loredana Balsamello, is a friendly, energetic, and knowledgeable local expert who will provide a great introduction to the city of Catania and a cultural journey through the cuisine of the island.

SWEETS OF CATANIA EXPERIENCE WITH CASA MIA TOURS

tel. 346/8001746; www.casamiatours.com; 3-hour tours at 10am or 4pm Mon.-Sat. by appointment; from €290 for 2 people including tastings

During the morning or afternoon passeggiata, Casa Mia Tours takes guests on an adventure tasting your way through the city's typical pastry specialties. Tastings on the Sweets of Catania Experience may include cannoli, minne di Sant'Agata (sponge cake with ricotta cream), crispy sweet croccante (brittle) made with honey and almonds or sesame, chiacchiere (fried dough with powdered sugar), cocoa and star anise spiced cassatelle (sweet ravioli) from the town of Agira, and a rama di Napoli (chocolate almond bonbon) cookie. The tasting might finish off with gelato, Sicilian granita, or a glass of local wine.

STREATY

Piazza del Duomo; tel. 351/5133552; www.streaty. com/city/street-food-tours-in-catania; group tours available morning and evening; from €44 per person (tastings included)

Let local experts lead the way on a street food tasting tour in Catania: Streaty mainly offers 3-hour group walking tours, but can arrange private tours upon request. Guests have the option to book the Friday or Saturday evening street food tour through the backroads of the city, or the morning program, which includes a visit to the fish market, on Tuesdays and Saturdays. These programs are unfortunately not suitable for guests with vegan or vegetarian dietary restrictions.

ENTERTAINMENT AND EVENTS
The Arts
TEATRO MASSIMO BELLINI

Via Giuseppe Perrotta, 12; tel. 095 /730-6111; www. teatromassimobellini.it; box office 9am-12:30pm Mon., Wed., and Fri.; tickets €10-20

Named for Vincenzo Bellini, the early-19th-century Catanian-born opera composer, the Teatro Massimo Bellini is Catania's main theater. The Sicilian Baroque theater opened with a performance of Bellini's masterpiece opera, *Norma,* in 1890, and has been the driving force of Catania's cultural scene for over 130 years. The glamourous, plush, deep

1: Faraglioni dei Ciclopi **2:** Cotumè cooking lesson

red interiors and arched arcades also boast a ceiling fresco by 19th-century artist Ernesto Bellandi, and four tiers of box suites. The 1,200-seat theater hosts operas, operettas, dance performances, and jazz concerts, and is also home to Catania's symphonic and chamber orchestras.

Festivals and Events
★ FESTA DI SANT'AGATA
Piazza del Duomo; www.festadisantagata.it; Feb. 5; free

Catania's annual festival to celebrate Sant'Agata attracts around one million people, making it one of the largest and most popular religious festivals in the world. Devotees dressed in white robes carry the statue through the city on their shoulders, and watching the grand procession of Sant'Agata's silver reliquary as it makes its way through the streets, you'll grasp the importance of the saint to the city. Although the saint is cherished all year round, the celebration is a reminder to pray and give thanks on the occasion her silver statue's carefully removal from her chapel inside the Duomo. The best places to view the procession are in the Piazza del Duomo and along Via Etnea. In addition to this procession through the streets, there are fireworks, concerts, general revelry and debauchery, and a parade of cannalori (candle-bearing carts carried by representatives of the Medieval guilds of the city).

If traveling to the city of Catania during the first week of February, be prepared for crowds and higher rates, and make sure to reserve accommodations well in advance and to call ahead to set up reservations for restaurants and tours.

RICCI WEEKENDER
Various venues around Catania; tel. 334/9197095; www.ricciweekender.com; first weekend of Sept.; ticketed events €40-50

Imagine a music festival that also has amazing food and wine, and you've got a good understanding of Ricci Weekender. This small annual festival by a team of entreprenuers, chefs, and DJs, with unique event locations including parks and former factories.

SHOPPING
NELSON SICILY
Via Crociferi, 50; tel. 095/836-1634; www. nelsonsicily.com; 10am-2pm and 4pm-9pm daily

Nelson Sicily was founded in 2013 by Giovanni Previti. Today, they ship hard-to-find natural and organic Sicilian wines all over the world from their headquarters on Via Crociferi in Catania.

FOLK
Via S. Michele, 17/19; tel. 392/207-5505; www. magdamasano.it; 10am-1:30pm and 5pm-8:30pm Tues.-Sat.

Folk is a carefully curated contemporary design shop with a great selection of ceramics, artisan crafts, jewelry, handbags, home décor, and clothing, all made by small producers in Sicily.

FOOD
In this region, between the Ionian Sea and steep Mount Etna, the local cuisine is a healthy mix of fresh seafood and hearty meat dishes, sweet pastries made with almonds and ricotta cream, and precious bright green pistachios added into both sweet and savory recipes whenever possible. The pride and joy of Catania is of course **Pasta alla Norma,** named for Vincenzo Bellini's famous opera and made with tomato sauce, fried eggplant, a sprig of fresh basil, and grated ricotta salata cheese on top.

Catania also has a vibrant street food culture, stemming from the need for quick, cheap food to feed the masses, further driven by the late-night dining needs of a dense student population. Try **cipollata,** thinly sliced pancetta wrapped around a long spring onion; **cipollina,** baked puff pastries filled with tomato, onion, mozzarella, and ham; or **scacciata,** savory pies made with fresh

Catania's Patron Saint

Sant'Agata, the beloved patron saint of Catania, is also the patron of breast cancer patients, rape victims, nurses, and bakers, and the people of Catania have long prayed to her to protect them from eruptions from Mount Etna, fires, and earthquakes. Even if you aren't able to see her silver reliquary in the **Cattedrale di Sant'Agata**, only reliably on display during February's **Festa di Sant'Agata**, representations of Sant'Agata here are hard to miss. This is not only because they seem everywhere you look, but because the martyr is often—jarringly—depicted carrying her own breasts on a platter.

This striking image is based on the brutal nature of the saint's martyrdom. It's said that in the year AD 251, her breasts were cut off when she refused to marry a Roman prefect, in order to preserve her chastity and devotion to God. This legend has even found its way into Catania's signature sweet, the **minne di Sant'Agata,** an almond marzipan and sponge cake shaped like a breast, filled with sweet ricotta cream and garnished

Festa di Sant'Agata

with a candied cherry on top. You can try this suggestive (and delicious) treat at local bakeries like **Prestipino Duomo** (page 348) or **Pasticceria Savia** (page 349).

tuma sheep's milk cheese and anchovies. More daring foodies may want to try some of Catania's many meat-based street snacks, including **polpette di cavallo** (horse meatballs), **arrusti** (mixed grilled meats, including donkey steaks, veal, pork ribs, and lambchops), **sanguinaccio** (pork blood sausage), and **zuzzo** (a mysterious meat jelly). You'll find the best vendors along **Via Plebiscito**, or in **Piazza Stesicoro**, near the Roman amphitheater.

Fine Dining
SAPIO

Via Messina, 235; tel. 095/097-5016; www. sapiorestaurant.it; 7:30pm-11pm Tues. and Sat., 12:30pm-2pm and 7:30pm-11pm Wed.-Fri. and Sun.; tasting menus from €80-110 per person

Sapio is an exciting addition to the city's array of more casual eateries. At the age of 26, in 2019, chef Alessandro Ingiulla earned the city of Catania its very first Michelin star. The tasting menu at Sapio dazzles guests with

innovative seasonal dishes such as red mullet stuffed with chickpea puree and calamari or the duck breast with fermented red turnip greens, hazelnuts, and yogurt.

Wine Bars
★ RAZMATAZ

Via Montesano, 17/19; tel. 095/311893; www. razmatazcatania.it; noon-2am Tues.-Sun.; dishes €5-12

Razmataz is a winemaker's wine bar. This popular foodie destination is often filled with wine producers from Mount Etna and features seasonal meat and fish dishes with a homemade feel. The heated outdoor space and the cozy dining room are perfect for any time of year. Try their grilled sausages, lemon leaf-wrapped meatballs, or the off-menu specialty of gnocco fritto (fried dough puffs) and thinly sliced Sicilian mortadella for a perfect make-your-own sandwich platter paired with a bottle of wine from Etna.

Bistros
UZETA BISTRO SICILIANO

Via Penninello, 41; tel. 095/250-3374; www.uzeta.it;
7pm-2am Tues.-Sun.; €10-20

Stop by Uzeta for a typical Sicilian meal paired with great drinks and good company, with a menu of tapas-style bites and authentic regional specialties such as arancini, pasta with local donkey-meat ragù, and a baccalà (salt cod) dish with oranges and fennel.

Trattorie
ME CUMPARI TURIDDU

Piazza Turi Ferro, 36/38; tel. 095/715-0142; www.
mecumparituriddu.it; 7pm-1am Mon.-Sat., noon-1am
Sun.; €10-20

Me Cumpari Turiddu is one of the most celebrated restaurants in Catania, where you'll feel like you've just walked into a friend's vintage dining room. For Sunday lunch and daily dinners, they serve simple traditional Sicilian cuisine with a touch of elegance. Stemming from the stories and old recipe book of their nonna, as well as playing with typical street food dishes from all over the island, they make it a point to highlight Slow Food-certified ingredients and pair them with an all organic and natural wine list.

MM TRATTORIA

Via Pardo, 34; tel. 095/348897; www.facebook.com/
mmtrattoria; noon-2:30pm and 8pm-11pm Mon.-Sat.;
€20

After a walk through the outdoor fish market, stop by Mm Trattoria for a seafood lunch. This small bistro with indoor seating offers local fish and seafood dishes, pastas, and regional dishes from the Catania area. Reservations are recommended.

Cafés and Light Bites
PRESTIPINO DUOMO

Piazza del Duomo, 1; tel. 095/320840; www.
prestipinoduomo.com; 7am-midnight daily; €5

The perfect spot for people-watching, with a large outdoor seating area in the Piazza del Duomo, this newly renovated, historic coffee bar is a local staple for a quick espresso or leisurely aperitivo. Try their candied orange peels dipped in chocolate or the city's specialty dessert, minne di Sant'Agata, a miniature version of a Sicilian cassata sponge cake with almond marzipan, sweet ricotta cream, powdered sugar glaze, and a bright red candied cherry on top (symbolizing Saint Agatha's breasts).

arancini at Pasticceria Savia

I DOLCI DI NONNA VINCENZA

Piazza S. Placido, 7; tel. 095/715-1844; www. dolcinonnavincenza.it; 9am-7pm Mon.-Sat., 9:30am-2pm Sun.; €5

Originating in the 1930s in the village of Agira, this historical pastry shop has carried on the traditions of preparing sweet Sicilian confections such as buccellati, amaretti, nocatole, cannoli, gelo di caffe, and croccante. It's a great place to track down local specialties such as chocolate rame di Napoli cookies and rosoli sweet liquors. If you run out of time, you can stock up on products from an outpost shop inside the Catania airport.

PASTICCERIA SAVIA

Via Etnea, 300-304; tel. 095/322335; www.lnx.savia. it; 7:45am-9:30pm Tues.-Sun.; €5

Founded in 1897 by Angelo and Elisabetta Savia, Pasticceria Savia is the top destination in Catania to find a perfectly crispy fried arancino rice ball. This pastry shop, located across from the Villa Bellini park, offers traditional sweets such as cannoli, minne di Sant'Agata, fruit-shaped marzipan bites, sfince di San Giuseppe ricotta-filled cream puffs, and rum-soaked babà cakes. The busy bar is filled with sweet and savory treats for a one-stop-shop afternoon snack, and table service is available outside.

BARS AND NIGHTLIFE

Catania home to a large student population and is filled with cocktail bars, pubs, and cafés, guaranteed to entertain visitors late into the night. Weather permitting, youthful, lively crowds spill out into the streets and town squares. The nightlife is concentrated around **Via Gemmellaro** and **Via Santa Filomena,** just one block east of the main avenue, Via Etnea.

Cocktail Bars

★ **OLIVA.CO COCKTAIL SOCIETY**

Via delle Scale, 3; tel. 349/1732075; www.olivaco.it; 6pm-2:30am daily; €8

This Manhattan-style speakeasy cocktail bar is the only hot tip you need to find the best cocktail in town. The elite bartenders are real artists who can prepare traditional drinks or passionately interact with guests to discuss the gamut of the world of spirits and mixology. The drink list includes classic cocktails such as the negroni, Manhattan, penicillin, or an old-fashioned, as well craft beers and specialties made with homemade infusions. The staff is friendly, the vibe is pure old-school New York, and the music can't be beat. Oliva.Co is located on a small backstreet just down the steps from Via Umberto I.

VERMUT

Via Gemmellaro, 39; tel. 347/6001978; www. facebook.com/vermutcatania; 11am-2am daily; €10

Vermut is a cocktail bar that specialized in Sicilian wines, vermouths, amari, and digestivi. This is the hot spot for a night out on the town in Catania. On weekends, crowds from this small bar pour out into the street and it becomes the perfect place to meet up. When it gets busy, make sure to stop by the cash register to pay for your drink before heading to the bar to order. Indoor seating is available and small bites can be ordered to go along with your drinks.

KITSCH

Via Antonino Di Sangiuliano, 286; tel. 095/2865503; www.facebook.com/kitschbistrot; noon-3pm and 7pm-1am Mon., noon-3pm and 6pm-1am Tues.-Sun.; drinks €5-8

Kitsch is one of Catania's finest cocktail bars. Nestled on the steep terraced street of Via Sangiuliano, you'll be able to burn off some calories just in time to sip a classic cocktail like a Sazerac or one of Antonio's special concoctions from their Carta Siciliana.

Wine Bar
PAMOCHÃ

Via Gemmellaro, 46; tel. 095/3788588; www. pamocha.it; 6pm-2am Tues.-Sun.; 4 small sandwiches €6-9, bruschette €5-9

The name Pamochã derives from the words "pane, mortadella, e champagne"—or bread, salami, and everyone's favorite bubbly wine.

This bar serves bite-size gourmet sandwiches, bruschetta, raw seafood platters, European oysters, and caviar paired with champagne, wine, and cocktails.

Live Music
MONK JAZZ CLUB

Via Scuto, 19; tel. 340 /122-3606; www.facebook. com/MonkClubCatania; hours vary; most events free with purchase of drinks

Notable Italian and international jazz performances are regularly hosted at Monk and their schedule of events can be found on their Facebook page. Reservations are recommended and can be organized by phone or by emailing centroculturalemonk@gmail. com.

ACCOMMODATIONS
Under €100
OSTELLO DEGLI ELEFANTI

Via Etnea, 28; tel. 095/2265691; www. ostellodeglielefanti.it; €16

Centrally located inside a historic 17th-century palazzo, this hostel is an economical option, with rooms ranging from shared mixed dorms for up to 10 guests, to small rooms for up to 4 guests, to private rooms with double or single beds. All bunkbeds are equipped with a reading light, and there's free Wi-Fi, 24-hour reception, laundry service (€4), free breakfast from 8am-9:30am, and access to a rooftop terrace. The helpful LGBTQ-friendly staff can assist solo travelers with navigating the city, and this is a great place to meet new people if you're traveling solo. When the city explodes with visitors in February for the Sant'Agata festival and hotel prices skyrocket, the rooftop of this hostel just happens to be one of the best views in town to watch the procession coming down Via Etnea.

CASA D'ARIA

Via Pietro Antonio Coppola, 14; tel. 335/771-3186; www.casadaria.it; €55

These creatively decorated, affordable apartments are around the corner from the Teatro Massimo Bellini in the historic center of Catania. Owner Daria Laurentini designed the eight stylish apartments to showcase traditional Sicilian artistry with a modern twist. Each unit includes a simple kitchenette for preparing coffee or small meals, and with room for 2-4 guests, they are a steal. The 312-square-foot (29-square-m) penthouse apartment has an adjoining rooftop terrace and seasonal hot tub. (Call or email ahead for reservations.) In 2020, the building was updated with a small private elevator to help guests get to the third floor.

€100-200
PALACE CATANIA

Via Etnea, 218; tel. 095/250-5111; www.gruppouna.it/ esperienze/palace-catania; €110

This four-star hotel is a great location for business conferences and special events. The 94 elegant bedrooms and suites are appointed with classic dark oak furniture, white linens, traditional majolica tiling, televisions, and air-conditioning. All private bedrooms and suites are equipped with Wi-Fi, minibars, and Culti bath products designed especially for the Gruppo Una hotel group. An Italian-style breakfast at the hotel includes savory and sweet options, egg dishes, coffee, tea, juices, and gluten-free products. Grab a drink at the Etnea Roof Bar for a spectacular view of the city.

★ QUATTRO CANTI SUITES

Via Antonino Di Sangiuliano, 293; tel. 095/312432; www.quattrocantisuites.com; €119

The elegant Quattro Canti Suites hotel is the perfect place to stay in the center of Catania's busy downtown. The four bright, modern guestrooms and suites are all located on the ground floor of a former convent. Each suite is appointed with modern furnishing and a refined style, equipped with Wi-Fi service, mini bar, coffee maker, and a tea kettle, guaranteed for a peaceful and welcoming stay.

ASMUNDO DI GISIRA

Via Gisira, 40; tel. 095/097-8894; www. asmundodigisira.com; €170

This boutique hotel combines luxurious living and eccentric art. The 11 guest rooms are decked out with Italian furnishings from the 1930s and 1960s. Located in Piazza Giuseppe Mazzini, which many believe to be the most beautiful square in Catania, each of the six exceptional Art Rooms have their own unique theme, from the epic *Story of the Moors* to the legend of Colapesce, a Sicilian boy who loved swimming so much he turned into a half-man, half-fish. There are an additional five Neoclassical Rooms to choose from, each with its own private balcony. Asmundo di Gisira serves up a delicious organic breakfast that can be enjoyed on the breathtaking terrace right in the historic center of the city.

INFORMATION AND SERVICES

Check out the **Visit Catania** (www. visitcatania.co) and **City Map Sicilia** (www. citymapsicilia.it/en/catania) websites for help finding accommodations, city sights, and dining recommendations.

- **Tourist information:** Informazioni Turistiche Catania; Via Vittorio Emanuele II, 172; tel. 095/742-5573; www.comune. catania.it; 8am-7pm Mon.-Sat., 8:30am-1:30pm Sun.

- **Hospital:** Presidio Ospedale Garibaldi-Centro, Piazza Santa Maria di Gesù, 5; tel. 095/759-1111; www.ao-garibaldi.catania.it/presidio-osp-garibaldi; open 24 hours

- **Police:** Polizia di stato questura catania, Piazza Santa Nicoletta, 8; tel. 095/736-7111; www.questure.poliziadistato.it/catania; 8am-6:30pm Mon.-Fri.

- **Post office:** Poste Italiane; Via Santa Maria del Rosario, 17; tel. 095/250-2150; www.poste.it; 8:20am-7pm Mon.-Fri., 8:20am-12:30pm Sat.

- **Pharmacy:** Farmacia Caltabiano Dr. Mauro Marcello; Piazza Stesicoro, 36; tel. 095/327647; 8:30am-1pm and 4:30pm-8pm Mon.-Fri.

GETTING THERE

With Sicily's largest airport, Aeroporto di Catania Fontanarossa, located just south of the city, most travelers to Catania are likely to arrive by plane. That said, if you're planning a trip around the whole island of Sicily, the island's second-largest city is connected to its train, bus, and highway networks, but infrastructure here is still less efficient than it should be. Trains heading north up the Ionian coast, toward Taormina and beyond, tend to be relatively fast and cheap, while a bus might be a better bet for traveling through the south and interior, toward Palermo. For the ultimate in flexibility, consider renting your own car.

The easiest way to travel from Palermo to Catania is by driving, hiring a private driver, or by direct bus service. Train service will connect Palermo and Catania, but the bus is faster. Catania is easily reached from Taormina and Syracuse by following the A18/E45 coastal highway that runs from Messina south to Catania and connects to SS114 for those heading all the way down to Syracuse. Taormina is often a stop for major cruise lines such as Norwegian Cruise Lines, which dock in the cruise terminal near Via Vittorio Emanuelle II in the port of Messina and smaller boats that arrive from Taormina (20 minues) in the bay of Giardini Naxos.

Though the **Cruise Port** (Terminal Crociere Sporgente Centrale; tel. 957/465-114; www.cataniacruiseport.com) at **Porto di Catania** is a frequent Mediterranean cruise stop, no ferries from Catania to mainland Sicily were in operation at the time of writing.

By Air
AEROPORTO DI CATANIA-FONTANAROSSA
Via Fontanarossa; tel. 095/7239111; www.aeroporto. catania.it

Catania-Fontanarossa Airport is Sicily's largest, with flights to and from over 70 destinations including **Rome** (1 hour 15 minutes; €65), **Naples** (1 hour; €60), and **Bari** (1 hour; €40), as well as many other European destinations outside Italy. This single-terminal airport is wheelchair accessible, with a coffee bar, one full-service restaurant, and a self-service cafeteria, as well as a tabacchi, newsstand, duty-free shop, and small kiosks selling souvenirs.

From the airport, travelers can get to Catania city by taxi, train service, or bus. **Taxis,** available at the taxi stand right outside the Arrivals hall, will cost around €25 each way for the 10-minute, 2.6-mile (4.3-km) drive. To schedule an airport transport or other private driving services in advance, contact **Sunny Sicily** (www.sunnysicily.com). **Trenitalia** (tel. 668/475475; www.trenitalia. com) runs a train service from the airport to Stazione Catania Centrale at least twice an hour, which takes 10-30 minutes depending on the number of stops (€2-3). Finally, **AMT** (www.amt.ct.it; €4), which operates Catania's bus system, run Alibus 457 from the airport to Catania Centrale every 25 minutes or so 5am-midnight, a 30-minute ride. There is also 1-hour 25-minute bus service from Fontanarossa to Taormina provided by **Etna Trasporti** (tel. 095/532716; www. etnatrasporti.it; €6).

If you prefer your own wheels, **rental cars** can be picked up at the Catania airport from companies such as **Hertz** (www.hertz. com; tel. 095341595), **Enterprise** (www. enterpriserentacar.it; tel. 095346893), and other smaller providers. Note that though a car can be useful for the wider region of northeastern Sicily, driving and parking in Catania can be difficult.

By Train
STAZIONE CATANIA CENTRALE
Piazza Papa Giovanni XXIII, 2; www.rfi.it/it/stazioni/catania-centrale.html

The main transit station in Catania is located 1 mile (1.5 km; a 20-minute walk) northeast of the Piazza del Duomo, along the SS114 coastal road. Regular, convenient train services to **Taormina-Giardini** (1 hour; €5), **Syracuse** (1 hour 30 minutes; €8), **Messina Centrale** (2 hours; €9), **Milazzo** (2 hours 45 minutes;

€10), and **Palermo** (3 hours; €13.50) are provided by **TrenItalia** (www.trenitalia.com). It's also possible to travel by train to Catania from **Naples** (8 hours; from €30) and **Salerno** (7.5 hours; from €30), though with cheap domestic flights, this is only advisable for those with time to spare. Tickets can be purchased inside the station or online and must be time stamped before boarding. Bathrooms are available on the train and in the main stations, and there are usually plenty of taxis outside the station waiting to take you to the city center, or take **Alibus L-EX** (www.amt.ct.it; tickets €1 valid for 90 minutes, available at local tabacchi, or purchase onboard with cash) to Piazza del Duomo, a 10-minute ride.

It's also possible to reach the slopes of Mount Etna from Catania via the **Ferrovia Circumetnea** train (www.circumetnea.it), which stops at various points around the volcano on its crescent-shaped, 70-mile (110-km) route. It leaves from the Borgo Metro Station (Via Etnea, 668), about 1 mile (1.5 km) north of Villa Bellini.

By Bus
AUTOSTAZIONE - CATANIA BUS STATION
Via Archimede and Viale della Libertà

The main bus station is located across the roundabout from the Catania Centrale train station, accessible via taxi, Alibus L-EX, or a 20-minute walk from Piazza del Duomo. Ticket offices a block away, along Via D'Amico. Routes across Sicily are operated by several companies, including **SAIS** (Via D'Amico, 181; tel. 095/536-168; www.saisautolinee.it), connecting Catania to **Palermo** (2 hours 45 minutes; €14), and **Interbus** (tel. 935/22-460; www.etnatrasporti.it) connecting Catania to **Syracuse** (1 hour 10 minutes; €5-8) and **Taormina** (1 hour 10 minutes; €4-7). SAIS and **Flixbus** (tel. 123/99-123; www.flixbus. com) run buses from Catania to **Naples** (9 hours; from €29) and **Bari** (10 hours; from €29). Tickets must be purchased online or from the ticket office before boarding.

By Car

Sicily's eastern coast, from Messina on the island's very northeastern tip, to Syracuse in the south, is easy to navigate thanks to the coastal **SS114/E45** road. From **Taormina,** the city of Catania is located due south (34 mi/55 km; 50 minutes); from **Syracuse,** take the E45 north, and after passing Catania-Fontanarossa Airport, continue toward the city center (40 mi/65 km; 50 minutes). From **Palermo,** (120 mi/200 km; 3 hours) you'll follow the **E90** coastal highway east toward Messina, before eventually heading inland on the **A19.** Stay alert; construction and detours are common on these rural roads.

Once arrived in Catania, the city's compact city center, with frequent one-way roads, pedestrianized streets, and relatively busy traffic makes driving a hassle. That said, it can be useful to have your own transport to make day trips to the surrounding areas, especially Mount Etna, more flexible. **Parking** on the street, with spots indicated by white and blue lines, is theoretically possible, but in practice open spots in the city center are hard to find and often limited to 1 hour. The paid parking lot at **Parcheggio Borsellino AMT** (Via Cardinale Dusmet) is one of the most convenient, located just behind the Porta Uzeda city gate that leads into Piazza del Duomo; expect to pay around €20 per day. Or, inquire with your accommodation about options for parking.

GETTING AROUND
By Bus and Metro

Though many of Catania's sites are located in the city center, it may be useful to take a bus, operated by **AMT** (tel. 095/751-9111), to the airport, train and bus stations, or Spiaggia San Giovanni Licuti. Tickets cost €1 and are good for transfers for up to 90 minutes, or buy a €4 ticket for the day. They can be purchased on board (with cash) or at tabacchi, newstands, and kiosks throughout the city.

The city also currently has one Metro line, also operated by AMT, with plans to expand it. Though there is one centrally located station under Piazza Stesicoro, it mostly runs to the outskirts of the city from there and won't be of much use to tourists. The one exception is the Borgo station, where you can board **Ferrovia Circumetnea,** which circumvents the Mount Etna volcano. Tickets (€1 for 90 minutes) are good for both buses and the Metro system.

By Taxi

In case you find yourself wanting a taxi to your accommodation after a night out in Catania's vibrant bar scene, or to get to the beach or back to the train station or airport, there are taxi ranks outside the train station and on Piazza del Duomo, or call **Radio Taxi Catania** (tel. 095/330966). Rates are reasonable, about €25 to the airport and generally less than €10 for rides around town.

By Car

Though a car or private driver (try **Sunny Sicily;** www.sunnysicily.com) is useful for the region surrounding Catania, it is not necessary for getting around the city center, which is compact and crowded enough to make driving and parking a nuisance.

On Foot

The historic city center of Catania is best explored on foot. Use the Piazza del Duomo as your starting point and you'll find many of the main city sights are located within a 15-minute walk. The website and app www.gpsmycity.com offers self-guided walking tours and itineraries with downloadable maps highlighting the palaces, churches, and monuments of the city.

Taormina

One of Sicily's top destinations, Taormina is a picturesque town perched on the dramatic outcrop of Monte Tauro with some of the most beautiful sea views in all of Sicily. Founded by the Greeks in the fourth century BC, who gave it its famous Greek theater, it was taken over by the Romans in the third century AD, who quickly saw its potential as an elite retreat. Like much of Sicily, Taormina was conquered by the Byzantines, Arabs, and eventually the Spanish, all of whom left their mark on this small town's architecture. It's a perfect town to explore on foot before a late afternoon aperitivo in the checkered-tiled central square, Piazza IX Aprile.

You certainly won't be alone in admiring Taormina's beauty. You can find praise for it in the poetry of Ovid, the diaries of Goethe, and the witticisms of Oscar Wilde, and a list of famous visitors to Taormina reads like a who's who of Hollywood and the literati. Today, the impeccably preserved Teatro Antico is brought back to life in the summer months with concerts and performances. Then there's the beach: An aerial tram connects the town with the breathtaking coast below. Save time to explore Isola Bella, a tiny, landscaped island connected to Taormina by a thin strip of sand, with views of the immense, turquoise sea from every angle.

Taormina's famed picture-perfect scenery means it is home to several four- and five-star hotels, as well as Michelin-starred fine-dining locations. If luxury is what you want, this is the place to treat yourself. The city does become very crowded in summer, when the beautiful nearby beaches and the small streets of the town are packed with travelers. Beat the crowds and visit in autumn and winter when hotel prices drastically drop, and you'll be able to tour the town's medieval streets almost all by yourself.

ORIENTATION

The town of Taormina is not large. It was once surrounded by large city walls, and walking through the old town from the arched gate of **Porta Catania** in the west, down the main street of Corso Umberto, to **Porta Messina** in the east takes only 15 minutes. All along

view of Taormina

Taormina

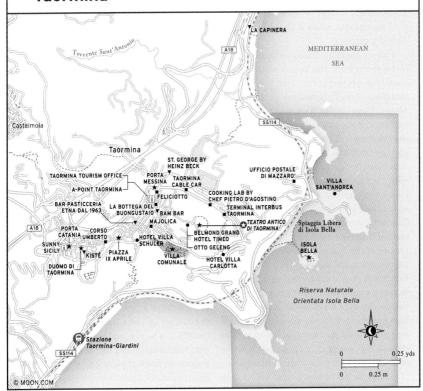

Corso Umberto you can find souvenir shops, boutiques, cafés, and bakeries. The small vicoli (side streets) shooting off the main avenue are also worth exploring to find additional restaurants and shopping that may possibly be less crowded.

Piazza IX Aprile is the main town square in the center of Corso Umberto, filled with open-air cafés perfect for an afternoon aperitivo with a beautiful panoramic view of the Ionian Sea. The Teatro Antico di Taormina, located 1,300 feet (400 m) off the main strip, is certainly the highlight, but just walking around the beautifully preserved old town, with its medieval buildings and churches and checkered-tile squares, is a treat. Taormina's sights can be explored in half a day, but with

the incredible options for accommodations and dining, you might just want to stay awhile. At the bottom of Monte Tauro are beaches and the tiny Isola Bella island, accessible by cable car, and longer stretches of golden sand await a short drive south of the city.

SIGHTS
★ Teatro Antico di Taormina

Via del Teatro Greco, 1; tel. 0942/23220; www. parconaxostaormina.com; daily 9am-4pm daily Nov.-Feb., 9am-5pm Mar. and Oct., 9am-6:30pm Apr., 5pm-10pm May, 5pm-9:45pm June, 9am-7pm July-Aug., 9am-6pm Sept.; €10, reduced rates €5

The ancient Greek theater is by far the most important stop for any trip to Taormina. It was built in the third century BC by the

Greeks using mostly red bricks, and they used it for musical and stage performances. It was later renovated by the Romans to host gladiator games, when it could hold up to 10,000 spectators.

Though there are many antique theaters in southern Italy, the Teatro Antico's size, excellent preservation, and spectacular location—literally carved out of the rock of Monte Tauro—make it unique. It's clear the natural surroundings were incorporated into the planning of this theater's stage, orchestra, and auditorium, which all dramatically overlook the Ionian Sea in one direction, with views of Mount Etna in the other. The iconic remains of the Corinthian columns were raised back up only in the 1860s, when Taormina was firmly situated as a destination on the European Grand Tour. Another unique feature of the Teatro Antico is that today, it serves much the same function as it did thousands of years ago, making it very easy to take a seat in the auditorium and imagine the works of Aeschylus or Aristophanes being performed. These days, the theater is frequently used for theatrical performances during the summer months; visit www.adituscu lture.com for a schedule of events.

Access to the theater comes with a map and audio guide, which takes you through a prescribed route and gives context to ruins, such as the portico, where eventgoers would have purchased drinks and snacks during intermissions. It also includes entrance to the small Antiquarium museum, with objects found at the site.

Duomo di Taormina

Piazza Duomo, 1; tel. 0942/23123; www.comune. taormina.me.it; 8:30am-8pm daily; free

Taormina's principle Catholic church, also known by its full name, the **Basilica Cattedrale di San Nicolò di Bari,** dates to the 13th and 14th centuries. Parts of the cathedral are more recent, most notably its 17th-century doors, surrounded by elaborately carved columns decorated with the images of 22 saints. The building itself is a relatively modest, squat structure, made of stone imported from Syracuse, with an angular, medieval, almost fortress-like shape that has been admired by visitors as illustrious as Oscar Wilde, Johannes Brahms, Alexander Dumas, Guy de Maupassant, and Richard Wagner. The interior walls are whitewashed with supporting columns of rose-colored marble, and there is a beautiful gilded portrait of Christ behind the altar.

In front of the Duomo, the three-tiered marble **Fontana di Piazza Duomo** is topped by the symbol of Taormina, the half-human, half-horse crowned minotaur.

Villa Comunale

Via Bagnoli Croci; www.comune.taormina.me.it; 8am-6pm daily; free

Taormina's Villa Comunale is an urban oasis, filled with palm trees, magnolias, hibiscus, and several purely decorative Victorian garden buildings. It originally belonged to Lady Florence Trevelyan, the British noblewoman known best for purchasing the island of Isola Bella in 1890. It was constructed as a typical English garden, and she meticulously cared for the land and filled it with rare tropical plants that thrived in the Sicilian climate. Since 1992, the park has been in the care of the municipality of Taormina. Travelers visiting the ancient Greek theater should make a point to take the additional 5-minute detour to Villa Comunale for some peace and quiet, away from the bustling streets of the historic city center.

Isola Bella

tel. 0942/620664; 9am-6pm Tues.-Sun.; €4

The tiny island of Isola Bella was originally gifted to the town of Taormina in 1806 by King Ferdinand I. In the late 1800s, it was acquired by Florence Trevelyan, a rich British noblewoman, who built lush tropical gardens and a private home there. In 2011, the island became the site of the Museo Naturalistico

---

1: Teatro Antico di Taormina 2: Spiaggia Libera di Isola Bella

Regionale di Isolabella, a kind of natural museum managed by the World Wildlife Fund for Nature that welcomes visitors who pay a daily entrance fee. Connected to the city of Taormina with a narrow sandy strip of land, Isola Bella and the surrounding bay within the Ionian Sea has become the iconic image of this stunning coastal city. The island can be reached on foot after taking the 3-minute cable car ride down from the town of Taormina.

BEACHES

Within the city of Taormina, beachgoers can enjoy the convenient free and public coastline down by the bay in view of Isola Bella, or head out of town to reach the sand beaches in **Giardini Naxos** to the south. Lidi, or beach clubs with amenities for paying guests like lounge chairs, umbrellas, restrooms, and restaurants, are scattered along the coast.

SPIAGGIA LIBERA DI ISOLA BELLA
Mazzarò; open 24 hours; free

This lovely pebbled beach can be found in the neighborhood of Mazzarò, at the foot of Taormina, facing the bay in which Isola Bella is located. The picturesque islet, crystal-clear water, and the spectacular location, nestled at the foot of Monte Tauro, make this a wonderful, if crowded, place to swim. In addition to the free beach, the **Lido Mendolia Beach Club** (Via Nazionale; tel. 0942/625258; www.mendoliahotel.com; 9am-6:30pm daily; two sun beds and an umbrella €40) is located nearby for those who want to relax with a few more amenities. From the city center of Taormina, this beach can be accessed by taking the cable car down to Mazzarò.

SPIAGGIA DI GIARDINI NAXOS
Via Naxos, Giardini Naxos

The beaches of Giardini Naxos, about 4 miles (7 km) south of Taormina, are considered among Sicily's best, not just for a relaxing day by the sea, but also for their well-known nightlife scene. With 2.5 miles (4 km) of mostly sandy beaches to choose from, you can

throw down a towel in the free spiaggia libera, or splash out on a lido (likely cheaper than some of the beach clubs closer to Taormina). With a youthful crowd, this is the perfect place to catch a late-night beach party.

Though the 10-minute drive from Taormina might seem simple, in the summer months there's traffic and parking is difficult. Consider taking a taxi, which will cost approximately €20 one-way (taxi stations available at Taormina's train station and in Piazza Vittorio Emmanuele, off Corso Umberto). Interbus (www.interbusonline.com) also runs frequent buses between Taormina and Giardini-Naxos (a 10-20-minute ride, 2-4 times per hour; €2); buses leave Taormina from the Interbus terminal, not far from the Teatro Antico, and drop off near the Garden da Nino restaurant (Lungomare Tysandros, 74) in Giardini Naxos.

SPORTS AND RECREATION
Tours
SUNNY SICILY
Salita Ciampoli, 3/A; tel. 338/5296915; www.sunnysicily.com

Sunny Sicily is an English-speaking private driver service based in Taormina and Syracuse that offers luxurious yet affordable airport transfers, half-day and full-day experiences, and cultural tourism options. Their service can be especially useful for wine tasting visits, multi-day sightseeing itineraries, and transportation for groups and family trips.

Hiking
PARCO FLUVIALE DELL'ALCANTARA
Via Nazionale, 5, Motta Camastra; tel. 0942/985010; www.parcoalcatnara.it; 9am-7pm daily; €1.50 entrance fee for guests using the stairs to reach the river; €8 at the private entrance with access to the elevator

Escape the crowds of Taormina with a refreshing trip to the Parco Fluviale dell'Acantara, a protected 30-mile (50-km) natural area that's carved into dramatic gorges by runoff from Mount Etna and the nearby Nebrodi Mountains. Impressive basalt columns and rock formations left over from volcanic eruptions add to the stunning natural landscape. Your first stop should be the **visitor center** (tel. 0942/989925) on Via dei Mulini in the tiny town of Francavilla di Sicilia, where you can learn about opportunities for river rafting, swimming, and hiking. Visitors can pay extra to access an elevator down to the river.

To arrive at the Parco Fluviale dell'Alcantara from Taormina, take Via Luigi Pirandello/SP10 on to Via Nazionale/SS114, following on to SS185 to Motta Camastra (12.8 mi/20.6 km; 35 minutes). A taxi will cost approximately €20 one-way.

Cooking Classes
COOKING LAB BY CHEF PIETRO D'AGOSTINO
Via Pirandello, 61; tel. 338/1588013; www. pietrodagostino.it/en/cooking-lab; 10am-1pm by reservation only; €120 plus taxes for group classes, €200 per person for private courses
Join a cooking class with one of Taormina's top chefs. Chef Pietro D'Agostino offers hands-on cooking programs for a minimum of eight participants on topics such as bread and pasta, innovative aperitivo, and personalized celebration menus. Adult programs, team building, and children's cooking classes can be organized in the Cooking Lab school kitchen in the city center of Taormina.

SHOPPING
MAJOLICA - UNIQUE HANDMADE CERAMICS
Via Bagnoli Croci, 6; tel. 327/407-5883; www. majolicataormina.com; 9:30am-8pm daily
Take a piece of Sicily home with you from this small ceramics shop, filled with handmade plates, serving platters, olive oil bottles, vases, coffee sets, and home décor featuring traditional designs including prickly pears, florals, fish, Moor's heads, citrus, and more.

Everything is produced right here in the shop by owner Maria and her sister Elvira.

FELICIOTTO
Corso Umberto, 5; tel. 0942/23280; www.feliciotto. com; 10am-10pm daily
This fresh and unique concept store stands out among the souvenir shop-lined streets of Taormina. The minimalistic shop is curated with cutting-edge Italian and international designer brands, niche streetwear lines, vinyl records, sunglasses, and sneakers. Feliciotto often hosts in-store events featuring art exhibitions, pop-up shops, and DJ sets.

LA BOTTEGA DEL BUONGUSTAIO
Via di Giovanni, 17; tel. 0942/625769; 9am-9pm daily
Since 1987, the Bottega del Buongustaio has been a staple in Taormina for all the best homemade preserves, wine and spirits, pastas, local honey, chocolates, marzipan fruit, and all kinds of typical Sicilian food products. This specialty food store has everything you'll want to take home with you after a trip to Sicily.

FOOD
Taormina is synonymous with luxury, from the accommodations to the food, so when budgeting for your trip to Sicily, save a little room for an extravagant meal in Taormina if you can. Reservations to most of the fine-dining restaurants below are essential.

Cafés and Light Bites
BAM BAR
Via di Giovanni, 45; tel. 0942/24355; 7am-11pm Tues.-Sun.; €3.50
Rosario Bambara's Bam Bar is the foremost stop for a quick coffee and a sweet treat in Taormina's historic center. His famous seasonal granitas include flavors such as Avola almond, pistachio, lemon, white fig, watermelon, and coffee. Order your granita with a fresh dollop of whipped cream and a fluffy brioche bun on the side for dipping.

BAR PASTICCERIA ETNA DAL 1963

Corso Umberto, 112; tel. 0942/24735; www. pasticceriaetna.com; 8am-midnight daily summer, 8am-9pm daily fall-spring; €5

This is the best old-school coffee shop in town. Bar Pasticceria Etna is a tiny store that has been serving up the best almond-based cookies, marzipan fruit, chocolate-dipped orange peels, and cannoli since 1963. Their dedication to Sicilian pastry traditions and friendly service has remained unchanged after all this time.

Fine Dining
KISTÉ

Via S. Maria de Greci, 2; tel. 333/371-1606 www. kiste.it; 12:30pm-2:30pm and 7:30pm-10:30pm Tues.-Thurs. and Sat.-Sun., 12:30pm-2:30pm and 7:30pm-1am Fri.; tasting lunch menu €35, 5 courses €65, 8 courses €80, à la carte options €18-25

Kisté is a new and approachable restaurant from chef Pietro D'Agostino, his partner Morena, and his two sisters. Located in the heart of the city center, inside the 15th-century Casa Cipolla, Kistè offers "easy gourmet" food for all, with the same high-quality ingredients and know-how you would expect from one of the city's best chefs.

LA CAPINERA

Via Nazionale, 177; tel. 094/2626247; www. pietrodagostino.it/la-capinera; 12:30pm-2:30pm and 7:30pm-10:30pm Tues.-Sun. Sept.-June, 7pm-10:30pm Tues.-Sun. July, 7pm-10:30pm daily Aug.; 6-course seafood tasting menu €75, 9-course tasting menu €90, wine tastings €36-60, à la carte antipasti €23-37, main courses €27

Chef Pietro D'Agostino's one-star Michelin restaurant, La Capinera, is a romantic fine-dining destination on Taormina's Spisone beachfront. The natural blue and white interiors, solid oak handcrafted tables, and beautiful sea-facing terrace exude the same essence of history and magic that chef D'Agostino puts into each of his elegantly plated dishes.

OTTO GELENG

Belmond Grand Hotel Timeo, Via Teatro Greco, 59; tel. 0942/6270200; www.belmond.com; 8pm-10pm Thurs.-Sat.; tasting menus for all guests at the table €150 per person, vegetarian menu €120 per person

This intimate fine-dining restaurant was named for the German artist who painted picturesque landscapes and was responsible for the boom in tourism here in Taormina during the late 1800s. Chef Roberto Toro's exclusive eight-table restaurant is located on the secluded Greek Theatre Terrace of the Belmond Grand Hotel Timeo, right in the heart of the historic city center. Chef Toro's meticulous dishes creatively reinterpret the flavors of Sicily in an atmosphere reminiscent of a dreamy vintage Italian villa. Otto Geleng earned a coveted Michelin star just one year after opening. Reservations can be booked online or organized through the hotel's concierge. Dress code: elegant.

ST. GEORGE BY HEINZ BECK

The Ashbee Hotel, Viale San Pancrazio, 46; tel. 0942/23537; www.theashbeehotel.it/st-george-restaurant; 7:30pm-10pm Wed.-Mon.; pasta dishes €35, main courses €45, 5-course tasting menu €130, 7-course tasting menu €160, wine pairings €40-90

Chef Heinz Beck's haute cuisine restaurant in Taormina quickly joined his impressive repetoire of Michelin-starred restaurants speckled throughout Italy. With 30-year-old chef Delfo Schiaffino commanding the kitchen, the St. George restaurant serves up a modern and revisited style of Sicilian cooking to the distinguished guests of the Ashbee Hotel and to nonguests.

ACCOMMODATIONS

Taormina is home to several notable high-end hotels with romantic accomodations, pools, and in-house dining options that will make you wish you never have to leave. In the height of summertime, from July-September, hotels tend to fill up; reserving as early as possible is highly recommended to secure a coveted spot at one of these sought-after locales.

€100-200
HOTEL VILLA CARLOTTA
Via Pirandello, 81; tel. 0942/626058; www. hotelvillacarlottataormina.com; €182
This independent four-star boutique hotel is more reasonable than other accommodations in Taormina. It features rooms, suites, and private villas with balconies or terraces, a rooftop restaurant, lush gardens, pool, and extraordinary views of Mount Etna and the sea.

€200-300
HOTEL VILLA SCHULER
Piazzetta Bastione, Via Roma, 16; tel. 0942/23841; www.hotelvillaschuler.com; €262
Hotel Villa Schuler is a traditional Sicilian villa hotel that has been around since 1905. This charming and sophisticated four-star hotel is conveniently situated right in the historic center within a botanical park with awe-inspiring panoramic views. Perfect for guests visiting Taormina without a car. Expect old-world hospitality from this charming third-generation family-owned villa.

Over €300
★ BELMOND GRAND HOTEL TIMEO
Via Teatro Greco, 59; tel. 0942/6270200; www. belmond.com; €450
Since 1976, Belmond has been an iconic luxury hotel group with properties in the most exclusive locations around Italy and throughout the world. The Grand Hotel Timeo is situated right next to Taormina's ancient Teatro Greco with priceless sweeping views of the Mount Etna volcano and the breathtaking Isola Bella in the Ionian Sea below. Apart from their stunning accommodations, the Literary Terrace & Bar of Belmond's Grand Hotel Timeo is one of the best places for an aperitivo al fresco, and the outdoor swimming pool, spa center, Timeo restaurant, and Michelin-starred Otto Geleng are not to be missed.

VILLA SANT'ANDREA
Via Nazionale, 137; tel. 0942/6271200; www.belmond.com; €475

This sister hotel of the nearby Grand Timeo is also operated by the Belmond luxury hotel group. At Villa Sant'Andrea, guests can take advantage of the restaurant and spa, private sun terraces, and just relax poolside. Follow the terraced tropical gardens down to Taormina's striking pebbled beach, in view of Isola Bella. Their concierge team can organize private sailing excursions upon request.

INFORMATION AND SERVICES
- **Visit Sicily:** Official tourism office located in Messina; tel. 0942/23243; www.visitsicily.info; strtaormina@regione.sicilia.it
- **Tourist information:** Taormina Tourism Office, Palazzo Corvaja, Piazza Santa Caterina; tel. 0942/23243; 8:30am-2pm and 3:30pm-6:30pm Mon.-Fri., 9am-1pm and 4pm-6:30pm Sat.-Sun. Dec.-Jan.
- **Post office:** Ufficio Postale di Mazzaro'; Piazza della Funivia, 1, Mazzarò; tel. 0942/626193; www.poste.it; 8:20am-1:45pm Mon.-Fri., 8:20am-12:45pm Sat.
- **Pharmacy:** Farmacia British; Piazza IX Aprile, 1; tel. 0942/625866; 8:30am-2pm and 2:30pm-8:30pm Mon.-Sat., 9am-1pm and 4pm-8pm Sun.
- **Hospital:** St. Vincent Sirina; Contrada Sirina, Sirina; tel. 0942 5791

For information on the nearby **Gole Alcantara Botanical and Geological Park,** visit A-Point Taormina (Corso Umberto - Palazzo Corvaja; tel. 0942/24564; 9am-1pm Mon.-Tues., 9am-1pm and 3:30pm-6:30pm Wed., 9am-1pm Thurs.-Fri.).

GETTING THERE
By Car
From Catania or the Catania Fontanarossa Airport, head north on the **E45** highway toward Taormina and Messina. The 41-mile (66-km) drive will take just over 1 hour. Most of the historic center of Taormina has been transformed into a pedestrian zone; ask your accommodation what they recommend

for parking. The main parking garage, **Parcheggio Lumbi** (follow signs for parking on approach to Taormina; €13.50 daily rate), is located outside the historic center but offers a free shuttle bus service into town.

By Train
STAZIONE TAORMINA-GIARDINI
Via Nazionale, 43, Villagonia; www.trenitalia.com
The closest train station for Taormina is shared between the city of Taormina and the beach town of Giardini Naxos to the south. Guests arriving with public transportation will need to take a 10-minute taxi ride up the hill to reach the city center (€15); there is a taxi stand outside the station. Taormina-Giardini can be reached by train service from **Trenitalia** (www.trenitalia.com) from **Messina Centrale** (1 hour; €5), **Catania Centrale** (35 minutes; €5), **Syracuse** (2 hours; €10), and **Milazzo** (1 hour 40 minutes; €8). Tickets can be purchased inside the station or online and must be time stamped at the station before boarding.

By Bus
TERMINAL INTERBUS TAORMINA
Piazza Luigi Pirandello
Bus services to Taormina are provided by **Interbus** (tel. 0942/625301; www.interbus.it). Typical routes include **Catania Fontanarossa Airport** (1 hour 25 minutes; €8.20), **Catania** (1 hour 15 minutes; €5.10),

and **Messina** (1 hour 45 minutes; €4.30). The Interbus Terminal is more conveniently located than the train station, just behind the Teatro Antico di Taormina.

GETTING AROUND
The best way to explore the city of Taormina is on foot, along with the cable car from the main town down to Isola Bella. Avoid having a car in Taormina if at all possible, since the historic city center is mostly blocked off for pedestrian-only access.

By Cable Car
TAORMINA CABLE CAR
(Funivia mazzarò Taormina)
Via Luigi Pirandello, 3; tel. 0942/23906; www. gotaormina.com/en/taormina/cable_car.html; departs every 15 minutes, 8:45am-8pm Mon., 7:45am-8pm Tues.-Sun.; one-way ticket €3, full-day €10
Taormina's gondola cable car provides service from the city down the hill to Isola Bella beach in only 2 minutes. The station in Taormina can be reached on a 3-minute walk from the Porta Messina city gates.

By Taxi
If you need a taxi to Giardini Naxos, you'll find taxi ranks at Stazione Taormina-Giardini and in Piazza Vittorio Emmanuele, or call **Taxi Messina** (tel. 35/586-1290; www. taximessina.com).

Mount Etna

Soaring to 10,990 feet (3,350 m), nearly two and a half times higher than Mount Vesuvius, Mount Etna is Europe's highest active volcano and one of the most active in the world. Its eruptions date back at least 3,500 years; the most devastating major eruption in recent history took place in 1992, lasted four months, and required local authorities to use dynamite to divert the intense lava flows. Called "Mongibeddu" in Sicilian and often referred

to as "Mother Etna," the volcano's name stems from the Greek word "aitho," meaning "to burn." Mount Etna is inseparable from Sicily's folklore and myths; in Roman mythology, the god of fire, Vulcan, used Mount Etna as his metal workshop, and it was believed that sparks flew from the volcano whenever his wife Venus, the goddess of love and beauty, was unfaithful. Although Mount Etna still regularly belches smoke, occasionally dusts

Mount Etna

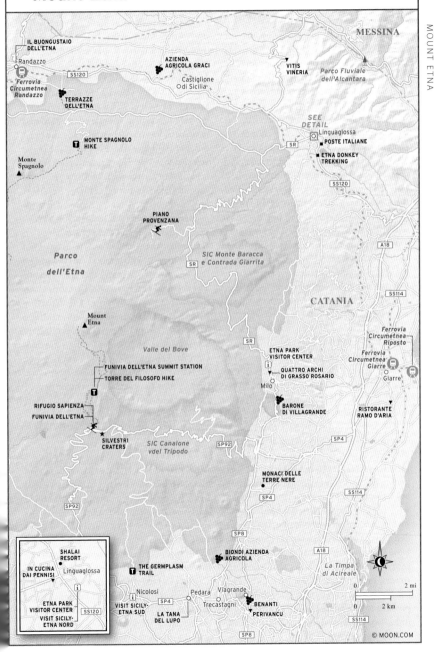

MESSINA

IL BUONGUSTAIO DELL'ETNA

Randazzo

SS120

AZIENDA AGRICOLA GRACI

Castiglione Odi Sicilia

VITIS VINERIA

Parco Fluviale dell'Alcantara

Ferrovia Circumetnea Randazzo

TERRAZZE DELL'ETNA

SEE DETAIL

Linguaglossa

SR

POSTE ITALIANE

MONTE SPAGNOLO HIKE

ETNA DONKEY TREKKING

Monte Spagnolo

SS120

PIANO PROVENZANA

A18

Parco dell'Etna

SIC Monte Baracca e Contrada Giarrita

SR

SS114

CATANIA

Mount Etna

Ferrovia Circumetnea-Riposto

Valle del Bove

SR

Ferrovia Circumetnea Giarre

FUNIVIA DELL'ETNA SUMMIT STATION

TORRE DEL FILOSOFO HIKE

ETNA PARK VISITOR CENTER

QUATTRO ARCHI DI GRASSO ROSARIO

Giarre

Milo

RIFUGIO SAPIENZA

FUNIVIA DELL'ETNA

BARONE DI VILLAGRANDE

RISTORANTE RAMO D'ARIA

SILVESTRI CRATERS

SIC Canalone vdel Tripodo

SP92

MONACI DELLE TERRE NERE

SP4

SP4

SS114

SP92

SP8

SHALAI RESORT

IN CUCINA DAI PENNISI

Linguaglossa

BIONDI AZIENDA AGRICOLA

A18

La Timpa di Acireale

ETNA PARK VISITOR CENTER

VISIT SICILY-ETNA NORD

SS120

THE GERMPLASM TRAIL

Nicolosi

SP4

Pedara

Viagrande

Trecastagni

BENANTI

0   2 mi

VISIT SICILY-ETNA SUD

LA TANA DEL LUPO

PERIVANCU

0   2 km

SP8

SS114

© MOON.COM

the city of Catania with ash, and has minor eruptions every few months, it is considered safe to visit, keeping in mind that trekking to the summit requires a guide.

The volcano is protected by 60,000-acre (24,000-hectare) **Parco dell'Etna** (www.parcoetna.it), a landscape ranging from lush green valleys and citrus orchards to mountainous volcanic craters. With such a vast area to cover, it's wise to divvy up the mountain into slopes—south, east, and north. The microclimates of the different slopes and the mineral-rich, fertile soil lend themselves to abundant agricultural production and to growing some of the most interesting wine in Italy. Though the mountain may seem forbidding, there are actually many small villages at the volcano's base, living in its shadow, with quaint, rustic agriturismo farm stays and luxurious modern resorts built in old wine presses or with black lava stones from the area. Mount Etna is a pilgrimage for wine lovers, outdoor adventurers, and the farthest south you're likely to ski within the boundaries of Europe.

ORIENTATION

When planning a trip to Mount Etna, try to divide the volcano up into slopes. You may find that a winery you want to visit on the south slope and a hotel near Randazzo, on the north slope, might be too far apart.

The **south slope** is most accessible from Catania: A drive up to Viagrande, one of the main towns on this slope, takes only 25 minutes. This is the best place to start trekking experiences, especially to the volcano's summit, but also offers some great vineyard tours and wine tastings. At the **Rifugio Sapienza** resort in the commune of Nicolosi, the Funivia dell'Etna provides access to ski slopes from November-March/April, a leg up to hikes, and tourist amenities including parking, bathrooms, tour guides, shops, bars, and snack stands for food and supplies. Note that it's impossible to access the summit of Mount Etna unless you're on a guided tour.

The **east slope** offers excellent dining,

wine tasting, and overnight stays. Towns on the **north slope,** such as Randazzo and Linguaglossa, are slightly larger, while smaller Castiglione di Sicilia is considered one of the most beautiful villages in Sicily. The east and north slopes are most accessible from Taormina, with the closest town, Linguaglossa, a 35-minute drive away; from Catania, making your way to Randazzo will take about an hour. This area is notable for its wide selection of wineries, trattorias, and wine bars, but travelers who enjoy the great outdoors will love this lush green side of the volcano, too. The Piano Provenzana ski resort is located in Linguaglossa, with its own cable car and amenities, but as the higher elevations on this side of the volcano are covered in hardened lava from eruptions in the 1990s, it's considered less scenic and therefore less popular.

Though the simplest way to get around Mount Etna is with a rental car; booking a tour or a private driver are other great options. There's also the **Ferrovia Circumetnea** (www.circumetnea.it) train route departing from Catania in the south and making a half-circle around the volcano, ending up at Riposto, some 20 miles (30 km) north of Catania. Though not the fastest way to travel, the train is scenic, and may make sense if you find it stops somewhere convenient to your Etna itinerary.

TOP EXPERIENCE

★ HIKING

Parco dell'Etna is crisscrossed by dozens of hikes, from low-intensity walks to advanced treks. It's possible to do many of these hikes self-guided, but if you want to reach the summit of Mount Etna, you'll need to do so with a guide. This regulation was put in place in 2013—understandable when you consider the very real risk of hikers falling into an active volcano. Fortunately, there are plenty of options available, from old-fashioned hikes to night excursions and donkey treks, and if hiking isn't your priority, you can always just take the cable car 8,200 feet (2,500 m) up the slope for a bucket-list view. Find additional trail maps and hiking information online at www.parcodelletna.it, www.myetnamap.it, and www.unescoparcoetna.it.

Mount Etna can be hiked year-round, keeping in mind that from October-April there can be snow and low temperatures, while August will be extremely hot and crowded. Beat the heat by avoiding hikes during the middle of the day July-August. Any time of year, hikers on Mount Etna should wear layered clothing, a wind and water-resistant jacket, sturdy hiking boots, and bring plenty of water and snacks. For summer visits, pack sunscreen, insect repellant, a hat, and sunglasses. In winter, check the weather before traveling: You may want to pack insulated pants, a warm jacket, a hat, gloves, and lip balm to protect from the wind.

The volcano's hiking hub is **Rifugio Sapienza** (Piazzale Rifugio Sapienza, Nicolosi; tel. 095/915-321; www.rifugiosapienza.com) on Etna's south slope, where you'll find parking (about €3.50 per day), trailheads, all manner of tour companies, hotels, restaurants, and other amenities. For a price, you can also hop on the panoramic **Funivia dell'Etna** cable car (Stazione Partenza Piazzale Funivia Etna Sud, Nicolosi Nord; tel. 095/914-141; www.funiviaetna.com; 9am-4pm daily; €67 combined ticket with a walking guide at the top of the mountain or €30 for only the cable car ride). Though quite expensive, the 10-minute ride itself is breathtaking, and it helps you to avoid a 1.5-hour, not terribly interesting walk from Rifugio Sapienza to the summit station.

Guided Treks

Hiring a private guide or joining a group tour is recommended for exploring Mount Etna to the fullest—and required to get to the 10,990-foot (3,350-m) summit. A knowledgeable guide will tell you all there is to know about the area's fascinating volcanic history.

GO ETNA

tel. 366/3592490; www.go-etna.com/excursions/etna-summit-trekking; group rate €120 per person

This 8-hour moderate trekking experience begins at Rifugio Sapienza, where you will board the cable car before taking a 4WD vehicle up to the Valle del Bove crater to see the lava flow from the major eruptions in 1992 and 2001. You'll trek through ancient lava flows to the highest point possible on Mount Etna. Go Etna's group excursions are led by

hiking on Mount Etna

English-speaking guides and can be booked from April-October. Private tours with hotel transportation can be arranged upon request.

ALPINE GUIDE ETNA NORTH

Piazza Attilio Castrogiovanni, 19, Linguaglossa; tel. 095/7774502; www.guidetnanord.com

The Gruppo Guide Etna Nord association offers a range of trekking for exploring the hidden natural treasures of Mount Etna. Their 5-6-hour private excursion leaves from Piano Provenzana on Etna's north slope, stopping at the craters and heading up to eruptive vents created in 1923, at 5,883 feet (1,793 m) above sea level. This easy-moderate trek requires a sturdy pair of boots, wind/rain protectant clothing, and a hat. A more advanced full-day trek (7-8 hours) with snowshoes is offered in winter and springtime.

FUNIVIA DELL'ETNA GUIDED WALK

Stazione Partenza Piazzale Funivia Etna Sud, Nicolosi Nord; tel. 095/914141; www.funiviaetna.com; 9am-4pm daily; €67 combined ticket with a walking guide at the top of the mountain, €30 cable car ride only

The Funivia dell'Etna offers the only certified excursion on the south slope, taking guests from the cable car's summit station and to the summit using off-road vehicles and some trekking. The entire round-trip journey, including the cable car, takes about 2 hours.

South Slope

TORRE DEL FILOSOFO HIKE

Distance: *4 miles (6 km) round-trip*
Time: *about 2 hours round-trip*
Trailhead: *Funivia dell'Etna Summit Station*
Information and Maps: *www.parcoetna.it*

This relatively moderate hike from the summit station of Funivia dell'Etna takes you about as close to the summit as you can get without a guide. Walking on the same makeshift road used by vehicles to get to the summit, which looms ominously to your left, you'll pass otherworldly craters created by eruptions in the early 2000s, some of them

still steaming decades later. About halfway through, you'll reach the tower for which the hike is named, an observation tower built on the site of what was said to be the shelter built by the Greek philosopher Empedocles. Not much is left of the tower, which was built too close to the summit to last for long. The pinnacle of the hike is the impressively large Barbagallo Craters, which can be walked around in their entirety.

Note that it is possible to hike from Refugio Sapienza and avoid the €30 round-trip cable car ride. The path up the mountain, near where you board the cable car, is fairly obvious. To do this, add approximately 3 hours and 3 miles (5 km) to your round-trip hike.

SILVESTRI CRATERS

Distance: *0.6 miles (1 km) round-trip*
Time: *45 minutes round-trip*
Trailhead: *SP92, Nicolosi*
Information and Maps: *www.mapcarta.com*

Not far from Rifugio Sapienza, these two smaller craters at an elevation of about 2,300 feet (700 m) were formed by an eruption in 1892. They're a great option for travelers with kids, or those who don't have the time for the 7-hour guided hike to the top of Mount Etna and back. You'll enjoy 360-degree panoramic views from the top of the lunar landscape; the lower crater, just south of the SP92 road that winds up the volcano, can be traversed in about 30 minutes on a leisurely, slightly uphill 0.25-mile (0.4-km) walk. The upper crater, on the north side of the SP92, is reachable via a steeper climb; hikers can also continue to Monti Calcarazzi (add 20 minutes and 0.6 mi/1 km round-trip), a mountainous area created by an eruption in the 18th century.

The black surface, arid landscape, and lack of coverage make this a very hot walk in the summer; start out early to beat the heat. Not recommended to visit after dark.

THE GERMPLASM TRAIL

Distance: *0.7 miles (1.2 km) round-trip*
Time: *1 hour round-trip*
Trailhead: *Via del Convento, 45, near the Monastero di San Nicolò L'Arena in Nicolosi*
Information and Maps: *www.parcoetna.it*

The Germplasm Trail is specially designed to stimulate all five of your senses, featuring plaques along the way to help you identify notable native plants. One of the easier routes on the volcano, this basic 1-hour hike is wheelchair accessible and includes rest areas with benches, bathrooms at the entrance, and signage in Braille for visually impaired visitors.

North Slope
MONTE SPAGNOLO HIKE

Distance: *3.4 miles (5.5 km) each way*
Time: *2 hours 30 minutes round-trip*
Trailhead: *Pirao Etna Nord, 20-minute drive southeast of Randazzo*
Information and Maps: *www.parks.it or www.myetnamap.it*

On the northern slope, a 20-minute drive from Randazzo, this moderate trail with a 750-foot (230-m) elevation gain passes lava tunnels created in 1981, with beautiful views of the mountainous area north of Mount Etna. At the hike's highest elevation (4,700 ft/1,440 m), you'll find the Rifugio Monte Spagnolo, a picturesque stone hut for hikers spending the night on the mountain.

OTHER SPORTS AND RECREATION
Jeep and Donkey Tours
ETNA DISCOVERY

tel. 095/780-7564; www.etnadiscovery.it/etna-jeep-tour-half-day-en; 4-hour programs at 9am and 3pm; €60 per person

This half-day tour of Mount Etna includes round-trip transporation from your hotel or meeting point. Your four-hour Jeep Tour will be led by an expert tour guide. Off-roading adventures include a tour of a lava tube and a walk around the crest of the craters.

DONKEY TREKKING

Piano Provenzana; tel. 349/306-5136; www. etnadonkeytrekking.com; office 9am-8pm daily; 1-hour experiences from €25 per person

Take a ride through Mount Etna on these beautiful Ragusano-breed donkeys. Various 1-4-hour excursions are available year-round. Winter programs (Nov.-Apr.) include rides through snow-covered woods, vineyards, and olive groves.

Skiing

There are two locations for skiing on Mount Etna (www.etnasci.it), giving skiers the unique opportunity to hit the slopes in the middle of the Mediterranean. Day passes cost €15-35, and equipment can be rented at either Rifugio Sapienza or Piano Provenzana. Etna's high elevation means there can be snow year-round, with enough for skiing from November-March, sometimes into April.

RIFUGIO SAPIENZA

Rifugio Sapienza-Montagnola, SP92, Nicolosi; tel. 095/915321; www.etnasci.it; 9am-3:30pm daily year-round; adult day pass €30

The slopes of Rifugio Sapienza, on the south slope of Mount Etna, stretch between 6,200-8,500 feet (1,900-2,600 m); five ski trails overlooking the Gulf of Catania and the smoking summit range from easy to intermediate. A six-seater cable car provides access to the slopes, and Etna Tourism Services offers ski and snowboard rentals (tel. 095/780-7740).

Traveling for 1 hour by car from Catania, follow SP10 north to SP92 into Nicolosi until you spot signs for Etna Sud. The **Autolinea AST** bus service (tel. 095/7461096) also departs from Catania Centrale at 8:15am and returns at 4pm from the resort (€3).

PIANO PROVENZANA

Via Provenzana, Piano Provenzana, Linguaglossa; tel. 095/643094; www.etnasci.it; 9am-4pm daily year-round; adult day pass €35, children's ticket €30

This resort is on the north slope of Mount

Etna near the town of Linguaglossa at 5,900-7,500 feet (1,800-2,300 m), with amazing views of the Ionian Sea. There are 6.4 miles (10.3 km) of slopes available for skiing and snowboarding, though due to hardened lava on this side of the mountain from relatively recent eruptions, the runs at Piano Provenzana tend to be open less. Equipment rentals are offered by La Capannetta (tel. 328/912-9666). From Taormina, it's a 30-mile (50-km) drive of just over an hour, though expect it to take longer on twisty, sometimes snowy roads. From Linguaglossa, follow signs for Etna Nord - Piano Provenzana.

★ VINEYARD VISITS AND WINE TASTING

Mount Etna is home to over 150 wineries; with so many to choose from, the ones featured here are all exclusively local, rather than extensions of larger wineries. Reservations are required for all tastings in this area; walking into a winery for a tasting unscheduled is unusual. Keep in mind that September-November is harvest season, meaning smaller winemakers will have less time to receive visitors. It is not expected to purchase after a tasting, though wines are often available to buy or ship back home.

Wine Tours

Consider a private driver to take you to Etna's wineries, to avoid worrying about navigating mountain roads after your tasting.

ETNA WINE SCHOOL

www.etnawineschool.com; info@etnawineschool. com; half-day programs from €120 per person, full day €220
The half-day expert-led programs at the Etna Wine School include a visit to a single winery, while full-day programs include two wine estates and guided wine tastings. Founder Benjamin North Spencer is a U.S.-born writer and Wine & Spirits Education Trust-certified expert, and his book, *The New Wines of Mount Etna,* is a great resource for wine lovers visiting this area. Reservations

must be made in advance; premium tastings, lunches, and transportation can be added for an extra fee.

SUNNY SICILY ETNA WINE TOUR

Sunny Sicily, Piazza S. Antonio Abate, 7, Taormina; tel. 338/5296915; www.sunnysicily.com/tour/ etna-wine-tour; 7-8-hour full-day experience; from €135 per person
Treat yourself to a full day of wine tasting with your own friendly English-speaking luxury chauffeur. This experience includes door-to-door service to and from your hotel and a visit and tasting at two of Etna's top wineries.

South Slope
BENANTI

Via Giuseppe Garibaldi, 361, Viagrande; tel. 095/789-0928; www.benanti.it; daily visits by appointment only; Wine & Culture Experience €50 per person
The Benanti family is among the most respected wine producers on Etna, and the only one to have vineyards on all four of its slopes. Their vineyard in Viagrande is one of the most popular, well-organized, professional, and efficient on the mountain. Visitors can purchase wine on site and take part in tours of the 19th-century estate, including the historic palmento wine press, 100-year-old Nerello Mascalese and Nerello Cappuccio vines, and wine tastings and food pairings inside a cozy country house.

BIONDI AZIENDA AGRICOLA

Via Ronzini, 55a, Trecastagni; tel. 347/501-1310; www. ibiondi.com; by appointment only; €30 per person
Ciro and Stef Biondi took over these 17th-century vineyards in the commune of Trecastagni in 1999, and are now ranked among the leading natural wine producers on Mount Etna. Their high-quality wines focus on sustainability and respect for the territory. Guests can enjoy 90-minute tastings of 4-5 wines paired with local cheese, meats,

1: wine tasting at Benanti 2: vines at Terrazze dell'Etna

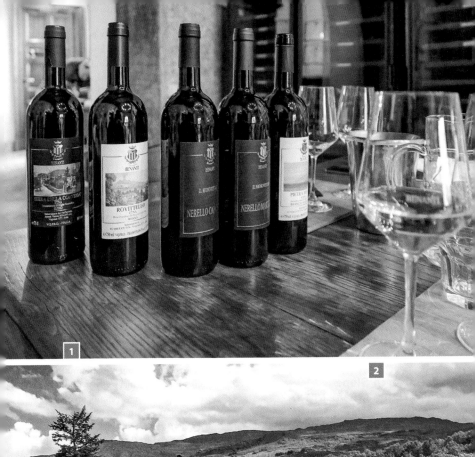

and accompaniments, right in the middle of terraced vineyards. Biondi is one of the most accessible wineries on Mount Etna's southern slope, 30 minutes from Catania by car.

East Slope
BARONE DI VILLAGRANDE

Via del Bosco, 25, Milo; tel. 095/708-2175; www. villagrande.it; by appointment only 11am-3:30pm and 6:30pm-10pm daily; tastings from €30 per person

Located at 2,300 feet (700 m) above sea level on the eastern side of the Mount Etna volcano, the Barone di Villagrande property has been owned by the Nicolosi Asmundo family since 1727. For the last 10 years, Marco and Barbara have been producing fine organic wines from the family vineyards overlooking Taormina. Their noble and historic 18th-century country manor also includes a Wine Resort, restaurant, and pool nestled between the vineyards, which host wine tastings, dinners, and overnight stays. It's 1 hour from Taormina and 35 minutes from Catania via the E45 coastal highway.

North Slope
TERRAZZE DELL'ETNA

Località Bocca d'Orzo, Randazzo; tel. 328/617-5952; www.terrazzedelletna.it; Mon-Sat by appointment only; €20-35

Since 2008, the Bevilacqua family has cultivated the land of the Contrada Bocca d'Orzo estate. Their 89 acres (36 ha) include terraced Nerello Cappuccio, Nerello Mascalese, Carricante, chardonnay, pinot noir, and Petite Verdot vineyards, as well as chestnut forests and olive groves. Terrazze dell'Etna in Randazzo can be reached with a scenic, 1-hour mountain drive from Taormina.

AZIENDA AGRICOLA GRACI

SP7, Contrada Arcuria, Passopisciaro; tel. 348/701-6773; www.graci.eu; by appointment only; €45 per person with tasting of 5 wines

Alberto Aiello Graci has been making wine on his 5-acre (2-ha) family property since 2004. His high-density vineyards are planted

at an altitude between 2,000-3,300 feet (600-1,000 m) above sea level and focus solely on indigenous grape varietals, set between towering lava stone walls. The certified organic wines are fermented using only wild yeasts. The Graci vineyards can be reached via a 1-hour ride from Taormina, passing through the charming hilltop village of Castiglione di Sicilia.

FOOD

Due to Mount Etna's fertile volcanic soil, this part of the island offers exceptional agricultural produce, including foraged mountain greens, stone fruit, world-famous pistachios, wild mushrooms, flavorful extra virgin olive oil, local cheeses, and pork products and salami made from the black pigs who thrive in the mountainous landscape. As this is one of Sicily's most famous winemaking regions, high-quality local wines will be readily available in restaurants, grocery stores, and markets.

Rustic farm stays and restaurants will be speckled throughout the mountainous region, and most winery visits will offer food pairing options or a even full lunch with advanced notice, but most of the restaurants, bars, markets, pharmacies, and gas stations are clustered in the town centers. Always stock up on food or snacks (maybe even a picnic!) before embarking on an outdoor adventure.

South Slope
PERIVANCU

Via Vincenzo Bellini, 18, Viagrande; tel. 095/7894698; www.perivancu.it; 8:15am-1:45pm and 5pm-8:30pm Mon.-Tues., 8:15am-2pm Wed. and Sun., 8:15am-1:30pm and 5pm-8:30pm Thurs.-Sat.; €10

Get a taste of Mount Etna and stock up on food to pack along with you on a hike or take home at the end of your trip. This small alimentari specialty foods store and deli has been family-run since 1926 and features regional delicacies such as cured meats and cheeses, seasonal vegetables and fruit grown on the volcano, foraged mountain mushrooms, local honey, marmalades, and pesto, as well as a selection of wine and spirits from the area. Perivancu is located just 10 minutes south of the Benanti winery.

LA TANA DEL LUPO

Corso Ara di Giove, 138, Pedara; tel. 095/7800303; www.ristorantelatanadelupo.it; 7:30pm-11pm Mon., 7:30pm-11pm Wed.-Sat., 12:30pm-2:30pm and 7:30pm-11pm Sun.; €10-18

Only 25 minutes from the center of Catania in a small village between Nicolosi and Trecastagni, La Tana del Lupo is a casual tavern specializing in delicious meat dishes. The restaurant was completely renovated inside of a traditional palmento winemaking press. Like any reputable restaurant on Mount Etna, their extensive wine cellar takes center stage.

East Slope
★ RISTORANTE RAMO D'ARIA

Ramo d'Aria: Etna Country Hotel, Viale delle Provincie, 261, Giarre; tel. 334/639-9145; www.ramodaria.it; 7:30pm-10pm with one rotating day closed per week; main courses €14-16

Nestled in a lush green lemon grove, this resort restaurant offers affordable contemporary dining on the eastern side of Mount Etna. Fresh seasonal dishes feature traditional Sicilian flavors of the land and sea using local artisanal ingredients such as pistachios, ancient wheat varieties, and local mountain cheeses, guaranteed to dazzle the palate of any food and wine lover.

QUATTRO ARCHI DI GRASSO ROSARIO

Via Francesco Crispi, 9, Milo; tel. 095/955566; www.4archi.it; 7pm-midnight Mon.-Tues. and Thurs.-Fri., noon-midnight Sat.-Sun.; €15-25

At Quattro Archi, owner Saro Grasso and chef Lina Castorina proudly follow the philosophies of Slow Food. They work directly with small producers and select top-quality ingredients, always striving to provide good

old-fashioned down-home Sicilian cuisine and wood-fired pizza in their rustic osteria. Milo can be reached by car in 45 minutes from Taormina or Catania.

North Slope
IL BUONGUSTAIO DELL'ETNA

Via Umberto, 8, Randazzo; tel. 320/976-0623; www.buongustaiodelletna.com; 9:30am-midnight daily; meat and cheese platters €5-15

Treat yourself to one of this deli's epic meat and cheese charcuterie platters, piled high with salsiccia secca with wild fennel, pistachio salame, fresh provola, smoked scamorza, ricotta al forno, and a tasting of oil-preserved mushrooms, honey, and marmalades. Or, take one of their gourmet sandwiches along with you for a late-night snack once you get back to your hotel after a long day of wine tasting. Randazzo is accessible from Taormina in 1 hour, driving along the E45 highway to the SS1120.

VITIS VINERIA

Via Tenente Tornatore, Castiglione di Sicilia; tel. 380/630-4756; www.bottegavitis.com; noon-2:30pm and 7pm-10:30pm Fri.-Sun.; antipasti €20, mains €14

A cozy night on the volcano is not complete without a few hours spent in a local wine bar. Located in the picturesque mountainside town of Castiglione di Sicilia, the selection of wines physically packed into every shelf, cantina, nook, and cranny of this tiny vineria is unparalleled. Test out seasonal specialties like wild mushroom soup, hefty hamburgers, and local cured meat and cheese platters. Castiglione di Sicilia is accessible by car from Taormina in 45 minutes via SS114 to SS185 and SP7.

★ IN CUCINA DAI PENNISI

Via Umberto I, 11, Linguaglossa; tel. 095/643160; www.facebook.com/daipennisi; 9am-11pm Tues.-Sun.; €35

This hidden culinary treasure is located in the small mountain town of Linguaglossa. Saro and Lina Pennisi have partnered with the

Shalai boutique hotel to revamp their historic family store into a butcher shop with its own contemporary bistro right in the middle of the cases of meat and sizzling grills. Dishes arrive at the table served on wooden boards, steakhouse-style. Guests arriving from Taormina can reach Linguaglossa by car in 30 minutes by following the E45 to SS120.

ACCOMMODATIONS

With choices ranging from eco-lodges to luxury accommodations and rustic farm stays, a night or two spent on Mount Etna will give guests the additional time needed for exploring the volcano and visiting wine producers without the need to drive back to Taormina or Catania. Resorts will often have their own in-house restaurant for a convenient and relaxing meal.

South Slope
ETNA BOTANIC GARDEN
Via Trinità, 34, Mascalucia; tel. 337/955493; www. etnabotanicgarden.com; €60

Plan an escape to this garden oasis on the southern slope of Mount Etna. The rustic manor house sits on a 3-acre (1-ha) property filled with citrus orchards and botanical gardens. Choose from their two rooms or six apartments, enjoy a poolside break and their excellent organic breakfast, or cook for yourself in the kitchenette-equipped cottages.

RELAIS SAN GIULIANO
Via Giuseppe Garibaldi, 280, Viagrande; tel. 095/9891671; www.relais-sangiuliano.it; classic rooms from €135 and family suites €200-260

Add a little glam to your trip to Mount Etna. This 12-room dimora storica noble country home can host up to 31 people. The lush gardens, gorgeous swimming pool, sun terrace, spa, fitness center, and restaurant are especially equipped for couples and families. A perfect pick at the foot of Mount Etna, stylishly designed to provide a relaxed family atmosphere. Pets are welcome, too!

East Slope
★ MONACI DELLE TERRE NERE
Via Monaci, Via Pietralunga, Zafferana Etnea; tel. 095/7083638; www.monacidelleterrenere.it; from €330

Monaci delle Terre Nere is the place where slow living and luxury meet. The 60-acre (25-ha) estate includes carefully renovated historic farmhouses, the main 18th-century manor house, and sustainably built villas and suites. Each space celebrates its original elements, such as exposed wood-beamed ceilings and lava-stone walls. Owner Guido Coffa considers himself a custodian of the land, and his passion for sustainability and respect for the natural surroundings shines through in every aspect of this magical paradise. The mountainside manor house can be reached by car in 35 minutes from Catania and 40 minutes from Taormina.

North Slope
SHALAI RESORT
Via Guglielmo Marconi, 25, Linguaglossa; tel. 095/643128; www.shalai.it; €112

After a day of outdoor adventures, treat yourself to a little rest and relaxation. In Sicilian dialect, "Shalai" means full of joy, and that's exactly what you'll experience in this elegant and contemporary resort. This 13-room boutique hotel is located in the historic center of Linguaglossa. Candle-lit spa treatments are available in the wellness center, and the resort restaurant is not to be missed. Linguaglossa can be reached by car in 35 minutes from Taormina or 50 minutes from Catania.

INFORMATION AND SERVICES

The online resource **My Etna Map** (www. myetnamap.it) and its printed maps were created in partnership with the Visit Sicily tourism board to help travelers discover the territory around Catania and the Mount

1: a tasty meal at Vitis Vineria **2:** villa at Monaci delle Terre Nere

Etna volcano. The guide includes seasonal itineraries, points of interest, and restaurant and hotel recommendations. Free printed maps can be found in many hotels, restaurants, cafés, and travel agency offices in the area.

There are many visitor centers throughout the Mount Etna area, including several run by Parco dell'Etna and a few others run by Visit Sicily.

- **Etna Park Visitor Centers:** www.parcoetna.it; Via A. Manzoni, 21, Fornazzo/Milo, tel. 338/2993077; Piazza Annunziata, 5, Linguaglossa, tel. 095/643094

- **Visit Sicily - Etna Sud:** Via Martiri d'Ungheria, 36/38; tel. 095/911505; www.visitsicily.info

- **Visit Sicily - Etna Nord:** Piazza Annunziata (corner of Via Marconi), Linguaglossa; tel. 095/643677; www.visitsicily.info

OTHER SERVICES

- **Police:** Polizia Di Stato; Via Sottotenente Manchi, 6, Randazzo; tel. 095/921222; www.questure.poliziadistato.it

- **Hospital:** Azienda Sanitaria Provinciale Di Catania: Piazza Ospedale, 1, Randazzo; tel. 095/921056; open 24 hours

- You'll find **pharmacies** in major towns like Viagrande, Linguaglossa, and Randazzo

- **Post office:** Poste Italiane, Viale Tommaso Fazello, 13, Linguaglossa; tel. 095/643663; www.poste.it; 8:30am-1:30pm Mon.-Fri., 8:30am-12:30pm Sat.

GETTING THERE AND AROUND

Though there is some public transportation to Mount Etna, including a slow (but scenic) train route, the best way to explore Mount Etna is with your own rental car. Most wineries or outdoor excursions will require you to arrive at a set meeting point somewhere on the mountain. Hiring a private driver is

another good option, especially for vineyard visits.

By Car and Private Driver

The south and east slopes are easily reached by car from **Catania** (25 minutes) and **Taormina** (1 hour). The north slope is most accessible via a scenic, 1-hour drive through the mountains from Taormina. The state roads and highways from Taormina and Catania are easy to navigate, but keep in mind that many roads in the Etna area are unmarked, unlit, and fairly dangerous for driving at night or during inclement weather. Allow more driving time than you think you need, and keep in mind that gas stations and restaurants are scarcely distributed around the perimeter of the volcano. When visiting wineries or country accommodations, double-check with your host for driving directions; often, they will even meet you at a central location so you can follow them to the destinations.

Though you may want to avoid driving in some of the tiny, narrow streets of mountainside towns, parking is for the most part easy, clearly signed, and rates generally cheap or even free. **Refugio Sapienza** and the Funivia dell'Etna is a 1-hour, 21-mile (35-km) drive from Catania and just over an hour (34 mi/55 km) from Taormina. Parking here costs €3.50 per day and is free after 5pm.

Private driver **Sunny Sicily** (Piazza S. Antonio Abate, 7, Taormina; tel. 338/5296915; www.sunnysicily.com) provides chauffeur services and organizes tours including vineyard visits on Mount Etna, with round-trip transportation from Taormina or Catania.

By Train
FERROVIA CIRCUMETNEA
Via Caronda, 352a, Catania; tel. 095/541111; www.circumetnea.it; approximately 6am-6pm daily; tickets range in price depending on distance, with discounted rates on round-trip services

This railway connects Catania with Riposto, traveling clockwise from the provincial capital city heading west along the south, west, north, and half of the east slope around Mount Etna for 69 miles (111 km). Unfortunately, it does not make a full round-trip loop back to Catania. Departing from the Catania Borgo (Via Caronda, 352a) Metro station, the journey from beginning to end of the line lasts about 3 hours (€8 one-way, €13 round-trip) and stops along the way in towns such as Randazzo and Linguaglossa. They offer two special itineraries: the Il Treno dei Vini dell'Etna train and Wine Bus service, to discover Etna's best wineries; or the Treno su Due Ruote trip, which allows you to board the train with a bicycle and get off at the destination of your choice.

A short train ride with **Trenitalia** (www.trenitalia.com) can also be helpful to return to Catania's without circling the volcano on the way back. Train service departs from the Giarre-Riposto station (Piazza Giuseppe Mazzini, 6, Giarre) for Catania Centrale (Piazza Papa Giovanni XXIII, 2, Catania) throughout the day (20-40 minutes; €3.40-8.50). This trip can also be taken in the opposite direction with the Trenitalia service to Giarre-Risposto and the Circumetnea scenic train on the way back to the Catania Borgo station.

By Funicular
FUNIVIA DELL'ETNA
Stazione Partenza Piazzale Funivia Etna Sud, Nicolosi Nord; tel. 095/914141; www.funiviaetna.com; 9am-4pm daily; €30 round-trip
Even though it's expensive, you should think about taking the cable car up the Mount Etna volcano even if simply just for the 10-minute ride and the exceptional panoramic views, departing at the 6,305-foot (1,923-m) base and arriving at 8,215 feet (2,504 m). Cable cars depart continuously every few minutes all day long. At the top of the mountain there is a chalet bar, café, and gift shop where visitors can purchase refreshments and enjoy the panoramic views from Taormina to the Aeolian Islands on a clear day.

During the winter season (Dec.-Mar.), the Etna cable cars run daily for sightseeing or snowshoers, with the final departure at 4pm. For summer excursions, the final uphill departure is at 3:30pm. By telephone reservation only, the Funivia dell'Etna offers an additional Sunset Excursion on Monday, Tuesday, and Thursday, departing at 5:30pm. The shop at the cable car entrance has coat and shoe rentals available, which may be helpful when the top of the volcano remains covered in snow even in summertime.

The Aeolian Islands

The seven volcanic islands of the Aeolian archipelago erupted from the sea off Sicily's northeastern coast some 700,000 years ago; today, Stromboli, on its eponymous island, still erupts every 30 minutes on average all year round. Now the Isole Eolie, as they're called in Italian, are best known as a summer holiday destination, often visited on sailing excursions and multi-day island-hopping adventures. They offer a unique mix of geological and archeological cultural sights, fine-dining options, outdoor adventures, luxurious hotels, beautiful beaches, and hidden rock coves. They're accessible mainly from the port town of Milazzo in northern Sicily, but it's also possible to visit them by ferry from Palermo, and from Naples on mainland Italy as well.

Nearby, on Sicily's very northern tip, the provincial capital Messina is mostly considered a stopover for travelers who choose to drive or take the train from the Italian region of Calabria, the "toe" of Italy's "boot." Milazzo, however, where most visitors to the Aeolian Islands will catch the ferry, is a vibrant town with a stunning smooth pebble beach, a long green mountain cape overlooking the Aeolian Islands, and a lively culinary scene and aperitivo culture, especially during the summer months.

PLANNING YOUR TIME

There is so much to do in Sicily that the less-visited northern part of the island, from Cefalù in the west to Taormina in the east, is often best passed up in favor of all the wonders farther south. But the magnificent Aeolian Islands are seven notable exceptions.

The logistics of getting to the archipelago and their relaxed vibe mean that a day trip is not a good option; it takes at least five nights to get the full Aeolian experience, a mix of relaxing at resorts, eating delicious food, vineyard visits, long beach days, and outdoor adventures. In a pinch, two nights added on to a Palermo or Taormina trip might be just enough to feel worthwhile. Note that the Isole Eolie are very seasonal, and many restaurants and hotels close in the off-season, opening only from **April/May-October.**

Lipari is the largest island and main transportation hub. **Salina** and **Stromboli** are great for day trips, while **Panarea** and **Vulcano** are often visited as part of a boat tour or island-hopping holiday. **Alicudi** and **Filicudi** are the most rustic of the "seven sisters." With fewer amenities, these islands are often overlooked by travelers pressed for time.

For more information on planning your trip to the Aeolian Islands, **Loveolie** (www.loveolie.com) is the official tourism website, providing history, information, and recommendations for accommodations, dining, and excursions.

GETTING THERE

The only way to get to the Aeolian Islands is by boat. The archipelago's main hub is the largest island, Lipari, but it's also possible to get directly to most of the other islands from Sicily, or even from mainland Italy. There are two types of boats: slower **ferries,** which include the option to take along a motorino scooter or car; and faster **hydrofoils,** built for passenger service only.

In Sicily, the principal port of departure to the Aeolian Islands is **Milazzo,** on the island's northern coast. Milazzo can be reached by trains operated by Trenitalia (www.trenitalia.com) from Catania (3 hours 20 minutes; €9), Taormina (2 hours; €7.80), and Palermo (2 hours 20 minutes; €12.40). After arriving at Stazione di Milazzo, you'll need a taxi to reach the Terminal Aliscafi Milazzo-Isole Eolie in the Porto di Milazzo, about 2.5 miles (4 km) away. Another option is to drive: from Taormina, it's a 1-hour drive (53 mi/86 km); from Catania, it's a 1-hour 40-minute drive (81 mi/130 km); and from Palermo, it's a 2-hour 10-minute drive (120 mi/200 km). Take your car with you on the ferry (to Lipari, Vulcano, or Salina), or leave your car at one of many parking lots near the port, including **Garage del Porto** (Via Giorgio Rizzo, 82; tel. 348/263-5179; www.garagedelportomilazzo.com). Parking costs around €12 per day.

By Ferry

Siremar (090/364-601; www.siremar.it) connects the Aeolian Islands from Sicily and Campania with large traghetto ferry services.

Daily ferry services are available from **Milazzo** to the Aeolian Islands with most of them connecting through Lipari. Prices ranging from €10-18 for one-way service with an additional €53-85 surcharge for automobiles and €23-37 for motorbikes. Ferries depart to Alicudi (3 hours) and Filicudi (2 hours, 15 minutes) twice per day, to Lipari (1 hour) 13 times, to Salina (1 hour, 35 minutes) 11 times, to Vulcano 10 times per day, and to Panarea (2 hours) or Stromboli (1 hour, 10 minutes) 4 times per day. The Siremar ticket office is located in the ferry terminal at the **Port of Milazzo** (Via dei Mille, 23; tel. 090/928-3415); tickets can be purchased in the ferry terminal office, but in summer season it's always recommended to purchase your tickets in advance online.

Siremar ferry services to the Aeolian Islands are also available from **Naples,** though only on Wednesday and Friday. Prices for the approximately 15-hour journey start from around €40 each way, or from €120 with

The Aeolian Islands

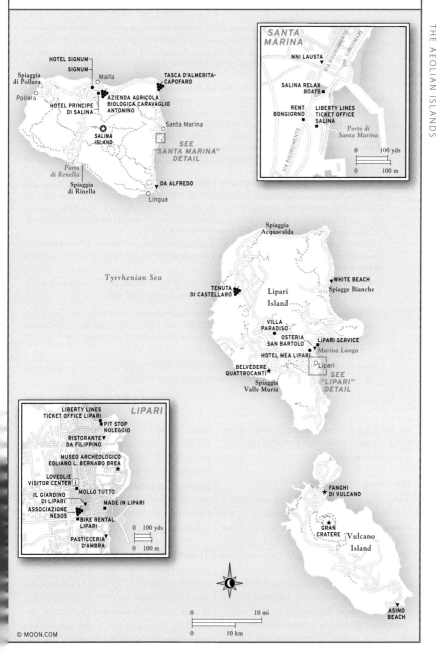

© MOON.COM

Crossing to Sicily: The Train on a Ferry

With cheap, two-hour flights to Palermo and Catania from Naples and Bari, taking the train is certainly not the most effective way to get to Sicily. But those who opt for a train are in for a unique (if not very speedy) experience. Despite ongoing discussion of building a bridge to connect Calabria and the island, this is not expected to happen anytime soon, so trains between the two are loaded onto a ferry.

For more than 50 years, **Caronte & Tourist** (https://carontetourist.it/en) has operated ferries across the Strait of Messina for up to five million passengers per year. Southern Italy's somewhat unreliable infrastructure is certainly tested by the process of dividing the train up into segments and loading them onto the ferry, meaning delays are common. However, being on a train on top of a ferry is one of a kind. Although the ferry ride itself is quite short (20 minutes), passengers are allowed to exit the train and enjoy the crossing from the ferry deck. Traditionally, the journey is commemorated with an arancino (fried rice ball), and the ones sold from the ferry concession stand for €2.50 are quite delicious.

Ferries arrive and depart from **Stazione Villa San Giovanni** (Viale Italia; tel. 090/364601) in Villa San Giovanni in Calabria, and from **Porto di Messina** (Via Vittorio Emanuele II, 27; tel. 090/601-3209; www.porto.messina.it) in Sicily. The train then continues toward the Stazione Messina Centrale (Piazza della Repubblica). Ferries leave every 40 minutes during the day (5:20am-11:20pm) and every 1 hour 20 minutes at night (1:40am-4:40am).

Buses between Calabria and Sicily are also boarded on ferries, and Caronte & Tourist provides passenger and car ferry service, too. Below is a breakdown for travelers who prefer to avoid flying and have some time on their hands.

- **Train:** Trains run by Trenitalia (tel. 668/475-475; www.trenitalia.com) connect Naples to Palermo (9 hours 25 minutes; from €35) and Catania (8 hours; from €30).

- **Bus:** Autoservici Salemi (tel. 0923/981-120; https://autoservizisalemi.it/en/home-2; from €27) runs buses from Bari to Catania (8 hours 20 minutes) and Palermo (11 hours 20 minutes), while Flixbus (tel. 123/99-123; www.flixbus.com; from €29) provides bus service from Naples to Catania (9 hours 15 minutes).

- **Car and passenger:** The passenger ferry costs €2.50 per person one-way, while most vehicles will cost €39 one-way (fare includes up to five passengers).

the surcharge for automobiles. Timetables and ticketing information can be found online at www.directferries.com.

By Hydrofoil

This is the most convenient way to reach the archipelago. **Liberty Lines** (formerly Ustica Lines; www.libertylines.it) serves all of the islands with quick and efficient aliscafo hydrofoil ferries (for passengers only—no cars or motorbikes). There are frequent crossings from **Milazzo**'s Terminal Aliscafi Milazzo-Isole (Via Luigi Rizzo; tel. 340/9023731; 45 minutes-3 hours depending on the island; from €19), **Messina**'s Molo d'imbarco Rizzo (Via Luigi Rizzo; tel. 347/0095781; 1.5-2.5

hours; from €30), and **Palermo**'s Calata Marinai d'Italia harbor (on the opposite side of the Via Francesco Crispi and SS113; tel. 091/324255; 3-5 hours; from €36). Note that crossings are more limited in the off-season, especially from Messina and Palermo, and ferries may be delayed or canceled by rough conditions.

Traveling Between the Islands

Frequent ferries (operated by **Siremar**) and hydrofoils (operated by **Liberty Lines**) connect all the islands year-round, though some islands are more connected than others; for example, Lipari, as the largest island, has connections to all of the six other Aeolian

Stopover in Milazzo

Many people just pass through Milazzo en route to the Isole Eolie, but if you find yourself with time to kill here before your ferry, don't be too disappointed. This seaside town is overlooked by the dramatic **Castello di Milazzo** (Sal. Castello, Salita Castello; tel. 090/922-1291; www. comune.milazzo.me.it; 9am-1:30pm and 4:30pm-8:30pm daily May-Sept., 9am-6:30pm daily Oct.-Apr.; €5). Its population of 31,000, known as the Milazzese, like to refer to their town as the "Milan of the south." The pace of life here is slow: There's always time for aperitivi with friends and dinners out.

BEST BEACH

Spend a few hours walking along the cape overlooking the Gulf of Milazzo, or enjoy some fun in the sun at **Spiaggia Milazzo** (Via Spiaggia di Ponente, 124; open 24 hours; free). You can rent sunbeds and umbrellas from **Horizon Milazzo** (Via Tono, 71; tel. 320/191-9900; www. horizonmilazzo.it).

WHERE TO EAT AND DRINK

Treat yourself to a meal at up-and-coming **Ristorante Balice** (Via Ettore Celi, 15; tel. 090/738-4720; www.baliceristo.com; 7:30pm-10:30pm Mon. and Wed.-Fri., noon-2:30pm and 7:30pm-10:30pm Sat., noon-2:30pm Sun.), enjoy Milazzo's best granita at **Bar Dama Francesco** (Via Cesare Battisti, 4; tel. 090/928-4066), or sip on an aperitivo at **Pane Mortadella e Champagne** (Via Francesco Crispi, 87; tel. 090/922-3260).

Islands. Travel times and fares range from 25 minutes and €15 on a hydrofoil (from Alicudi to Filicudi) to 4 hours and €40 on a ferry (from Alicudi to Vulcano). Unless you're traveling with your own vehicle, you're most likely to find yourself on a hydrofoil, which are generally quicker, cheaper, and more frequent than the ferries. There are Liberty Lines ticket offices on every island; visit their easy-to-navigate website (www. libertylines.it) for the complete set of time-tables and fares.

It's also possible (though much more expensive) to travel by private sailboat or yacht; especially at the main ports of Lipari or Salina, you'll find boat tour companies right in the port to organize trips.

GETTING AROUND

Most of the islands are small enough to be explored by foot, or by renting a bicycle or motor scooter. For short trips, taxis are usually available, especially in the towns. It's also possible to bring your own vehicle to Lipari, Vulcano, and Salina by ferry, and many of the islands also have their own public bus systems, though service is somewhat limited.

LIPARI

Lipari is the largest of the Aeolian Islands, covering an area of 14 square miles (37 square km). It's easily reached in 1 hour via hydrofoil from Milazzo, or in 4 hours on a ferry from Palermo in summertime. Most visitors to this central island hub arrive in the port and promptly take off on another ferry to another island—but they're missing out. Although there are few options right in the harbor for a delightful granita, glass of wine, or quick shopping spree, the magic of Lipari is only truly discovered beyond the port.

The fairly hilly landscape has great views of the nearby island of Vulcano and Mount Etna on mainland Sicily; traversed by motorino scooter, rental car, or e-bike, you'll pass coastal vineyards, smooth pebbled beaches, and the pristine white cliffs, once quarries where 200 tonnes of pumice stone were extracted each year. Beyond the coast, Lipari slowly reveals more secrets, from fascinating

1

2

3

museums on archeology and volcanology to trekking and excursions through old volcanic craters. Enjoy fresh and simply prepared island food featuring seasonal vegetables and native capers speckled throughout as many dishes as possible. Lipari's diverse range of wild rocky coastlines and sand beaches and its central location in the archipelago offer enough for more than a day trip.

Orientation

Ferries to Lipari arrive in the in the main port, **Marina Lunga,** right in the central town (also named Lipari) on the southern side of the island. Though many restaurants, bars, cafés, shops, and accommodations are located in walking distance of Lipari town, there are amazing options for swimming, wine tasting, dining, and overnight stays scattered across the island. Taxis available near the port can be helpful for reaching your accommodation if you are planning to stay the night, or rent a scooter or car to venture out to the beaches near **Canneto** and **Acquacalda.** The hilly landscape and dramatic coastline are also great for trekking experiences, and the island is easy to navigate on its main perimeter roads, the **SP179** and **SP180.**

Sights

MUSEO ARCHEOLOGICO EOLIANO L. BERNABÒ BREA

Via Castello, 2; tel. 090/988-0174; www.facebook. com/museoLipari; 9am-7:30pm daily; €6, guests 18-25 €3, first Sun. of month free

The Bernabò Brea Museum is located inside the angular 15th-century walls of the Castle of Lipari, about 10 minutes' walk south of the port on the coast. During the construction of the castle, many important artifacts were uncovered, leading the builders of the time to realize there were digging into what was once the center of Neolithic life on the island. Many of these finds are now housed in the

1: sailing between the Aeolian Islands
2: wildflowers growing on the Aeolian Islands
3: the picturesque island of Lipari

archaeological museum, made up of six pavilions housing prehistoric and classical objects collections across the islands, and exhibits related to volcanology and paleontology. This regional museum is dedicated to its late director, Italian archaeologist and prehistoric expert Luigi Bernabò Brea, one of Italy's most famous archaeologists.

BELVEDERE QUATTROCCHI

SP179, 3, Quattropani; open 24 hours; free

Located 2.5 miles (4 km) west of the central town of Lipari, this scenic overlook along the SP179 is a great place to catch the sunset, admire the dramatic rock formations off the coastline, or spot the difficult-to-access Spiaggia Valle Muria beach below.

Beaches

Lipari's shorelines are a mix of soft white sand, smooth black stones, and rustic swimming spots. For the rockier beaches, especially if you're traveling with children, consider bringing water shoes, and be sure to bring along everything you many need for your beach day, including sunscreen, swimwear, drinking water, and of course a few snacks or a picnic lunch.

SPIAGGIA VALLE MURIA

Pianogreca; open 24 hours; free

One of the closest beaches to Lipari town is also one of the island's hardest to access, but Spiaggia Valle Muria is worth the trek. It's a 25-minute walk down a steep mountain path leading to this bare rocky beach, where a local named Barni sometimes sells refreshments out of a cave-like hut. Otherwise, it is imperative to bring everything you will need for a beach day here, including extra drinking water, sunscreen, and maybe a beach umbrella. To get here, follow the SP179 to the panoramic Quattrocchi viewpoint, and then make a sharp right, following the sign for Pianogreca, a 10-minute drive. At the end of the road, leave your car or motorbike and begin the hike down to the beach. The only other way to get here is to hire a boat and anchor offshore.

SPIAGGE BIANCHE

Contrada Ghiozzo, Canneto; tel. 338/523-9290; open 24 hours; free

Considered one of the most beautiful beaches on the island, with comfortable sandy shores, dramatic white pumice stone cliffs, and warm turquoise waters, Spiagge Bianche is a busy spot in summertime, when it fills up with sunbathers, families, and endless rows of beach umbrellas. The **White Beach** lido club (www.whitebeachlipari.com; €25 for one umbrella and two beach beds) is a great option for beachgoers who want more amenities, and even hosts DJ sets and beach parties. Rentals can be reserved ahead of time through their website. Spiagge Bianche in Canneto can be reached by car from Lipari in 15 minutes along SP180 from Lipari town, or via public bus (Guglielmo Urso; www.ursobus.it; tel. 090/9811026; €2.30) from the main port.

SPIAGGIA ACQUACALDA

SP179, Acquacalda; open 24 hours; free

The smooth black stone beach of Acquacalda on the north coast of Lipari overlooks the nearby islands of Salina and Panarea, the perfect spot for catching the sunset. There are no public facilities here in Acquacalda, but the nearby **Naghet Cafè** (Via Giuseppe Mazzini, 29/32; tel. 366/595-1145; 10am-10pm daily) is a great place to stop for a coffee, cold beer, granita, snack, or bathroom break. Spiaggia is a 20-minute, 6-mile (10-km) drive from Lipari town on the SP180. Since the stone beach is black, it becomes very hot in summertime, so bring along a beach towel or blanket as well as water shoes to move around more easily.

Vineyard Visits and Wine Tasting
TENUTA DI CASTELLARO

Via Caolino; tel. 345/4342755; www. tenutadicastellaro.it; by reservation only; €35 per person

Located at 1,100 feet (350 m) above sea level, the Tenuta di Castellaro winery offers vineyard visits and tastings with an incredible sunset view. You'll be able to try three wines with food pairings from their underground wine cellar, the largest in the Aeolian Islands. They also have three minimalist-chic accommodations available on the property to rent (starting at €200/night).

Guided Tours
ASSOCIAZIONE NESOS

Corso Vittorio Emanuele II, 24; tel. 331/5660771; www.nesos.org; group tours from €15 perperson, private guides €120-180 per day

Flavia Grita and her team at Nesos offer expert-led trekking excursions, hikes, nature walks, bird-watching, and foraging experiences on all of the Aeolian Islands. On Lipari, you can Join Flavia and her trusted donkey on nature walks through old volcanic craters, mountains, and vineyards. They also offer guided hikes and cycling excursions for all levels, with stops for swimming and a picnic.

Boat Rentals
LIPARI SERVICE

Via Francesco Crispi; tel. 090/988-6156; www. lipariservice.it; €70-160 per day for 8 guests

Since 1989, Lipari Service has offered motorboat rentals for 8-20 guests with seasonal rates, and the option to hire a captain. They can also arrange sailing trips, yachts, or catamarans to make the most of your adventures in the Aeolian Islands.

Shopping
MADE IN LIPARI

Via Giuseppe Garibaldi, 6; tel. 333/9733398; www. instagram.com/madeinlipari; May-Oct.

In the heart of Lipari town, at Daniela Billi's chic artisan boutique, you'll find tasteful handmade jewelry, clothing, bags, and shoes.

1: Spiaggia Acquacalda **2:** vineyards on Lipari
3: Spiaggia Valle Muria

MOLLO TUTTO

Corso Vittorio Emanuele II, 80; tel. 090/9812491; www.mollotuttoshop.com; 8:30am-1pm and 4:30pm-9pm daily

Lipari is the headquarters of this casual nautical-themed brand, whose carefree island life motto is "throw it all away." All the T-shirts, tote bags, sweatshirts, and backpacks here are created by fashion designer Natalie Rossi.

Food and Drinks
★ OSTERIA SAN BARTOLO

Via F. Crispi, 109; tel. 090/896-1317; www. sanbartolovineriaedispensa.com

Husband-and-wife team Danilo Conti and Luisa Fernanda Mendoza opened Osteria San Bartolo in summer 2020, serving up simple coastal dishes, innovative cocktails, and the best wine on the island, right on the Marina Lunga harbor.

RISTORANTE DA FILIPPINO

Piazza Giuseppe Mazzini; tel. 090/981100; www. filippino.it; 11:30am-3pm and 7pm-11pm daily; €30-50

Open for over 100 years, Ristorante da Filippino is a classic choice for traditional dining in Lipari. Located near the castle, this large informal restaurant offers a large selection of local seafood dishes, authentic Sicilian cooking, and a beautiful open-air terrace. The restaurant is still managed by Bernardi family, and it remains to be a reliable choice for classic Mediterranean cuisine on the island.

PASTICCERIA D'AMBRA

Via Salita San Giuseppe, 5; tel. 090/6019225; www. facebook.com/pasticceriadambra; 7am-midnight daily; €5

Take an afternoon break at Pasticceria d'Ambra in Marina Corta near the port of Lipari. The d'Ambra brothers are ready to welcome you with a refreshing Aperol Spritz aperitivo, fresh fruit granita, a traditional Sicilian cannoli, or a few bomboloni fritti fried donuts in their small family-run bar with outdoor seating overlooking the water.

IL GIARDINO DI LIPARI

Via Nuova, Strittu Longu; tel. 339/3299029; www. ilgiardinodilipari.com; 6:30pm-2:30am daily in summer; cocktails €10-12, antipasti €8-15, mains €12-24

Enjoy chic hand-crafted cocktails, dinner, and live music in Luca Cutrufelli's tropical garden lounge, where you can lay back on a lawn chair under the lemon trees with a gin fizz in hand. Il Giardino di Lipari is located just a 10-minute walk from the port of Lipari.

Accommodations
★ VILLA PARADISO

Contrada Cugna; tel. 339/1405583; www.villa-paradiso-sicily.com; from €50

Claudio Cafarella is a charming Messina native who owns this group of cozy hillside guesthouses. They have a beautiful terrace where guests can meet up for aperitivo or dinners, but it's also a great place for solo travelers. The houses are all equipped with a small kitchenette, private terrace, and interiors decorated with vintage and recycled furnishing. Most of the bungalows are attached to one another, but there are also some more private options. Villa Paradiso is located on the top of the mountain near the district of Pianoconte, easily reachable with a quick motorino ride from the port of Lipari. It is not recommended to stay here without any mode of transportation. Scooters can be rented directly through Villa Paradiso upon request.

HOTEL MEA LIPARI

Via Paolo Borsellino e Giovanni Falcone; tel. 090/9812077; www.hotelmealipari.it; from €100

Aeolian Islands expert and luxury hotelier Sarah Tomasello is waiting to welcome you to Lipari. Take your cocktail poolside at one of their two swimming pools and enjoy the panoramic view of Lipari's Marina Lunga. All the rooms of this refined four-star boutique hotel have their own private terrace.

1: Osteria San Bartolo 2: Hotel Mea Lipari 3: Villa Paradiso

Their professional staff can help guests organize dinners, excursions, and spa treatments, and can connect you with many of the local beach clubs on the island. Hotel Mea is easily reached on foot from Lipari's harbor.

Information and Services

- **Loveolie Visitor Center:** Via Vittorio Emanuele, 165; tel. 090/981-2894; www.loveolie.com/en/salina
- **Hospital:** Ospedale Civile di Lipari; Via S. Anna; tel. 090/98851; www.asp.messina.it
- **Pharmacy:** Pharmacy Cincotta: Via Giuseppe Garibaldi, 60; tel. 090/9811472

Getting There

The main port on Lipari is **Marina Lunga,** tucked into a natural harbor just off the island's main town of Lipari, where you'll find a Liberty Lines ticket office (tel. 090/981-2448; www.libertylines.it) for hydrofoils to all the other Aeolian islands, as well as numerous options for private boat tours and rentals. Lipari is the main travel hub for the archipelago, with crossings from Milazzo approximately 15 times per day (about 1 hour; from €12).

Getting Around

Perhaps the best way to get around Lipari is zipping between the mountain and the sea on a scooter or e-bike. Clearly marked taxi services are available for hire near the port, but be warned that prices can be high; for example, two people with luggage from the ferry port to Canneto will be €15. There are also bus routes run by **Guglielmo Urso** (www.ursobus.it; tel. 090/9811026; €2.30) linking Lipari town to the rest of the island's coast; check the bus information kiosk in town for schedules and fares.

- **Car and Motorino:** Pit Stop Noleggio; Via T. M. Amendola, 42; tel. 090/988-0344; www.pitstopnoleggio.it; 8:30am-7pm daily
- **E-Bikes:** Bike Rental Lipari; Via Stradale Pianoconte, 5; tel. 368/7535590; www.bikerentalipari.com; €25-35 per day

- **Taxi:** Taxi Service da Simone; tel. 333/3143066

★ SALINA

Nicknamed "Isola Verde," or Green Island, Salina is the Aeolian port of call for lovers of food, wine, and exceptional resorts. It's also the land of Malvasia wine, a fruity yet herbaceous golden grape that was anciently referred to as the "nectar of the Gods," first imported by the Greeks to the island of Salina around 588 BC. This island is central enough for day trips to the other Aeolian islands, but its luxurious fine dining, wineries, and accommodations mean many of its guests never want to leave.

Santa Marina, the main port of the island of Salina, is a small commune with only 900 residents that can be explored on foot in less than half an hour, with a clean beach next to the harbor and several restaurants, cafés, and boat tour offices. On the southeastern coast of the island, **Lingua** is a small fishing village with pebbled beaches, a lighthouse, and the picturesque 18th-century Vallone Zappini bridge. On the north-central coast, **Malfa** is named for immigrants from Amalfi on the Italian mainland, who relocated here in the 17th century. It's known for the production of Malvasia grapes, and has the island's second (and even smaller) ferry port. Finally, don't miss a stop in **Pollara,** made famous by the 1994 film *Il Postino,* which boasts one of the best beaches in the archipelago.

Winery Visits and Tastings
TASCA D'ALMERITA - CAPOFARO
Via Faro, 3; tel. 090/984-4330; www.tascadalmerita. it/tenuta/capofaro; by reservation only at 10:30am, 3pm, and 5pm May-Oct.; €30-120 per person

Capofaro is one of the Tasca d'Almerita winemaking family's most picturesque estates, located on the edge of Salina near a mid-19th-century lighthouse. A tasting of their Malvasia wines can be paired with light dishes from the resort restaurant (reservations required). Capofaro can be reached with a 10-minute drive or taxi ride along SP182 from the Santa Marina port.

AZIENDA AGRICOLA BIOLOGICA CARAVAGLIO ANTONINO

Via Provinciale, 33; tel. 339/8115953; www.
caravaglio.it; by reservation only 6pm Apr.-Oct.; €15
per person

Nino Caravaglio is an innovative and hard-working organic wine producer responsible for the very first dry Malvasia wine in the Aeolian Islands, something that could be enjoyed throughout a meal instead of as a sweet after-dinner drink. Nino's vineyards span 30 different plots over 50 acres (20 ha) of land, a great place for a relaxing, no-frills wine tasting. Ninety-minute visits (reservations required) include a tasting of four wines along with a tour of the cellar and overview of wine-making practices and the personal stories of this winery. Caravaglio's winery is located 10 minutes (4 mi/6 km) northwest from Santa Marina in the district of Malfa.

Beaches
SPIAGGIA DI POLLARA

Via Massimo Troisi; open 24 hours; free

The amphitheater-shaped beach in Pollara, which served as the location of the mid-1990s film *Il Postino,* is located underneath a cliff on the northwest corner of Salina. It's accessed by a steep staircase, which means it's not accessible for travelers with mobility issues. Just off the shore, the 115-foot-high (35-m-high) faraglione volcanic rock formation emerges from the sea, said to be the remains of a volcanic crater submerged over 100,000 years ago. There are no amenities available at this beach, so prepare to bring everything you will need for the day and stop off at a bar for a refreshment and bathroom break before heading down to the sea.

SPIAGGIA DI RINELLA

SP182; open 24 hours; free

The sand and stone-lined free public beach of Rinella is located on the southern coast of Salina. This is the most well-equipped beach on the island, with tabacchi shops, grocery stores, cafés, and a pizzeria, all within walking distance from the shore.

Boat Rentals
SALINA RELAX BOATS

Via Lungomare, Santa Marina Salina; tel.
345/216-2308; www.salinarelaxboats.com; from €25
per person

With three kiosks on the island of Salina, the Salina Relax Boats company organizes daily group boat trips to all the Aeolian Islands, exclusive private boat excursions, boat and dinghy rentals with a skipper, island transfers, nautical charters, and mini cruises. Their affordable pricing, professional English-speaking staff, and easy booking process makes them a great choice.

Food
DA ALFREDO

Via Vittorio Alfieri, 11, Piazza Marina Garibaldi,
Lingua; tel. 090/984-3075; www.facebook.com/
daalfredosalina; 9:30am-5:30pm daily Apr.-Oct.;
granita €3, pane cunzato from €9-13

This casual and fun café features some of the best granita on Salina, as well as huge pane cunzato (open-faced sandwiches topped with tuna, olives, sun-dried tomatoes, arugula, and capers). This is a great place to people-watch near the Lingua beachfront and take a break from the fierce Sicilian summer sun with a cold beer and light lunch. Reservations recommended in July and August.

NNI LAUSTA

Via Risorgimento, 188, Santa Marina; tel.
090/984-3486; www.nnilausta.it; noon-3pm and
7pm-11pm daily; €9-14

Fresh local seafood plays a starring role in this inviting Mediterranean restaurant. Pull up a seat under the pergola in Nni Lausta's cozy patio garden and enjoy a delicious fish-centric meal at this casual beach tavern near the port of Santa Marina Salina.

★ SIGNUM

Via Scalo, 15, Malfa; tel. 090/9844222; www.
hotelsignum.it/en/signum-restaurant/the-kitchen;
12:30pm-3:30pm and 7:30pm-10pm daily
Easter-Oct.; tasting menus €120-140 per person

Celebrated island native chef Martina

Caruso's exceptional restaurant has been awarded with one Michelin star, and it continues to be one of the top destinations for fine dining in the Aeolian Islands. Located in the Hotel Signum resort, chef Caruso's cuisine is an extension of her heart and soul, featuring mesmerizing dishes like fried red mullet with ginger broth and black olives, breaded barbecue spatula (scabbard) fish with almonds and "leche de tigre" ceviche sauce, and caper-infused desserts.

Accommodations

★ HOTEL PRINCIPE DI SALINA

SP182, 3, Malfa; tel. 090/984-4415; www. principedisalina.it; from €170

This four-star luxury accommodation nestled in the lush vegetation of the Isola Verde boasts a relaxing geothermal pool. Hotel Principe di Salina can organize cooking classes, private events, and personalized travel itineraries for your trip to Salina. Their 12 rooms with private terraces and sea views are perfect for catching the sunrise or sunset overlooking the nearby islands of Stromboli and Panarea.

HOTEL SIGNUM

Via Scalo, 15, Malfa; tel. 090/9844222; www. hotelsignum.it; Easter-Oct.; from €200

Hidden away in the green paradise of Salina, this four-star boutique hotel offers an infinity pool overlooking the Gulf of Malfa, a library, a wellness center, a bar, and one of the very best restaurants on the island. The concierge service is at your disposal to organize mountain excursions, boat trips, and wine tastings. The port of Malfa and nearby Spiaggia dello Scario beach are accessible on foot.

Getting There

Ferries to Salina arrive at the **Porto di Santa Marina,** just off the island's main town on the western side of the island, as well as at **Porto di Renella** on the south coast, both of which

---

1: boating off the island of Salina 2: the winemaking estate of Tasca D'Almerita – Capofaro 3: dessert at Da Alfredo 4: seafood pasta

have a Liberty Lines (www.libertylines.it) ticket office (Santa Marina: tel. 090/9843003; Rinella: tel. 090/9809170). Though not as busy as Lipari, Salina's ports are well connected with the other Aeolian Islands and the Sicilian mainland, with hydrofoils to Lipari (20 minutes, 6 sailings daily; €9), Milazzo (1.5 hours, 3 sailings daily; €23); and even Palermo (3.5 hours, 1 sailing daily; €50), though less frequently and in summer only.

Getting Around

The island of Salina covers 10 square miles (26 square km), making it the second largest in the archipelago after Lipari. You can explore the island of Salina on a scooter from **Rent Bongiorno** (Via Risorgimento, 222; tel. 090/984-3409), located in the main port. It should be fairly easy to find taxis in the major communes of Santa Marina and Malfa, or call **Taxi Salina di Daniela** (Via Risorgimento, 81, Santa Marina; tel. 333/616-7491) to organize transfers in advance. But while the other Aeolian islands offer more in terms of exploring on your own, Salina is the island where you treat yourself, and after getting to your accommodation, you may not need to move around much. Check with your hotel or resort to see if they can provide or organize island transfers.

STROMBOLI

The nearly 5-square-mile (13-square-km) Aeolian Island of Stromboli is made up of one of the only three remaining active volcanoes in all of Italy. The red neon lava spurting from the volcano is seen best in the evenings, but white-and-gray smoke puffs out of Stromboli all day long, following rhythmic eruptions that occur every 20-30 minutes, almost like clockwork. In 1950, Stromboli gained international fame when Roberto Rossellini's *Stromboli: Terre di Dio,* starring Ingrid Bergman, was filmed on the island.

The volcano takes up most of the island, except for two extremely small coastal villages: Stromboli, on the northeastern coast; and Ginostra to the west. Several companies offer

Island Hopping in the Aeolian Islands

Once you arrive in the Aeolian Islands, you'll want to see them all, and ferries and boat tours make it easy to do so. Smaller than their sister islands of Lipari, Salina, and Stromboli, the rustic islands of Panarea, Alicudi, Filicudi, and Vulcano can be visited on a short excursion.

VULCANO

The 8-square-mile (3-square-km) island of Vulcano is the closest of the Aeolian Islands to mainland Sicily. Its main attraction is the still-active **Gran Cratere** (Riserva Naturale Isola Vulcano), a 1,600-foot-wide (500-m-wide) volcanic crater located at 2,740 feet (385 m) above sea level, best explored on a self-guided, 4.7-mile (7.5-km), 90-minute hike, following signs for the crater from the port. Add a bit of luxury to your time on the island at **Fanghi di Vulcano** thermal springs (Via Riccardo Conti, 20; www.vulcanoterme.com/terme_fanghi_centenari.html; €3 entrance fee), accessible with a short walk from the ferry port, or spend an afternoon relaxing at **Asino Beach** club (Str. Serra - Pirrera, 11; tel. 324/984-5382; www.asinobeach.it).

PANAREA

Panarea is the smallest of the Aeolian Islands, clocking in at only 1.3 square miles (3.4 square km). One of its highlights is diving in the **Cala Junco** bay with **Eolo Sub Panarea** dining center (Va Ditella; tel. 338/824-2725; www.eolosub.it; from €35).

FILICUDI

There's no need for any mode of transportation here on Filicudi: everything can be discovered on foot or by sea. You can take a 1-hour walk (3 mi/5 km) to the **Spiaggia di Pecorini a Mare** (Località Pecorini a Mare) for a refreshing dip.

ALICUDI

The farthest flung of the islands, Alicudi is also the most rustic. There is no pharmacy or post office, and barely any restaurants, only a sprinkling of bed-and-breakfasts, walking distance from the main port. All the buildings on the island are staggered up a steep hill; the islanders often refer to the location of their house based on how many steps it takes to get to it (anywhere up to 600). Check out the **Giardino dei Carrubi** (Via XXIV Maggio; tel. 380/783-6666; www.facebook.com/giardinocarrubi; from €98) for an affordable overnight stay that doesn't require trekking all the way up the hill.

nighttime excursions and boating adventures to view the nighttime eruptions.

Beaches
FICOGRANDE

Via Marina; open 24 hours; free

This black volcanic pebble coast is the only beach on Stromboli where you'll find restaurants, beach bar kiosks, and beach chair and umbrella rentals. It's located near the tourist port, where ferries arrive, and slightly downhill from the town of Stromboli. Although there are no public restrooms at this beach,

the cafés and bars along the main strip allow paying guests to use their facilities.

Volcano Tours

Hikes to the top of Stromboli are strictly regulated. Although it is possible to hike the volcano independently, hikers aren't permitted higher than 1,300 feet (400 m) up the 3,012-foot (918-m) volcano unguided. The hike is also enhanced with a professional guide, who can provide additional information and the

1: Porto di Ginostra 2: town of Stromboli
3: Stromboli volcano

added security that comes from knowing you won't be accidentally walking into a crater. The ascent takes around 3 hours, and most hikes begin in the late afternoon or early evening, so as to arrive at the crater when the regular eruptions glow neon red against the dark sky.

STROMBOLI ADVENTURES
Via Roma, 17; tel. 339/532-7277; www. stromboliadventures.it; 10am-7pm daily; from €30

Unforgettable experiences led by Stromboli Adventures's alpine guides take guests extremely close to Stroboli's active craters at night. Departing from Stromboli town center, the night trekking excursions can reach heights of over 2,950 feet (900 m) above sea level to view the projectile, firework-like glowing eruptions. Allow at least 6 hours for this moderate hike.

Trekkers should be in good health and used to walking as well as equipped with the proper recommended gear, including a mandatory helmet (provided), flexible non-slip shoes or trekking boots, long pants, headlamp, an extra T-shirt plus a windbreaker and sweatshirt or fleece, electric flashlight, 1.5 to 2 liters of water per person, and snacks. All equipment can be hired from **Totem Trekking** (Piazza di San Vincenzo, 4; www.totemtrekkingstromboli. com; tel. 090/986-5752).

BARTOLO AMICI DEL MARE
Via Picone, Stromboli; tel. 338/416-2580; 9am-10pm daily; from €30 per person

The best way to admire the eruptions of Stromboli's volcano is at night, and even more so from a safe distance at sea. These night excursions take guests out to sea to view the puffs of smoke, ash, and red incandescent eruptions near the blackened "sciara del fuoco" volcanic cliff, without having to spend several hours trekking up the volcano on foot. Evening tours of the volcano last about an hour, while the sunset trip ranges from 2-3 hours, including a stop for an aperitivo in Ginostra.

Hiking
SCIARA DEL FUOCO HIKE
Distance: *5 miles (8 km) round-trip*
Time: *3-4 hours round-trip*
Trailhead: *Near Spiaggia Lunga, in Piscità, approximately 1 mile (2 km) northwest of Stromboli town*

The hike to this popular, 400-mile viewpoint, with a stunning views of Stromboli's eruptions at night (if at a distance), is the highest hikers can go unguided. It's a switchbacking trail

eruption on the Stromboli volcano

up the coast, with the **Osservatorio** restaurant (Via Mulattiera Salvatore Di Losa) about halway up (more celebrated for its panoramic views than its food). With the loose volcanic soil and some steep sections, hikers should be well-equipped with proper hiking shoes, water, and warm clothing, especially if hiking at night (in which case you'll need a headlamp). All this gear and more can be bought and rented from Totem Trekking in Stromboli town Center.

Food and Drinks
RISTORANTE PUNTA LENA

Via Marina, 8, Stromboli; tel. 090/986204; www. ristorantepuntalena.business.site; 12:15pm-2:30pm and 8pm-midnight Mon.-Tues. and Thurs., 8pm-midnight Wed., noon-2:30pm and 8pm-10:30pm Fri.; €25

When arriving from the port of Stromboli, Ristorante Punta Lena is located at the very beginning of the Ficogrande beach. This Michelin-recognized seafood restaurant with a beautiful terrace overlooking the sea serves dishes like octopus salad, marinated anchovies, gnocchi with olives, capers and amberjack, and pasta with wild fennel and cured bottarga tuna roe.

MARANO

Via Vittorio Emanuele, Stromboli; 8:30am-1pm and 5pm-8pm Mon.-Sat., 9am-1pm Sun.

Stop in this Italian deli and wine shop in the center of Stromboli for delicious sandwiches and snacks to pack for a hike or beach day.

Getting There
Stromboli has two ports: the **Porto di Stromboli** (Liberty Lines ticket office: tel. 090/986-003), on the eastern coast, and the smaller **Porto di Ginostra** (tel. 331/597-9914) to the west, mostly used by trekking companies accessing the volcano at night. One of the archipelago's main attractions, Stromboli is well-connected to the other islands, as well as to Milazzo and even Palermo in summer.

Getting Around
Stromboli is small enough to explore on foot, though to travel between the towns of Stromboli and Ginostra, you'll need to take a boat or arrive in the port by ferry service, since there is no road connecting the two towns. Ferry service provided by Liberty Lines (www.libertylines.it; €7.80) from Stromboli to Ginostra takes about 10 minutes.

Island-style electric golf cart taxi services are available when arriving in the port of Stromboli. **Paolo Taxi** (tel. 327/0916421; €10) is one of the more popular companies providing services helping guests get around the island and transport luggage.

Syracuse and Southeastern Sicily

Itinerary Ideas 399

Syracuse...............402

Around Syracuse.......417

Ragusa 424

The southeastern corner of Sicily is a unique

blend of luxurious Baroque architecture, ancient archeological sites, windswept sand beaches, and top-notch food and wine.

Take a glimpse into Sicily's Greek history in Syracuse, or Siracusa in Italian, the region's largest city, whose Neapolis Archaeological Park is filled with remnants of its long, complicated past. The capital of the Greek colony Magna Grecia, which covered all of Sicily and Southern Italy, Syracuse was once the Mediterranean's most powerful city, even defeating Athens in battle in 413. Described by the Roman scholar Cicero as "the greatest Greek city and the most beautiful of them all," Syracuse is not to be missed. Feel free to mix history with indulgence: The streets of Ortigia, a neighborhood on a small island south of

Highlights

Look for ★ to find recommended sights, activities, dining, and lodging.

★ **Parco Archeologico della Neapolis:** Syracuse's archaeological park is home to countless ancient Greek treasures, including the limestone Quarry of Paradise and the Ear of Dionysius cliffside grotto (page 402).

★ **Island of Ortigia:** The tiny, 0.6-square-mile (1.5-square-km) island of Ortigia is the oldest part of the city of Syracuse, packed with restaurants, shops, historic monuments, and lovely places to swim (page 404).

★ **Noto's Baroque Architecture:** Among a wealth of Spanish-influenced Baroque towns in this part of Sicily, Noto stands out (page 420).

★ **Villa Romana del Casale:** The precious remains of a luxurious Roman villa more than merit a day trip to inland Sicily (page 427).

★ **Wine Tasting in Ragusa:** Learn about the top winemaking families, grape varietals, and Sicily's only DOCG-classified wine with a tasting trip through the fertile vineyards in the province of Ragusa (page 428).

★ **Chocolate in Modica:** While under Spanish rule, Modica adopted a specialized cold-processing Aztec technique to grind cacao beans, and you can really taste the difference (page 434).

Syracuse and Southeastern Sicily

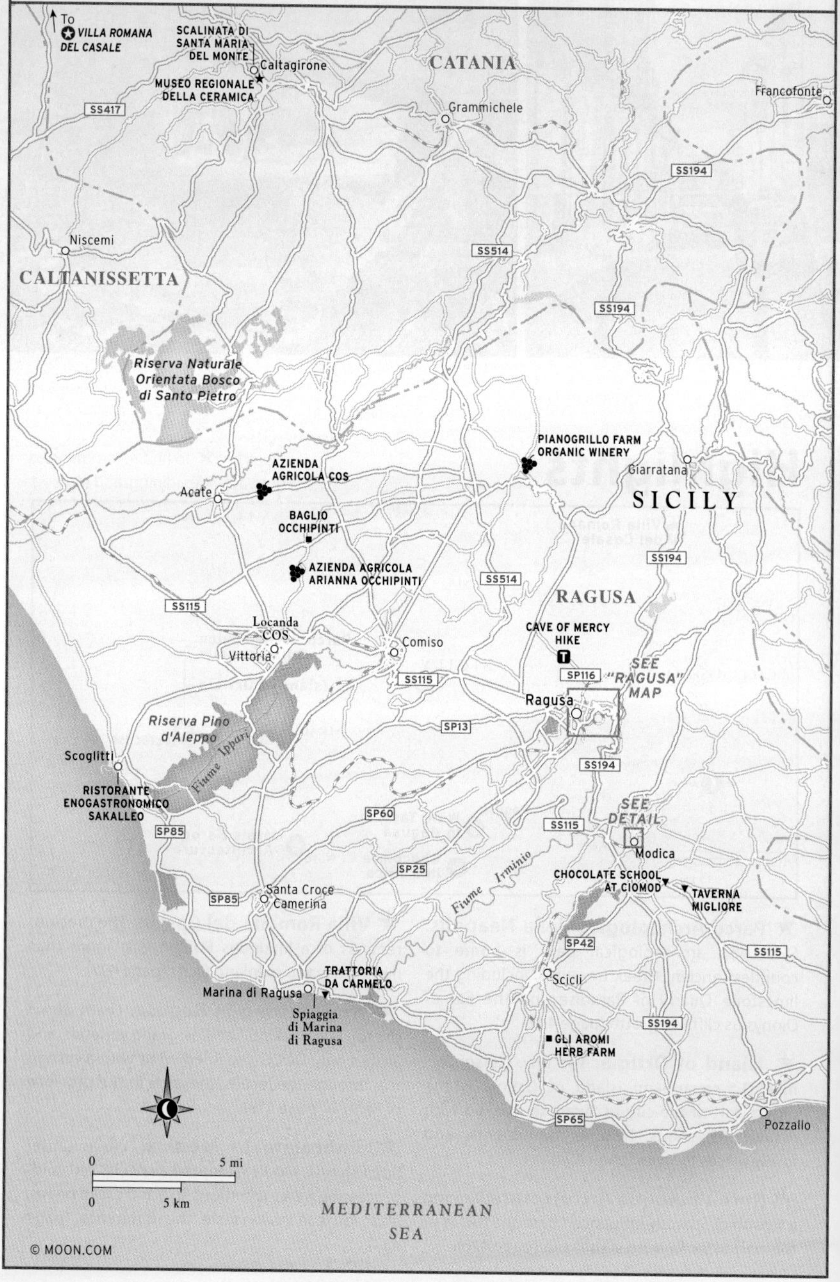

To
★ VILLA ROMANA
DEL CASALE

SCALINATA DI
SANTA MARIA
DEL MONTE
Caltagirone

CATANIA

Francofonte

MUSEO REGIONALE
DELLA CERAMICA

SS417

Grammichele

SS194

Niscemi

SS514

CALTANISSETTA

SS194

Riserva Naturale
Orientata Bosco
di Santo Pietro

PIANOGRILLO FARM
ORGANIC WINERY

Giarratana

AZIENDA
AGRICOLA COS

SICILY

Acate

BAGLIO
OCCHIPINTI

SS194

AZIENDA AGRICOLA
ARIANNA OCCHIPINTI

SS514

RAGUSA

Locanda
COS

SS115

Vittoria

Comiso

CAVE OF MERCY
HIKE

SS115

SP116

SEE
"RAGUSA"
MAP

Ragusa

Riserva Pino
d'Aleppo

SP13

Fiume Ippari

Scoglitti

RISTORANTE
ENOGASTRONOMICO
SAKALLEO

SS194

SEE
DETAIL

SP60

SP85

Modica

SS115

SP25

CHOCOLATE SCHOOL
AT CIOMOD

TAVERNA
MIGLIORE

SP85

Santa Croce
Camerina

Fiume Irminio

SP42

SS115

TRATTORIA
DA CARMELO

Scicli

SS194

Marina di Ragusa

Spiaggia
di Marina
di Ragusa

GLI AROMI
HERB FARM

0   5 mi

0   5 km

SP65

Pozzallo

MEDITERRANEAN
SEA

© MOON.COM

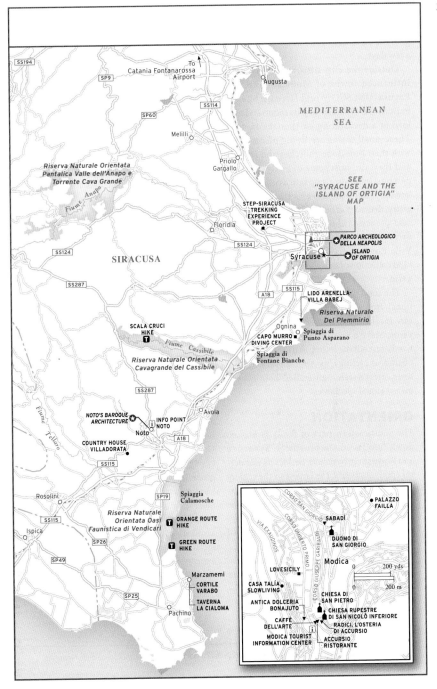

SS194
SP9
To
Catania Fontanarossa
Airport
Augusta
SS114
SP60
MEDITERRANEAN
SEA
Melilli
Priolo
Gargallo
Riserva Naturale Orientata
Pantalica Valle dell'Anapo e
Torrente Cava Grande
Fiume Anapo
Floridia
STEP-SIRACUSA
TREKKING
EXPERIENCE
PROJECT
SEE
"SYRACUSE AND THE
ISLAND OF ORTIGIA"
MAP
SS124
SS124
PARCO ARCHEOLOGICO
DELLA NEAPOLIS
SIRACUSA
Syracuse
ISLAND
OF ORTIGIA
SS287
SS115
LIDO ARENELLA-
VILLA BABEJ
A18
Riserva Naturale
Del Plemmirio
SCALA CRUCI
HIKE
Fiume Cassibile
Ognina
Spiaggia di
Punto Asparano
CAPO MURRO
DIVING CENTER
Spiaggia di
Fontane Bianche
Riserva Naturale Orientata
Cavagrande del Cassibile
SS287
Fiume Telluro
Avola
NOTO'S BAROQUE
ARCHITECTURE
INFO POINT
NOTO
Noto
A18
COUNTRY HOUSE
VILLADORATA
SS115
Rosolini
SP19
Spiaggia
Calamosche
Riserva Naturale
Orientata Oasi
Faunistica di Vendicari
ORANGE ROUTE
HIKE
SS115
Ispica
SP26
GREEN ROUTE
HIKE
SP49
Marzamemi
CORTILE
VARABO
SP25
TAVERNA
LA CIALOMA
Pachino

CORSO SAN GIORGIO
PALAZZO
FAILLA
VIA EXAUDINOS
CORSO UMBERTO PRIMO
CORSO GIUSEPPE GARIBALDI
SABADÌ
DUOMO DI
SAN GIORGIO
Modica
0   200 yds
0   200 m
LOVESICILY
CASA TALÍA
SLOWLIVING
CHIESA DI
SAN PIETRO
ANTICA DOLCERIA
BONAJUTO
CHIESA RUPESTRE
DI SAN NICOLÒ INFERIORE
CAFFÈ
DELL'ARTE
RADICI, L'OSTERIA
DI ACCURSIO
MODICA TOURIST
INFORMATION CENTER
ACCURSIO
RISTORANTE

Syracuse, are lined with shops, restaurants, cocktail bars, and specialty food markets guaranteed to keep you occupied for at least a few days.

Outside the city, discover the Spanish-influenced towns of Modica, Noto, and Ragusa, UNESCO World Heritage Sites rebuilt in the 18th-century Baroque style following a devastating earthquake in 1693. These small towns are living pieces of art with their limestone churches and palaces, and they also host some of Sicily's top restaurants. In Modica, pop into as many chocolate shops as possible to experience the crisp, gritty, delicious crunch of the town's famous cold-processed chocolate. And a few hours' drive inland, the isolated fourth-century Villa Romana del Casale and its one-of-a-kind collection of mosaics are certainly worth a trip.

The food and wine scene here is exceptional, from crudo plates of fresh seafood, to rare local cheeses and small artisanal vineyards. Make a reservation for a winery visit, hands-on cooking lesson, extra virgin olive oil tasting, or cycling trip. Almost every city and town offers a seemingly endless bounty of its own regional specialties.

ORIENTATION

The southeastern part of Sicily is broken down into two main provinces, **Syracuse** and **Ragusa.** In Syracuse, besides its wonderful eponymous city, the largest in the region, you'll find the Baroque town of **Noto,** picturesque small villages, and great **beaches.** The province of Ragusa also includes its eponymous town, as well as the chocolate capital of **Modica** and hillside **wineries.**

In the inland town of Piazza Armerina, northwest of Ragusa, the **Villa Romana**

del Casale is technically in the province of Catania, and a 1.5-hour drive from that city as well as its airport. But the villa makes for a great day trip from Syracuse, Ragusa, and even Agrigento in western Sicily as well. To the south, the town of **Caltagirone** is known for its ceramics.

PLANNING YOUR TIME

The city of **Syracuse** can be explored in a weekend, but the surrounding provinces of Syracuse and **Ragusa** require at least three days. Syracuse is a great choice for visitors to Eastern Sicily who want to beat the crowds of Mount Etna and Taormina. You'll likely need a **rental car** or to hire a **private driver** in this part of Sicily. There is sparse access to public transportation, even if each town is fairly compact and walkable once you get there. The main highway in the eastern part of Sicily is the **A19.**

The nearest airport is **Catania Fontanarossa Airport,** only an hour drive north of Syracuse. Pick up your rental car and drive south; Syracuse, particularly the neighborhood of **Ortigia,** is a great place to base yourself for a few days, taking day trips to the surrounding towns, wineries, and beaches. Syracuse and Ragusa are definitely busiest in **July-August,** but they're equally enjoyable in the **low season,** especially September-October, when the weather is still just warm enough to take a swim and eat al fresco. In general, accommodations, tours, and cooking lessons here should be reserved in advance; most restaurants welcome walk-ins, but calling a day before to book a table may help you avoid disappointment, especially in summertime or around December 13, when all of Syracuse celebrates the festival of their patron saint, **Santa Lucia.**

Previous: Modica; a Baroque street in Noto; Latomie del Paradiso in Parco Archeologico della Neapolis.

Itinerary Ideas

THREE DAYS IN SOUTHEASTERN SICILY

With a home base on the island of **Ortigia,** off **Syracuse,** you can reach many of the incredible surrounding cities like **Modica, Noto,** and **Ragusa** in less than 2 hours. Take a trip back to Greek and Roman times with a walking tour of the **Parco Archeologico della Neapolis** and taste your way through Modica's famous chocolate shops and the **Vittoria winemaking region** with enough time in between for shopping, swimming, and nights out on the town.

Day 1: Syracuse

1 Start your day on the island of Ortigia in **Piazza Duomo** with a cappuccino and cornetto before popping into the main cathedral, the Duomo di Siracusa.

2 Walk 10 minutes, past the sixth-century Tempio di Apollo on Via Cavour, until you reach the **Mercato di Siracusa,** where you can browse for local goodies.

3 At the northern end of the market, stop by **Fratelli Burgio** for a leisurely lunch featuring impeccable Sicilian meat and cheese platters (taglieri).

4 In the afternoon, visit the ancient **Parco Archeologico della Neapolis,** a 10-minute taxi ride or 30-minute walk north into central Syracuse via Corso Gelone. You'll need a few hours to explore all the stunning sites, including a Greek theater, Roman amphitheater, and mysterious grotto.

5 After a long day of sightseeing, grab some pizza at **Piano B,** across the bridge from Ortigia.

Day 2: Beach Day and Cooking in Modica

Be sure to reserve your intimate cooking class with **LoveSicily** in Modica in advance to ensure an unforgettable dinner experience.

1 Start your morning back in Ortigia's outdoor market and pick up some famous sandwiches and homemade cheeses from **Caseificio Borderi** to bring along with you to the seaside.

2 Relax for a few hours on the local public beach, the **Spiaggia di Cala Rossa.** Enjoy a refreshing swim and, when you get hungry, a picnic lunch. (If you prefer a beach with a few more amenities, head over to Solarium Nettuno, where the beach beds and onsite restaurant means there's no need to bring a picnic.)

3 Afterward, grab your rental car and take the 1-hour drive southwest on E45 to explore the Baroque town of Modica and sample its famous chocolate at **Caffè dell'Arte.**

4 Meet chef Katia from **LoveSicily** for a cooking lesson and dinner at her home in Modica.

5 In the evening, drive back to Ortigia and, if you're feeling up for it, stop in for a craft beer or custom cocktail at **BOATS,** in view of the Tempio di Apollo.

Day 3: Ragusa

Be sure to reserve your visit to the **Arianna Occhipinti** winery, and a cooking class at sister property **Baglio Occhipinti,** in advance.

Itinerary Ideas

DAY ONE	DAY TWO	DAY THREE
1 Piazza Duomo	1 Caseificio Borderi	1 Azienda Agricola Arianna Occhipinti
2 Mercato di Siracusa	2 Spiaggia di Cala Rossa	2 Baglio Occhipinti
3 Fratelli Burgio	3 Caffè dell'Arte	3 Caffè Sicilia
4 Parco Archeologico della Neapolis	4 LoveSicily	4 Ristorante Don Camillo
5 Piano B	5 BOATS	5 Enoteca Solaria

© MOON.COM

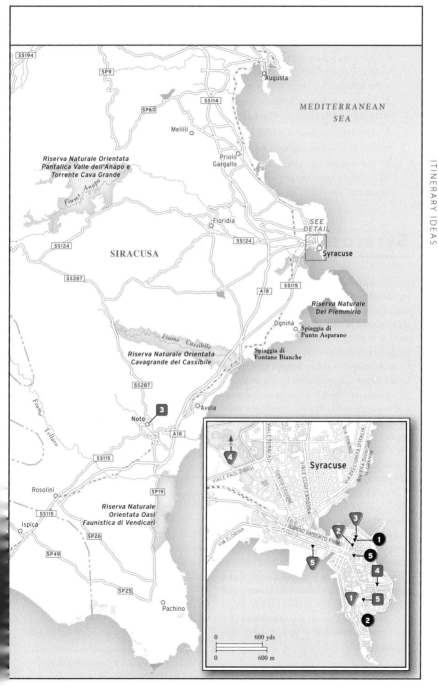

1 After breakfast at your hotel, take a 1-hour 45-minute drive west on SS194 into the province of Ragusa for a morning with the island's most fascinating young female winemaker at **Azienda Agricola Arianna Occhipinti.**

2 After the wine tour at Arianna's, drive 5 minutes north on SP68 to her sister's country home at **Baglio Occhipinti.** Fausta Occhipinti will welcome your group for a private, homemade Sicilian lunch with organic products grown on the property.

3 On the way back to Syracuse, stop by the Baroque town of Noto, a 90-minute drive on SS115, for a tasting of Sicily's best desserts from chef Corrado Assenza at **Caffè Sicilia.**

4 Finish up the road trip with a 30-minute drive north on E45 back to Ortigia. Treat yourself to a fine-dining meal at the historic **Ristorante Don Camillo.**

5 On your last night, enjoy a nightcap at Sicily's best natural wine bar, **Enoteca Solaria.** Take a final peek at the city's stunning Duomo cathedral lit up at nighttime, just around the corner.

Syracuse

Founded by the Ancient Greek Corinthians in 734 BC, Syracuse's architecture, enticing atmosphere, and incredible food and wine all ooze with history. Though today Syracuse runs at a much slower pace than the other Sicilian metropolises of Palermo and Catania, in its heyday it was the biggest city in the Greek Empire, as evidenced by the wealth of well-preserved Greek theaters, stone quarries, and ancient caves in Parco Archeologico della Neapolis. A few millennia later, the locals are friendly and welcoming, large open piazzas are filled with light, and bright limestone monuments immediately capture the hearts of visitors.

The golden, atmospheric heart of Syracuse, the island of **Ortigia,** is southeast of the main city, just over a narrow channel across the Santa Lucia. Known as the old city or città vecchia, Ortigia has it all, from ancient ruins to luxurious palaces, treasured jewels of Renaissance art, and a vibrant shopping and dining district, all within an area of only a half square kilometer. The romantic views along the coastline and sunlit piazzas make it a perfect home base while visiting the southeastern corner of Sicily.

SIGHTS
Central Syracuse
★ **PARCO ARCHEOLOGICO DELLA NEAPOLIS**

Via del Teatro Greco; tel. 093166206; www. aditusculture.com/biglietti; 9am-7pm daily; adults €10, reduced rates €5, first Sun. of the month free, joint ticket with Museo Archeologico Regionale €13.50, limited free parking available

Located in the northern part of the city center, Syracuse's Neapolis Archaeological Park is home to the most diverse collection of Greek ruins in Sicily, attesting to the city's importance to the Greek, and later the Roman, world. This 86-acre (35-ha) area boasts Greek and Roman theaters as well as various structures and sites related to everyday life for the ancients, built between the fifth century BC-third century AD. Each element on its own is worth a trip, but to take in most of the archaeological park, you'll need at least three hours. The **ticket office** can be found near the corner of Via Cavallari and Viale Augusto; you'll also find a café onsite.

The first site you'll see after leaving the

1: Cattedrale di Siracusa **2:** Fontana di Diana on Ortigia **3:** Orecchio di Dionisio

ticket office is the third-century **Anfiteatro Romano,** used for horse races and brutal gladiator competitions, and flooded for mock navy battles. Continuing north, the massive **Teatro Greco,** dating back to the fifth century BC, presents a stark contrast to the later Roman structure. Enlarged and rebuilt by Hieron II, the Greek tyrant king of Sicily, in the third century BC, it was built to host more peaceful events, such as public meetings and early Greek plays by classic dramatists like Aeschylus, Epicharmus, and Phormis. From May-July, they still offer Greek tragedy performances in the same place they could have been seen more than 2,000 years ago (tickets from €30); visit www.indafondazione.org for the schedule and more details.

Nearby, the **Orecchio di Dionisio** (Ear of Dionysius) is a 213-foot-long, 75-foot-high (65-m-long, 23-m-high) grotto sliced into the cliffside, so named by the Italian painter Michelangelo Merisi da Caravaggio for its exceptional natural acoustics. Finally, you'll see the **Latomie del Paradiso** (Quarry of Paradise), where limestone was excavated to construct the metropolis you see around you today. On a grim note, the quarries were also used to hold more than 7,000 prisoners from the war between Syracuse and Athens. Today, the white stone landscape is overgrown with vegetation, fragrant Mediterranean plants, and citrus trees.

BASILICA SANCTUARIO MADONNA DELLE LACRIME
Via del Santuario, 33; tel. 0931/21446; 7am-1pm and 3pm-8pm daily; free

The massive, more than 300-foot-high (100-m-high) white spire of this modern sanctuary is hard to miss, one of the most striking buildings in Syracuse's skyline. About a block east of the Parco Archeologico della Neapolis, the conical stone structure is a relatively recent addition to the cityscape, built in the 1960s.

MUSEO ARCHEOLOGICO REGIONALE PAOLO ORSI
Viale Teocrito, 66; tel. 0931/489511; www.aditusculture.com/biglietti; 9am-2pm Sun., 9am-7pm Tues.-Sat.; €8, joint ticket with Parco Archeologico della Neapolis €13.50

Browse through prehistoric, Hellenistic, and Roman artifacts in one of Europe's top archeological museums. Inaugurated in 1988, this prestigious museum was named after Paolo Orsi, the Italian archeologist and researcher who laid the groundwork for excavations, from the prehistoric through Byzantine eras, in southeastern Sicily. This thoroughly modern museum is a great supplement to the Parco Archeologico della Neapolis. Look for the famous Landolina Venus, a graceful (now headless) sculpture of the Greek goddess.

CATACOMBE DI SAN GIOVANNI
Largo San Marciano, 3; tel. 0931/1561472; 9:30am-12:30pm and 2:30pm-5:30pm daily

Carved at the site of the city's ancient limestone aqueducts, this sacred burial ground with its labyrinth of underground tunnels has been used as a funeral chapel to ensure the transition of Syracuse's dead on to their eternal life for centuries. San Giovanni's Basilica and Crypt of San Marciano were built in the sixth century by the Byzantines and restored by the Normans in the 12th century. Beneath the 17th-century Basilica di San Giovanni, the church and its catacombs are only accessible on guided tours (30-40 minutes), which can be booked from the ticket office. The catacombs also feature ancient inscriptions related to the oldest nativity scene in the world as well as the first reference to Santa Lucia, the patron saint of Syracuse.

★ Island of Ortigia
Nestled in the Ionian Sea southeast of central Syracuse, the island of Ortigia is the oldest part of the city. Its sun-kissed principle square, **Piazza Duomo,** is home to Syracuse's

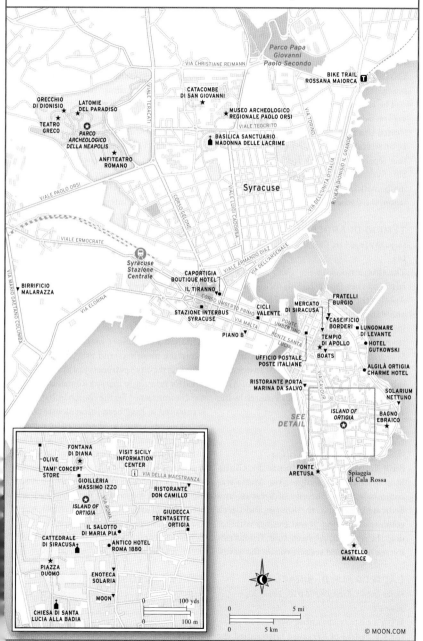

Syracuse and the Island of Ortigia

Parco Papa
Giovanni
Paolo Secondo

VIA CHRISTIANE REIMANN

BIKE TRAIL
ROSSANA MAIORCA

CATACOMBE
DI SAN GIOVANNI

ORECCHIO
DI DIONISIO

LATOMIE
DEL PARADISO

MUSEO ARCHEOLOGICO
REGIONALE PAOLO ORSI

VIA TORINO

TEATRO
GRECO

PARCO
ARCHEOLOGICO
DELLA NEAPOLIS

VIALE TEOCRITO

BASILICA SANCTUARIO
MADONNA DELLE LACRIME

VIALE TERACATI

RIVIERA DIONISIO IL GRANDE

VIA DELL'UNITÀ D'ITALIA

ANFITEATRO
ROMANO

VIALE PAOLO ORSI

Syracuse

VIALE LUIGI CADORNA

CORSO GELONE

VIALE ERMOCRATE

Syracuse
Stazione
Centrale

VIALE ARMANDO DIAZ

VIA DELL'ARSENALE

VIA MARIO GAETANO COLUMBA

BIRRIFICIO
MALARAZZA

CAPORTIGIA
BOUTIQUE HOTEL

IL TIRANNO

VIA ELORINA

CORSO UMBERTO PRIMO

CICLI
VALENTE

MERCATO
DI SIRACUSA

FRATELLI
BURGIO

STAZIONE INTERBUS
SYRACUSE

VIA MALTA

PONTE
UMBERTINO

CASEIFICIO
BORDERI

LUNGOMARE
DI LEVANTE

PIANO B

PONTE SANTA
LUCIA

TEMPIO
DI APOLLO

HOTEL
GUTKOWSKI

UFFICIO POSTALE
POSTE ITALIANE

BOATS

ALGILÀ ORTIGIA
CHARME HOTEL

VIA CAVOUR

RISTORANTE PORTA
MARINA DA SALVO

SOLARIUM
NETTUNO

SEE
DETAIL

ISLAND OF
ORTIGIA

BAGNO
EBRAICO

FONTE
ARETUSA

Spiaggia
di Cala Rossa

CASTELLO
MANIACE

FONTANA
DI DIANA

VISIT SICILY
INFORMATION
CENTER

OLIVE

TAMI' CONCEPT
STORE

VIA DELLA MAESTRANZA

GIOILLERIA
MASSIMO IZZO

RISTORANTE
DON CAMILLO

VIA ROMA

ISLAND OF
ORTIGIA

GIUDECCA
TRENTASETTE
ORTIGIA

IL SALOTTO
DI MARIA PIA

CATTEDRALE
DI SIRACUSA

ANTICO HOTEL
ROMA 1880

PIAZZA
DUOMO

ENOTECA
SOLARIA

MOON

0   100 yds

0   100 m

CHIESA DI SANTA
LUCIA ALLA BADIA

0   5 mi

0   5 km

© MOON.COM

main cathedral, the **Duomo di Siracusa.** Its main shop-lined avenue, **Corso Matteotti,** and the peripheral road that surrounds it, **Lungomare di Levante Elio Vittorini,** are lined with ancient ruins. Catch a sunrise from the waterfront, where you'll find **Fonte Aretusa** (a mythical fresh water spring), **Castello Maniace,** and the small public beach.

The island is accessible by car or on foot via the side-by-side **Ponte Santa Lucia** or **Ponte Umbertino** bridges, and you'll see a **bronze statue** as you're crossing the channel that separates the island from the rest of the city. Syracuse is the hometown of the Greek mathematician and physicist Archimedes, to whom the statue is dedicated.

TEMPIO DI APOLLO

Largo XXV Luglio; tel. 0931/175-6232; open 24 hours; free

The inscriptions on the sixth-century BC ruins of this Doric temple dedicate it to Apollo, the Greek god of archery, music, and dance, although there are records stating it was actually dedicated to his twin sister Artemis. It's possible to see the layers of Syracuse's history here: starting with ancient Greece, the temple was later transformed into a Byzantine church, then into an Arab mosque, and finally back into a church by the Normans.

FONTANA DI DIANA

Piazza Archimede; open 24 hours; free

Built in 1907, this sculpture by Giulio Moschetti and his sculptor son Mario was commissioned by the city of Syracuse and dedicated to Diana, the Roman and Greek goddess of hunting. It features her with her dog, the river god Alpheus, four Tritons riding sea horses, and sea serpents in the waves.

CATTEDRALE DI SIRACUSA

Piazza Duomo, 5; tel. 0931/65328; 9am-5:30pm daily; €2

With a history spanning over 2,500 years, the Cathedral of Syracuse (also called the Chiesa Cattedrale della Natività di Maria Santissima, or just il Duomo), is the main landmark in the oldest part of this magnificent city, as well as Syracuse's main cathedral. Built on the location of the ancient Greek temple of Athena, dating back to the fifth century BC, it was transformed into a basilica by the Byzantines, into a mosque by North African Muslims, and changed back into a basilica by the French Normans. The earthquake of 1693 damaged the basilica and its facade; the stunning one you see today, featuring the Virgin Mary, Saint Peter, and Saint Paul, was rebuilt in the Baroque style. Uniquely, the original doric columns of the Greek temple were preserved into the design of the cathedral's interior, where the massive, weathered structures evoke a sense of hushed awe.

CHIESA DI SANTA LUCIA ALLA BADIA

Via Pompeo Picherali, 4; tel. 0931/65328; 11am-4pm Tues.-Sun.; free

The main attraction of the Chiesa di Santa Lucia is *The Burial of Saint Lucy* oil painting by Italian Renaissance master Caravaggio. Depicting mourners and gravediggers surrounding the city's patroness just after she was killed for refusing to marry a Roman soldier, it was commissioned for the church in 1608 and is rumored to have been miraculously completed in only a month. The domed limestone church itself dates back to the middle of the 15th century and also contains two wooden crucifixes from the 14th century, Baroque doorways, frescoes, and 18th-century painted tiles. Note that the painting is often moved out of the church to be used in special exhibitions. Try the online chat service at Secret Siracusa (www.secretsiracusa.it) to help find out where this magnificent painting is currently located.

FONTE ARETUSA

Largo Aretusa; open 24 hours; free

1: Lungomare di Levante **2:** papyrus growing in Fonte Aretusa

The Fonte Aretusa is important to a Greek myth, in which Arethusa, a nymph, inadvertently bathed in a stream, not knowing it was the river god Alpheus. Discovering this, she fled, Alpheus pursuing her until the goddess Artemis transformed Arethusa into this fountain to save her from the river god. Today, this beautiful natural fountain on the southwestern coast of Oris one of the very few places in Europe where papyrus grows in abundance.

BAGNO EBRAICO/MIKVEH

Via G.B. Alagona, 52; tel. 0931/21467; 10am-10pm daily; €5

This ancient mikveh, or traditional Jewish bath, was only discovered in 1989, when renovating the palace above it. It could be the oldest Jewish ritual bath in Europe, dating back to the seventh century. The three pools, located 59 feet (18 meters) underground, contained pure spring water used by the Jewish community for religious purification rituals. The Jewish population here was once the most important, oldest, and richest in all of Sicily. Although the city of Syracuse no longer has a synagogue, there is still a Jewish Quarter, or Giudecca, located in southeastern Ortigia, between Via della Meastranza and Via Larga.

CASTELLO MANIACE

Via Castello Maniace, 51; tel. 0931/450-8211; www. comune.siracusa.it; 11am-6:45pm daily; €4

The dramatic location of Ortigia's golden limestone, 13th-century castle made it a great place to defend the island and the city of Syracuse as a whole, and today it's the perfect place to stroll the substantial ramparts, with views of the sea. Inside is a small municipal museum that educates visitors on the castle's Norman-era history.

SPORTS AND RECREATION

Though you can find some lovely walks and beaches in the city of Syracuse itself, the surrounding area is filled with panoramic views and some of the region's most beautiful unspoiled nature, including the **Cavagrande** and **Vendicari Nature Reserves,** a one-hour drive southwest and 40 minutes south of Syracuse respectively.

Tours
AGAVE TRAVEL CREATIVE

www.agavetravelcreative.com; info@ agavetravelcreative.com

Agave Travel Creative pairs you with an English-speaking guide for an incredible itinerary deeply rooted in cuisine and culture. Founder Marcello Baglioni curates unforgettable experiences in southeastern Sicily, from private guided visits to archeological sites to visiting almond orchards, olive groves, and forgotten villages. You may have an art historian, archeologist, or cultural guide at your side to help you discover hidden gems, whether you are looking for a sunset sail around the island of Ortigia, an in-depth pizza-making lesson, or a private wine or olive oil tasting. Multi-day itineraries can be completely customized to your special requests to unlock all of Sicily's secrets.

STEP - SYRACUSE TREKKING EXPERIENCE PROJECT

Traversa Sinerchia, 20; tel. 335/808-6973; www.step-Syracusetrekking.it; two or more guests can join a group tour for €65 per person

STEP highlights the natural aspects of southeastern Sicily with outdoor adventure programs, including a 7-hour hiking trip to see the waterfalls in the Cavagrande Nature Reserve (including lunch and a break for swimming), or a 4-hour visit to the bird sanctuary and old tuna factory at the Vendicari Nature Reserve.

Hiking and Cycling
CICLI VALENTE

Corso Umberto, 38; tel. 0931/60618

Mountain, e-bikes, and city bicycles can be rented from Cicli Valente, near the Ponte Umbertino bridge. Rentals come equipped with a lock and repair kit for €10/day;

helmets can be rented for an additional €3/day. Discounted rates are available if renting the bicycles for longer than one week.

BIKE TRAIL ROSSANA MAIORCA

Cycling Distance: *9 miles (14 km) round-trip*
Cycling Time: *About 2 hours round-trip including stops*
Trailhead: *Monumento ai Caduti war memorial, Piazza Cappuccini, 5*
Information and Maps: *Pacer mobile app and www.mypacer.com/routes*

Cyclists and runners will love this off-the-beaten-path coastal excursion, named for the daughter of Sicilian champion free diver Enzo Maiorca. The Rossana Maiorca bike path was built on the abandoned railway stretch, once connecting the industrial area of Targia with the city. Although the bike path is fairly short, fascinating views along the way are worth a stop or two. The trail begins at the Monumento ai Caduti war memorial, about 1 mile (2 km) northeast of Ponte Santa Lucia, and leads past Greek quarries, World War II bunkers, fascinating rock formations, the ruins of the rail station, and a tonnara tuna factory. Bring a swimsuit: Off of the main path, side roads lead down to secret coastal swimming spots. The gravel paths are suitable for runners and any type of bicycle.

Beaches

Syracuse and the surrounding region boast many sandy beaches, in contrast to the rocky ones often found in the rest of Sicily. In Syracuse proper, most of the beaches are located around the island of Ortigia.

SPIAGGIA DI CALA ROSSA

Lungomare d'Ortigia; open 24 hours; free
A highlight of Ortigia's clean and clear coastline is the public beach located on the eastern side of the island, convenient for a quick dip on warm days, which occur throughout most of the year. The sandy beach is speckled with small stones, shells, sea glass, and pieces of colorful ceramic tiles, so water shoes may be beneficial for small children. It can be reached with a short staircase leading down from Ortigia's main peripheral road, Lungomare di Levante Elio Vittorini.

SOLARIUM NETTUNO

Belvedere San Giacomo, Via della Mestranza; tel. 393/915-8801; solariumnettunoortigia.business.site; 9am-7pm daily May-Sept.; €30-40 for an umbrella with two sunbeds
For those who want a little more comfort during their time on the seaside, the Solarium Nettuno is a small beach club with private access to the crystal blue sea below. The lido deck is one of the best places to lay out on a beach bed underneath an umbrella. Enjoy perks like their bar and restaurant services, stationed lifeguards, freshwater showers, bathrooms, and a shaded gazebo area. Reservations are recommended.

Cooking Classes
CASA MIA TOURS

tel. 346/8001746; www.casamiatours.com; by reservation only; group lessons €150 per person, private lessons €175 per person
To delve deep into the local culture, there's nothing quite like cooking in someone's home. This Sicilian cooking adventure starts in Ortigia's historic outdoor food market. With your host, you'll pick up ingredients for the lesson and create the menu while browsing. Guests are then welcomed into the elegant warmth of their host's home overlooking the Ortigia harbor. The experience includes a coffee or welcome aperitivo, a hands-on cooking lesson, and lunch paired with local bread, olive oil, and Sicilian wine. Contact Casa Mia for information and availability. Five-hour cooking lessons and lunch experiences in Ortigia can be organized for 2-6 people and should be booked at least one month in advance, especially from May-September.

Beaches Beyond Ortigia

Although Ortigia has its own wonderful beaches just a few meters from its bustling streets and fascinating monuments, sometimes you want a more peaceful and secluded place to take a dip. From the Plemmirio Nature Reserve down to the coastal hamlet villages of Arenella, Ognina, and Fontane Bianche, the coast here offers a range of places to swim, sun, and relax, all within half an hour from the heart of Syracuse.

RISERVA NATURALE DEL PLEMMIRIO
Via del Corindone, 31; tel. 0931/449310; www.plemmirio.eu; open 24 hours
A 20-minute, 9-mi (14-km) drive south of Syracuse on SS115 and SP58, the protected Plemmirio Nature Reserve was the dreamy location of country villas for Syracuse's wealthy in the 19th and 20th centuries. In addition to 4 miles (6 km) of stone quarry-lined coastline, Plemmirio is known for its excellent diving: You might spot shrimp, octopuses, parrot fish, amberjack, red scorpion fish, and even dolphins. Visit the **Capo Murro Diving Center** (Porticciolo di Ognina, Via Capo Ognina; tel. 331/324030; www.capomurrodivingcenter.it; 8:30am-8:30pm daily; from €40) for guided diving excursions.

LIDO ARENELLA - VILLA BABEJ
Traversa Renella, Arenella; tel. 0931/715025
Also a 20-minute drive from Syracuse (7mi/12 km on the SS1115), umbrellas and sun beds (€12) can be rented from Arenella's lido (9am-7pm daily), and there are also free sandy and rocky beaches a few meters south of the beach club. This wide fine-grained sand beach is also equipped with slides for guests with special needs as well as stationed lifeguards.

SPIAGGIA DI PUNTO ASPARANO
Traversa Capo Ognina, Ognina; tel. 0931/464657; www.syracuseturismo.net; open 24 hours; free
A bit farther south (25 minutes, 9 mi/14 km on SS115), try this rocky beach with crystal-clear water surrounded for a more tranquil beach day.

SPIAGGIA DI FONTANE BIANCHE
Viale dei Lidi; open 24 hours; free
Farthest south (30 minutes, 10.5 mi/17 km on the SS115), this is the best-equipped beach on Syracuse's coastline. Sun beds and umbrellas can be rented (€20-40), and beachgoers also have access to restaurants, bars, bathrooms, and boat rentals. The white sand and calm, clean, warm, turquoise water are great for families.

FESTIVALS AND EVENTS

ORTIGIA SOUND SYSTEM MUSIC FESTIVAL
Via Castello Maniace, 51; www.ortigiasoundsystem.com; late July; full night pass €75
At the end of July, Ortigia transforms itself into a huge dance party; this international electronic music festival combines contemporary performances with Mediterranean tradition. Ticketed boat parties (€33), late night DJ sets (starting at €10 per person), and large concerts are organized in various locations around the island, with the main stage at the **Castello Maniace**.

FESTIVAL OF SANTA LUCIA (Festa di Santa Lucia)
Piazza Duomo, 5; www.siciliainfesta.com; Dec.13-20; free
This celebration for Syracuse's patroness, Santa Lucia, takes place annually in December. Santa Lucia is a symbol of light, rebirth, and devotion to the people of Syracuse. The holy martyr was tortured and killed because she refused to marry a Roman

soldier in the year 304. Her legend begins one December 12 in the 17th century, when the island was suffering from famine and a ship filled with wheat mysteriously arrived at the port in the middle of the night. Desperate citizens boarded the ship and took the grains home to be cooked immediately, without even grinding them first. The Syracusans credited Santa Lucia for saving them from starvation, since the boat arrived on her birthday. The symbolic sweet wheatberry dish cuccia is still eaten to this day in her honor.

The main celebration occurs on December 13, when the 16th-century silver statue of Santa Lucia is paraded through the streets upon the shoulders of men wearing green berets. Keep in mind when traveling to Syracuse in December that the city will be buzzing with festivities and all reservations should be made well in advance. Apart from the main celebrations on December 13, the festival week includes additional events such as special church services and concerts.

SHOPPING
Island of Ortigia
GIOILLERIA MASSIMO IZZO
Piazza Archimede, 25; tel. 093/122301; www. massimoizzo.com; 4pm-8pm Mon., 9am-1pm and 4pm-8pm Tues.-Sat.

Take a peek into the magical underwater world of Massimo Izzo's flagship jewelry boutique. His creative designs, inspired by Greek myths and marine creatures as well as Sicily's Baroque heritage, have been featured in publications such as *Vogue* and *Marie Claire*. Massimo's each piece of original jewelry is made right here in Syracuse.

GIUDECCA TRENTASETTE ORTIGIA
Via della Giudecca, 37; tel. 349/083-7461; www. facebook.com/giudeccatrentasetteortigia; 10am-1pm and 3pm-8pm daily

Everything you'll want to bring home from Ortigia can be found in this boutique: ceramic vases, beautiful clothing, holiday décor, hand-painted postcards and stationery, ceramic serving platters, Sicilian wine, and

hard-to-find liquors. The friendly staff will help you select the best olive oils, spices, and dinnerware, or you can browse for gorgeous dresses and unique bags.

TAMI' CONCEPT STORE
Via Cavour, 13; tel. 0931/465926; www.tamishop.com; 4pm-8:30pm Mon., 10am-1:30pm and 4pm-8:30pm Tues.-Sat., 11am-1:30pm and 4pm-8:30pm Sun.

This concept store is a great spot to find a gift before leaving Ortigia. It's filled with cookbooks, clothing, tote bags, kitchen gadgets, stylish office accessories, and a line of children's products. TAMI' also carries a selection of natural wine and beer. Make sure to pop into their sister shop, Olive, for local food products.

OLIVE
Via Cavour, 27; tel. 0931/095391; www.tamishop.com; 4pm-8:30pm Mon., 10am-1:30pm and 4pm-8:30pm Tues.-Sat., 11am-1:30pm and 4pm-8:30pm Sun.

Olive is the carefully curated sister store of TAMI', just down the street. Specialty food products like sea salt from Trapani, chocolate from Modica, and extra virgin olive oils from Ragusa all tell the story of the culinary landscapes of Sicily.

FOOD
Central Syracuse
★ PIANO B
Via Cairoli, 18; tel. 0931/66851; www.pianobsyracuse. com; 7pm-midnight Tues.-Sun.; pizzas €10-18

Eat at Piano B for artisanal pizzas made with top level seasonal ingredients at affordable prices just three blocks north of the island of Ortigia. Friedrich Schmuck's pizzas are inspired by the flavors and techniques of his childhood split between Rome, the Dolomites, and Ortigia. Since opening in 2011, they've expanded their menu, now offering options like naturally leavened and gluten-free dough. Piano B was recognized by *Gambero Rosso* among the top Pizzerias of Italy and as the Pizza of the Year in 2020. *Cronache di Gusto* named Piano B the Best Pizzeria in Sicily in 2018.

IL TIRANNO

Caportigia Boutique Hotel, Viale Montedoro, 78; www.iltiranno.it; 7:30pm-11pm daily, Sunday lunch Oct.-May; mains €18-32

The fine-dining restaurant located inside the Caportigia Boutique Hotel offers à la carte options and innovative tasting menus from young chef Valentina Galli. Their philosophy is based on technique, creativity, and the selection of the best ingredients.

Island of Ortigia

MERCATO DI SIRACUSA

Via Trento, 21; 8am-1pm Mon.-Sat.

The best way to introduce yourself to a new city is a quick trip through the local outdoor food market. Learn how the Syracuseni eat! The outdoor market in Ortigia is lively and approachable, with fresh, local seafood not found elsewhere, like spatola, costardelle, and sea urchin. Friendly vendors smile and sing as they announce their wares and welcome tourists to their shops. Small stands sell Sicilian spices, herbs, nuts, and dried fruit, and the local tomatoes are among the best on the island; take home as many sun-dried ones as you can carry, along with a packet of wild fennel seeds and some salt-cured capers. At the end of the market, specialty food shops showcase local cheeses, like primo sale, pecorino, Ragusano, ricotta, and mozzarella.

CASEIFICIO BORDERI

Via Emmanuele de Benedictis, 6; tel. 329/985-2500; www.facebook.com/CaseificioBorderi; 7am-3:30pm Mon.-Sat.; sandwiches €10

You know those big sandwiches that everyone has been talking about? This is where you get them. While walking through Ortigia's outdoor market, look for the people waiting in line, jump in, and enjoy an abundance of small samples while watching Signor Andrea Borderi work his magic. He creates jam-packed customizable deli sandwiches filled with sliced mozzarella, arugula, potatoes and crushed garlic, olives, lemon zest, sun-dried tomatoes, chili peppers, and everything else you can dream of. Plan on sharing—the

sandwiches are truly huge—and save room for their fresh mozzarella di bufala and Sicilian primo *sale* cheese with pistachios. This friendly family has been serving the best sandwiches in town since 1930.

FRATELLI BURGIO

Piazza Cesare Battisti, 4; tel. 0931/60069; www.fratelliburgio.com; 7:30am-3pm daily; mains €7-12

This third-generation Italian deli is situated at the end of the Ortigia outdoor food market. Stop by for a casual lunch or pick up some goodies from their exceptional selection of hard-to-find Sicilian meats and cheeses in the salumeria. Fratelli Burgio prepares their own line of specialty food products in small glass jars that are easy to travel with. Treat yourself to a few of their top sellers, like caponata, sweet and sour onions, pickled chili peppers, wild fennel pâté, and peperonella spicy chile paste.

MOON

Via Roma, 112; tel. 334/257-1002; www.moonortigia.com; 7pm-11:30pm Wed.-Mon.; €8-15

"Move Ortigia Out of Normality" is a vegan restaurant and bar in the heart of Ortigia. Their fresh and seasonal menu is alluring even for non-vegans. The apple caponata and smoked eggplant ravioli offer their own twists on Sicilian classics while still sticking to high-quality farm-to-table values. MOON often hosts live DJ sets and parties throughout summertime.

RISTORANTE PORTA MARINA DA SALVO

Via dei Candelai, 35; tel. 0931/22553; www.ristoranteportamarina.it; noon-2:30pm and 7:30pm-10:30pm Tues.-Sun.; €15-22

Cozy up in this simple but chic restaurant for some of Ortigia's best seafood dishes. The vaulted stone ceilings dating back to the 1400s, elegantly plated dishes, and

---

1: fresh artichokes from Mercato di Siracusa
2: cheese from Caseificio Borderi **3:** vegan ravioli at MOON

professional front-of-house service give the place a luxurious feel while keeping prices affordable. Chef Salvo Di Mauro and his son Giancarlo tell their family stories through their dishes. Enjoy lunch or dinner in this inviting dining space, right in the heart of Ortigia's historic center.

RISTORANTE DON CAMILLO
*Via delle Maestranze, 96; tel. 0931/67133; www.
ristorantedoncamillo.it; 12:30pm-2:30pm and
8pm-10pm daily; tasting menu €60*

Founded in 1985 by Camillo and Giovanni Guarneri, Don Camilo has continued to be the mecca of old-school dining in Ortigia. The dining room was constructed from the remains of a religious building that collapsed during the earthquake of 1693. A great spot for a classic Sicilian meal with outstanding formal and friendly service.

BARS AND NIGHTLIFE
Central Syracuse
BIRRIFICIO MALARAZZA
*Via Gaetano Mario Columba, 49; tel. 340/654-5668;
www.birramalarazza.it; 8pm-midnight Fri.-Sat.*

This spot has been serving artisanal beer made with Sicilian ingredients since 2014. Pull up a barstool in the tap room to taste craft beers like their blonde ale, session IPA, Saison, amber ale, or rye. Pair your beers with one of their classic house-made sandwiches for a low-key night out in Syracuse.

Island of Ortigia
★ ENOTECA SOLARIA
*Via Roma, 86; tel. 0931/463007; www.
enotecasolaria.com; 11am-2:30pm and 6pm-midnight
Tues.-Sat.*

Elisa Merlo and her husband Gianfilippo Russo have been running the top natural wine bar in Sicily since 1987. Enjoy hard-to-find natural Sicilian wines by the glass or the bottle from Vini Scirto, Cantina Giardino, Eduardo Torres Acosta, Etnella, and Frank Cornelissen. The curated wine list also includes international wines and top-level,

classic Italian bottles like Barolo, Brunello di Montalcino, and Sassicaia. Bruschetta topped with caponata, wild fennel pâté, or cured anchovies and charcuterie boards with Sicilian salami and cheese pair perfectly with a bottle—or two or three. You'll never want to leave this place.

BOATS
*Via dell'Apollonion, 5; tel. 339/111-0294; www.
facebook.com/boatsortigia; 7pm-1am Sun., 6pm-1am
Tues.-Thurs., 6pm-2am Fri.-Sat.*

"Based On A True Story" is one of a very few truly amazing cocktail bars in Sicily. The cozy speakeasy-style bar welcomes locals and tourists for live music, specialty drinks, and a friendly inclusive atmosphere, just across from the Tempio di Apollo. Owners Giulio Messina and Simone Di Stefano work closely with bar consultant Mattia Cilia to offer the best mixed drinks in town, along with artisanal beers, natural wines, and a menu of small bites. Signature drinks change with the seasons, from the Sterling Silver Irish coffee in winter to the Medusa's Skin, a riff on a classic Manhattan. Incredible nonalcoholic options are offered all year round.

ACCOMMODATIONS
Central Syracuse
CAPORTIGIA BOUTIQUE HOTEL
*Viale Montedoro, 76; tel. 0931/580576; www.
hotelcaportigia.com; rooms and suites from €89*

This luxurious five-star hotel is conveniently located just across the bridge from the island of Ortigia. Business travelers, tourists, and families will find everything they need including high-speed Wi-Fi and rooms accessible for people with disabilities. The comfortable rooms are tastefully decorated with Italian ceramics, artisanal wooden furniture, and contemporary textiles. The hotel concierge can organize breakfasts, aperitivo and dinners, wine-tasting events, bicycle rentals, and information for touring the city.

Island of Ortigia
IL SALOTTO DI MARIA PIA
Via Roma, 45; tel. 339/435-4520; www.
ilsalottodimariapia.it; €105
This cozy home away from home is located in
an early 20th-century palace. There's friendly
service, quirky vintage décor, and morning
breakfast is served in a beautiful basket filled
with pastries and fresh fruit at your doorstep.
The Maria Pia and Paola suites have double
beds and views of the cathedral, while the
Suite bedroom is equipped with a double bed
and its own private terrace.

ANTICO HOTEL ROMA 1880
Via Roma, 66; tel. 0931/465630; www.algila.it; €138
The Antica Hotel Roma was founded in
1880, right betwen the cathedral and the
Archbishop's Palace in the heart of Ortigia. Just
steps away from the Piazza Duomo, this perfectly central hotel is a great find. The stairwell
of the hotel showcases the remains of part of
the Doric Temple of Minerva, and simply furnished hotel rooms are available for 1-4 guests
all with their own balconies. The Garden Suite
and Spa has a built-in sauna and overlooks the
hotel's internal courtyard garden.

ALGILÀ ORTIGIA CHARME HOTEL
Via Vittorio Veneto, 93; tel. 0931/465186; www.algila.it; €188
Algilà Ortigia Charme Hotel was built on the
street where all the 14th-century noblemen
of Syracuse once lived. Set in a historic building restored by architect Manuel Giliberti,
it's designed with traditional Sicilian décor,
antique furniture, and bright ceramics.
Rooms and family suites are available for 2-7
guests. Classic, Superior, and Deluxe rooms
and suites offer guests a city or sea view. The
Deluxe Spa option includes access to a private
sun terrace equipped with a hydro-massage
hot tub overlooking the sea.

★ HOTEL GUTKOWSKI
Lungomare di Levante Elio Vittorini, 18; tel.
0931/465830; www.guthotel.it; from €220
The bright and airy rooms of this boutique
hotel are a perfect home base for a short holiday in Syracuse. The Hotel Gutkowski consists of two fully renovated 19th-century
pastel periwinkle palazzi. The cozy hotel
rooms and two-person apartments can include upgrades with terraces and sea-facing
views overlooking the coastal promenade
on the east side of the island. The modern
Bistro Gutkowskino is open 7pm-midnight
Monday-Saturday.

INFORMATION AND SERVICES
Syracuse is a very well-serviced city, with an
easy-to-find array of pharmacies, post offices,
healthcare services, and tourist information
centers. In addition to the main Visit Sicily
information center, **Visit Ortigia** (www.
visitortigia.it) and **Secret Siracusa** (www.
secretsiracusa.it) offer information on sightseeing, restaurant and hotel recommendations, transportation.

- **Visit Sicily Information Center:** Via
  Maestranza, 33; tel. 0931/464255; www.
  visitsicily.info; 8:30am-1:30pm Mon.-
  Tues. and Thurs.-Fri., 8:30am-1:30pm and
  2:45pm-5:45pm Wed.
- **Post Office:** Ufficio Postale Poste Italiane,
  Via Trieste, 3, Ortigia; tel. 0931/796051;
  www.poste.it; 9am-1pm and 3:30pm-
  6:30pm Mon.-Fri.
- **Pharmacy:** Farmacia Lo Bello, Viale
  Regina Margherita, 16; tel. 0931/65001;
  www.farmacialobello.com; 8:30am-1pm
  and 4pm-8pm Mon.-Fri., 9am-1pm Sat.
- **Hospital:** Ospedale Umberto I, Via
  Giuseppe Testaferrata, 1, Syracuse; tel.
  800/013-009; www.asp.sr.it; open 24 hours
- **Police Station:** Commissariato di
  Syracuse Ortigia, Via Vittorio Veneto, 154;
  tel. 0931/481411; www.poliziadistato.it;
  open 24 hours

GETTING THERE
The best way to get here is to fly into the
Catania Fontanarossa Airport, and then travel
south by train, bus, or rental car.

By Air
CATANIA FONTANAROSSA AIRPORT
(Aeroporto di Catania Fontanarossa)
Via Fontanarossa, Catania; tel. 095/7239111; www. aeroporto.catania.it

The airport in Catania is located 45 minutes north of Syracuse. This single-terminal airport is wheelchair accessible, with a coffee bar, one full-service restaurant, and a self-service cafeteria located in the terminal, as well as a tabacchi, newsstand, duty-free shop, and small kiosks selling souvenirs. Long-term, short-stay, and handicap parking spaces are available onsite.

Catania Fontanarossa Airport is one of the main airports in Sicily, with flights arriving and departing from over 70 destinations including **Roma Fiumicino** (1 hour 15 minutes; €65), **Naples** (www.volotea.com; 1 hour; €60), **Bari** (1 hour; €20) and many other European destinations outside Italy.

Syracuse can be reached by car from the Catania Airport by following the A19 highway south to E45 and SS114, a 41-mile (66-km) trip. **Rental cars** can be picked up at the Catania airport from Hertz (www.hertz.com; tel. 095/341595), Enterprise (www.enterpriserentacar.it; tel. 095/346893), and other small rental providers. **Taxis** (tel. 328/8434403) will cost around €80 each way. For airport transports and other private driving services, contact **Sunny Sicily** (www.sunnysicily.com); luxury transfers to Syracuse cost around €125. **Interbus** also provides transportation from the Catania airport to the city of Syracuse (www.interbus.it; 1 hour 15 minutes; €6.50).

By Train
SIRACUSA STAZIONE CENTRALE
Piazzale della Stazione Centrale, 21; tel. 0931/69650; www.rfi.it/it/stazioni/Syracuse.html

The main transit station in Syracuse is located off of Via Francesco Crispi, 0.9 miles (1.5 km) north of the bridge connecting Syracuse and Ortigia, a straight ride or walk along Via Corso Umberto I. Convenient train services from Catania Centrale (1 hour 30 minutes; €8), Modica (1 hour 45 minutes; €9), and Ragusa (2 hours; €10) and are provided by **Trenitalia** (www.trenitalia.com); to reach Syracuse from Palermo, you'll first need to travel to Catania (3 hours; from €16), and then board a train to Syracuse from there. Tickets can be purchased online or in the station, and must be time stamped at the station before boarding. Bathrooms available on the trains and in the main stations.

By Bus
STAZIONE INTERBUS SYRACUSE
Piazzale del Stazione, 11; tel. 0931/66710; www. interbus.it

Interbus provides frequent service from Catania Airport (1 hour 15 minutes; €6.50), Catania bus station (1 hour 25 minutes; €6.50), Noto (1 hour; €4), Palermo Centrale (3 hours 15 minutes; €14), and Taormina (1 hour 15 minutes; €6.50). The main stops in Syracuse include Corso Umberto, 196 (near the Syracuse train station), Via Paolo Orsi (near the Neapolis Archeology Park), or the main Interbus station.

By Car
From **Catania-Fontanarossa Airport** (50 minutes; 40 mi/65 km), take the A19 highway, following E45 and SS114 toward Floridia/SS124. From **Catania** (45 minutes; 40 mi/65 km), take the A18 highway, following RA15 Tangenziale di Catania and continue on to the NSA339 Catania-Syracuse highway. Continue along the SS114 Orientale Sicula toward Syracuse. From **Palermo** (3 hours; 164 mi/265 km), the main A19 highway from Palermo-Catania cuts diagonally through the island. When you reach the RA15 Tangenziale di Catania, continue along NSA339 from Catania-Syracuse until you reach the SS114 state road to Syracuse. There is often construction on the highway, so giving yourself extra time if cross the island by car.

Once you have arrived in Syracuse, **Parking Talete** (Lungomare di Levante Elio Vittorini; open 24 hours) is a convenient open-air parking garage in Ortigia. A camera at the parking gate automatically registers your license plate as you enter the garage. Before departing, enter your license plate number into the self-serve kiosk machine and pay per hour or approximately €10 per day depending on your stay. In the off-season, parking here is often free.

Otherwise, keep an eye out for clearly marked blue parking spots, which can be paid for by the hour at nearby kiosks (€1.50/hour). White parking spaces will be free, but make sure to check all nearby signs closely before leaving your car. Do not park in a yellow marked spot since these are generally restricted to residents only.

GETTING AROUND

The best way to enjoy Syracuse, especially Ortigia, is **on foot.** The farthest you may find yourself walking from Ortigia, where most of the restaurants and accommodations are concentrated, is about 30 minutes to the Parco Archeologico della Neapolis.

Taxis can be hailed at Piazza Pancali in front of the Tempio di Apollo or arranged by your hotel. There is a fleet of minibuses operated **by Sd'A Trasporti** (www.siracusadamare. it; single ride ticket €1), but most tourists don't find much need for it. Driving around the city is not recommended; the old city has very narrow streets and the parking situation is difficult.

Sunny Sicily (tel. 338/5296915; www. sunnysicily.com) is an English-speaking private driver service based in Syracuse, with luxury Mercedes-Benz E, S, and V-class vehicles. The founder, Paolo Gallo, and his team of expert local drivers provide much more than just chauffeur services; their passion and knowledge of the island is unparalleled. Airport transfers, half-day and full-day transports perfect for wine-tasting, or multi-day sightseeing itineraries all around Sicily can be easily arranged through their website.

Around Syracuse

Outside its namesake historic city, the province of Syracuse offers so much more: Heading south, you'll discover beautiful countryside villages, wild nature reserves, and exceptional sandy beaches. A tour through southeastern Sicily is not complete without a visit to the late Sicilian Baroque town of Noto to enjoy almond pastries and the series of noble palaces and monumental treasures, and save time to enjoy a meal in the small fishing hamlet of Marzamemi. Travelers interested in outdoor adventures can opt to spend full-day excursions hiking, swimming, and bird-watching in the Vendicari or Cavagrande nature reserves. Following the coastline, these untouched natural escapes offer a chance to breathe in fresh Sicilian mountain air.

RISERVA NATURALE ORIENTATA CAVAGRANDE DEL CASSIBILE

Take a break from eating and drinking your way through Sicily with a half-day adventure to the majestic Cavagrande Nature Reserve (Contrada Monzello di Pietre SN, Avola; tel. 393/181-8900; www.cavagrandedelcassibile. com; recommended to visit before 5:30pm; free), about an hour south of Syracuse. Formed by the Cassibile River, this secluded valley, with 6,700 acres (2,700 ha) of protected land, is filled with rushing streams, wild flora and fauna, and hiking paths around the Laghetti di Avola lakes. Visit the Riserva Naturale Orientata Cavagrande del Cassibile for a hike, picnic break, or a swim.

Hiking
SCALA CRUCI HIKE
Distance: *2.5 miles (4 km) round-trip*
Time: *1 hour*
Trailhead: *In front of the Cava Grande Ra Za Gina pizzeria, near the Laghetti di Cavagrande parking lot*
This challenging hike includes switchbacks with a 948-foot (289-m) altitude gain. After following along the Cassibile River, the trail leads to the largest of Cavagrande's lakes, Laghetti Principali, to finish up at the Cavagrande waterfalls. Bring water shoes and a swimsuit along for swimming, and wear appropriate hiking shoes and long pants, if possible, to protect yourself from any brush along the trail.

Getting There and Around
From **Syracuse** (45 minutes; 25 mi/40 km), take Viale Ermocrate onto SS124. Follow signs for Noto to SS287. Turn left toward Avola onto SP4 and follow this road to the nature reserve. From **Noto** (35 minutes; 12 mi/20 km): Take SS115 to the Circonvallazione di Avola and follow the signs for Avola. Drive along SP4 for about 15 minutes to arrive at the nature reserve. A 7-hour full-day hiking excursion or a 4-hour swimming trip to the Cavagrande nature reserve can be organized in the Cavagrande **STEP - Syracuse Trekking** (tel. 335/808-6973; www.step-syracusetrekking.it).

RISERVA NATURALE ORIENTATA OASI FAUNISTICA DI VENDICARI
The stunning Vendicari Nature Reserve (Contrada Vendicari, Noto; tel. 0931/468879; www.riserva-vendicari.it; 8am-7pm daily; free) stretches for 5 miles (8 km) over 1,420 acres (575 ha) of untouched beaches, wetlands, and the remains of salt pans and the Tonnara of Bafuto factory, where tuna and mackerel were caught after mating, before they could return to the open sea. Enjoy the diverse flora and fauna of this beautiful natural area, from salt water succulents, prickly juniper, and wild orchids to ducks, geese, swans, turtles, foxes, hedgehogs, and porcupines.

Hiking
ORANGE ROUTE
Distance: *2.7 miles (4.4 km) one-way*
Time: *45 minutes one-way*
Trailhead: *Main entrance of Vendicari*
This moderately difficult hike passes by Vendicari Beach, the tonnara tuna factory, and several bird-watching observation cabanas, to finish at Calamosche Beach. Toward the end of the hike there is a series of steps to climb down that might be difficult for people with mobility issues.

GREEN ROUTE
Distance: *3 miles (5 km) one-way*
Time: *45 minutes-1 hour one-way*
Trailhead: *Cittadella dei Maccari*
This moderately difficult hike passes by the remains of a sixth-century Byzantine village known as the Cittadella dei Maccariin to the south of the park before ending up at the Tonnara di Bafuto.

Beaches
From north to south, the sand beaches along the coast of the Vendicari Nature Reserve are: Spiaggia Eloro, Marianelli, Calamosche, Vendicari, and San Lorenzo.

SPIAGGIA CALAMOSCHE
northern end of the nature reserve along the Ionian Sea
Make sure to visit the exotic sandy Calamosche Beach positioned in a small bay among the migratory homes of thousands of visitors including flamingos (in spring and autumn) and sea turtles (in May). The nature reserve is a tranquil oasis and careful attention should be considered when observing the area's incredible wildlife. In 2005, the Legambiente Blue Guide named Calamosche the most beautiful beach in Italy.

Getting There and Around
The extensive area of the Vendicari Nature

Taste of Marzamemi

Marzamemi is a quaint fishing hamlet near an old tonnara tuna processing factory with a population of just over 350 people, one hour south of Syracuse and 30 minutes south of Noto. It's the perfect place to stop for a bite to eat in between adventures in the coastal nature reserves. Here are two of the best places to eat in this picturesque 10th-century Arab village:

CORTILE ARABO
Piazza Villadorata Marzamemi; www.cortilearabo.it; 12:30pm-2:30pm and 7:30pm-10:30pm Wed.-Sun., 7:30pm-10:30pm Mon.-Tues.; antipasti €14, mains €15-20, tasting menus €75-85 plus €35 for wine pairings
This chic and charming osteria di mare is nestled inside a typical central sandstone courtyard with three entrances, as required by traditional Islamic urban design. Fabulous dishes feature flavors of the sea like oysters, sea urchin, raw anemones, red shrimp, sardines, cured anchovies, swordfish, and smoked needlefish. Every dish intricately celebrates the flavors of the island with raw preparations directly from the sea, low-temperature cooking techniques, and wood ovens burning local carob and olive branches.

TAVERNA LA CIALOMA
Piazza Regina Margherita, 23; tel. 0931/841772; www.tavernalacialoma.it; 1pm-3pm and 7:30pm-11pm daily; antipasti €16, pasta dishes €15, mains €20
La Cialoma may be the most "Instagrammable" of all open-air Sicilian courtyards. Their vintage tableware, teal wooden chairs, and hand-sewn colorful textiles are simply iconic. The dishes at Lina Campisi's family-run restaurant highlight the local tradition of tuna fishing, featuring bottarga, salted anchovies, handmade pastas, and vegetables grown nearby in Pachino. Signora Lina's daughter Chiara Fronterrè and her husband Totò run the kitchen, while the youngest son Davide manages the front of house and their 400-label wine program. Request a table in their additional sea-view dining area.

Reserve runs down along the coast of the province of Syracuse, with four entrances equipped with parking lots at along the SP51: Vendicari, Calamosche, Eloro, and Cittadella.

From **Syracuse** (40 minutes; 26 mi/42 km), Take the E45 highway from Viale Ermocrate and SS124, heading south toward Noto. Take the exit for Noto/Polizia Stradale and continue on SP59, SP19, and Contrada Vendicari to reach the nature reserve.

TOP EXPERIENCE

NOTO
Come for the Sicilian Baroque architecture, stay for the sweet almond treats. Under an hour south of Syracuse, nestled at the foot of mountains, the town of Noto is surrounded by hills covered with olive, almond, and citrus groves, and dense wild evergreen shrubs. The

southern coast of Sicily is its main almond producing region, which means here in Noto you'll find almonds that actually taste like almonds! Don't leave Noto without tasting almond gelato, almond granita, cassata cakes, or almond milk drinks.

This area has always been affected by strong seismic activity. The new city of Noto was rebuilt following the major earthquake of 1693 that completely destroyed the area now known as Noto Antica. Today, Noto is considered the Capital of Baroque, recognized as a UNESCO World Heritage Site in 2002. Just off Corso Vittorio Emanuele, the main avenue of the centro storico, the narrow streets are filled with typical Baroque architecture, from the churches to the golden limestone palaces. Many buildings are lavishly decorated, with gargoyles and wrought-iron trimmed balconies. Noto is a must-see on a

☆ Baroque Noto Walking Tour

Chiesa di San Francesco d'Assisi

This tour of Noto's Baroque buildings demonstrates the wealth and opulence of this city's layered past.

- Starting on the eastern side of the town, begin your walking tour of Noto at King Ferdinand I's golden limestone **royal gate** (Porto Ferdinandea o Reale, 9, Largo Porta Nazionale; open 24 hours; free).

- Heading two blocks west on the main avenue, Corso Vittorio Emanuele, you will reach the grand staircase of the **Chiesa di San Francesco d'Assisi** (Corso Vittorio Emanuele, 142; free). This church was built in the 1700s and includes a Franciscan monastery and rococo-style stuccoes.

- Crossing back over the Corso Vittorio Emanuele, the next stop is the **Palazzo Ducezio** municipal hall (Corso Vittorio Emanuele; 10am-1:30pm and 3pm-6pm daily; €2). The palace was designed by Noto native architect Vincenzo Sinatra, featuring the oval-shaped Sala dei Specchi (Hall of Mirrors), neoclassical frescoes, and a panoramic rooftop terrace.

- Turn right on Via Papa Giovanni XXIII toward Noto's main Roman Catholic **cathedral,** named for Saint Nicholas, in Piazza del Municipio. Pass the tourists sitting on the steps as you make your way up to admire the extravagant Baroque and neoclassical facade including a bell tower, clock, Corinthian columns, statues of saints, and the green doors at the main entrance.

- Just around the back corner of the cathedral is **Palazzo Nicolaci di Villadorata,** located on the corner of Via Corrado Nicolaci and Via Cavour (10am-7pm Mon.-Sat., 10am-1pm and 2:30-6pm Sun.; €4). Built as a private home in 1737, the recognizably Baroque facade features curved wrought iron balconies adorned with sculptures of sea creatures, winged horses, half-eagle hippogriffs, and sphinxes. The €4 entrance fee grants visitors access to a select few of the 90 rooms of this palace.

- Continue following Via Cavour west and take a left on Via Giovanni Bovio to reach the **Chiesa di San Domenico** (5am-10pm daily; free) in Piazza XVI Maggio. This Roman Catholic church and monastery is a quintessential example of 18th-century Sicilian Baroque design. The marble altars, stuccoed domes, and Doric and Ionic columns of the facade are complemented by the lush sculpted landscaping in the piazza.

trip to southeastern Sicily and can be enjoyed even with a half-day visit.

Sights
CATTEDRALE DI NOTO
Piazza del Municipio; diocesinoto.it; 9am-8pm daily; free

The pleasingly symmetrical, impressive limestone Cattedrale di Noto, with its column-lined facade and golden central dome, is a more staid example of Sicilian Baroque building. Among many of the buildings to be rebuilt after the devastating earthquake of 1693, it is commonly referred to as the Chiesa Madre or Duomo, signifying that it is the most important church in the town. Its reached by a wide, grand staircase and is relatively simple and un-ornamented, with a timeless, monumental design. Inside, the timeless simplicity continues, with white walls adorned by golden carvings and frescoes. The cathedral is dedicated to San Nicolò, a Christian saint from Greek times.

PALAZZO CASTELLUCCIO
Via Camillo Benso Conte di Cavour, 10; tel. 0931/838881; www.palazzocastelluccio.it; open to guided visits 11am-7pm Wed.-Sun. Nov.-Mar., 11am-7pm daily Apr.-Oct.; general admission €12, guided visits €25, children under 12 free

Built in 1782 for the Marquis Corrado di Lorenzo del Castelluccio, the palace stands out among a plethora of Baroque-style buildings in Noto. You'll find a neoclassical theme, late-18th-century frescoes, and intricate flooring throughout the 54,000-square-foot (5,000-square-m) palace—making it one of the largest noble residences in the area. This palace has only been open to the public since 2018. One-hour guided tours of this private historical monument include access to the palace living rooms on the main floor. Reservations are recommended.

Festivals and Events
INFIORATA FLOWER FESTIVAL
Via Corrado Nicolaci, 1; www.facebook.com/ Infiorata; third Sun. of May

The Infiorata Flower Festival and the Baroque historical parade in Noto is an annual celebration of spring. Since 1980, natural mosaics have been laid out on the town's main avenue every May to create a handmade tapestry of tiny colorful flower petals.

Food
★ CAFFÈ SICILIA
Corso Vittorio Emanuele, 125; tel. 0931/835013; www.caffesicilia.it; 8am-9pm Tues.-Sun. winter and spring, 8am-11pm summer and fall, closed Nov. and Jan. 8-Mar. 15; cannolo €3, cassatina €4, gelato €5

Although there are several amazing pastry shops in Noto, the most famous is Caffè Sicilia, chef Corrado Assenza'a fourth-generation gourmet pastry shop, featured in an episode of Netflex's *Chef's Table*. Located across from the Cattedrale di Noto, Caffè Sicilia has been making artisanal handmade desserts for over a century. Celebrated around the world, Assenza has become an iconic figure in modern-day Sicilian cuisine, a passionate, curious pastry chef who continues to make torrone nougat candies, granita with fluffy brioche buns, crisp ricotta cream-filled cannoli, small cassatine marzipan cakes, and other Sicilian sweets the same way his ancestors did. His respect for local the farmers and products, such as almonds, honey, and pistachios, is unparalleled.

RISTORANTE CROCIFISSO
Via Principe Umberto, 48; tel. 0931/571151; www. ristorantecrocifisso.it; 12:30pm-2:30pm and 8pm-11pm Thurs.-Tues.; entrees €14-22, 8-course tasting menu €60 without wine pairings

This is a sleek and modern fine-dining restaurant. Chef Marco Baglieri's carefully crafted dishes are an homage to the food and wine of the region, highlighting exceptional ingredients like ancient Sicilian grains, piacentino ennese and caprino girgentano specialty Sicilian cheeses, local meat, seafood, and plant-based dishes.

RISTORANTE MANNA

Via Rocco Pirri, 19; tel. 0931/836051; www. mannanoto.it; 12:30pm-2:30pm and 7:30pm-10:30pm Wed.-Mon.; €40-60

Roberta Assolari, Manuela Alberti, and chef Gioacchino Brambilla have created a smart and modern bistro within a newly restored classic Sicilian Baroque-style shell. The restaurant has a casual and tastefully designed chic feel to it.

Accommodations

SAN CARLO SUITES

Corso Vittorio Emanuele, 127; tel. 347/662-0548; www.sancarlosuites.com; €160

This seven-room bed-and-breakfast is located on Noto's main avenue, directly above the famous Caffè Sicilia. Tasteful rooms are decorated with modern furniture and original majolica tile flooring. Their reception team can help plan guided tours, excursions, and wine tastings. The view of the Basilica of San Nicolò is also perfect for for viewing the annual Infiorata Flower Festival in May.

COUNTRY HOUSE VILLADORATA

Contrada Portelle; tel. 392/2022910; www. countryhousevilladorata.it; seasonal prices from €339

Built in a renovated 18th-century farmhouse with its own palmento mill, this four-star farmhouse hotel is made up of three guest rooms, a suite, a filtered freshwater outdoor pool, and dining. The 50-acre (20-ha) property includes a working organic farm producing olives, almonds, citrus, and biodynamic wine.

Information and Services

- **Info Point Noto:** Corso Vittorio Emanuele, 135; tel. 339/481-6218; www. infopointnoto.it; 10am-6pm daily

Getting There and Around

After arriving in Noto, the quaint city is best explored **on foot.** The best Baroque churches, palaces, restaurants, shops, and cafés are all located on or near the main avenue, **Corso Vittorio Emanuele.**

From the **Catania-Fontanarossa Airport,** it's a drive of just over an hour (57 mi/92 km). From **Syracuse,** the drive takes less than half an hour (24 mi/38 km). From **Modica,** the drive takes 45 minutes (22 mi/36 km). Visitors can park in the Parcheggio Centrale (Via Camillo Benso Conte di Cavour; tel. 349/084-5075; www. parcheggionoto.it), a 4-minute walk from the Noto Cathedral.

NOTO TRAIN STATION

Piazza Stazione, 5

Noto is also accessible by train and bus. **Azienda Siciliana Trasporti** (www. aziendasicilianatrasporti.it) runs about four buses a day from Syracuse, a journey of about an hour (from €3); the train, operated by **Trenitalia** (www.trenitalia.com; from €2), takes around 35 minutes. From Modica, the train takes about an hour (from €5.60). The station is located a 15-minute walk south of the city center.

SYRACUSE AND SOUTHEASTERN SICILY
AROUND SYRACUSE

1: Cattedrale di Noto **2:** can't-miss desserts from Caffè Sicilia

Ragusa

Located just west of Syracuse, the province of Ragusa is home to several extraordinary Baroque cities, all built after the devastating earthquake that destroyed much of the region in 1693. Today, this part of the island is frequented by travelers looking for culture, architecture, Sicilian culinary specialties, incredible wines, and a coastline of golden-sand beaches. The city of Ragusa and its historic district of Ragusa Ibla, along with Modica, belong to the Late Baroque Towns of the Val di Noto UNESCO World Heritage Site, preserving Sicilian Baroque architecture and deep-rooted food and wine culture.

Ragusa Ibla is the oldest district of the historic center of the capital city. Located in the eastern part of town on a hilltop 1,300 feet (400 m) above sea level, it is the perfect place to enjoy panoramic views of Ragusa's rural countryside. Its Duomo di San Giorgio is a textbook example of the splendid Sicilian Baroque style of architecture from the 17th and 18th centuries.

The province of Ragusa has one of the best food and wine scenes in all of Sicily, from wineries to Michelin-starred restaurants. And the coastline of Ragusa is perfect for a summer holiday away from the crowds of other, more popular Sicilian beaches.

SIGHTS

Central squares in Ragusa include the **Piazza della Repubblica** and **Piazza Duomo,** located only a 10-minute walk away from each other. From Piazza Duomo where the Baroque Duomo di San Giorgio is located, **Corso XXV Aprile** runs east toward the Giardino Ibleo, a manicured public garden.

Duomo di San Giorgio

Salita Duomo, 13; Ragusa Ibla; tel. 0932/220085; www.duomosangiorgioragusa.it; 10am-1pm and 3:30pm-7pm Fri.; 10am-1pm and 3:30pm-7:30pm Sat.-Thurs.; free

The Church of Saint George is the Chiesa Madre or principle duomo church in the heart of Ragusa and one of the best expressions of the Sicilian Baroque style of architecture, with an extravagant, wedding cake-like facade ornamented by curlicues and stained glass. The single tower features both a bell and a clock. Inside, the extravagance continues with gilded décor and a life-size statue of St. George on a rearing horse. The Festa di San Giorgio is celebrated every year here during the last weekend of May or first weekend of June. Explore the religious relics of the city at the **Museo San Giorgio** (Salita Duomo, 15; 9:30am-12:30pm and 3:30pm-6pm daily, Sat.-Sun. only Nov.-Apr.) right next door.

Giardino Ibleo

Piazza Giovan Battista Hodierna, Ragusa Ibla; tel. 0932/652374; 10am-10pm Mon.-Fri., 10am-1am Sat.-Sun.

This city park was originally built as the gardens for the town's main villa. With a stunning panoramic view of the surrounding mountains, the manicured park includes three main churches, archeological excavations, and a monument dedicated to fallen war heroes. As you wander through the paths of this 3.7-acre (1.5-ha) park, the lawns are filled with laurel bushes, oleander, and bougainvillea, and the main Avenue of the Palms is lined with 50 date palms and pink blossoming judas trees.

FOOD

Start your day in Ragusa with a piece of **perpetua cake,** a croissant, or a homemade brioche bun and a cup of granita made from local pizzuta almonds. For lunch, look for a slice of **scacce ragusane** (stuffed Sicilian flatbread) layered with tomato, eggplant, and **caciocavallo** cheese, or the fluffy Palermitan **sfincione** topped with breadcrumbs, slow-cooked tomato **estratto** (paste), and onions.

Ragusa

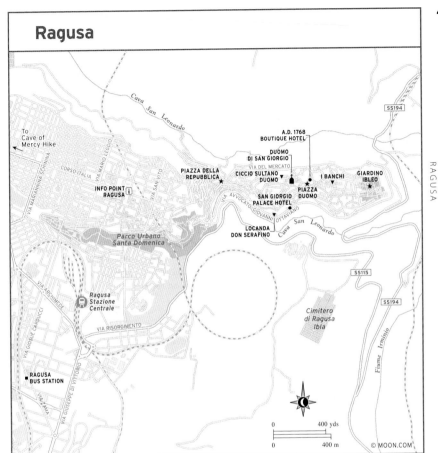

I BANCHI

Via Orfanotrofio, 39, Ragusa Ibla; tel. 0932/655000;
www.ibanchiragusa.it; breakfast 8am-12:30pm,
lunch 12:30pm-3pm, aperitivo 3pm-7:30pm, dinner
7:30pm-midnight daily; pizzas €10, mains €10-16,
family-style tasting menus €20-50, cocktails €8

A celebration of house-made bread, wine, and exceptional Sicilian olive oil led by chef Peppe Cannistrà, a protégé of Ragusa's top Michelin-starred chef, Ciccio Sultano. This smart-casual restaurant's kitchen features the best of Sicilian baked goods, seasonal meat and fish dishes, chef's tasting menus, artisanal cocktails, oysters, and charcuterie platters served throughout the day.

★ CICCIO SULTANO DUOMO

Via Capitano Bocchieri, 31, Ragusa Ibla; tel.
0932/651265; www.cicciosultano.it/en/restaurant;
tasting menus €90-160, wine pairings €28-50,
à la carte dishes €30-39, cover charge €12 per
person included with a minimum order of two
courses

Celebrated and world-renowned as the best chef in Sicily, Ciccio Sultano's love for his homeland, respect for small artisan producers, and exceptional interpretation of classic Sicilian flavors shine through in his innovative and perfectly plated dishes. This stylish two-Michelin-starred fine-dining restaurant is located just steps from the Duomo di San

Giorgio in the heart of Ragusa Ibla. His elegant dishes are a poetic journey through Sicily. Absolutely worth a trip to Ragusa, just to eat here.

LOCANDA DON SERAFINO

Via Avvocato G. Ottaviano 13, Ragusa Ibla; tel. 0932/248778; www.locandadonserafino.it; tasting menus €70-165, 3-course lunch menu €55, à la carte dishes €30-40

The imaginative menu in chef Vincenzo Candiano's Locanda Don Serafino was awarded one Michelin star in 2020. The restaurant is built in the caves of the converted warehouse of the Chiesa dei Miracoli in the historic center of Ragusa Ibla. With over 1,700 different labels, their wine cellar is one of the best in all of Sicily.

ACCOMMODATIONS

★ SAN GIORGIO PALACE HOTEL

Via Avvocato Giovanni Ottaviano; tel. 0932/686983; www.sangiorgiopalacehotel.it; from €65

This four-star hotel was built in a renovated 18th-century building, just an 8-minute walk from the Duomo di San Giorgio. The 108-foot-long (33-m-long) stone tunnel entrance leads guests up to the reception with a private elevator, and the panoramic views of the Vallata di Santa Domenica from the San Giorgio Palace Hotel are unparalleled. The newly restored rooms are modestly decorated for a comfortable stay right in the heart of Ragusa Ibla.

A.D. 1768 BOUTIQUE HOTEL

Via Conte Cabrera, 6; tel. 0932/663133; www.1768iblahotel.it; from €110

This contemporary Baroque four-star boutique hotel features eight rooms and two suites, located in the noble Palazzo Arezzo di Donnafugata, overlooking Piazza Duomo in Ragusa Ibla. La Carretteria, the hotel's ancient carriage house stables, are now open to the public and can be used by guests of the hotel for a place to enjoy a buffet breakfast or a break during the day.

INFORMATION AND SERVICES

The website **Scale del Gusto** (www.scaledelgusto.it) features special events in Ragusa and Ragusa Ibla including tastings, workshops, guided tours, demonstrations, masterclasses, outdoor dinners, and artistic exhibitions.

- **Info Point Ragusa:** Via Giacomo Matteotti, 79, Ragusa; tel. 0932/191-1883; www.infopointragusa.it; 9:30am-7:30pm Mon.-Fri., 9:30am-6pm Sat., 9:30am-1:30pm Sun.

GETTING THERE AND AROUND

Most will likely arrive in Ragusa by **car,** but it is also possible to get here by **train and bus.** Once you arrive, park your car and check out the city **on foot.**

By Car

From **Syracuse,** Ragusa is a 1-hour 30-minute drive southwest (50 mi/80 km); from **Catania-Fontanarossa Airport,** it's also 1 hour 30 minutes, a 65-mile (105-km) drive. From **Modica,** Ragusa is only 25 minutes away (10.5 mi/17 km).

By Train
RAGUSA STAZIONE CENTRALE

Piazza Gramisci, 1; www.rfi.it/it/stazioni/ragusa.html

The main transit station in Ragusa is located within walking distance of the historic town center. Convenient train services from Modica (25 minutes; €2), Noto (1 hour 30 minutes; €7), and Syracuse (2 hours; €10) are provided by **Trenitalia** (www.trenitalia.com), and tickets can be purchased online or from the 24-hour automated machines in the station.

By Bus
RAGUSA BUS STATION

Via Zama, 53; tel. 331/687-7678

Ragusa can be reached by **Interbus** (tel. 0931/66710; www.interbus.it) from Catania Airport (1 hour 40 minutes; €9) or the

Catania bus station (1 hour 50 minutes; €9). Timetables and fares from Ragusa to Modica (25 minutes), Noto (1 hour 50 minutes), and Syracuse (2 hours 45 minutes) are posted on the Azienda Siciliana Trasporti (AST; www.aziendasicilianatrasporti.it) website. A walk from the main bus station in Ragusa to the center of Ragusa Ibla will take about 45 minutes.

The AST city bus runs from the main bus station to the Giardino Ibleo in Ragusa Ibla (€1.20 tickets valid for 90 minutes).

AROUND RAGUSA

In the mountains around Ragusa, treat yourself to an afternoon of wine tasting in the hills surrounding Vittoria, a small town in the province of Ragusa, and hire a private driver to take you there. Cerasuolo di Vittoria wines are the only DOCG certified wines in all of Sicily. Their perfect blend of indigenous frappato and nero d'avola grapes creates a balanced cherry-red colored wine with hints of black currant, pepper, and tobacco. Visits to all vineyards in the area are by appointment only and should be scheduled with as much advanced notice as possible. Outside Ragusa, you'll also find good hiking, a great beach, and some excellent restaurants.

★ Villa Romana del Casale

SP90, Piazza Armerina; tel. 0935/687667; www.villaromanadelcasale.it; 9am-10pm daily; €10, free Mar. 8 for International Women's Day

Despite being relatively remote, this luxurious, sprawling Roman villa near Piazza Armerina in the central province of Enna is one of the island's most visited tourist destinations. Built in the fourth century AD as a private-hunting-lodge-cum-grand-estate for an unknown Roman aristocrat, Villa Romana del Casale was named a UNESCO World Heritage Site in 1997. It's especially famous for its intricate mosaics, considered some of the finest and best preserved of their kind in the world.

Over an estimated 150 years of occupation, the villa was expanded upon multiple times, each time getting larger and grander, until the complex measured some 38,000 square feet (3,500 square m). It was thought to be damaged by the Vandals in the fourth century AD, and more or less abandoned after the destruction of the nearby town of Piazza Armerina by the Normans in the 11th century, followed by a landslide that had the silver lining of protecting Villa Romana del Casale from the elements over the centuries. Archeological excavations began in the 1800s and miraculously revealed this one-of-a-kind, luxurious Roman estate.

Today you can explore thermal baths, the living areas for the unknown owner and his guests (including a throne room), and a lovely courtyard. The site is now almost entirely covered with wooden planks to preserve the precious collection of mosaics, most famously the Room of the Gymnasts, which features nine female athletes exercising in costumes resembling modern-day bikinis, as well as depictions of hunting expeditions and the mythical adventures of Hercules and Odysseus. With so much to see, and so many interpretive signs to read, allow 2-3 hours to visit this site. There's a restaurant and restrooms on site, or venture to nearby Piazza Armerina, a 10-minute (4-mi/6-km) drive away, which has a few good places to eat.

You can hire one of a number of qualified guides at the entrance to the villa (tours from €60), or organize a full-day trip including the ceramics city of Caltagirone with your own private driver via Sunny Sicily (www.sunnysicily.com; tel. 338/5296915; from €65 per person). On a self-guided trip, Villa Romana del Casale can be reached on a half-day excursion from Syracuse (2 hours; 90 mi/150 km), Catania (90 minutes; 60 mi/100 km), Ragusa (90 minutes; 60 mi/100 km), or Agrigento (90 minutes; 60 mi/100 km).

From Catania, the scenic drive will take about 1 hour 30 minutes, traveling west along SS417 to SS125 and SS177 toward Piazza Armerina. The 1-hour 45-minute drive northwest from Ragusa and Modica will also pass through the ceramic city of Caltagirone via SS115 to SS514 and SS683, continuing on to Piazza Armerina by following SS124 to SS117. From Agrigento, the 1-hour 25-minute drive northeast along SS640 to SP42 and SP15 will pass through Sicily's "entroterra" countryside. A full-day trip to visit the Villa Romana del Casale and the ceramics city of Caltagirone can be organized by Sunny Sicily (www.sunnysicily.com; tel. 338/5296915; from €65 per person).

★ Vineyard Visits and Wine Tasting

AZIENDA AGRICOLA ARIANNA OCCHIPINTI

SP68 Km 3, 3, Vittoria; tel. 0932/186-5519; www. agricolaocchipinti.it

Arianna Occhipinti is an unassuming and fierce leader in the natural winemaking world. She started studying winemaking at 16 years old with her family at the COS winery in Vittoria. Always focusing on naturally produced wines in her home region of Ragusa, she grew from a single-hectare property to become a spearhead in a new generation of Sicilian winemaking. Her goal is to make high-quality wines from her frappato, nero d'avola, moscato, and albanello vines. A visit to the Azienda Agricola Arianna Occhipinti winery in the Contrada Bombolieri will include a walk through the vineyards, an overview of production activities, and a tasting accompanied by local cheese, olives, and extra virgin olive oil from the property.

AZIENDA AGRICOLA COS

SP3, Km 14, 300, Vittoria; tel. 0932/876145; www. cosvittoria.it

Giusto Occhipinti and the whole team at COS winery in Vittoria are passionate people who love their land and strive to make wines with a true expression of the terroir of southeastern Sicily. They started with experimenting on family vineyards in the 1980s and have grown to be one of the most reputable Sicilian wine producers. Their Cerasuolo di Vittoria blend of native frappato and nero d'avola grapes is

one of the best examples of this DOCG wine. Winery visits and tastings explore COS's natural values and ancient techniques of winemaking with barrels and clay amphorae.

PIANOGRILLO FARM ORGANIC WINERY

Contrada Pianogrillo, 8, Chiaramonte Gulfi; tel. 338/819-3102; www.pianogrillo.it

The hilltop town of Chiaramonte Gulfi is located in Ragusa's DOC Vittoria winemaking region in southeastern Sicily. One of the highlights of this area is Pianogrillo's beautiful contrada filled with 170 acres (70 ha) of olive trees, most of which are 800-900 years old. The farm also has its own small agricultural museum and ancient wine cellar. The owner, baron Lorenzo Piccone Pianogrillo, is a true Renaissance man—a kind, multitalented, passionate artist and farmer. At his family farm, visits can be organized for a winery tour that includes a tasting of homemade products like his exceptional tonda iblea extra virgin olive oil, local cheeses, and house-made nero ibleo salami.

Hiking

CAVE OF MERCY HIKE (Cava della Misericordia)

Distance: 4 miles (6 km)

Time: 4-hour full loop trail

Trailhead: Located between Ragusa and Giarratana along SP116

Information and Maps: www. circuitodellecaveiblee.it/en/cava-della-misericordia-2

Eight miles (13 km) north of Ragusa, take a quiet afternoon walk through the lush valleys and grasslands of the Cava della Misericordia. This gorge and its limestone quarries are located along the tributary of the Irminio River within the Valley of Misericordia in the Hyblaean Mountains. **Uncovered Sicily** (www.uncoveredsicily.com; tel. 338/872-6610; 4-hour excursions for €180/group) organized guided tours.

1: Pianogrillo Farm Organic Winery 2: Casa Mia Tours cheesemaking experience

Cooking Classes
CASA MIA TOURS

tel. 346/8001746; www.casamiatours.com; from €300 for 2 people including tastings, transportation not included

Visit a small, family-run farm for a morning cheesemaking experience with Casa Mia Tours in the province of Ragusa, where Frisona cows graze freely. Trace the entire journey of the milk from the stables all the way to the creamery where cheeses, such as provola, caciocavallo, tuma, and ricotta, are made right before your eyes. At the end of demonstration, guests enjoy a cheese tasting along with other local specialties, like bread, olive oil, and cured meats. Contact Casa Mia Tours to reserve this program.

Beaches
SPIAGGIA DI MARINA DI RAGUSA

Lungomare Andrea Doria, Marina di Ragusa; open 24 hours; free

The coastline in the province of Ragusa spans 37 miles (60 km) running from Pozzallo to Scoglitti. The central Marina di Ragusa beach is a great place to enjoy a seaside break, conveniently located just a short drive from the city of Ragusa (25 minutes), Modica (40 minutes), or the winemaking area of Vittoria (30 minutes). The golden-sand beaches are not overcrowded on weekdays and offer options at lido beach clubs like **Lido Azzurro 1953 Da Serafino** (tel. 0932/239522; www.locandadonserafino.it) where guests can enjoy a delicious seafood meal and rent daily beach beds and umbrellas (May-Sept., €30 for two beds and one umbrella). The Marina di Ragusa beach was awarded the Bandiera Blu recognition for its clean and clear waters and features amenities like stationed lifeguards, a volleyball court, bars, gelaterias, restaurants, showers, and bathroom facilities.

Food
VOSSIA IL MARE

Via Benedetto Brin, 2, Marina di Ragusa; tel. 0932/734101; www.vossiailmare.it; 12:30pm-3pm and 7:30pm-11pm Thurs.-Tues., 7:30pm-11pm Wed.; mains €12-20

This restaurant, just 650 feet (200 m) from the sea, features plates of fresh pesce crudo and bottles of natural wine. Dishes like ruby red shrimp, oysters on the half-shell, golden saffron pasta, and perfectly pink langoustines bring a burst of color to the white and blue dining room. This casual Sicilian nautical-themed restaurant is a perfect choice for a light seaside lunch in the Marina di Ragusa.

TRATTORIA DA CARMELO

Lungomare Andrea Doria, Marina di Ragusa; tel. 0932/239913; www.facebook.com/trattoriadacarmelo; 12:45pm-2:45pm and 7:30pm-11pm Tues., 12:30pm-3pm and 7:30pm-11pm Wed., 12:30pm-3pm and 7:45pm-10:30pm Thurs., 12:45pm-3pm and 7:30pm-11pm Fri.-Sat., 12:45pm-3pm and 7:30pm-10pm Sun.; mains €12-22

Here you'll find simple coastal cuisine featuring Sicilian ingredients like sea urchin, swordfish, Mediterranean red tuna, or sea bass. Stop by for the freshest seafood in a local trattoria with an elegant dining area overlooking the sea.

RISTORANTE ENOGASTRONOMICO SAKALLEO

Piazza Camillo Benso Conte di Cavour, 12, Scoglitti; tel. 0932/871688; 1pm-2:30pm and 8pm-10:30pm daily; antipasti €35, mains €45-55

Fresh fish from the boat to your plate. This small trattoria highlights simply prepared seafood like plentiful plates of raw langoustines and oysters on the half-shell, octopus, tuna carpaccio, and red shrimp, as well as excellent pasta dishes and fish entrees.

Accommodations
BAGLIO OCCHIPINTI

Contrada Fossa di Lupo; tel. 349/394-4359; www.bagliocchipinti.com; from €120

This hotel is located in an authentic family country house dating back to 1860, in the beautiful Sicilian countryside in the province of Ragusa. The manor house is composed of five living rooms, 12 bedrooms with en suite

Ceramics of Caltagirone

Caltagirone, technically in the province of Catania but equidistant from Catania and Ragusa, is known as Sicily's city of ceramics. Its name derives from the Arabic words "qal'at-al-jarar," the "castle of jars," or similarly "qal'at al Ghiran," meaning "rock of the vases." The town's ceramic techniques date back to the introduction of the potter's wheel to Sicily, brought by the Greeks during the eighth century BC. Add the influence of Arab glazing techniques, and you get the ceramics that are still commonly produced here today.

TRADITIONAL SICILIAN CERAMICS AND THE LEGEND OF THE MOOR'S HEAD VASE

The most common traditional ceramic you'll see in Caltagirone comes from a rather brutal, and very typically Sicilian, story. The head-shaped vase known as the Moor's head, or teste de moro, originates in an 11th-century legend, in which a beautiful young girl fell in love with a handsome Moorish man from her balcony. When she discovered that her lover was already married, with a family back home, she cut off his head and filled it with basil sprouts to be left out on her balcony as a sign of his infidelity. Many ceramics shops throughout Sicily feature a pair of vases representing these young lovers.

For a ceramic sight in Caltagirone that's much less gory, visit the **Scalinata di Santa Maria del Monte,** a ceramic tile-lined 142-step staircase in the center of town.

WHERE TO BUY CERAMICS

Caltagirone is completely filled with ceramic shops, most of which have a showroom in the center of town and a larger workshop on the outskirts of town. A few of the most notable include **Giacomo Alessi** (Corso Principe Amedeo di Savoia, 9; tel. 0933/221967; www.giacomoalessi. com), **Ceramiche Nicolo Morales** (Corso Principe Amedeo di Savoia, 28; tel. 393/971-4113; www.ceramicmorales.com; 10am-1pm and 3pm-7pm daily), and **Crita Ceramiche** (Via Sfere, 17; tel. 340/512-4624; www.critaceramiche.com; 9am-7pm Mon.-Sat.). If you can't make it to Caltagirone or prefer to shop from home, unique hand-crafted ceramics from **Maremoro** are available to purchase online (www.ceramichemaremoro.com).

LEARN MORE

While in Caltigione, visit the **Museo Regionale della Ceramica** ceramics museum (Via Giardini Pubblici; tel. 0933/58418; 9am-6:30pm daily) for a great introduction to the city and the history of ceramic production in this area, with a small but interesting collection from the 17th-18th centuries.

GETTING THERE

From Catania, drive along SS192 and SS416 to SS180, exiting at the Caltagirone Sud turnoff and following SS417 to SP196 on to Via Sfere and Via Roma to arrive in the Piazza del Municipio in Caltagirone. From Ragusa and Modica, take a 1-hour drive northwest on the SS514 to SS683 to Via Noto in Caltagirone.

When arriving in Caltagirone, leave your car parked along Via Roma and walk toward the Scalinata di Santa Maria del Monte staircase. For additional information about visiting Caltagirone, contact the **Caltagirone Visit Sicily Tourism Office** (Via Volta Libertini, 4; tel. 0933/53809).

bathrooms, and a large fully equipped kitchen. The main living room is in the restored palmento winery press and has floor-to-ceiling windows toward the courtyard baglio, and an enormous old fireplace. The kitchen is original, with a wood-burning oven and a large stone sink. The bedrooms are spacious and luxuriously furnished in a vintage style, all equipped with en suite bathrooms decorated with old, traditional ceramics. All rooms are equipped with heating and air-conditioning. Guests are treated to a healthy organic breakfast spread every morning.

Cooking classes are available upon request; dishes may include scacce ragusane (folded pizzas), arancini, fresh pasta, and Sicilian cannoli. You'll be welcomed with a glass of wine, a walk through the garden to collect vegetables, and a six-course dinner.

LOCANDA COS

Azienda Agricola COS, SP3, Km 14, 300; tel. 0932/876145; www.cosvittoria.it; from €300

Locanda COS is a true wine-lovers hideaway. This ancient 18th-century house is located in the heart of Vittoria in southeastern Sicily. The villa is surrounded by vineyards, a garden, a maze, and a swimming pool, and has a great view of the sunset. There are six suites and two large rooms around the main tower. Three of the suites also have large private terraces overlooking the family vineyards. Meals are not included in the booking. The accommodations have built-in heating, air-conditioning, and Wi-Fi.

MODICA

Like many towns in the region, the two areas that make up Modica, Modica Alta and the valley of Modica Bassa, were rebuilt in Sicily's famous Baroque architectural style after the infamous 17th-century earthquake. During these years, Sicily was under Spanish rule, and you can taste a remnant of the Spanish colonies in South America here in Modica, which adopted the specialized Aztec cold-pressing technique of grinding cacao beans to make chocolate without melting the sugar. Spend a day stopping in and out of Modica's famous chocolate shops and laboratories while discovering the hidden backstreets of the town, built into a steep slope. The city is characterized by terraced houses clinging to the rocks and stunning Baroque churches. A short walk down the town's high street, Corso Umberto I, will lead you past architectural gems, shops, and restaurants.

Sights
DUOMO DI SAN GIORGIO

Corso S. Giorgio, Modica Alta; tel. 932/941279; 8am-12:30pm and 3:30pm-7pm daily; free

This 18th-century Baroque cathedral is the principle duomo of Modica. Like many of the important monuments in southeastern Sicily, the reconstruction of the cathedral took place following the devastating series of earthquakes in the Val di Noto in 1542, 1613, and 1693. It

interior of Chiesa di San Pietro

was renovated by the same Syracusan architect, Rosario Gagliardi, who created the San Giorgio duomo in Ragusa. Look for the *Eventi del Vangelo e della vita di San Giorgio* painting by Girolamo Alibrandi, known as the Raphael of Sicily; the temple dedicated to Saint George; a marble statue of the Madonna della Neve; and a magnificent white-and-gold pipe organ. Plan your visit to the duomo at noon to witness the cathedral's floor sundial.

CHIESA DI SAN PIETRO

Corso Umberto I, 159A; tel. 0932/941074;
9am-12:45pm and 3:30pm-7:15pm Mon.-Sat.

The 18th-century Baroque Church of Saint Peter is located front and center on the main avenue in Modica Bassa. Dedicated to the patron saint, this church features statues of the 12 apostles, three main naves with Corinthian columns, and a large central staircase starting on Corso Umberto I. Take a break from chocolate tastings and peek into this church to see the marble *Madonna di Trapani* and the wooden *San Pietro e il Paralitico* by Palermitan sculptor Benedetto Civiletti.

CHIESA RUPESTRE DI SAN NICOLÒ INFERIORE

Via Clemente Grimaldi, 691, Modica Bassa; tel.
0932/752897; 10am-1pm and 4pm-7pm daily; €2
entrance fee

Hidden away on a backstreet in Modica Bassa, the small church of San Nicolò Inferiore showcases one of the most significant collections of rock art in southeastern Sicily with roots dating back to the Middle Ages. It was only discovered in 1987, then only being used as a private storage garage. The church itself is carved from the rocks, and excavations uncovered a series of tombs, late medieval Byzantine frescoes, and late Norman and Swabian artwork.

Cooking Classes
★ LOVESICILY

Via Ritiro, 7; www.lovesicily.com; 10am lunch
programs, 5pm evening classes

While visiting Modica, spend a few hours with Katia Amore to discover the world of Sicilian cooking in her private home overlooking the San Giorgio Cathedral. Options for classes include pasta-making, cooking with Modica's famous chocolate, and traditional Sicilian cooking using local ingredients. All classes can be taught in English or Italian and begin with a short introduction to Sicilian culinary history and traditions. The experience lasts about three hours, including a welcome coffee or aperitivo, hands-on cooking lesson, and a meal paired with wine. Lessons can be booked all year round depending on availability, for a minimum of two people.

GLI AROMI HERB FARM

Contrada Santa Rosalia, Scicli; tel. 342/061-6781;
www.gliaromi.it; 7am-noon and 2pm-6pm Mon.-Fri.,
7am-noon Sat. Apr.-Oct., 7am-noon and 2pm-5pm
Mon.-Fri., 8am-noon Sat. Nov.-Mar., farm visits
8am-noon

Located 20 minutes (6 mi/10 km) south of Modica, Enrico Russino's herb farm is one of the most precious gardens in all of Sicily. You may feel like you are driving into the middle of nowhere, but it will be worth it. Upon arrival, you'll be amazed by this family-run plant nursery. The company produces over 200 varieties of native Sicilian and tropical plants including colorful sage, thyme, lavender, rosemary, chamomile, passion fruit, and geraniums.

The **Emotional Olfactory Journey** (6pm; €30 per person) is a multisensory tour of the property through smell, sight, touch, and taste. The group weaves their way through ornamental, aromatic, and medicinal plants including unique fields of pineapple sage, lemon thyme, stevia, orange geranium, and bergamot mint with Enrico's wealth of knowledge and undeniably passionate guidance before ending the experience with a light aperitivo.

Entertainment and Events
FESTA DI SAN GIORGIO

Historic center of Modica; weekend following Apr. 23

☆ Modica's Chocolate and the Legacy of Spanish Rule

For more than 200 years, from 1554-1860, Sicily was ruled by the kings of Spain. In addition to cultural, architectural, and culinary influence, Spanish rule meant products such as cocoa beans, corn, peppers, and tomatoes were introduced to the region. In Modica, the history of chocolate making dates back to the 18th century, when letters regarding Spanish trade routes were discovered by a local noble family. These documents contained a recipe revealing the secrets of Aztec chocolate-making.

Using simple tools, chocolate makers began experimenting and creating their own method. What makes Modica's chocolate so unique is the way they crush the sugar, grind the cocoa beans by hand, and combine the two ingredients at less than 104°F (40°C), without melting the cocoa butter. This process, inspired by the Aztecs, helps to preserve all the beneficial nutritional and aromatic properties of the beans. The grainy consistency and crisp sugar crystals speckled through each bite make Modica chocolate immediately identifiable. These typical characteristics and the complex Aztec process have been awarded with IGP (Indicazione Geografica Protetta) recognition. The streets of Modica are lined with chocolate shops, including some historic producers who have been working with ancient techniques since the 1800s.

ANTICA DOLCERIA BONAJUTO

Corso Umberto I, 159; tel. 0932/941225; www.bonajuto.it; 9am-midnight daily; chocolate bars from €2.90-5, chocolate lab group tours and tastings €8 per person by reservation only

Antica Dolceria Bonajuto is world renowned for 150 years of chocolate production, making it the oldest chocolate factory in Sicily. In the heart of Modica's centro storico, six generations of family history are preserved in this tiny sweets shop, in the same location where Francsco Bonajuto opened the doors in 1880. It's now under the loving care of Pierpaolo Ruta, and in addition to their immense menu of artisanal chocolate bars are local specialties like cannoli, hot chocolate, panatigghi chocolate meat pies, and honey-poached orange peels called aranciata.

SABADÌ

Corso San Giorgio, 105; tel. 0932/191-2327; www.sabadi.it; 9:30am-7:30pm daily; 50g chocolate bars €4

Simone Sabaini moved from northern Italy's Veneto region to Modica in 2008 with the hopes

Visit during the patron saint festival of San Giorgio, when the festive procession follows the saint through the streets of Modica Alta and on to Modica Bassa. Spectators enjoy a triumphant firework show and a grand procession. The impressive highlight of this joyful event are the men known as "Sangiorgiari" who carry the symbolic saint at a fast pace to simulate the gallop of his horse.

Food
TAVERNA MIGLIORE

Via Modica Ispica, 95; tel. 0932/948669; www. tavernamigliore.it; 12:45pm-2:30pm and 7:45pm-10:45 Tues.-Sat., 12:45pm-2:30pm Sun.; mains €14-24

Innovative dishes originating from quintessential home cooking. Chefs Lorenzo Ruta and Giorgetta Abbate take their guests on a sensorial journey in this restored natural stone country house surrounded by vegetable gardens. Seasonal menus feature playful dishes like a stuffed pasta with marinated squid. The 50-seat restaurant serves creative fare at an affordable price point.

ACCURSIO RISTORANTE

Via Clemente Grimaldi, 41; tel. 0932/941689; www.accursioristorante.it; 12:30pm-2pm and 7:30pm-10:30pm Tues.-Sat., 7:30pm-10:30pm Sun.; 4-course tasting menus €90, 8 courses €130 per person

of creating a high-quality organic chocolate in a city filled with multigenerational historic chocolate shops. Sabadì uses four types of natural sugar cane, highly rated Ecuadorian cacao, and Slow Food Presidium-certified specialty ingredients like mandarin oranges from Ciaculli, white pepper from Sarawak, and fleur de sel from Trapani. He is taking the international market by storm with an incredible product, packaged with style.

CAFFÈ DELL'ARTE
Corso Umberto I, 114; tel. 0932/943257; www.caffedellarte. it; 7am-1pm and 3:30pm-9pm Mon.-Sat., 7am-1pm and 4:30pm-midnight Sun.; 100g bars €1.50
For nearly 50 years, Ignazio, along with his wife Gina and their children, have had their family chocolate shop right in a prime location at the center of Corso Umberto I in Modica. Their chocolates are produced following the ancient Modican traditions.

CHOCOLATE SCHOOL AT CIOMOD
Casa Ciomod, Via Nazionale Modica Ispica; tel. 0932/455412; www.ciomod.com
Just outside town, Innocenzo Pluchino welcomes you into his country home test kitchen for an immersion in the world of artisanal chocolate-making. His passion and dedication to the craft shine through in every product: The attention to detail with cocoa sourcing, innovative packaging, creative branding, and especially the high-quality ingredients all go hand in hand with the level of care that Innocenzo brings to this project. In Chocolate School, guests learn all about the history of Modica's chocolate, the origins and the production of cocoa, and the nutritional value, and can create a bar of chocolate to take home with them. Contact Casa Ciomod for reservations, pricing, and availability.

Beautiful Modica is known for its chocolate.

Michelin-level fine dining, since 2016, in the heart of Modica. Chef/restaurateur Accursio Craparo is known as "the chef of two Sicilies" regarding his experience traversing the island from Sciacca to Modica. The dishes at Accursio are inventive, modern, and clean, always showcasing the quality of ingredients and romanticism of his deep connection to many sides of this island. As a great connoisseur of sparkling wines, you'll find an exceptional selection of bubbly on his wine list.

RADICI, L'OSTERIA DI ACCURSIO
Via Clemente Grimaldi, 55; tel. 331/236-9404; www.accursioradici.it; 12:30pm-2:30pm and 7:30pm-10:30pm Mon., Wed., Fri.-Sat., 7:30pm-10:30pm Sun., Tues., Thurs.; entrées €12-15, desserts €6
A casual offshoot from Modica's top chef and restaurateur, at Radici chef Accursio Craparo experiments with dishes drawing on home cooking and Sicilian street food while always honoring local farmers and fishermen. He dissects and reinterprets the flavors, aromas, and essences of traditional dishes like caponata, sfincione, panzerotto, and granita in an osteria setting.

Accommodations
PALAZZO FAILLA
Via Blandini, 5; tel. 0932/941059; www.palazzofailla. it; from €82

Spend the night in a 10-room 18th-century aristocratic palace on the town's quieter side in Modica Alta. The rooms are furnished with original ceramic tiled floors, antique vases, framed portraits, and Persian rugs. Guests are treated to a seasonal breakfast spread of cheeses, cakes, and freshly baked bread. Hotelier Giorgio Failla and Palermitan chef Francesco Mineo invite guests into the hotel's restaurant, Locanda del Colonnello, to experience creative and seasonal Sicilian dishes like saffron-infused sardine linguine and smoked porkbelly from the nearby Hyblaean Mountains.

CASA TALÍA SLOWLIVING

Via Exaudinos, 1/9; tel. 0932/752075; www.casatalia. it; from €140

This charming bed-and-breakfast has 11 rooms, all including a panoramic view of the Baroque town. Owners Marco Giunta and Viviana Haddad are architects from Milan. Every inch of the rooms, guest houses, secret gardens, and terraces were renovated and upcycled creating something fresh, dreamy, and Mediterranean with a vintage feel. Their Buendia guest house is a duplex for five guests carved out of the stone walls. The Mandorlo and DolceVita guest houses even have their own pools. Their "slow living" philosophy savors the moment and allows their guests to slip into another world from their daily routines and atmospheres.

Information and Services

- **Modica Tourist Information Center:** Corso Umberto I, 1431; tel. 346/655-8227; www.comune.modica.gov.it/site/ufficio-turistico; 9am-1pm and 3pm-7pm Mon.-Sat.

Getting There and Around

Modica is located 35 minutes from **Noto** (21 mi/35 km), 1 hour from **Syracuse** (45 mi/72 km), and 15 minutes from **Ragusa** (10 mi/16km), making it a convenient stop on a road trip through the southeastern corner of Sicily. Once arrived in Modica, it's easy to get around **on foot. Uncovered Sicily** (www.uncoveredsicily.com; tel. 338/872-6610; 4-hour excursions €180/group) runs guided walking tours.

The bus, operated by **Azienda Siciliana Trasporti** (www.aziendasicilianatrasporti.it), takes 2 hours 40 minutes from Syracuse (from €7) and 40 minutes from Ragusa (from €2).

MODICA TRAIN STATION

From Ragusa, train service with Trenitalia takes 24 minutes (www.trenitalia.com; €2); from Noto, it's a 1-hour train ride (€5.60); From Syracuse, it's 1 hour 50 minutes (€8.40). It's a bit of a hike up to Modica's city center, a 25-minute walk (1 mi/2 km), but taxis are usually at the ready for the 6-minute drive.

Background

The Landscape

The Landscape. 437
Plants and Animals. 439
History 441
Government
  and Economy. 449
People and Culture 450

There area known as Southern Italy is generally thought to comprise eight of Italy's 20 Italian regions, roughly making up the foot of Italy's boot. The regions featured in this book are Campania, home to Naples and the Amalfi Coast; Puglia, at the heel; and Sicily, the roughly triangular-shaped island off the peninsula's toe.

GEOGRAPHY

Roughly the size of Colorado, the long, boot-shaped Italian peninsula was formed millions of years ago in the Cenozoic Era, when tectonic

plates underneath Europe and Africa slowly collided and transformed the earth's surface. Over the past million years, alternating warm and glacial periods shaped the terrain and formed mountain ranges, valleys, lakes, and rivers, and geographic features as diverse as Alpine peaks, active volcanoes, hot springs, and desert-like settings.

The region of Campania is the third most populous of Italy and covers an area of 5,247 square miles (13,590 square km), with a coastline of about 217 miles (350 km) on the Mediterranean Sea. It is bordered by the regions of Lazio to the northwest (where Rome is located), Molise directly to the north, Puglia to the northeast, and Basilicata to the east and south. Its coastline and two large gulfs are divided by the Sorrentine Peninsula, with the Gulf of Naples to the north and the Gulf of Salerno to the south. The Gulf of Naples is home to the islands of Capri, Ischia, and Procida.

Moving northeast, the 7,500-square-mile (19,000-square-km) region of Puglia (sometimes referred to by its anglicized name, Apulia) is bordered by a stunning, almost 500-mile-long (800-km-long) coastline. The large sub-peninsula known as the Salento protrudes out to the south, bordered by the Adriatic Sea to the north and the Ionian Sea to the south. The bay that forms the arch in the foot of the Italian peninsula is known as the Gulf of Taranto. Puglia is relatively flat compared to the rest of the Italian peninsula, with the exception of the mountainous Gargano Promontory to the north.

To the southwest, passing over the "toe" regions of Basilicata and Calabria, you'll reach Sicily, separated from the mainland by the thin Strait of Messina (only about 1 mi/3 km wide at its narrowest point). Covering 10,000 square miles (26,000 square km), the island's 930-mile (1,500-km) coastline (longer if you include the sub-archipelagos of the Aegadian and Aeolian Islands) is bordered by the Tyrrhenian Sea to the north, the Ionian to the east, and the Mediterranean to the south. The mountainous island is dominated by the behemoth that is Mount Etna, standing guard over the eastern side of the island.

Volcanoes and Volcanic Islands

Almost no part of Southern Italy has not been touched by volcanic activity, from **Mount Vesuvius,** the massive volcano that soars 4,203 feet (1,281 m) above the city of Naples, to the even larger Mount Etna (10,922 ft/3,329 m), the largest active volcano in Europe. These volcanoes are only parts of long volcanic chains, stretching along the coastline west of Naples to the islands of Ischia and Procida, and north along Sicily's east coast to the Aeolian Islands, which include the famous volcanos of Stromboli and Vulcano. This volcanic area comprises active, dormant, and extinct volcanoes. Because of centuries of volcanic activity, Southern Italy has always been prized for its rich soil and productive farming.

CLIMATE

The weather throughout Southern Italy is mostly warm and Mediterranean—characterized by hot, dry summers and mild, rainy winters—though there are some variations: Temperatures are generally milder the closer you are to the coast, and higher-elevation areas tend to be cooler and receive more precipitation. Average temperatures throughout the region range from 37-61°F (3-16°C) in winter, 43-72°F (6-22°C) in spring, 54-86°F (12-30°C) in summer, and 45-81°F (7-27°C) in fall. Of the three regions, Campania is typically the mildest, Puglia tends the driest, and Sicily is the hottest—though the island has the best chance of more than a dusting of snow, due to the high elevation of Mount Etna.

If you're planning a seaside holiday, the

Previous: Valle dei Templi in western Sicily.

beach season usually begins around April or May and continues through October in most coastal areas. The air and sea temperatures are the warmest during July and August, with an average water temperature of about 78.8°F (26°C).

ENVIRONMENTAL ISSUES

Italy's environmental concerns range from poor building practices in earthquake-prone areas to air and water pollution. Over the past decade, seasons have begun to stray from their clockwork patterns and people have started to recognize the greater variability. Summers aren't just hot, they can be excruciating; rainless summer seasons are extending into longer and longer periods of severe drought; and local TV broadcasts advise viewers throughout July and August on how to avoid sunstroke and heat exhaustion.

A waste management crisis in the 1990s and 2000s also led to an epidemic of illegal toxic waste dumping in Italy, especially in a region northeast of Naples. Unfortunately, the practice is very profitable and difficult to stop. Harmful chemicals and other forms of pollution found in agricultural products from the region have raised concerns, from residents to international trade partners, that still persist to this day.

Plants and Animals

The diverse natural landscape of Southern Italy supports rich and varied wildlife and plant life, though cultivation of agriculture since at least Roman times has deprived the region of much of its former biodiversity over the centuries.

TREES

Deforestation has been an issue throughout Southern Italy for millennia, as the region has been inhabited and cultivated for centuries. Still, the mountainous slopes of the Sorrentine Peninsula and the surrounding areas are home to thick forests with many different types of trees, including pine, oak, beech, and chestnut, and occasionally, you'll also see palm trees and the iconic umbrella pines on the Amalfi Coast, introduced to the area in Roman times. The noci di Sorrento are a variety of walnut typically found on the Sorrento coastline, while unique trees in Puglia include the Aleppo Pine and the holm-oak, and some of the oldest chestnut trees in Europe exist in the mountainous, inland, forested areas of Sicily.

Limone Costa d'Amalfi and Limone di Sorrento

Though citrus trees like mandarin and orange are also common in the area, the lemons of the Amalfi Coast and Sorrentine Peninsula are world famous. Two types of lemons are grown in the area, the limone Costa d'Amalfi and the limone di Sorrento, and these two varieties have garnered the IGP (Indicazione Geografica Protetta) status, which indicates a protected product unique to a geographic area. The limone Costa d'Amalfi is noted for its tapered shape, very bright and medium-thick peel, and intense aroma. It is rich in essential oils and the pulp is juicy with a moderate acidic level, making it popular for use in creating the classic limoncello liqueur as well as in traditional cooking.

Along the Sorrento coastline you'll find the limone di Sorrento, a slightly smaller and more oval-shaped lemon compared to the Sfusato Amalfitano. The juice has a higher acidity level and is rich in vitamin C. The peels are also extremely fragrant and are used to create excellent limoncello and lemon sweets.

Olives

Olive trees are typical at lower elevations along the Sorrentine Peninsula and Amalfi Coast, where groves climb nearly vertically up and down terraces on the mountain slopes, but it is Puglia that reigns supreme in olive production, producing around 40% of the country's olive oil. Their silvery green leaves are a common sight driving through the hills of Puglia. During autumn harvest you can spot the black and green nets placed below the trees to catch the olives.

PLANTS AND FLOWERS

Plants and flowers grow in abundance in the Campania area: Wildflowers fill the mountainsides with color and their sweet scent starting in the spring. You'll see many varieties of orchids, as well as cyclamen, crocuses, freesias, lilies, poppies, valerian, lavender, honeysuckle, buttercups, geraniums, and even wild garlic. Bright bursts of bougainvillea in various shades of purple and pink dot the area along with delicate wisteria in the spring. Jasmine grows particularly well here and fills the early summer air with a divine scent. Along rugged slopes you'll see the characteristic wisps of green and yellow of the many broom plants. Herbs grow wild here, including rosemary, thyme, oregano, and sage.

Drier Sicily and Puglia are less known for their wildflowers; in Puglia, the distinctive maquis is the most common vegetation, a scrubland-like landscape made up of dense, fragrant evergreen shrubs.

Though the region is not as well known for its wine as areas like Tuscany, this is changing; grapevines and vineyards are common throughout the area; especially in the dry, hilly landscape of Puglia. They also can be found in the most unlikely places, spread vertically along terraces on the Amalfi Coast or the slopes of Mount Etna.

MAMMALS

Throughout Southern Italy, it's possible to find wild boar, foxes, hare, weasels, martens, porcupines, hedgehogs, and roe deer, though the latter have been hunted nearly to extinction, especially in Puglia. Both Puglia and Sicily were once home to a species of wolf that has also sadly been eradicated.

However, you're more likely to encounter the mules and donkeys traditionally used as pack animals in the area, outfitted with metal baskets to carry their loads—which in the summer may be tourists' suitcases. Sheep and goats are also common; you'll hear the tinkling of their bells before you see them making their way along the mountainside. Wild goats occasionally pick their way carefully along the rocky, steep cliffs.

REPTILES

Out in the countryside, you're sure to happen across lizards and geckos sunning themselves or darting across your path. There are snakes in rural areas, most commonly long, dark, and nonpoisonous, but keep an eye out for vipers, which have a triangular head, lighter color, and smaller size. They'll stay away from you and are only defensive when startled.

SEA LIFE

The Mediterranean is home to a variety of sea life, integral to coastal life throughout Southern Italy. Occasionally, dolphins can be spotted jumping alongside boats, especially in the early morning, and fin whales migrate off the coast of Sicily. The Tyrrhenian, Ionian, Adriatic, and Mediterranean Seas are home to many different types of fish, from the tiny alici (anchovies), to large tuna in the deeper waters off the coast, as well as squid, octopus, and sea urchin. While swimming, you might run into a jellyfish (medusa), an unpleasant experience, but not dangerous. Locals are keen to spot jellyfish and will likely alert you if they have been seen in the area. If you are stung, you can find creams or lotions that offer relief at any local farmacia (pharmacy).

BIRDS

The cry of seagulls is a familiar sound in the coastal regions, where you'll see colonies perched on rocks along the shore or high atop rugged cliffs on the islands. It's also not unusual to see falcons and other birds of prey gently gliding through the air. At night, you may hear the calls of owls, especially in the mountaintop villages of the Amalfi Coast.

Many types of migratory birds pass through the area in the spring and autumn, on the way to breeding grounds in northern Europe or winter nesting areas in Africa. It's possible to see greater flamingoes in some coastal areas of Puglia and Sicily.

History

MAGNA GRAECIA
(8th-4th Centuries BC)

Inhabited since Paleolithic times (Matera, in the province of Basilicata, is thought to be one of the oldest continuously inhabited settlements in the world), Southern Italy was home to many ancient Italic and Phoenician tribes, colonized by the Greeks to become what was later called by the Romans Magna Graecia: a densely populated, strongly Hellenized coastal area stretching from Puglia to Sicily and north to Calabria. Major Greek settlements throughout the area included Neapolis (modern-day Naples); Poseidonia, now called Paestum; Akragas, later Agrigento, where the magnificent remains now known as Valle dei Templi can still be found; and Taras, now Taranto. Syracuse was Magna Graecia's most important city, powerful enough to even defeat the Athenians in the Peloponnesian War in the fifth century BC.

At its height, the cities of Magna Graecia were among the most prosperous and influential in the ancient world. The Greek settlers brought language, alphabet, religious customs, and the administrative system of the polis to the region. Frequently interacting (and often squabbling) with native Italic tribes, including the Etruscans, the decline of Magna Graecia began when the Roman republic began its expansion southward, first conquering Neapolis in 327 BC.

ROMANS
(4th Century BC-6th Century AD)

After taking over the area around Neapolis (Naples) in the fourth century BC, Roman expansion continued slowly southward, arriving in Taras (Taranto) in 272 BC; evidence of the Via Traiana, an ancient Roman road built by Emperor Trajan that stretched to Brindisi, can still be seen in Puglia. The main obstacle to Roman domination at the time were the Carthaginians, led by the renowned general Hannibal, who stacked up many important victories including at the Battle of Cannae in Puglia in 216 BC. Only Syracuse, leveraging its power, prosperity, and alliances with the Carthaginians, retained some sort of Greek independence a bit longer, but it too was eventually sacked and conquered in 212 BC.

Over the following centuries, Southern Italy became almost completely Romanized. Roman ruins are still visible throughout the region, especially in Naples, where Roman ruins lie just below modern-day streets, and of course in Pompeii and Herculaneum. In many cases, the Romans built upon or repurposed Greek constructions, seen especially in the amphitheater in Taormina, which went from hosting plays by famous Greek writers to being filled with water to stage fake naval battles. The territories of Puglia and Sicily were considered important breadbaskets for the Roman empire, producing large quantities of wheat, olive oil, and wine.

Romans seemed to find much of the same appeal in the area around the Amalfi Coast, including the island of Capri, that people do today, building lavish residences such as Villa Jovis. Villa Romana del Casale in inland Sicily is another fine example of an over-the-top, palatial Roman dwelling.

Roman Decline

The Roman cities of Pompeii and Herculaneum around the base of Mount Vesuvius thrived until the violent eruption of the volcano in AD 79 completely destroyed the cities. **Constantine** (AD 272-337) moved the capital to Constantinople (modern-day Istanbul) in AD 312, which led to the split of the Roman Empire. Though the eastern half survived for another 1,000 years in the guise of the **Byzantine Empire** (whose influence can be seen in many buildings across the region that survive today, especially in Palermo's main cathedral and its rival in nearby Monreale), the west could not stop the Vandals, Franks, and Visigoths from pouring over the Alps in the north. The western Roman Empire officially came to an end in AD 476, with some sources indicating that the last emperor, Romulus Augustulus, died at the Roman villa that once stood where the Castel dell'Ovo stands in Naples today.

Despite persecution, **Christianity** grew and eventually became an officially recognized religion, with the first Christian temples built on the sites of former Greek and Roman buildings, which later formed the foundations (literally) on which many other churches in the area were built.

MIDDLE AGES
(6th-13th Centuries AD)

After the fall of the Western Empire, Italy was subject to repeated foreign invasion. **Lombards** founded their capital in Pavia, followed by the **Franks** and **Charlemagne** (742-814), eventually crowned Holy Roman Emperor. The Lombards then moved south and vied for control of much of the region. **Saracen** pirates landed in Sicily, Puglia, and Campania, and **Normans** built impressive fortifications all along the Southern Italian coast. The **Byzantine Empire** continued to fight for control of the area after taking Naples in the sixth century; Naples would continue on as an independent duchy under Byzantine influence until the 12th century. Salerno grew in prominence during the late Middle Ages under the Lombards. After the Duchy of Benevento was moved to Salerno in 774, the city thrived as a center of culture and art.

From the 9th-11th century, Sicily was dominated by the Arabs, who established an Islamic caliphate on the island, and also managed to establish temporary footholds on the Italian mainland at various times throughout their rule, including the Emirate of Bari. But it's still on Sicily where Islamic influence is most deeply felt, from buildings like the Palazzo Normanni's peculiar mix of Byzantine, Arab, and Norman architecture, to regional dishes like couscous not seen elsewhere in Italy. The Arabs also introduced new irrigation techniques and brought crops like oranges, lemons, and pistachios.

The Normans eventually expelled all of the Muslims from Sicily, in the course of conquering the rest of Southern Italy between the 10th-11th centuries. Sicily was conquered in 1071, and Naples was the final territory to fall in 1139. What came to be called the **Kingdom of Sicily,** which then included most of what we call Southern Italy today, including modern-day Campania, Puglia, and Sicily, went on to become one of the most powerful and wealthy states in Europe at the time. The Normans were relatively tolerant rulers for the time, for the most part allowing Southern Italy's mix of Arabs, Jews, and Christians to coexist, and most of the fortified castles seen throughout the region, perhaps most notably the Castel dell'Ovo in Naples, owe their construction to the Norman period.

Many of these castles were later expanded upon by the Swabians, who took over in 1194, not without resistance from many parts of Southern Italy. The Swabian King of Sicily, Frederick II of the Hohenstaufen dynasty from Germany, has a mixed legacy: He founded the University of Naples in 1224, promoted a literary movement known as the Sicilian School from his court in Palermo, and constructed lasting buildings like the Castel del Monte in Puglia. But he also expelled all Muslims who remained from the kingdom, and got into the conflict with the Roman

Catholic papacy, which eventually led to the Hohenstaufens's ouster.

Independent Republics

In the fray of the early Middle Ages many cities managed to form independent republics. Along with Venice, Genoa, and Pisa, Amalfi became one of the most powerful maritime republics of Italy. The peak of the **Duchy of Amalfi** stretched from the 10th-11th century, when the republic included much of the Amalfi Coast and its trading ships crisscrossed the Mediterranean, traveling as far as Africa, Constantinople, and Jerusalem. Many of the richly decorated churches and sprawling estates, like the Villa Rufolo in Ravello, date from this period. The Duchy of Amalfi was sacked by the Republic of Pisa in 1137, which was the beginning of the area's decline as powers shifted to the cities of Salerno and Naples.

ANJOU AND ARAGONESE RULE
(13th-15th Centuries)

Upon Frederick II's death in 1250, there was something of a power vacuum in Southern Italy, eventually filled by the Angevins of France, who were hand-selected by Pope Urban IV (who had long opposed Swabian rule) to take over. The Kingdom of Sicily was divided in two when Charles I of Anjou arrived in the region in 1266 and was crowned king. This was the beginning of a centuries-long period in which Sicily and Naples would be unified, divided, and reunified again as the area passed hands between different ruling dynasties. After decades of squabbling, the island of Sicily went to Frederick II of Aragon, while Charles II (descendent of Charles I) ruled the **Kingdom of Naples,** which included the area that is now called Puglia.

The ruler of the French Angevin kingdom set about developing Naples as an intellectual and artistic European capital, with efforts continued by his grandson, Robert of Anjou (1275-1343). During this time, the coastal cities of Puglia, including Otranto, were often besieged by the Turks, though they never quite managed to secure a foothold in the area. The Angevins redoubled the fortifications built by the Normans and Swabians to provide Apulian towns with more protection.

In the early 15th century, the Angevin dynasty's internal family squabbles led the Aragonese to attempt an attack. After a bloody battle, Alfonso of Aragon conquered Naples in 1442, arriving triumphant in early 1443. Aragonese rule only lasted a little over half a century, though, and was marked by near constant turmoil: The Aragonese rulers were widely disliked, but it was a vibrant period for the arts and learning in Naples and the surrounding region, attracting notable Renaissance poets and painters. The regions of Puglia and Sicily were largely left out of these cultural awakenings due to their relative geographical isolation

SPANISH RULE
(16th-17th Centuries)

By the end of the 15th century, both France and Spain were vying for the Kingdom of Naples. The French first took control in 1501 but power passed to Spanish King Ferdinand III by 1504. This began about 200 years of Spanish rule in both Naples and Sicily (though the kingdoms officially remained separate), largely under the Hapsburg dynasty. This was a key period for Naples, which very quickly grew into one of the largest cities in Europe. Overcrowding and poverty became significant issues, contrasting with the high achievements in art and architecture.

This was a time of relative peace and prosperity for Puglia, which had been suffering incursions from the Ottoman Empire and other seafaring invaders on its shores on and off for centuries. A decisive defeat of the Ottomans at the Battle of Lepanto in 1571 freed up cities like Lecce to build magnificent Baroque churches and cityscapes. The Spanish rule was also characterized by the introduction of goods and products from the country's burgeoning empire—notably including chocolate in Sicily—and punctuated by a series of revolts to oppressive taxes. A 1647 uprising led by young fisherman Tommaso Aniello (called Masaniello, 1620-1647) turned into a citywide uprising that lasted until the leader's assassination on July 16, 1647. Capitalizing on the disorder, the French attempted to take back Naples, but by 1648 order was restored under a new Spanish viceroy.

By the second half of the 17th century, the situation in both kingdoms was deteriorating. In 1656, the plague hit the region in full force, killing more than half of the population in Naples alone. A strong earthquake in 1688 caused significant destruction in the historic center of Naples, setting the city's recovery back even further. Meanwhile, devastating earthquakes and eruptions of Mount Etna rocked eastern Sicily in the late 17th century and destroyed much of Catania and other nearby towns. It was during this period, when corruption took hold of much of the region, that criminal groups formed and grew in power, forming the roots of the modern-day Sicilian Mafia.

THE BOURBONS
(18th Century)

After the tumultuous Spanish period, the 1700s brought great changes to Southern Italy. During the War of the Spanish Succession (1701-1714), as the Austrian Habsburg and Bourbon families fought over the Spanish Empire, Naples was ceded to Austria in 1707, which also later gained control of Sicily in 1720. The Austrian viceroyalty rule lasted only until 1734, however, when the Bourbon King Charles VII (future Charles III, King of Spain) conquered Naples and set about transforming it into a European capital. Grand urban plans and a focus on public works marked the Bourbon era, including the rebuilding of much of the earthquake- and eruption-devastated region of eastern Sicily in the era's trademark Baroque style.

Under Charles VII, and later his son Ferdinand IV, Naples became one of the finest cities in Europe, and arts and theater flourished in the region, along with new industries, like silk, porcelain, and ceramics. Meanwhile, in Puglia, a unique, humble form of construction began to pop up in the countryside: The conical huts known as trulli actually developed as a way to avoid taxes, as they were built without mortar and easy to dismantle.

Rediscovering Pompeii and Herculaneum

During Bourbon rule, Herculaneum was accidentally rediscovered in the construction of yet another royal residence. The first real exploration of the archaeological site began in 1738. In 1748 Pompeii was rediscovered after an intentional search for the ancient city. The treasures uncovered were highly valued by the kings of Naples and extremely influential to the neoclassical movement.

Naples garnered attention across Europe, and the first tourists began to arrive on the Grand Tour, a popular tour across Europe that was an integral part of an aristocratic and upper-class education in the 18th century. After visiting Florence, Venice, and Rome, many travelers continued to Naples to appreciate the fine music, art, and cultural experiences, as well as to marvel at the ancient temples in Paestum, walk among the ruins of Pompeii and Herculaneum, and eventually travel farther south to see the Greek and Roman ruins at Taormina, Catania, Syracuse, and Agrigento. By the early 1800s, especially after the rediscovery of the Grotta Azzurra in 1826, the allure of Capri and Amalfi as international travel destinations had begun.

PARTHENOPEAN REPUBLIC AND UNIFICATION
(19th Century)

At the end of the 18th century, the wave of revolutionary ideas of the French Revolution arrived in Southern Italy. When Marie Antoinette—who was the sister of King Ferdinand IV's wife Maria Carolina—was beheaded in 1793, the revolution became very personal to the Bourbon rulers of Naples. After battling with the French, the king and queen escaped to Palermo, which was then under the protection of the British, and remained the base of the British military operations against Napoleon in the Mediterranean until 1814. Meanwhile, the French established the Parthenopean Republic in 1799. This was a short-lived moment of confusion, which ended after only six months when a counter revolution lead by the Bourbons ousted the republic and brutally executed republican sympathizers.

Despite the return of the Bourbon monarchy, the beginning of the 19th century in Naples was a period of turmoil. The French returned in 1805, this time more successfully. In 1806, Napoleon made his brother Joseph Bonaparte king of Naples, a role that was passed to Napoleon's brother-in-law Joachim Murat in 1808. The French were never fully embraced by the Neapolitans, and when the French lost power in 1815 the Neapolitans welcomed Ferdinand IV back to rule as Ferdinand King of the Two Sicilies.

Resurgence and Restoration

The Bourbon family continued to rule Southern Italy for first half of the 19th century, another period of great unrest, when a nationalist movement, known as the **Risorgimento** (Resurgence), began to spread across Italy, aiming to unite the peninsula against foreign domination. **Giuseppe Garibaldi** (1807-1882) was one of the movement's great leaders, and Southern Italy posed a major hurdle to unification. The **Kingdom of the Two Sicilies** was overseen by Bourbon monarchs who ruled from their capital in Naples. Garibaldi set off from Genoa with a ragtag team of volunteers who were able to capture Palermo and the rest of Sicily with little violence. Campania was tougher, but the Bourbons eventually surrendered Naples, and the Kingdom of the Two Sicilies was incorporated into the Kingdom of Italy.

But the effort to unite Italy into one cohesive nation did not stop there. At the time of unification, the differences in development and prosperity between the northern and southern halves of the country were significant. After years of being under feudal rule while the rest of Italy developed into small nation states resembling modern republics, the north was far ahead in terms of road and railroad construction, agriculture and industry, living conditions, and educational systems. Many of these disparities persist to this day.

WORLD WAR I
(1914-1919)

Newly united Italian citizens were challenged by the tumultuous onset of World War I, with leaders and intelligentsia divided on which side to join until the Allies offered to expand the country's territory into lands that were then under Austrian control. Predicting a short conflict, Italy did little to prepare, equip, or train their army and its leadership, leading to a major defeat at the 1917 **Battle of Caporetto.** The ensuing campaign against the Germans and Austro-Hungarians was long, bloody, and of little strategic import, with more than 650,000 Italians dead and more than a million wounded by 1919.

FASCISM
(1920-1945)

In the grim postwar period, droves of Italians emigrated to the United States, Argentina, and Australia, many embarking from Naples. Conditions for those who remained were poor, with little food and much discontentment with the unfulfilled promises of war. The Russian revolution caused a stir among workers worldwide, including in Italy, and frustration against the liberal government grew.

Amid the unrest, **Benito Mussolini** (1883-1945), a former Socialist Party newspaper editor, came to prominence, spreading fascism that relied heavily on widely circulated, successful propaganda. Mussolini announced a march on Rome in October 1922, and in response, King Emmanuel III promoted him to prime minister.

Historical Timeline

10th millennium BC	Earliest evidence of inhabitation of Matera.
8th century BC	Greek settlers arrive in Southern Italy; founding of Syracuse, which went on to become Magna Graecia's most important city.
7th century BC	Greek city of Neapolis (modern-day Naples) is founded.
560-450 BC	Three large Greek temples are built in Paestum.
413 BC	Syracuse, allied with Sparta, defeats Athens in the Peloponnesian War.
4th century BC	Seven temples built in Akragas, modern-day Agrigento, on the site now known as Valle dei Templi.
3rd century BC	Romans arrive in Campania and establish settlements.
272 BC	Taras (Taranto) conquered by the Romans.
212 BC	Syracuse, Sicily's last Greek stronghold, falls, putting all of Sicily under Roman control.
AD 109	Emperor Trajan builds the Via Traiana, connecting important areas of Puglia to Rome.
AD 27-37	Emperor Tiberius rules Roman Empire from his lavish Villa Jovis on Capri.
AD 79	Violent eruption of Mount Vesuvius destroys Roman cities of Pompeii and Herculaneum.
5th century	Campania area is ruled by Byzantines, Goths, and Lombards.
9th-11th centuries	Sicily under Arab rule.
10th-11th centuries	The Republic of Amalfi reaches its peak.
1071	Normans conquer Sicily, expelling the Islamic Caliphate from the island.
1139	Naples becomes part of the Norman kingdom that already includes Amalfi and Salerno.
1240-1250	Swabian Emperor Frederick II builds Castel del Monte in Puglia.
1266	Angevin dynasty gains control of Naples.
1302	Charles I of Anjou splits the Kingdom of Sicily from the Kingdom of Naples.
1442	Alfonso of Aragon conquers Naples and begins the Aragonese dynasty in Naples.

Order was restored for a time, until the elections of 1924 and the assassination of socialist politician Giacomo Matteotti, who criticized corruption and the authoritarian government. With Matteotti's prominent death to serve as an example, fascists in Parliament encountered little resistance when turning Italy into a virtual dictatorship. Large-scale public works projects kept workers employed, and propagandized cinema and radio glorified Mussolini's achievements. This was a time when Puglia and Sicily were very much returned to their roots as a breadbasket for the nation, with Mussolini pushing the regions to ramp up their agricultural production. Worried about the potential challenge the Mafia might present to his regime, the dictator also made

1504	Naples becomes a colony of Spain and two centuries of Spanish rule begin.
1693	Devastating earthquakes rock Catania and much of eastern Sicily.
1734	Bourbon dynasty begins in the Kingdom of Naples.
1738	Herculaneum is rediscovered, and 10 years later Pompeii is found again.
1752	Construction begins on the massive Reggia di Caserta royal palace.
1787	Goethe visits Sicily, making it a mandatory stop on the European Grand Tour.
1799	Parthenopean Republic established after bloody revolution in Naples; King Ferdinand IV flees to Palermo.
1815	Bourbons take back control of Naples.
1832	Construction begins on the Amalfi Coast Road.
1860	Garibaldi's Expedition of the Thousand lands in Sicily, hoping to unite the Kingdom of the Two Sicilies with the Kingdom of Italy.
1861	Italian city-states and regions unify into a single nation governed by a constitutional monarchy.
1943	Operation Avalanche, also known as the Landing of Salerno, during World War II takes place on September 9.
1943	Naples is liberated from German occupation September 27-30.
1945	The Surrender of Caserta is signed at the Reggia di Caserta on April 29, ending the Italian campaign of World War II.
1946	Italians choose to become a democratic republic in national referendum.
1952	Sassi di Matera evacuated due to poor living conditions.
1962	First Lady Jacqueline Kennedy spends a summer vacation on the Amalfi Coast and visits Capri.
1997	The Amalfi Coast, Pompeii, Herculaneum, and the Reggia di Caserta are listed as UNESCO World Heritage Sites.
2019	Matera named European Cultural Capital.
2022	Island of Procida is named the Italian Capital of Culture.

some progress cracking down on organized crime in the Italian south.

WORLD WAR II
(1939-1945)

Under Mussolini, Italy invaded Ethiopia and sided with Francisco Franco in the Spanish Civil War, leading to an ill-fated alliance with Hitler in World War II. Once again unprepared, Italy's military and civilian casualties were greater than during World War I, suffering demoralizing defeats in North Africa and the Balkans.

By the time U.S. and British troops landed in Sicily in July 1943, Mussolini and the Axis powers' decline was evident, but Germany wasn't ready to give up the fight, brutally struggling against Allied advances up the peninsula after the **Landing of Salerno** on September 9, 1943. After a four-day popular uprising in Naples against German forces, the allied troops arrived on October 1 for the **Liberation of Naples.**

Mussolini was shot attempting to escape to Switzerland in April 1945, but his authoritarian, conservative ideals remain popular among a small segment of Italians.

The Most-Bombed City in Italy

Industrial cities like Bari, Brindisi, and Taranto were all major bombing targets during World War II, but it was Naples, with more than 200 air strikes between 1940-1944, that was the most-bombed Italian city of the war. The approximate civilian toll ranges from 20,000 to 25,000. During bombing raids, the city's residents fled to the underground areas of the city, which can now be visited on Napoli Sotterranea (Naples Underground) tours. To cap it all off, Mount Vesuvius erupted in 1944 (its last major eruption), destroying towns around the volcano as well as planes from the United States Army Air Forces (USAAF) 340th Bombardment Group, based near Naples at the time.

The **Surrender of Caserta** was signed at Reggia di Caserta on April 29, 1945. This written agreement ended the Italian campaign of World War II and formalized the surrender of German forces in Italy.

POSTWAR AND CONTEMPORARY TIMES
(1946-Present)

A 1946 referendum was held to decide whether the Italian government would be a monarchy or democracy. A majority of Italians voted for democracy (although Naples as a city voted for the monarchy), leading to the adoption of a new constitution and the establishment of the **Italian Republic;** Sicily was one of five regions that retained its status as an autonomous region. Italy's recovery from the war was slow, and Naples had a significant uphill battle to rebuild from the extensive damage. In particular, the city of Matera, in the province of Basilicata, became a symbol of the poverty and squalid living conditions in Southern Italy. However, by the late 1950s and 1960s, Naples, along with much of Italy, began a period of growth. Postwar recovery was also hindered by the prevalence of the Mafia throughout the region. Industrialization was slower in Southern Italy than in other areas as well, which led to high unemployment and mass emigration, this time largely to the north of Italy and throughout Europe.

Largely untouched by the war, the Amalfi Coast and island of Capri quickly became popular tourist destinations in the 1950s and '60s. Capri offered the epitome of the la dolce vita, attracting the jet-set crowd of movie stars, royalty, and other rich celebrities.

Starting in the 1990s, political leaders in Southern Italy began a war on corruption and criminality as well as a focus on preserving and enhancing the region's historic treasures. The region has seen a remarkable transformation and is now one of Italy's top tourist destinations. Redevelopment has reached Sicily and Puglia as well, with unemployment in Sicily falling from 23% in 1990 to 11% in 2005, though these regions still tend to have less tourist infrastructure than Campania to the north.

Government and Economy

GOVERNMENT

Italy is a parliamentary republic, governed by a head of state (president), legislative branch (Parliament), executive branch (prime minister), and judicial branch. The country is divided into 20 regions, including Campania, Puglia, and Sicily, which have a great deal of control over their own legislation; Sicily, which is one of five regions in Italy with special autonomy, has a greater degree of individual legislative, administrative, and financial power.

The city of Naples serves as the capital for Campania, which reelected in center-left regional president Vincenzo De Luca in 2020. In Puglia, Bari is the capital, and President Michele Emiliano of the Democratic Party was elected to his second term in 2020, while Sicily (whose capital is Palermo) tends to be more center-right. Nello Musumeci has been the Sicilian president since 2017.

ECONOMY

Italy's economy is the world's eighth largest, but there are significant economic disparities between various Italian regions. The gap between the Northern and Southern Italian economy, evident since Italian unification in the late 19th century, has deep roots, from a feudalistic social system that retained its hold of Southern Italy to the dominance of the Mafia in the region. It is estimated that 70% of unemployed Italians reside in the southern part of the country. That said, this economic disparity is beginning to change, with a GDP growing at almost double the rate of Northern Italy's, and increased investment in infrastructure and tourism.

Campania, Puglia, and Sicily are all known for their agricultural production, from canned tomatoes and pasta, to buffalo mozzarella and Burrata di Andra, to olive oil produced in Puglia. All three regions are noted for their wine, including unique volcanic wines grown on the slopes of Mount Etna and marsala, a fortified wine from western Sicily.

Industry

Besides agriculture, other industries include high-end automotive production like the Alfa Romeo facilities outside Naples, and the shipping and aerospace industries. Naples, Taranto, and Palermo are major ports for cargo transport and some of the Mediterranean's busiest port cities. Traditional crafts play a smaller yet integral part of the regional economy, from ceramics, to coral carving, to woodworking, all keeping the nation's "Made in Italy" movement going strong.

Fishing remains a major industry, source of income, and way of life for many coastal cities in Southern Italy, who bring in significant yields of sardines, anchovies, and mussels.

Tourism

Italy is the fifth most visited country in the world and attracted more than 94 million visitors in 2019, before a steep drop-off due to COVID-19 travel restrictions. Though still less visited than Rome, Venice, or Tuscany, Campania, Puglia, and Sicily are in the top 10 most popular destinations in Italy. Tourism still tends to be more well organized in Campania than Puglia or Sicily, but the latter regions record a notable increase in visitors every year.

Some cities have been taking a deeper look at how to handle the mass influx of tourists, especially on the Amalfi Coast, from establishing a set route for visiting popular sites like Pompeii, revisiting ferry schedules, and investigating other ways to help visitors get around the island more easily. Cultural initiatives like Slow Tourism are designed to address the impact of overtourism, encouraging travelers to slow down and get a deeper understanding of the places they visit.

People and Culture

DEMOGRAPHY

Italy as a whole has more than 60 million inhabitants; of the regions covered in this book, Campania is home to about 5.8 million people, Apulia to 4 million, and Sicily to 5 million. Naples is Italy's third-largest city, with 3.1 million inhabitants; the largest cities in Puglia and Sicily, respectively, are Bari (320,000 inhabitants) and Palermo (680,000 inhabitants). The average life expectancy is relatively high, 85 years for females and 80 for males, with a median age of 45.5 and plenty of people pushing 100.

IMMIGRATION

Until the late 20th century, Italy was often more associated with emigration than immigration. Today, foreign-born residents make up close to 9 percent of the total population, with the largest immigrant communities coming from African countries (including Morocco), Romania, Albania, Poland, and China. Many move to Rome or cities in Northern Italy to find jobs as day laborers, builders, cleaners, dishwashers, and caretakers. You'll find second-generation immigrations working as chefs in fusion restaurants, attending schools, or appearing on TV quiz shows or the news.

Immigration from Syria and sub-Saharan Africa to Europe has become a crisis, leading to a wave of anti-immigrant sentiment and policy. Though Italians generally favor legal immigration, it's a hot political issue.

RELIGION

Catholicism is the dominant religion in Italy, though the country is growing more secular. That doesn't stop almost every town from celebrating its patron saint with festivals each year.

Islam, Buddhism, and Orthodox Christianity are also growing in Italy. In Naples, the Jewish community dates to the first century under Roman control of the city. The 15th-16th centuries brought much persecution, with all Jews being forced to leave in 1541. In the 19th century, the community grew thanks to the thriving branch of the Rothschild family bank in Naples. Today the Jewish community of Naples is only around 200 people.

LANGUAGE

Modern Italian derives from Latin. Dante Alighieri (1265-1321) was the first to codify and utilize the dialects spoken during the Renaissance, but there is a big difference in the accent you'll hear in the north and the one you'll hear in Rome and central Italy, or farther south around Naples and the Amalfi Coast, Puglia, or Sicily.

Neapolitan

In Naples and much of Southern Italy, your ear will pick up a highly expressive and unique dialect called Neapolitan. Though it's not officially a language and isn't taught in school, the dialect sounds distinctly different from Italian even though it shares a great deal of vocabulary. The pronunciation of Neapolitan is what largely sets it apart, although there are significant grammatical differences as well. The dialect can even be almost incomprehensible to Italian speakers. Yet one thing Neapolitans excel at is the use of highly demonstrative gestures, which is a seemingly integral part of communication in the area. Stay long enough and you'll likely find yourself gesturing to communicate as well. The Neapolitan dialect is indelibly linked with the cultural history of Naples, thanks to an especially rich musical, theatrical, and literary heritage that is still appreciated around the world today.

Griko

A remnant of Magna Graecia, there are a few small communities in Southern Italy, especially Puglia, where Griko, an Italian-Greek dialect, is still spoken. This precious connection to Southern Italian history is unfortunately endangered, with only 40,000 or so remaining speakers.

Sicilian

Spoken in Sicily, Calabria, and the southern part of Puglia, Sicilian is distinct enough from standard Italian to be considered its own separate language. The story of the Sicilian dialect is the story of the island itself, influenced by Ancient Greek, Arabic, Norman, Germanic, and Spanish languages. Some Sicilian words sound so different from standard Italian, even native speakers may find themselves scratching their heads: Bor example, standard Italian B's are often turned into B's in Sicilian, and double L's become D's. Today, there are estimated to be over five million Sicilian speakers worldwide.

LITERATURE AND PHILOSOPHY

Southern Italy and the surrounding areas have been important cultural centers since ancient Greek and Roman times. Many of the adventures in Homer's *Odyssey* are associated with locations across Southern Italy, including the Faraglioni dei Ciclopi, off Sicily's eastern coast. South of Paestum, the town Elea (Velia) was home to the Greek philosopher Parmenides, founder of Eleaticism, an important pre-Socratic school of philosophy that also counted philosopher and mathematician Zeno of Elea as a member. Naples was later a center of Epicureanism, a school of philosophy arguing that pleasure or happiness is the chief good in life. The great Greek mathematician, Archimedes, was born in the Italian town of Syracuse.

Classic and Renaissance Literature

Roman orator Cicero lived and worked in western Sicily for several years, and Roman writer and natural philosopher Pliny the Elder

was among the many victims of the eruption of Mount Vesuvius in AD 79 that destroyed Pompeii and Herculaneum. His nephew, **Pliny the Younger,** wrote two letters to the great historian Tacitus describing the eruption of Vesuvius and death of his uncle; the letters serve as remarkable pieces of historical evidence of the tragic events. The Roman poet **Virgil** (70-19 BC), author of the epic poem *The Aeneid*, is also associated with Naples, from the legend of the egg he placed below the Castel dell'Ovo to the mysterious allure of his supposed tomb west of Naples (in fact, it is not his tomb at all).

Naples was a place of pilgrimage for other writers, including Dante Alighieri (1265-1321), Francesco Petrarca (1304-1374), and Giovanni Boccaccio (1313-1375), who lived there for years and used the city as the setting for *The Decameron* and later works. A literary community known as the Sicilian School, founded in the 13th century, had a marked influence on writers like Dante; their poetry is credited with the coining of the term Doce Stil Novo, or "sweet new style," and helping in the creation of the modern Italian language. Influential philosopher and theologian **San Tommaso d'Aquino** (St. Thomas Aquinas) also lived and worked in Naples in the 13th century.

Contemporary Writers

Sicily's most famous writer is probably Giuseppe Tomasi di Lampedusa, whose novel, *The Leopard,* takes place during the Risorgimento movement to unite the Italian peninsula. On the lighter side, Sicilian author Andrea Camilleri's Inspector Salvo Montalbano series, written between 1994-2020, are tremendously popular across Italy and have been adapted into an extremely popular TV series. Other recent examples of Southern Italian authors include Neapolitan writer **Roberto Saviano,** who gained fame for his stories of the Camorra crime syndicate; and bestselling author **Elena Ferrante,** whose Neapolitan novels have captivated readers around the world.

VISUAL ARTS

Architecture

With its remarkable churches, royal palaces, and castles, Southern Italy has an incredibly rich architectural heritage. Below many cities lie ancient Greek and Roman ruins, where you can walk down Roman streets and see ruins of markets as well as a theater where performances were once held. Above the ancient city, layer upon layer of history has creates modern-day cities like Naples and Palermo.

GREEK AND ROMAN RUINS

The region of Southern Italy is home to many remarkable ancient architectural treasures. Just south of Salerno at Paestum you can see some of the best preserved ancient **Greek temples** and explore the Greek and Roman ruins of the ancient city. The archaeological sites of Pompeii and Herculaneum offer the rare chance to walk through ancient Roman towns, and Villa Jovis on Capri is the once-lavish villa where Emperor Tiberius ruled the Roman Empire. In Sicily, the sites of Selinunte, Segesta, and Valle dei Templi offer Greek ruins as spectacular as any you might find in Athens, and Villa Romana del Casale is another sprawling example of an elite ancient Roman's country home.

FORTIFIED CITIES

Centuries of turmoil gave the entire coastal region a great deal of defensive architecture, such as **castles,** from the Castel dell'Ovo in Naples to Castel del Monte in Puglia. Many of these fortifications were built in the tumultuous Norman and Swabian periods, when areas of Southern Italy frequently changed hands and rulers needed to protect their lands from foreign invaders.

GOTHIC AND BAROQUE CHURCHES

In Naples, the Complesso Monumentale di San Lorenzo Maggiore is a fine example of **Gothic architecture.** Many churches in throughout Southern Italy were remodeled during the Baroque period, from the Duomo di Amalfi to the Cattedrale di Salerno. Destructive 17th-century earthquakes in Sicily gave builders of the time an opportunity to rebuild towns like Noto and Modica in the Baroque style, and the Apulian city of Lecce is particularly known for its Baroque architecture.

ROYAL PALACES

Southern Italy is home to many splendid **royal palaces.** In the 17th century, Domenico Fontana (1543-1607) designed the grand Palazzo Reale on the waterfront in Naples, and later Ferdinando Fuga (1699-1782) added the lavish court theater inside. Next came a royal palace in Capodimonte, now the Museo e Real Bosco di Capodimonte, which was built in 1738 in the hills above Naples by the Bourbon King Charles VII as a royal palace for hunting. The jewel in the crown of royal Campania's palaces is the Reggia di Caserta, a masterpiece of 18th-century architecture designed by prominent architect Luigi Vanvitelli (1700-1773). It is one of the largest palaces in Europe, with 1,200 rooms and truly immense monumental gardens.

In Palermo, the Palazzo dei Normanni is a stunning example of a royal residence, first constructed in the ninth century but renovated and expanded through the centuries.

Painting

For a glimpse of incredible frescoes and pictorial decorations from the ancient world, a stroll through the ruins of Pompeii and Herculaneum is a one-of-a-kind experience. Many fine examples of frescoes uncovered at the archaeological sites are on display at Museo Archeologico Nazionale in Naples. You can go back even further in time at the Museo Archeologico Nazionale in **Paestum,** as you admire the Tomb of the Diver, a rare example of an ancient Greek burial tomb with painted figures.

The **Neapolitan School** of painting only began in the 17th century. In 1606, Caravaggio (1571-1610) arrived in Naples, and though he only spent about eight months in the city, his stay created a lasting impression on many artists of the day, including Battistello Caracciolo (1578-1635). In Naples, you'll find impressive works by Caravaggio, including *The Seven Works of Mercy* at the Pio Monte della Misericordia, *Martirio di Sant'Orsola* (*The Martyrdom of Saint Ursula*) at the Gallerie d'Italia (likely his final painting), and other works at the Museo di Capodimonte. In addition, you'll find many paintings in churches and museums in Naples by local artists who were inspired by Caravaggio's dramatic use of chiaroscuro, defined by its strong contrast between light and dark.

Also very active in the 17th century, the noted Italian painter Luca Giordano (1634-1705) was born in Naples and contributed his lively and particularly colorful style to many churches. Exploring the city's churches, you'll also find masterpieces by local artist Francesco Solimena (1657-1747), who was the most important painter in the 1700s in Naples. In addition to the churches in Naples, head to the Museo di Capodimonte to explore an extensive collection of paintings from the 13th-18th centuries.

By the 19th century, painting styles had become decidedly more naturalistic and romantic, and the **Posillipo School** of painters were drawn to the natural beauty of the Gulf of Naples. Domenico Morelli (1823-1901), a leading artist of the 19th century, was known for his fine historical and religious paintings. He was also an influential professor at the Accademia di Belle Arti di Napoli (Naples Academy of Fine Arts) and later its president. Morelli was the designer of the mosaics depicting the Triumph of Christ and the Twelve Apostles on the facade of the Duomo di Amalfi.

In the 1970s, the **Transavanguardia movement,** an Italian version of neo-expressionism, was developed by a group of artists in Naples, including Francesco Clemente and Mimmo Paladino. Visit the Madre (Museo d'Arte Contemporanea Donnaregina) museum in Naples to see fine

examples of their work as well as pieces by other top Italian and international artists from the past 50 years.

Decorative Arts and Crafts

The creative talents of generations of artisans have always brought an artistic touch to daily life in Sicily. A strong artisan tradition still thrives in the dramatic Baroque-influenced **presepe** (nativity), still hand crafted in Naples, and the intricate **intarsia** (inlaid woodwork) in Sorrento.

Ceramic production is traditional in the entire area, especially terra cotta ceramics in Sicily. Since ancient times, **coral** and **cameo** carving has been a tradition in the Gulf of Naples, especially in Torre del Greco, located between Naples and Pompeii.

Famous for producing European porcelain, Capodimonte flourished under Bourbon control of Naples. The Real Fabbrica di Capodimonte (Royal Factory of Capodimonte) produced remarkable porcelain pieces from 1743-1759, and many fine examples can be seen at the Museo di Capodimonte in Naples. After the Real Fabbrica di Capodimonte was transferred to Madrid, **porcelain production** continued to be a popular local craft throughout the 18th century. Some small factories still produce pieces in the Capodimonte style today.

MUSIC, THEATER, AND DANCE
Music

Nothing captures the spirit of Naples quite like traditional Neapolitan songs. The city's contributions to musical history began in the 16th century, when many important conservatories were founded. During the baroque period, Alessandro Scarlatti was the founder of the Neapolitan school of opera and was known for his operas and chamber cantatas. Known as the "conservatory of Europe," Naples was noted not only for its many important composers, such as Domenico Cimarosa, but also for attracting other famous composers like the young

Mozart, who was smitten with the city, as well as Gioachino Rossini. Opened in 1737, the Teatro di San Carlo is the oldest continuously active opera house in the world.

Starting in the 1800s, traditional Neapolitan popular songs, called canzone napoletana, took center stage. Songs like "O Sole Mio," "Torna a Surriento," and "Funiculì Funiculà" became internationally known and are just as popular today. Neapolitan tenor Enrico Caruso had great success in America and was an important ambassador of opera and Neapolitan song around the world. Later, the recordings of Renato Carosone had an international success with songs like "Tu Vuò fà l'Americano," which was later performed by Sophia Loren in the movie It Started in Naples with Clark Gable. In Naples, you can enjoy a live performance of iconic Neapolitan songs at Napulitanata (www.napulitanata.com).

Nineteenth-century opera composer Vincenzo Bellini, best known for his opera Norma, was born in Catania, in Sicily. And, though the song "Nel Blu Dipinto Di Blu" may not sound familiar, you may know it better than you think: This is the full name of the song "Volare," which was written by Apulian musician Domenico Modugno, who was born in Polignano a Mare.

Theater

Naples's theatrical heritage is rich: Eduardo Scarpetta (1853-1925) was one of the most notable theatrical actors and writers working in the Neapolitan dialect from the end of the 1800s to the beginning of the 1900s. He created an artistic dynasty that was continued by his son Eduardo de Filippo (1900-1984) and siblings, Peppino and Tatiana de Filippo.

Eduardo de Filippo was extremely active as an actor, playwright, screenwriter, and author, considered one of the most important Italian artists of the 20th century.

Naples wouldn't be Naples without Totò (1898-1967), one of the most characteristic and entertaining actors, often considered the most popular Italian comedian of all time. Neapolitan through and through, Totò first gained success as a stage actor before appearing in many films from the 1940s-1960s, many of which are still regularly aired on TV. One of the classics is Totò, Peppino e la Malafemmina, featuring Totò and Peppino de Filippo and including the beautiful song "Malafemmena," written by Totò.

A Southern Italian tradition, it's still possible to take in the unique experience of puppet opera (opera dei pupi) in Palermo, an artform that emerged in the region in the early 19th century. Though there are only a few performers keeping this theatrical tradition alive, a visit to the Museo Internazionale delle Marionette Antonio Pasqualino is a great way to get some background on opera dei pupi and find out where you can see one in action.

Dance

Popular throughout Southern Italy, the Tarantella is a folk dance, with regional variations connected to cities and towns throughout the region. Dating back to the 1700s, it's a lively and flirtatious dance typically performed by couples or groups of couples, and accompanied by tambourines and castanets. You can see performances of the dance in Sorrento at the Sorrento Musical or the Tarantella Show at the Cinema Teatro Armida.

Essentials

Transportation

GETTING THERE
By Air

The **Aeroporto Internazionale di Napoli** (NAP; Viale F. Ruffo di Calabria; tel. 081/789-6111; www.aeroportodinapoli.it), also referred to as the Capodichino airport, is the Naples International Airport, located about 3.7 miles (6 km) northeast of Naples city center. Although it's not a large airport, it handles more than 10 million passengers a year and is the main airport for Naples and the region of Campania, including travelers

Transportation 455
Visas and Officialdom . . 461
Festivals and Events 463
Recreation 464
Food 465
Shopping 468
Accommodations 468
Health and Safety 470
Conduct
    and Customs 471
Practical Details 472
Traveler Advice 476

Coronavirus in Southern Italy

At the time of writing in April 2021, Southern Italy was moderately impacted by the effects of the coronavirus, but the situation was constantly evolving. Throughout Italy, numbers of cases are constantly monitored, and zones with varying levels of closures are instituted to manage and reduce the spread. Zone yellow has the lightest restrictions, while zones orange and red indicate more closures and restrictions. Face masks and social distancing are the norm throughout the region, but keep in mind that even as restrictions ease, some towns and cities may continue to require face masks both indoors and outdoors. Be prepared to follow local regulations, including possible curfews, and to wear masks on public transportation, ferries, and trains.

Now more than ever, Moon encourages its readers to be courteous and ethical in their travel. We ask travelers to be respectful to residents, and mindful of the evolving situation in their chosen destination when planning their trip.

BEFORE YOU GO

- Check local websites (listed below) for **local restrictions** and the **overall health status** of the destination and your point of origin. If you're traveling to or from an area that is currently a COVID-19 hotspot, you may want to reconsider your trip.

- Get **vaccinated** if your health status allows, and if possible, take a **coronavirus test** with enough time to receive your results before your departure. Some destinations may require proof of vaccination or a negative COVID test result before arrival, along with other tests and potentially a self-quarantine period, once you've arrived. Check local requirements and factor these into your plans.

- If you plan to fly, check with your airline, the Ministero della Salute, and your government's health authority for updated **travel requirements.** Some airlines may be taking more steps than others to help you travel safely, such as limited occupancy; check their websites for more information before buying your ticket, and consider a very early or very late flight to limit exposure. Flights may be more infrequent, with increased cancellations.

visiting the Amalfi Coast, Sorrentine Peninsula, and the islands of Capri, Ischia, and Procida.

Naples is home to the region's largest airport, but the **Aeroporto di Palermo Falcone e Borsellino** (PMO; Cinisi; tel. 800/541-880; www.aeroportodipalermo.it), **Aeroporto di Catania-Fontanarossa** (CTA; Via Fontanarossa; tel. 095/723-9111; www.aeroporto.catania.it), and **Aeroporto Internazionale di Bari** (BRI; Viale Enzo Ferrari; tel. 080/580-0200; www.aeroportidipuglia.it) are regional hubs, to which you can occasionally find connecting flights that may be cheaper or more convenient than flying to Naples.

FROM NORTH AMERICA

Direct flights from the United States to Naples are very limited, but **United** (www.united.com) offers one daily direct flight from Newark to Naples during the peak travel season, from the end of May through the beginning of October. However, there are more than 50 daily nonstop flights from the United States to Italy, with most landing in Rome or Milan. There are many connecting flights daily from Rome and Milan to Naples. **Alitalia** (www.alitalia.com), **Delta** (www.delta.com), **American** (www.aa.com), **United** (www.united.com), and **Air Canada** (www.aircanada.com), along with

---

Previous: countryside around Camporeale.

- Check the website of any museums, archaeological sites, and other venues you wish to patronize to confirm that they're open, if their hours have been adjusted, and to learn about any specific visitation requirements, such as mandatory **reservations** or **limited occupancy.**

- Pack **hand sanitizer, a thermometer,** and plenty of **face masks.** Many businesses offer hand sanitizing and temperature stations at the entrance. Be prepared to have your temperature taken before entering businesses or getting on a ferry.

- Assess the risk of entering crowded spaces, joining group tours, and taking public transit.

- Expect general disruptions. Events may be postponed or cancelled, and some tours and venues may require reservations, enforce limits on the number of guests, be operating during different hours than the ones listed, or be closed entirely. Restaurants may also be required to collect your name and contact information in the event that contact tracing is required.

RESOURCES

- **Ministero della Salute** (www.salute.gov.it): Italy's health ministry offers the latest news on the COVID-19 situation in Italy as well as travel information and restrictions. The pages offering coronavirus information are all available in English.

- **Immuni** (www.immuni.italia.it): This app was created by the Italian government and Ministero della Salute to alert people who may have come into contact with someone who tests positive for COVID-19. The app uses Bluetooth technology and does not collect your personal information for privacy.

- **Italia** (www.italia.it): Italy's national tourist office offers updated information on traveling to Italy, tips for how to travel responsibly, and COVID-19 updates for tourists

- **World Health Organization** (www.who.int/emergencies/diseases/novel-coronavirus-2019/travel-advice): Visit the World Health Organization for global information on the pandemic and travel.

their European partners, operate most of the flights from major North American cities to destinations in Italy, with connecting service to Naples.

To reach Palermo, Catania, or Bari from North America, you'll likely need a connecting flight as well, likely in Milan or another European hub. Flights are offered by many of the same airlines listed above.

FROM EUROPE AND THE UK
Alitalia (www.alitalia.com) operates most domestic flights within Italy to Naples, Bari, or either of the major Sicilian airports. Direct flights are available from most major cities across Italy as well as from more than 80 European and international cities. There are many direct flights from

London, Paris, Frankfurt, and Amsterdam via **Air France** (www.airfrance.com), **BA** (www.britishairways.com), or **Lufthansa** (www.lufthansa.com). Low-cost airlines like **EasyJet** (www.easyjet.com), **Vueling** (www.vueling.com), and **Ryanair** (www.ryanair.com) also fly from many major European cities.

FROM AUSTRALIA AND NEW ZEALAND
There are no direct flights from Australia or New Zealand to Southern Italy, or even to larger cities like Rome. **Quantas** (www.qantas.com), **Emirates** (www.emirates.com), and **Etihad** (www.etihad.com) operate daily departures to Italy from Sydney, Melbourne, and Perth. Most flights require a transfer in

Dubai or Abu Dhabi, and total travel time is around 24 hours. Travelers from Auckland can transfer in Australia with the above airlines or fly **Qatar** (www.qatarairways.com), **Korean Air** (www.koreanair.com), and **Emirates** on single-stop flights with transfers in Hamad, Seoul, or Dubai. You will then need to catch a connecting flight to reach Campania, Puglia, or Sicily. The low-cost airline **flydubai** (www.flydubai.com) based in Dubai offers direct flights from Dubai to Naples.

FROM SOUTH AFRICA

There are no direct flights from South Africa to Southern Italy, but **Alitalia** flies direct between Johannesburg and Rome in about 10 hours. From Rome, you will need to catch a connecting flight. You can fly from Durban, Cape Town, and Johannesburg to Rome with **Ethiopian Airlines, Qatar, Emirates,** and **Turkish Airlines** with a transfer in that airline's respective hub.

By Train

Though Europe has a good train network, travel between countries can still be slow. Traveling to Southern Italy by train will likely require arriving in Naples first, though it is possible to take the train from Rome or Milan to destinations in Puglia. There are daily overnight departures from Paris to Naples onboard the **Thello** (www.thello.com); for the most comfortable experience, purchase a berth in one of the sleeping cabins. There are also many trains from northern European cities to Naples, often with a transfer in Milan or Rome. Single tickets can be purchased through www.trenitalia.it. A rail pass from **Eurail** (www.eurail.com) or **Rail Europe** (www.raileurope.com) can be worthwhile if you're traveling to many European countries.

Due to massive government investment in high-speed trains over the last 10 years, traveling to Naples or Salerno from major cities like Milan, Rome, Florence, and Venice is fast, easy, and convenient. Trains are comfortable, clean, have Wi-Fi, and food and drink is served onboard. The state-owned **Trenitalia** (www.trenitalia.com) and private **Italo** (www.italo.it) both provide frequent daily departures to the Napoli Centrale station in Naples and to Salerno. The Trenitalia **Frecciarossa** (red arrow) service is slightly more expensive and frequent, making it popular with business travelers. Journey times vary significantly, depending on the type of train and number of stops or transfers, but the high-speed direct journey time to Naples is about 1 hour 15 minutes from Rome, about 3 hours from Florence, about 5 hours from Venice, and about 4 hours 30 minutes from Milan. Salerno's train station is also served by both Trenitalia and Italo trains, with the travel time taking 35-40 minutes more than to Naples. Buy your tickets in advance online or at the train station.

Trenitalia also operates local and intercity trains throughout Italy, to hubs in Puglia and Sicily. These are slower and make more stops, but tickets are fairly cheap, a very affordable way to reach Southern Italy from destinations across Italy.

By Bus

Buses are an inexpensive, if much slower, alternative to trains. **Flixbus** (www.flixbus.com) is the main company offering bus service to and from many points throughout Italy. Buses seat around 40 passengers with one-way tickets starting as low as €4.99 and going up to €50 for longer journeys. All are equipped with free Wi-Fi, electrical outlets, restrooms, and baggage storage.

By Boat

Naples is one of the busiest ports in Italy, handling a large number of ferries, cruise ships, and commercial vessels daily. Many of the cruise ship companies offering Mediterranean cruises stop in Naples, usually at the Stazione Marittima. Naples is well connected by ferries from destinations across Italy, including Sicily and Sardinia, as well as destinations around the Mediterranean. Ferries from around the Gulf of Naples, such as Sorrento and Capri, arrive at either the Molo Beverello near the Stazione Marittima or the Calata Porta di Massa. Ferries from Ischia, the Aeolian Islands, and Ponza also arrive at the Mergellina port in Naples.

Farther south, Salerno continues to grow as a popular cruise ship destination. Ferry service also connects many ports around the Mediterranean to Salerno. Ferry service to the Amalfi Coast and Capri is also available seasonally from April-October. Palermo is also a common port of call for cruise ships.

By Car

It's usually possible to travel across the borders of countries that are members of the European Union without a document check, under the **Schengen Agreement.** But recent issues with immigration mean some governments have reinstated a bit more control. Entering Italy usually isn't a problem, but leaving Italy can be trickier as border officials check incoming vehicles.

Italy's **highways** (autostrade) are generally very good. Drivers collect tickets at booths as they enter the network and pay tolls in cash or credit, based on distance traveled, upon exiting. **Autostrade** (www.autostrade.it) manages highways and provides real-time traffic information in English. Signage should be familiar to international drivers; to review the rules of the Italian road, visit the **Italian Office of Tourism** (www.italia.com).

GETTING AROUND
By Plane

The advent of cheap domestic airlines throughout Italy makes them a pretty hard option to pass up for people traveling between Campania and Sicily, or Puglia and Sicily. Tickets for the 1-hour flight from Naples to Palermo can be bought for as little as €17, with about a dozen departures per day on providers like easyJet (www.easyjet.com) and Volotea (www.volotea.com). From Bari, it's a 1-hour 10-minute flight to Palermo (from €17), with many flight options to choose from.

By Train

Trenitalia (www.trenitalia.com) operates frequent train service between Naples and many other Italian hubs daily, with travel times varying wildly depending on the type of train. Traveling by train to Sicily (which involves loading the train onto a ferry at Vila San Giovanni) usually takes between 8-10 hours, while getting to Puglia takes 5-6 hours. Though most cities and large towns and Sicily and Puglia are fairly well connected by train, cheap domestic flights may be a better option for travelers with limited time hopping from region to region.

The **Circumvesuviana train** line operated by EAV (www.eavsrl.it) connects Naples with the archaeological sites of Pompeii and Herculaneum as well as Sorrento.

By Car and Scooter

Cars can be rented from **Avis** (www.avisautonoleggio.it), **Europcar** (www.europcar.com), **Sixt** (www.sixt.com), **Maggiore** (www.maggiore.com), **Hertz** (www.hertz.com), and other companies upon arrival at pretty much any airport in the region, as well as from rental offices located in most cities and larger towns, or with smaller local companies along the Amalfi Coast. **Skyscanner** (www.skyscanner) and **Kayak** (www.kayak.com) can help find the best rental prices.

Cites like Naples and Palermo are famous for their chaotic traffic, and driving in the city is not for the timid. Given the extensive public transportation systems, challenging parking, and the **limited traffic zone** (ZTL) in the historic centers, getting around by car in cities is not recommended. It's best to park at a supervised lot and continue to explore the city via public transportation.

Roads in Sicily and Puglia are fairly easy to drive (though inland Sicily is famous for seemingly perpetual construction and detours), but the Amalfi Coast Road is famous for its twists and turns. It's not the easiest to negotiate and parking is limited, so getting around the area by car can be more of a hassle than it's worth. Scooters are a popular choice because they're easier to maneuver along the winding road and are usually easier to park as well. That said, renting a car for your time in Sicily or Puglia can be a great option, offering maximum flexibility and the chance to discover tiny villages and beautiful countryside off the beaten path.

RULES AND DOCUMENTATION

You'll need a **passport** and a **driver's license** if you plan to rent a scooter or car. (Specify automatic transmission for cars if you're unfamiliar with manual drive.) For U.S. citizens, an **international driver's permit** is not required but can help you avoid confusion if you're pulled over. It's available from **AAA** (www.aaa.com) for $20. The **minimum driving age** in Italy is 18. Police and Carabinieri frequently set up control posts along roads and randomly stop cars. The **blood alcohol limit** in Italy is 0.5, which is lower than in the United States and UK (both 0.8) but is on par with most European nations.

DRIVING TIPS

Whether you rent a car or scooter, always get the maximum insurance. Anything can happen on Italian roads, especially the ones around Naples, Palermo, and the Amalfi Coast. Most cars are manual transmission, so be sure to request or reserve automatic if you're not comfortable tackling the mountains and tight curves of the Amalfi Coast with a stick shift.

In contrast to the relaxing atmosphere in much of Southern Italy, drivers in the area are usually in a hurry. Passing is a very common practice. If traffic seems to want to move faster than you're comfortable, find a straight section to slow down or pull over to let traffic pass. Naturally, if you're the one passing, pay extra careful attention to the curves, taking advantage of the mirrors placed on the side of the road in especially tight curves for guidance. Scooters, motorcycles, and cyclists can appear very suddenly around curves, so it's best for drivers who are unfamiliar with the road to go with the flow of traffic.

By Bus

Regional bus systems provide fairly good connections to most towns and cities throughout Southern Italy, and are often the only option for public transportation when trains are not an option. On the **Amalfi Coast,** buses are operated by **SITA SUD** (www.sitasudtrasporti.it), with Amalfi as the central hub. For the **Sorrentine Peninsula,** buses are operated by both **SITA SUD** (www.sitasudtrasporti.it) and **EAV** (www.eavsrl.it). While you're in Naples, you can get around on public buses operated by **ANM** (www.anm.it). The large bus transit network covers the city center day and night.

There are myriad bus companies operating in various regions of Sicily, but some of the most common are **Interbus** (www.interbus.it) and Azienda Siciliana Trasporti, or **AST** (www.aziendasicilianatrasporti.it). In Puglia, **Ferrovie Sud Est** www.fseonline.it) offers some of the most extensive routes.

In areas with a high level of tourist infrastructure, taking a bus geared more toward travelers than local commuters may actually make more sense. **City Sightseeing** (www.city-sightseeing.it) hop-on hop-off buses operate in Naples and run between Amalfi, Ravello, and other spots on the Amalfi Coast.

For the most part, tickets for city bus systems must be **validated** upon boarding the bus; this is done with a small machine located near the driver. Controllers do occasionally check passengers and will fine anyone without a ticket. Daily and multiday travel cards are available in most areas and can be more convenient and affordable than single tickets.

By Boat

Ferries are the most comfortable and scenic modes of transportation between destinations in the Gulf of Naples and Gulf of Salerno, and can also be an exciting way to travel between

Naples and Palermo. **Travelmar** (www. travelmar.it) and **Alicost** (www.alicost.it) are the main ferry companies connecting Salerno, the Amalfi Coast, Capri, and Sorrento. On the Amalfi Coast, ferry service runs between most major towns from April through the beginning of November.

The Naples port (www.porto.napoli.it) is very large and offers frequent ferry connections to destinations around the Gulf of Naples, though service is reduced during the winter months. Palermo's port (www.adsppalermo.it) is located on the western side of the city and is the point of arrival and departure for ferries from Naples (operated by GNV, www.gnv. it; or Tirrenia, https://en.tirrenia.it), as well as international destinations and hydrofoils to the Aeolian Islands in the summer. Ferries to the Aeolian Islands operated by Liberty Lines (www.libertylines.it) and Siremar (https://carontetourist.it) also depart from Milazzo and Messina. To get to the Aegadian Islands, you'll need to depart from Trapani or Marsala (ferries also operated by Liberty Lines).

You can purchase tickets in advance online from most ferry companies, which is a good idea during the busy summer months. Tickets are also available to purchase before boarding from ticket booths in the ports.

By Taxi

In many Italian cities, rather than hailing a cab from the street, you'll find them stationed at taxi stands near large squares, at the train station, and near the port, 24 hours a day. They usually have signage that indicates whether cars are free or in service. Usually, especially in larger cities, taxis operate 24 hours, and vehicles for special-needs passengers are available.

Taxi fares in most heavily touristed areas may be more expensive than you'd expect, especially on weekends and at night. They're usually calculated according to time and distance, though places like the Amalfi Coast have set fares for common destinations. It is essential to notify the driver before departure that you want the fixed-rate fare.

Visas and Officialdom

PASSPORTS AND VISAS

United States and Canada

Travelers from the United States and Canada do not need a visa to enter Italy for visits of 90 days or fewer. All that's required is a passport valid at least three months after your intended departure from the European Union.

EU/Schengen

Citizens from all 27 countries belonging to the European Union as well as citizens of the non-EU member states of the European Economic Area (EEA) and Switzerland can travel visa-free within the European Union. A passport or National Identity Card is all that is needed for entering Italy.

UK

After the United Kingdom's exit from the European Union, all UK citizens can enter Italy with UK passport without a visa for visits of fewer that 90 days within any 180-day period. Check your passports in advance as they must be less than 10 years old and valid for at least 6 months beyond your travel dates.

Australia and New Zealand

Visas are not required for Australian or New Zealand citizens who visit Italy for 90 days or fewer within any 180-day period in the Schengen Area (European Union). New Zealanders between the ages of 18 and 30 can apply for a special working holiday visa at the Italian Embassy in Wellington.

South Africa

Visas are required to visit Italy from South Africa and can be obtained through **Capago** (tel. 087/231-0313; www.capago.eu). The application process begins online and requires stopping into one of the visa application centers located in Cape Town, Durban, Sandton, and Pretoria. Getting a visa takes two weeks and there is a fee.

Electronic Registration

In 2023, a pre-travel electronic registration system (European Travel Information and Authorization System, or ETIAS) is planned for travelers from Schengen visa-waiver countries like the UK and United States. If traveling in or after 2022, be sure to check with the state department or foreign affairs ministry in your home country for more information.

CONSULATES

The majority of foreign embassies and consulates in Italy are located in Rome. However, the **U.S. Consulate General in Naples** (Piazza della Repubblica, Naples; tel. 081/583-8111; https://it.usembassy.gov/embassy-consulates/naples) offers passport and emergency services for U.S. citizens. There is also a U.S. Consulate in Palermo (Via Giovan Battista Vaccarini, 1). For emergencies, call the consulate at 081/583-8111, which is a 24-hour hotline. For help with **lost or stolen passports,** you can apply in person for same-day emergency passports at the consulate in Naples. The consulate is closed during Italian and U.S. holidays. For emergencies while abroad or to report lost or stolen passports, call the **U.S. Department of State** (tel. 1-888/407-4747 from the United States, 1-202/501-4444 from other countries; 8am-8pm EST Mon.-Fri.).

CUSTOMS

Travelers entering Italy are expected to declare any cash over €10,000 and are prohibited from importing animal-based food products into the country. Duty-free imports for passengers from outside the European Union are limited to one liter of hard alcohol, two liters of wine, 200 cigarettes, 50 cigars, and 250 grams of smoking tobacco.

Bags are likely to be heavier upon leaving Italy than they were when you packed. U.S. citizens are limited to $800 worth of goods deemed for personal use. Anything over that amount must be declared and will be taxed. Fresh fruit and vegetables, cheese, and animal-based products are not allowed into the United States. Further details regarding what can and cannot be imported into the country are available from the **U.S. Department of State** (www.state.gov).

Canadian regulations are fairly lenient and allow cheese, herbs, condiments, dried fruits, baked goods, and candies; for a complete list, visit the **Canadian Border Services Agency** (www.cbsa-asfc.gc.ca). Australian regulations are particularly stringent, and customs officers go to great lengths to avoid contamination. All fruit, vegetables, and meat products are forbidden. Fake designer goods will also be confiscated and may lead to a fine. Consult the **Australian Department of Immigration and Border Protection** (www.border.gov.au) for a complete list of items that need to be declared upon entry.

Festivals and Events

From moving religious processions to gastronomic events, festivals offer a unique chance for visitors to experience local life and traditions in Italy. There are many festivals throughout the year in this region. Here are a few highlights to mark on your calendar.

NAPLES
FESTA DI SAN GENNARO
Sat. before the first Sun. in May, Sept. 19, and Dec. 16
The patron saint of Naples is celebrated three times a year with important religious festivals complete with processions and miracles.

NAPOLI PIZZA VILLAGE
June
The traditional Neapolitan pizza is celebrated in this fun food festival that takes over the waterfront in Naples.

SORRENTO
EASTER HOLY WEEK
Good Friday
Easter is a major holiday in Italy, and in Sorrento you can see two impressive processions through town.

AMALFI COAST
Positano
FERRAGOSTO
Aug. 15
While Ferragosto is a national holiday, it is also a religious festival celebrating the Assumption of the Virgin Mary in the main church of Positano. Watch the traditional processions and spectacular fireworks displays over the sea. **Maiori** hosts a similar celebration.

FESTA DEL PESCE
Last Sat. in Sept.
Seafood enthusiasts will love the annual Fish Festival held in Positano on the Spiaggia di Fornillo.

Amalfi
FESTIVAL OF SANT'ANDREA
June 27 and Nov. 30
The biggest festivals of the year in Amalfi are dedicated to Sant'Andrea, the town's patron saint and protector. Don't miss seeing the incredible running of the statue of the saint up the steps of the Duomo di Amalfi at the end of the procession.

NEW YEAR'S EVE
Dec. 31
Amalfi rings in the new year with a massive firework display over the harbor and music in Piazza Duomo that lasts well into the early hours of the morning.

Ravello
RAVELLO FESTIVAL
June-Aug.
Called the City of Music, Ravello hosts an important music and performing arts festival every year with concerts and other events.

PUGLIA
Bari
FESTA DI SAN NICOLA
Dec. 3-6 and May 7-9
Faithful and secular alike gather together to celebrate their patron saint twice each year with music, processions, fireworks, and traditional feast day foods.

SICILY
Palermo
ZAGARA FESTIVAL
Mar. and Oct.
This three-day, semi-annual festival celebrating the zagara citrus flower takes place in the University of Palermo's Botanical Garden.

BALLARÒ BUSKERS
end of Oct.
Artists, bands, clowns, acrobats, jugglers, and

dancers take to the streets of Palermo's Ballarò neighborhood, creating a lively atmosphere with music, parades, and other performances.

Catania
FESTA DI SANT'AGATA
Feb. 5
One of the largest and most popular religious festivals in the world, the grand procession of Sant'Agata's silver reliquary through the sites of Catania is a sight to see.

Syracuse
ORTIGIA SOUND SYSTEM MUSIC FESTIVAL
end of July
An international electronic music festival in the timeless city of Syracuse.

Recreation

HIKING

Outdoor enthusiasts will find plenty of hiking opportunities on the Amalfi Coast, summitting the volcanic slopes of Mount Etna or Mount Vesuvius, or in one of Sicily or Puglia's stunning national parks. Make sure to wear hiking boots, or at least closed-toed shoes with support. Most hikes include a significant change in altitude, so do be prepared for a lot of steps and steep walking up or down, and bring layers for changes in temperature, especially if you're hiking Mount Etna. However, the fine views are a wonderful compensation for the effort.

BEACHES

Beaches are among the biggest draws to Southern Italy. Like the rugged and mountainous landscape, most beaches here are rocky and often tucked away in scenic spots along the coastline, with a few sandy exceptions in Puglia and Sicily. It's a good idea to pack water shoes or flip-flops to make walking on the beaches and wading into the sea more comfortable.

Going to the beach in Italy might be a different experience from what you're used to at home. Beaches are divided into two areas, one that is free and the other where you must pay to gain access. The free areas are called spiaggia libera, literally meaning free beach, where you can simply throw down a towel and enjoy swimming. However, if you see rows of sun beds and umbrellas neatly lined up, that is a stabilimento balneare, or a private beach club. To access those beach areas, you will need to rent a sun bed and umbrella for the day. The rental also includes beach services that vary depending on the size of the stabilimente balneare, but usually you'll have access to changing rooms and showers. Most stabilimenti balneari will also offer snack bar and drink options, or even complete seaside restaurants. Given the rocky nature of the beaches, renting a sun bed and having beach services is certainly the most comfortable way to enjoy a relaxing day at the beach.

WATER SPORTS

Water sports are not as popular in Southern Italy as might be expected, but there are some great experiences to be had, such as kayaking, scuba diving, windsurfing, or renting a boat of your own to cruise around Capri or the Sicilian archipelagos, the Aegadian or Aeolian Islands.

Food

ITALIAN EATERIES
Restaurants

Sit-down eateries in Italy are usually known as **ristoranti, trattorias,** and **osterie.** Trattorias and osterie are often more rustic, older, and cheaper. More popular in Naples and Palermo, an osteria has fewer items on the menu and rarely strays from tradition. While the style can change from seaside restaurants to city dining, a ristorante is often more expensive and elegant, with uniformed waiters, a wine cellar, and nicer table settings, with more likelihood to play with new flavors, ingredients, and variations on old recipes. Though continuous food service throughout the day is not the norm—usually all three types of eateries close between lunch and dinner—during the summer months in more touristy areas like the Amalfi Coast and Capri, you can usually find a handful of restaurants in the main piazzas that are open from lunch through dinner.

Pizzerias and Street Food

With the strong Neapolitan pizza tradition, you don't have to go far to find an excellent pizzeria, especially in Naples, and with other regional variations like focaccia barese or sfincione, a Palermitan cross between pizza and focaccia. Pizza is on the menu in many restaurants, or visit pizzerias or street food stands dedicated just to making pizza.

The most popular street food in Naples also happens to be pizza. Both **pizza al taglio** (pizza by the slice) style and **pizza fritta** (fried pizza) are available in small food shops from midmorning onward. But it's in Palermo that the Southern Italian genius for street food really comes alive. In the open-air markets of Sicily's capital, you can find everything from arancine (fried rice balls often filled with a meat or cheese sauce) to pane con le milza (a veal sandwich). Across the island, Catania has its own share of street food specialties, too.

Bakeries and Pasticceria

Fornaio (bakeries) are often the first businesses open in the neighborhood, to supply locals with all types of bread, buns, and sweets, usually priced by weight. **Pasticceria** shops are entirely dedicated to sweets; they open early in the morning and remain busy until midafternoon. If combined with a coffee bar, they may be open all day and late into the night.

The tradition of pastries is strong in the entire area, and there are unique varieties of cakes and sweets to be found from Naples to convents in Palermo. In Naples, don't miss the classic sfogliatella, a shell-shaped pastry with flaky crust and citrus-infused ricotta filling. On the Amalfi Coast, try lemon-infused sweets like the delizia al limone, a cake with lemon filling and topped with a lemon cream. In Capri, you'll often find torta Caprese: a rich flourless almond and chocolate cake. Sicily is known for its pastries filled with almond paste, made fresh from the nuts that grow right on the island, as well as marzipan. In Puglia, look for pasticciotto, a cream-filled shortcrust pastry.

Coffee Bars

Coffee bars and cafés open nearly as early as bakeries; in the morning, locals come for an espresso or cappuccino and **cornetto** (croissant), a cheap and tasty breakfast. While at the coffee bar, remember that the counter service, where most locals eat and drink, is cheaper and faster. Sitting at table to linger over your coffee and pastries will cost more than standing inside, but the experience may be worth it. If you're sitting at a **café** in Capri's Piazzetta or the Piazza Duomo in Amalfi, you can expect prices to be higher than what you'd pay at a small bar tucked away on a small street. In other words, you'll pay for the view and atmosphere, and the tables outside are usually filled with tourists. In Sicily and Puglia, coffee bars often add a little indulgence to their caffeine fix, for example in caffè leccese (a coffee with almond syrup) or granita di caffè, which combines the beloved Sicilian iced dessert with delicious coffee.

MENUS

Italian menus are divided into **antipasti** (starters), **primo** (first course), and **secondo** (second course), distinct and served in order. Antipasti are meant to whet the appetite; try local specialties like prosciutto and mozzarella di bufala (buffalo milk mozzarella) or alici (anchovies) fried or marinated and share them with the table to try more options.

The primo, usually pasta or risotto, can be any of hundreds of traditional pasta shapes, served with vegetable, meat, or fish sauces. Pasta with seafood is featured at many restaurants, especially on the coast and islands. Risotto is often served with a simple yet beautiful lemon infusion, or with seafood and crustaceans. In places like Bari, you can see people making pasta in the streets by hand, the most homemade pasta you're likely to eat outside your own kitchen.

While it's fine to order just one course, try to leave room for the secondo, which can include meat or fish cooked rare (al sangue), medium rare (cotta), or well done (ben cotta). Typical **contorni** (sides), ordered separately, include grilled vegetables or roasted potatoes. It's worth checking out daily specials, often listed on a separate menu.

DRINKS

Italy is known for its natural spring water, which Italians drink more of per capita than any other people in the world. Water usually does not come free at Italian restaurants, and you'll asked by your waiter whether you want **acqua** (water) **frizzante** (sparkling) or **naturale** (still), sometimes with a choice of brands (around €3/liter). **Acqua del rubinetto** (tap water) in Italy is regularly tested by authorities and safe to drink, but rarely will be an option while dining.

Most restaurants have a decent **wine** list of local, regional, and international bottles. House wine is also generally very good. It can be ordered by the glass or in different-sized carafes.

Most Italians end lunch with an **espresso** and usually conclude dinner with a **digestivo** (digestif). The latter is some kind of high-grade alcoholic spirit infused with a variety of fruits or herbs and reputed to help digestion. The most famous of these in the area is limoncello, a very strong lemon-infused liqueur. It is served ice-cold in small glasses and is sipped. Each area has its typical digestivo options to try, including other citrus fruits, wild fennel, or licorice liqueurs on the Amalfi Coast, and the rucola liqueur infused with arugula (rocket) made on Ischia. **Soft drinks** are widely available but are not often seen on Italian restaurant tables.

REGIONAL AND SEASONAL SPECIALTIES

The Mediterranean is never far away in Southern Italy, meaning **seafood** is the top regional specialty that you'll find on nearly every menu. Yet that doesn't mean you won't find anything you'll like if you don't care for seafood or are vegetarian or vegan. The regional cuisine is divided into mare (sea) and terra (land), reflecting the sea and the mountainous setting as well as the area's strong agricultural tradition. The majority of dining spots, even ones specializing in seafood, will have primi and secondi options highlighting seasonal vegetables and meat as well.

If you do enjoy seafood, you are in for some excellent gastronomic experiences, as it is fresh and prepared in an unfussy way that highlights the natural flavors. You'll often find spaghetti or linguine with vongole (clams) or cozze (mussels). Pasta with freshly caught fish is another classic, as is grilled or baked fish for a second course. Cetara, a small fishing village on the Amalfi Coast, is noted for alici (anchovies), which are prepared in a variety of ways. Squid and octopus are also popular, and are served fried as an appetizer, prepared with pasta or potatoes, and grilled or stuffed for secondi. Even if you've not tried squid or even ricci (sea urchins), it's well worth stepping out of your comfort zone to try local seafood specialties.

Vegetables and legumes are important parts of the traditional Southern Italian diet, especially when it comes to home cooking. Cheap, healthy, and ubiquitous vegetables like zucchini, chickpeas, beans, and eggplants are essential parts of la cucina povera, or poor cooking, the culinary ethos inextricable from the identity of most of Puglia and Sicily. Vegetables appear on menus very seasonally, from artichokes and asparagus in the spring to zucchini, eggplant, and peppers in the summer, and pumpkin and broccoli in the autumn. Other notable seasonal specialties include Amalfi Coast chestnuts and almonds in Sicily and Puglia.

Nothing compares to **pizza in Naples,** where it is truly a gastronomic art form. Be sure to try the classic pizza Margherita topped with tomatoes, mozzarella, basil, and olive oil. Or go even more traditional by enjoying the pizza marinara with tomatoes, oregano, garlic, extra virgin olive oil, and no cheese. Of course, you'll find plenty of options for toppings at most pizzerias.

No visit to the Amalfi Coast region is complete without trying the local lemons. It's an easy task since the famous lemons cultivated in the area are incorporated into many of the regional specialties. Squeeze lemons over your fresh fish or salad, enjoy traditional lemon desserts, and finish off your meal with a chilled glass of limoncello, a lemon-infused liqueur.

HOURS

Restaurants are typically open 12:30pm-2:30pm for lunch and 7:30pm-10:30pm for dinner; Italians tend to eat later, especially in the summer, waiting for the sun to go down and for cooler temperatures. Most eateries close one day a week, except during the peak of summer, and many take an extended break from January to March in the coastal areas and islands. Reservations aren't usually necessary, but to guarantee a seat at especially popular eateries it's wise to book ahead or to arrive early or late. Bakeries open before sunrise and close in the midafternoon, while coffee bars remain open all day long and pizzerias and gelaterie stay open late.

TIPPING

While tipping is generally not required in much of Italy, in the Amalfi Coast area it's traditional leave a small tip. Rounding your bill up or leaving €3-5 behind after a good meal is one way to show appreciation. The other way to express gastronomic gratitude is with words. Italians are proud of their cuisine and compliments are always welcome. Customers at coffee bars often leave a low-denomination coin on the counter.

Shopping

Shopping is a fun local experience as the majority of family-owned shops are dedicated to one thing, like shoes, hats, books, clothing, or furniture, or materials like leather, ceramics, or paper. These shops are true treasures in Campania, where you can often see artisans at work painting ceramics on the Amalfi Coast, carving wood in Sorrento, or creating traditional presepe (nativity) figures in Naples.

There are department and flagship stores in the center of bigger cities like Naples, Salerno, Bari, and Palermo, but they attract as many tourists as locals, who shop more at malls and outlets.

SHOPPING ETIQUETTE

Italians entering a shop (or bar) nearly always greet shopkeepers with buongiorno or buonasera (good morning/good evening), and acknowledge them once more upon leaving with a grazie (thank you) or arrivederci (good-bye), whether or not they've bought something. It's certainly okay and even encouraged to browse in Italian shops, and shopkeepers are generally helpful, professional, and appreciate being asked how an object was made.

SHIPPING ITEMS HOME

If something larger than your suitcase catches your eye, stores, especially ones selling ceramics, can often arrange for shipment back to your home, usually for about 10 percent of the purchase price.

HOURS

Even more so than restaurants, family-owned stores and smaller businesses nearly always close in the early afternoon, as well as on Sundays and Monday mornings. However, larger stores and those located in heavily trafficked areas have continuous hours. If you're shopping in Naples, Salerno, and on Ischia, do plan on shops closing mid-afternoon for a break. However, if you're in Amalfi, Positano, Sorrento, or Capri, you'll find shops open daily and with continuous hours. If you're traveling off season, many shops on the Amalfi Coast and Capri close for a period after Christmas through early spring, but the length of time varies from a couple of weeks to a month or longer. Just keep in mind that from early January through March many shops will be closed in those areas. This is not the case in larger cities like Salerno and Naples.

Accommodations

MAKING RESERVATIONS

The Amalfi Coast and Capri are among the most popular travel destinations in Italy, and though Sicily and Puglia are still lesser visited among overseas tourists, they are tremendously popular summer destinations for Italians and other Europeans. So, accommodations can fill up very quickly, despite the large number of options in tourist-focused areas. If you have your eye on a particular hotel for its features or views, it's wise to book ahead of time, especially if you're going to be

traveling from July to August. Yet even during the shoulder seasons certain hotels can be booked up many months ahead of time, especially if the rates are relatively reasonable. Keep in mind that many hotels or B&Bs might only have a handful of rooms and are relatively small compared to large chain hotels in other parts of the world.

Accommodations in Naples, Salerno, Palermo, and other large cities are open throughout the year, but most hotels in rural and beach resort areas. This may be the entire winter season from November to March or for a shorter period from January to March. Some smaller B&Bs will operate year-round, or you will find vacation apartment rentals available throughout the winter season in these areas.

Choosing a holiday destination can be a challenging task, with so many fine options in Southern Italy. If you're planning a visit of only a few days, choose a central location with easy access to public transport connections. If you're staying longer, a visit to a smaller town on the Amalfi Coast, or to a masseria (farm stay) in rural Puglia, can be a highlight of a trip to Italy.

HOTELS

Like in other parts of the world, Italian hotels are graded on a system of one to five stars based on amenities and services. Breakfast is usually included, and most hotel rooms include en suite bathrooms. It's possible to book online; most hotels have multilingual websites. A **passport** or ID card is required when checking in, and smaller hotels often have a "leave the key" policy in which keys must be left and retrieved whenever entering or leaving the accommodation. Expect to be charged a city **hotel tax** of €1.50-5 per guest/per day depending on the number of stars and accommodation type. (Kids younger than 10 are exempt.) Some towns only collect the city hotel tax seasonally from April to November, while others charge you year-round. The city tax is usually required to be paid in cash when you leave.

HOSTELS

Hostels (ostelli) in Italy aren't just for young travelers; they provide clean accommodation as well as a sense of community for a good price, and most include private or semi-private rooms in addition to dormitories. Bathrooms are often shared, but some private rooms may have en suite baths. Expect higher than usual hostel rates in locations like Positano.

BED AND BREAKFASTS AND APARTMENTS

Italy boasts thousands of B&Bs, a great option to mingle with owners for a truly local stay. Another option is to rent an **apartment** or **villa** through **Airbnb** (www.airbnb.com) or **VRBO** (www.vrbo.com), an especially good choice and usually affordable for those traveling in large groups, and it allows you to prepare your own meals and enjoy other amenities of fully equipped housing. A word to the wise if you're considering a short-term vacation rental on the Amalfi Coast: Be sure to check for the number of stairs to access the property. Though most hotels have easy access or elevators available, many private residences or villas may require climbing a significant number of steps to reach them. If number of steps or access information is not indicated on the website where you're searching, it's a good idea to ask in advance before booking if there are steps and how many. It is far better than arriving to your vacation rental and finding a daunting flight of stairs to navigate daily.

Health and Safety

EMERGENCY NUMBERS

In case of a **medical emergency,** dial **118.** Operators are multilingual and will provide immediate assistance and ambulance service. The **U.S. Consulate General in Naples** (tel. 081/583-8111) offers U.S. citizens phone access any time for matters regarding illness or emergencies of any sort. **Carabinieri** (112), **police** (113), and the **fire department** (115) also operate around the clock.

POLICE

The law enforcement in Italy is divided into different agencies. The two main agencies are the polizia and the Carabinieri, who are responsible essentially for the same duties. The Carabinieri are a military corps that perform both military and civilian police duties, whereas the polizia is the more customary civilian police force. Either one can help in an emergency situation because they both handle law enforcement duties, investigations, and traffic incidents. The polizia tend to be more involved in patrolling the Autostrade (highways), yet both forces also perform periodic and random traffic stops. If you are driving and see the polizia or Carabinieri on the side of the road flag you to stop, be prepared to show your documents and vehicle registration or rental information. The Carabinieri uniforms are black with a red stripe on the pants while the vehicles are dark blue, also with red stripe details. Polizia uniforms are gray and blue, and their vehicles light blue and white.

Although you're less likely to encounter them while sightseeing, the Guardia di Finanza are another military police force who are responsible for policing financial and drug crimes. They are usually outfitted in gray uniforms and the vehicles are also gray. On a city level, the vigili urbani, which are part of the polizia municipale (municipal police), are usually on hand in every town to help with traffic, parking violations, and local law enforcement.

MEDICAL SERVICES

Italian medical and emergency services are relatively modern and are ranked fourth in the world by the World Health Organization. First aid can be performed by all public hospitals, and urgent treatment is entirely free of charge. A symbolic copayment is often required for non-life-threatening treatment but does not exceed €30. The emergency medical service number is **118.** If you can't wait, go directly to the pronto soccorso (emergency room) located in most hospitals.

For the most part, vaccines are not required for entering Italy, but a flu shot can prevent unnecessary time in bed if you're visiting in winter, and at the time of writing, health authorities were discussing allowing travelers who had received a COVID-19 vaccination to enter the EU as early as summer 2021. Check the latest vaccine guidelines and restrictions for travel with your local health authority as well as Italian and European health departments.

PHARMACIES

A pharmacy is called a farmacia in Italian, and they are recognizable by their green neon signs. They are very common in cities and even smaller town centers. If a pharmacy is closed, you can always find a list of the closest open ones posted in the window. Pharmacists can be very helpful in Italy and provide advice and nonprescription medicine for treating minor ailments. You'll also find practical items such as toothbrushes, sunscreen, baby food, and dietary foods like gluten-free products along with automated prophylactic vending machines out front.

CRIME

Italian cities are safe, and muggings and violent crime are rare. The Amalfi Coast area and much of coastal and rural Puglia and Sicily are very safe. Of course, you'll want to keep an eye on your personal items, but even petty crimes are rare.

Though Naples and Palermo have a reputation regarding organized crime, violent crimes are usually restricted to the local Mafia and generally do not affect tourists. Petty crime is the main issue, as in any large city in the world. Being street savvy is your best defense against thieves. Most petty criminals work in teams and can be quite young. Crowded train stations and public transportation are ideal places for thieves. Leave the eye-catching jewelry and expensive accessories at home and opt for a cross-body bag, carried in front, that closes well. It's best to keep wallets and other valuables in a front pocket or locked in a hotel safe. Distribute what you carry with you in different front pockets, or even better, use a money belt and leave out just the cash that you need to be easily accessible for the day. Keep smart phones and cameras out of sight as much as possible, and always keep a close eye on your bags.

If you're driving in Naples or Palermo, it's best to park your car in an attended parking garage rather than on the street. Be sure to lock the vehicle and leave no valuables in the car.

Before traveling, make a photocopy of your passport and other vital documents and call your credit card company immediately if your wallet is stolen. If you are the victim of a pickpocket, have a bag snatched, or have issues with car theft, report it within 24 hours to the nearest police station. You'll need a copy of the police report (denuncia) in order to make an insurance claim.

Conduct and Customs

LOCAL HABITS

Many of the most noticeable Italians habits are related to food: strict mealtimes, almost always eaten sitting down—you'll hardly ever see Italians eating on the go. Breakfast is generally light to save room for lunch and dinner, served at 1pm and 8pm. When eating out, Italians usually divide the bill between friends, and each person buys his or her own drink. Drinking is generally considered part of a meal, rather than with the intention of intoxication.

Though most etiquette in Italy will feel fairly familiar to most travelers, one exception is cutting in line, which is a frequent occurrence. If you don't defend your place, you may be waiting all day, and don't expect an orderly line while waiting to get on the bus or other forms of transportation. Often there is an order to a queue based upon order of arrival. If you're unsure, you can ask who is the last in a waiting group and then remember that your turn is after that person.

GREETINGS

Italians' interactions with friends and acquaintances often involve physical contact, and kisses on both cheeks are common (though a handshake is just as acceptable). However, these traditions have largely been put on hold, or replaced with an elbow bump greeting, as a precaution because of COVID-19. Conversation in public spaces, from the café or square, is unhurried; the proliferation of the cell phone has only fueled Italians' passion to communicate, and in some cases has led to an overreliance that can be witnessed on public transportation and sidewalks of Italian cities.

ALCOHOL AND SMOKING

In Italy, alcohol can be consumed in public and purchased by anyone over 18. Attitudes toward alcohol are relaxed, and excessive drinking is rare. Smoking has been banned in bars, restaurants, and public spaces since 2005, and the number of smokers in is falling, though you'll still see plenty of people smoking in outdoor spaces, including seating outside restaurants.

DRUGS

Italy's geographical position between Europe and North Africa and extensive coastline mean smuggling of drugs including heroin, cocaine, hashish, and synthetic drugs is a problem here. Hashish (derived from cannabis and mixed with tobacco), is the most common drug here, and most dealers aren't too pushy, while cocaine or amphetamines may be present at discos and nightclubs. Cannabis has been decriminalized for decades, but harder drugs are illegal. Though personal use of cannabis in public will not lead to arrest, it's not worth the risk of a fine or warning.

DRESS

Style is second nature to Italians. It can be easy to feel out of place when surrounded by their more formal attire and attention to detail when it comes to appearance. Clothing is generally elegant and fits well; to fit in style-wise, think about packing your Sunday best for the trip, or doing some shopping to pick up some of that easy Italian elegance.

That being said, style on the coastal areas is more relaxed than many Italian cities. People are often dressed resort-chic, including a lot of linen for both men and women, flowing summer dresses to keep cool, and handmade sandals or leather loafers. And while the skimpy Speedo-style swimsuits for men and the proliferation of bikinis on the beach might give the idea of a relaxed beach vibe everywhere, Italians cover up when leaving the beach. It's not appropriate, or even allowed in many towns, to walk around in only swimwear except on the beach. A beach cover-up and flip-flops are fine for getting from your accommodation to the beach, but you won't see Italians dining anywhere except a beachside restaurant in a beach cover-up.

At Places of Worship

It is assumed travelers will dress more conservatively when visiting churches in Italy. Though modest dress codes are not as strictly enforced in this region as in other parts of Italy, if you are revealing too much skin you might be denied entry. Even if a sign isn't posted, it's polite to avoid going into churches while wearing short skirts or shorts, or bare midriffs or shoulders. For women, it can be handy to carry a scarf to cover your shoulders while visiting religious sites during the summer months.

Practical Details

WHAT TO PACK

Traveling to an area famous for its many steps can quickly make you regret packing those extra five pairs of shoes; it's probably best to err on the side of packing light, and to leave expensive watches and jewelry at home, especially if you'll be spending time in Naples. Finally, it's a good idea to email yourself a copy of your passport and any important credit card codes or customer service numbers as backup in case you lose your wallet or bag.

Luggage: Wheeled suitcases can be bumpy going on Italy's cobblestone streets, but it's often still worth it to avoid carrying heavy bags. Bring a backpack or handbag with zippers for daily excursions, and a money belt can be useful for cash and valuables.

Paperwork: You'll need your passport and a driver's license if you plan on renting your own transportation.

Clothing, shoes, and accessories: Bring comfortable shoes and clothes for long days of walking, and layers, especially in spring and fall, when mornings and evenings can be chilly. Bring at least one fancier outfit for nicer restaurants or clubs, and clothes that cover knees and shoulders to visit places of worship. You'll thank yourself for bringing flip-flops to the rocky beaches. If you have very sensitive feet, consider packing a pair of water shoes. You might not win style awards, but being comfortable on your beach holiday is more important. Pack some beach coverups for seaside dining and getting to and from the beach. Sunglasses and hats are useful for sunny summer days. For hiking and walking, a good pair of supportive athletic shoes will be fine, and you can save space by leaving your hiking boots at home.

Toiletries and medication: You can pick up most normal toiletries and common medications like aspirin at Italian pharmacies, but pack a high-SPF sunscreen, which can be quite costly in seaside locations. If you take medication, make sure to bring enough, and a copy of your prescription in case you need a refill. **Hand sanitizer** is now a must while traveling and is especially useful on the go. **Face mask** regulations can change from town to town and may be required on public transportation, so it's helpful to always have one on hand. Tuck several **travel tissue** packs into your bag, as it's not uncommon to find bathrooms without toilet paper.

Electronics: Voltage is 220 in Italy and plugs have two round prongs. Pack a U.S.-to-European **travel adapter,** which are harder to find once you're in Italy; that said, many hotels supply them to guests free of charge. A portable battery charger can prevent phones and other devices from going dark while out and about during the day. Digital photographers will definitely want to bring extra memory cards, too.

LAUNDRY AND LUGGAGE STORAGE

If you need to do laundry while traveling, keep in mind that laundromats are often small and offer washing services as well as dry-cleaning options. Self-service laundromats can be hard to find, but they are available as a budget-friendly option or if you're traveling light. Luggage storage can make day trips and transfers easy if you're staying in multiple places. In general, look for deposito bagagli (luggage storage) signs and be sure to check on timing as some locations only offer storage during the day.

MONEY
Currency

The euro has been Italy's currency since 2000. Banknotes come in denominations of €5, €10, €20, €50, €200, and €500 (which is currently being phased out). Denominations are different colors and sizes to facilitate recognition. Coins come in €0.01, €0.02, €0.05, €0.10, €0.20, €0.50, €1, and €2 denominations; these also vary in color, shape, and size.

Currency Exchange

Fluctuation between the dollar and euro can have a major impact on expenditures. One dollar is now worth roughly €0.85. To obtain euros, you can exchange at your local bank before departure, use **private exchange** agencies located in airports and near major monuments, or simply use **ATMs** in Italy. Banks generally offer better rates but charge commission, while agencies charge low commission but offer poor rates. Certainly the easiest and best option is to withdraw the cash you need from ATMs as you go.

ATMs and Banks

ATMs are easy to find and use throughout Italy, providing instructions in multiple languages and accepting foreign debit and credit cards. Before withdrawing cash in Italy, ask your bank or credit card company about fees; **Charles Schwab** is one of the few financial institutions that does an international fee. Italian banks also charge a small fee for cardholders of other banks using their ATMs.

The maximum daily withdrawal at most banks is €500, and banks are generally open weekdays 8:30am-1:30pm and

2:30pm-4:30pm. Be aware of your surroundings when withdrawing cash late at night or on deserted streets.

Debit and Credit Cards

Debit and credit cards are ubiquitous in Italy, and recent legislation meant to encourage cashless transactions has removed monetary limits. Yet it's still best not to assume you can use a card absolutely everywhere, and to contact your bank before leaving to let them know about your trip, so your card doesn't get frozen. Do plan on always having some cash on hand for transactions like bus tickets or small purchases, as not all small businesses are equipped to process cards. However, you can use credit cards at most museums, restaurants, and shops. It's useful to have a card with a chip-and-PIN system, the most common form of bank card in Italy. Credit cards often provide the most advantageous exchange rates, with a 1-3 percent commission fee per transaction.

Sales Tax

There's a value-added tax (IVA) of 22 percent on most goods, but visitors who reside outside the European Union are entitled to **tax refunds** (www.taxrefund.it) on all purchases over €154.94 on the same day within stores that participate in the tax-back program. Just look for the **Euro Tax Free** or **Tax Free Italy** logo, have your passport ready, and fill out the yellow refund form. You'll still have to pay tax at the time of purchase, but you are entitled to reimbursement at airports and refund offices. Forms must be stamped by customs officials before check-in and brought to the refund desk, where you can choose to receive cash or have funds wired to your credit card. Lines move slowly and it's usually faster to be refunded at private **currency exchange agencies** such as **Forexchange** (www.forexchange.it) in Naples. They facilitate the refund process for a small percentage of your refund. All claims must be made within three months of purchase.

COMMUNICATIONS
Telephones

To call Italy from outside the country, dial the **exit code** (011 for the United States and Canada), followed by **39** (Italy country code), and the number. All large Italian cities have a 2- or 3-digit **area code** (081 for the city of Naples and surrounding areas and 089 for the province of Salerno), and numbers are 6-11 digits long. Landline numbers nearly always start with a zero, which must be dialed when making calls in Italy or calling Italy from abroad. Cell phone numbers have a 3-digit prefix (347, 390, 340, etc.) that varies according to the mobile operator, and cell phone numbers are 10 digits long total. Numbers that start with 800 in Italy are toll-free, 170 gets you an English-speaking operator, and 176 is **international directory assistance.**

Most smart phones, such as iPhones, Samsung Galaxy, and Google Nexus devices, will work in Italy, but rates vary widely. Before leaving, check whether your company offers an international to avoid unexpected bills. You can also visit a mobile shop on arrival in Italy to purchase an Italian SIM card from operators like **Wind** (www.wind.it), **Tim** (www.tim.it), and **Vodafone** (www.vodafone.it). You need a passport or photo ID to purchase a SIM card, but this is a cheap option that usually allows the most generous use of minutes and data. Or, save on charges by connecting to Wi-Fi whenever possible—in hotels, bars, and many other places throughout the region.

Wi-Fi

Many towns in Italy have free Wi-Fi networks that make it simple to stay connected throughout a journey, as do train operators, airports, and hotels. You must register to access Wi-Fi and there are often time and traffic limits.

Postal Services

Yellow **Poste Italiane** (tel. 800/160-000; www.poste.it) offices range from larger branches, usually open weekdays 8:30am-7pm, to smaller branches, open from about 8:30am-1:30pm. A postcard to the United States costs €2.40 as long as it doesn't exceed 20 grams and remains within standard dimensions. The cost of sending letters and other goods varies according to weight; just know that it may take many weeks for your items to reach their destination. Some tabacchi (tobacco shops) also have standard francobolli (stamps) available for purchase. Mailboxes are red and may have slots for international and local mail, so take a close look before mailing.

OPENING HOURS

Opening hours can vary based on the season and location throughout the region of Campania. In larger cities, you can expect to find many shops, especially smaller ones, closed in the afternoons around 1:30pm-4:30pm. Shops often close on Monday morning as well, especially during the winter, while in more popular tourist spots will be open daily and offer continuous hours from April to October.

Shop hours also vary significantly by season. In the top tourist spots, shops will likely be open daily and continuous hours during the summer months, with extended evening hours from July to August. Hours will be shorter over the winter months, and some shops may close entirely in beach resort areas for a period after Christmas or for the entire winter period.

Restaurants will often close one day a week, possibly Monday, Tuesday, or Wednesday. In the coastal areas and islands, restaurants will usually be open daily in August or for the entire summer period, but will close for much or all of the winter season.

Nothing is worse than arriving at a museum you are eager to visit and finding it closed. Many major museums in close on Monday or Tuesday; be sure to check the website before visiting to avoid disappointment.

PUBLIC HOLIDAYS

Public holidays in Italy usually mean that banks and offices will be closed. It also means that grocery stores will be closed, or open for reduced hours. In addition to public holidays, each town has one or more days dedicated to celebrating its local patron saint. Though this usually doesn't impact the hours of banks or public offices, you may sometimes find that shops keep more limited hours. However, along the Amalfi Coast, on the islands and other peak tourist spots, you will find all restaurants and shops open during the summer months and for public holidays.

- **January 1:** Capodanno (New Year's Day)
- **January 6:** Epifania (Epiphany)
- **Pasqua** (Easter Sunday)
- **Pasquetta** (Easter Monday)
- **April 25:** Festa della Liberazione (Liberation Day)
- **May 1:** Festa del Lavoro (International Worker's Day)
- **June 2:** Festa della Repubblica (Republic Day)
- **August 15:** Ferragosto (Assumption Day)
- **November 1:** Tutti i Santi (All Saints' Day)
- **December 8:** Immacolata (Immaculate Conception)
- **December 25:** Natale (Christmas)
- **December 26:** Santo Stefano (St. Stephen's Day)

WEIGHTS AND MEASURES

Italy uses the metric system. A few helpful conversions:

- 5 centimeters = about 3 inches
- 1 kilogram = a little more than 2 pounds
- 5 kilometers = around 3 miles

Celsius is used to measure temperature; room temperature is about 20°C (68°F). When summer temperatures break the 35°C (95°F) barrier, head to the beach early in the day and spend the hottest midday hours indoors as many Italians do.

Italy is on **Central European Time,** six hours ahead of the U.S. East Coast and nine ahead of the West Coast. Military/24-hour time is frequently used (i.e., 13:00 for 1pm and 20:15 is 8:15pm). Italians order dates by day, month, and year, which is important to remember when booking hotels and tours.

TOURIST INFORMATION
Tourist Offices

You'll find tourist offices in most major destinations, where city travel cards, maps, and event information can be obtained, though Sicily tends to have the least infrastructure for tourists among the three regions covered in this guide. Hours vary but most are open nonstop from 9:30am until around 6pm during the tourist season, with more limited hours during the winter months. Staff are usually multilingual and can help put you in touch with local guides, order tickets, or get directions. Tourist offices are located in the city center and are usually well indicated with signs.

Maps

Maps are available at most tourist offices and at newsstands and bookstores, though small towns are usually quite easy to navigate, with one or two main streets or piazzas, and a maze of little passageways weaving through the town. Often a quick glance at a map is enough to orient yourself and memorize major landmarks and sights. Studying maps and getting an idea of the layout of each city beforehand will make getting around easier once you arrive.

Finding the name of a street you're standing on is simple, but finding that same street on a map can be tricky. Often, it's quicker to locate a piazza or a nearby cathedral, museum, or monument. Also, asking for directions is the best way to start a conversation with a stranger and learn something new. One of the most enjoyable experiences in Southern Italy is putting away the map and simply meandering through town. You'll happen across moments of daily life and experience the joy of discovering quiet spots.

Traveler Advice

ACCESS FOR TRAVELERS WITH DISABILITIES

For a country with predominantly historic buildings that were not designed to be wheelchair-accessible, Italy has been making great strides to improve accessibility in airports, train stations, hotels, and sights. However, not all historic churches and sights, or even restaurants, are wheelchair-accessible, so it's always a good idea to call in advance before visiting to confirm. Calling ahead is also a good idea because some sights offer wheelchair access, but it must be reserved.

The Amalfi Coast presents many barriers for travelers with disabilities or mobility issues simply due to the mountainous setting and many steps involved in navigating the towns along the coastline. The historic centers of Naples, Sorrento, Palermo, Catania, Syracuse, Taormina, and Lecce have many pedestrian-only areas, but the cobblestone streets can present challenges for travelers with disabilities. Yet cultural sightseeing, particularly in Naples and Sorrento, is well ahead of the curve in Italy. It's safe to say that nearly all museums are accessible and offer special services.

Though the uneven terrain and large stone streets of the archaeological sites of Pompeii and Herculaneum present challenges, there are new initiatives to make them both more accessible. **Pompeii** has a special route called Pompeii per tutti (Pompei for everyone) that leads through a specially designed 2.2-mile (3.5-km) tour of the ruins, with ramps to make it more manageable. While it's a fantastic endeavor, you'll still want to keep in mind that you're entering an archaeological site; there are ramps or slopes of more than 8 percent at times, as well as stretches of ancient and uneven pavement and certain points that may present challenges for wheelchair users to move independently. **Herculaneum** is a much smaller site than Pompeii and offers wheelchair-accessible ramps and walkways to enter the ancient city. Movement within is, again, somewhat challenging given the uneven terrain and steps required to enter some of the houses. **Paestum** has some barrier-free paths through its archaeological park as well as wheelchair access to all areas of the museum.

Turismo Accessibile (www.turismo accessibile.org) provides detailed information on accessibility in Naples, yet much of the information is only available in Italian. **Sage Traveling** (www.sagetraveling.com) is a travel company specializing in disabled travel. In the Naples area, the company offers a number of day tours that are wheelchair-friendly, including tours to Pompeii, Herculaneum, Sorrento, Capri, and the Amalfi Coast.

TRAVELING WITH CHILDREN

Italians go crazy for kids, and if you're traveling with a baby or toddler expect people to sneak peaks inside the stroller or ask for the name, age, and vital statistics of your child. Restaurants and hotels generally welcome young travelers, and some high-end accommodations offer babysitting services for parents who want to sightsee on their own. Not all restaurants offer booster seats or high chairs, but many will create half-size portions (mezza porzione) for small appetites. Tickets to museums and public transportation are usually discounted for children under 12, and are free for kids under 6.

Strollers

Keep in mind that steps, and often a lot of them, are hard to avoid on the Amalfi Coast, which can make getting around with a stroller challenging. You're going to want a lightweight and easy-to-fold stroller in order to navigate steps. For infants and young children, baby wraps, carriers, or a hip seat can be helpful to make handling the steps a little easier. Be sure to check the number of steps required to reach your accommodation.

The archaeological sites like Pompeii, Herculaneum, and Paestum can also be challenging to navigate with a stroller. Herculaneum is a much smaller site to cover, yet offers all of the intriguing aspects of ancient Roman life to capture the interest of young visitors. A tour guide can also help bring the history to life for children in fun and engaging ways.

Beaches

Most of the beaches in this area have pebbles or are rocky, so a pair of beach shoes will keep little feet safe and can help make the beach experience more enjoyable for the whole family. (Adults will want water shoes or flip-flops for the beach as well.) Hiring a boat or booking a boat excursion is a family-friendly way to explore the coastline and islands, allowing you to stop and swim in beautiful coves and older kids to explore the rugged coastline and little grottoes.

Managing the Heat

During the hot days of summer, do like the Italians do and head to the beach in the morning. Then, return to your accommodation for a midafternoon break during the hottest part of the day to rest up for evening adventures. You'll find that most Italian children have later bedtimes, especially during the summer, and it's normal for families to be out to dinner late, even with young children. With some advance planning, it's hard for kids not to love Italy. Involving them as much as possible in the journey will help leave an impression they'll never forget.

FEMALE TRAVELERS

Women travelers may find that Italians in general are less shy about staring than they may be accustomed to at home. This may make women feel uncomfortable, but for the most part, men in Southern Italy are respectful. The stereotype of Italians and their wandering hands is uncommon here and would be looked upon as shameful by the locals. Advances are usually not aggressive and can simply be ignored. Enter a shop, bar, or other public space if unwanted attention threatening; if harassment persists, call the police (113) from a crowded area. In Naples and Palermo, women should be more aware of their surroundings at all times and avoid unlit streets and train stations at night. Having a cell phone handy is a wise precaution, and periodically keeping in touch with family back home never hurts. Hotels will be happy to order a taxi or make reservations whenever necessary.

SENIOR TRAVELERS

Italy's high life expectancy (83) and median age (47) means visiting seniors may feel right at home, and there's a general respect for older people. You'll see that the steps of the Amalfi Coast and cobblestone streets in the centro storico don't stop local seniors from getting around. They just take the slow and steady approach and stop to chat along the way. Take a cue from them and enjoy sightseeing at a relaxed pace. If mobility and steps are problematic, be sure to check on the number of steps at your accommodation and confirm there is an elevator. Nearly all hotels have elevators, but smaller accommodations and B&Bs may not.

Special Discounts

People over age 65 are entitled to discounts at museums, theaters, and sporting events, as well as on public transportation and for many other services. With a CartaFRECCIA card from Trenitalia, over-60s traveling by train receive a 30 percent discount off the base price on all tickets. It's free to apply for the CartaFRECCIA on the Trenitalia website (www.trenitalia.com).

LGBTQ TRAVELERS

Though Italy was one of the last European countries to enable civil unions for same-sex couples, violence against LGBTQ people is rare (although cases of physical and verbal harassment in Naples do occasionally make headlines). In modern Italy, it's not uncommon to see same-sex couples holding hands. Capri has long been known for its open community and appeal for gay travelers. For LGBTQ nightlife, your best bet is Naples, though the scene is more modest than in other large cities in Italy like Rome or Milan. The Mediterranean Pride of Naples (www.napolipride.org) parade and festival take place in June or July in the streets of Naples. In recent years, the coastal town of Gallipoli in Puglia has become something of a LGBTQ mecca in the summer season.

TRAVELERS OF COLOR

Over the last few decades, Italy has become increasingly diverse, with growing communities of Eastern Europeans, Asians, South Americans, and Africans. Still, the country's population is 92 percent Italian, though that group itself is comprised of many different cultural, linguistic, and historical subgroups. In an area where travelers arrive from all corners of the world, most Italians are welcoming to travelers of color. However, it's a good idea to keep in mind that Italians are known for staring, which isn't something just reserved for travelers. Although this cultural quirk makes some people uncomfortable, blatant discrimination is rare. That said, growth in immigration from African countries has led to an increase in anti-immigration sentiment across the country, and an uptick in incidents of racial violence. If you think you've been refused service based on race, report the incident to local police or Carabinieri, who treat all acts of racism seriously.

Resources

Glossary

A

aeroporto: airport
albergo: hotel
alcolici: alcohol
alimentari: grocery store
aliscafo: hydrofoil (high-speed ferry)
ambasciata: embassy
analcolico: nonalcoholic
aperitivo: appetizer
aperto: open
arrivo: arrival
autista: driver
autobus: bus
autostrada: highway

B

bagaglio: suitcase
bagno: bathroom
banca: bank
bibita: soft drink
biglietteria: ticket office
biglietto: ticket
buono: good

C

calcio: soccer
caldo: hot
cambio: exchange
camera: room
cameriere: waiter
carta di credito: credit card
cartolina: postcard
cassa: cashier
cattedrale: cathedral
centro storico: historic center

chiesa: church
chiuso: closed
città: city
climatizzato: air-conditioned
coincidenza: connection (transport)
consolate: consulate
contante: cash
conto: bill

D E

destinazione: destination
discoteca: disco
dogana: customs
duomo: cathedral
edicola: newsstand
enoteca: wine bar
entrata: entrance
escursione: excursion

F G

farmacia: pharmacy
fermata: bus/subway stop
ferrovia: railway
fontana: fountain
forno: bakery
francobollo: stamp
gratuito: free
grazie: thanks

L

letto: bed
libreria: bookshop
limone: lemon
lontano: far
lungomare: waterfront

M N O

macchina: car
mare: sea
mercato: market
metropolitana: subway
moneta: coin
monumento: monument
mostra: exhibition
museo: museum
negozio: shop
orario: timetable
ospedale: hospital
ostello: hostel

P Q R

palazzo: building
panino: sandwich
parcheggio: parking lot
parco: park
partenza: departure
passeggiata: walk
pasticceria: pastry shop
pasto: meal
periferia: outskirts
piazza: square
polizia: police

ponte: bridge
prenotazione: reservation
prezzo: price
quartiere: neighborhood
ristorante: restaurant

S T

sconto: discount
soccorso: assistance
spiaggia: beach
spuntino: snack
stabilimento balneare: seaside beach club
stazione: station
strada: road
tabaccherie: tobacco shop
teatro: theater
torre: tower
traghetto: ferry
trattoria: restaurant (casual)
treno: train

U V

uscita: exit
via: street
viale: avenue

Italian Phrasebook

Many Italians in touristy areas like the Amalfi Coast, and in larger cities, have some knowledge of English, ranging from managing basic communication to being fully fluent. Of course, whatever vocabulary they lack is compensated for with gesticulation. It is, however, more rewarding to attempt to communicate in Italian, even a little bit, and your efforts will often be greeted with encouragement from locals.

Fortunately, Italian pronunciation is straightforward. There are 7 vowel sounds (one for *a*, *i*, and *u*, and two each for *e* and *o*) compared to 15 in English, and letters are nearly always pronounced the same way. Consonants will be familiar, although the Italian alphabet has fewer letters (no j, k, w, x, or y). If you have any experience with French, Spanish, Portuguese, or Latin you have an advantage, but even if you don't, learning a few phrases is simple and will prepare you for a linguistic dive into Italian culture. Inquiring how much something costs or asking for directions in Italian can be a little daunting, but it's also exciting and much more gratifying than relying on English.

PRONUNCIATION
Vowels

a   like *a* in *father*
e   short like *e* in *set*
é   long like *a* in *way*
i   like *ee* in *feet*
o   short like *o* in *often*, or long like *o* in *rope*
u   like *oo* in *foot*, or *w* in *well*

Consonants

b	like *b* in *boy,* but softer
c	before e or i like *ch* in *chin*
ch	like *c* in *cat*
d	like *d* in *dog*
f	like *f* in *fish*
g	before e or i like *g* in *gymnastics* or like *g* in *go*
gh	like *g* in *go*
gl	like *ll* in *million*
gn	like *ni* in *onion*
gu	like *gu* in *anguish*
h	always silent
l	like *l* in *lime*
m	like *m* in *me*
n	like *n* in *nice*
p	like *p* in *pit*
qu	like *qu* in *quick*
r	rolled/trilled similar to *r* in Spanish or Scottish
s	between vowels like *s* in *nose* or *s* in *sit*
sc	before e or i like *sh* in *shut* or *sk* in *skip*
t	like *t* in *tape*
v	like *v* in *vase*
z	either like *ts* in *spits* or *ds* in *pads*

Accents

Accents are used to indicate which vowel should be stressed and to differentiate between words with different meanings that are spelled the same.

ESSENTIAL PHRASES

Hi Ciao
Hello Salve
Good morning Buongiorno
Good evening Buonasera
Good night Buonanotte
Good-bye Arrivederci
Nice to meet you Piacere
Thank you Grazie
You're welcome Prego
Please Per favore
Do you speak English? Parla inglese?
I don't understand Non capisco
Have a nice day Buona giornata
Where are the restrooms? Dov'è il bagno?
Yes Sì
No No

TRANSPORTATION

Where is...? Dov'è...?
How far is...? Quanto è distante...?
Is there a bus to...? C'è un autobus per...?
Does this bus go to...? Quest'autobus va a...?
Where do I get off? Dove devo scendere?
What time does the bus/train leave/ arrive? A che ora parte/arriva l'autobus/ treno?
Where is the nearest subway station? Dov'è la stazione metro più vicina?
Where can I buy a ticket? Dove posso comprare un biglietto?
A round-trip ticket/a single ticket to... Un biglietto di andata e ritorno/ andata per...

FOOD

A table for two/three/four... Un tavolo per due/tre/quattro...
Do you have a menu in English? Avete un menu in inglese?
What is the dish of the day? Qual è il piatto del giorno?
We're ready to order. Siamo pronti per ordinare.
I'm a vegetarian. Sono vegetariano (male) / Sono vegetariana (female)
May I have... Posso avere...
The check please? Il conto per favore?
beer birra
bread pane
breakfast colazione
cash contante
check conto
coffee caffè
dinner cena
glass bicchiere
hors d'oeuvre antipasto
ice ghiaccio
ice cream gelato
lunch pranzo
restaurant ristorante

sandwich(es) panino(i)
snack spuntino
waiter cameriere
water acqua
wine vino

SHOPPING
money soldi
shop negozio
What time do the shops close? A che ora chiudono i negozi?
How much is it? Quanto costa?
I'm just looking. Sto guardando solamente.
What is the local specialty? Quali sono le specialità locali?

HEALTH
drugstore farmacia
pain dolore
fever febbre
headache mal di testa
stomachache mal di stomaco
toothache mal di denti
burn bruciatura
cramp crampo
nausea nausea
vomiting vomitare
medicine medicina
antibiotic antibiotico
pill/tablet pillola/pasticca
aspirin aspirina
mask maschera
thermometer termometro
I need to see a doctor. Ho bisogno di un medico.
I need to go to the hospital. Devo andare in ospedale.
I have a pain here... Ho un dolore qui...
Can I have a facemask? Posso avere una maschera?
She/he has been stung/bitten. È stata punta/morsa.
I am diabetic/pregnant. Sono diabetico/incinta.
I am allergic to penicillin/cortisone. Sono allergico alla penicillina/cortisone.

My blood group is...positive/negative. Il mio gruppo sanguigno è... positivo/negative.

NUMBERS
0 zero
1 uno
2 due
3 tre
4 quattro
5 cinque
6 sei
7 sette
8 otto
9 nove
10 dieci
11 undici
12 dodici
13 tredici
14 quattordici
15 quindici
16 sedici
17 diciassette
18 diciotto
19 diciannove
20 venti
21 ventuno
30 trenta
40 quaranta
50 cinquanta
60 sessanta
70 settanta
80 ottanta
90 novanta
100 cento
101 centouno
200 duecento
500 cinquecento
1,000 mille
10,000 diecimila
100,000 centomila
1,000,000 un milione

TIME
What time is it? Che ora è?
It's one/three o'clock. E l'una/sono le tre.
midday mezzogiorno
midnight mezzanotte

morning mattino
afternoon pomeriggio
evening sera
night notte
yesterday ieri
today oggi
tomorrow domani

DAYS AND MONTHS

week settimana
month mese
Monday Lunedì
Tuesday Martedì
Wednesday Mercoledì
Thursday Giovedì
Friday Venerdì
Saturday Sabato
Sunday Domenica
January Gennaio
February Febbraio
March Marzo
April Aprile
May Maggio
June Giugno
July Luglio
August Agosto
September Settembre

October Ottobre
November Novembre
December Dicembre

VERBS

to have avere
to be essere
to go andare
to come venire
to want volere
to eat mangiare
to drink bere
to buy comprare
to need necessitare
to read leggere
to write scrivere
to stop fermare
to get off scendere
to arrive arrivare
to return ritornare
to stay restare
to leave partire
to look at guardare
to look for cercare
to give dare
to take prendere

Suggested Reading

HISTORY AND CULTURE

Beard, Mary. *The Fires of Vesuvius: Pompeii Lost and Found.* This is an excellent look at life in Pompeii, written in a compelling narrative style that brings the history of the ancient city to life.

D'Acierno, Pellegrino, and Stanislao G. Pugliese, eds. *Delirious Naples: A Cultural History of the City of the Sun.* A fascinating selection of essays on an interdisciplinary range of topics by Neapolitan and American scholars, artists, and writers.

Goldsworthy, Adrian. *Cannae: Hannibal's Greatest Victory.* A deep dive into what's now considered one of the greatest tactical victories in military history, this book offers a snapshot of the battle between Rome and Carthage for the Italian peninsula.

Hazzard, Shirley. *The Ancient Shore: Dispatches from Naples.* Celebrated Australian writer Shirley Hazzard first visited Naples in the 1950s, beginning a lifelong love affair with the city. This volume brings together her many writings on Naples.

La Capria, Raffaele. *Capri and No Longer Capri.* This intriguing portrait of Capri by an Italian novelist and screenwriter blends the island's history with personal tales and beautiful descriptions of Capri.

Levi, Carlo. *Christ Stopped at Eboli*. The stunning memoir of anti-fascist Italian writer Levi's exile to remote Southern Italy, in what is now Basilicata, exposing the extreme poverty and resilience of the people who lived there.

Lewis, Norman. *Naples '44: A World War II Diary of Occupied Italy*. This is a classic look at Naples during World War II by noted British writer Norman Lewis, famous for his travel writing, who was stationed in Naples in 1944 as an Intelligence Officer.

Lima, Chiara. *Mamma Agata: Traditional Italian Recipes of a Family That Cooks with Love and Passion in a Simple and Genuine Way*. Both a cookbook and the story of a family dedicated to traditional cooking on the Amafi Coast, this book will enchant you with its photos and help you re-create the delicious recipes in your own home.

Munthe, Axel. *The Story of San Michele*. The memoir of Swedish-born doctor Axel Munthe was a bestseller when it was published in 1929 and offers a captivating glimpse into his life and his beloved Villa San Michele on Capri.

Phelps, Daphne. *A House in Sicily*. A memoir written by an Englishwoman who inherits a house in Taormina, turns it into a guesthouse, and goes on to host some of the most esteemed writers and artists of the day, from Tennessee Williams to Henry Faulkner.

Saviano, Roberto. *Gomorrah*. Saviano provides a frightening and unforgettable insider's account of the inner workings of the Camorra, the organized crime network in the Naples area.

Simeti, Mary Taylor. *Bitter Almonds: Recollections and Recipes from a Sicilian Girlhood*.

This incredible true story follows a young girl sent to live in a cloister in Erice, Sicily, who learns the secret pastry recipes so treasured by the nuns by watching them bake. The book includes over 40 traditional pastry recipes.

FICTION

Adler, Elizabeth. *The House in Amalfi* and *Sailing to Capri*. International bestselling author Elizabeth Adler has brought a charming combination of romance, intrigue, and love of travel to her two novels set on the Amalfi Coast and Capri. This is fun and light travel reading for a beach holiday.

Camilleri, Andrea. *The Shape of Water*. The first book in Camilleri's famous Inspector Montalbano series is a fast-paced, hard-boiled detective thriller set in a small seaside Sicilian town.

de Lamartine, Alphonse. *Graziella*. Published in 1852 and based on firsthand experiences of French writer Alphonse de Lamartine in Procida, the novel is the story of an ill-fated relationship between a young French man and poor young woman named Graziella, the granddaughter of a fisherman.

di Lampedusa, Giuseppe Tomasi. *The Leopard*. Set during the Italian Risorgimento, when Giuseppe Garibaldi arrived in Sicily with the hope of uniting Italy into one kingdom, this historical novel is considered one of the best books ever written by a Sicilian author.

Ferrante, Elena. *Neapolitan Novels: My Brilliant Friend, The Story of a New Name, Those Who Leave and Those Who Stay, The Story of the Lost Child*. This four-part novel follows a captivating friendship between two young girls and throughout their lives, set in the Naples area—with parts of the first book, *My Brilliant Friend*, taking place on Ischia.

Her latest novel *The Lying Life of Adults,* is also set in Naples.

Mazzoni, Jan. *Dreamland and Other Stories.* A collection of 15 short stories based in the Amalfi Coast in the 1980s.

Puzo, Mario. *The Sicilian.* Thought of as the sequel to Puzo's *The Godfather,* this book follows Michael Corleone as he gets mixed up with a Sicilian bandit named Salvatore Guiliano, who has gotten on the bad side of the Cosa Nostra.

Sontag, Susan. *The Volcano Lover.* A compelling historical novel about Sir William Hamilton, British Ambassador to the Kingdom of Naples from 1764-1800, his wife Emma Hamilton, and her scandalous affair with Lord Nelson.

Walpole, Horace. *The Castle of Otranto.* Considered by many to be the first Gothic novel, published in 1764, this colorful story follows Manfred, lord of the eponymous Apulian castle, on a series of dramatic adventures following what was meant to be his son's wedding day.

Webb, Katherine. *The Night Falling.* Set in 1920s Puglia, Webb's historical novel is a study of the economic inequality rampant in the area in the early 20th century, following an Italian emigrant returning from America as he renovates an old palace.

Suggested Films

L'Avventura (1960) Michelangelo Antonioni. This well-known Italian film about a beautiful woman who goes missing has a particularly famous scene set in the Aeolian Islands, but Sicily shines as a setting throughout the movie.

Cinema Paradiso (1988) Giuseppe Tornatore. A beloved film set in a small Sicilian village, following a young man's love of the movies on his journey to becoming a filmmaker in his own right.

L'Oro di Napoli (1954) Vittorio De Sica. Meaning "The Gold of Naples," this film is a tribute to the city by Italian director and actor Vittorio De Sica. Composed of six episodes, the film features some of the most iconic names in Italian film, including Totò, Eduardo De Filippo, and Sophia Loren.

It Started in Naples (1960) Melville Shavelson. This fun love story features the great duo of Clark Gable and Sophia Loren. Despite the title, the movie was filmed mostly on Capri and shows off the island as it was in the '60s.

Only You (1994) Norman Jewison. This romantic comedy with Robert Downey Jr. and Marisa Tomei follows a grand tour from Venice to Rome and Positano. The poolside scenes in Positano were filmed at the Le Sirenuse hotel.

The Godfather Trilogy (1972, 1974, 1990) Francis Ford Coppola. Almost synonymous with Sicily in many people's imaginations, this trio of films about an Italian-American crime family is considered among the best movies of all time.

The Talented Mr. Ripley (1999) Anthony Minghella. A movie adaptation of Patricia Highsmith's 1955 novel, this thriller has the powerhouse cast of Matt Damon, Jude Law, and Gwyneth Paltrow. For the film, Procida was used for the novel's fictional seaside town of Mongibello, with scenes also shot in Positano.

A Good Woman (2004) Mike Barker. Based on *Lady Windermere's Fan* by Oscar Wilde, this captivating film set in the 1930s features Helen Hunt and Scarlett Johansson. Filmed on the Amalfi Coast.

Si Accettano Miracoli (2015) Alessandro Siani. Neapolitan actor and director Alessandro

Siani shot this film on the Amalfi Coast, with much of the filming taking place in the peaceful town of Scala near Ravello.

Wonder Woman (2017) Patty Jenkins. The stunning cave city of Matera was used as the fictional home of Diana, princess of the Amazons, before she leaves to help the outside world fight the evil plot of Ares, god of war.

Internet and Digital Resources

TRAVEL AND TOURIST TIPS

www.incampania.com
The official tourist website for Campania is a great place to start looking for inspiration, with information on the landmarks, museums, culture, gastronomy, and natural landscape of the region.

www.scabec.it
Scabec (Società Campania Beni Culturali) is a society dedicated to preserving and sharing Campania's cultural heritage through organizing and promoting events, concerts, and exhibitions throughout the region.

www.viaggiareinpuglia.it
The official tourist website for Puglia is smartly designed and easy to navigate, a great resource for planning your itinerary in this special Italian region.

www.visitsicily.info
Sicily's official tourism website is full of useful information, with an especially useful, up-to-date list of events happening across the island.

TRANSPORTATION

www.skyscanner.com, www.kayak.com, www.momondo.com

These flight aggregators help find the cheapest fares. Momondo often pulls in the lowest fares, but they all can offer great savings and simplify planning as well as offering hotel and car-rental services.

www.rome2rio.com
Door-to-door transportation details with distances, departures times, and prices for planes, trains, buses, and ferries. There's also a carbon emissions estimate for the ecologically inclined.

www.seatguru.com
Learn your legroom options and read unbiased advice on where to sit on a flight. The database includes all major airlines, along with diagrams, photos, and descriptions of Airbus and Boeing interiors.

www.jetlagrooster.com
Avoid jet lag by creating a personalized sleep plan for a smooth transition between time zones. Just log on 3-4 days before departure and follow their recommended bedtimes.

www.italo.com, www.trenitalia.com
These are the sites of Italy's high-speed rail operators. Tickets can be printed at home or saved on mobile devices. If your trip is still

months away, sign up for the Italo newsletter and receive monthly travel offers.

www.autostrade.it
Drivers can calculate mileage (in kilometers) and toll costs for planned routes. Rest areas are listed, as are the cheapest gas stations. It's also useful for traffic alerts and brushing up on the rules of the Italian road.

ACCOMMODATIONS
www.airbnb.com, www.booking.com, www.slh.com
Search for B&Bs, apartments, or boutique hotels. Sites include realistic visuals, plus advice and reviews from people who have traveled before you.

www.tripadvisor.com
Get feedback and user ratings on sights, services, and hotels. Comments are detailed and often highlight inconveniences like a bad view or small bathroom.

www.xe.com
Calculate what a buck is worth and know exactly how much you're spending. The site's sister app is ideal for the financially conscious and allows travelers to track expenditures on the go.

APPS
Alitalia
Italy's main airline has an app with flight status, boarding information, and baggage claim info.

Trenitalia, Italo
Italy's two train companies offer English-language apps with timetables, the latest train status information, and the ability to purchase tickets via the apps.

Moovit
This excellent app covers transportation for the entire area, including trains, metro, buses, funicular trains, and ferries. Offline maps of Naples's train and Metro lines are available to download.

Google Translate
This helpful dictionary and translation app helps travelers decipher and pronounce Italian.

The Weather Channel
Here you'll find the latest reliable weather information and forecasts for the Amalfi Coast area.

Index

A

accommodations: 468–469; Naples 70–72; Palermo 302–303; see also specific place
Aci Trezza: 343–344
Acquacalda: 381
adapter, electronic: 24, 473
Aegadian Islands: 20, 274, 326–327
Aeolian Islands: 20, 21, 332, 375–393; map 377
Aeroporto del Salento: 241
Aeroporto di Catania-Fontanarossa: 23, 332, 351–352, 398, 416, 456
Aeroporto di Palermo Falcone e Borsellino: 23, 274, 304, 456
Aeroporto di Reggio Calabria: 267
Aeroporto Internazionale di Bari: see Bari International Airport
Aeroporto Internazionale di Napoli: 23, 73, 455
Agrigento: 32, 274, 322–329
Agriristories Ristorante: 265
Airbnb: 469
air travel: 23, 455–458, 459; Naples 73; Palermo 304; see also specific place
Albergheria: 271; accommodations 302–303; food 295; sights 282–283
Alberobello: 28, 206, 235–240
alcohol: 471–472
Alessandro di Camporeale: 32, 310
Alicudi: 376, 390
Alighieri, Dante: 450
Amalfi: 19, 26, 98, 141–157; map 144–145
Amalfi Coast: 18–19, 21, 26, 28, 120–177; maps 100–101, 106–107, 122–123
Amalfi Coast Road: 31, 99
Amalfi Lemon Experience: 33, 149
Amphitheater (Pompeii): 26, 84
anchovies: 21, 33, 166
Andria: 28, 225–227
Anfiteatro Romano (Syracuse): 404
Anfiteatro Romano di Catania: 342
animals: 440–441
Anjou and Aragonese Rule: 443
Antiquarium: 80
apartment rentals: 469
A' Piscaria: see Pescheria di Catania
arancine: 34, 296
archaeological sites: 13, 16, 27, 78–87, 87–92, 177–180, 321, 322–324
architecture: 27, 452
Arco Naturale: 181, 183, 193

Arco Naturale to Belvedere di Tragara Walk: 132, 188–189
Arienzo beach: 123, 127
arrusti: 347
Asino Beach: 390
Aspromonte National Park: 268
ATMs: 473–474
Auditorium Oscar Niemeyer: 162
Avenue of Immensity: 160
Awaiting Table Cookery School: 246
Azienda Agricola Arianna Occhipinti: 428

B

babbalucci: 296–297
Baglio Occhipinti: 430–432
Bagno Ebraico/Mikveh: 408
Baia Verde: 253–254
baked goods: 34, 68, 465
Ballarò: see Mercato di Ballarò
Ballarò Buskers: 290–291, 463–464
banks: 473–474
Bari: 19, 206, 210–220; map 211
Bari, vicinity of: 220–240
Bari International Airport: 206, 219, 456
Bari Stazione Centrale: 219
Bari Vecchia: 211
Barletta: 223–225
Barletta-Andria-Trani: 206
Barone di Villagrande: 370
Baroque architecture: 15, 21, 27, 241–249, 419–423, 452
Bar Pasticceria Etna dal 1963: 360
bars/nightlife: Naples 69–70; Palermo 300–301; see also specific place
Basilica Cattedrale di San Nicolò di Bari: 356
Basilica Cattedrale di San Sabino: 213
Basilica Cattedrale di Sant'Agata: 253
Basilica Cattedrale San Nicola Pellegrino: 221
Basilica di San Martino: 239
Basilica di San Nicola: 27, 213
Basilica di Santa Croce: 30, 246
Basilica of the Crucifix: 143
Basilica Sanctuario Madonna delle Lacrime: 404
Basilicata region: 267–268
Bastinone Santo Stefano: 229
Battistero di San Giovanni in Fonte: 49
Battle of Caporetto: 445
beach clubs: 29
beaches: 11, 29, 464; Aegadian Islands 327; Aeolian Islands 381–382, 387, 390; Agrigento

324; Amalfi 143, 146–147; Amalfi Coast 130; Bari 214; Capri 186–188; Catania 343–344; Cefalù 313; Gallipoli 253–254; Mondello 307; Otranto 250; Polignano a Mare 229, 232; Positano 126–129; Ragusa 430; Salento, the 254–255; Sorrento 113–114; Syracuse 409; Syracuse, vicinity of 410, 418; Taormina 358; Trapani 317

bed and breakfasts: 469; see also accommodations

Belvedere Castellammare del Golfo: 318

Belvedere della Migliera Walk: 132, 189

Belvedere di Tragara: 189

Belvedere Quattrocchi: 381

Belvedere Santa Lucia: 237

Bike Trail Rossana Maiorca: 409

biking: Naples 59; Syracuse 408–409

BIPOC travelers, advice for: 478

birds: 440–441

Bisso Bistrot: 295, 299

Blue Grotto: see Grotta Azzurra

boating: 14, 131, 147, 148, 191–193, 308, 382, 387

BOATs: 414

Bomerano: 129

Borbonika Napulitan Restaurant: 69

Borgo Egnazia: 28, 234

Borgo Marinari: 52–53

Brindisi: 30, 206, 241

Brindisi Airport: see Aeroporto del Salento

busiate con pesto trapanese: 317

business hours: 467, 468, 475

bus travel: 24, 458, 460; Naples 74, 76, 77; Palermo 305; see also specific place

Byzantine Empire: 442

Byzantine New Year: 150–151

C

caciocavallo cheese: 424

Café and Snack Bar (Pompeii): 84

Caffè dell'Arte: 435

Caffè Sicilia: 421

Calabria region: 267–268

Cala dell'Acquaviva: 207, 255

Cala Junco bay: 390

Cala Mosca: 319

Cala Petròlo: 318

Caltagirone: 398

Camigliatello Silano: 268

Campania Artecard: 39, 79, 89

Camporeale: 310–311

Camporeale Day: 310

Canneto: 381

Capo: accommodations 303; bars/nightlife 300–301; entertainment/events 289; food 295, 299–300; shopping 292; sights 283

Capodichino: see Aeroporto Internazionale di Napoli

Capodimonte: 37; sights 49–50

Cappella dei Crociati: 168

Cappella Palatina: 50, 283

Capri: 18, 21, 98, 180–201; map 181

car travel: 24, 31, 459, 459–460; Naples 75, 77; Palermo 305, 306; see also specific place

Caruso Roof Garden Restaurant: 67

Casa e Bottega: 135

Casa Grotta Nei Sassi: 261

Casamicciola Terme: 57

Casa Noha: 260–261

Casa Stagnitta: 277, 294

Caseificio Borderi: 412

Castel dell'Ovo: 37, 52–53

Castel del Monte: 27, 227–228

Castellammare del Golfo: 318

Castello Arabo Normanno: 318

Castello Aragonese (Ischia): 57

Castello Aragonese (Otranto): 30, 249

Castello Carlo V: 243

Castello del Gallipoli: 253

Castello della Zisa: 271, 283

Castello di Arechi: 170–171

Castello di Barletta: 223

Castello di Milazzo: 379

Castello di Trani: 221

Castello di Venere: 317

Castello Maniace: 406, 408, 410

Castello Normanno-Svevo: 213

Castello Ursino: 341–342

Castel Nuovo: 50

Castel Sant'Elmo: 37, 53, 56

castles: 452; see also specific castle

Catacombe dei Cappuccini: 271, 283

Catacombe di San Gaudioso: 58

Catacombe di San Gennaro: 58

Catacombe di San Giovanni: 404

Catania: 20, 21, 30, 330–353; maps 333, 335, 338–339

Catania-Fontanarossa airport: see Aeroporto di Catania-Fontanarossa

Cattedrale Basilica Santa Maria Assunta in Cielo: 231

Cattedrale di Maria Santissima Della Bruna e Sant'Eustachio: 261

Cattedrale di Monreale: 32, 309–310

Cattedrale di Noto: 420, 421

Cattedrale di Palermo: 283

Cattedrale di Salerno: 27, 168, 170

Cattedrale di Sant'Agata: 30, 336, 337, 347

Cattedrale di Siracusa: 406

Cattedrale di Sorrento: 108–109

Cavagrande Nature Reserve: 408

Cave di Murgia – Chiesa Rupestri di San Falcione Hike: 264

Cave of Mercy Hike: 428
Cefalù: 271, 311–314
Cefalù Medieval Laundry: 313
Central Baths (Herculaneum): 90
Central Baths (Pompeii): 83
centro storico (Lecce): 242–243
centro storico (Naples): 37; accommodations
    70–71; bars/nightlife 69–70; entertainment/
    events 60; food 64–65; maps 44–45; shopping
    62–63; sights 42–49
centro storico (Palermo): 20, 271
centro storico (Polignano a Mare): 229
centro storico (Salerno): 168
centro storico (Sorrento): 26, 108, 109
Centro Visite Jazzo Gattini: 264
ceramics: 62, 134, 151–152, 163–164, 173, 359,
    431, 453
Certosa di San Martino: 37
Certosa e Museo di San Martino: 56
Cetara: 21, 166
Chiaia: 37, 38
Chiesa della Badia di Sant'Agata: 341
Chiesa di Gesù Nuovo: 46
Chiesa di San Cataldo: 277, 281
Chiesa di San Domenico: 420
Chiesa di San Francesco d'Assisi: 420
Chiesa di San Gennaro: 126
Chiesa di San Matteo: 243
Chiesa di San Nicola di Patara: 239
Chiesa di San Pietro: 433
Chiesa di San Pietro Barisano: 262
Chiesa di Santa Caterina d'Alessandria: 277
Chiesa di Santa Chiara: 245
Chiesa di Santa Lucia Alla Badia: 406
Chiesa di Santa Maria Assunta: 26, 123–125
Chiesa di Santa Maria dell'Ammiraglio: 281
Chiesa di Santo Stefano: 182, 189
Chiesa Madre di San Giorgio: 238
Chiesa Monumentale di San Michele: 186
Chiesa Rupestre di San Nicolò Inferiore: 433
Chiesa Rupestri di San Falcione: 262, 264
Chiesa Rupestri di San Nicola dei Greci e
    Madonna Delle Virtù: 262
chiese rupestri: 261
children, traveling with: 477
chocolate: 434–435
cipollata: 346
cipolline: 34
Cisternino: 239
City Hall (Palermo): 281
climate: 438–439
Cloister of Paradise: 143
clothing: 472
coffee bars: 465–466
colatura di alici: 166
Colonna di Sant'Oronzo: 245

Colossus of Barletta: 223
communications: 474–475
Complesso Monumentale di Santa Chiara: 27,
    46, 48
Complesso Monumentale di Sant'Andrea: 143
consulates: 462
cooking classes: 162, 191, 246, 286, 288, 344, 359,
    409, 430, 433
corals: 163, 453
cornetto: 465
Corona Trattoria: 300
coronavirus: 23, 456–457
Corso Matteotti: 406
Corso Umberto: 355
Corso Vittorio Emanuele: 271
Cotognata Leccese: 34, 247
Cous Cous Fest: 319
crafts: 453
credit cards: 474
Cre.Zi. Plus - Cantieri Culturali Alla Zisa: 290
crime: 471
Cripta del Peccato Originale: 262
crocchè: 297
crowds, tips for avoiding: 21, 22
Crypt of Sant'Andrea: 143
cucina povera: 34, 292
currency: 473
customs: 462
customs, cultural: 471–472
cycling: see biking

D
Da Ferdinando: 127
dance: 454
Dante Alighieri: 450
debit cards: 474
decorative arts: 453
Decumano Inferiore: 88
Decumano Massimo: 88
demography: 450
disabilities, access for travelers with: 476–477
discounts for senior travelers: 478
Domenico Modugno Statue: 229
donkey tours: 367
drinks: 466
drugs: 472
Duchy of Amalfi: 443
Duoglio: 130, 146
Duomo (Ostuni): 239
Duomo di Amalfi: 26, 27, 141, 143
Duomo di Cefalù: 311
Duomo di Lecce: 245–246
Duomo di Napoli: 25, 27, 37, 48–49
Duomo di Otranto: 249–250
Duomo di Ravello: 28, 158
Duomo di San Giorgio: 424, 432–433

Duomo di Siracusa: 406
Duomo di Taormina: 356

E

Easter: 149–150, 463
economy: 449
Egadi Islands: *see* Aegadian Islands
emergency numbers: 470
Enoteca Picone: 301
Enoteca Solaria: 414
entertainment/events: Naples 60–61; Palermo
    288–291; *see also specific place*
environmental issues: 439
Erice: 317
espresso: 466
Etna Sud: 374

F

Faraglioni: 29, 183, 187, 193
Faraglioni dei Ciclopi: 343
Faro di Punta Palascia: 250
fascism: 445–447
Favignana: 326–327
Ferragosto: 133, 463
Ferrante, Elena: 451
Ferrovia Circumetnea: 364, 374–375
ferry travel: 24, 458–459, 460–461; Naples 74–75;
    Palermo 305; *see also specific place*
Festa del Carmine: 61
Festa della Bruna: 264
Festa del Pesce: 133, 463
Festa di San Costanzo: 191
Festa di San Gennaro: 61, 463
Festa di San Giorgio: 433–434
Festa di San Nicola: 214, 216, 463
Festa di Sant'Agata: 346, 347, 464
Festa di Sant'Antonio: 191–192
Festa di Santa Rosalia: 290
Festival of San Matteo: 171, 173
Festival of San Pantaleone: 163
Festival of Santa Lucia: 410–411
Festival of Sant'Andrea: 150, 463
festivals/events: 463–464; Naples 61; Palermo
    290–291; *see also specific festival*
Ficogrande: 390
Filicudi: 376, 390
films, suggested: 485–486
flowers: 440
Foggia: 207
Foggia Airport: 231
Fontana dell'Amenano: 337
Fontana dell'Elefante: 337
Fontana del Sebeto: 53
Fontana di Diana: 406
Fontana di Piazza Duomo: 356

Fontana di Sant'Andrea: 143
Fontana Greca: 253
Fontana Pretoria: 281
Fonte Aretusa: 406, 408
food: 33–34, 465–467; Naples 64–69; Palermo
    292–300; *see also specific place*
football (soccer): 59
Forio: 57
fornaio: 465
Foro Italico: 32, 285
fortified cities: 452
Forum (Pompeii): 78, 80–82
Forum Baths (Pompeii): 83
Francesco Pantaleone Arte Contemporanea:
    289–290
Franco's Bar: 137
Fratelli Burgio: 412
free beaches: 29
frittola: 297
Funicolare Centrale: 77
Funicolare di Chiaia: 77
Funicolare di Montesanto: 77
Funivia dell'Etna: 365, 375

G

Galleria Borbonica: 52
Galleria d'Arte Moderna Palermo: 281
Galleria Umberto I: 25, 37, 52
Gallipoli: 20, 206, 252–258
Gambarie: 268
Garibaldi, Giuseppe: 445
gay travelers, advice for: 478
geography: 437–438
Germplasm Trail: 367
Giardini di Augusto: 181, 182–183
Giardini Naxos: 358
Giardini Poseidon Terme: 57
Giardini Pubblici Giuseppe Garibaldi: 246
Giardino dei Carrubi: 390
Giardino della Kolymbetra: 31, 324
Giardino Ibleo: 424
Giardino Inglese: 271, 285
glossary: 479–480
Gothic architecture: 27, 452
government: 449
Gran Caffè: 154
Gran Caffè Gambrinus: 25, 67
Gran Cratere: 390
Gravina di Matera: 259
Green Route: 418
greetings: 471
Griko language: 450–451
Grotta Azzurra: 185–186, 193
Grotta Bianca: 193
Grotta del Genovese: 326–327
Grotta della Poesia: 30, 207, 254

Grotta di Matermania: 189
Grotta Verde: 193
Grotte di Castellana: 206, 235
Guidaloca: 319

H

Hall of the Augustals: 90
handmade pasta: see orecchiette
Herculaneum: 13, 18, 27, 37, 39, 87–92, 444; map
    88
high season: 22
hiking: 464; Aeolian Islands 392–393; Amalfi 147;
    Amalfi Coast 32, 132; Capri 188–191; Cefalù
    313; Matera 262, 264; Mount Etna 12, 32,
    364–367; Mount Vesuvius 32, 94; Positano
    17, 129–130; Ragusa 428; Syracuse 408–409;
    Syracuse, vicinity of 418, 418–419; Taormina
    358–359
Historical Regatta of the Ancient Maritime
    Republics: 150
history: 21, 441–448
holidays: 475
hostels: 469; see also accommodations
hotels: 469; see also accommodations
House of Menander: 83
House of Neptune and Amphitrite: 90
House of the Deer: 90
House of the Faun: 84
House of the Tragic Poet: 84
House of the Vetii: 84
House of Venus in the Shell: 83–84

IJK

Il Parco della Salute: 285
Il Re di Girgenti: 328
Il Rivellino: 253
immigration: 450
industry: 449
Infiorata Flower Festival: 421
information/services: Naples 72; Palermo 303; see
    also specific place
intarsia (inlaid woodwork): 113, 114, 117, 453
Ischia: 57
I Segreti del Chiostro: 34, 294
Isola Bella: 355, 356, 358
itineraries, suggested: 23, 25–32; Naples 40–42;
    Palermo 275; see also specific place
jeep tours 367
Kalsa: 271; accommodations 302; bars/nightlife
    300–301; food 294–295; shopping 291–292;
    sights 277, 281–282
Karol Wojtyla Airport: see Bari International
    Airport
kayaking: 32, 147, 148; Amalfi Coast 32; Naples 32,
    59; Positano 130–131; Sorrento 32, 114

Kingdom of Sicily: 442
Kolymbetra Gardens: see Giardino della
    Kolymbetra

L

La Capinera: 360
La Loggia: 271; accommodations 302; bars/
    nightlife 300–301; entertainment/events
    288–289, 289–290; food 293–294
La Marinella: 146
La Martorana: 32, 277, 281
landscape: 437–439
language: 450
L'Antica Pizzeria da Michele: 33, 65
La Praia dei Nacchi: 327
Large Theater (Pompeii): 83
La Rocca hike: 313
Latomie del Paradiso: 404
La Tonnara di Scopello: 318–319
laundry: 473
Lavatoio Medievale Fiume Cefalino: 313
La Zisa: 271
Lecce: 15, 20, 27, 30, 206, 241–249; map 242
lemons: 33, 467
Le Sirene: 146
Levanzo: 326–327
Le Vie dei Tesori: 291
LGBTQ travelers, advice for: 478
Lido Adria: 214
Lido Arenella - Villa Babej: 410
Lido Cala Paura: 232
Lido San Francesco: 214
Li Galli Islands: 125–126
limoncello: 33, 439, 466
limone Costa d'Amalfi: 439
limone di Sorrento: 439
Lingua: 386
Lipari: 376, 379–386
literature: 451
Locorotondo: 238
LoveSicily: 433
low season: 22
Luciano Faggiano: 243
Luci d'Artista: 171, 173
Luci in Valle: 323
luggage storage: 473
lungomare (Salerno): 168, 171
Lungomare di Bari: 214
Lungomare di Levante Elio Vittorini: 406
Lungomare Franco Battiato: 336
Lupanar: 83

M

Madre: 49
Magna Graecia: 441

Malfa: 386
mammals: 440
maps: 476
Marettimo: 326–327
Marina Corricella: 57
Marina di Praia beach: 123, 127, 129
Marina Grande (Amalfi): 146
Marina Grande (Capri): 180, 187
Marina Grande (Procida): 57
Marina Grande (Sorrento): 18, 105, 108, 114, 130
Marina Lunga: 381
Marina Piccola (Capri): 29, 130, 181, 187–188
Marina Piccola (Sorrento): 105–120, 113–114
Marsala: 20, 274, 322–323
marsala wine: 34, 322–323
Martina Franca: 239
Marzamemi: 419
masserie: 207
Matera: 20, 21, 206, 259–267; map 260
Matera Film Festival: 264–265
medical services: 470
menus: 466
Mercato del Capo: 286
Mercato di Ballarò: 32, 286, 295
Mercato di Siracusa: 412
Mercato Vucciria: 32, 286, 293
Mergellina: 37, 53
Messina: 332
Milazzo: 376, 379
minne di Sant'Agata: 347
Modica: 22, 398, 432–436
Molo Pennello: 141
Mondello: 271, 306–309
money: 473–474
Monreale: 274, 309–310
Monte Solaro: 18, 180, 186, 189
Monte Spagnolo Hike: 367
Monte Tiberio: 180
Monumento al Marinaio d'Italia: 241
MOOM: Matera Olive Oil Museum: 261
Mount Etna: 12, 20, 30, 33, 332, 362–375; map 363
Mount Vesuvius: 18, 37, 92–95, 438
Museo Archeological Romano Santa Maria
    Assunta: 124–125
Museo Archeologico (Agrigento): 324
Museo Archeologico Eoliano L. Bernabò Brea: 381
Museo Archeologico Nazionale (Naples): 25, 37,
    42, 78, 83
Museo Archeologico Nazionale (Paestum):
    179–180
Museo Archeologico Nazionale di Taranto: 258
Museo Archeologico Provinciale: 168, 170
Museo Archeologico Regionale Paolo Orsi: 404
Museobottega della Tarsialignea: 113
Museo Cappella Sansevero: 48
Museo Civico (Catania): 342

Museo Civico (Naples): 50
Museo Civico Torre di Ligny: 315–316
Museo Correale di Terranova: 109
Museo della Carta: 26, 143
Museo dell'Opera: 48
Museo dell'Opera del Duomo: 158, 160
Museo del Novecento: 53
Museo del Teatro Romano: 245
Museo del Tesoro di San Gennaro: 49
Museo di Capodimonte: 37, 38
Museo Diocesano (Amalfi): 143
Museo Diocesano (Catania): 337
Museo Duca di Martina: 56
Museo e Real Bosco di Capodimonte: 50
Museo Internazionale delle Marionette Antonio
    Pasqualino: 282, 288–289
Museo Mandralisca: 311, 313
Museo Medievale: 171
Museo Nazionale di Reggio Calabria: 267–268
Museo Regionale Conte Agostino Pepoli: 316
Museo Regionale della Ceramica: 431
Museo San Giorgio: 424
music: 453–454
Musma: Museo della Scultura Contemporanea
    Matera: 261
Mussolini, Benito: 445

N
Naples: 18, 21, 25, 35–77; accommodations 70–72;
    bars/nightlife 69–70; entertainment/events
    60–61; food 64–69; information/services 72;
    itineraries, suggested 40–42; maps 38–39, 41,
    43–44, 54–55; planning tips 38–40; shopping
    61–64; sports/recreation 59; transportation
    73–77
Naples Card: 39
Napoli Centrale Stazione: 37, 73
Napoli Pizza Village: 61, 463
Napoli Sotterranea: 37, 49
Napoli Sotterranea, L.A.E.S.: 49
nativities: see presepe
Neapolitan language: 450
Neapolitan pizza: 12, 26, 33, 66, 467
Neapolitan School of painting: 452–453
New Year's Eve: 463
nightlife: see bars/nightlife
Nocelle: 129
NO Mafia Memorial: 283
Noto: 15, 22, 27, 398, 419–423

O
olive oil: 34, 226
olive trees: 440
Orange Route: 418
orecchiette: 34, 215

Orecchio di Dionisio: 404
Ortigia, Island of: 22, 404–408; map 405
Ortigia Sound System Music Festival: 410, 464
Orto Botanico dell'Università di Catania: 343
Orto Botanico dell'Università di Palermo: 282
Osteria degli Spiriti: 247
osterie: 465
Ostuni: 239
Otranto: 30, 206, 249–252

PQ

packing tips: 24, 472–473
Paestum: 16, 27, 177–180; map 178
painting: 452–453
Palaestra: 90, 92
Palazzo Abatellis: 282
Palazzo Ajutamicristo: 291
Palazzo Biscari: 341
Palazzo Castelluccio: 421
Palazzo dei Normanni: 27, 32, 282–283
Palazzo Ducezio: 420
Palazzo Morelli: 238
Palazzo Nicolaci di Villadorata: 420
Palazzo Reale: 25, 37, 50, 52
Palazzo Sovrana: 302
Palermo: 20, 21, 32, 269–306; accommodations
    302–303; bars/nightlife 300–301;
    entertainment/events 288–291; food
    292–300; information/services 303; itineraries,
    suggested 275; maps 272–273, 276, 278–279;
    planning tips 274; shopping 291–292; sports/
    recreation 285–288; transportation 304–306
Palermo, vicinity of: 306–314
Palermo Stazione Centrale: 271, 304–305
Palombaro Lungo: 261
Panarea: 376, 390
pane cunzatu: 317
panelle: 34, 297
pani cà meusa: 297
Parco 2 Giugno: 213–214
Parco Archeologico della Neapolis: 22, 402, 404
Parco Archeologico di Ercolano: 89
Parco Archeologico di Paestum: 177, 179
Parco Archeologico di Pompei: 78
Parco dell'Etna: 364
Parco Fluviale dell'Alcantara: 358–359
Parco Nazionale del Gargano: 206, 207, 230
Parco Nazionale dell'Alta Murgia: 228
Parco Nazionale della Sila: 268
Parco Nazionale del Vesuvio: 93–94
Parco Regionale della Murgia Materana: 259,
    262, 264
parks: Bari 213–214; Catania 342–343; Lecce 246;
    Palermo 285; Trani 221
passports: 22–23, 461–462
Pasta alla Norma: 346

pasticceria: 465
Pasticceria Maria Grammatico: 34, 320
Pasticceria Pansa: 154
pastori: 62
Pathway of the Gods: 17, 32, 129–130, 132
people of color travelers, advice for: 478
Perivancu: 370–371
perpetua cake: 424
Pescheria di Catania: 20, 30, 33, 341
pharmacies: 470
philosophy: 451
phrasebook: 480–483
Piano B: 411
Piano Provenzana: 367–368
Piazza Anfiteatro: 78
Piazza Bellini: 42, 69, 277
Piazza Dante: 69
Piazza dei Mulini: 122, 133
Piazza del Duomo (Catania): 30, 336, 337
Piazza del Plebiscito: 37, 52
Piazza Duomo (Amalfi): 26, 141
Piazza Duomo (Ravello): 158
Piazza Duomo (Syracuse): 404–408
Piazza Flavio Gioia: 141
Piazza IX Aprile 355
Piazza Porta Marina Inferiore: 78
Piazza Pretoria: 32
Piazza Sant'Oronzo: 243, 245
Piazza Sedile del Campo: 170
Piazza Sedile di Portanova: 168, 170, 173
Piazza Stesicoro: 347
Piazza Tasso: 108, 109
Piazza Universita: 342
Piazza Vittorio Veneto: 173
Piazzetta (Capri): 18, 181
pizza al taglio: 465
pizza fritta: 34, 465
pizza Margherita: 66
Pizzaria La Notizia: 69
pizzerias: 465
planning tips: 18–24; Naples 38–40; Palermo 274;
    see also specific place
plants and animals: 439–441
Pliny the Younger: 451
police: 470
Polignano a Mare: 28, 206, 229, 232–235
Pollara: 386
polpette di cavallo: 347
Pompeii: 13, 18, 26, 27, 37, 39, 78–87, 444; map
    80–81
Ponte Borbonico: 229
Ponte de Piedra: 258
Ponte Girevole: 258
Ponte Papa Giovanni Paolo II: 253
Ponte Santa Lucia: 406
Ponte Tibetano della Gravina: 264

Ponte Umbertino: 406
porcelain: 453
Porta Catania: 354
Porta Ercolano: 78
Porta Garibaldi: 337
Porta Marina: 78, 79, 86
Porta Messina: 354
Porta Rudiae: 243
Porta San Biagio: 243
Porta Uzeda: 337
Porta Vecchia: 229
Porto di Catania: 336
Porto di Messina: 378
Porto di Napoli: 24, 74–75
Porto di Napoli (Lecce): 243
Porto di Palermo: 305
Posillipo School of painting: 453
Positano: 19, 26, 98, 120–141; map 124–125
postal services: 474–475
Praiano: 98, 123, 126
presepe: 62–63, 453
Prestipino Duomo: 348
Procida: 57
Profumi di Positano: 134
public transportation: Naples 75–77; Palermo
      305; see also specific place
Puglia: 19–20, 21, 28, 30, 202–268; maps 205–206,
      208–209
Punta Barcarello: 307
Punta Carena beach: 188, 193
Punta Raisi: see Aeroporto di Palermo Falcone e
      Borsellino
Quanto Basta: 247–248
Quattro Canti: 32, 271, 277, 302

R
Ragusa: 22, 398, 424–432; map 425
Ravello: 19, 28, 98, 158–167; map 159
Ravello Concert Society: 162
Ravello Festival: 160, 162–163, 463
Razmataz: 347
reading, suggested: 483–485
Reale Cappella del Tesoro di San Gennaro: 49
recreation: see sports/recreation
Reggio Calabria: 267–268
religion: 450
reptiles: 440
reservations: 468–469
restaurants: 465; see also food
ricci di mare: 33, 233
Ricci Weekender: 346
Rifugio Sapienza: 364, 365, 367
Rinascente: 294
Rione Aia Piccola: 237
Rione Monti: see Zona Trulli Rione Monti
Riserva Naturale del Plemmirio: 410

Riserva Naturale di Capo Gallo: 307
Riserva Naturale Orientata Cavagrande del
      Cassibile: 417–418
Riserva Naturale Orientata dello Zingaro: 319
Riserva Naturale Orientata Oasi Faunistica di
      Vendicari: 418–419
Riserva Naturale Orientata Torre Salsa: 324
Risorgimento: 445
Ristorante Don Camillo: 414
Ristorante Garden: 164
Ristorante La Scogliera: 328
Ristorante Marina Grande: 152
Ristorante Ramo d'Aria: 371
ristoranti: 465
Riviera dei Ciclopi: 343–344
road trips: 31, 207, 318–319
Rolex Capri Sailing Week: 191
Roman Amphitheatre (Lecce): 30, 245
Romanesque architecture: 27
Roman history: 441–442
Rose Terrace: 160
royal gate (Noto): 420
royal palaces: 452; see also specific palace
ruins: see archaeological sites

S
safety: 470–471; Palermo 274
Sala dell'Armeria: 50
Salento, the: 21, 29, 30, 206, 240–258
Salerno: 19, 28, 98, 167–177; map 169
sales tax: 474
Salina: 376, 386–389
Saline di Trapani e Paceco: 316–317
salt: 316–317
Salt Museum: 317
San Ferdinando: 37; accommodations 71;
      entertainment/events 60–61; shopping 63, 65,
      67; sights 50–52
San Giovanni in Fiore: 268
sanguinaccio: 347
Santa Croce beach: 130, 146–147
Santa Marina: 386
Sant'Angelo: 57
San Tommaso d'Aquino: 451
Santuario di San Michele Archangelo: 230
Santuario di Santa Maria dell'Isola di Tropea: 268
Santuario di Santa Rosalia: 306–307
Sassi di Matera: 27, 259
Sassi di Matera Living Nativity Scene: 265
Sasso Barisano: 261
Sasso Caveoso: 16, 259, 260–261
Savelletri: 28, 233
Saviano, Roberto: 451
scacce ragusane: 424
scacciata: 346
Scala Cruci Hike: 418

Scala dei Turchi: 32, 324
Scalinata di Santa Maria del Monte: 431
Scaturchio: 65
Sciara del Fuoco hike: 392–393
Scogliera di Cala Rossa: 327
scooter travel: 459–460; see also specific place
Scopello: 318–319
sea life: 440
sea urchin: see ricci di mare
Segesta: 27, 274
Selinunte Archaeological Park: 27, 274, 321
senior travelers, advice for: 478
sfincione: 297, 424
sfogliatelle: 34, 68
shipping: 468
shopping: 468; Naples 61–64; Palermo 291–292;
    see also specific place
shoulder seasons: 22
Sicilian language: 451
sightseeing passes: Herculaneum 89; Naples
    39–40; Pompeii 79
Silvestri Craters: 366
Sinagoga de Scolanova: 222
Siracusa Stazione Centrale: 416
skiing: 32, 367–368
Small Theater (Pompeii): 83
smoking: 471–472
soccer: see football (soccer)
Solarium Nettuno: 409
Sorbillo: 65
Sorrento: 18, 26, 98, 105–120; maps 100–101,
    110–111
Spaccanapoli: 25, 37, 38, 46
Spiagge Bianche: 382
Spiaggia Acquacalda: 382
Spiaggia Calamosche: 418
Spiaggia dei Gradoni: 250
Spiaggia della Purità: 253
Spiaggia della Rotonda: 268
Spiaggia di Cala Dogana: 327
Spiaggia di Cala Rossa: 409
Spiaggia di Cefalù: 313
Spiaggia di Fontane Bianche: 410
Spiaggia di Fornillo: 28, 127
Spiaggia di Giardini Naxos: 358
Spiaggia di Lama Monachile: 28, 29, 229, 232
Spiaggia di Marina di Ragusa: 430
Spiaggia di Mondello: 307
Spiaggia di Pecorini a Mare: 390
Spiaggia di Pollara: 387
Spiaggia di Porto Badisco: 255
Spiaggia di Porto Selvaggio: 255
Spiaggia di Punto Asparano: 410
Spiaggia di Rinella: 387
Spiaggia di San Giuliano: 317
Spiaggia di San Vito Lo Capo: 319

Spiaggia di Torre dell'Orso: 254–255
Spiaggia di Vignanotica: 230
Spiaggia e Piscina Naturale di Marina Serra: 255
Spiaggia Grande (Positano): 26, 127, 130
Spiaggia Libera di Isola Bella: 358
Spiaggia Michelino: 268
Spiaggia Milazzo: 379
Spiaggia Pane e Pomodoro: 214
Spiaggia San Giovanni Licuti: 343
Spiaggia San Vito: 232
Spiaggia Valle Muria: 381–382
sports/recreation: 32, 464; Naples 59; Palermo
    285–288; see also specific place
SSC Napoli: 59
Stabian Baths: 82–83
Stadio Diego Armando Maradona: 59
Stano: 265
Stazione Catania Centrale: 336, 352
Stazione Marittima di Salerno: 168
Stazione Villa San Giovanni: 378
stigghiole: 297
Strada delle Orecchiette: 216
street food: 15, 34, 286, 296–297, 465
strollers: 477
Stromboli: 376, 389–393
Synagogue Museum of Sant'Anna: 222
Syracuse: 22, 394–417, 398, 402–417; maps 396–
    397, 400–401, 405
Syracuse, vicinity of: 417–423

TU

Taormina: 20, 332, 354–362; map 355
Taranto: 258
tax: 474
taxis: 461; Naples 77; Palermo 306; see also specific
    place
Teatro Antico di Taormina: 355–356
Teatro Bellini: 60
Teatro Biondo Stabile: 289
Teatro di San Carlo: 60–61
Teatro Giuseppe Verdi: 168, 171
Teatro Greco: 404
Teatro Massimo: 289
Teatro Massimo Bellini: 344, 346
Teatro Politeama Garibaldi: 288–289
Teatro Romano: 342
telephones: 474
Tempio di Apollo: 406
Temple of Athena: 179
Temple of Concordia: 31, 323
Temple of Diana: 313
Temple of Hera: 179
Temple of Neptune: 179
Temple of Segesta: 321
Tenuta Sallier de La Tour: 32, 310–311
Terme Della Rotonda: 342

Terrace of Infinity: 28, 160
Terra Murata: 57
theater: 454
timeline, historical: 446–447
tipping: 467
Torre a Mare watchtower: 129
Torre del Filosofo hike: 366
Torre Museo: 160
Torre Normanno Sveva: 239
tourism: 449
tourist information: 476; Naples 72; Palermo 303;
    see also specific place
train travel: 23, 378, 458, 459; Naples 73–74;
    Palermo 304–305; see also specific place
Trani: 221–223
Transavanguardia movement: 453
transportation: 455–461; Naples 73–77; Palermo
    304–306; see also specific place
Trapani: 20, 274, 313–320; map 315
trattorias: 465
Trattoria Terra Madre: 237–238
trees: 439–440
Trellis House: 90
Tremiti Islands: 206, 231
Tropea: 268
trulli: 27, 236–237
Trullo Church: 237
Trullo Siamese: 237
Trullo Sovrano: 237
Uzeta Bistro Siciliano: 348

V

vaccines: 456–457, 470
Valle dei Templi: 16, 20, 27, 31, 274, 322–324
Valle delle Ferriere: 132, 147
Valle d'Itria: 238
Vallone dei Mulini: 109
Vendicari Nature Reserve: 408
Via dei Mulini: 122, 133
Via dei Rufolo: 160, 162
Via della Libertà: 291
Via del Sale: 316
Via Etnea: 336
Viale delle Ginestre: 78
Viale Enrico Caruso: 109
Viale Pasitea: 122, 133
Via Lorenzo d'Amalfi: 141
Via Lucana: 259
Via Maqueda: 271
Via Marina Grande: 120, 122
Via Mercanti: 168, 170, 173
Via Migliera: 189
Via Plebiscito: 347
Via Positanesi d'America: 127
Via Roma: 163

Via Ruggero Settimo: 291
Via San Francesco: 163
Via San Gregorio Armeno: 25, 63
Via Stabiana: 78
Vieste: 231
Villa Athena: 328
Villa Bellini: 30, 336, 342–343
Villa Cimbrone: 28, 158, 160
Villa Comunale (Naples): 53
Villa Comunale (Salerno): 168, 170
Villa Comunale (Sorrento): 26, 109
Villa Comunale (Taormina): 356
Villa Comunale (Trani): 221
Villa dei Papiri: 89
Villagio di Babbo Natale: 265
Villa Giulia: 285
Villa Jovis: 27, 181, 183, 185, 193
Villa Malaparte: 189, 193
Villa of the Mysteries: 26, 84
Villa Pottino: 291
Villa Romana del Casale: 398, 427–428
Villa Rufolo: 158, 160
Villa San Michele: 181, 186
Virgil: 451
visas: 22–23, 461–462
Vittorio Emanuele: 168
volcanoes and volcanic islands: 438; see also
    Mount Etna; Mount Vesuvius; Stromboli;
    Vulcano
Vomero: 37, 38; bars/nightlife 70; food 69; sights
    53–56
VRBO: 469
Vucciria: see Mercato Vucciria
Vulcano: 376, 390

WZ

walking: see hiking
walking tours: Matera 259; Noto 420; Palermo
    286, 288; Pompeii 80; Salerno 170
Waterfront, Chiaia, and Vomero: 37;
    accommodations 71–72; food 67, 69; map
    54–55; shopping 63–64; sights 52–53
water sports: 464; Amalfi 147; Mondello 308;
    Positano 130–131; Sorrento 114; see also
    specific place
weights and measures: 475–476
Wi-Fi: 474
wine tasting: 30–31, 33–34, 131, 225, 246–247,
    310–311, 322–323, 368, 370, 382, 386–387, 428
women travelers, advice for: 478
World War I: 445
World War II: 447–448
Zagara Festival: 282, 290, 463
Zona Trulli Rione Monti: 236–237
zuzzo: 347

List of Maps

Front Map
Southern Italy: 2–3

Discover Southern Italy
chapter divisions map: 19

Naples and the Ruins
Naples and the Ruins: 38–39
Itinerary Ideas: 41
Naples Overview: 43
Centro Storico: 44–45
San Ferdinando, Waterfront, and Vomero: 54–55
Pompeii: 80–81
Herculaneum: 88

Sorrento, Capri, and the Amalfi Coast
Sorrento, Capri, and the Amalfi Coast: 100–101
Itinerary Ideas: 106–107
Sorrento: 110–111
Amalfi Coast: 122–123
Positano: 124–125
Amalfi: 144–145
Ravello: 159
Salerno: 169
Paestum: 178
Capri Town: 181

Puglia and the Best of the South
Puglia and the Best of the South: 204–205
Two Days in Puglia: 208–209
Bari: 211
Puglia's Wild North: 230
Lecce: 242
Matera: 260

Palermo and Western Sicily
Palermo and Western Sicily: 272–273
Itinerary Ideas: 276
Palermo: 278–279
Trapani: 315

Catania, Northeastern Sicily, and the Aeolian Islands
Catania, Northeastern Sicily, and the Aeolian Islands: 333
Itinerary Ideas: 335
Catania: 338–339
Taormina: 355
Mount Etna: 363
The Aeolian Islands: 377

Syracuse and Southeastern Sicily
Syracuse and Southeastern Sicily: 396–397
Itinerary Ideas: 400–401
Syracuse and Island of Ortigia: 405
Ragusa: 425

Photo Credits

Trips to Remember

CHILE

ECUADOR
& THE GALÁPAGOS ISLANDS

EGYPT

GREEK ISLANDS & ATHENS

ISLAND ESCAPES WITH TIMELESS VILLAGES, SCENIC HIKES, AND LOCAL FLAVORS

ICELAND

WITH A ROAD TRIP ON THE RING ROAD

JAPAN

PLAN YOUR TRIP, AVOID THE CROWDS, AND EXPERIENCE THE REAL JAPAN

TRIP OF A LIFETIME

MACHU PICCHU

MOROCCO

PORTUGAL

PRAGUE, VIENNA & BUDAPEST

ROME, FLORENCE & VENICE

Epic Treks

CAMINO DE SANTIAGO

SACRED SITES, HISTORIC VILLAGES, LOCAL FOOD & WINE

BEEBE BAHRAMI

Drive & Hike

APPALACHIAN TRAIL

THE BEST TRAIL TOWNS, DAY HIKES, AND ROAD TRIPS IN BETWEEN

TIMOTHY MALCOLM

Drive & Hike

PACIFIC CREST TRAIL

THE BEST TRAIL TOWNS, DAY HIKES, AND ROAD TRIPS IN BETWEEN

CAROLINE HINCHLIFF

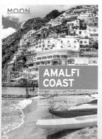

Get inspired for your next adventure

Follow **@moonguides** on Instagram or subscribe to our newsletter at **moon.com**

#TravelWithMoon

MAP SYMBOLS

═══ Expressway	○ City/Town	ⓘ Information Center	♠ Park
═══ Primary Road	◉ State Capital	🅿 Parking Area	⚐ Golf Course
═══ Secondary Road	⊛ National Capital	⚲ Church	✛ Unique Feature
┄┄ Unpaved Road	✪ Highlight	❦ Winery/Vineyard	Waterfall
╌╌╌ Trail	★ Point of Interest	⚑ Trailhead	Λ Camping
┈┈┈ Ferry	• Accommodation	Ⓡ Train Station	▲ Mountain
┄┄ Railroad	▾ Restaurant/Bar	✈ Airport	⛷ Ski Area
═══ Pedestrian Walkway	▪ Other Location	✗ Airfield	Glacier
═══ Stairs			

CONVERSION TABLES

°C = (°F - 32) / 1.8
°F = (°C x 1.8) + 32
1 inch = 2.54 centimeters (cm)
1 foot = 0.304 meters (m)
1 yard = 0.914 meters
1 mile = 1.6093 kilometers (km)
1 km = 0.6214 miles
1 fathom = 1.8288 m
1 chain = 20.1168 m
1 furlong = 201.168 m
1 acre = 0.4047 hectares
1 sq km = 100 hectares
1 sq mile = 2.59 square km
1 ounce = 28.35 grams
1 pound = 0.4536 kilograms
1 short ton = 0.90718 metric ton
1 short ton = 2,000 pounds
1 long ton = 1.016 metric tons
1 long ton = 2,240 pounds
1 metric ton = 1,000 kilograms
1 quart = 0.94635 liters
1 US gallon = 3.7854 liters
1 Imperial gallon = 4.5459 liters
1 nautical mile = 1.852 km

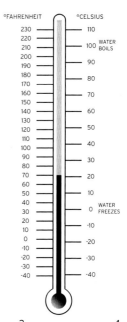

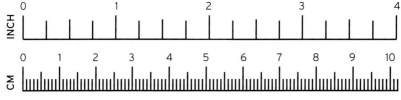

MOON SOUTHERN ITALY

Avalon Travel
Hachette Book Group
1700 Fourth Street
Berkeley, CA 94710, USA
www.moon.com

Editor: Megan Anderluh
Managing Editor: Hannah Brezack
Graphics and Production Coordinator: Darren Alessi
Cover Design: Faceout Studio, Charles Brock
Interior Design: Domini Dragoone
Moon Logo: Tim McGrath
Map Editor: Kat Bennett
Cartographers: Mark Stroud (Moon St Cartography, CO), John Culp, Kat Bennett

ISBN-13: 978-1-64049-453-4

Printing History
1st Edition — March 2022
5 4 3 2 1

Text © 2022 by Linda Sarris & Laura Thayer.
Maps © 2022 by Avalon Travel.
Some photos and illustrations are used by permission and are the property of the original copyright owners.

Front cover photo: Otranto Salento Apulia Puglia, Italy © Luca Antonio Lorenzelli / Alamy Stock Photo
Back cover photo: soup with mussels, tomatoes and red beans © Photosimysia | Dreamstime.com

Printed in Malaysia for Imago